Cybernetics and Systems Theory in Management:
Tools, Views, and Advancements

Steven E. Wallis
Foundation for the Advancement of Social Theory, USA
Institute for Social Innovation, Fielding Graduate University, USA

Information Science REFERENCE
INFORMATION SCIENCE REFERENCE
Hershey · New York

Director of Editorial Content: Kristin Klinger
Senior Managing Editor: Jamie Snavely
Assistant Managing Editor: Michael Brehm
Publishing Assistant: Sean Woznicki
Typesetter: Carole Coulson, Kate Griffin, Sean Woznicki
Cover Design: Lisa Tosheff
Printed at: Yurchak Printing Inc.

Published in the United States of America by
Information Science Reference (an imprint of IGI Global)
701 E. Chocolate Avenue
Hershey PA 17033
Tel: 717-533-8845
Fax: 717-533-8661
E-mail: cust@igi-global.com
Web site: http://www.igi-global.com/reference

Library of Congress Cataloging-in-Publication Data

Cybernetics and systems theory in management : tools, views, and advancements / Steven Wallis, editor.
p. cm.

Includes bibliographical references and index.
Summary: "This book provides new models and insights into how to develop, test, and apply more effective decision-making and ethical practices in an organizational setting"--Provided by publisher.

ISBN 978-1-61520-668-1 (hbk.) -- ISBN 978-1-61520-669-8 (ebook) 1. Management. 2. Cybernetics. 3. System theory. I. Wallis, Steven, 1960-
HD31.C93 2010
658.001'13--dc22

2009043364

British Cataloguing in Publication Data
A Cataloguing in Publication record for this book is available from the British Library.

Table of Contents

Detailed Table of Contents

Alex and David Bennet offer solid research that is cogent and well presented. Their approach interweaves emerging understandings of the human brain with multiple forms of knowledge, theory, cybernetics, and complexity to gain new insights into the decision-making process. Their clear and effective definitions provide readers with a solid foundation for exploring the new frontier of neurology as it relates to human behavior and organizational effectiveness. By viewing the decision-making process through multiple points of view. We learn what is going on from the view of inside the decision-maker, as well as the view from outside the decision-maker. And, significantly, we begin to understand the importance of the pattern similarity between inside the human brain and the surrounding environment. Only by understanding the complex relationships between mind, environment, and the spectrum of theories available to the decision-maker can we move toward the ability to make more effective decisions in complex situations.

This chapter presents a wealth of thought-provoking ideas. With depth and precision, Richardson explores opportunities for drawing insightful connections between complexity theory and management theory. And, to the purpose of advancing management science, he describes three schools of thought for applying complexity to organizations: metaphor, neo-reductionism, and critical pluralism. Taken as a set, these three schools present a range of possibilities for engaging, thinking, and applying complexity in management. From an applied perspective, Richardson suggests that managers (and other members of organization) should, to some extent, become philosophers. That is to say managers should spend some time contemplating deep questions from multiple perspectives. This view is combined with a new challenge for managers to find the openness needed to address deep questions and the courage to do so in humility and collaboration with others.

In this readable and thought-provoking work, Hodgson offers timely insights into decision-making theory. He addresses the difficult issue of decision making from a nonlinear perspective in a profound way. First, he revisits von Foerster's idea that the only decisions we can make are those that are actually about undecidable questions. Because, in a sense, the easy decisions have already been made for us by our way of framing them. Then, Hodgson introduces the rich idea of "decision integrity." This approach requires that the decision maker should understand the relationship between learning and deciding, as well as addressing important ethical concerns. An understanding of cybernetic feedback and systemic relationships is required for this big picture approach – which has intriguing implications for practice.

Most managers seem to work from a perspective of Cartesian reduction. Such management often involves the use of simple, linear, models such as the classic organizational chart. In this chapter, Donald Mikulecky shows how this approach is ultimately ineffective. This rich collection of concepts and insights are combined to challenge the reductive philosophy that has trapped managers in the Cartesian mode of thought. While all managers create mental models, Mikulecky effectively argues that the habit of Cartesian reduction has led managers to "manage the model" rather than manage the real complex system in which they are embedded. By updating our philosophical foundations, Mikulecky suggests a path towards more complete understanding, and more effective management practices. Advancing "relational systems theory," this chapter suggests a more effective approach is for managers to identify the complex causal relationships as a way to understand and manage the real system more effectively.

The focus of this section is to provide scholars with a suite of methodologies for conducting research that are innovative, rigorous, and effective. The methods suggested here will prove very useful for scholars who want to develop, apply, and advance theoretical models toward greater insight and effectiveness. Individually, each of these chapters contains ideas that will have a profound effect on the larger paradigm of management science. Together, they have the potential to shape that science for a decade or more.

In this chapter, the authors describe their participation in a process of academic and managerial collaboration for benchmarking best practices in business. This is an important new approach with major implications in several areas. First, in response to calls for more engagement between academic and business circles, this chapter provides an example that scholars and practitioners should both follow. Second, this chapter helps researchers answer the call for better theory by providing a useful process for gathering data and buidling theory. That process suggests the opportunity for creating more complex theory – grounded in a new paradigm of conscious and purposeful collaboration between business and academia. Third, Schiele and Krummaker point the way for academia to develop theory that is more relevant to business. And, this process results in the creation of theory that is more likely to work in practice. Importantly, this chapter sets a standard for "next generation" case study research by overcoming many of the biases and limitations of existing case study methodology.

Working to understand complex and systemic nature of disruptive organizational change requires metatriangualtion – the use of multiple lenses to better understand a complex situation. Lewis applies a set of lenses in a case study analysis to investigate the implementation of Advanced Manufacturing Technology (AMT). In an excellent example of this kind of metatheoretical approach, she describes that change through four separate lenses and identifies "paradox" as an important and common theme. Lewis provides a useful description of management practices that will support these change efforts. Finally, this chapter provides readers with suggestions for future research. One important direction is found in the difference between linear change theories, and change theories of plurality and paradox. These suggestions open the door for further innovation and advancement in the theory and practice of organizational change.

Citing the need for better metatheory as a prerequisite for the development of better theory, Mark uses a metatheoretical discourse to gain a clearer view of management theory. He describes four general forms of transformational management theory; and, importantly, Mark steps out of the either-or debate between the benefits of self vs. organization, or top-down vs. bottom-up theories of management. In doing so, he transcends those debates to integrate and extend the extremes by looking through the metatheoretical lens of relationality. This broad and radical reframing of management theory will be very useful to scholars studying corporate social responsibility, spiritual leadership, ethics, sustainability, and more. Management scholars will find this list of concepts very useful as they frame and reframe their investigations. Edwards' chapter is more purposefully metatheoretical than most in this book. And, as such, provides a useful guide for scholars interested in exploring the newly revived (and more rigorously applied) metatheoretical conversation.

In response to specious claims of revolutionary improvements in management theory, this chapter investigates the relationship between Kuhnian paradigmatic revolution and the objectively measured, inter-propositional structure of theory. Here, propositional analysis is applied to determine the formal robustness of a set of theories spanning 1,500 years of history. The results show that increasing robustness seems to be a useful predictor of Kuhnian paradigm revolution. This, in turn, suggests that scholars who are interested in developing revolutionary theories should develop theories with a high level of formal robustness. Further, these results suggest that the measure of robustness may be an effective tool in evaluating the potential efficacy of theories. This chapter has profound implications for the advancement of management science toward true paradigmatic revolution.

Section 3
Cybernetics and Organizational Evaluation

In this section of the book, our focus is two-fold. First, these chapters present new and intriguing ideas for advancing cybernetics and systems theory. As such, they are more suited for advanced thinkers. Second, the chapters in this section suggest innovative forms of organization analysis. For researchers, this section provides new lenses for investigating organizations.

Taking note of some fundamentals of complexity theory (including logical openness, cybernetics, and coherence), we see human social systems as multiple systems or collective beings that are generated by human elements simultaneously interacting in different ways. To manage complexity, Minati, presents his approach: Dynamic uSAge of Models (DYSAM). DYSAM is a meta-approach that should be of great use to scholars investigating complex systems because it provides a framework for integrating approaches, models, and theories. The goal of DYSAM is to represent every aspect of the system at all of its levels. Intriguingly, DYSAM investigates the acquisition of properties, rather than investigating the changes to the values of existing properties of existing systems. This approach is used to gain new insights into growth, development, sustainability, non-reductionist management techniques, and emergence.

In this chapter we are treated to a deep and challenging exploration of knowledge cybernetics. Yolles' approach begins with the ideas of Stafford Beer, and adds the insights from Eric Schwarz, then extends those ideas to create a more complete model of socially viable systems (SVS), which is capable of modeling more complex social relationships than previously possible. His model is then applied as a social frame of reference to understand organizational patterning, personality type, and knowledge profiling. Maurice shifts the conversation on knowledge cybernetics from one of epistemology to one of ontology – an important step. And, in the process, extends and deepens Beer's viable systems model (VSM) developing a lateral ontology (where a systems is understood as a contextual domain consisting of sub-contextual domains or sub-systems) and transverse ontology (relating to emergence and higher-order control of the system) to better understand and redefine the paradigm and develop new tools for analyzing organizations for their system pathologies.

Section 4
Multiple Levels and New Perspectives

For decades, the "micro-macro question" has haunted the social sciences as large. In management theory, as well, the question persists: "Does the individual control the group, or does the group control the individual?" Such questions raise serious questions of agency and effectiveness in business organizations. By understanding the relationships between multiple levels (data, theory, individuals, teams, departments, organizations, nations) we may be able to increase our human and organizational efficacy at all levels. Yet, despite the apparent importance of the topic, these questions remain unanswered. In this section, we look at multiple levels of interaction from DNA to work teams – views that promise new paths of research for management scholars.

In contrast to the traditional understanding of evolution guided by external forces of selection, Dr. Riegler investigates how a cybernetic theory of evolution suggests that evolution is channeled by internal constraints based on the reciprocal dependencies of the genetic material. In short, where the normal view is "top-down," Dr. Riegler provides us with a new, "bottom-up" view of evolution. This Batesonian view of evolution challenges, and perhaps compliments, the more common approach of understanding evolution in terms of "fitness landscapes" by developing a better understanding of an "epigenetic landscape." This new view lets us realize how our top-down view may easily skew our understanding of management and the creative change in work teams. Indeed, by gaining the ability to understand developmental paths, we may gain the ability to predict the development of a team, or an organization.

Dr. Hansson takes a new approach to the question of human agency with an investigation into the nature of human interaction in organizations. While some authors consider how supervisors acquire agency at the expense of employees, Hansson avoids such dualisms by investigating from a dialectical perspective – where both employees and supervisors gain agency through the process of social co-construction. He investigates the combination of individual and social influences to develop a new theory of learning object creation. Interestingly, he finds support for these views by applying an innovative research technique involving a facilitated group working both live and networked, so the researcher can capture interactions as well as reflections. These insights into social construction shine a new light onto an age-old question – and open the door for a new path of investigation.

Section 5
Metamodelling and Mathematics

Just as metatheory is the analysis of theory (to gain greater insights into theory), so too metamodelling and mathematics are used to gain better insights into modeling. The similarity is not a coincidence. Computer models are the dynamic software equivalent of management theories discussed in the previous chapters. In this final section of the book, we explore innovative advances in mathematics and computer modeling. The contributions of the brilliant scholars in this section suggest exciting opportunities to develop more effective computer models. After all, there can be a synergistic benefit where better computer models can lead to better management theories, and better management theories can lead to better computer models.

This author uses Petri nets to develop metamodelling insights into multi agent systems. He considers multiple levels of interactions of agents, their interfaces, and the related environment. He presents examples from inter-personal cooperation, inter-organizational negotiations, supervisor-system relationships, supervised-agents, and relationships in an environment of limited resources. This last (limited resources) is of particular importance, as limited resources will limit productivity and is often a cause of conflict. His results suggest opportunities for understanding paths for avoiding conflict and improving productivity in a wide variety of situations.

In this chapter, the author accepts an impressive challenge – to improve our ability to predict the accuracy of models. He shows how alternative approaches to prediction (deterministic and probabilistic) are limited. His approach looks at the model parameters as, "…time-varying but bounded variables, which are characterized by an interval of real numbers. Since the model parameters are intervals, the predicted system's response at any instant is not anymore a real number but an interval of real numbers. The set of predicted intervals at different instances generates a tube through time called *wrapping envelope*." This innovative metamodelling approach can be used to identify (and so limit) modeling error. In short, he opens the door for the creation of more effective models.

Readers are presented with the problem of "subset selection" (or, variable selection) – that arises when attempting to model the relationship between a topic of interest and the multiple, potential explanatory variables. This kind of problem is common in many decision-making or strategic planning situations where there is no easy answer; indeed, there are multiple possible answers with no way to be sure which one might be best. These authors submit new, simple, variable selection criteria. Their ambitious goal is to select the smallest number of decision-making criteria that can be used without losing **any** explanatory power. Their approach is tested with chemical processes, manpower allocation, housing prices, corporate profitability, supervisor performance, and more. The potential importance of this approach should be evident to anyone who has had to make a difficult decision.

Foreword

UNITY-IN-DIVERSITY

I have always enjoyed works whose very processes of creation, whose manners of presentation or re-presentation, embody the very same principles that they try to espouse. It is this reflexive aspect that is certainly at the heart of cybernetic and systemic enterprises. Appreciation of this process-oriented reading is also one way to enjoy this book, edited by Steven Wallis, *Cybernetics and Systems Theory in Management: Tools, Views and Advancements*.

With a background in cybernetics and systems, and teaching courses in this area, I often get asked questions such as "what is THE key principle that is at the heart of a cybernetic, or a systems (while related, these are not necessarily the same) approach. Now this is a difficult question to address directly since, you could say, that while at its core, cybernetics and systems approaches are about interconnectedness and a resultant emergence of those "things" that are interconnected, the very notion of a core is somewhat antithetical to cybernetic understanding. This indeed seems paradoxical –but perhaps, then, the need for paradox is itself a core concept. That is, if interconnectedness is "at the heart" would our very specification of that (any one thing being at the heart) deny the very idea of interconnectedness? Think about it. Take your time, catch your breath. Perhaps play with Gregory Bateson's play with logical types.

So, in doing some serious play with cybernetic and systems approaches, we recognize that we may choose one core idea as a starting point but we need immediately repair the cleavage that we have created in our world(s) by making the distinction (Heinz von Foerster and George Spencer-Brown certainly invited to us to recognize how we make distinctions!) that we do, by connecting it back with that which we distinguished it from. Not so easy, is it, to continually remind ourselves to do this! A distinction-relation couplet may work as a continual process.

I mention these issues since one reading of this important edited volume is to recognize the fundamental value of the systems idea of Unity-in-Diversity. Rather than feel that all chapters in a book that connects cybernetics and systems theory to management must be in total agreement about what cybernetics and systems theory "is," we can appreciate the family resemblances (also noting the link to Wittgenstein's very idea of family resemblances) that form the ways of making connections. What are the manners of connection that allow for apparently different perspectives to be part of a greater whole? And what is that greater whole whose "wholeness" rests on maintaining those differences – that variety - rather than losing them? And how are these two questions themselves interconnected? It is no coincidence that the European Union makes use of this very systemic principle of Unity-In-Diversity in its mission- allowing for retaining the integrity of cultural differences, while still retaining the integration that allows for a Union to become a Union.

The notion of Unity-In-Diversity is so critical here in reading this book because it invites us to both appreciate the cybernetic ideas that are developed and advanced, while at the same time opening up to question whether these are the exact same cybernetic approaches that are "shared" by all. It invites to appreciate looking for connections, while at the same time thinking about how we make connections across differences, to create a unity – a unity that thrives on maintaining variety. Steve Wallis, in describing his read of the book he has put together, commented that perhaps it is a made up of a "team of rivals" – but they are rivals in a collaborative sense, maintaining the differences AND maintaining the connections. These surface when we think about systems theory, systems practice, and the relationship between systems theory and practice – and it is this relationship which can be seen to be a major contribution of this book.

One of the interesting tensions that has been a major conversation of the professional organization, the American Society for Cybernetics (which is much more international than its name would suggest) is that of how we offer definitions of cybernetics. As a former president of that society, it is a question I have been asked many times – as have other presidents. At the web site of that organization, Stuart Umpleby (another former president) offers a very cybernetic response to this question (http://www.gwu.edu/~asc/cyber_definition.html) by telling a story of how different critical definitions came to be those offered. It is a story of Unity-In-Diversity of its own self-definition. So we have, among others, Stafford Beer's "science of effective organization," Gordon Pask's "art and science of manipulating defensible metaphors," in addition to W. Ross Ashby's "the art of steersmanship," Gregory Bateson's "a branch of mathematics dealing with control, recursiveness and information," and the oft-recognized (but frequently misunderstood) one of Norbert Wiener – "the science of control and communication in the animal and the machine."

There is an important side note here – particularly within the theme of Unity-In-Diversity, and terribly important for how we read this book – the misunderstanding that is frequently made of Wiener's definition rests upon how we usually think of control. Wiener was very careful to choose the word IN, so control is a property of a system's internal operations, rather than control OF, which would imply control from outside the system. Hence, concerns with SELF-regulation become paramount in cybernetics. Indeed, this recognition of the important distinction between control IN rather than control OF was of major importance to Warren McCulloch, one of the key figures in the development of cybernetics, in his recollection of the many sources of cybernetics.

In my own work, I have also noted that in many ways, cybernetics can be seen as a most Eastern of Western philosophical positions, foregrounding relational understanding and taking seriously questions of the relationship between the observer and that which is observed – a manner of understanding that fits nicely with many of the chapters in this volume. There is a reliance on processes of mutual relationships – building on the very idea of the Circular Causal and Feedback Mechanisms in Social and Biological Systems that were the basis of the seminal Macy Conferences (see the wonderful accounts of these conferences by Steve Heims, *The Cybernetics Group*, and Jean-Pierre Dupuy, *The Mechanization of Mind*, for more about this).

This is a book, then, that invites exploring many different kinds of critical mutual relationships. And, out of that frame of mutualities, it is a book that invites asking profound questions about the very assumptions that form the basis for those parts whose particular "partness" may derive from their very relationship.

Of course, the chapters are not just about cybernetics and systems theory. They are about how to connect ideas of cybernetics and systems to how we enact management processes. The notion of tools for management rings loudly here – it is even part of the subtitle. But what does it mean to think about tools from a cybernetic perspective? Might the tools also be "things to reflect with, together with others," for example – so what emerges from the use of those tools could also be new questions about what kind of organization we may be "managing" (or even, what using diverse metaphors of "managing" do to how we think about our organization and its constitutive relationships).

Often, the framework within which questions and issues of management cybernetics is done is one of management (or leadership, for that matter) being an "application" of cybernetics. Cybernetic principles are taken as the "given" and the organization the scene of their application, with the principles being unchanging. But in a book such as this, which is about meta-theory as much as management, we are encouraged to rethink the very paradigmatic basis for anything being "applied" – which privileges, to be sure, the theory. Instead, what a volume like this encourages us to do is to think of cybernetics (or systems) and management as mutually intertwined – as theory and practice. Cyberneticians can learn as much about cybernetics, or systems theorists about systems, from seeing how those managers who describe themselves as coming from a cybernetic perspective enact those ideas in practice. Indeed, their very use may alter the theory and the theoretical frames. What we are encouraged to do here is to change the way that we view the relationship between theory and practice – and perhaps, as Will McWhinney has noted (in his *Paths of Change*, among other places), allow this recogntion to become the basis for a meta-praxis. Perhaps a movement away from the idea of "applied" to the idea praxis, as some in this volume could be seen to encourage, signals such a shift.

But this is just one of many mutualities offered by this book that we need take seriously. Understanding theory and practice as intertwined, to be sure, is a good starting point. Yet so is the relationship between management and what it might often be distinguished from – for example, leadership. How are management and leadership interconnected in a mutually informing relationship? Might even asking that question allow us to see, in a deeply systemic way, managing as a property of a whole system, rather than what one individual does? And what are the consequences of that systemic approach?

This volume also, including in its introduction, a recognition of different "theories" of systems at play here. Steven Wallis very nicely uses this recognition as a way to assert the importance of meta-theory as part of the cybernetic and management program (with managers and designers being meta-theorists too, in the strong sense that Don Schön implies in his Reflective Practitioner). Yet, in the same way that concepts at the same logical type might be mutually related, such as theory and practice, management and leadership, we might look at how concepts at different logical types, such as theory and meta-theory, mutually inform each other – challenging notions of fixed hierarchies of meaning in a delightfully cybernetic way. In other words, we are invited to look at how a context that might ordinarily allow for making meaning of events within it, might also be questioned (and then perhaps altered) by those very "situated" events.

Continuing, we are invited to consider mutualities of praxis and meta-praxis – and perhaps, meta-theory and meta-praxis, and maybe even, crossing over a boundary, meta-praxis and theory. In so doing, since complexity is also a key theme of this book (for example, the chapter by Kurt Richardson), considering the mutual relationship between complexity and simplicity – how each requires the other – can also be of "use" in managing and beyond. Perhaps it is the design of the very reflective space to consider these relationships – again, out of the frame of Unity-In-Diversity –that can be a valuable "tool" emerging from the interconnection of the authors here.

Gregory Bateson, in *Mind and Nature*, and elsewhere, invites us to consider the "patterns that connect" as a hallmark of his cybernetic thought and practice. In this volume, several key themes (and questions!) emerge out of the chapters and the spaces in between them. We have the themes, so important to a management cybernetics, of innovation, and of creativity AND the relationship between innovation and creativity. How do we create space for the new, the novel, while still maintaining the integrity of our identity – whether it be our personal identity or what we value as our organization's or our community's identity?

And then we have theme of an evolutionary approach to questions of success of our managing process. Might we, in evaluating managerial moves, consider how we know if these strategies, innovations, etc. work? How do we learn along the way by carefully considering what "works" means? And might this be different when viewed from different perspectives within the system? And how is "withinness" itself understood from different perspectives – questions of boundary construction, as well as the relationship between openness and closedness, are essential to consider in the diverse ways invoked in this volume. Thus, we recognize that systems are not open or closed, as absolutes, but that that very idea is contingent upon the kind of operation or relationship we are considering – open to energy, but closed to organization, perhaps, which is at the heart of ideas of autopoiesis.

We have themes of complexity (what are the networks of interconnection, and when are they, and what are the opportunities afforded by understanding how complexity "works"), of undecidability (what are judgment-making processes and how are these interwoven with our ways of dealing with and embracing uncertainty), of modes of collaboration (how do we forge ways of knowing and doing together, that open up space for emergence), of paradox (how do we recognize when our worlds collide – and how that opens up opportunity for reflection on the very basis of frames for those worlds), and of the deeply epistemological concerns of constructivism (how do we individually and collectively come to create world(s) from our experience and come to "know" our world(s) as participants).

And then what happens when we consider all of these themes as a whole system of concepts - interrelated, an ecology of ideas, in Geoffrey Vickers' sense. Looking at the interrelated themes of this book as an ecology of ideas, we might ask – What does it mean to understand managing from the point of view of complexity AND what does it mean to understand complexity from the point of view of managing?

Underscoring all of this is that woven throughout is the distinction between, and the relationship between, first order and second order cybernetics. We have concerns of our observed worlds (first order) folded into how we as observers are part of that which we are observing – what Heinz von Foerster so cleverly referred to as Observing Systems (second order). This distinction/relationship couplet invokes a management cybernetics that immediately becomes a reflective and collaborative practice. The different authors have different takes on precisely how, and when, this plays out – but, again, that is what makes the Unity-in-Diversity theme so appealing, as, from the introduction on through the entire volume, we are invited to appreciate what we see through our lens (whether the lens be a paradigmatic or an everyday frame lens), while at the same time recognizing what our lens allows us to see AND what it obscures.

We might even, then, in linking systems theory and cybernetics to managing, as this volume does, become aware of the very metaphors we use for knowledge creating processes in organizations. Anne Salmond, in writing about cross-cultural conceptions of knowledge, notes the difference between landscape metaphors of knowledge (which perhaps our idea of a "lens" invites) and which also implies having "perspectives" of a ground that is inexhaustible, with Maori metaphors of knowledge that speak to its exhaustibleness and destructibility. What are the consequences of the metaphors we rely on – which brings us back nicely to Gordon Pask's cybernetics as the art and science of manipulating defensible metaphors.

One final question we might ask of ourselves in reading this book is what are the consequences of our particular "lens" and, at another level, the consequences of relying on "seeing" as a path to managing knowing.

This is book that asks us to ask such questions about how we think and act in working with others.

Frederick Steier
Fielding Graduate University, USA;
University of Southern Florida, USA

***Frederick Steier** is currently on the faculty of the Department of Communication at the University of South Florida, where he previously served as Director of Interdisciplinary Studies Programs. He is also a Scientist-in-Residence at the Center for Learning, at the Museum of Science and Industry (MOSI) in Tampa, Florida. He received his Ph.D. in Social Systems Sciences from the University of Pennsylvania. A member of the Board of Trustees of the American Society for Cybernetics, he is also on the editorial board of the journal* Cybernetics and Human Knowing, *where he has served as Praxis editor. His research focuses on systemic approaches to the design, understanding, and transformation of, social systems of diverse kinds, with special attention to issues of learning and quality of life. He has also focused on cybernetic methodologies, including cybernetic approaches to action research. He is the editor of the volume,* Gregory Bateson: Essays of an Ecology of Ideas *(Imprint Academic, 2005).*

Preface

In management science, as with the broader social sciences, theories appear to be of limited efficacy and not fully appreciated by the business world. Even when we set our specific theories aside and rely on the benefits of a general education, the results are mixed. While no one denies the benefits of a general business education, that same education has also been implicated in corporate scandals such as the downfall of Enron. From these issues, one might imagine a **crisis of confidence** for management studies.

Yet, while the fortunes of business rise and fall, there is something different happening here. We management theorists are not a corporation, we are a community dedicated to advancing knowledge, and we are part of a science. And, the science continues to advance; sometimes in small steps, sometimes in great paradigmatic leaps. Instead of shutting down our science (like a business might close its doors) the realization of our limitations has inspired calls for more theory, improved theory, and more innovative theory – all in an attempt to reach beyond the horizon of our own limited comprehension. This book is informed by those calls while realizing that there is the need for something more.

To ask for a better theory without providing a better understanding of how theory emerges, is like asking a garden to provide a more bountiful harvest – without providing more light, fertilizer, and water. **The underlying prerequisites are simply not in place to support success.** We are doing more of the same thing while expecting different results. To facilitate a shift in thinking, my approach in instigating this project was to encourage the investigation of theory itself. Only by developing new ideas into the creation, structure, testing, and application of management theory can our science be expected to gain the metatheoretical insights needed to develop better theory. Since metaphorically theory can be understood as a lens through which we view the world, this approach asks for the creation of new lenses, and the re-arranging of existing lenses, to better understand the manager's world.

When looking at a drop of water, a magnifying glass might show dots where the naked eye saw nothing. If we arrange multiple lenses, one in line with another, we have a greater opportunity for learning because we have created a microscope. And, importantly, we gain an improvement in resolution by 100 times or more. Now those dots are seen to be living creatures (and we have enabled the emergence of a new branch of the biological sciences). This is the highest purpose of theory – making clear what was once invisible. Where management science contains many theoretical lenses for viewing the manager's world, this book is about applying the lenses of systemic thinking to better understand the lens of management theory. **In this process, we hope to dramatically improve our ability to make sense of the world and our organizations.**

The next section contains a brief overview of the primary lens (management theory) and secondary lenses (cybernetics and systems theory) from which this book emerges. An additional sub-section will provide a brief overview of theory and metatheory. The following sections will then describe the usefulness of the book, the target audience, brief descriptions of the sections and chapters of this book, and the impact this book will have on some fields of study.

FROM MANAGEMENT TO METATHEORY

While the roots of management studies reach back to Weber's studies on bureaucracy (and beyond), a reasonable starting point may be found in Taylor's analyses of workflow in the beginning of the 20th century. The field has grown steadily ever since with most universities providing courses and programs in management at the undergraduate and graduate level. From those original time and motion studies, management studies have extended to include communication, entrepreneurship, strategy, ecology, sustainability, neurology, leadership, decision-making, best practices, organizational change processes, ethics, marketing, and knowledge management (just to name a few).

Given the recent studies questioning the efficacy of management theory, and the related call for new and better theory, the greatest challenge for management science is to develop theories that may be reliably applied in practice for incontestably efficacious results. As we move toward that goal, an intermediate step is to develop theories that will provide us with general and specific understandings of the many aspects found in the field of management.

While new theories are continually emerging, our view of theory creation has (for the most part) remained the same – mired in the traditions of the past century. For example, Mintzberg has suggested that we use intuition and avoid paying conscious attention to the process by which we make our theories. In contrast to this intuitive approach, there is a growing interest in grounded theory, whose proponents suggest that theory building should be accomplished through rigorous and specific methodology. Somewhere in the middle are the vast majority of the social scientists who apply a certain level of academic rigor that appears to be acceptable to editors and reviewers (although that rigor seems to result in theory that is insufficient for practitioners).

With this proliferation of theories and paradigms (criticized by Donaldson, among others), there exists the increased opportunity to examine the field of management. This is best accomplished by using lenses that are specifically adapted for understanding the complexity and systemic relationships that exist within and between the many paradigms of management studies. In this book, we purposefully adopt such a view by looking at management theory through the lenses of cybernetics and systems theory. It is important, always, to know what kind of lenses we are using. One would not, for example, choose to wear reading glasses to view distant mountains!

Cybernetics

As the practice of management is (to a large extent) about moving toward individual and organizational goals, one lens that does seem well adapted to understanding management is cybernetics. The term is derived from the Greek "kybernetes" or "steersman" and the general focus is to understand why and how systems move toward their goals – through an understanding of communication, feedback, and control. Founded by Norbert Weiner, Cybernetics began in the middle of the 20th Century and the field has developed over the decades, impelled by pioneering work such as von Bertalanffy (primarily in biology), von Neumann (cellular automata), and Ashby (including his law of requisite variety for system control). By the late Seventies, second-order cybernetics emerged with the work of Foerster (self reference), and Maturana (autopoiesis and cognition).

The field of cybernetics has grown to include investigations into artificial intelligence, robotics, control systems, simulation, and more. Stafford Beer was a leading figure in bringing cybernetics into the realm of management theory, particularly with his Viable System Model. And, more recently, Stuart

Umpleby has been an influential figure in the field with his work on social cybernetics and cybernetics in management theory. In management theory, concepts from cybernetics are part of studies in communication, learning organizations, self-organizing teams, and others. The cybernetic approach suggests the opportunity to integrate and so better understand the relationships **between** the many aspects of management theory (e.g. communication).

Systems Theory

Many cyberneticists also conducted investigations in the more general realm of systems theory (for example, Ashby's studies of complex systems). General systems theory was advanced by the likes of von Bertalanffy (philosophy of systems), Gerard (in neurology), and Boulding (economics and social science). The work of Prigogine in self-organizing systems is particularly notable as is the development of complex adaptive systems theory by Holland, Gell-Mann and others. Systems theory has emerged to inform a variety of fields including catastrophe theory, chaos theory, context theory, complexity theory, and complex adaptive systems theory. More recently the work of Checkland has proved influential with investigations of messy systems in the field of management. In management, systems theory supports a wide variety of perspectives such as "systems thinking" (promoted by Senge and others).

Derived from the Greek "sunistánai" relating to how things stand together. Systems theory has proved to be an important perspective in studying management by the simple yet important idea that things (including processes, objects, actions, and individuals) can best be understood in relation to other things. These systemic interrelationships support our ability to understand the human condition and take more effective action. This systemic approach suggests the opportunity to better understand the interrelationships **within** the field of management theory (e.g. the structure of communication theory).

Theory and Metatheory

Broadly, a theory might be understood as conceptually similar to a schema, model, mental model, or metaphor – a lens to see the world. All so-called "facts" are understood to be valid only in terms of the theoretical lens through which the researcher views the undifferentiated world. That is why, for example, two people can look at the same situation and come to two different conclusions – they are viewing the world through different lenses. As social scientists, we may have a heightened awareness of our lenses because an important part of our work is the process of making lenses (in our research and writing) and helping others to try on different lenses so that they too may understand the world in new ways (in our classrooms).

This perspective of perspectives may be understood as the theory of theory, or metatheory. In past years, it should be noted, metatheory was given a bad name when it was applied to the creation of speculative over-arching theories. As our conversation of metatheory in the 21st Century gains momentum, however, the metatheoretical perspective is better understood as relating to the study of theory (including the rigorous development of new theories), and the critical analysis of theory (including methods of creation, structure, testing, validation, falsification, and application).

However, as suggested above, most scholars have not employed a specific metatheoretical methodology. Developing theory without a guiding metatheory is akin to managing a business "by the seat of the pants;" purposefully eschewing formal education and conscious reflection. This is not to say that intuition is irrelevant – only that we need to differentiate between intuition, theory, and action, if we are to understand how they are interrelated and enable ourselves to become more effective in scholarship and practice.

In short, it should be noted that our understanding of lens making is, itself, a lens. More philosophically than metaphorically, the theory is what frames the epistemological validity of the knowledge, while metatheory frames the ontological validity of the theory. And, as theory guides practice, we need to understand the relationship between these aspects of our management science paradigm if we are to gain indisputably effective insights into practice.

FROM PRACTICE, TO THEORY, AND BACK AGAIN

The practice of management is fraught with uncertainty. As the business world grows increasingly chaotic due to the parallel growth in global uncertainty (e.g. economic collapse), the need for useful theory of management transcends our need as academicians to add another brick to the ivory tower. We must rise above our personal and academic interests to serve the greater good. A few publications that have addressed this issue recently include "*Great Minds in Management*" (Hitt & Smith, Eds.), "*Engaged Scholarship*" by Andrew Van de Ven, and the forthcoming "Emerging Perspectives on Metatheory and Theory," a special issue of the "*Integral Review.*" This higher-level conversation is expected to support academicians as they strive to advance theory. That advance, in turn, is expected to provide long-awaited improvements in practice.

Cybernetics and systems theory show great potential for advancing how we understand the process of management. And, it is interesting to note, the growing influence of cybernetics and systems theory does not seem to be a "fad of the year;" rather, there is continual growth as scholars investigate ways of thinking systemically. Organizations such as ISCE, NECSI, and Plexus, seek to develop our understanding of systems and investigate the relationship between complexity and management. Some universities, such as Fielding, build entire doctoral programs around a systems approach. And, consulting firms such as Human Systems Dynamics Institute and the Mountain Quest Institute to consciously apply systemic perspectives to organizational analysis and development. This is not the "big boom" of an overnight fad. Rather, systemic thinking has been expanding for decades – with no signs of slowing.

Yet, the call for better theories is only partially answered by applying cybernetics and systems theory to management science. While this book certainly presents innovative theories, the authors go one step further by engaging in a conversation that essentially metatheoretical.

WHO SHOULD READ THIS BOOK

This book is primarily directed toward those who seek an innovative understanding of management theory. This book will be useful for management scholars who draw (or would like to draw) on ideas from cybernetics and systems theory. In this book, they (and, to some extent, researcher in the broader social sciences) will find innovative tools to support rigorous and effective research.

Professors will want to use this book to provoke rich and interesting discussions among advanced undergraduate students because systems thinking is increasingly common in management studies. And, for graduate students, this book will be of interest because the innovative chapters in this book will suggest new directions for study. Students might find some parts of this book challenging. However, if they persist, they will be amply rewarded by cutting-edge insights and an understanding of the conversation that is occurring at the border between systems thinking and management science. Many chapters also suggest specific and exciting directions for future research. Those interested in computer modeling will likewise find intriguing opportunities to advance their abilities and investigations.

Scholar-practitioners, particularly managers and consultants who are thinking at the doctoral level, will gain useful insights into practical management. Additionally, they will gain new tools and new insights that will challenge many preconceived notions.

Scholars who are interested in, and challenged by, interdisciplinary studies will also find this a useful book because the systemic approaches used by these authors can be applied usefully to find links between, and to integrate, a variety of fields and disciplines. In addition to the focus on management science, this book will also be of interest to those whose focus is directed more specifically toward cybernetics and/or systems theory. Finally, readers with an interest in theory of theory or metatheory will find this book a useful resource.

A TASTE OF THE BOOK

In this section, we introduce the layout of the book, along with a few key ideas from each chapter. This "amuse bouche" is intended to whet the intellectual appetite of the reader and provide some idea of where the reader may want to focus his or her reading at a level that cannot be found in a mere table of contents. Due to the linear nature of the printing process, the chapters are necessarily in order. Be sure to read the detailed table of contents for alternative orders for these chapters.

Chapter 1

Alexander and Kathia C. Laszlo present a very readable chapter, highlighting the challenges faced by businesses in the 21st century. In this they take note of critical global issues and opportunities for evolutionary change. Importantly, they make a convincing call for new perspectives, based on a systems view, to support the development of improved management theories and practices. A critical part of that perspective is the need to address knowledge management as a "provocative invitation to engage in the purposeful and conscious evolution of knowledge management as a future creating activity." This exciting challenge is worthy of deep consideration by academics and practitioners, alike.

These authors make clear the inadequacy of existing measures of business success. Must 'success' refer only to wealth, growth, and power? Or, are there alternative measures? Alexander and Kathia press toward the idea of "sustainable stewardship," a process of caring for and creatively cultivating a wide variety of resources. The ten forms of capital described in this chapter represent a ten-dimensional, interrelated, understanding of what success could be in the emerging century.

They frame 'business as usual' as the simple compliance with legal requirements. Yet, as recent global events have shown, it is possible for most businesses to be in compliance, while we all suffer an economic collapse. Clearly, something more is needed. The Laszlo's begin by describing multiple stages of corporate responsibility, from business as usual – to the level where an organization might achieve a true practice of dynamic sustainability. However, they do not stop with sustainability. Indeed, their far-sightedness suggests something more – an additional level of internal and external dynamic equilibrium which organizations should endeavor to attain.

The Laszlo's brilliantly illustrate the how interdependence is a more reasonable law of nature than survival of the fittest. In this, they challenge us to move toward syntony – a conscious realization of meta-stability in consonance with the larger co-evolutionary process. This conscious relationship with the dynamic environment presents a bold challenge for theory and practice.

Chapter 2

In their chapter on Leaders, Decisions, and the Neuro-Knowledge System, Alex and David Bennet offer solid research that is cogent and well presented. Their approach interweaves emerging understandings of the human brain with multiple forms of knowledge, theory, cybernetics, and complexity to gain new insights into the decision-making process. Their clear and effective definitions provide readers with a solid foundation for exploring the new frontier of neurology as it relates to human behavior and organizational effectiveness.

Increasing levels of change, uncertainty, and complexity in the business world make the idea of simple, deterministic, decision-making a thing of the past. Instead of seeking simple decisions, the Bennet's suggest that decision-makers should recognize they are on a "decision journey," a journey of discovery that will simultaneously result in expected and unexpected outcomes. The cybernetic feedback process relating to these decisions (and the results) is an important key to understanding effective decision-making in terms of the situational context, the theories of the decision-maker, and the knowledge created in the process.

Alex and David address the issue of decision-making through combining multiple points of view. We learn what is going on from the view of inside the decision-maker, as well as the view from outside the decision-maker. And, significantly, we begin to understand the importance of the pattern similarity between inside the human brain and the surrounding environment. Our brains naturally anticipate the outcome of our decisions. By understanding this predictive power of the cortex, we can gain new insights into decision-making. Leaders have the opportunity to become more effective decision-makers by understanding the resonance between the complex human brain and the complex decision environment.

To some extent, we are both enabled and impeded by the "invariant forms" of patterns stored in our brains. While these forms (such as facial recognition) are frequently useful (it is easy to recognize our friends), they may also lead to poor decisions. For example, when we think we recognize a friend and it turns out to be a stranger. This insight has profound implications for leaders. For example, if a CEO sees an increase in commodity prices, her mental patterns might suggest those prices represent a short-term bubble (suggesting one course of action), or a long-term trend (suggesting a different course of action). In short, the same 'facts' might appear to make different kinds of sense to different people depending on what theories they hold in their heads. Only by understanding the complex relationships between mind, environment, and the spectrum of theories available to the decision-maker can we move toward the ability to make more effective decisions in complex situations.

Chapter 3

The chapter by Kurt A. Richardson is less academic and more accessible. If you have an interest in management theory as it relates to complexity theory, this is the place for you to start. Despite the conversational tone of the author, this chapter presents a wealth of thought-provoking ideas. With depth and precision, Kurt explores opportunities for drawing deeper, more insightful connections between complexity theory and management theory. And, to the purpose of advancing management science, Kurt provides three frames for thinking about complexity thinking.

The first is the path of metaphor; this is one where flexible ideas are more casually acquired and the manager must trust intuition for successful implementation. The second path is neo-reductionism where ideas from cybernetics, complexity, and systems thinking are used to develop new conceptual tools for managers. Those tools would be carefully developed, purposefully chosen, and rigorously applied. The third path, critical pluralism, represent an interweaving of the first two – and also adds the importance of critical reflection, open mindedness and humility.

Taken as a set, these three schools present a range of possibilities for engaging, thinking, and applying complexity in management. Importantly, Richardson's framing has implications that extend beyond complexity and systems thinking out to the broader range of management science. By bracketing our thinking as schools of thought we may engage each school in a more precise manner and so work more purposefully toward the advancement of management along multiple, intertwined, paths.

From an applied perspective, Richardson suggests that managers (and other members of organization) should, to some extent, become philosophers. That is to say he/she should spend some time contemplating deep questions from multiple perspectives. For a 'simple' example, every manager must make decisions based on what he/she believes to be true. Yet, in philosophy, the nature of truth is still an open question. For managers, developing a new understanding of truth might inspire an entire organization toward greater trust, improved communication, and a clearer sense of purpose. This does not make the managers' life any easier. Instead, it presents a new challenge for managers to find the openness needed to address deep questions and the courage to do so in humility and collaboration with others.

Chapter 4

Decision Integrity and Second Order Cybernetics is the chapter by Anthony Hodgson. This readable and thought-provoking work offers timely insights into decision making theory. Hodgson addresses the difficult issue of decision making from a nonlinear perspective in a profound way. First, he revisits von Foerster's idea that the only decisions we can make are those that are actually about undecidable questions. Because, in a sense, the easy decisions have already been made for us by our way of framing them.

Then, Hodgson introduces the rich idea of "decision integrity." This approach requires that the decision maker should understand the relationship of learning to deciding, as well as addressing important ethical concerns. The discussion of decision integrity includes an investigation into uncertainty and risk, as well as "integration." This last idea requires that the decider must expand her approach to include the bigger picture, rather than the most immediate concern.

The idea of looking at the "big picture" is not only about gathering more information. There are also special, temporal, and structural concerns to consider in the light of cybernetic feedback and understanding of systemic relationships. The big picture approach has intriguing implications for practice. For example, if a manager faces a simple decision, the immediate implication is that he should expand his understanding of the broader implications until he crosses the boundaries of any objective framework and experiences the decision as difficult or impossible.

Anthony's many, wonderfully interwoven, ideas are integrated and more easily understood through the use of a mathematical language based on Spencer-Brown's laws of form. This symbolism can be used to describe the structure of undecidable questions and the relationship between the decider and the decision field. This understanding opens the door for insights into self-reference, "second order management" and a variety of challenging and useful opportunities for practical application.

Chapter 5

Most managers seem to work from a perspective of Cartesian reduction. Such management often involves the use of simple, linear, models such as the classic organizational chart. In this chapter, Donald C. Mikulecky shows how this approach is ultimately ineffective.

He begins with a historical narrative that touches on important concepts of complexity, cybernetics, and biology. Usefully, he includes a particular focus on long-undervalued insights from Robert Rosen, particularly the idea that every organization has a metabolism and is, to some extent, self-repairing. This rich collection of concepts and insights are combined to challenge the reductive philosophythat has trapped managers in the Cartesian mode of thought.By updating ourphilosophical foundations, Mikulecky suggests a path towards more complete understanding, and more effective management practices.

While all managers create mental models, Mikuleckyeffectively argues that the habit of Cartesian reduction has led managers to "manage the model" rather than manage the real complex system in which they are embedded. Where simple modelsare used to identify simple cause and effect, no organization is really that simple. The simpler the model used by the manager, the more the manager loses in terms of his or her ability to manage effectively.

This author builds on Rosen's work in theoretical biology to investigate how an understanding of complex causality may be used to help us understand a system more effectively than using linear causality. To advance this conversation, Mikulecky notes the importance of using multiple forms of Aristotelian causality. This approach encourages managers to avoid asking the reductionist question of, "How?" that leads to answers that are simple, linear, and inaccurate. Instead, readers are shown the importance of asking, "Why?" that leads to richer, more complex, and more accurate understanding of complex causal relationships.

Advancing "relational systems theory," this chapter suggests a more effective approach is for managers to identify the complex causal relationships as a way to understand and manage the real system more effectively. Managers who attempt to "manage the model" instead of the real complex system may find themselves inhibiting the effective functioning of the organization.

Chapter 6

Holger Schiele and Stefan Krummaker take case study research to an impressive new level in their chapter on Consortial Benchmarking. In this, the authors describe their participation in a process of academic and managerial collaboration for benchmarking best practices in business. There are four steps to this process: Preparation (the forming an academic-industry consortium), Kick-off workshop (where academics present relevant theory, the consortium chooses what firms to be studied, both sides create questionnaire), Benchmark visits (the members of the consortium visit firms, conduct interviews, share insights), and Final meeting (collate and discuss results and prepare final report). The key distinguishing feature of consortial benchmarking is that practitioners are involved as co-researchers, not just as objects of analysis.

This is an important new approach with major implications in several areas. First, in response to calls for more engagement between academic and business circles, this chapter provides an example that scholars and practitioners should both follow. And, importantly, this process will result in benefits for all participants. Practitioners can expect to improve their business operations without being trapped in obscure and abstract academic theory. Academicians will also benefit as they can expect, through their participation, to acquire sufficient material for multiple publications. Also, the opportunity presents itself for both sides to use scholar-practitioners to facilitate the process because they, as high-level consultants, speak the language of academia as well as the language of business.

Second, this chapter is goes beyond answering the call for more and better theory. These authors explain a better process for building that theory. On a deeper level, the opportunity also exists for creating more complex theory – grounded in a new paradigm of conscious and purposeful collaboration between business and academia. Third, Holger and Stefan point the way for academia to develop theory that is more relevant to business. And, this process results in the creation of theory that is more likely to work in practice.

Importantly, this chapter sets a standard for "next generation" case study research by overcoming many of the biases and limitations of existing case study methodology.

Chapter 7

Recognizing the complex and systemic nature of disruptive organizational change, Marianne W. Lewis writes on the Systemic Paradoxes of Organizational Change. Her interesting and effective approach employs metatriangualtion – the use of multiple lenses to better understand a complex situation.

Lewis applies these lenses in a case study analysis to investigate the implementation of Advanced Manufacturing Technology (AMT). In an excellent example of this kind of metatheoretical approach, she describes that change through four separate lenses and identifies a common theme between them – paradox. It should be noted at this point, that paradox is a foundational concept of systems thinking, as may be illustrated by the relationship between stability and change. So, in identifying and investigating paradox, Marianne is conducting an important exploration at the core of our science.

At this point, some authors might be satisfied to conclude their chapter with some quip about the universe being founded on paradox; Lewis, however, does not stop here. Moving boldly forward, she presents a compelling metaframework for understanding organizational change in terms of multiple paradoxes (cognitive, action, and institutional). Further, Marianne provides a useful description of management practices that will support these change efforts.

This chapter is written with great clarity, nuance and insight. And, while not neglecting personal reflection, is written in perfect academic form. Finally, this chapter provides readers with suggestions for future research. One important direction is found in the difference between linear change theories, and change theories of plurality and paradox. These suggestions open the door for further innovation and advancement in the theory and practice of organizational change.

Chapter 8

The engagingly written and provocative chapter by Mark G. Edwards notes the failure of corporate management, and strives to provide a useful guide for management theorists interested in purposefully and effectively advancing their science. Citing the need for better metatheory as a prerequisite for the development of better theory, Mark uses a metatheoretical discourse to gain a clearer view of management theory. He describes four general forms of transformational management theory – as that theory suggests groundbreaking, whole-system change. The pre-conventional form is seen as primarily egocentric and focused on top-down management methods. Conventional management theory is similarly top-down, but the focus has shifted to an organizational-centric view. Post conventional management is framed as community-centric and employing bottom-up philosophies of change. Finally, integrative forms of management theory are suggested as glocal-centric and reciprocal between top and bottom (and other areas).

Importantly, Mark steps out of the either-or debate between the benefits of self vs. organization, or top-down vs. bottom-up theories of management. And, in doing so, transcends those debates to integrate and extend the extremes by looking through the metatheoretical lens of relationality.

This broad and radical reframing of management theory will be very useful to scholars studying corporate social responsibility, spiritual leadership, ethics, sustainability, and more. His collection of ideas, some necessarily abstract, provides an extensive list of concepts and definitions that management scholars will find very useful in framing their own investigations. Edwards' chapter is more purposefully metatheoretical than most in this book. And, as such, provides a useful guide for scholars interested in exploring the newly revived (and more rigorously applied) metatheoretical conversation.

Chapter 9

In Thomas Kuhn's influential "Structure of Scientific Revolutions," he suggests that a paradigm revolution is one where there is a major improvement in theory and practice. This kind of shift is as large as the difference between Newton and Einstein, or between Ptolemy and Copernicus. Following this idea, some scholars (and some popular management authors) claim that their work represents a paradigmatic revolution of Kuhnian proportions. Despite these claims, studies have shown more failure than success in business process reengineering (BPR), total quality management (TQM), and other methods and theories. This contradiction between claims of effective theory and the limitation of actual results has led to a loss of legitimacy for the social sciences in general and to management programs in particular.

These specious claims are possible for three reasons. First, because Kuhn did not describe exactly how much change constitutes a revolution. Second, because Kuhn focused on the ability of objective empirical analysis to advance a paradigm, rather than the structure of theory for that purpose. This chapter explores the structure of theory as an indicator for paradigm revolution and so provides a reliable frame of reference for future claims.

Another issue is the question of comparability between theories of physics and theories of management. Importantly, this chapter finds that theories of physics and theories of management are legitimately comparable if we focus on the structure of those theories as determined by the level of interrelationship between co-causal propositions. This is an important consideration because we have no theories in the social sciences that can be unequivocally described as "revolutionary." Therefore, to determine what constitutes a legitimately revolutionary structure of theory in the social sciences, we must analyze theories from physics to understand how they evolved toward revolutionary status.

Having identified the common ground between social and physical science, this chapter investigates the structure of theory by applying "propositional analysis" to determine the formal robustness of a set of theories spanning 1,500 years of history. The results show that increasing formal robustness seems to be a useful predictor of paradigm revolution. This, in turn, suggests that scholars who are interested in developing revolutionary theories should develop theories with a high level of formal robustness. Further, these results suggest that practitioners may be able to choose the more effective theory from among a set of theories based on the robustness of the theory. While there is certainly room for additional studies, this chapter has profound implications for the advancement of management science toward true paradigmatic revolution.

Chapter 10

Gianfranco Minati begins by taking note of some fundamentals of complexity theory including logical openness, cybernetics, coherence, and a constructivist approach that is a refreshing contrast to the objectivist approach. He sees human social systems as multiple systems or collective beings that are generated by human elements simultaneously interacting in different ways.

To manage complexity, Minati, presents his approach of Dynamic uSAge of Models (DYSAM). Usefully, DYSAM is a meta-approach that should be of great use to scholars investigating complex systems because it provides a framework for integrating approaches, models, and theories. The goal of DYSAM is to represent every aspect of the system at all of its levels.

Rather than investigating the changing values of existing systems, DYSAM relates to thc acquisition of properties that may then exhibit those changing values. In Minati's chapter, this approach is used to gain new insights into growth, development, sustainability, non-reductionist management techniques, and emergence.

Among other insights, Minati suggests that the study of management, and management theory, should not be limited to reductivist models. For example, a simulation that seeks to model only how agents optimise a single condition would be understood as far too limited to derive the kind of revolutionary insights needed to obtain quantum leaps in the field of management science. Minati's suggestions have profound implications for simulation modelling; and, they imply important new directions for the broader community of management scholars. Further theoretical developments relate to modelling processes of emergence by using meta-structures and meta-structural analysis.

Chapter 11

Maurice I. Yolles presents a deep and challenging exploration of knowledge cybernetics. His approach begins with the ideas of Stafford Beer, and adds the insights from Eric Schwarz. Maurice then extends those ideas to create a more complete model of socially viable systems (SVS) – based on the idea of circular causality, and capable of modeling more complex social relationships than previously possible. His model is then applied as a social frame of reference to understand organizational patterning, personality type, and knowledge profiling.

Maurice shifts the conversation on knowledge cybernetics from one of epistemology to one of ontology – an important step. And, in the process, extends and deepens Beer's viable systems model (VSM) developing a lateral ontology (where a systems is understood as a contextual domain consisting of sub-contextual domains or sub-systems) and transverse ontology (relating to emergence and higher-order control of the system) to better understand and redefine the paradigm and develop new tools for analyzing organizations.

Importantly, this new model can be applied to understand a variety of system pathologies that might be found within an organization. Pathologies that might pass unrecognized, even in collaborative change processes. Some applications of knowledge cybernetics have been applied to create successful empirical studies in organizational coherence, organizational pathology, and cultural mapping. Therefore, researchers should realize that this is a well-developed model and, as such, should be applied and tested in research projects. One approach might be to apply this model to case studies, and later move into fieldwork. Testing this model provides an excellent opportunity for researchers seeking to make their mark on the academic world.

Chapter 12

Alexander Riegler presents a new look at an old theory. Recognizing some shortcomings in our current understanding of evolution, he outlines a specifically Batesonian view of evolution. For example, where a "fitness landscape" relates to the optimization of an organism by increasing levels of fit, an "epigenetic landscape" serves to illustrate a developmental pathways for the organism, based on the interrelationships within the DNA. These pathways are understood as purposeful – a more useful description than "random mutation."

In contrast to the traditional understanding of evolution guided by external forces of selection, Dr. Riegler investigates how a cybernetic theory of evolution suggests that evolution is channeled by internal constraints based on the reciprocal dependencies of the genetic material.

For management theory, importantly, if we understand evolution as occurring only through external influences, we may transfer that point of view to organizations. Such a view might suggest that a work-team's ability for creativity, evolution, and change is influenced only by some external force – a manager imposing his will on the team. Instead, by understanding evolution as occurring because of interrelationships between bits of genetic material, we may gain new insights into how the cybernetic, self-organizing, interactions of employees, supports creativity, and change.

Indeed, by gaining the ability to understand developmental paths, we may gain the ability to predict the development of a team, or an organization.

Chapter 13

Thomas Hansson takes a new approach to the question of human agency with an investigation into the nature of human interaction in organizations. Where other theories present confusing views, (such as Vygotsky's stages of human development, ideas around learning objects, and general action theory), He identifies how self-management, self-awareness, and professional thinking combine to develop new systemic views for understanding the interrelationships between individuals and groups. An important part of his approach is avoiding a dualistic point of view (for example, where increasing the agency of a manager can only occur at the expense of the employees). And, instead, looking at the manager and the employees as working in a dialectical relationship – one that is generative.

Dr. Hansson finds support for these views by applying an innovative research technique involving a facilitated group working both live and networked, so the researcher can capture interactions as well as reflections. He investigates the combination of individual and social influences to develop a new theory of learning object creation. Importantly, he finds that they are created in a purposeful way as well as non-purposefully. These insights into social construction shine a new light onto an age-old question – and open the door for a new path of investigation.

Chapter 14

František Čapkovič uses Petri nets to develop metamodelling insights into multi agent systems. He considers multiple levels of interactions of agents, their interfaces, and the related environment. He presents examples from inter-personal cooperation, inter-organizational negotiations, supervisor-system relationships, supervised-agents, and relationships in an environment of limited resources. This last (limited resources) is of particular importance, as limited resources will limit productivity and is often a cause of conflict. His results suggest opportunities for understanding paths for avoiding conflict and improving productivity in a wide variety of situations.

Chapter 15

Kyarash Shariari takes on an impressive challenge – to improve our ability to predict the accuracy of models. He shows how alternative approaches to prediction (deterministic and probabilistic) are limited. His approach looks at the model parameters as, "...time-varying but bounded variables, which are characterized by an interval of real numbers. Since the model parameters are intervals, the predicted system's response at any instant is not anymore a real number but an interval of real numbers. The set of predicted intervals at different instances generates a tube through time called *wrapping envelope*." This innovative metamodelling approach can be used to identify (and so limit) modeling error. In short, he opens the door for the creation of more effective models.

Chapter 16

Nicholas Nechval, Konstantin Nechval, Maris Purgailis, and Uldis Rozevskis combine their creative and mathematical talents to investigate the problem of "subset selection" (or, variable selection) – that arises when attempting to model the relationship between a topic of interest and the multiple, potential explanatory variables. This kind of problem is common in many decision-making or strategic planning situations where there is no easy answer; indeed, there are multiple possible answers with no way to be sure which one might be best.

These authors submit new, simple, variable selection criteria. Their ambitious goal is to select the smallest number of decision-making criteria that can be used without losing **any** explanatory power. Their approach is tested with chemical processes, manpower allocation, housing prices, corporate profitability, supervisor performance, and more. The potential importance of this approach should be evident to anyone who has had to make a difficult decision.

ALTERNATIVE ORDERS

You, the reader, may want to pick and choose among these chapters, read one or two sections, or read the book cover-to-cover. Alternatively, depending on your interests, you may want to consider reading these chapters in one of many possible sequences. Here are some alternative foci for reading this book. These are, of course, mere starting suggestions and readers are encouraged to blaze their own trails!

If you are more interested in cybernetics, particularly at a higher level of thought, you might be more interested in chapters 4, 11, and 12. Chapter 5 might also be of interest. If your interest is more focused on systems theory, the chapters of greater interest might be 3, 10, and 12. Of additional interest might be 1 and 11. For those who are interested in metatheory, chapters 8 and 9 will be of greatest interest; followed by 7 and 3. Some have an interest in the logical/mathematical approach, while others feel uncomfortable while reading numbers and formulae. For the former, I would recommend chapters 4, and 10 - while chapters 14, 15, and 16 are highly mathematical. For the latter, chapters 1, 2, 3, 6, 7, 8, and 11. Chapters 5 and 9 are somewhere in the middle.

On the subject of scale, chapter 2 is focused at the level of neurology and decision-making while chapter 5 relates to the individual decision maker. Chapters 6 and 10 address the organizational level while 4 and 6 look at relationships between organizations. Chapter 11 spans individual learning and organizational diagnosis, while chapter 1 reaches from individual to global-scale systems. Chapters 12,13, and 14 provide innovative view across levels. Finally, 3, 8, 9, 12 are focused more on concepts, theory, and metatheory.

There are a few, more tightly focused, topics that may also be of interest to readers. Again, these are meant as starting-places for exploration; you will find many related ideas in other chapters (for such is the nature of systems sciences). The failure of classical management theory is implicit through much of the book. Some additional focus on this topic may be found in chapters 1, 5, 8, and 9.

Those who are interested in Knowledge Management you may want to begin with 1, 2, and 11. The limits of knowledge are noted in 3, and 4, while decision-making is an important part of 2, and 4. A closely related topic is the investigation of the decision maker as an integral part of the decision environment; this idea is discussed in 4, and 5. If you are interested in the highly intriguing idea that we may understand information as a form of energy, you should read 2 and 12.

You may have an interest in the idea of evolution. If so, chapter 12 provides an intriguing cybernetic view of evolution. Chapter 1 discusses the purposeful evolution of organizations while 9 investigates the evolution of theory. Finally, is your interest is in growth and development, you will find interesting readings in chapter 1, 2 and 6; and an interesting challenge in chapter 3. Some additional ideas are suggested in chapters 10 and 11.

These groupings should not be taken as a suggestion that these authors are in full agreement on all of the concepts in their chapters. Indeed, their approaches, ontologies, and epistemologies may be very different. Therein lies the opportunity for new insights to emerge and new opportunities for present themselves.

CONTRIBUTION AND IMPACT

This book will impact management science, cybernetics, systems theory, computer modeling, and the nascent field of metatheory. Additionally, this book is expected to impact research methodology and, if practitioners are able to rise to the challenge, there may be meaningful impacts in the practical application of these theories. As may be inferred, this book also supports a mission to accelerate the advancement of the social sciences. This book has a strong "focus on the future" to suggest innovation directions that will inform the work of scholars for the next decade or more. Metatheory is the "new world" for the 21st century. Not, I hasten to add, a continent inhabited by indigenous people doomed to be exploited; instead, this is a new collaborative world, waiting to emerge.

Among these chapters are some ideas that are fairly straightforward, and others that are quite complex. The reader who looks at those complex ideas and thinks, "this is too difficult to use in research or to be applied in practice" is asked to consider one last challenging idea; the idea that such complex approaches may be necessary if we are to develop theories and methodologies for practical management. That is to say, simple theories may be effectively applied to improve our understanding the physical world. For example as Ohm's law is used to understand the interrelationship between (only) three aspects of volts, amps, and ohms. It may be, in contrast, that a truly useful theory of the social sciences will require dozens of aspects. This is a challenging concern, to be sure. However, we are scientists; we are here to be challenged.

CONCLUSION

In this project, it has been my honor as editor to open a space, an attractor, where authors are allowed and encouraged to reach their highest level of intellectual expression and advance our interrelated fields of study. This includes presenting their most innovative ideas in the writing style that best expresses their personal voices. As editor, I am privileged to support these authors and their pursuit of bold insights that serve to advance our understanding of management science. While every effort has been made to maintain high academic standards, authors have not been required to fit every academic convention of style. This emphasis of boldness over baby-steps – of adherence to high standards over adherence to a standard style – is part of what makes this book a worthy read. We are moving consciously toward a revolution in management science – and it is not possible for the paradigm to remain the same while undergoing change.

These chapters represent a variety of epistemologies, ontologies and methodologies. The reader must decide among this "team of rival ideas" which are the most worthy of advancement and adoption. I encourage the reader to enjoy the interplay of ideas, both complimentary and contradictory; because it is that relationship between ideas that opens the human mind to creative insights. Therefore, in the same sense that this book, as a project, opened a space for authors to develop new ideas, the chapters presented here generate openings for the emergence of powerful new ideas in the minds and conversations of the readers.

Steven E. Wallis, PhD
Foundation for the Advancement of Social Theory, USA
Institute for Social Innovation, Fielding Graduate University, USA

Section 1
Applications in Practice and Theory

Chapter 1
Emerging the Evolutionary Corporation in a Sustainable World:
Toward a Theory Guided Field of Practice

Alexander Laszlo
Syntony Quest, USA

Kathia C. Laszlo
Tecnológico de Monterrey, Mexico

ABSTRACT

This chapter explores the emerging direction of business strategy as expressed by the theoretical construct of evolutionary advantage. It begins with a backward look at the major forms of business knowledge as they developed over the last century, turning subsequently to consideration of mainstream frameworks for strategic analysis, and offering, as a compelling alternative, the emerging notions of evolutionary development and it's corollary, evolutionary leaning. Through application of the praxis known as Evolutionary Systems Design, it is shown how an organization may cultivate strategies for sustainable success. Such strategies, based on a redefinition of that which constitutes success, foster dynamics of organizational change that reinforce life affirming, future oriented and opportunity increasing patterns of change over positions of power for both internal and external clients. The implication, therefore, is that this theoretical framework forms the emerging basis for sustainable value creation in the context of twenty-first century organizational dynamics.

INTRODUCTION

The tides of change constantly surface new currents in the world of business. The confluence of ecological, economic and energetic crises that have (de) formed contemporary civilization at the beginning of this century herald the end of the Era of Mindless Waste and the business leadership practices associated with it. Not even the notions of *Sustainability* and *Sustainable Development* are up to the task of providing a coherent roadmap for a globally interconnected and interdependent civilization. In theory, both these concepts are systemic and relational, but in contemporary mainstream business practice

DOI: 10.4018/978-1-61520-668-1.ch001

they tend to be employed in ways that are neither *systemic* nor *relational*. Our hypothesis for why this is the case is that they are still built on the worldviews and dominant paradigms of the past century — seeking to 'fix' situations and 'solve' problems — and therefore are already hopelessly out of date. At best, such notions serve management theory as guideposts for the prevention of business induced global civilizational collapse of the sort described by Jared Diamond in his 2005 book on *Collapse* (see also Tainter, 1990). However, it is precisely a failure to contemplate the systemic and relational aspects of business that most impact (and stand to be impacted by) the interdependency of the grids that hold our world together: from our energy grid to our financial grid to our communication grid. It is the interlocked nature of these grids that creates the confluence of crises and the implication of collapse.

Contemporary business theory often tends to foment Sustainability As Usual (SAU) by providing action frameworks that do little beyond bolstering these grids given the unconditional dependence of our societies upon them. Such orientations do nothing to create new dynamics in business and business leadership; new ways of fostering the legacy by which we will be remembered, of stewarding the abundance of our living environment, of relating considerately to each other, and of creating new habits of mind and heart. Beyond sustainability lies the domain of life affirming, future creating, opportunity increasing leadership; of learning to embody new ways of thinking, doing, making and being that we incorporate in our essence so as to enact a new narrative of life. For example, The Natural Step framework developed by Karl-Henrik Robèrt (Robèrt, 1997) alludes to "the other side" of sustainability through the construct of the 'Resource Funnel' with increasing constraints heading into sustainability and increasing opportunity for thriving and abundance in an emergent phase beyond (van Gelder, 1998).

No longer is it sufficient to seek the static positional advantage offered by classical Porterian analysis in order for a corporation to develop with dignity. In fact, it is not enough even to learn to read the patterns of change that shape the organization in it's environment (and which in return are shaped by it). Without a doubt, such business acumen is essential to contemporary change management leadership in the business world, but unless an organization is dedicated to evolutionary value creation, it's ability to navigate the currents of change in life-affirming directions will be compromised. This chapter explores the conceptual bases evolutionary value creation and the principles and perspectives required to bring it into management practice.

BACKGROUND

This book is testament to the complexity of business challenges in the 21st century. Societies all around the world are currently experiencing a period of rapid and extensive transformation. The signs of change are pervasive, and the rate of change is itself changing and accelerating, speeding contemporary societies toward a critical threshold of stability (*C.f.*, Diamond, 2005) and engulfing the corporation in a confusing blur of strategic choice. Global flows of information, energy, trade, and technology are swept up in massive economic reforms and political reorientations with the result of creating a disorienting and disrupting vortex of political and economic change on both local and global levels.

Humanity is poised to transit to a new kind of society, one that is as different from the society we leave behind as the grasslands were from the caves or the settled villages of antiquity from life in nomadic tribes. However, the countervailing tendencies in this dynamic are strong given the atavistic attraction for those in positions of political and economic power to keep things just as they are. And yet, as a species, we find ourselves in the position of conscious choice — of being able to leave behind the geo-political system of nationally based industrial societies created at the dawn of the first industrial revolution in favor of an interconnected socio-economic system created by the growing impact of information, the globalization of business and government, and the ever greater demands on an increasingly over-burdened and fragile planetary biome. All that is needed is a new vision of the world, different premises of what constitutes sustainable value creation, and a more socially, environmentally, *and* financially attuned basis of value exchange.

A World in Transition

Patterns of existence have seldom changed in any single lifetime as significantly as they are changing now. Today, anyone who has reached mid-life will have witnessed the aftermath of a world war, the coming of the information and communications age, the shift from a bi-polar superpower dominated world to a uni-polar hyperpower dominated world to an emerging multi-polar patchwork of regional power bases, and with it the opportunity to replace a world dominated by the polarization of military-might with one led by an economy with intensifying 'coopetition' for information, technologies, and markets. However, this opportunity has its dangers, and they are only now starting to be both incontrovertible and ineluctable.

There are three main dimensions of change that characterize the global transition (for more on this concept, see Korton, 2006; Meadows, 1999; and Macy, 2006). One is the dimension of communication or information processing capacity; the second is the dimension of business and government in the expression of individual and collective self-organization; the third is the dimension of planetary life support systems that are being steamrolled by the pressures of a burgeoning humanity. And like it or not, at the dawn of the 21st century we're experiencing 3D change with all three dimensions going global as the rules of the game that define the nature of power, wealth and sustainability change and become redefined.

Power can no longer be legitimized simply by the authority of an office or organization, and wealth is shifting away from such tangible items as gold, money, and land. The emerging basis for both power and wealth is more flexible and intangible than ownership of position or of material; it is being formed around the power and ownership of know-how, know-why, and care-why — in short, of knowledge management. The transition toward a knowledge-based society is felt in all domains of existence — in politics and in business, and even in private life. The impacts are due to the way we are now accessing, processing, and transmitting information. Indeed, the fact that information can be so quickly transmitted and processed from anywhere in the world to anywhere else has changed the horizons of time and space in the context of our social interactions.

Along with the rise in information processing capacity, we are witnessing a rise in business enterprises and international and intergovernmental organizations that span the globe. As a matter of fact, the globalization of business (that has developed in direct relation to the globalization of communication and information processing technologies) has done the most to change the way we interact as companies, nations, and regions. Until the last few decades, governments were the principal, if not the only, actors on the global scene. Today, things are quite different. The approximately 180 national governments and roughly 10,000 international or intergovernmental organizations are joined by a thousand or more business corporations as major global players. The fact is that the leading domestic industries of the 1950s have grown into the multinationals of the 1960s and '70s and the transnationals and globals of the '80s and '90s. Since growth is no longer the new frontier for business or government (unless we choose either political parasitism or corporate cannibalism as empire expanding tactics), new dimensions of progress in the 21st century will, of necessity, be along the lines of sustainable development, or more precisely, of evolutionary development.

The actual extent of globalization in the business world is seldom fully recognized. The confluence of production, commerce, the technologies of control and information, and the changing political scene have provided major industrial and financial enterprises with the opportunity and the means to span the world. The globalization of leading manufacturing enterprises was accomplished by the globalization of trade and service companies and paralleled by financial markets operating "round the clock and round the world." The exchange market has become the most global of all business sectors, with worldwide rates, instantaneous electronic banking and arbitrage, and a daily turnover estimated easily in excess of US$700 billion (E. Laszlo, 2002).

The global economic depression of the last years of the first decade of the 21st century surfaces another systemic aspect of the globalization of business and finance: that of the inherent fragility of complex dynamic systems that continue to complexify without sufficient means of diversification and integration. What was hailed as a "global economic crisis" in 2008 and 2009 was little more than the full expression of a crisis that had characterized most of the world for many prior decades. People of less developed nations and even of the socio-economically disenfranchised portions of over-developed nations have lived with the crisis as a fact of life for years. It is only when the vested interests of the commercially ruling elite of the world are impinged upon that the situation is finally recognized as a crisis. They tend to be buffered from the misery of the majority by insular media exposure and a distancing of worldviews and life experiences. However, in a world of such highly coupled interdependence as the one in which we currently live, insularity is the functional equivalent of blindness. Taking a big-picture perspective, Daniel Pinchbeck describes what happened to humanity in scathing terms:

Electronic culture created soulless replacements for connective rituals — television supplanted tribal legends told around the fire; "fast food" consumed in distraction took the place of a shared meal. We substituted matter for Mater, money for mother's milk, objects for emotional bonds. (Pinchbeck, 2006, p. 322)

Such a strident admonition should not be taken as a condemnation of humanity nor even of capitalism but rather as a warning lest the excesses of consumerism take a greater toll on our civilizational composure. The challenges of information and knowledge management have become global, not only for business and government, but for education, extended families, and any sort of geographically disperse community. The challenges come both in terms of the volume and relevance of information among those who have ready access to the increasing number of channels of information flows with ever increasing width and flow rates, and to those who do not have ready access to these major arteries and the pressure this puts on a global civilization to maintain cohesion. Such issues relate to the long-term sustainability of current patterns of production and consumption and spill over into deeper questions of planetary well-being.

3RD GENERATION KNOWLEDGE MANAGEMENT

There is little question as to the fact that today, more than ever, business is a key shaper of the emerging global society. In this context, the relevance of knowledge and the need for approaches to manage it have become critically apparent in the business world. In fact, in a survey of chief

Figure 1. Business knowledge for evolutionary corporations (Adapted from Laszlo and Laszlo, 1997)

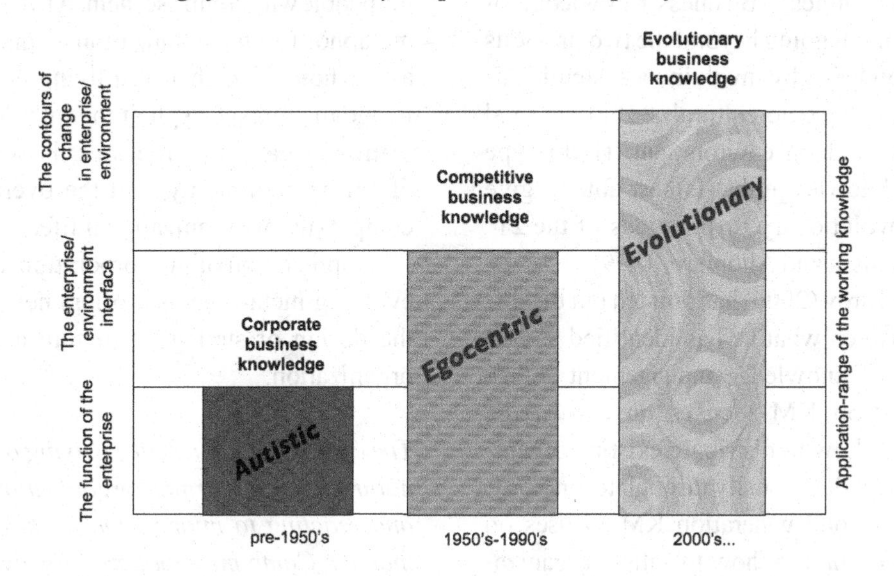

executives, knowledge management was put second on their "must do" list after globalization (TFPL, 1999, p. 3).

Knowledge has always been relevant for good business performance. However, the kind of knowledge relevant to the development and maintenance a healthy competitive edge has changed over time (see Figure 1). During the first half of the 20th century, successful companies focused on improving their internal processes since production and managerial operations needed to become more efficient. The principles of Scientific Management, as developed by Frederick W. Taylor and disseminated in his widely influential 1911 book by that name, provide an example of this type of Business Knowledge of the First Kind — what we call *corporate business knowledge.* But increases in competition and expansion of the economy made it necessary to focus beyond the enterprise itself in order to learn more about one's market, one's industry, one's consumers. This is Business Knowledge of the Second Kind — *competitive business knowledge* that is contextual and that uses benchmarks and best practices as references points for "dog eat dog" strategic positioning. The work of Michael Porter on competitive advantage is a typical example of business knowledge of the second kind with greatest impact in the 1980's. These two kinds of business knowledge tend to use metaphors that refer to business as a jungle (i.e., survival of the fittest; eat or be eaten), warfare (i.e., war room strategy, guerrilla tactics), and the machine (i.e., efficiency and efficacy at any cost; humans as replaceable parts) (Solomon & Hanson, 1983), all of which derive from a reductionistic scientific paradigm.

The challenges and opportunities emerging from a rapidly changing global environment demand that we go beyond these conceptions. Knowledge, and the processes of its acquisition, generation, distribution and utilization, has become the main source of value creation in the world today. But science, as a knowledge creation enterprise, is itself evolving and transcending reductionistic and mechanistic conceptions. For this reason, it is important that contemporary knowledge management be grounded in the most recent scientific thought — in particular, in the sciences of complexity (such as chaos theory and complexity theory, and general evolution theory and dynamical systems theory) which provide the foundations for a new understanding of how complex dynamic systems *evolve*. What we see emerging now is an *evolutionary business knowl-*

edge that constitutes a Business Knowledge of the Third Kind in going beyond the two previous types of knowledge by involving a systemic understanding of the socio-cultural and bio-physical dynamics of the global environment. It is this type of business knowledge that is best able to give rise to the evolutionary corporations of the 21st century (Natrasss and Altomare, 1999).

Mark McElroy (2000) has pointed out the differences between what he has identified as two generations of knowledge management (KM). First generation KM focuses on *knowledge sharing* — on how to distribute existing organizational knowledge, usually through technology. In contrast, second generation KM focuses on *knowledge creation* — how to satisfy organizational needs for new knowledge, usually through processes of learning and value creation. In other words, first generation KM is about imitation (focusing on standards and benchmarks) while second generation KM is about innovation. This second generation is linked to the convergence that McElroy noted between first generation KM, organizational learning, and complexity theory as applied to business: all three areas have individual developmental paths but they share similar and complementary goals. And as Senge (1993) and others have pointed out, the process of learning has become one of the main sources of sustainable competitive advantage.

However, it is a particular mode of learning that is especially valuable for knowledge creation and innovation: learning through collaboration, which in the business world has been adapted and applied as "organizational learning." The view of the organization as a machine in which humans are replaceable "resources" deadens the human spirit — the emotive, intuitive, and moral aspects of being — from organizational life and assumes this corporate machine to be a static and sterile system. And yet, the fact is that organizations are human activity systems (Checkland, 1981) that, like any other form of community or society, reflect the purposes, values, expectations and feelings of the people who comprise them. A more appropriate metaphor for the organization — and for society as a whole — is that of a living ecosystem: an image that makes explicit the interdependencies of multi-organismic processes, the sentient nature of life in community, and the overall dynamic complexity of organizational life.

Appreciation of the corporation as a complex evolving meta-organism offers new insights for the design of strategy, structure and processes organization.

The company that acts like a living organism will naturally be a learning organization absorbing and reacting to information in an evolutionary manner. Companies that are conceived of as machines, rather than living organisms, are unlikely to be aware of external shifts in public opinion or be sensitive enough to their key relationships, because they will not be sensitive to the unexpected" (McIntosh, Leipziger, Jones, & Coleman, 1998, p. 74-75).

This appreciation manifests as corporate citizenship (McIntosh, Leipziger, Jones, & Coleman, 1998), a concept that has gained weight as a performance benchmark among global enterprises. It is an important illustration of how Business Knowledge of the Third Kind includes issues of socio-ecological responsibility in corporate strategies that ensure thriving and robust business ecosystems. We are not talking about information for the sake of compliance, here; we are talking about knowledge for the purpose of innovation (for more on the subject of information and knowledge, meaning, and knowledge management, see Laszlo & Laszlo, 2002).

In a highly interconnected world, the field of knowledge management (KM) faces the challenge of making concrete and relevant contributions for the betterment of society and not only for promotion of competitive advantage for business. This involves a research agenda through which, first, KM can foster Business Knowledge of the Third

Figure 2. Evolving KM (knowledge management)

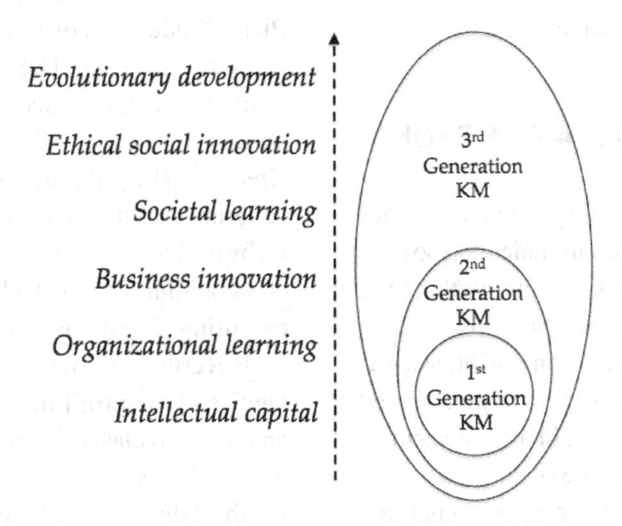

Kind for the expansion of a corporate citizenship agenda and the emergence of evolutionary learning corporations; and second, KM can make significant contributions for the creation of human, social, and environmental capital required for evolutionary development.

Departing from McElroy's descriptive scheme for defining first and second generation KM (McElroy, 2000), we have proposed a third generation of KM that is no longer descriptive, but rather, prospective (Laszlo & Laszlo, 2002). We suggest that KM involve an exploration of *what should be* presented as a provocative invitation to engage in the purposeful and conscious evolution of knowledge management as a future creating activity. This prospective and somewhat prescriptive suggestion responds to the need for ethical social innovation with explicit commitment to evolutionary development (see Figure 2).

Third generation KM is relevant both within and beyond the sphere of business. And yet, it is correlated with the need for Business Knowledge of the Third Kind to support the evolution of business, the development of strong corporate citizenship, and the emergence of thriving business ecosystems (K.C. Laszlo, 2003). Given that global business operations are changing the world, the idea is that this change be for the good.

Essentially, third generation KM is about the democratization of knowledge, about citizen involvement and the expansion of the boundaries of what traditionally has been considered education in order to give rise to an authentic learning society at both regional and global levels. It is not so much about the accumulation and application of knowledge through know-how anymore, but more about the creation of shared meaning through know-why and care-why. It is based on a new way of thinking, informed by a planetary ethic and a different way of living from what it is now favored by mass media commercialization. In the final analysis, KM has both the potential and the responsibility to contribute to the emergence of a sustainable global civilization. But is it the business of business to engage in this dimension of KM? Without a doubt, the answer is yes — provided business is considered a part of, rather than separate from, issues of our planetary well-being and global welfare. But before considering the big-picture implications and the long-term consequences of the role business plays in a world in transition, let's take a more in-depth look at how business is being affected, and stands to affect, the contemporary global macroshift.

FROM *BAU* TO *SAU* ... AND BEYOND

The fact that business is going global as our information processing and communication powers span the world is a necessary outgrowth of the linear evolution of consumer culture. To keep pace with the ever increasing extension and intensification of shopping lifestyles — now hypertrophied through the Internet — it would almost seem as though the universal objective of corporate marketing departments were to sell you something you don't yet know you need. Unfortunately, the question of How Much is Enough has become drowned out in the clutter of overstimulation. In a 1992 book by that name, Alan Durning notes that, "measured in constant dollars, the world's people have consumed as many goods and services since 1950 as all the previous generations put together" (Durning, 1992, p. 38). Clearly, there is no denying that the way of life under materialist consumer-based capitalism is wasteful. Durning (1992) calls on Victor Lebov who, in the years immediately following the end of the Second World War, commented on how

... our enormously productive economy ... demands that we make consumption our way of life, that we convert the buying and use of goods into rituals, that we seek our spiritual satisfaction, our ego satisfaction, in consumption. ... We need things consumed, burned, worn out, replaced, and discarded at an ever increasing rate. (Durning, 1992, p. 21-22)

Already in the 1950s, this pattern, this defining but defaming profile of the contemporary human being, emerged and caused Lebov and others to take pause. More than half a century later, some of us are *still* waking up to this reality, although many more of us are in deep (and usually highly remunerative) denial. Like Lebov and Durning, Pierre Pradervand of *Vivre Autrement,* has called for simpler living. The contribution of simpler living to the emergence of a new, more syntonious culture — one of the sort Paul Ray's Cultural Creatives (Ray, 2000) could bring forth — is a sobering yet vitalizing antidote to the ills brought on by ever more powerful information processing and communications technologies coupled with engulfing global business dynamics.

Nevertheless, to consider "competitive advantage" and the profit motive it supports as *ills* is anathema to classical management theory. But is it really heresy or is there more to it? What about the third dimension of the global transition mentioned earlier; ecological sustainability? All these facts and figures about the Global Problematique, with those "signs of change" that include new and disturbing phenomenon like acid rain, all sorts of pollution, disappearing habitats and with them, the extinction of species "at an alarming rate" — even the threat of globally decimating devastation from either accidental or purposeful misuse of the tens of thousands of today's actively armed weapons of mass destruction (be they biological, chemical, or nuclear) — are linked to the explosion of business and information in the last 200 years. In fact, it is the way business is conducted, and the way information is harnessed and put to use, that helps create these evolutionarily dissonant and unsustainable patterns of existence.

Brian Nattrass and Mary Altomare (1999) note that business, information, and environment can all get along — provided we get our act together:

The emerging conflict of humanity with the rest of the natural world need not be inevitable if we use our insight, muster our forces globally, and act now. A small yet growing number of leading business people from around the globe have heard and understood the warnings of our cultural look-outs, those scientists, shamans, and other people of wisdom, whose vision can pierce the mists of the future more clearly than most of us.

It is these perceptive business people who have made a remarkable discovery: if we align the business economy with the economy of nature, there are still great profits to be made — profits made in ways that enhance rather than endanger the future of life on Earth. (Nattrass & Altomare, 1999, p. 4)

According to Nattrass and Altomare, these new ways of aligning the business economy with the economy of nature, of enhancing the future of life on Earth, involve new business acumen:

It is no longer sufficient to be a smart organization, one that can scan the commercial environment, detect variations, and react accordingly. If we restrict ourselves to reacting to signals when it comes to human impact on the natural environment, we may well end up focusing our organizational resources just on minimizing the pain of irreversible damage. Our business organizations need to become conscious of the evolutionary role business plays in the future of the planet and to take responsibility for that role. (Nattrass & Altomare, 1999, p. 13)

So it seems that business need become conscious of the evolutionary role it play as change agent in our socio-cultural and bio-physical environments and as shaper of possible futures. Laszlo and Laugel (2000) stress that "seeing the whole and understanding the dynamics of change in complex situations is fast becoming a business imperative ... it requires being a good 'evolver'" (p. xiv). Leadership along these lines is taken "by declaring a future others may not see as possible, and get[ting] alignment in the organization so that actions forward that future" (Laszlo & Laugel 2000, p. 124). To gain this type of business acumen, old ideas about what constitutes good business practice need be reconsidered. For example, another aspect of interaction that is being redefined and even re-invented along the lines of "power" and "wealth" discussed earlier is the notion of what constitutes *success* in the business world. Corporate success, it would seem, is an unquestioned objective. Robert Theobald (1997) begins *Reworking Success* with the familiar cliché, "You cannot argue with success." For many, if a company is among the Fortune 500 or Global 2000 it is clearly successful, but even if it is a household name, we rarely consider what constitutes success, let alone how it is defined and measured.

Theobald (1997) points out that many people see corporate behavior as a serious national problem in the US. He presents data in which *only* 22% of those surveyed think that competition motivates corporate behavior, while 70% think greed is the motivating factor — a finding of the sort to which David Korten gave voice in a 2002 article called "From Mindless Greed to Civil Society: Restoring an ethical culture and challenging a world consumed with the love of money" (Korten, 2002). Business practices in the United States have been going through numerous changes in past decade ... from the rapid growth and subsequent crash of the dotcom bubble, to the scandals of Enron, Arthur Anderson and others, to terrorists attacks that crippled the US economy. Undoubtedly, success is not as simple a concept as used to be thought.

From a classical Darwinian perspective, the criteria by which to differentiate one corporation from another in terms of success would come down to which business showed evidence of an expanding market share, or a faster and more consistent rising stock price, or a larger profit margin. Under criteria such as these, the most financially profitable corporation with superior market domination would be seen as most successful.

But Darwin is dead and his theories, while never having been legitimately applied to the sphere of social dynamics, are now clearly no longer valid (Laszlo & Laszlo, 2009). The bottom line is that,

...a series of random genetic mutations is not likely to have produced all the complex species indicated

by observation and the fossil record within the time that was available for biological evolution on this planet. ... In any case, if random mutation and natural selection require more time to produce viable species than the fossil record indicates, then Darwin's theory, if not quite mistaken, is at least incomplete" (Laszlo, 1999, p, 50).

... in our day the consequences of social Darwinism go beyond armed aggression to the more subtle, but in some ways equally merciless, struggle of competitors in the marketplace. . . . States and entire populations are relegated to the role of clients and consumers and, if poor, dismissed as marginal factors in the equations that determine success in the global marketplace. (E. Laszlo, 2002, p. 51)

Fortunately, these equations are changing. Koestenbaum (in Labarre, 2000) points out that "an evolutionary transformation of who we are, how we behave, how we think, and what we value" (Labarre, 2000, p. 226) is necessary to resolve the paradox between business as usual (BAU) and the contemporary global challenges that call for social and environmental responsibility. He connects this evolutionary transformation to the basic human quest for meaning, purpose, and fulfillment which have been left behind in the mad dash by 'homo economicus' toward a mechanized nirvana. Unless such issues of purpose and meaning are addressed, people cannot make intelligent decisions come Monday morning — much less develop a long term strategy toward sustainability. Human depth makes business sense, he argues, and it is precisely the depth required to move to a broader perspective that advances the wellbeing of individuals, societies, ecosystems *and* future generations. "The more you understand the human condition, the more effective you are as a business person" (Labarre, 2000, p. 224). As the evolution of consciousness draws us ever more along the lines of 'homo universalis' (see Hubbard, 1998), Koestenbaum's framing expands such that the more we understand the interconnected nature of the universe, the more competent we are as shapers of sustainable and evolutionary organizations.

To a large extent, corporate citizenship is expressed through the framework of corporate social responsibility (CSR) and the increasingly refined metrics associated with it. Since this a business term specifically dedicated sustainability management (as distinct from sustainable management), it is worth being clear on what is meant by sustainability and sustainability management in order to get a better handle on CSR. To the rigorous thinker who seeks integrity between the theoretical contsructs of management and their practical application, the term sustainability management falls short of the systemic and relational issues at hand. These involve heart, spirit, creativity and innovation — not just management.

The term *sustainability stewardship* is a more life affirming, future creating and opportunity increasing expression. It is worth stipulating the meaning of this term as rigorously as possible without losing relevance to its ultimate applicability.

A process of development (individual, corporate, or societal) can be said to be socially and ecologically sustainable if it involves an adaptive strategy that ensures the evolutionary maintenance of an increasingly robust and supportive environment.

- *Sustainability stewardship* is the responsible caretaking and creative cultivation of resources — social, cultural, financial, and natural — to generate stakeholder value while contributing to the well-being of current and future generations of all beings.

This type of framework allows organizations to set objectives that identify the opportunities for increasing the dynamic stability and self-sufficiency of individual, community and societal interests. It would serve to indicate the areas of socio-economic potential that could be developed to the advantage of all the stakeholders involved — both human and non-human and both those who benefit from the system at present, as well as those who stand to benefit from the system in the future.

Management perspectives that truly address sustainability stewardship are systemic, regardless of the label we use for them or how they are popularly known. However, as Figure 3 illustrates, the sustainability learning curve in business and industry is a steep one. Most businesses are only at the 1st Stage of compliance with governmental laws and industry standards with regard to social justice and environmental responsibility. However, a sizable portion of businesses around the world — including transnationals and global organizations — prefer to pay the fines associated with non-compliance than to engage in what often appears to be more onerous and expensive changes to their operations. Nevertheless, it is fair to say that most organizations seek to comply with the law and this, therefore, represents business as usual (BAU) practices.

To move beyond compliance to the 2nd Stage on the sustainability learning curve, organizations must incorporate a business ethic that reflects a corporate consciousness built on conservation. To conserve resources, to protect both social and environmental wellbeing and keep them from further degradation, this needs be part of the vision and values statement of organizations that operate at the 2nd Stage. The shift to the 3rd Stage involves a further change in business consciousness; from conserving to restoring. When an organization views its business as inextricably involved in restoring living systems (from inner city neighborhoods to polluted rivers and lakes), it has reached the 3rd Stage on the sustainability learning curve. The 4th Stage implies an inflection. No longer are business strategies dedicated to making the best of what is; they are now oriented to changing relationships so that the full abundance of a community (be it human or natural — or both) be restored to levels of thriving that may have eroded or disappeared in recent history. This is the level of true sustainability — where the load place upon the biome in which an organization operates does not exceed its carrying capacity. However, many organizations that reach this stage on the sustainability learning curve do so with the same paradigmatic mindset that guides the operations based on Competitive Business Knowledge or even Corporate Business Knowledge (see Figure 1). As a result, they tend to be oriented just to bringing green products and services to market at a profit, regardless whether they are truly future oriented, life affirming or opportunity increasing. Much of the effort at this stage is dedicated to "solving the problems" of sustainability by providing "technological fixes" to non-systemic concerns.

The 5th Stage on the sustainability learning curve is definitely not the final stage. It is merely the last stage currently defined. To reach it, the organization must undergo yet a further intensification of consciousness. It must position itself as a creative force in the world, contributing to the increased vitality and robustness of the ecosystem in which it operates. The fuzzy guiding principles by which such organizations set their strategic compass involve being:

- **Future oriented.** This does not mean ignoring the past or disavowing tradition and heritage. Quite the contrary, in involves creating a coherent and integral path from past to future. But the point is that the destination is arrived at through innovation, not through seeking to recapture some glorious golden past of organizational success. Neither is it oriented to affirming or maintaining the status quo. Strategy is set with an evolutionary eye.
- **Life affirming.** This means that both the products and the processes of the organization are non-destructive of life and the ecosystem services upon which they depend. The organization does not engage in utilitarian strategies that sacrifice the interests

Figure 3. The sustainability learning curve

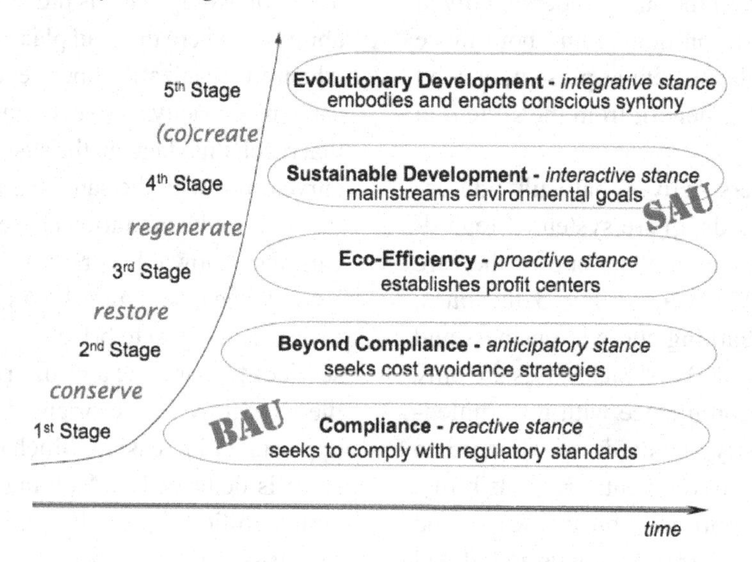

of a few for those of the many (or vice-versa, as is more common in actual practice). This ethic applies to dealings with both external as well as internal clients.

- **Opportunity increasing.** To the extent that business strategy creates more opportunity to have more opportunities, it can be said to be opportunity increasing. This builds directly on the work of Karl-Henrik Robèrt and The Natural Step framework that he developed (see Nattrass and Altomare, 1999). Rather than just leveling off both the demands on the natural environment created by business practices and the rate at which ecosystem services are being diminished in the hope of stabilizing human activity within sustainable parameters of the planet's carrying capacity, the idea is to operate in such a way as to create an ever more robust and supportive environment.

The sustainability learning curve represents a strategic path for business leadership to pursue value creation with integrity. The strategic vision it implies should not be limited by the horizon of the 5th Stage and notions of evolutionary development. This is merely the current event horizon of business theory on issues of sustainability and sustainable development. As we move further along this path, new horizons will open as deeper understanding of the systemic and relational complexity of sustainable stewardship emerge.

Solomon (1999) suggests that certain myths and metaphors about the roles of business present negative stereotypes that are commonly used not only by an unreflective consumer base, but also by strategically minded business people. A win/loose premise coupled with the profit motive have lead to a single bottom line criteria for measuring success: financial gains. Not any more, though. The emerging metric, an example of 3rd generation KM informed by Business Knowledge of the Third Kind, suggests a triple bottom line: financial profits, social profits, and environmental profits—equally considered and equally emphasized. To focus beyond the bottom line does not necessarily imply forgetting about the "profit motive." However, it does mean transcending it toward a mode of wealth creation that pursues personal, social and ecological gains in addition to financial results. Ultimately, "the gift of working for sustainability is its meaningfulness" (Paul Hawken in Nattrass & Altomare, 1999, p. 203). For organizations that begin to raise their sights to the horizon of corporate citizenship, success is a desirable pattern to be pursued more than a desirable end state to be obtained. As a result, corporate strategy is reformulated to include planning cycles that extend somewhat beyond the next fiscal quarter. To this end, strategy can best be defined as "the art of bringing values and resources together to influence and shape the future" (Moore, 1997). (For a more extensive exposition on business strategy and emerging trends in strategic analysis, see Laszlo & Laszlo, 2004.)

Now Michael Porter has a lot to say on the subject of strategy. Unfortunately, most of it is framed in Business Knowledge of the Second Kind and couched in Darwinian terms of corporate rivalry and survival of the fittest. The notion of competitive advantage as presented in his widely read books of the 1980s seems to confer what Hao Ma has called *positional* advantage, in contrast to *kinetic* advantage (Ma, 2000). Positional advantage relates to the assessment that a corporation will make of its strengths, weaknesses, opportunities, and threats in relation to what it perceives to be its direct intra-industry rivals. However, as Porter points out, "the more benchmarking that companies do, the more *competitive convergence* you have — that is, the more indistinguishable companies are from one another." As an alternative, he goes on to suggest how "*Strategic positioning* attempts to achieve sustainable competitive advantage by preserving what is distinctive about a company. It means performing *different* activities from rivals, or performing *similar* activities in different ways" (Porter, 1996, p. 2). What Porter describes as "sustainable competitive advantage" has little to do with the notion of sustainability in terms of the triple bottom line as considered by the evolutionary corporation. In fact, it amounts to little more than a strategy for '*sustained* (not sustainable) competitive advantage' exclusively in terms of financial profits. Likewise, his concept of strategic positioning is little more than a dynamic form for obtaining positional advantage through a series of steps of the sort described by Constantinos Markides in his article on "A Dynamic View of Strategy" (Markides, 1999, p. 62). Markides summarizes these steps as follows:

- Find a unique strategic position in your current industry
  - Compete in this position by becoming better than your industry competitors
    - Search for new strategic positions
    - Manage old and new positions simultaneously
    - Make transition from your old position to the new position
  - Compete in this position by becoming better than your industry competitors
- Jump into a different industry — repeat the process.

Kinetic advantage, then, is what we want. Actually, no, it isn't. It falls short, as well. The fact is that kinetic advantage is only a category of which Porter's notion of strategic positioning represents one form. According to Ma, it relates to an action oriented ability that allows a firm to function more effectively and efficiently, conferring an advantage that gives a company an edge in what it actually does by allowing the company to perform its value-adding activities more effectively and/or efficiently than its rivals (Ma, 2000). In other words, it turns out to be a type of dynamic strategy along the lines considered by Markides.

So, within the framework of Business Knowledge of the Second Kind, static or competitive advantage is seen to be conferred upon companies that pursue relativistic jostling strategies for positional advantage or, in the case of dynamic or sustained competitive advantage, that pursue effort optimizing strategies for kinetic advantage. In either case, corporate strategy leaves 3rd generation KM pristine and untouched. What these approaches are missing is a framework that confers *evolutionary advantage* on the corporation which pursues sustainability in terms of the triple bottom line.

EVOLUTIONARY ADVANTAGE

The dynamic patterning process of change management initiatives that embrace evolutionary advantage are essentially future creating. By drawing on 3rd generation KM within a framework of Business Knowledge of the Third Kind, evolutionary advantage holds implications for corporate survival beyond those conferred by reliance on either the static or dynamic strategic positioning initiatives of popular orientations that seek to establish competitive advantage.

Strategic evolutionary advantage incorporates notions that promote collaboration over competition, linking rather than ranking, power to empower instead of power over others, and win-win rather than conquest and dominate relations. These are not antithetical to the fundamental axioms upon which business is based (if one can abstract to a common set of characteristics that inhere in the concept of "business culture" in its most generic and pervasive form). The fact is that competition makes sense under conditions of unbounded independence, but when there are no more new frontiers into which to expand, no more countries to colonize or people to conquer, then conditions of interdependence and mutual interest promote cooperation above and beyond (though not to the exclusion of) competition. In business, as in nature, community means that "every species ... directly or indirectly, supplies essential materials or services to one or more of its associates" (Dice, 1962, p. 200). Such a conception of community brings with it deeper insights, such as "... the notion of life as self-directed movement. Nature is not at war, one organism with another. Nature is an alliance founded on cooperation" (Augros & Stanciu, 1987, p. 129). Ruthless competition never was the law of nature. If it had been, we would never have witnessed the rise of multi-cellular organisms. Similarly, in a world of great interrelations, tight interconnections, and deep interdependencies among and between businesses, it makes as much sense to take a cold and calculating "survival of the fittest" attitude to the international market place as it would to let the cells in the toes of an infected foot struggle to survive as best they can. The pretense of such attitudes is that if we help those in need it will only weaken the entire system, but as we clearly know by direct systemic analogy, not taking care of the overall health of our body leads to certain disease and probable death. Life in our global village is no longer akin to that of independent amoebae in a vast sea of possibility. Our shared resources and common destinies have woven us into a geo-political body whose every move affects all of its constituents.

In essence, strategic evolutionary advantage seeks to situate the corporation in a flow of value exchange that both nourishes society and the environment in which it is embedded and is nourished by them. It is built on the foundations of Natural Capitalism, as described and championed by Paul Hawken and others (Hawken, Lovins, & Lovins, 1999). The notion of sustainability to which it adheres is not the linear conception of being able to continue doing what you are doing for longer than any of your competitors. That, in fact, is not sustainability but 'sustained ability'—a different beast altogether! In other words, to sustain something is to keep it in existence, as in a note that a singer is able to sustain (until they run out of air), whereas to engage in a strategy for sustainability is to learn how to play improvisational jazz through listening, responding, improvising, innovating, actively learning and interactively creating (a process which never need run out).

Alfonso Montuori (1989) helps us understand why the new realities of the evolutionary corporation might suggest competencies closer to those of the jazz player than the orchestral musician: "everything an artist produces, how s/he shapes the silence, and our interpretation of it, is a product of a historical period, which both enriches and constrains" (Montuori, 1989, p. 145). Nowadays, organizations that make a difference in this world tend more often to be ones that explore opportunities to create new patterns and processes as they appear, rather than ones that *only* know how to sustain a pattern or process that already exists. Gordon Rowland (1992) reinforces this point by suggesting how this stylistic difference in musical metaphor relates to ways people work together within organizations. He notes that "teams resembling jazz ensembles are more capable of meeting today's challenges than teams resembling orchestras" (Rowland, 1992, p. 19). According to Rowland, we are living in a world that more and more demands the ability to work flexibly and loosely together in ways that combine rational thought, technical skill, creativity and intuition. Rather than "following the score" that is handed to us, the challenges of sustainable survival in the business world more frequently asks us to improvise around a basic theme.

Strategic evolutionary advantage involves new vision, a new ethos, and new leadership skills. Take, for example, the new shared leadership that project-based work teams display. To describe it, we use a set of images presented in a televised corporate advertisement. The commercial begins with a classical music quintet performing a beautiful piece of chamber music. The black of the tuxes, gowns, and music stands of the two violinists, violist, cellist, and flutist created a nice contrast with the all white space in which they played. And they played beautifully, weaving their melodies together in a harmony of classical counterpoint. Then, all of a sudden, a basket ball came sailing in from off stage, bounced once, and landed right in the cellist's lap! The startled cellist stopped playing immediately as did the other musicians who all stared incredulously at the basket ball. The cellist looked at his companions, shrugged once, got up and began dribbling the ball. The other musicians glanced at each other briefly, put down their instruments, and got up to join the now former cellist. They all moved off to the right, their instruments and stands quickly forgotten and fading out of view. Soon the five of them were passing the basket ball back and forth in ways that would have made the Harlem Globe Trotters green with envy. As when they were playing music, their motions seemed to flow in a graceful harmony of interdependence and partnership. Then, just as they were really getting into it, a trapeze bar swung in from off stage and almost hit the former flutist in the head, but in the last minute she reached up and grabbed it. The others stopped to look at her, the one with the basket ball just letting it drop and roll off. She looked back at her partners, shrugged once, and began to swing, and as she did, the others moved with her as one, the scene fading out as the commercial ended.

This little story illustrates the phenomenon of "syntony" within a group — an idea central to evolutionary advantage, meaning to tune in and consciously align oneself with the evolutionary flows of one's milieu (A. Laszlo, 2008). All five "players" acted in unison, although each did their own thing. And when something in their environment changed, they neither ignored nor reacted against it, but instead immediately adapted to it. They didn't have to stop for long discussions of the pros and cons of one course of action or another, to analyze, plan, or argue the strengths and weaknesses of one option over another, and they didn't have to go off to training seminars to learn how to deal with change. They learned together, "on the job" as it were, and in dynamic interaction with each other and their environment. Wouldn't it be wonderful if corporations and business units were able to cope with uncertainty and change like this group did? Actually, it wouldn't. The people in that story demonstrated the essence of syntony — of harmonizing with, and tuning to, each other — but they did so only *among themselves*. They were totally out of syntony with their environment. Whenever they were challenged by a change in their environment, they simply shrugged and adapted *to* it. In short, they reacted. Where were they going with this pattern of adapting to anything that came their way? While they may have been very much in syntony with each other — fluidly co-creating consonant patterns of behavior among themselves — they did not go the extra step required of true systems of syntony: they did not co-create *with* their evolving environment. In short, they had no strategy to secure evolutionary advantage, and this story is typical of most organizations pursuing strategies of competitive advantage.

In terms of the strategies involved, evolutionary advantage emphasizes the triple bottom line as a standard according to which ten dimensions of capital are generated. These are:

1. Natural capital (the raw materials we use as input in our industrial processes and the affordances[1] they provide)
2. Manufactured capital (the finished products to which we ascribe market value)
3. Financial capital (the monetary representation of market value)
4. Technological capital (the implements and methods of doing or making that extend human capability)
5. Intellectual capital (the knowledge and know-how that support human activity and innovation)
6. Human capital (the health and well-being of a productive population)
7. Social capital (the coherence and functionality of relationships in a community and the foundation of trust that underlies them)
8. Cultural capital (the lifeways and traditions that characterize a society or social group)
9. Ecosystemic capital (the biodiversity and biotic robustness of a bioregion)
10. Evolutionary capital (the potential for a course of action to be opportunity increasing)

By and large, classical conceptions of competitive advantage focus on the generation of manufactured capital, occasionally including intellectual capital in its purview. Evolutionary advantage, by contrast, considers all ten dimensions. For example, Electrolux is a an industry leader in the manufacturing of water and energy efficient appliances, including solar-powered lawn mowers, and dishwashers that use only 15 liters of water per cycle compared to 40 liters in most conventional machines. The company constantly sets waste reduction goals, such as, in 2002, to reduce waste by 35%, water usage by 25%, and to cut emissions significantly by the end of 2002 (Makower, 2002, p.1). This example serves to highlight the feasibility of keeping sight of the triple bottom line in the cultivation of a sustainable survival strategy: not only did the company increase its overall profit margins, but it did so in a way that gives back to the environment and is socially responsible through its concern for future generations.

The pursuit of evolutionary advantage is already being observed in more mainstream companies such as Toyota. Toyota's hybrid car, the Prius, is an example of a product that is 'green' without compromising product use or functionality. It was launched in the US market in 2000, representing an energy efficient car that is best used for city driving where pollution is worst (Makower, 2002, p.7). The marketing strategy used by Toyota is low-key. They are a generally quiet company, not making a big splash about their sustainability drive. They pursue a more results oriented type management style than in-your-face image projection that is ahead of (and possibly detached from) true corporate identity.

Interface, the carpet company that has set for itself the goal of becoming the first name industrial ecology, is another excellent example of the successful pursuit of evolutionary advantage. Their mission statement suggests that they will "lead by example and validate by results in profits, leaving the world a better place than when we began and we will be restorative through the power of our influence in the world" (Interface Inc., 1997). They truly walk their talk by even having an environmental position statement. The company has set a continuous improvement goal for 2005 to reduce energy consumption per unit of production by 15% from their 1996 baseline, as well as to reduce the consumption of raw materials in operations by reusing rather than disposing of byproducts and recycling whenever reusing is not possible, thereby striving to approximate zero emissions in their operations. This is clearly a company that has taken their sustainability goals seriously and makes every effort possible to achieve those goals through company policies and practices. They follow James Moore's previously mentioned definition of strategy as "the art of bringing values and resources together to influence and shape the future." However, the issue of how to set one's sustainability goals and in what direction to influence the shape of the future remain key issues in the pursuit of sustainable evolutionary advantage. The key lies in the pattern to which sustainable evolutionary advantage gives rise. Being able to identify this pattern requires a basic evolutionary literacy, and being able to articulate strategy that forwards it results in sustainable evolutionary development.

CONCLUSION

Management theory must incorporate systemic and relational constructs of sustainability for corporate strategy to be effective beyond issues of either survival or domination. Through concepts such as evolutionary development it is possible to provide ways of "doing more with less" — by increasing the abilities of organizations to resourcefully adapt with their environments in ways that change as their environment changes — but that remain constant in their maintenance of viable environments in which to operate. In order for this concept of evolutionary development to be equally in service of business, humanity, and the ecosystems of our planet, it must assure that both the products and the processes of change are:

1. Socially desirable
2. Culturally acceptable
3. Psychologically nurturing
4. Economically sustainable
5. Technologically feasible
6. Operationally viable
7. Environmentally friendly
8. Generationally sensitive
9. Capable of continuous learning

By monitoring all these aspects simultaneously, a process of development (individual, corporate, or societal) can be said to be sustainable if it involves an adaptive strategy that ensures the evolutionary maintenance of an increasingly robust and supportive environment. Sustainable development strategies that seek to do so set objectives that identify the opportunities for increasing the dynamic stability and self-sufficiency of an individual, a group, or a society by indicating the areas of socio-economic potential that could be developed to the advantage of all the stakeholders involved — both human and non-human and both those who benefit from the system at present, as well as those who stand to benefit from the system in the future. This is the very essence of evolutionary development, and through it, an organization may sustain a pattern of mutual adaptation in interaction with its socio-cultural and bio-physical environment that confers strategic evolutionary advantage (Laszlo & Laszlo, 2004).

Sustainability, in essence, is an inside job. The search for solutions to the challenges faced in common by all people will not be successful if limited to an outward quest for answers in the domains of science, technology and business — that is to say, without including the human factor as the essential ingredient in every consideration. The moral and ethical responsibility of the leader of integral development for long-range systemic sustainability is, in the first place, a commitment to the well-being of all living things in our planet as well as to their descendants. No longer can we afford the luxury of ignoring the secondary impacts of our technologies and the undesirable consequences of our paradigms. To be sustainable, we need business leaders who draw upon a systemic and relational framework to incorporate perspectives that are systemic, humanistic and ethical at the heart of all that they do to advance their cause.

Systemic inquiry in management theory tends to contribute most to the evolution of consciousness and, through actionable models such as those derived from evolutionary systems design, to ways of engaging in conscious evolution. Advanced research on evolutionary leadership for development begs contemplation of what lies beyond sustainable development, from business as usual (BAU) to sustainability as usual (SAU) and beyond. The relational and systemic aspects of sustainability are the very factors that lead it out of its homocentric and chronocentric parameters and into a reference system of integral evolutionary development. In this sense, systemic sustainable development is evolutionary, and it is with this sense that contemporary management theory most need be infused.

REFERENCES

Augros, R., & Stanciu, G. (1987). *The new biology: Discovering the wisdom in nature.* Boston, MA: Shambhala.

Checkland, P. (1981). *Systems thinking, systems practice.* New York: Wiley.

Diamond, J. (2005). *Collapse: How societies choose to fail or succeed.* New York: Viking.

Dice, L. R. (1962). *Natural communities.* Ann Arbor, MI: University of Michigan Press.

Durning, A. T. (1992). *How much is enough?* New York: Norton.

Hawken, P., Lovins, A., & Lovins, L. H. (1999). *Natural capitalism: Creating the next industrial revolution.* New York: Little, Brown & Co.

Hubbard, B. M. (1998). *Conscious evolution: Awakening our social potential.* Novato, CA: New World Library.

Interface Inc. (1997). *Interface sustainability report.* Corporate publication. See also the online version of this report at http://www.interfacesustainability.com.

Korten, D. (2002, May). From mindless greed to civil society: Restoring an ethical culture and challenging a world consumed with the love of money. *Opportunity Knocks, 9.*

Korten, D. (2006). The great turning: From empire to Earth community. *YES! A Journal of Positive Futures, 38,* 12-18.

Labarre, P. (2000, March). Do you have the will to lead? *Fast Company.*

Laszlo, A. (2008). *Evolving with heart: Dancing the path of syntony.* Manuscript.

Laszlo, A. (2009). The nature of evolution. *World Futures, 65*(3), 204–221. doi:10.1080/02604020802392112

Laszlo, A., & Laszlo, K. C. (2004). Strategic evolutionary advantage (S.E.A.). *World Futures, 60*(1-2), 99–114. doi:10.1080/725289195

Laszlo, C., & Laugel, J. F. (2000). *Large-scale organizational change: An executive's guide.* Woburn, MA: Butterworth-Heinemann.

Laszlo, E. (1999). *Holos — The fabulous world of the new sciences: Explorations at the leading edge of contemporary knowledge.* Unpublished manuscript.

Laszlo, E. (2002). *Macroshift: Navigating the transformation to a sustainable world.* San Francisco: Berrett-Koehler.

Laszlo, K. C. (2003). The evolution of business: Learning, innovation, and sustainability for the 21st century. *World Futures, 59*(8), 655–664.

Laszlo, K. C., & Laszlo, A. (2002, October). Evolving knowledge for development: The role of knowledge management in a changing world. *Journal of Knowledge Management, 6*(4), 400–412. doi:10.1108/13673270210440893

Ma, H. (2000, January). Of competitive advantage: Kinetic and positional. *Bryant College Journal.*

Macy, J. (2006, September). The great turning as compass and lens. *YES! A Journal of Positive Futures, 38.*

Makower, J. (2002, December). Follow the leaders: How consumer product companies burnish their green credentials. *The Green Business Letter.*

Markides, C. (1999, Spring). A dynamic view of strategy. *Sloan Management Review,* 55–63.

McElroy, M. W. (2000). *Managing for sustainable innovation.* Unpublished manuscript.

McIntosh, M., Leipziger, D., Jones, K., & Coleman, G. (1998). *Corporate citizenship: Successful strategies for responsible companies.* London: Financial Times Pitman Publishing.

Meadows, D. (1999). *Leverage points: Places to intervene in a system.* Hartland, VT: The Sustainability Institute.

Montuori, A. (1989). *Evolutionary competence: Creating the future.* Amsterdam: J. C. Gieben.

Moore, J. F. (1997). *The death of competition: Leadership and strategy in the age of business ecosystems.* New York: Harper Business.

Nattrass, B., & Altomare, M. (1999). *The natural step for business: Wealth, ecology, and the evolutionary corporation.* British Columbia: New Society Publishers.

Pinchbeck, D. (2006). *2012: The return of Quetzalcoatl.* New York: Tarcher/Penguin.

Porter, M. (1996, November/December). What is strategy? *Harvard Business Review.*

Ray, P., & Anderson, S. R. (2000). *The cultural creatives: How 50 million people are changing the world.* New York: Harmony Books.

Robèrt, K. H. (1997). *The natural step: A framework for achieving sustainability in our organizations.* Cambridge, MA: Pegasus Innovations in Management Series.

Rowland, G. (1992, November/December). Do you play Jazz? *Performance & Instruction.*

Senge, P. (1993). *The fifth discipline: The art and practice of the learning organization.* New York: Doubleday Currency.

Solomon, R. C. (1999). *A better way to think about business: How personal integrity leads to corporate success.* New York: Oxford University Press.

Solomon, R. C., & Hanson, K. R. (1983). *Above the bottom line: An introduction to business ethics.* New York: Harcourt Brace Jovanovich.

Tainter, J. A. (1990). *The collapse of complex societies.* Cambridge, MA: Cambridge University Press.

TFPL. (1999). *Skills for knowledge management: A briefing paper.* London: TFPL, Ltd.

Theobald, R. (1997). *Reworking success: New communities at the millennium.* Stony Creek, CT: New Society Publishers.

van Gelder, S. (1998, Fall). The natural step: The science of sustainability. *YES! A Journal of Positive Futures, 7*, 50-54.

ENDNOTE

[1] The notion of 'affordances' relates to qualities inherent in a situation or in an object's sensory characteristics that permit specific kinds of uses. For example, a button, by being slightly raised above an otherwise flat surface, suggests the idea of pushing it. A lever, by being an appropriate size for grasping, suggests pulling it. A chair, by its size, its curvature, its balance, and its position, suggests sitting on it.

Chapter 2
Leaders, Decisions, and the Neuro-Knowledge System

Alex Bennet
Mountain Quest Institute, USA

David Bennet
Mountain Quest Institute, USA

ABSTRACT

Every decision-maker has a self-organizing, hierarchical set of theories (and consistent relationship among those theories) that guide their decision-making process. In support of this thesis the authors explore the following: (1) the development of invariant hierarchical patterns removed from the context and content of a specific situation; (2) the connections among values, beliefs, assumptions and those patterns (a personal theory); and (3) the robustness of those patterns and connections in a complex decision situation. These focus areas are addressed through the following chapter sections: baseline definitions; surface, shallow and deep knowledge; the decision-making process; decision-making viewed from outside the decision-maker; decision-making viewed from inside the decision-maker; anticipating the outcome of actions; hierarchy as a basic property of the decision-making system; advanced decision-making: the cortex; and final thoughts. It is also forwarded that the workings of our mind/brain provide a model for decision-making in a complex situation.

INTRODUCTION

This chapter focuses on (1) the development of invariant hierarchical patterns removed from the context and content of a specific situation; (2) the connections among values, beliefs, assumptions and those patterns (a personal theory); and (3) the robustness of those patterns and connections in a complex decision situation. It is forwarded that every decision-maker has a self-organizing, hierarchical set of theories (and consistent relationships among those theories) that guide their decision-making process. Further, the decision-making process within the mind/brain can serve as a model for the decision-making process we must now learn in order to deal with complex situations in a complex world.

To support this thesis, we first provide baseline definitions for information and knowledge,

DOI: 10.4018/978-1-61520-668-1.ch002

then introduce the concepts of Knowledge (Informing) and Knowledge (Proceeding) before discussing surface, shallow and deep knowledge with specific reference to decision-making. The decision-making process is then introduced, and decision-making explored as viewed from both outside and inside the decision-maker. We then focus on anticipating the outcome of actions and hierarchy as a basic property of the internal and external decision-making processes. Finally, we build an understanding of the human cortex, and relate this understanding to the generation of neuro-knowledge.

We begin.

BASELINE DEFINITIONS

Embracing Stonier's description of information as a basic property of the Universe—as fundamental as matter and energy (Stonier, 1990; Stonier, 1997)—we take information to be a measure of the degree of organization expressed by any non-random pattern or set of patterns. The order within a system is a reflection of the information content of the system. Data (a form of information) would then be simple patterns, and while data and information are both patterns, they have no meaning until some organism recognizes and interprets the patterns (Stonier, 1997; Bennet and Bennet, 2008b). Thus knowledge exists in the human brain in the form of stored or expressed neuronal patterns that may be activated and reflected upon through conscious thought. This is a high-level description of knowledge that is consistent with the operation of the brain and is applicable in varying degrees to all living organisms.

For purposes of this paper the brain consists of an atomic and molecular structure and the fluids that flow through this structure. The mind is the totality of the patterns in the brain created by neurons, their firings and their connections. These patterns include all of our thoughts. Neuronal (and the prefix neuro-) refers to any of the impulse-conducting cells that constitute the brain, spinal column, and nerves.

As a functional definition, knowledge is considered *the capacity (potential or actual) to take effective action in varied and uncertain situations* (Bennet & Bennet, 2004), and consists of understanding, insights, meaning, creativity, judgment, and the ability to anticipate the outcome of our actions. Knowledge itself is neither true nor false, and its value in terms of good or poor is difficult to measure other than by the outcomes of its actions. Hence, good knowledge would have a high probability of producing the desired (anticipated) outcome, and poor knowledge would have a low probability of producing the expected result. For complex situations the quality of knowledge (from good to poor) may be hard to estimate before the action is taken because of the system's unpredictability. After the outcome has occurred, the quality of knowledge can be assessed by comparing the actual outcome to the expected outcome.

We consider knowledge as comprised of two parts: Knowledge (Informing) and Knowledge (Proceeding) (Bennet & Bennet, 2008b). This builds on the distinction made by Ryle (1949) between "knowing that" and "knowing how". Knowledge (Informing), or $Kn_{I,}$ is the *information (or content)* part of knowledge. While this information part of knowledge is still generically information (organized patterns), it is special because of its structure and relationships with other information. Kn_I consists of information that may represent understanding, meaning, insights, expectations, theories and principles that support or lead to effective action. When viewed separately this is information even though it *may* lead to effective action. It is considered knowledge when used as *part of the knowledge process*.

Knowledge (Proceeding), Kn_P, represents the *process* and *action* part of knowledge. Kn_P is the process of selecting and associating or applying the relevant information (Kn_I) from which specific actions can be identified and implemented, that is, actions that result in some level of anticipated effective outcome. There is considerable precedence for considering knowledge as information or a product of a process versus an outcome of some action. For example, Kolb (1984) forwards in his theory of experiential learning, knowledge retrieval, creation and application requires engaging knowledge as a process, not a product. The process our minds use to find, create and semantically mix the information needed to take effective action is often unconscious and difficult to communicate to someone else (and thus could be described as tacit).

A theory is considered a set of statements and/or principals that explain a group of facts or phenomena to guide action or assist in comprehension or judgment (American Heritage Dictionary, 2006). While a written theory could be considered information, when used by a decision-maker to guide action it would be considered knowledge. Further, while in its incoming form it is Knowledge (Informing) as it is complexed with other information in the mind of the decision-maker it may become part of the process that is Knowledge (Proceeding).

We now look at our definition of the term leader. Today leader is used in many different ways; almost everyone acts as a leader in some context or situation. For example, Cleveland (2002) sees the growth rate of leaders in the USA in the same light as the growth rate of knowledge:

I have tried several times to count the number of leaders in the USA. In the mid-1950s, because I was publisher of a magazine I wanted them to buy, I counted 555,000 "opinion leaders." A 1971 extrapolation of that figure came out at about a million. Seven out of ten of these were executive leaders of many kinds of organizations; this "aristocracy of achievement" was estimated in 1985 at one out of every two hundred Americans. After that I gave up: the knowledge revolution keeps multiplying the number of Americans who take the opportunity to lead, at one time or another, on one issue or another, in one community or another ... The galloping rate of growth of complexity means that a growth curve of the requirement for leaders if anyone were clever enough to construct such an index would show a steeper climb than any other growth rate in our political economy. (Cleveland, 2002, p.6)

For purposes of this paper, *leaders are individuals who create, maintain and nurture their organization* so that it creates and makes the best use of knowledge and the full competencies of all workers to achieve sustainable high performance. Further, it is acknowledged that leaders emerge and make decisions at every level of the organization.

SURFACE, SHALLOW AND DEEP KNOWLEDGE

Building on the terms "shallow" and "deep" that have historically been used to describe knowledge, we now consider knowledge in terms of a continuum moving from surface knowledge, through shallow knowledge, to deep knowledge (Bennet & Bennet, 2008c). Surface knowledge answers the questions of what, when, where and who. It involves visible choices that require minimum understanding. Examples would be following personnel procedures as spelled out in a manual, or filling out a short-form tax return. Much of everyday life such as light conversations, descriptions and even some self-reflection can be considered surface thinking, and learning that creates surface knowledge. Facts, data, concepts and information memorized for quizzes and tests (without a deeper understanding of purpose and underlying meaning) would fall into this category.

Shallow knowledge is surface knowledge coupled to a strong understanding of causal relationships and a deeper level of meaning, with that meaning typically related to a situation and implying some level of action. To make meaning requires context. Since social interactions such as conversations and dialogue help convey context, shallow knowledge emerges and expands as decision-makers learn and interact in the course of everyday practices. For example, organizations who embrace the use of teams and communities facilitate the mobilization of knowledge and creation of new ideas as individuals interact in these groups. Shallow knowledge frequently addresses the "how" (and sometimes "why") of understanding a situation.

Deep knowledge about a situation involves understanding the situation, sensitivity to the patterns within the situation, and the meaning of those patterns and their relationship to potential actions. It also includes the ability of the decision-maker to shift frames of reference as the context and situation shifts. This requires a large amount of Knowledge (Proceeding) to know when and how to take effective action (and often "why"). The source of deep knowledge lies in an individual's creativity, intuition, forecasting experience, pattern recognition, and *their theories and the use of those theories*. In other words, this is the area of the expert whose unconscious has learned to detect patterns, evaluate their importance, and anticipate the behavior of situations that are too complex for the conscious mind to comprehend. The development of such knowledge requires intense and persistent focus, interest, and experience to a specific area of learning, knowledge and action.

Taken together surface, shallow, and deep knowledge represent concepts that leaders and managers can use to aid in better decision-making. Routine decisions made in organizations occur at the surface level. Decisions requiring deep knowledge are much fewer, and tend to be more critical to the organization's survival and performance. Understanding knowledge in terms of surface, shallow and deep levels can help decision-makers recognize the scope and depth of knowledge needed and/or available to maximize problem solving, decision-making, and action in simple, complicated, or complex situations. See Figure 1.

Thinking about knowledge in terms of three levels can also help leaders and managers tailor knowledge capture and learning experiences to improve knowledge sharing and retention. For example, surface knowledge involves facts, data, simple concepts and other information that can be memorized, and applied, captured and stored in technology systems for processing and reference. To share and retain shallow knowledge the focus is primarily through social interactions such as conversations, dialogues, and thc flow of ideas that emerge in communities and teams. Shallow knowledge would also reside at the technician level where some understanding, meaning, and problem-solving are essential and how work is done is understood, but "why things behave the way they do" may not be understood. To share and retain deep knowledge, the focus on learning from effortful practice and lived experience would suggest the need for an organizational learning strategy which might include mentoring, apprenticeships and leadership development programs.

Note that we have separated knowledge into three levels only for ease of comprehension. Clearly knowledge exists at all levels in a continuum from surface down to the deepest expertise (world-class experts) in any given area, with deep knowledge building on shallow knowledge, and shallow knowledge building on surface knowledge.

THE DECISION-MAKING PROCESS

Every decision is a guess about the future and involves values, beliefs, assumptions, incoming information from the environment, and the internal information and knowledge of the decision-maker. The decision-making process refers to the purposeful selection from one or more alternative actions in order to achieve a desired outcome. Mid-twentieth century theories such as Theory X, Theory Y, Theory Z, Charismatic and Trans-

Figure 1. Characterization of organizational knowledge needs (Adapted from Bennet & Bennet, 2008c)

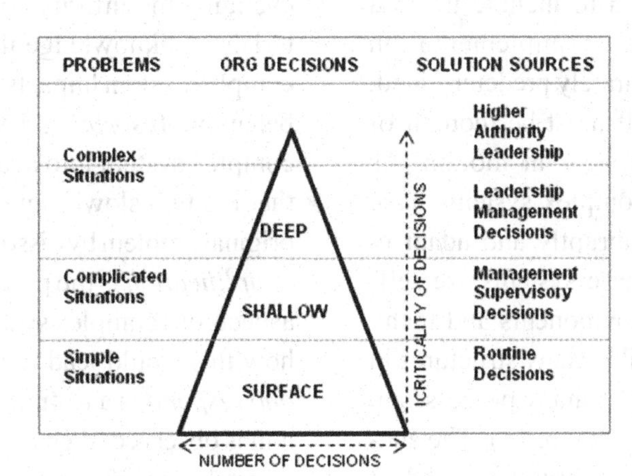

formational Leadership, General Systems Theory, and Organizational Linking Pins heralded the beginning of a shift in decision-making. This shift moved leadership and management theory away from the absolutism of hierarchical control based on ownership, societal status, and positional power to the recognition of knowledge as power (Bennet & Bennet, 2004). Representing power and authority, knowledge and information were held close and protected by leaders and managers throughout the latter part of the twentieth century.

By the dawn of the twenty-first century, the explosion of communications technologies was well underway, and the global world was advancing through the age of information into the age of knowledge. Today everything moves farther, faster and is intertwined among people, societies and technologies. While some levels of complexity have existed throughout history, this explosion of information, communication velocity, and networking coupled with the competitive nature of organizations has produced an increasingly complex environment. In other words, complexity begets complexity. As the futurist Peter Schwartz confirms, "... complexity and turbulence in the world at large [are] facts of life, looming larger and larger in people's concerns until today there is hardly anyone unaffected by them" (Schwartz, 2003, p. 2). We call this environment CUCA, that is, increasing Change, rising Uncertainty, growing Complexity and the ubiquitous Anxiety being driven by that change, uncertainty and complexity (Bennet & Bennet, 2004).

Traditional decision theory was built on an implied causal or deterministic connection between the decision that was made and the end result. This meant that there was a relatively closed system with feedback loops between a decision, the action taken, and the result achieved. However, this approach does not work with complex systems, where causes are difficult or impossible to identify and there may be no predictable end results from a decision. Thus the theory of decision-making is coevolving right along with the environment (Bennet & Bennet, 2008a). As Buchanan describes,

> *...executives and scholars recognize that conventional theories of management, forged in the era of industrialization, vertically integrated companies, and relatively impermeable institution borders, can no longer cope with the immensely complex organizations that have emerged during two decades of rising globalization and decentralization. (Buchanan, 2004, p. 71)*

When dealing with a complex system, the decision strategy may need to include internal support mechanisms for an implementation journey that cannot be accurately predetermined. The decision journey itself must be thought of in terms of a complex system in motion. As Auyang describes, such complex systems have the capability to change abruptly and adapt to external environments. These systems are self-organizing, "have many components and many characteristic aspects, exhibit many structures in various scales, [and] undergo many processes in various rates …(Auyang, 1998, p. 13). The success of this ability to change abruptly and adapt to external environments is highly dependent on the self-organization, the robustness, and the reaction time of the adaptive elements built into the decision strategy.

The term "decision journey" is used to emphasize that there is rarely, if ever, a single decision involved to move a complex system toward a desired outcome. More likely, there will be several decision sets and sequences. For each perturbation of the system (whether internal or external) unexpected results may emerge, which then call for other decisions, and perhaps shifts in the decision strategy. As decisions are made, actions taken, and the system changes emerge, so, too, will the expected outcome change. While a desired outcome may be initially identified, a cone of acceptable outcomes may be more practical as the system—entangled with its environment—interacts with changes effected by the decision-maker. For example, system perturbations may be caused by any, or a combination of, actions or mechanisms such as structural adaptation, boundary management, absorption, simplification, sense and respond, amplification, and seeding (Bennet & Bennet, 2008a).

Structural adaptation is the ability to change the internal structure of a complex system in response an external perturbation. *Boundary management* is influencing a complex system by controlling its boundary conditions. For example, changing the information, funding, people, materials and knowledge that goes into or out of a complex system impacts its internal operation and behavior. *Absorption* is the action that brings the complex system into a larger complex system so that the two slowly intermix, thus resolving the original problem by dissolving the original system. *Simplification* is the process of identifying which aspects of a complex system can be simplified and how this would lead to the desired result. *Sense and respond* is a testing approach where the system is observed, then perturbed, and the response studied. *Amplification*—closely coupled to sense and respond—is the evolutionary approach where a variety of actions are taken to determine which ones will succeed. The successful ones are then used in similar situations (the process of amplification) as long as they yield the desired result. *Seeding* is the process of nurturing emergence, that is, finding the right set of parallel actions to move the system in the right direction.

Cybernetic decision-making and management with continuous feedback from the system's behavior is essential when predictions of results are not possible due to either the internal complexity of the system or to the uncertainty and variability of its environment. What is needed could be considered part of a theory of sustainability management. As part of such a theory we propose sustainable decision-making where the decision-maker's belief system is to nurture the movement and direction of the organization or situation in concert with an evolving decision journey. To be successful and ensure that the most effective actions are taken requires the decision-maker to utilize multiple frames of reference consistent with their personal theory. This was discussed in a new theory of the firm based on the Intelligent Complex Adaptive System organizational model (Bennet & Bennet, 2004).

DECISION-MAKING VIEWED FROM OUTSIDE THE DECISION-MAKER

The decision-making process begins with a situation that is both context sensitive and situation dependent, and with three sets of information that start the learning process: (a) theories, values, beliefs, and assumptions internal to the decision-maker, (b) memories related to the situation at hand, and (c) incoming information from the external environment. The decision-maker creates knowledge by reflecting upon and comprehending the interactions among (a), (b) and (c) above, complexed with knowledge related to potential actions available and applicable to the situation at hand. This represents a problem-solving aspect of decision-making. Out of this process comes understanding, meaning, insights, perhaps creative ideas, and anticipation of the outcome of potential actions (that is, knowledge).

Frequently, there are a number of potential actions that may result in the desired outcome relative to the situation at hand. Assuming three potential actions and their forecasted outcomes, the decision-maker evaluates each decision option in terms of the science and the art of decision-making. The *science* of decision-making refers to the use of logic, reductionist thinking, analysis, cost-benefit investigations, linear extrapolation, and—where feasible—simulations, trade-off analysis, and probability analysis. The *art* of decision-making refers to the intuition, judgment, feelings, imagination, and heuristics which come mostly from the unconscious. Combining these two approaches to understanding the forecasted outcomes, the decision-maker selects the decision which either objectively or intuitively (or both) is expected to have the highest probability of success in achieving the desired goals and objectives. As can be seen, much thought is spent in anticipating the outcome of specific actions. This is discussed from the mind/brain perspective later in this chapter.

A "good" decision in a complex situation would result in an expected outcome that would fall within a cone of acceptable results. As part of the decision journey, implementation of such a decision requires continuous feedback loops to update the complex situation's response to management actions. It would most likely be necessary to guide the complex situation's movements by a series of corrective actions or nudges to keep the situation heading in the desired direction.

The above paragraphs provide an external viewpoint to complex decision-making. [For a deeper layer of detail on complex decision-making see Bennet & Bennet, 2008a.] We now look at decision-making from what happens inside the mind/brain of the decision-maker. This discussion will be a high-level overview since there is much that is unknown about the neural details of decision-making.

DECISION-MAKING VIEWED FROM INSIDE THE DECISION-MAKER

The similarities between decision-making in a complex adaptive situation introduced above and the internal workings of the mind/brain are striking. In the brain of the decision-maker, thoughts are represented by patterns of neuronal firings. Recall that the brain stores information in the form of patterns of neurons, their connections, and the strength of those connections. These patterns represent thoughts, images, beliefs, theories, emotions, etc. Although the patterns themselves are nonphysical, their existence as represented by neurons and their connections *are* physical, that is, composed of atoms, molecules and cells.

If we consider the mind as the totality of neuronal patterns, then we can consider the mind and the brain to be connected in the sense that the neural patterns cannot exist without the brain, yet the brain would have no mind if it had no patterns. It may be helpful to consider the following metaphor: the mind is to the brain as waves of the ocean are to the water in the ocean (Bennet & Bennet, 2008b). Even this is simplified because surrounding the neurons are continuous flows of blood, hormones and other chemicals which have complex interactions within the brain and the body (Church, 2006; Pert, 1997). The power of the metaphor derives from the relationship between the neuronal network patterns used to represent the external (and internal) world of concepts, thoughts, objects and their relationships, and the physical neurons and other material in the brain. To get some idea of the density and intricacies of the brain, consider the following: "A piece of brain tissue the size of a grain of sand contains a hundred thousand neurons and one billion synapses (connections), all talking to one another" (Amen, 2005, p. 20). A single thought might be represented in the brain by a network of a million neurons, with each neuron connected to 10,000 other neurons (Ratey, 2001).

A decision is the result of recursive interactions between external information and internal information of relevance to the problem at hand, what we call the process of associative patterning (Bennet & Bennet, 2006; Byrnes, 2001; Stonier, 1997). Consider the following description of how the brain creates patterns of the mind. In the quote below, neuroscientist Antonio Damasio uses the term "movie" as a metaphor for the diverse sensory images and signals that create the show and flow (patterns) we call mind. The quote also brings out a few of the large number of semi-independent systems in the brain that work together to make sense of our external environment.

Further remarkable progress involving aspects of the movie-in-the-brain has led to increased insights related to mechanisms for learning and memory. In rapid succession, research has revealed that the brain uses discrete systems for different types of learning. The basal ganglia and cerebellum are critical for the acquisition of skills—for example, learning to ride a bicycle or play a musical instrument. The hippocampus is integral to the learning of facts pertaining to such entities as people, places or events. And once facts are learned, the long-term memory of those facts relies on multi-component brain systems, whose key parts are located in the vast brain expanses known as cerebral cortices. (Damasio, 2007, pps. 63-64)

We learn by changing incoming signals (images, sounds, smells, sensations of the body) into patterns (of the mind and within the brain) that we identify with specific external concepts or objects. These incoming neuronal patterns have internal associations with other internal patterns that represent (to varying degrees of fidelity) the corresponding associations in the external world. The intermixing of these sets of information (patterns), what is referred to as semantic mixing (Stonier, 1997) or complexing, creates new neural patterns that represent understanding, meaning, and the anticipation of the consequences of actions, or, in other words, knowledge. We represent external reality through the creation and association of internal patterns of neuron firings and connections. Thus associative patterning is the way the mind/brain creates knowledge.

The mind/brain/body is essentially a self-organizing, cybernetic, highly complex adaptive learning system that survives by converting incoming information from its environment into knowledge (the capacity to take effective action) and then using that knowledge. The mind, brain and body are replete with feedback loops, control systems, sensors, memories, and meaning-making systems made up of about 100 billion neurons and about 10^{15} interconnections. It is self-organizing because there is no central subsystem that "controls" the mind, brain or body.

ANTICIPATING THE OUTCOME OF ACTIONS

The process of storing sequences of patterns or memories are one way the mind/brain anticipates the outcome of actions. In 1949 the Canadian psychologist Donald Hebb explained learning and memory as a result of the strengthening of synapses (connections) between neurons in the brain. In other words, when connected neurons *fire simultaneously*, their synaptic connections become stronger (Begley, 2007). This has become known as Hebb's rule: learning takes place when pairs of neurons fire in coincidence. Although an oversimplification, the colloquial version is *neurons that fire together wire together*. One implication of Hebb's rule is the ease with which we can remember sequences of information. As Begley describes this process, "... traveling the same dirt road over and over leaves ruts that make it easier to stay in the track on subsequent trips" (Begley, 2007, p. 30). For example, we remember songs or stories (especially ones we sing or hear over and over again) much better than isolated or disconnected facts. This is also why memory of information can be improved by repeating the information over and over. In other words, the more often we recall what we have learned the better we will recall it in the future.

From another perspective, the rule is, "use it, or lose it" (Christos, 2003, p. 95). While the pattern may stay in memory if it is not repeated (used), it could prove very difficult to retrieve. Freud suggested that there are separate sets of neurons for perception and memory. The neural networks concerned with perception create fixed synaptic connections and by doing so ensure the accuracy of our perceptual capability. On the other hand, neuronal networks concerned with memory make connections that change in strength as we learn. This is the basis of memory and of higher cognitive functioning (Kandel, 2006).

We never see the same world twice; the brain (as distinct from a computer) does *not* store exact replicas of past events or memories. Rather, it stores invariant *representations*. These forms represent the basic source of recognition and meaning of the broader patterns (Hawkins, 2004). In an email titled "Very Interesting Stuff" that made its way across the Internet, landing on a lot of websites dedicated to humor, there is an anonymous entry that begins: "Don't delete this just because it looks weird. Believe it or not, you can read it." Reading the following text (from an anonymous source) begins to demonstrate the power of patterns stored as invariant forms.

I cdnuolt blveiee that I cluod aulaclty uesdnatnrd what I was rdanieg. The phaonmneal pweor of the hmuan mnid Aoccdrnig to rscheearch at Cmabrigde Uinervtisy, it deosn't mttaer in what oredr the ltteers in a word are, the olny iprmoatnt tihng is that the first and last ltteer be in the rghit pclae. The rset can be a taotl mses and you can still raed it wouthit a porbelm. This is bcuseae the huamn mnid deos not raed ervey lteter by istlef, but the word as a wlohe. Amzanig huh?

According to Hawkins, "...the problem of understanding *how* your cortex forms invariant representations remains one of the biggest mysteries in all of science" (Hawkins, 2004, p. 78). This isn't for lack of trying; "no one, not even using the most powerful computers in the world, are able to solve it" (Hawkins, 2004, p.78). Nobel laureate Eric Kandel describes this process:

By storing memories in invariant forms, individuals are able to apply memories to situations that are similar but not identical to previous experiences. Cognitive psychologists would describe this as developing an internal representation of the external world, a cognitive map that generates a meaningful image or interpretation of our experience. (Kandel, 2006, page 298)

In summary, the ability to anticipate the future stems from the brain remembering the patterns associated with past experiences and their outcomes. When a new experience or situation is encountered, the brain tries to match it with past experiences and then identifies the probable outcome based on those prior experiences. A series of these similar experience-outcome events generates a belief, frame of reference, or mind-set that is likely to drive the decision-maker's choice of what action(s) to take. While this system is robust with a high level of trustworthiness, it is not perfect. Because of the uniqueness of context and content of a situation coupled with the complexity of a situation, there is always the danger of oversimplifying and relying on largely unconscious beliefs learned from past—no longer applicable—experiences. As the world changes more rapidly, old decision rules or theories may be inappropriate and outdated. Complexity creates many unique states, each of which may have to be independently explored from a decision-maker's perspective. This foreshadows the need for each decision-maker to consciously create and apply a set of theories that respond to their decision space.

HIERARCHY AS A BASIC PROPERTY OF THE DECISION-MAKING SYSTEM

The brain stores patterns in a hierarchical and nested fashion. Recall that thoughts are represented by patterns of neuronal firings, their synaptic connections and the strengths between the synaptic spaces. As introduced earlier, from the viewpoint of the mind/brain, any knowledge that is being "re-used" is actually being "re-created" and—especially in an area of continuing interest—most likely complexed over and over again as incoming information is associated with internal information (Stonier, 1997). Further, if Knowledge (Informing) is different, there is a good chance that Knowledge (Proceeding) will be different, that is, the *process* of pulling up, integrating and sequencing associated Knowledge (Informing) and semantically complexing it with incoming information to make it comprehensible (and usable and applicable) is going to vary. In essence, every time we apply knowledge (Informing and Proceeding) it is to some extent new knowledge because the human mind—unlike an information management system—*unconsciously tailors what is emerging as knowledge to the situation at hand* (Edelman & Tononi, 2000).

As Marchese points out, another characteristic of this process is that when you see a picture, only about 20 percent of what you are seeing is brought into your brain; the other 80 percent of that image comes from information, ideas and feelings *already in your brain* (Marchese, 1998). The point is that the mind/brain doesn't store memories like a computer; that is, storing an exact replica of everything coming in. The mind/brain stores the *core* of the picture, what was referred to above as an invariant form (Hawkins, 2004). This particular phenomenon of relating external and internal forms of experience is called "appresentation" (Marton & Booth, 1997), and is an example of the mind's search for meaning. As Moon explains, "Appresentation is the manner in which a part of something that is perceived as an external experience can stimulate a much more complete or richer internal experience of the 'whole' of that thing to be conjured up" (Moon, 2004, p. 23). The reader experienced this in our earlier example of "Very Interesting Stuff."

Exploring this further, if you see your friend from the side or back you can usually recognize who they are since your mind has stored an invariant core basic memory that includes major features of that person (Begley, 1996; Hawkins, 2004). When you see your friend, your mind is filling in the blanks and you recognize the incoming image as your friend. There is a robustness in the way the brain *stores* invariant core memories. If it takes a million neurons to create a specific pattern (the core part of incoming information), the brain may set aside 1.4 million neurons with their connections as space for that pattern, providing a looseness to account for future associative changes, or dying cells (Hawkins, 2004). Thus for this particular pattern you could lose tens of thousands of brain cells and still have significant aspects of the invariant core memory available for future retrieval via re-creation. The brain stores the *meaning* or essence of the incoming information; it does not store every detail. If it did, it would be overwhelmed with data and information.

This phenomenon also explains the resilience of beliefs, frames of reference and mental models since a memory cannot simply be erased by the desire to do so.

At the same time you catch sight of your friend and are smiling, getting ready to call out and wave, you may be swatting gnats away from your eyes, shivering from a soft breeze, registering the dark clouds moving in from the west, feeling hunger pains in your stomach, and sensing a soreness in your little toe from tight shoes, etc. The brain is multidimensional, simultaneously processing visual, aural, olfactory and kinesthetic sensory inputs and, as discussed above, combining them with mental thoughts and emotional feelings to create an internal perception and feeling of external awareness (Bennet & Bennet, 2006). Thus, as introduced above, the brain is simultaneously identifying and storing core patterns from incoming information, with some more important to the situation at hand than others. In other words, there is a *hierarchy of information* where hierarchy represents "an order of some complexity, in which the elements are distributed along the gradient of importance" (Kuntz, 1968, p. 162). This hierarchy of information is analogous to the physical design of the neocortex, "a sheet of cells the size of a dinner napkin as thick as six business cards, where the connections between various regions give the whole thing a hierarchical structure" (Hawkins, 2004, p. 109).

In a hierarchy the dominant structural element may be a central point such as in a circular structure, or have an axial symmetry. Wherever the central point (dominant structure) is located, each part is determined by where it is located in relation to that central point. While it is true that in a radial version of hierarchy the entire pattern may depend directly on an open center, most hierarchies consist of groups of subordinate hierarchies who in turn have groups of subordinate hierarchies, with each group having its own particular relation to the dominant center point (Kuntz, 1968). The core pattern stored in the brain could be described as a pattern of patterns with the possibility of both hierarchical and associative relationships to other patterns.

The mind/brain develops robustness and deep understanding derived from its capacity to use past learning and memories to complete incoming information and, instead of storing all the details, *it stores only information meaningful to the this individual mind/brain*. This provides the ability to create and store higher level patterns while simultaneously semantically complexing incoming information with internal memories, adapting the resulting patterns to the situation at hand. Through these processes—and many more that are not yet understood—the brain supports survival and sustainability in a complex and unpredictable world. For example, recent studies of world-class chess players have shown that experts examined the chessboard patterns (not the pieces) over and over again, looking at nuances, generally "playing with" and studying these *patterns*. Ross noted that their ability to chunk patterns (put into a hierarchical form) for ease of memory and retrieval was a significant part of their success (Ross, 2006). These world-class players can recognize as many as 50,000 different and hierarchically related chess patterns.

As a brief summary, our brain receives patterns from the outside world, stores them as memories, and makes predictions by combining what it has seen before and what is happening now. In particular, the cortex has a large memory capacity and is constantly predicting what we will see, hear, and feel, usually occurring in the unconscious. The reason this is possible is because our cortex has built a model of the world around us, a hierarchical and nested structure of the cortex that "stores a model of the hierarchical structure of the real world" (Hawkins, 2004, p. 125).

ADVANCED DECISION-MAKING: THE CORTEX

There are six layers of hierarchical patterns in the architecture of the cortex. For a deeper discussion of these levels we draw on the extensive work of Hawkins (2004). Using what he describes as the memory-prediction model of the cortex, Hawkins (2004) has developed a framework for understanding intelligence. The cortex's core function is to make predictions. A comparison of what is happening and what was expected to happen is part of the prediction process. In order to do this, there are not only avenues of incoming patterns but feedback paths, that is, information flowing from the processing area of the brain (the highest levels of the hierarchy) back to the lowest levels of the hierarchy that first received the input from the external world.

While only documented for the sense of vision, it appears that the patterns at the lowest level of the cortex are fast changing and spatially specific (highly situation dependent and context sensitive) while the patterns at the highest level are slow changing and spatially invariant. For example, since the light receptors in the retina are unevenly distributed and the cells in the cortex are evenly distributed, the retinal image relayed to the primary visual area of the cortex is highly distorted. Through the use of probes it has been discovered that at the lowest level of the cortex any particular cell responds only to a tiny part of the visual input coming into the retina. Each neuron at this level has a "so-called receptive field that is highly specific to a minute part of your total field of vision" (Hawkins, 2004, p. 112). Further, each cell at this level also appears to be fine-tuned to specific kinds of input patterns which change with every fixation. (A fixation occurs approximately three times a second as the eyes make a small, quick movement (a saccade) and then stops.)

In contrast, when probes are used at the higher fourth level of the cortex, some cells that become active *stay active*. As Hawkins explains,

> *... we might find a cell that fires robustly whenever a face is visible. This cell stays active as long as your eyes are looking at a face anywhere in your field of vision. It doesn't switch on and off with each saccade ... cells have changed from being rapidly changing, spatially specific, tiny-feature recognition cells, to being constantly firing, spatially nonspecific, object recognition cells. (Hawkins, 2004, p. 113)*

What this conveys is the presence of higher-order patterns as incoming sensory information flows up from the lowest level to the highest level of the cortex, and then back down in a continuous feedback loop. Further, our example represents only the visual sense, yet *all* the senses (visual, auditory, somatic, etc.) are interconnected, acting as one associated whole, part of a "single multibranched hierarchy" (Hawkins, 2004, p. 119). This affirms that a decision-maker's ability to anticipate expected outcomes is based on the patterns of his experience, that is, incoming sensory information is integrated with stored information in its invariant form as it moves up through the hierarchical structure of the cortex, with each level a representation (stored in invariant form) of the information patterns beneath it in the hierarchy. Now, add the presence of feedback loops from the higher-order patterns to the lower-order patterns and you have a continuously self-organizing system that relies heavily on its invariant forms that do not change easily.

Let us look at this process from the viewpoint of the four modes of Kolb's experiential learning model (concrete experience, reflective observation, abstract conceptualization and active experimentation) (Kolb, 1984). You have a situation. You experience the situation. Out of that experience you have a set of information (the first and lowest level pattern in the prefrontal cortex), and all the details (in the form of information) that have come into your mind/brain/body. Then you reflect on the situation, and that reflection process is one of assembling and integrating all of the incoming information (thus creating second-level patterns). The third level of patterns is created in the comprehension phase and where not just understanding and meaning (started in the reflection process) are generated, but also insight, creative ideas, judgment and anticipating the outcome of various actions. In your mind, you already have certain invariant patterns which represent past beliefs, experience, values and other previous assumptions that exist in the top level of the hierarchy in your cortex. Those patterns that already exist are matched with the patterns created at levels 1, 2 and 3, and through that learning process create high-level invariant forms. You've thrown away all of the excess information and are looking at the core meaning of the incoming information from the situation at hand. You have now generated neuro-knowledge that presents avenues for taking action to achieve the desired situation. Here is where the highest level of invariant forms—theories, beliefs and assumptions—are used to select the best action to take. This information is passed back down the hierarchical levels which then supplies the details of the solution that drive the actions that are anticipated will change the situation.

FINAL THOUGHTS

As we move from simple to complex problems, and from an industrial to information to knowledge-based society, decision-makers must create and apply the best knowledge they can. Understanding this decision process requires good definitions—a clear understanding of information and knowledge—and how the mind/brain through patterns (thoughts) and actions is able to learn, make decisions, and anticipate the outcome of actions. As a result of the significant neuroscience findings over the past 15 years, we are beginning to learn just how this occurs.

In our discussion of information and the three levels of knowledge—surface, shallow and deep—we explored how knowledge is created. Through anticipating the outcome of actions the decision-maker can recognize the role of the mind in using theory, frames of reference, meaning and forecasting to make decisions in a complex environment. Sustainable decision-making through continuous learning and feedback loops was introduced—demonstrating the need for a spectrum of theories to support flexible and sustainable decision journeys.

There is a resonance between the current decision environment and the workings of the mind/brain. Theories that are invariant forms at the highest hierarchal level of the prefrontal cortex significantly influence decision-making. These invariant theories are continuously integrated across complementary sensing modes (visual, auditory, somatic, etc.) and through a downward feedback loop provide the decision-maker with the capacity to anticipate the outcome of actions. The larger the number of and connections among invariant forms developed through experience and learning, the more robust the spectrum of theories available to the decision-maker which offer (1) a greater potential for adaptable decision-making, and (2) a higher probability of achieving the expected outcome. Thus the workings of our mind/brain provide a model for decision-making in a complex situation.

REFERENCES

Amen, D. G. (2005). *Making a good brain great.* New York: Harmony Books.

American Heritage Dictionary 4th Ed. (2006). Boston: Houghton Mifflin Co.

Anonymous. (n.d.). Appeared in numerous emails to authors and is available on dozens of Internet sites. Retrieved April 5, 2009, from http://www.gamedev.net/community/forums/topic.asp?topic_id=375056

Auyang, S. Y. (1998). *Foundations of complex-system theories in economics, evolutionary biology, and statistical physics*. New York, NY: Cambridge University Press.

Begley, S. (2007). *Train your mind change your brain: How a new science reveals our extraordinary potential to transform ourselves*. New York, NY: Ballantine Books.

Bennet, A., & Bennet, D. (2004). *Organizational survival in the new world: The intelligent complex adaptive system*. New York, NY: Elsevier.

Bennet, A. & Bennet, D. (2006). Learning as associative patterning. *VINE: The journal of information and knowledge management systems, 36* (4).

Bennet, A., & Bennet, D. (2007). *Knowledge mobilization in the social sciences and humanities: Moving from research to action*. Frost, WV: MQIPress.

Bennet, A., & Bennet, D. (2008a). The decision-making process for complex situations in a complex environment. In F. Burstein & C.W. Holsapple, (Eds), *Handbook on decision support systems*. New York, NY: Springer-Verlag.

Bennet, D. (2006). Expanding the knowledge paradigm. *VINE: The journal of information and knowledge management systems, 36* (2).

Bennet, D. & Bennet, A. (2008b). Engaging tacit knowledge in support of organizational learning. *VINE: The journal of information and knowledge systems, 38* (1).

Bennet D. & Bennet, A. (2008c). The depth of KNOWLEDGE: Surface, shallow and Deep. *VINE: The journal of information and knowledge management systems, 38*(4/December).

Bennet, D., & Bennet, A. (2009), Associative patterning: The unconscious life of an organization. In J.P. Girard, (Ed.), *Building organizational memories*. Hershey, PA: IGI Global.

Buchanan, M. (2004). Power laws and the new science of complexity management. *Strategy + Business, 34*(Spring), 70-79.

Byrnes, J. P. (2001). *Minds, brains, and learning: Understanding the psychological and education relevance of neuroscientific research*. New York, NY: The Guilford Press.

Christos, G. (2003). *Memory and dreams: The creative human mind*. New Brunswick, NY: Rutgers University Press.

Church, D. (2006). *The genie in your genes: Epigenetic medicine and the new biology of intention*. Santa Rosa, CA: Elite Books.

Cleveland, H. (2002). *Nobody in charge: Essays on the future of leadership*. San Francisco, CA: Jossey-Bass.

Damasio, A. (2007). How the brain creates the mind. In Bloom, F.E. (Ed.), *Best of the brain from Scientific American: Mind, matter, and tomorrow's brain* (pp. 58-67). New York: Dana Press.

Edelman, G., & Tononi, G. (2000). *A universe of consciousness: How matter become imagination*. New York: Basic Books.

Hawkins, J., & Blakeslee, S. (2004). *On intelligence: How a new understanding of the brain will lead to the creation of truly intelligent machines*. New York: Times Books.

Kandel, E. R. (2006). *The neuroscience of adult learning: New directions for adult and continuing education*. San Francisco: Jossey-Bass.

Kolb, D. A. (1984). *Experiential learning: Experience as the source of learning and development*. Upper Saddle River, NJ: Prentice-Hall.

Kuntz, P. G. (1968). *The concept of order*. Seattle, WA: University of Washington Press.

Marchese, T. J. (1998). The new conversations about learning: Insights from neuroscience and anthropology, cognitive science and workplace studies. *New Horizons for Learning*. Retrieved January 19, 2008, from www.newhorizons.org/lifelong/higher_ed/marchese.htm

Marton, F., & Booth, S. (1997). *Learning and awareness*. Mahwah, NJ: Erlbaum.

Moon, J. A. (2004). *A handbook of reflective and experiential learning: Theory and practice*. New York: Routledge-Falmer.

Pert, C. B. (1997). *Molecules of emotion: A science behind mind-body medicine*. New York: Touchstone.

Ratey, J. J. (2001). *A user's guide to the brain: Perceptions, attention, and the four theaters of the brain*. New York: Pantheon Books.

Ross, P. E. (2006). The expert mind. *Scientific American*, (August): 64–71. doi:10.1038/scientificamerican0806-64

Schwartz, P. (2003). *Inevitable surprises: Thinking ahead in a time of turbulence*. New York: Penguin Group, Inc.

Stonier, T. (1992). *Beyond information: The natural history of intelligence*. London: Springer-Verlag.

Stonier, T. (1997). *Information and meaning: An evolutionary perspective*. London: Springer-Verlag.

Chapter 3
Exploring the Implications of Complexity Thinking for the Management of Complex Organizations

Kurt A. Richardson
ISCE Research, USA

ABSTRACT

This article is an attempt to explore the implications of the emerging science of complexity for the management of organizations. It is not intended as an introduction to complexity thinking, but rather an attempt to consider how thinking 'complexly' might affect the way in which managers do their jobs. This is achieved in a rather abstract way with some theory, but I hope the general message that there is no one way to manage comes through loud and clear, and that management is as much an art as it is a science (and always will be). In a sense complexity thinking is about limits, limits to what we can know about our organizations. And if there are limits to what we can know, then there are limits to what we can achieve in a pre-determined, planned way.

INTRODUCTION

This article is an attempt to explore the implications of the emerging science of complexity for the management of organizations. It is not intended as an introduction to complexity thinking, but rather an attempt to consider how thinking 'complexly' might affect the way in which managers do their jobs. This is achieved in a rather abstract way with some theory I'm afraid, but I hope the general message that there is no one way to manage comes through loud and clear, and that management is as much an art as it is a science (and always will be). In a sense complexity thinking is about limits, limits to what we can know about our organizations. And if there are limits to what we can know, then there are of course limits to what we can achieve in a pre-determined, planned way. Complexity thinking offers us a rigorous and scientific explanation as to why to some degree we are helpless and that surprise is inevitable, as well as provide some tools for thought that help us manage our inevitable shortcomings and limitations. In a way, accepting that we have limitations, and that we can never have

DOI: 10.4018/978-1-61520-668-1.ch003

complete control over the future evolution of our organizations, is rather emancipating. Complexity thinking is about the middle ground between extremes, and so although managers are to a degree helpless and at the mercy of the 'system', it certainly does not follow that there are not many opportunities to affect organizational behavior in desirable, semi-planned, ways.

The first section explores the difference between the view that organizations are complicated and the view that organizations are complex. This distinction leads to very different conclusions about what we can mean by the term 'management theory'. This first section is a little philosophical so I hope it doesn't scare anyone off! Linear (complicated) thinking is often rather superficial and simplistic, whereas nonlinear (complex) is more sophisticated and often requires more time to do properly. Complexity thinking actually requires us to spend a little more time thinking and a little less time working.

The next section presents and discusses an important concept in complexity thinking: incompressibility. It is this very notion that denies the possibility of a nice and neat theory of organization that managers might learn and execute. I'm sorry – being a good manager is always going to be a challenging job; there's no easy way out!

The penultimate section considers three schools of thinking within the complexity community followed by a brief discussion of how each school might inform management activity. Some concluding remarks will be offered to close the article, but first let's consider what we might mean by labeling an organization 'complex'.

WHAT IF ORGANIZATIONS WERE MERELY COMPLICATED?

What if human organizations were *complicated* rather than *complex*? The simple answer to this question is that the possibility of an all-embracing Theory of Management would almost certainly exist. This would make management very easy indeed as there would be a book of theory (*The Management Bible* – it would probably challenge the current all-time bestseller in sales!) that would tell the practicing manager what to do in any given context. The means of achieving effective and efficient organizational management would no longer be a mystery. But what is it about the concept of 'complicated' that makes this scenario plausible? Why has the possibility of a final management theory not been realized yet, given the millions of man-hours and published pages devoted to the search? Why does approaching organizations as 'complex' rather than 'complicated' deny us of this possibility?

A very common (but incomplete) description of a complex system is that such systems are made up of a large number of nonlinearly[1] interacting parts. By this definition the modern computer would be a complex system. A modern computer is crammed full of transistors which all respond nonlinearly to their input(s). Despite this 'complexity' (sic) the average PC does not show signs of emergence or self-organization; it simply processes (in a linear fashion) the instruction list (i.e., a program) given to it by its programmer. Even the language in which it is programmed is rather uninteresting. Although there are many programming languages, they can all be translated into each other with relative ease. Technically this is to say that computer languages are *commensurable* with each other. A line of code in C# can be translated into Visual Basic very easily – the one line of C# code may require more lines of VB code to achieve the same functionality but it can be done in the vast majority of cases. The universal language into which all such languages can be translated without loss is called 'logic' (more accurately, Boolean, or even binary, logic). More often though, if a programmer wants to use a language very close to the universal language of computing, *assembly* is used as this at least contains concepts that are more easily read by mere mortal programmers (although the domain knowledge – microelectronics – needed to program in assembly is a major requirement). This is then translated (without loss) into machine code (which is based on Boolean logic) – writing sophisticated programs directly in the language of the 0s and 1s of Boolean logic is nigh on impossible. The computer cannot choose the way it interprets the program, it cannot rewrite the program (unless it is programmed to in a prescribed manner), and it cannot get fed up with running programs and pop to the pub for a swift pint! So, what is it about the modern computer that prevents it from being labeled a *complex* system, but rather a *complicated* system?

The critical element is *feedback*. It is the existence of nonlinear feedback in complex systems that allows for *emergence*, *self-organization*, *adaptation*, *learning* and many other key concepts that have become synonymous with complexity thinking – and all the things that make management such a challenge. It is not just the existence of feedback loops that leads to complex behavior. These loops must themselves interact with each other. Once we have three or more *interacting* feedback loops (which may be made up from the interactions of many parts) accurately predicting the resulting behavior via standard analytical methods becomes problematic (at best) for most intents and purposes. In a relatively simple complex system containing as few as, say, fifteen parts / components, there can be hundreds of interacting feedback loops. In such instances the only way to get a feel for the resulting dynamics is through simulation, which is why the computer (despite its rather uninteresting dynamics) has become so important in the development of complexity thinking. We say that the prediction of overall system behavior from knowledge of its parts is *intractable*. Basically, *absolute knowledge about the parts that make up a system and their interactions provides us with very little understanding indeed regarding how that system will behave overall*. Often the only recourse we have is to sit back and watch. In a sense the term complex system refers to systems which, although we may have a deep appreciation of how they are put together (at the *microscopic* level), we may be completely ignorant of how the resulting *macroscopic* behavior comes about – i.e., complexity is about limits to knowledge, or our inevitable ignorance. Without this understanding of causality planning for particular outcomes is very difficult indeed. In the computer (which we will now class as a complicated system) causality is simple, i.e., low dimensional – few (interacting) feedback loops (although there are many millions of connections). In complex systems, causality is networked making it very difficult indeed, if not impossible, to untangle the contribution each causal path makes. It is hard enough to grasp the possibilities that flow from a small group of people let alone the mind-boggling possibilities that might be generated from a large multi-department organization. Maybe this is why a major part of management tends to be suppressing all these possibilities so that one individual might begin to comprehend what remains – departmentalization is an obvious example of a complexity reduction strategy.

Another unexpected property of complex systems is that there exist stable abstractions, not expressible in terms of the constituent parts, that themselves bring about properties different from those displayed by the parts. This sentence is a bit of a mouthful, but I have here succinctly described the process of emergence although in a rather awkward way. This is deliberate. More often than not emergence is portrayed as a process from which macroscopic properties 'emerge' from microscopic properties, i.e., the properties of the whole emerge from the properties of its parts. But this is an overly simplistic view of emergence. When recognizing the products of emergence, e.g., novel wholes, what is really happening is that we are abstracting (which essentially means information filtering, i.e., ignoring some information in favor of paying attention to some other information that comprises some kind of pattern) away from the description in terms of parts and interactions, and proposing a new description in terms of entities or concepts quite different from the constituent parts we started with – regarding an organization as a collection of interacting departments rather than a collection of individual people is the same process. These new entities have novel properties in relation to the properties the constituent parts have, i.e., whole departments do not act just like individual people, and 'team-ness' is not the same as 'person-ness'. What is even more interesting is that these supposed abstractions can interact with the parts from which they emerged – a process known as *downward causation*. I won't go into the problematic nature of the concept of emergence any further here – please refer to Richardson (2004) – suffice to say that the view that the process of emergence is captured by the expression "the whole is greater than the sum of its parts" is far too simplistic.

In specially idealized complex systems such as in cellular automata (see the Wiki link below) the parts are very simple indeed, and yet they still display a great deal of emergent phenomena and dynamical diversity. Complex systems which contain more intricate parts are often referred to as *complex adaptive systems* or CASs, in which the parts themselves are described as complex systems. The parts of CASs contain local memories and have a series of detailed responses to the same, as well as different, contexts / scenarios. They often have the ability to learn from their mistakes and generate new responses (by combining with other parts for example) to familiar and novel contexts. Because of this localized decision-making / learning ability such parts are often referred to as (autonomous) agents. There is a profound relationship between simple complex systems (SCSs), i.e., complex systems comprised of simple parts, and CASs, i.e., complex systems comprised of intricate agents. The Game-of-Life, a particularly well-known SCS, shows how a CAS can be abstracted, or emerges, from a SCS! Intuition might tell us that a CAS is an intricate SCS with something 'extra' added, something different that drives adaptive evolution. The Game-of-Life demonstrates that our intuition is, as is often the case in complexity thinking, too simplistic. If you are unfamiliar with the Game-of-Life, 'invented' by John Conway, then I recommend starting with the Wiki at http://en.wikipedia.org/wiki/Conway's_Game_of_Life. The Game-of-Life, and other cellular automata-like systems, offer an entertaining way to learn a great deal about complex systems dynamics, and to begin to develop a deep appreciation for the systems view of the world.

COMPLEXITY AND INCOMPRESSIBILITY

Cilliers (2005) introduces the idea of incompressibility:

We have seen that there is no accurate (or rather, perfect) representation of the system which is simpler than the system itself. In building representations of open systems, we are forced to leave things out, and since the effects of these omissions are nonlinear, we cannot predict their magnitude. (Cilliers, 2005, p. 13)[2]

It is this concept of incompressibility that leads us away from a managerial monism – a definitive theory of management – to a managerial pluralism (assuming organizations are complex rather than merely complicated) – in which many theories co-exist each with their own unique strengths and weaknesses. Restating Cilliers, the best representation of a complex system is the system itself, and any alternative representation of the system will be incomplete and, therefore, can lead to incomplete (or even just plain wrong) understanding. One must be careful in interpreting the importance of incompressibility. Just because a complex system is incompressible it does not follow that there are (incomplete) representations of the system that cannot be useful – incompressibility is not an excuse for not bothering. This is rather fortunate otherwise the only option available, once we accept the impossibility of an ultimate theory, is to have no theory at all – not a very satisfactory outcome (and contrary to what experience would tell us); I think I'd rather know something that is wrong rather than nothing at all. Knowing something and knowing how it is wrong is even better! Equally useful is knowing something that is wrong, but knowing why it is wrong.

Building on the work of Bilke and Sjunnesson (2001), Richardson (2005a) recently showed how Boolean networks (which are a type of SCS) could be reduced / compressed in such a way as to not change the qualitative character of the uncompressed system's phase space, i.e., the compressed system had the same functionality as the uncompressed system. If nothing was lost in the compression process, then Cilliers's claim of incompressibility would be incorrect. However, what was lost was a great deal of detail of how the different attractor basins (regions that describe qualitatively different system's behavior) are reached. Furthermore, the reduced systems are not as tolerant to external perturbations as their unreduced parents. This evidence would suggest that stable and accurate – although imperfect – representations of complex systems do indeed exist. However, in reducing / compressing / abstracting a complex system certain potential significant details are lost. Different representations capture different aspects of the original system's behavior. We might say that, in the absence of a complete representation, the overall behavior of a system is *at least* the sum of the behaviors of all our simplified models of that system. Richardson (2005a) concludes that:

Complex systems may well be incompressible in an absolute sense, but many of them are at least quasi-reducible in a variety of ways. This fact indicates that the many commentators suggesting that reductionist methods are in some way anti-complexity – some even go so far as to suggest that traditional scientific methods have no role in facilitating the understanding complexity – are overstating their position. Often linear methods are assessed in much the same way. The more modest middle ground is that though complex systems may indeed be incompressible, most, if not all, methods are capable of shedding some light on certain aspects of their behavior. It is not that the incompressibility of complex systems prevents understanding, and that all methods that do not capture complexity to a complete extent are useless, but that we need to develop an awareness of how our methods limit our potential understanding of such systems. (Richardson, 2005a, p. 380)

In short, all this is saying is that we can indeed have knowledge of complex organizations, but that this knowledge is approximate and provisional. This may seem like common sense, but it is surprising how much organizational knowledge is acted upon *as if* it were perfectly correct.

The suggestion that there are multiple valid representations of the same complex system is not new. The complementary law (e.g., Weinberg, 1975) from general systems theory suggests that any two different perspectives (or models) about a system will reveal truths regarding that system that are neither entirely independent nor entirely compatible. More recently, this has been stated as: a complex system is a system that has two or more non-overlapping descriptions (Cohen, 2002). I would go as far as to include "potentially contradictory" suggesting that for complex systems (by which I really mean any part of reality I care to examine) *there exists an infinitude of useful, non-overlapping, potentially contradictory descriptions*. Maxwell (2000) in his analysis of a new conception of science asserts that:

Any scientific theory, however well it has been verified empirically, will always have infinitely many rival theories that fit the available evidence just as well but that make different predictions, in an arbitrary way, for yet unobserved phenomena. (Maxwell, 2000, p. 18)

The result of these observations is that to have any chance of even beginning to understand complex systems we must approach them from many directions – we must take a pluralistic stance. This pluralist position provides a theoretical foundation for the many techniques that have been developed for group decision making, bottom-up problem solving, distributed management; any method that stresses the need for synthesizing a wide variety of perspectives in an effort to better understand the problem at hand, and how we might collectively act to solve it.

COMPLEXITY AND PLURALISM

The pluralism inherent in complexity thinking undermines the whole notion of a unified theory of complexity, i.e., theoretical monism. A simplistic view of unification would be similar to the example above about computer languages. Unification of this sort would suggest that if we work very hard indeed, eventually we will not only have at hand all the relevant laws of complexity, but that these different laws could be derived from *one* underlying principle. This is very much the basis of Theories of Everything (TOEs) in the physical sciences. Although there will exist a plurality of theories, they will all be coherent in that they can be expressed in terms of a more fundamental / general language (likely to be a form of mathematics) without any loss of detail. We might refer to this as *commensurable pluralism*. However, if we assume that a complex systems perspective provides a more appropriate basis from which to understand our surroundings, then we must address the issue of incompressibility. Incompressibility leads to a different sort of pluralism altogether; a pluralism in which the different theories / representations are not all reducible to a fundamental language without loss of detail – even if we agree that a theory of individual psychology is more fundamental (i.e., lower-level) than a theory of team dynamics, *all* team dynamics will never be described in terms of individual psychology only. In such a pluralism the different representations are generally incommensurable with each other (i.e., not expressible in terms of each other), and rather than leading to a coherent TOE, a patchwork of overlapping theories results. Within such *incommensurable pluralism* there will be opportunities for limited translations, reductions and simplifications, but a TOE will never result. In this situation the critical importance of context also becomes apparent. Each approach in the patchwork will be valid only for a certain range of contexts, and so matching theory to context becomes ever so important. However, a feature of complex systems is that context recognition is not a trivial exercise, as to define a context we must ignore some aspects of the situation of interest (as in the process of abstraction described above). Contexts which appear similar may actually be quite different, and so the process of matching theory to context is problematic at best, which again highlights the importance of approaching real world problems from many different directions. Furthermore, complex systems evolve (in a qualitative sense) and so fundamentally novel contexts emerge requiring new theoretical syntheses. If we assume that human organizations are best described as complex systems then this has quite profound implications for management science; implications that are at odds with traditionalist views.

The main criticism traditionalists have of the 'others' is that by refusing to focus management studies on a single perspective / theory, the potential political and influential clout of management academics has been vastly reduced. According to Pfeffer (1993):

Without a recommitment to a set of fundamental questions and without working through a set of rules to resolve theoretical disputes, the field of organization studies will remain ripe for a hostile takeover (Pfeffer, 1993, p. 558; emphasis added)

Donaldson (1995) built an entire book around this idea: *American Anti-Management Theories of Organization: A Critique of Paradigm Proliferation*. Donaldson's book is an indictment of existing management science which, he claims, has fragmented into competing paradigms. Donaldson argues that this profusion of perspectives is driven not by a genuine need to further the body of knowledge, but by a "push for novelty fuelled by individual career interests" typical of the academic environment[3]. He asserts that the resulting fragmentation of the field into mutually incompatible ideas has significantly weakened management science as an intellectual enterprise worthy of attention and support – I think this is confusing the marketing of theory with the process of theory development (the last thing we want to do is compromise the standards by which theory is developed for the sake of marketing).

Donaldson's book calls for building a unified theory of organizations. Clearly this is at odds with what has been discussed above. In my view, paradigm proliferation is healthy for management science – not a disease that needs to be eradicated – status quos are never maintained and are rarely healthy in the long term. Fragmentation is inevitable, but what we must learn to do better is work with this fragmentation rather than force a 'commensurable unification' upon it. Efforts to this end are readily apparent with the current trend for cross-disciplinary and multi-disciplinary research (which are themselves essential through the lens of complexity thinking). Such research will always be difficult by its very nature, and will not be overcome by pushing for a unifying framework, which will do no more than paper over the cracks (and in so doing severely limit our opportunities to develop richer understanding).

USING COMPLEXITY THINKING

In this section I will briefly outline three approaches for how complexity thinking might support organizational management. These different approaches are derived from three different schools of thinking within the complexity movement. These three schools are not isolated from each other, but themselves form a complex system of interrelationships. Despite their interdependence I still find it useful to divide the complexity movement into these divisions. The three schools / themes / divisions that I identify and discuss are: the neo-reductionists, the 'metaphorticians', and the critical pluralists.

The Neo-Reductionist School

The first theme is strongly associated with the quest for TOE in physics mentioned above, i.e., an acontextual explanation for the existence of everything. This community seeks to uncover the general principles of complex systems, likened to the fundamental field equations of physics[4]. The search for such over-arching laws and principles was / is one of the central aims of the general systems movement. Any such Theory of Complexity, however, will be of limited value. In Richardson (2005b) I suggest that even if such a theory existed it would not provide an explanation of every 'thing' in terms that we would find useful. If indeed such fundamental principles do exist they will likely be so abstract as to render them practically useless in the everyday world of human experience – a decision-maker would need several PhDs in pure mathematics just to make the simplest of decisions. I do not want to sound too critical here (I am an active contributor within this school of complexity) as we just need to consider how much valuable science has come out of the quest for a TOE. It clearly has been a highly motivating and productive idea. We just need to have realistic expectations for this way of doing science. It is quite likely that we would start to see diminishing returns if society (more specifically, funding councils) got too pre-occupied with this particular (reductionist) approach.

This complexity community makes considerable use of computer simulation in the form of bottom-up agent based modeling. The 'laws' such nonlinear studies yield provide a basis for a knowledge paradigm that is considerably broader than just bottom-up simulation, or any formal mathematical / computer-based approach for that matter.

The neo-reductionist school of complexity science is based on a seductive syllogism (Horgan, 1995 – perhaps meant semi-ironically

- **Premise 1:** There are simple sets of mathematical rules that when followed by a computer give rise to extremely complicated patterns.
- **Premise 2:** The world also contains many extremely complicated patterns.
- **Conclusion:** Simple rules underlie many extremely complicated phenomena in the world, and with the help of powerful computers, scientists can root those rules out.

Though this syllogism was definitively refuted in a paper by Oreskes, *et al.* (1994), in which the authors warned that "verification and validation of numerical models of natural systems is impossible," this position still dominates the neo-reductionist school of complexity in the (computational) social sciences. The recursive application of simple rules is certainly not the only source of complex behavior, and should not be seen as the only legitimate way to study complexity in human organizations (or anywhere else for that matter).

Despite all the rhetoric about reshaping our worldview, taking us out of the age of mechanistic (linear) science into a brave new (complex) world, many complexity theorists of this variety have actually inherited many of the assumptions of their more traditional scientific predecessors (they were very successful after all) by simply changing the focus from one sort of model to another, in very much the same way as some managers jump from one fad to another in the hope that the next one will be the ONE. There is no denying the power and interest surrounding the new models (e.g., agent-based simulation, genetic algorithms) proposed by the neo-reductionists, but it is still a focus on the model itself. Rather than using the linear models often associated with classical reductionism, a different sort of model – nonlinear models – have become the focus. Supposedly, 'bad' models have been replaced with 'good' models. This is a strategy we see in a wide variety of fields, not just the sciences. Although I myself do not have a great appreciation of the history of art, it does seem to me that new artistic ways of expression are more often thought of as 'different' rather than 'better' or 'worse'. I think this is a healthier attitude towards different methods.

The Metaphorical School

Within the organizational science community, complexity has not only been seen as a route to a possible theory of organization, but also as a powerful metaphorical tool (see, for example, Lissack, 1997, 1999; Richardson, *et al.*, 2005). According to this school, the complexity perspective, with its associated language, provides a powerful lens through which to 'see' organizations. Concepts such as *connectivity*, *edge-of-chaos*, *far-from-equilibrium*, *dissipative structures*, *emergence*, *epi-static coupling*, *co-evolving landscapes*, etc., facilitate organizational academics and practitioners in 'seeing' the complexity inherent in socio-technical organizations. The underlying belief is that the social world is intrinsically different from the natural world. As such, the theories of complexity, which have been developed primarily through the examination of natural systems, are not directly applicable to social systems (at least not to the practical administration of such systems), though its language may trigger some relevant insights to the behavior of the social world which would facilitate some limited degree of control over the social world.

Using such a 'soft' approach to complexity to legitimate this metaphorical approach, other theories have been imported via the 'mechanism' metaphor into organization studies; a popular example being quantum mechanics (see McKelvey, 2001 for an example). While new lenses through which to view organizations can be very useful (see Morgan, 1986 for an excellent example of this) the complexity lens, and the 'anything goes' attitude that sometimes accompanies this perspective, has been abused somewhat. My concern is not with the use of metaphor *per se*, as I certainly accept that the role of metaphor in understanding is ubiquitous and essential. Indeed, in Richardson (2005b) it is argued that in an absolute sense all understanding can be nothing more (or less) than metaphorical in nature[5]. The concern is with its use in the absence of criticism – metaphors are being imported all over with very little attention being paid as to the legitimacy of such importation – the organization as an organism being a popular current example. This may be regarded as a playful activity in certain academic circles, but if such playfulness is to be usefully applied in serious business then some rather more concrete grounding is necessary. As van Ghyczy (2003) warns, "Instead of being seduced by the similarities between business and another field, you need to look for places where the metaphor breaks down... [M]etaphors are often improperly used" (pp. 87-88).

I refer to this school of complexity, which often uncritically imports ideas and perspectives via the mechanism of metaphor from a diverse range of disciplines, as the *metaphorical school*, and its adherents, *metaphorticians*. It is the school that perhaps represents the greatest source of creativity of the three schools classified here. But as we all know, creativity on its own is not sufficient for the design and implementation of successful managerial interventions. Recently, Evan Davis, reporting for the BBC (UK), blamed the current financial meltdown of the world's markets on creativity and innovation. He concluded that we should not ban innovation, but at least be wary of it (Davis, 2009).

The Critical Pluralist School

Neo-reductionism with its modernistic tendencies can be seen as one extreme of the complexity spectrum, whereas *metaphorism* with its atheoretical acritical relativistic tendencies can be seen as the opposing extreme. In my view the complexity perspective (when employed to underpin a philosophical outlook) both supports and undermines these two extremes. What is needed is a middle path.

The two previous schools of complexity promise either a neat package of coherent knowledge that can apparently be easily transferred into any context, or an incoherent mish mash of unrelated ideas and philosophies – both of which have an important role to play in understanding and manipulating complex systems. In my opinion, not only do these extremes represent overly simplistic interpretations of the implications of complexity, they also contradict some of the basic observations already made within the neo-reductionist mold, i.e., there are seeds within the neo-reductionist view of complexity that if allowed to grow lead naturally to a broader view that encapsulates both the extremes already discussed as well as everything in between.

One of the first consequences that arise from the complexity assumption is that as we ourselves are less complex than the Universe (The Complex System), as well as many of the systems we'd like to control / affect, there is no way for us to possibly experience 'reality' in any complete sense (Cilliers, 1998, p. 4; see also the comments above regarding incompressibility). We are forced (by our very nature) to view 'reality' through (evolving) categorical frameworks that allow us to tentatively tiptoe our way through life with some vague direction in mind. The critical pluralist school of complexity focuses more on what we cannot explain, rather than what can be explained – it is a concern with limits, and how we take those limits into account when trying to understand the world around us. As such, it leads to a particular *attitude* towards models, rather than the privileging of one sort of model over all others. And, rather than using complexity to justify an 'anything goes' relativism, it highlights the importance of critical reflection in grounding our models / representations / perspectives in an evolving reality. The keywords of this school might be *pluralism*, *criticism*, *open-mindedness* and *humility*. Any perspective whatsoever has the potential to shed light on complexity (even if it turns out to be wrong, otherwise how would one know that it was wrong?), but at the same time, not every perspective is equally useful / applicable in any given context (try fixing your car with prayer rather than with a good mechanic). Complexity 'thinking' is the art of maintaining the tension between pretending we know something, and knowing we know nothing for sure; it is a state of mind rather than a particular perspective.

THE THREE SCHOOLS AND MANAGEMENT

Now that we have identified and discussed the three schools of complexity, how does each one contribute to the management of human organizations? The first one, neo-reductionism, is the easiest as it simply adds a new collection of analytical tools to the decision-makers tool set. These tools will probably impact the fields of management science and operations research the most, providing some very powerful tools to facilitate the decision-making process surrounding larger strategic questions. Indeed such models are ideal for exploring that class of question where individual behavior matters only as a contribution to group behavior. They will probably not contribute to rather more mundane day-to-day management activities – it is unlikely that the development of an agent-based model will help much in deciding if to promote someone or not, or whether to change the supplier for the hallway coffee machine (techniques such a causal mapping and multi-criteria decision analysis are 'complexity' tools better matched to such 'micro' questions). There are certain types of problems that can benefit from nonlinear analytical models and some problems that will not. This school of complexity seems to be the most visible at present, and is probably the easiest of the three to (attempt to) apply. Given the immense computational resources needed to utilize the neo-reductionist's tools, there is also a certain level of glamour and excitement associated with this sort of complexity application; this seems to have captured the imagination of the management world, even though the problems it can usefully be brought to bear on are limited.

The metaphorical school of complexity can certainly play a part in the day-to-day activities of management. Given that our personal worldviews determine to a large extent what we 'see' and how we 'manage' what we 'see', replacing / enhancing that worldview with a perspective that is rather more sensitive to the complexities that are inherent in daily experience, can have a profound effect. Richardson *et al.* (2005), for example, considers project management through the lens of complexity-inspired metaphors. It is difficult to fully appreciate the influence the widespread usage of complexity-inspired metaphors will have, but I would like to think that many of the shortcomings of the dominant command and control metaphor (which, unfortunately, has become rather more than a metaphor) will be mitigated. Of course, replacing one worldview with another creates as many new problems as it solves. It'll be interesting to see what these new problems will be. (Although, seeing management as a problem solving process is itself a feature of the command and control attitude).

The metaphorical school does not only legitimate the use of complexity-inspired metaphors though; it is often used to justify a fully blown pluralism in which anything goes. We have to be careful that our wish to explore all possibilities does not lead to chaos (and I don't mean this in the mathematical sense). Quoting van Ghyczy (2003) again, "It's tempting to draw business lessons from other disciplines – warfare, biology, music. But most managers do it badly" (p.87). I would also add the many academics also do this badly.

The critical pluralist school of complexity also has implications for all aspects of management, although it is possibly one of the hardest to 'teach'. It encourages not only management, but all participant members of an organization, to approach everything they do in a critical way and to maintain some (ontological) distance from their ideas, i.e., to not take our ideas of organization too seriously – use our ideas to guide, or initiate, our thinking about organizations, not to determine our thinking. Complexity 'thinking' is a particular attitude towards our ideas of the world and the world itself, not a particular tool / method, or even a particular language. The last school is rather more philosophical than the first two and is also the hardest to describe in any complete sense. To close the article I'd like to discuss briefly why I believe philosophy is important for organizational managers (and every sophisticated thinker for that matter). I hope it is already clear that I believe complexity science itself suggests the central importance of a philosophical attitude when considering the world we experience.

WHY PHILOSOPHY?

Managers seem reluctant to study philosophy. They're not alone. This is not particularly surprising given that many books on the subject are often devoid of any practical recommendations. However, when I talk about a philosophical attitude I'm not saying that we all need to go out and invest considerable time in penetrating obscure texts. Philosophy is a study of what underlies choice. In both management and research choices abound. Researchers have to choose which methodology they are to employ in understanding a particular aspect (which of course also has to be chosen) of management; the boundaries of the research study need to be chosen (which is strongly dependent upon research methodology), etc. Managers have to continually decide which information is required to make a particular decision; how to interpret that information for the purposes at hand, and even choose what the actual purpose might be, as well as what the issue is that needs to be decided upon (although, often this is done very much unconsciously without much attention to the actual framework within which they have been 'taught' to operate).

From the perspective of the researcher Hughes (1990) suggests that philosophy underpins the whole selection process because:

... every research tool or procedure is inextricably embedded in commitments to particular versions of the world and to knowing the world. To use an attitude scale, to take the role of a participant observer, to select a random sample, to measure rate of population growth, and so on, is to be involved in conceptions of the world which allow these instruments to be used for the purposes conceived. No technique or method of investigation (and this is true of the natural sciences as it is of the social) is self-validating: its effectiveness, that is its very status as a research instrument making the world tractable to investigation, is, from a philosophical point of view, ultimately dependent on epistemological justifications. Whether they may be treated as such or not, research instruments and methods cannot be divorced from theory; as research tools they operate only within a given set of assumptions about the nature of society, the nature of human beings, the relationship between the two and how they may be known. (Hughes, 1990, p. 11)

When managers choose to adopt a particular perspective, or set of procedures, or what issue to focus upon, these choices are philosophically equivalent to the researcher's selection of a particular methodology. Both sets of choices are underpinned by particular views of how the world we observe is constructed, and how it should respond to our actions upon it. More often than not we are unaware of the commitments that our choices imply. It is not a question we are often taught to ask. It is not a question we have evolved to be too concerned with either. Of course, researchers often spend some time on these concerns, because many of them have been taught to. However, many managers, as well as most of us at large, are very rarely concerned with the underlying assumptions upon which our choices made. If we were, we would be rather surprised as to the absurdity of some of our most cherished beliefs.

Philosophers often refer to the dominant worldview (or philosophy) of the average layperson as *naïve realism*. The 'naïve' part is possibly a poorly chosen label as it would seem to indicate that all of us who are not philosophers are a little daft, in that we have been so poorly misguided into ever believing that realism could possibly be a sensible way to view our surroundings. I think, given that much of our sensory and decision making equipment has evolved in a way that naturally leads to a kind of realism, perhaps we can be forgiven for not knowing any better. Maybe common sense realism is a more positive way of distinguishing a layperson's realism from a philosopher's realism.

Realism is based on a what-you-see-is-what-you-get (or WYSIWYG for those fluent in computer jargon) worldview, i.e., that our senses tell us accurately what the world is comprised of and how those parts interact – what-you-sense-is-what-there-is (WYSIWTI), if you like. The first implication of realism is that the way in which we 'see' the world is quite independent of what our senses, and our beliefs, guide us to 'see'. This is quite contrary to the quote given above which suggests that our senses and beliefs profoundly affect what we 'see'. If our senses are truly unbiased (as naïve realism suggests) then understanding the world around us simply becomes a process of map making. For this reason realism is often also referred to as *representationalism*.

A second implication of realism is to regard causality as a first order process, i.e., if a change in object A results in a change in object B we have a tendency to assume that such a correlation points to a causal mechanism – 'A caused B to ...' So not only do the objects A and B exist as such, they also affect each other directly. The 'existence' of A and B would seem to be a trivial matter especially when considering objects such as cars and computers, but what about concepts like 'consumer confidence' or 'social capital'? Furthermore, given WYSIWTI, the possibility that it is an unseen object C that affected A and B (or mediated the affect), or that two unrelated objects C and D affected A and B directly, or that the change in B resulting from a change in A was no more than a coincidence (and therefore not causal even if there was some correlation) are all scenarios that are omitted from a simplistically realist perspective. The natural sciences have developed tools to allow us to 'see' objects that remain 'unseen' with the naked eye, but even here any explanations offered must necessarily be based on what has been detected.

Quite often realism is associated with 'linearity', but this would be a mistake. The advent of the computer has allowed us to 'model' scenarios in which complicated loops of interaction can be represented and explored, a trick which the human mind seems woefully inept at doing. The main consequence of realism that concerns me here is that it leads to an overconfidence in what we have represented and analyzed as being exactly how the real world works. Quite clearly this is not a view devoid of merit. If it was then our capacity to successfully achieve anything would be very much lower than it actually is. Clearly, to a useful degree, realism produces some rather good results.

Given the successes of modern science, it is not surprising that realist viewpoints dominate

Western thought – it is a natural way to view things, and such impressive machines as computers have been built that surely prove the power of realist thinking. Relating this back to philosophy, the success of modern science is arguably the reason that philosophy has fallen by the wayside. If science leads to correct knowledge all the time, then what is the point of questioning its underlying assumptions; surely the way in which modern science and the realists view the world is how the world *is*? Each new management fad promises to provide the ultimate answers to the hard questions troubling practicing managers, which again encourages philosophical ignorance. Why bother thinking too hard if there is a framework 'out there' claiming to do the thinking for us?

Two of the big questions for philosophers are what objects *exist* and how can we *know* about those objects. Jargon-wise, the study of what exists is referred to as *ontology* and the study of how we come to know these objects of existence (the study of knowledge) is referred to as *epistemology*. These two areas of interest have been enthusiastically investigated for at least 2500 years, until very recently that is. The Newtonian view of the Universe leads to an 'exquisitely intricate timepiece' model, i.e., the Universe is a really big machine. As a big machine it can be taken apart, its parts can be studied in isolation, and knowledge of the whole can be accurately gleaned by summing together the knowledge of its component parts. In popular views of modern science, there is something referred to as the scientific method which guides us in the study of these parts. So ontologically the Universe is a big machine, and epistemologically we have the scientific method to give us knowledge of the Universe's parts and eventually the Universe as a whole.

What is often missed from popular views of modern science is that science does not always work very well, and that there is no such well-defined process called the scientific method. This may come as a surprise to the many opponents and critics of modern science, but most decent scientists are well aware of their chosen occupation's shortcomings. Questions of ontology and epistemology really haven't been answered to complete satisfaction, thus there is still very much a role for philosophy.

The famous physicist Louis de Broglie once said "May it not be universally true that the concepts produced by the human mind, when formulated in a slightly vague form, are roughly valid for reality, but that, when extreme precision is aimed at, they become ideal forms whose real content tends to vanish away?" (quoted in Cory, 1942, p. 268). This suggests that we should use scientific understanding (not knowledge) to guide our decisions, not determine them as such understanding is only correct in a "vague" sense. This is true of all understanding once we accept the limitations of the realist worldview. Rather than regarding our knowledge as faithful maps of reality we must see it as a potentially useful, but not necessarily so, caricature of reality, or as a metaphor. This follows from the fluid and complex nature of systemic boundaries as seen from the complexity perspective. Causality is complex, intricate, multi-ordered, and intractable (in an absolute sense). All this suggests a renewed concern with ontology and epistemology and therefore with philosophy. What is ironic is that, though it has taken a revolution in science (spurred by a technological revolution which resulted from the dogmatic application of realist thinking for the past 400+ years) to bring complexity to the fore, philosophers have been concerned with complexity for hundreds if not thousands of years. So if you do find the time, and are willing to put in the hard work often necessary to understand many philosophical writings, you may well be surprised with the nuggets of wisdom you will uncover in even the oldest texts. Fortunately we are blessed with 'Dummies Guides' to get us started!

SOME CONCLUDING THOUGHTS

The aim of this article was not to provide a full introduction to complexity science, but to consider the various ways in which it might inform managerial action in a general sense. There are various tools that have derived from complexity science that might be used in the analysis of certain managerial problems. However, it is the implications of complexity thinking for the 'managerial attitude' that I have focused on here as I believe the shift from a linear simplistic attitude to a nonlinear complex attitude is significantly more challenging than a simple switch from one framework / tool to another as is more common in our faddish modern world.

The concept of incompressibility discussed above would suggest that attempting to capture the complex systems-derived implications for organizational management in some short snappy conclusions would at best be a limiting exercise, and at worst rather irresponsible (even unethical!). However, in the hope that you have read the preceding pages and not just jumped to the conclusions, I will attempt to do just that with the knowledge that you will appreciate that this is a problematic exercise to say the least. The laws of complex organizational management, therefore, might be listed as follows:

1. **Just because it looks like a nail, it doesn't mean you need a hammer:** A complex systems view acknowledges that context recognition is problematic, and as such deciding what to do is not a simple exercise of repeating what you did the last time you were in the same situation. The chances are the situation is quite different.
2. **Decisions made by the many are often better than those made by a few:** A precursor to any decision has to be a thorough consideration (critique) from multiple perspectives (pluralism). This might be the application of a variety of different models, or simply just asking more than one person for their opinion. Such an approach quite naturally leads to creative thinking, and enables the development of a richer understanding concerning a context of interest before a decision is made. Beware, however, as "too many cooks may spoil the broth", and in situations where time is not readily available, the leadership of an individual may prove more effective than attempts at group decision making;
3. **Expect to be wrong (or at least not completely right):** There are limits to how pluralistic and critical our decision making processes can be. But even with all the time and resources in the world (and a commitment to do the 'right' thing), decisions can only be made based on our best current understanding, and that understanding will always be incomplete. Everything is connected to everything else. We can't consider everything so we construct artificial boundaries to help us make a decision – without those boundaries we are helpless, with them our responses are limited (but at least we have some responses!);
4. **Flip-flopping is OK:** Contrary to the beliefs of certain US politicians, being prepared and confident enough to change one's mind when it becomes clear that one's model is proving ineffective (and even counterproductive) is actually a virtue, not a sin. The complex organization evolves in unforeseeable ways, and as such we must be prepared to "move with the times". The simple act of making a decision (based on past experience) can change how the future unfolds. Don't make the mistake of escalating one's commitment in the face of mounting contrary evidence. Dogmatism is rarely an effective long term strategy.

These bullets may be common sense to the experienced manager (endowed with an innate understanding of human networks). I certainly hope so! What is particularly interesting about complexity science is that it provides a scientific way of making these points. Good science has a tendency to change what common sense is over time, and I am excited at the prospect of an emerging systemic common sense. The complex systems view really is a profoundly different way of understanding the world from what we in the West (primarily) have become accustomed to. My modest hope is that the systemic task of managing will be no less challenging, but may be a little less frustrating (oh, and that our companies' obligations change to stakeholders rather than mere stockholders, but that may be asking for far too much!).

REFERENCES

Bilke, S., & Sjunnesson, F. (2002). Stability of the Kauffman model. *Physical Review E: Statistical, Nonlinear, and Soft Matter Physics*, *65*, 016129. doi:10.1103/PhysRevE.65.016129

Cilliers, P. (1998). *Complexity and postmodernism: Understanding complex systems*. New York: Routledge.

Cilliers, P. (2005). Knowing complex systems. In K. A. Richardson (Ed.), *Managing organizational complexity: Philosophy, theory, and application* (pp. 7-19). Greenwich, CT: Information Age Publishing.

Cohen, J. (2002). *Posting to the Complex-M listserv*, 2nd September.

Cory, D. (1942). The transition from naïve to critical realism. *The Journal of Philosophy*, *39*(10), 261–268. doi:10.2307/2017517

David, E. (2009). *The rockets scientists of finance*. Retrieved April 29, 2009, from http://news.bbc.co.uk/2/hi/business/7826431.stm

Donaldson, L. (1995). American anti-management theories of organization: A critique of paradigm proliferation. *Cambridge Studies in Management, 25*. Cambridge, UK: Cambridge University Press.

Greenwich, CT: Information Age Publishing.

Horgan, J. (1995). From complexity to perplexity. *Science*, *272*, 74–79.

Hughes, J. (1990). *The philosophy of science*. Golden, CO: Longhand Press.

Lissack, M. R. (1997). Mind your metaphors: Lessons from complexity science. *Long Range Planning*, (April): 294–298. doi:10.1016/S0024-6301(96)00120-3

Lissack, M. R. (1999). Complexity: The science, its vocabulary, and its relation to organizations. *Emergence*, *1*(1), 110–126. doi:10.1207/s15327000em0101_7

Maxwell, N. (2000). A new conception of science. *Physics World*, August, 17-18.

McKelvey, W. (2001). What is complexity science? It is really order-creation science. *Emergence*, *3*(1), 137–157. doi:10.1207/S15327000EM0301_09

Morgan, G. (1986). *Images of organization*. Thousand Oaks, CA: Sage Publications.

Oreskes, N., Shrader-Frechette, K., & Belitz, K. (1994). Verification, validation, and confirmation of numerical models in the earth sciences. *Science*, *263*, 641–646. doi:10.1126/science.263.5147.641

Pfeffer, J. (1993). Barriers to the advance of organizational science: Paradigm development as a dependent variable. *Academy of Management Review*, *18*, 599–620. doi:10.2307/258592

Richardson, K. A. (2004). On the relativity of recognizing the products of emergence and the nature of physical hierarchy. In *Proceedings of the 2nd biennial international seminar on the philosophical, epistemological and methodological implications of complexity theory*, January 7th-10th, Havana International Conference Center, Cuba.

Richardson, K. A. (2005a). Simplifying Boolean networks. *Advances in Complex Systems*, *8*(4), 365–381. doi:10.1142/S0219525905000518

Richardson, K. A. (2005b). The hegemony of the physical sciences: An exploration in complexity thinking. *Futures*, *37*(7), 615–653. doi:10.1016/j.futures.2004.11.008

Richardson, K. A., Tait, A., Roos, J., & Lissack, M. R. (2005). The coherent management of complex projects and the potential role of group decision support systems. In K. A. Richardson (Ed.), *Managing organizational complexity: Philosophy, theory, and application* (pp. 433-458)

von Ghyczy, T. (2003, September). The fruitful flaws of strategy metaphors. *Harvard Business Review*, 86–94.

Weinberg, G. (1975). *An introduction to general systems thinking*. New York: John Wiley.

ENDNOTES

1 'Nonlinearly' simply means that the parts are constructed in a way such that the output from one particular part is not necessarily proportionate to its input. The weather system is an oft cited example in which small additions of energy don't necessarily lead to small changes in the system's behavior.

2 This statement risks conflating the concept of incompressibility with the problem of identifying a bounded description of a complex system. These two concerns are not equivalent; just because a particular system cannot be bounded easily is not what incompressibility is all about. Incompressibility derives from the interacting nonlinear feedback loops that exist even in well bounded complex systems, i.e., a bounded complex system is still incompressible.

3 Donaldson's argument may account for why certain perspectives are more dominant than others, it does not explain why there is a "profusion of perspectives" in the first place. I would tend to think that if there was even a whiff of an ultimate theory of management then I doubt that the "individual career interests" of academics could prevent its development. Maybe the fact that after all the effort that has gone into trying to find this elusive organizational theory of everything (OTOE) we still only have a 'profusion' suggests that a 'profusion' is the optimal situation, and that an OTOE does not in fact exist (or that it is at least way beyond the grasp of mere mortals).

4 It is likely that these two research thrusts, if successful, will eventually converge if it is assumed assume that some kind of complex systems representation of the Universe as a whole is valid.

5 Metaphor is the description of certain aspects of one thing in terms of certain aspects of another. If we consider the Universe to be one 'thing' then human knowledge is the partial representation of the Universe in terms of the 'things' that constitute human language. Language itself determines to a great extent what aspects of reality are promoted to the 'foreground' – i.e., what we pay attention to – and what aspects are demoted to the 'background' – i.e., what we ignore – in the same way that the fox metaphor – 'He is as cunning as a fox' – highlights a particular trait of an individual and compares it to the cunningness of the fox. At the same time traits like the fox's shyness, for example, are ignored. By describing knowledge as metaphor, the bias and limited nature of knowledge is explicitly acknowledged.

Chapter 4
Decision Integrity and Second Order Cybernetics

Anthony Hodgson
Decision Integrity Limited, UK

ABSTRACT

The rational worldview of management science has come to dominate decision theory. This chapter proposes that, despite its evident successes, this view of decision making is decreasingly effective in a global world which turns out to be unruly and unpredictable in critical areas. The result is an escalation of unintended consequences in business, public affairs and human ecology. Despite its success in some fields of management, we need to question the rational view which disconnects the observer from the observed. Decision integrity is proposed as a reflexive theory of decision making that incorporates the decision maker as part of the decision field. It requires stepping out of the observer/object paradigm of classical science and into the alternative paradigm of second order cybernetics. The decision maker is not simply an observer but also a participant who cannot abdicate from personal ethical considerations and ultimate responsibility even in the face of uncertainty.

INTRODUCTION

Man is the prisoner of his own way of thinking and of his own stereotypes of himself. His machine for thinking the brain has been programmed to deal with a vanished world. This old world was characterized by the need to manage things – stone, wood, iron. The new world is characterized by the need to manage complexity. Complexity is the very stuff of today's world. (StaffordBeer, 1975, p. 15)

DOI: 10.4018/978-1-61520-668-1.ch004

With the rise and adoption of management science as the primary worldview or metatheory in both commerce and public affairs there has emerged a largely unexamined fixation with rational decision making. Rational economic man has become the unit in modern management and mathematical decision analysis has become the dominant espoused basis of management.

A recent case is the 2008 financial crisis. The growth of markets for derivatives and more complex financial instruments was made possible by the development of mathematical methods for valuing these new constructs. These became the adopted norm across the banking sector. In this way the very idea of "hedging" was an attempt to eliminate the risks of uncertainty. There is a paradox here. As creatures of limited intelligence in an unstable world we form definable requirements that we hope to fulfil in what we believe to be a predictable world. Commerce has fixated our goal-seeking in the context of profit games. The application of science has identified some domains of relative predictability and they have been adopted as the official view bolstered by economic theory. Management science, over the last few decades, appears to have led us into an evolutionary trap. Kay (2008, p. 43) points out that "our abilities in pattern detection often lead us to observe systematic relationships where they do not exist, or confuse underlying causes with statistical noise." For example, people view economic behaviour in the context of equilibrium theory and anticipate the future accordingly. As we shall see, there are other models that predict different futures on the same data.

The implicit view of the operating environment is something like "this is what we want; this is what is going to happen in the world; so we know what we are going to do in that world in order to get what we want." Herein lays the trap. The world is continuously changing, it is complex and it throws out events and properties which are outside any range of prediction. Such events have been characterised as the phenomena of 'black swans'. (Taleb, 2007) The Black Swan theory refers to the implications of large-impact, hard-to-predict, and rare event beyond the realm of normal expectations.

We are part of this world, not separate from it and so of the same nature. When we rationalise ourselves and our world we are asserting something which at best is of limited consistency with how things really are. The perverse consequence of this is that the more we assert we understand the world, and so limit what we do, the more we find ourselves living with the unintended consequences of our decisions.

The above view can be applied to the individual, the group, the institution, the nation and the globe. From a management perspective we focus on the institution or organisation. Organisation management, dominated by the management sciences, has analysed and systematised situations to bring them under control to pursue goals such as "return to shareholders" or "public value."

However, the real world leaks out from the boundaries of rationality, springs surprises on us and confronts us with uncertainties. Indeed, on occasion, the world smashes through the very centre of institutional life and destroys jobs, companies, industries and even whole economies. Control should then be seen for what it is, a convenient half-truth.

We need probabilities to help us assess risks and narratives to guide us through uncertainties – and the general knowledge and judgement to know how to approach each particular situation. It is that general knowledge and judgement that has been so lacking in the financial follies of the last decade. (Kay, 2008, p. 43)

The kind of decision making that dominates in the "controlled world" does not match the behaviour of the "uncontrollable world." Effective decisions cannot be arrived at by rational analysis alone because the rationale is inherently a limited perspective. We need the half-truth this generates but we need an approach to deal with the missing unruly half. Kay points out; "We suffer, not just from ignorance of the future, but from a limited capacity to imagine what the future might be" (Kay, 2008, p 43).

Some thinkers and practitioners have made efforts to create alternative modes of perception, analysis and decision making more congruent with this unruly world beyond the veneer of socio-economic rationality. The International Futures Forum (2009), sums up its foundational work in addressing these issues in a text called *Ten Things to Do in a Conceptual Emergency*. This puts forward ten strategies that offer prospect for working towards the other half of truth not accessible to rational analysis. The following subset of five principles, summarised below, helps to frame the approach in this chapter.

- *Give up on the myth of control.* We have taken our ever more sophisticated models as a proxy for reality. But our models break down in the face of the real complexity and mystery of the world.
- *Trust subjective experience.* The implications for how we see the world and our place in it are critical for our understanding of it and our behaviour towards it and, more profoundly, as part of it.
- *Form and nurture integrities.* The traditional model of organisation is struggling. Start by replacing integration with the more flexible and adaptable notion of integrity.
- *Re-perceive the present.* We underestimate the importance of living more deeply and consciously in the present. We need to extend our habits of what counts as 'knowledge'.
- *Move beyond an enlightenment consciousness.* The subject-object split is the hallmark of the Enlightenment, the separation of self from the world. We need to recognise a new context.

In a conceptual emergency it is necessary to take a different approach to decision making than the one which dominates the current paradigm of management.

This chapter will bring together a number of theoretical perspectives from the diverse fields of strategic management, scenario planning, learning theory, cognition and induction, reflexive investment theory, and new organisational forms under the overarching notions of second order cybernetics. Decision integrity will be used as a term to embrace the synthesis in both theory and practice that emerges. This synthesis will be considered in the context that a large scale shift is occurring from the modern age, in which objectivist science has ruled, to the global age in which a higher variety science is emerging that allows for a greater number of variables in the way valid science will be conducted and which will acknowledge von Foerster's requirement that a theory of biology should be able to explain the existence of theories of biology.

New Context, Old Ways

A distinction can be made between a decision field and a decision process. The decision field is the context of decision, its environment and all the external factors that will have some bearing on the decision. The field is in the present but also has attached to it histories giving it momentum and futures in the sense of trends and emerging patterns. The decision process is how the human decision maker conducts himself or herself to investigate, assess and intervene in the decision field. Aspects of the decision process are unconscious, like habits of mind and a taken-for-grantedness of the nature of the decision field. Other aspects are designed according to disciplines and understandings and could be called the decision system. The decision system can also be viewed as the espoused theory (Argyris, 1990) of the decision makers.

Clearly, for successful outcomes, there needs to be sufficient correspondence between the decision process and the decision field, the latter usually being largely outside the control of the decision makers. For example, a market may be moving in a certain way which will prescribe the range of options for choice. In an expanding market the choices may be about investment in growth opportunities; in a shrinking market the choices may be about competitive strengthening or about exit strategies.

When the world is behaving in a reasonably predicable and forecastable way, then the decision process can be based on technical analysis, such as net present value or cost/benefit, and the outcomes will tend to be as hoped for. Indeed, accumulated successes in this way will become ingrained the generic type of decision process as the success formula for that world.

If the world is actually more complex, more interconnected and more uncertain than supposed then there is a mismatch between the decision process and the decision field. To be successful the appreciation of the decision field must keep up with changing circumstances. The decision system has to take into account an unruly rather than a predictable world. One of the more successful approaches to coming to grips with the uncertain world is scenarios planning (van der Heijden, 2005). The basic idea of scenario planning is to acknowledge that prediction and forecasting are rendered ineffective in a world where structural change is taking place and consider multiple possible futures Further, taking a systems view of the world where structure determines behaviour it follows that distinct possible futures will have different underlying structures. There will be essential discontinuities between them. No extrapolation of the behaviour of today's structure will give account of different structures emerging in the future. Each shift of structure has different behavioural outcomes over different time scales (Curry and Hodgson, 2008). So now our reading of the decision field is more sophisticated, allowing for alternate structural changes with their accompanying narratives. A scenario exercise, then, constructs several different "structures in the future" which then serve as a test bed for proposed strategies and policies. This kind of exercise can unearth hidden assumptions, challenge rigidity and stimulate option generation (Sharpe and van der Heijden, 2007). Hodgson (2007) has demonstrated how the structural differences between scenarios can be modelled using causal loop methods.

In a scenario exercise, environmental trends, uncertainties and potential discontinuities are converted to a set of future scenarios. The decision field is now more in correspondence to the realities. In the decision process strategies or options are proposed and prepared. These are tested as to success or failure in each scenario and overall improvements made in risk assessment, strengthening robustness and evaluating on options to pursue. This is the decision shaping stage. The problem comes at the choosing stage. The criteria used for evaluation, dominates by the ordered world paradigm, are largely first order analyses of using criteria like net present value, economic thresholds and so on. The practical outcome is that the even though the scenario work has transformed the perception of the decision field it has not changed the perception of the decision maker. The result is that the decision gets taken in the "business as usual" mode with at best only minor assimilation of the implications of the scenarios and consequently a massive reduction in the consideration of options. Both flexibility and anticipation are lost.

So the promising new way of viewing the decision field, scenarios, runs into the linear decision process of the previous phase. Hodgson (2007) points out that strategic thinking with scenarios in itself is also invaded by linear assumptions. The rules and practices of the decision process do not change to keep pace with the change in perception of the decision field or, worse, even prevent the construction of a valid scenario set.

So there are two obstacles to strategic decision making in the face of complexity and uncertainty. One is changing the perception of the decision field and the other the changing of the decision process. Out of the author's many experiences of encountering these difficulties two will serve to illustrate these difficulties. Both examples refer to a leading and historically successful major UK domestic retailer. The first example concerned developing a scenario set based on some agreed driving forces and uncertainties where the logic pointed towards a possible scenario of rapid internationalisation of retail competition. This provide very difficult to get management to accept and eventually was considered only if it was a remote possibility, say in three to five years time. Six months later a major domestic competitor was taken over by Wal-Mart, changing the market dynamics. The second example concerned a review of strategic expansion into a potentially lucrative Europe wide market. A successful scenario exercise provided several business streams with stimulus to create a tenfold increase in the number of options. Yet when taken to the decision stage there was no decision process that could handle the opportunities and activity collapsed back pretty much to "business as usual". Shortly after this the ownership of the company changed hands.

The constraint on decision making reflects the impact of management science. It is necessary to open up the boundaries of management thinking in both theory and practice. (Mitroff and Linstone, 1993). In the business as usual decision process, however intelligently and thoroughly carried out, the mental model of the decision maker is not treated as part of the system in question. It stands outside of it in the "observer distinct from the observed" mode. It is first order. "It is the principle of objectivity that the properties of the observer shall not enter into the description of his observation". (von Foerster, 1995, p. 3)

Decision as Learning

So although multiple structural anticipatory scenarios can help create mental conditions for revealing the hazards, they cannot deal with the framing of decisions in their context. The usual result is that decision makers, having engaged with the decision field as a set of scenarios, reach for the familiar tools of decision analysis and project the rational onto the unruly. In reaching for rules to give them the answer (say the optimum on their usual assumptions) they collapse the benefits of the scenario work. The fundamental incongruence between the complex uncertain nature of the decision field and the assumption limited algorithms of the decision process has been retained. Management lacks approaches to decision making congruent with and capable of incorporating the real value of scenario planning.

Some attempts to overcome this introduce systems thinking into the decision process. For example, system dynamics simulations of different scenarios through micro-worlds can create a game-like engagement with them and help engage the decision maker into a different frame of reference, one that has feedback on the consequences of the decision maker's choices compared to the usual one. (Langley, Morecroft & Morecroft, 2008)) This approach was clearly recognised as a step forward by de Geus (2007) in his discussion of the nature of play in learning and different process that is needed to switch from assimilative learning to accommodative learning as defined by Piaget. The treatment of decision making as a subjective learning process as well as an objective analytical process, points to a whole new approach to decision making under uncertainty.

The need for decision as learning is strengthened by considering the decision system in the context of cybernetics. Particularly relevant is the role of Ashby's Law of Requisite Variety (Ashby, 1960) in a guidance system. Let us suppose that the decision system has a primary goal. It might be to make money, to heal the sick, or to win a team game. The decision field has a quasi-infinite set of states or variables only some of which can be known and predicted. We have established the mismatch between the decision process and the decision field. Ashby's Law states in effect that the greater the variety of the context then the greater the need for variety in the guidance system. Stafford Beer summarised this as variety absorbs variety. This implies that the higher the variety (complexity) of the decision system, the larger the range of perturbations that can be accommodated or compensated. It leads to the somewhat counterintuitive observation that the decision system (individual or group) must have a sufficiently large variety of options in order to ensure a sufficiently small variety of outcomes in achieving the goal. This principle has important implications for practical situations: since the variety of perturbations a system can potentially be confronted with is unlimited, we should always try to increase its internal variety (or diversity), so as to be optimally prepared for any foreseeable or unforeseeable contingency; hence the importance of learning.

This challenge of linking the reframed decision field to the actual mental frame of the decision maker was clear to Pierre Wack, a key originator of scenario thinking. In making his final critique to Shell executives and planners of the state of strategic planning and especially the use of scenarios, he strongly affirmed the point that unless the decision maker himself or herself actually changes in the process of arriving at a choice then the exercise is useless. He names this "the gentle art of reperception". For Wack (1985a and 1985b), the shift in perception of the decision makers was an essential component of the decision system if scenario planning is to be successful. The decision maker needed to enact his or her intentions as a mental rehearsal in the context of the scenarios. To explore this further we need to consider how the interaction between decider and decision field can lead to shifts in the nature of strategies and decisions.

Long experience of helping executive and planning teams both to develop multiple scenario thinking and to frame strategy work to match process to external challenges has led the author to propose that the frame of decision making needs to move from decision maker as detached observer, through involved observation to self-aware involvement. In other words, to move from the classical scientific paradigm, through systems science to the emerging domain of second order cybernetics and the emerging understandings of embedded cognition, to a new resonance between the global decision field and the practiced decision processes. I will call this third stage of correlation, *decision integrity*.

DECISION INTEGRITY

What is a decision emerging from reperception? We must first distinguish between those kinds of decision which are delegatable to constructed systems (such as computer programmes) and those requiring the specific insight of human beings. In an age where more and more decisions are delegated to automated systems (which systems can often perform better than most human beings at some tasks), why are humans other than a temporary expedient only needed until all significant decisions can be delegated (Kurtzweil, 1990)? The necessity for the human being in decision making arises where there is a need for integrity. Integrity has several aspects to it. It implies integration in the sense of taking into account a whole picture in which the decision is framed in a wider context than that of the immediate concern. For example, regarding the long term implications not just the short term payoff. Also taken into account is the spatial and structural context of interconnections, linkages and feedbacks. So integrity implies the *big when* and the *big where*.

Integrity also involves an ethical dimension, a sensitivity to values, and a degree of consistency in relation to those values that transcend the optimising and satisfising (Simon, 1996) nature of the situation in question. In a complex world these two sides of integrity, the holistic and the ethical, often are in seeming contradiction. In a system where economics is dominant, the ethical is considered secondary and even itself "unethical" by viewpoints such as the Chicago school who assert there is only one social responsibility of business – to use its resources to engage only in activities designed to increase its profits (Friedman, 1979).

Another approach to decision making under uncertainty is that of risk mitigation. When faced with a set of uncertainties which cover a range of future states, some of which are unfavourable, then the uncertainties constitute a hazard. When we form an intent to act within that hazardous situation we are faced with a risk. The manner in which we deal with that risk will challenge us with an ethical dilemma. In a situation where the risk frame is more complex than a simple good/bad choice and the ethical frame is more complex than a simple right/wrong choice, then we are faced with a need for decision integrity. This is especially so when emergent circumstances present us with incalculable issues and destroy the rule book's validity.

The discussion so far would lead us to believe that as long as we can learn enough we can decide. But given the gap between the high variety of the decision field and the restricted variety of the decision system, there are increasing numbers of questions which are not decidable by those rules and assumptions. This leads us to make the step from first order to second order cybernetics.

In the first order mode, however intelligently and thoroughly carried out, the mental model of the decision maker is not treated as part of the system in question. It stands outside of it in the "observer distinct from the observed" mode. It is first order.

The Inseparability of Decision Maker and Decision Field

Von Foerster (1995) points out that it took some time in the early days of cybernetics for the idea that there is a limitation to the classical scientific paradigm in which the observer is separated from the observed. This paradigm dominates management science and decision analysis. The implication in management is that the properties of the decision maker shall not enter the analysis of the decision space. Breaking out of this paradigm to the view that the observer has to give account of him or herself in the system in question, creates a whole new perspective. He points out that "this perception represents a fundamental change not only in the way we conduct science, but also how we perceive of teaching, of learning, of the therapeutic process, of organisational management, and so on and so forth..." (von Foerster, 1995, p. 4). From this perspective, known as second order cybernetics, the decision maker is a participant in the world about which and within which decisions are being made.

Now von Foerster goes on to make a profound but simple observation that relates back to the introductory remarks about decision integrity. In the first order paradigm, decision analysis is considered independent of the analyst and so can be informed by the rules of analysis as to what the "optimum" decision is. Any non-quantitative judgement is based on an explicit or implicit moral code. By contrast, in the second order paradigm the decision maker is considered part of the system under decision and so can only tell himself or herself what the "best" decision is. This, von Foerster (1995) points out, is the origin of ethics and that ethics cannot be articulated as a code. The rewards of ethical action lie in the action itself.

In the paradigm where the decision maker is independent of the decision field, as in the mode of classical science, then the aim of decision framing and analysis is to render the initial question decidable. Von Foerster (1995) also points out that as well as this type of question there are other kinds of question that are in principle *undecidable*. Whether we recognise such questions and how we treat them if we do, is the crux of the matter.

This brings us to need to consider the mental model of the decision maker, and indeed for him or her to consider reflectively their own mental model. Clemson's (1984) treatment of management cybernetics is helpful in representing the basis of this issue. In his discussion of the operational unit in the context of Beer's VSM (viable systems model) he describes a set of relationships as shown in Figure 1.

Modified for decision making, the *decision environment* is the contextual field in which the decision is taken. This is also the high variety, unpredictable and unruly world upon which we impose our scientific or rational order. Within that environment and of considerably less variety is

Figure 1. An operational unit in viable systems b. nested nature of the levels

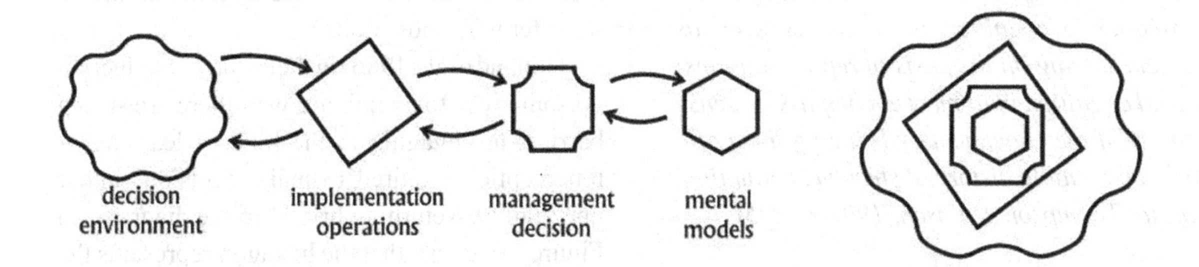

the *implementation operation* which is the vehicle of the decision. It could be an organisation or a project. It has a reciprocal relationship with the environment, acting upon it and being acted upon. This, in turn, is subject to a *management decision* that is an intervention by the decision maker. He or she is steering the ship, so to speak, also with a two way interaction based on a *mental model*. Interventions are of even less variety than the operations themselves and the feedback from the operations is highly filtered information. The variety of the decision system is less than that of the decided upon operation. The decision maker's approach to the steering action is therefore framed by the mental model of the decision maker, represented in Figure 1 as the hexagon. In other words, how they view the world is a determinant of the interventions made. This is also a two way relationship which may be static or dynamic. In the static mode, equivalent to Argyris's (1990) single loop learning, the main interaction between the mental model and the management intervention is error correction. In the dynamic mode, equivalent of Argyris's (1990) double loop learning the interaction is assumption revision implying an enrichment of the mental model. If this second order learning does not take place then there is a gap between 'espoused theory' and 'theory in use'. At either level the mental model is being enacted in its engagement with the decision field.

The mental model of the decision maker may be more or less sophisticated. It may be very complex but still linear. It may be informed by systems thinking and cybernetics and enriched with dynamic loops. In this case we could say that the decision system of manager/operation/environment is working in a frame of first order cybernetics. This offers some movement towards decision integrity in a complex interconnected world.

We can make a step towards the second order perspective if we realise that the different components in the above diagram are actually embedded in each other. In other words the mental model is embedded in the decision maker is embedded in the operation is embedded in the environment as shown in Figure 1. Thus we can see that the decider is actually part of the decision environment or decision field. The decision maker then is exercising a cognitive system which is not distinct from his or her history of action in the decision field. This perspective has much in common with the view that cognition is enactive. In this view representation is taken to be separated from action, whether the realism of construction of a mental model from external information or the idealism as the projection of a pregiven inner world. Varela, Thompson & Rosch (1991) consider the real situation to be a "middle way" between these two opposites. They state that we can

...situate cognition as embodied action within the context of evolution as natural drift provides a view of cognitive capacities as inextricably

linked histories that are lived, much like paths that exist only as they are laid down in walking. Consequently cognition is no longer seen as problem solving on the basis of representations; instead cognition in its most encompassing sense consists of the enactment or bringing forth of a world by a viable history of structural coupling. (Varela, Thompson & Rosch, 1991, p. 205)

From this perspective we acknowledge that the whole of the above cybernetic structure is itself enclosed in a meta mental model which might be considered as the world-view of the decider.

From the perspective of both second order cybernetics and enactive cognition, the separation of decider from decision field is a misleading construct. They are inseparably bound together and the pathway taken by the decider is reciprocally bound up with the decision field and the outcome of any decision.

Induction and Learning

The decision maker is actually more complex than just an observer. To take a decision is to commit to some interaction with the field of the decision and "bring forth a world." An investment decision places financial resources at the disposal of the situation the decision maker has been observing and analysing. From a systemic point of view, the decision maker is an integral component of the decision systems. Yet in judging the efficacy of decisions the dominant viewpoint taken is to exclude or bracket the decision maker and attribute (or blame) ineffective decisions on vague features of the decision maker and blame the decision analysis or the changed environment.

The perspective we are constructing here requires that we recognise, as does de Geus (2007), that decision making and learning are basically two ways of describing the same act. However, taking a perspective from learning theory gives us a different traction on how change of assumption might occur. We explore the proposition that reperception is pretty much the same mental action we refer to as induction.

Holland et al. (1986) in their study of induction go some way to explaining why there are strong barriers to engaging in the kind of learning or reperception required to make decisions under uncertainty. Returning briefly to the diagrams in Figure 1, we note that the hexagon represents the mental model of the decision maker. This mental model is a short hand for the cognitive patterning of the decision maker. Holland's approach has similarities to embedded cognition in that the emphasis is on the transactions between the learner and the environment. We encounter the world through transactions between our mental models and the behaviour of the world. When we improve our effectiveness in the world we have made a step of improved correspondence between the mental model and the world. In a quasi-infinitely complex environment, the extent of this correspondence is limited by the law of requisite variety which states that the variety in a control function must match that of the environment under control. For effective decisions there ideally needs to be a sufficient degree of structural equivalence between the mental model and the decision field.

Where we appear to be dealing with the world in a way where its behaviour matches our expectations, we codify and categorise the elements of the world. This correspondence is called by Holland et al. (1986) homomorphism. A homomorphism differs from an isomorphism which would require two situations to have equal variety in their equivalent structures. In that sense a homomorphism is a pragmatic approximation. We can link this to the first order view of the world where the homomorphism of the mental model becomes the subconscious assumption that we are the detached observer seeing the world as it really is. If nothing major contradicts this then we apply our categories and rules and so are in the world of single loop learning where deviations are treated as errors to be corrected rather than challenges to the deeper assumptions ingrained in the mental model.

To evoke the possibility of a shift from a first to a second order state of mind the homomorphism must be challenged by a shock or anomaly. We need to examine this effect in context.

The cognitive system can be viewed as a holarchy (Koestler, 1967). The most general level is H_0; within this are sub-holons H_1, H_2, and so on; and within any of these are further sub-levels $H_{1.1}$, $H_{2.1}$ and so on. H_0 establishes a general homomorphism based on a set of categories limited by rules and patterns. If these are in correspondence, they are able to predict future states of the environment or decision field. However, significant anomalies provoke new categories and rules that expand the predictive capability of the cognitive system. For example, a falling leaf, classified as "airborne" is observed to move from flower to flower and is re-categorised as "self-propelling" butterfly. In this way the variety of the cognitive system is expanded. This is a normal sensemaking activity.

However, in the face of high uncertainty there is another level of challenge which is "in spite of adjustments, things still don't make sense." New situations require new cognitive rules of interpretation. New rules can be considered in the context of decision making as "options in waiting."

New rules get a chance, typically, in situations where none of high-strength rules have their conditions satisfied. That is, new rules are tried in situations where the system does not know what to do. The generation of new rules is triggered by just such situations for just this purpose. The new rules fill new "niches" corresponding to domains in which the system has inadequate sets of rules, as revealed by its inability to make reliable predictions. (Holland et al., 1986, p. 79)

As an example, a good scenario set builds up in the mind of the decision maker at least two competing 'memories of the future' (Ingvar, 1985). What usually happens is that a trial sub-holon H_1 that might fit with the new realities detaches from the homomorphism H_0 and becomes a parallel competing cognitive orientation. As the "business as usual" becomes increasingly implausible through considering the scenario implications and the gathering of more indicative evidence, a flip occurs and H_1 becomes the new top level or inclusive homomorphism H_{00} with H_0 becoming a sub-holon. This is illustrated in the Figure 2.

The degree of shock delivered by the anomaly is critical. If it is too low, then it is subsumed in the current mental model. If it is too great then it leads to denial, rejection or even staying in a blind spot. The best opportunity for reperception is where the Stage 1 shock factor is intense enough to move

Figure 2. The process and stages of induction

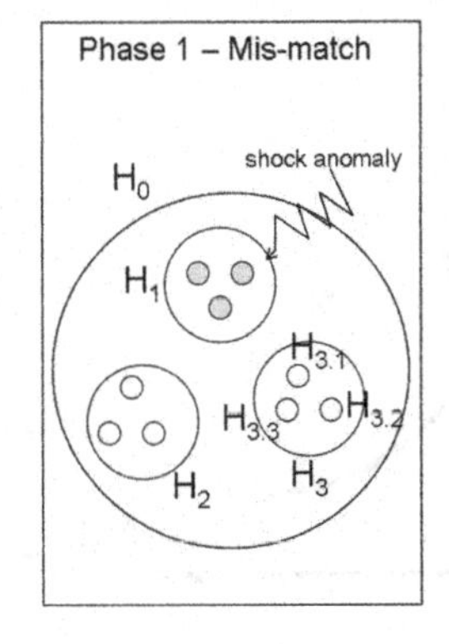

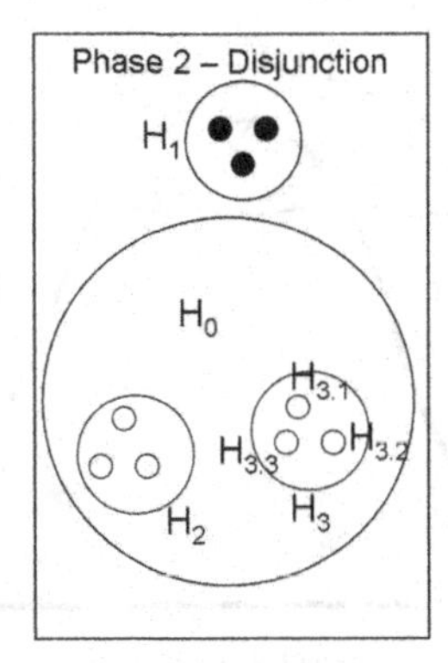

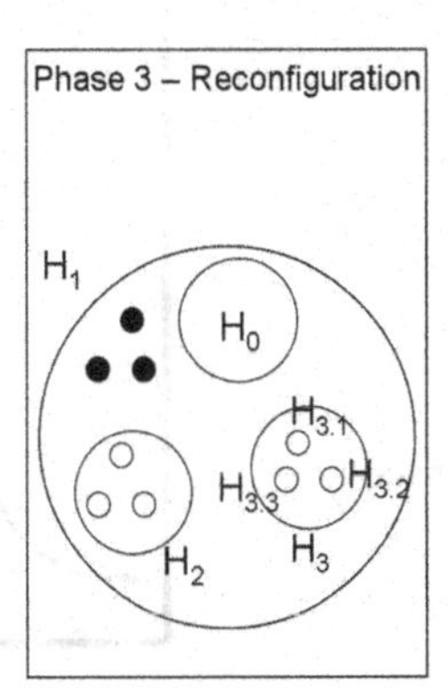

the mind to stage 2 and provoke a temporary crisis of "parallel competing homomorphisms" which then resolves into a Stage 3 reconfiguration of the holarchy. When the impact of the anomalous factor is at its optimum, Holland et al. (1986) call this "graceful entry" which is related to the degree to which the decision maker or learner admits of uncertainty and is willing to entertain alternate views. "The property of *gracefulness* is vital for inductive systems that are to operate in realistic, complex environments." (Holland et al., 1986, p. 78)

The critical factor in moving from stage 2 to stage 3 is the extent to which the decision maker is willing to play with possibilities. In using scenario method one of the most crucial steps is to get the subjects to entertain the scenarios, however unbelievable, and play with them as if they were real. This discovery by Arie de Geus became central to his efforts to change the paradigm of decision making to incorporate the role of reperception.

One characteristic of play, as the Tavistock Institute in London has shown, is the presence of a transitional object. For the person playing, the transitional object is a representation of the real world. A child who is playing with a doll learns a great deal about the real world at a very fast pace. (de Geus, 1988, p. 5)

The important distinction here is that, in the face of uncertainty, there are multiple representations of a possible reality that have not yet happened. The uncertainties have not yet been resolved by subsequent events.

The Notion of Undecidable Questions

The next stage in our hypothesis is to take further the implications that the decision system includes the decider. This is an issue of consciousness and its relationship to the properties of systems. Consciousness comes into consideration because we are now affirming learning as a function of the human decider and because there is an ethical dimension to choice. The properties of systems enters our considerations because, in a holistic decision system there is feedback or reflexivity. Reperception implies a change of consciousness and choice implies taking responsibility for the consequences of decisions.

It is necessary to break out of the type of science that believes that observer and observed

Figure 3. The positioning of graceful entry

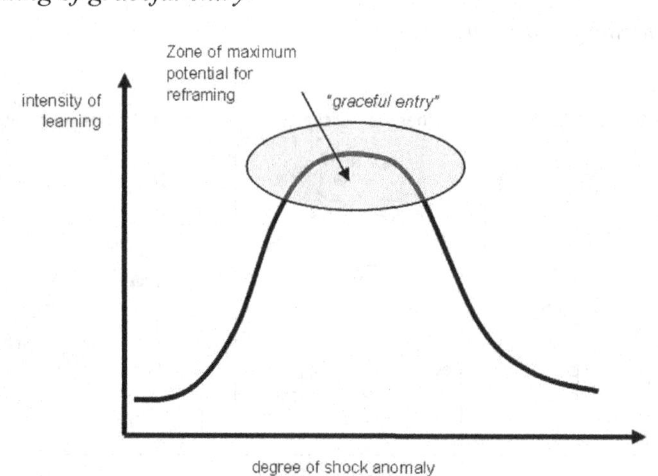

are distinct, separable and non-interactive and circularity is an incorrect viewpoint.

In contrast, the reflexive worldview leads to assertions like the following:

A implies B, B implies C, C implies A

or

A implies B, B implies A

or

A implies A

In other words the result is caused by itself. In terms of worldview we might say that the separation, made earlier in this chapter, between the decision process and the decision field is a false dichotomy. The decision process creates the decision field which creates the decision process.

An interesting example of this described by Umpleby (2007) is the reflexive view of George Soros in his approach to markets and wider social systems. Soros takes the view that in social systems there are two processes – one of observation and another of participation. Science generally only applies observation. Participation places the observer as also a player. It is therefore congruent with second order cybernetics. A second order view leads to quite different assumptions and actions. For example, the first order perspective and the second order perspective lead to quite different models of market behaviour.

The first order view of, say, a shares market is represented by a dynamic balancing causal loop in which as stock price goes up and becomes more expensive, it has an inhibiting effect on demand which, in turn, holds the price in check. In the second order view, the market is represented by a dynamic reinforcing causal loop in which as the stock price goes up the demand increases as buyers "follow the herd". This second order view is reflexive in the sense that it makes sense if the motivation to participate in the market gains is factored in as well as the supply demand balance.

The second order "game" of the decision maker is to read the biases and preconceptions of the various players in the social system. These actors, through enactive cognition are "bringing forth the world" of the game. However, those biases also filter out aspects of the situation and lead to gaps opening up between perception and reality. This eventually leads to instability and a reperception on the part of players which collapses the game system. For example, a credit bubble bursts or a political system collapses.

Umpleby (2007) raises the question as to how a second order framework would change the frame of reference of decision makers.

What would economics look like if beliefs in perfect information, rationality, and equilibrium were replaced with bias, interaction between cognition and participation, gaps between perception and reality, disequilibrium, and boom and bust cycles? (Umpleby, 2007, p. 7)

What is the nature of decision making in the context of an uncertain world in which the biases and actions of the decider is part and parcel of the uncertainty in the system? This also raises the question of ethics, an essential aspect of decision integrity. Von Foerster (1995) makes the point

Figure 4.

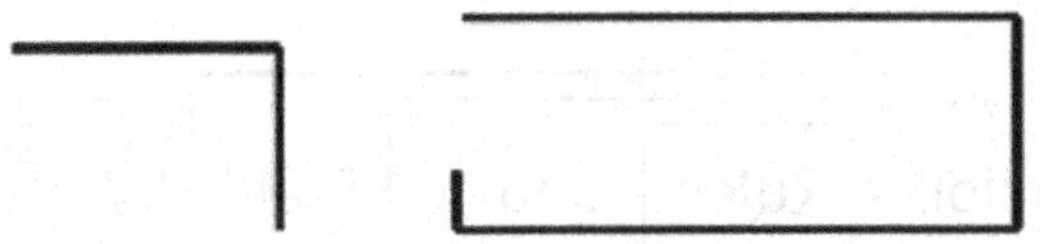

that only decisions about undecidable questions carry the quality of ethical responsibility. Where a question is decidable through rational analysis or "mathematical economics", then there is no real decision and the best we can hope for is some kind of application of a moral rule behind which the decision maker takes shelter. Faced with an undecidable question there is nowhere to shelter. In this latter case, responsibility must reside in the decision maker's action or choice itself. The reason that only *undecidable* questions demand *real* decisions is:

Simply because the decidable questions are already decided by the choice of the framework in which they are asked, and by the choice of rules of how to connect what we call "the question" with what we may take for an "answer." In some cases it may go fast, in others it may take a long, long time, but ultimately we will arrive, after a sequence of compelling logical steps, at an irrefutable answer: a definite Yes, or a definite No. (von Foerster, 1995, p. 7)

If we separate the decider from the decision field then decision rules can be applied to the field and, if sufficiently ingenious, the question and automatic selection of an answer is rendered decidable. But selecting is not true choosing. "Only those questions that are in principle undecidable, we can decide". (von Foerster, 1995, p. 7)

At this stage of the discussion we begin to come up against the limitations of language, especially the linear language of subject-verb-object. In systems thinking this limitation is generally overcome by the use of loop diagrams which, for example through arrows connecting variables, are able to state that an effect is influencing its cause as well being caused. There is another discipline that can express these ideas in a more general form.

Spencer-Brown (1969) developed a mathematical language he called the laws of form in which he based on the notions of distinction and self-reference. Distinction is represented by the first mark (Figure 4).

The mark splits a domain, say the decision field, into an inside and an outside. Self-reference is represented by the second mark which loops back on itself implying the basic second order relationship of "A implies A ". This type of structure is basic to biological systems which have the capacity of self-forming or autopoesis. This is also referred to as a reentrant system.

In this language the structure of decidable questions can be represented as shown in Figure 5.

This reads "*decision* is a function of a set of *rules* which determine a *result* within the decision *field* in the context of the *world*." This is topologically a nested structure.

The structure of undecidable questions can now be represented in Figure 6, showing the structural distinction.

For an undecidable question this reads "*decision* is a function of the *state* of the decision maker which determines a *choice* in the context of a decision *field* which is in *world* which itself includes the *state* of the decision maker." This is also expressed in the never-ending sentence: "The world context of the decision affects the state of the decision maker which determines a choice which is embedded in the decision field which is itself embedded in the world which affects….." In

Figure 5.

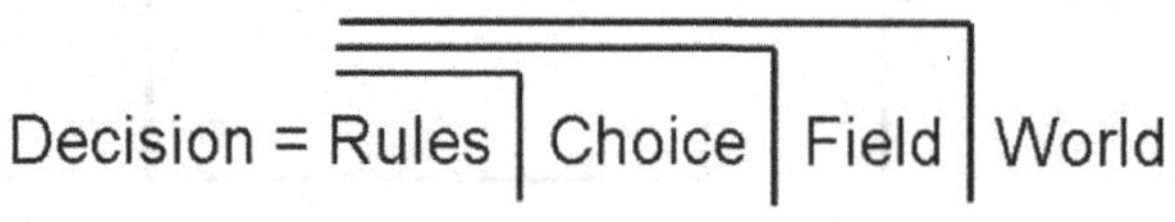

Decision = Rules | Choice | Field | World

Figure 6.

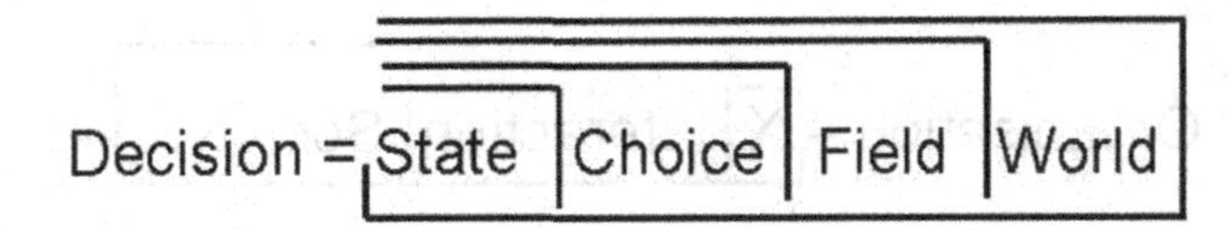

commenting on the general mathematical form of this nested and re-entrant relationship Kauffman (2008) points out that in essence

... the reentering mark would represent autonomy or autopoesis. It represents the concept of a system whose structure is maintained through the self-production of its own structure. This idea of a calculus for self-reference, and the production of a symbol for the fundamental concept of feedback at the level of second order cybernetics captured the imaginations of many people, and it still does! Here is the ancient mythological symbol of the worm ouroboros embedded in a mathematical, non-numerical calculus. (Kauffman, 2008, pp. 12-13)

All this takes us right back to the reentrant condition that the decider is part of the decision field. If the decider changes state then the decision field changes state and therefore both the practical options and their ethical implications come into the foreground. The induction theory of Holland et al. (1986) helps us to understand that there is a different operation of the cognitive system needed to deal with undecidable questions. But the cognitive system must also be recognised as a reentrant system. The implications of this are summarised by von Foerster like this:

... we are under no compulsion, not even under that of logic, when we decide upon in principle undecidable questions. There is no external necessity that forces us to answer such questions one way or another. We are free! The complement to necessity is not chance, it is choice! We can choose who we wish to become when we have decided on in principle undecidable questions. (von Foerster, 1995, p. 7)

... With this freedom of choice we are now responsible for whatever we choose. For some this freedom of choice is a gift from heaven. For others it is an unbearable burden: How can one escape it? How can one avoid it? How can one pass it on to somebody else? With much ingenuity and imagination, mechanisms were contrived by which one could bypass this awesome burden. With hierarchies, entire institutions have been built where it is impossible to localize responsibility. Everyone in such a system can say 'I was told to do X'. (von Foerster, 1995, p. 7)

The implications of this insight about choice are critical. Second order systems are participative and have the capacity of choice beyond any inherent rule system. This view simply does not fit the deterministic view of systems.

Locker (1997) takes a similar viewpoint in formulating Trans-Classical Systems Theory, TCST, which is a form of second order cybernetics. His approach also recognises that a true system can never be fully explained by its properties alone, but has to be considered in conjunction with the systems theory the designer already holds prior to designing the system. In this approach, observing and describing the system fuses with knowing and understanding it. Translating this into the arena of decisions we can suppose that the true nature of a decision field cannot be completely known by its description and analysis, but has to be considered in conjunction with the mental

Figure 7.

Organisation = X | Interaction | Society

model of the decision field that the decision maker holds prior to engaging with the act of choice. Thus any genuine decision system cannot avoid the question of the human being as the ultimate decision designer, and being humanly responsible within the decision field of concern. This is itself a system that is a mutually interactive engagement. As Markus-Ekkard Locker expresses it:

Whenever the observer enters into the system in concern he alters this system and himself. Thus in TCST, both the access system and the system in concern are changing and open systems that mutually interact with, and depend on one another. (Locker, 2006, p. 9)

ORGANISATIONAL IMPLICATIONS OF DECISION INTEGRITY

So far we have concentrated on the second order system {(decider)(decision field)}. But decisions are also taking place in contexts of multiple human beings in organisations. The system in question then becomes more complex. With regard to an organisation of human beings is it possible for there to be genuine decisions about undecidable questions? As pointed out earlier, generally our institutions are invented to avoid ethically responsible decisions and place them in a context of rules and frameworks in which everyone either is "told to do it" or "had no choice".

Reichel (2008), drawing on Luhman's social systems theory, has explored this question in his work on the paradox of second order cybernetics in a social context. He points out that the "next organisation" is an observation of the process of organising in the context of interaction in the context of society, represented in the notation of the Laws of Form as shown in Figure 7.

This reads "the next organisation is an observation of X in the context of interaction in the context of society. The X is the process of organising, with the mark from society pointing to a reentry, thus creating the self-reference of the next organisation." The process of organising is also a function in classical organisation theory as management, but in this case it raises the question what is second order management?

The restlessness Reichel refers to here is similar to what was referred to in the early part of this chapter as the unruliness of the real world. This second order cybernetic description sets a context for decision making where multiple deciders are involved. What is inside and what is outside is thus continuously negotiable and hence has no formal framework. Institutions to date have tended to be designed (organised) by sets of rules that are decidable questions - for example reporting structures, work force structural planning, functional hierarchies and so on. But the shape and nature of a perpetually self-reflective organisation falls into the category of undecidable questions. Thus managers (decision makers) in such an organisation are of necessity reflective learners. An example given is that of Wikipedia which is an autopoetic organisation that references on itself, its processes and goals, while at the same time ensuring sensemaking for all its members. Reichel points out that it is not only restless as regards its name and its boundary but also its goals. It is a teleogenic system, able to reframe its own purpose.

Building on Reichel's analysis of second order organisation we can make some attempts to formulate how this translates into the idea of collective decision making. This will place decision integrity in an organisational context.

- Decisions are a co-created production in a context of openness and peer review
- The boundaries of the decision field are continuously reshaped by the self-referential and reflexive nature of the shared consciousness
- Control over decisions is exercised by non-control, that is, handing the undecidable questions to the members of the organisation itself. Note that this is not the same as an abdication of choice or responsibility. It is rather a step to an existential recognition of the nature of collective intelligence and its shared responsibility

Reframing for Decision Integrity

How does this exploration of the structure of reentrant decision systems change the way we need to think about decisions on undecidable questions? There are a number of interconnected points.

a. The undecidable question, because of its inherent uncertainty, requires an ethical commitment that cannot be arrived at by applying business-as-usual rules whether they be financial or moral.
b. This also means that the decision maker's current mental model, which is a fixed holarchical structure of categories and subcategories, is an inadequate basis for his or her real decision.
c. Therefore a voluntary cognitive reconfiguration is an essential step to prepare the decision. This can be described by such terms as inviting reframing, reperception, induction or double loop learning in the context of reflexivity
d. For this to take place, the conditions of graceful entry have to be established with scope to "play" with an appropriate transitional object.

From this analysis we can now look at some of the implications for strategic management of the second order view represented by decision integrity. Strategy work in management weaves together understanding of the decision field (for example, the global market for energy) with the decision process (for example: how do we make the shift from fossil to renewable energy systems). An executive group or team running a business will form, from this weaving together, a decision system. This will include formal and informal components and be guided by explicit and tacit knowledge of the team members. The more long range their strategic concerns, the more the decision field will be filled with complexities and uncertainties and the more further strategic progress will confront them with undecidable questions.

To grapple with the decision field they may create a set of scenarios incorporating speculative narratives about trends and uncertainties recognising that the nature of their challenge is not a simple "yes or no". If they are to employ the scenario set and its supporting analysis effectively they will recognise that much of their usual economic analysis to arrive at conclusions, though necessary, is not the way to arrive at strategic choices.

Van der Heijden (2005) recognises over many years of observation and participation in high level strategy work that decisions are arrived at by a reflexive decision process which is essentially one of mutual learning.

The learning loop model shows the interwovenness of thinking and action. If action is based on planning on the basis of a mental model, then institutional action must be based on a shared mental model. Only through a process of conversation can elements of personal observation and thought be structured and embedded in the accepted and shared organisational theories-in-use. Similarly new perceptions of opportunities and threats, based on the reflection on experiences of actions playing out in the environment, can only become institutional property through conversation. (Van der Heijden, 2005, p. 43)

However, the reflexive mutual accommodation of strategic conversation is still a rarity in management. Management cultures are dominated by non-negotiable hierarchy and by the domination of powerful individuals who may seek advice but are not open to reflexive review of their biases and beliefs. The result is an absence of learning, a tendency to repeat previous mistakes, large scale external diseconomies and an absence of ethical decision making.

Managers practising decision integrity will reflect on their role more on the following lines, consistent with a second order viewpoint.

a. The recognition that I, the decision maker, am faced with undecidable questions that are nevertheless unavoidable
b. That this places me within, not outside, the system in which I am a manager and hence in the reflexive context
c. That I am inescapably faced with ethical dilemmas that cannot be reduced to moral rules. I must therefore make free choices and take responsibility
d. That any choice amongst options made are a function of my own state of mind and understanding in conjunction with my colleagues
e. That the nature of being in an organisation with mutual responsibility with others means that the essence of shaping a decision is dialogic and emergent as distinct from analytic and persuasive
f. That if my exploration of the nature of the decision field and its context (stimulated, for example, by a well crafted scenario set) does not alter my perceptions then I have not properly engaged with the decision task (the reperception issue). If the possible future worlds do not change me then I am still in the detached observer paradigm and failing in responsibility.

Von Foerster (1995) summarises the position this way:

With the essence of observing, namely the processes of cognition, being removed, the observer is reduced to a copying machine, and the notion of responsibility has been successfully juggled away. (von Foerster, 1995, p. 7)

The act of reperception is the antithesis of a copying machine. It is an act of induction, of learning. The support that framework-based decision making becomes a weakness in the face of undecidable questions. This weakness arises from ingrained subconscious mental patterns that are difficult to change. We think we are peering into the windscreen of the future but are actually fixated on the view in the rear view mirror. It usually takes the shock consequences of a bend in the road to realise that we have ceased learning. The point here is that our decision making needs to be, as well as consistent with the above six points, a learning process.

De Geus (1999) makes the point that,

... the real decision-making process is a learning process rather than the application of knowledge. Many at high levels of management are convinced they are there because of what they know and how they represent what they are. These statements were saying you're not there because of what you know. You're there because you're reasonably good at intuitively or otherwise finding your way to a learning process together with your colleagues, such that you learn and arrive at new conclusions that are more or less successful. (de Geus, 1999, p. 1)

There is an inherent psychological and cultural resistance to the proposition that real ethical decisions inevitably change the decision maker who cannot be abstracted from the decision system. In today's world of applied management science in fields such as financial management, the mathematisation of making money inevitably leads to breakdown both systemically and ethically. There are no "masters of the universe" because, in reality, the fallible human being has not actually been removed from the decision system. The abdication of responsibility to 'copying machines' has its unavoidable consequences. The factors which colour ethics and responsibility are buried in propaganda and kept there by greed and attachment to power over reality. But in actual fact the decision maker is never outside of the decision system.

Decision Integrity as a System

The proposition for management is, then, that decision theory should shift its attention from first order systems to second order systems in which the neurobiology and cognitive psychology of the decision maker is included in the decision system. The overall case is summarised in Figure 8. There is a new context for management which has higher complexity, higher uncertainty, dislocation and breakdown of the usual success formulae. There is also increasing moral hazard with destructions on a large scale from money to biological species. The dominant paradigm is one of management drawing on the current science paradigm as seen as an objective and detached measure of things. This is so ingrained that the "old ways" continue to be applied to try and solve the escalating problems.

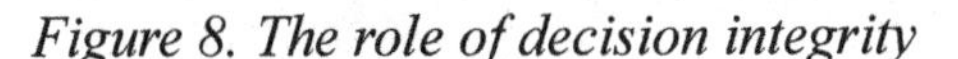

Figure 8. The role of decision integrity

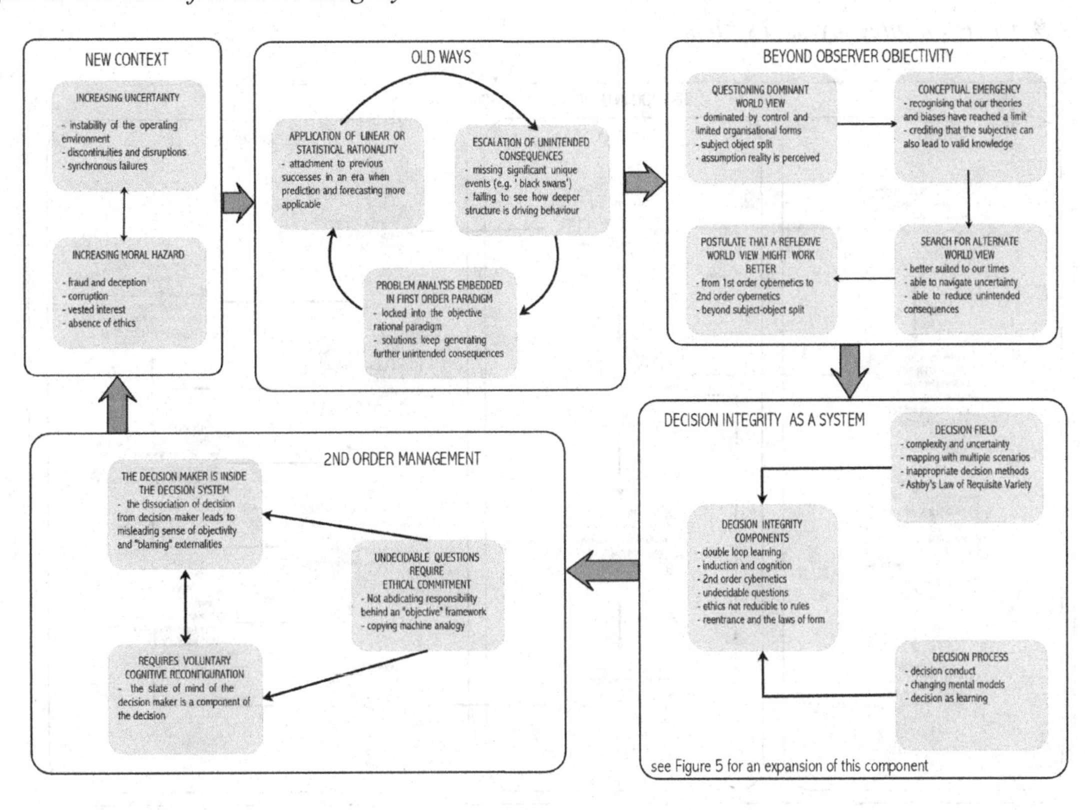

This leads to a questioning of the dominant world view and the suggestion that reflexive theories may offer better prospects. This entails a shift from first order cybernetics to second order cybernetics. Decision integrity is postulated as an approach that integrates a systems approach in a second order context and includes the ethics of the decision maker as a scientific component. This offers the prospect of changing the way difficult or undecidable questions are tackled. Better decisions will be made in the sense that they will lead to better short, medium and long term outcomes. Better as used here can be judged by a number of criteria; reduced unintended consequences, acceptance of responsibility by decision makers rather than abdication, fast learning when circumstances change. This, however, will require nothing less than a paradigm shift in management theory and practice.

Decision integrity as a system, summarised in Figure 9, requires an internal understanding of how the decision field "out there" and the decision process "in here" are one and the same system which is participative as well as observational. It also requires recognition that new organisational forms are emerging that are more congruent with the new second order paradigm and demand the shift to second order management. This will not be easy due to the deeply ingrained defensive routines in the current human organisational systems. It will require innovative applied research into fields such as embodied cognition, distributed cognition and next organisations.

Implications for Management and Governance

One conclusion from this exploration is that we have a legacy of applied management science that is incongruent with the increasingly unruly nature of the real world. Further, by carrying on with mis-matching decision processes we are

Figure 9. Decision integrity as a system

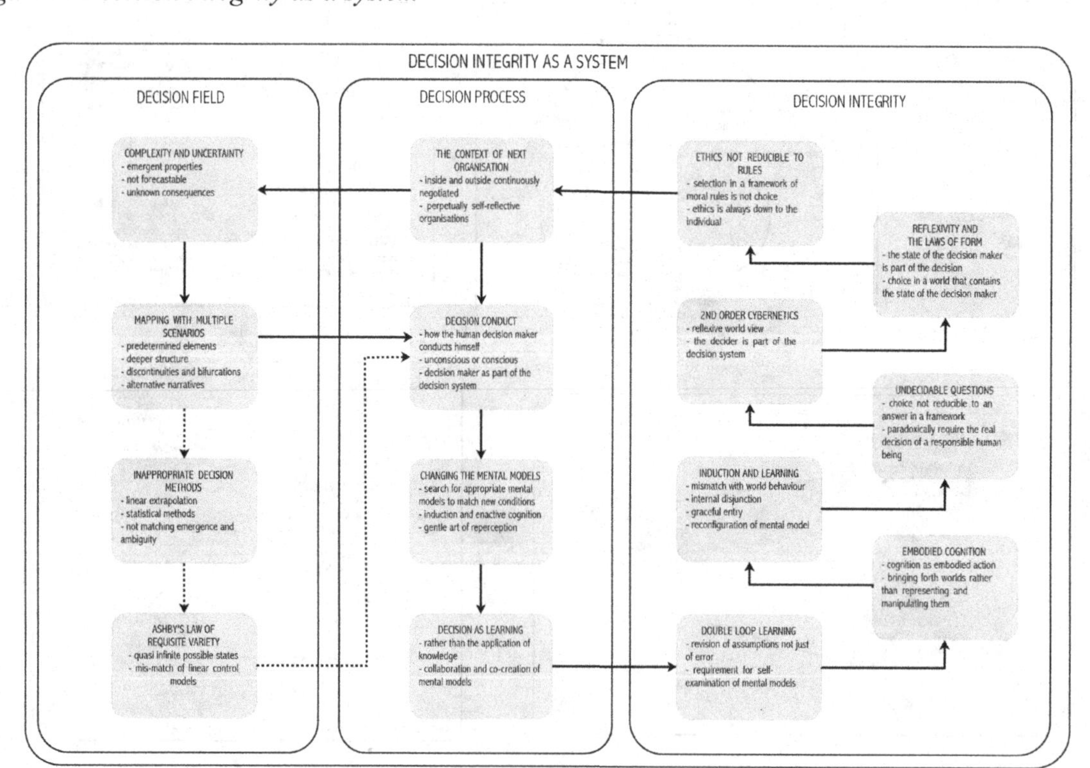

actually exacerbating the situation. In the new global era, continuing the objectification of the world assumes that we are not part of the world system, obscuring the reflexivity of our actions in the quest for control, certainty and predictability. Just as Newtonian science finds itself subsumed in a larger paradigm of relativity and quantum physics, so observer detached management science will find itself subsumed in a larger and more reflexive notion of that science. Discussion of this is beyond the scope of a single chapter but it is important to recognise that management science is not actually detached from the current transition to the global age. Albrow (1996) puts this in context by making the case that the era of modernity, which is deeply enmeshed in the objectivist science paradigm has come to the end of the road. The new situation is globality which confronts us with bigger and potentially more fatal issues of responsibility for limits and consequences of our decisions.

We do not need to cast aside the decades of development of management science; rather we need to assign them a diminished role and realise that the dominant paradigm of science itself needs reforming into a science which includes consciousness and the human quality as primary factors. Theoretical physicists like Goswami (1993) have made incursions into the idea of consciousness as a primary basis of a coherent quantum physics. The idea of decision integrity opens up a field for exploring self-aware management. The disciplines surrounding the idea of second order cybernetics and Trans-Classical Systems Theory (Locker, 1997) offer a potentially fruitful basis for reframing decision science.

Decision integrity, as a management capability can only be developed by its practice. It requires the courage to take decisions and ethical responsibility in the face of consciously recognised undecidable uncertainties. Where things are predictable and decision analysis is used there is no real choice in the sense of discriminative cognition because the answer falls out of the rules, not from a reflective human choice. Some differences between first order and second order decision making are summarised in Table 1.

The implications of this analysis are that, from the perspective of second order cybernetics, most decisions are not decisions at all but selections derived from systems which logically or computationally provide a "decidable" answer for a passive observer. Since the passivity of the observer is never-the-less subject to psychological biases, distortions of motivation and even deliberate corruption it is hardly surprising that we live in a society full of unintended consequences for which no one will take responsibility. There are not only consequences for decision outcomes of decision makers but also for the whole future of organisations and society. On the other hand, we also live in a time when forms of co-operation are reconfiguring social integrities beyond the forms of institution that combine classical power hierarchy and applied management science.

Table 1. Comparison of decision making in certain and uncertain situations

DECISIONS IN FORECASTABLE SITUATIONS	DECISIONS IN UNCERTAIN SITUATIONS
• Susceptible to decision analysis • Can be modelled with first order cybernetics or systems theory • Abdicates responsibility to "the system" or decision rules • Values are "mechanised" as impersonal moral (or immoral) rules and conditions • Consequences subsumed into the predictive tools and techniques • Skills of decision *analysis* predetermined or configured to give a calculable outcome • Error and failure are attributed to changes context and external circumstances	• Decision analysis insufficient • Requires shift to second order cybernetics • Requires decision maker to assume ethical responsibility • Values embodied in the personal ethics of the decision maker • Consequences continuously monitored in the act of observing the observer - reflexive • Skills of creative decision *thinking* and dialogue exercised by the decision maker • Error and failure are treated as feedback to the decision maker as learner

CONCLUSION

This analysis puts the whole of business practice and management education up for review. Equally, it opens up a whole new area of research possibilities which might be inspired by one of the prime originators of the second order cybernetics proposition. Heinz von Foerster's Biological Computer Laboratory which existed from 1958 to 1975, was a living example of applying reflexive dialog to the generation of ideas and the choice of research themes and programmes. (Umpleby, Anbari & Müller, 2007) It would be very timely that there should appear a new laboratory (probably with many virtual players) that would illustrate the same principles of highly innovative research directed towards the field we might describe as "Second Order Management".

The next organisation (Reichel, 2008) is emerging with some very different configurations and arrangements where a new kind of decision praxis is emerging which is better suited and matched to the unruly nature of the emerging world. The next organisation tends to include

- Open source collaboration
- Networks with little institutional structure
- Multiple motivational values (beyond the financial)
- Control exercised through trust (ethics) rather than rules
- Performance is emergent
- Management is vested in a founding community that is not necessarily a recognisable legal entity but a social integrity

In this emerging world we need to move from the idea of a certain organisation navigating through a world of uncertainty to a world in which *the enterprise itself is inherently uncertain.* Put simply, we are dealing with *uncertainty multiplied by uncertainty*! Being caught in our previous set of assumptions and world views drives us deeper into the conceptual emergency indicated in the introduction to this chapter. The way out of the emergency is to evolve our scientific worldview to a new level of insight and complexity.

In this world the scope and implications of undecidable questions is vastly expanded and it calls for a shift to a second order thinking and account of what decision making under uncertainty is. Decision integrity as discussed here a vital core component of understanding and guiding (perhaps even the word managing will be replaced by a better one) complex self-observing systems with the power to generate their own purposes.

REFERENCES

Albrow, M. (1997). *The global age.* Stanford, CA: Stanford University Press.

Argyris, C. (1990). *Overcoming organizational defenses: Facilitating organizational learning.* Boston: Allyn and Bacon.

Ashby, R. (1960). *Design for a brain: The origin of adaptive behaviour.* New York: John Wiley.

Beer, S. (1975). *Platform for change.* Chichester, UK: John Wiley & Sons Ltd.

Clemson, B. (1984). *Cybernetics: A new management tool.* Tunbridge Wells, UK: Abacus

Curry, A., & Hodgson, A. (2008). Seeing in multiple horizons: Connecting futures to strategy. *Journal Future Studies, 13*(1), 1–20.

de Geus, A. (1988). Planning as learning. *Harvard Business Review,* March-April.

de Geus, A., & Scharmer, C. (1999). *Every institution is a living system.* Retrieved December 31, 2008, from http://www.management.com.ua/cm/cm015.html de Geus, A. (2007). Learning together for good decision making. *Reflections, 8*(1), 28 -35.

December 31, 2008, from http://www.richardjung.cz/bert2.pdf.

December 31, 2008, from http://www.strategy-dynamics.com/products/oilprod.asp

Friedman, M. (1979, Sept. 13). The social responsibility of business is to increase its profits. *The New York Times Magazine*.

Goswami, A. (1993). *The self-aware universe – how consciousness creates the material world.* New York: Penguin Putnam.

Hodgson, A. (2007). Using Systems Thinking to Deepen Scenarios. *Systemist, 29*(2), 71–80.

Hodgson, A. (2007). Strategic thinking with scenarios. In S. Muralidaran (Ed.), *Business Environment Analysis* (p. 125). Hyderabad, India: Icfai University Press. Holland, J., Holyoak, K., Nisbett, R. & Thagard, P. (1986). *Induction: Processes of inference, learning and discovery.* Cambridge, MA: MIT Press.

Ingvar, D. H. (1985). Memory of the future: An essay on the temporal organization of conscious awareness. *Human Neurobiology, 4*, 127–136.

International Futures Forum. (2009). *Ten things to do in a conceptual emergency.* Axminster, UK: Triarchy Press.

Kaufmann, L. (2008). *Laws of form – An exploration in mathematics and foundations* (Rough Draft). Chicago: University of Illinois. Retrieved December 31, 2008, from http://www.math.uic.edu/~kauffman/Laws.pdf

Kay, J. (2008, Winter). Drowning by numbers. *RSA Journal.* London: Royal Society of Arts.

Koestler, A. (1967). *The ghost in the machine.* London: Hutchinson.

Kurtzweil, R. (1990). *The age of intelligent machines.* Cambridge, MA: MIT Press.

Langley, P., Morecroft, J., & Morecroft, L. (2008). *Oil producers microworld.* Retrieved

Locker, A. (1997). *The present status of general system theory, 25 years after Ludwig von Bertalanffy's decease.* Kutna Hora, Czech Republic: Centre for Systems Research. Retrieved

Locker, M. (2006). *Reviving paradoxes: Transclassical systems theory as meta-theory for a science-faith dialogue.* Bryn Mawr, PA: Metanexus Institute. Retrieved March 30, 2009, from http://www.metanexus.net/conferences/pdf/conference2006/Locker.pdf

Mitroff, I., & Linstone, H. (1993). *The unbounded mind: Breaking the chains of traditional business thinking.* New York: Oxford University Press.

Press.

Reichel, A. (2008). Observing the next organisation. *UK Systems Society: Systemist, 30*(2).

Sharpe, B., & van de Heijden, K. (2007). *Scenarios for success – Turning insights into action.* Chichester, UK: John Wiley & Sons Ltd.

Simon, H. (1996). *The science of the artificial.* Cambridge, MA: MIT Press.

Spencer Brown, G. (1969). *The laws of form.* London: Allen and Unwin.

Taleb, N. (2007). *The black swan: The impact of the highly improbable.* New York: Random House.

Umpleby, S. (2007). Reflexivity in social systems: The theories of George Soros. *Systems Research and Behavioral Science, 24*, 515–522. doi:10.1002/sres.852

van de Heijden, K. (2005). *Scenario planning – The art of strategic conversation.* Chichester, UK: John Wiley & Sons Ltd.

Varela, F., Thompson, E., & Rosch, E. (1991). *The embodied mind.* Cambridge, MA: MIT Press.

von Foerster, H. (1995). Ethics and second order cybernetics. *Stanford Humanities Review 4*(2), 308-319. Retrieved March 30, 2009, from http://www.stanford.edu/group/SHR/4-2/text/foerster.html

Wack, P. (1985a). Scenarios: uncharted waters ahead. *Harvard Business Review*, *63*(5), 73–89.

Wack, P. (1985b). Scenarios: Shooting the rapids. *Harvard Business Review*, *63*(6), 139–150.

Chapter 5
A New Approach to a Theory of Management:
Manage the Real Complex System, Not its Model

Donald C. Mikulecky
Virginia Commonwealth University Center for the Study of Biological Complexity, USA

ABSTRACT

An organization is defined by the performance of function which is different from the way the organization is put together by its designers. An example is a business. The organizational chart is a poor way of understanding what actually goes into performing a task. The problem arises because of misunderstanding about to how events are caused. There is not just one type of causality, but there are four distinct kinds leading to closed causal loops. The causal entailment allows us to identify "functional components" that do not correspond to entities in an organizational chart or its accompanying job descriptions. Functional components are defined in a specific context and are destroyed if that context is altered significantly. By comparing a relational analysis of organizational functions with the standard organizational chart and its intent for getting things done, many problems in management can be given an explanation and thereby be solved.

INTRODUCTION

There must be a reason for the call for new ideas in management theory. That reason lies, at least in part, in the failure of previous attempts to set down such a theory. This chapter will examine the misconceptions that led to those failures and how to proceed naturally using modern ideas resulting from the acknowledgement of those failures. It is significant that we are looking at cybernetics and systems theory for new ideas. Both cybernetics and systems theory have been with us for some time. The infiltration of all aspects of human culture by technology is becoming as much a way of life for our youth as automobiles were in my youth. Thus we are forced to ask whether we are looking in an empty barn for the horses that escaped when the door was left ajar. The answer lies in the semantics that frame the context for interpreting those words.

DOI: 10.4018/978-1-61520-668-1.ch005

There are two related areas where progress that has been made can be of great help to us. The first is in philosophy itself. Here we have many contributors to select from, but we can focus on a few who will provide us with the advances we need to cast management theory in a context dictated by these advances. First and foremost is the radical, but useful, idea that the philosophy we have been so enamored with since the 18th century enlightenment may have fallen behind the way we live and do things today. There are a number of ways to approach this need for updated philosophical foundations, but we will focus on three and among them, one in particular. George Lakoff, founder of the field of cognitive linguistics in the 1970's has provided us with an alternative view of philosophy (Lakoff and Johnson, 1999: Lakoff, 2008) that has come a very long way in a rather short time in the sense that it has been the source of or lends support to new ideas . In fact, much of the philosophical basis for Rosen's work is given a solid foundation by Lakoff in spite of their having no references to each other's work. Along with his challenges to traditional philosophy, we have Soros (2006) and earlier, at the University of Chicago where, as we will see, much of this unfolded, Leo Strauss (1964).

It is necessary that this chapter has to be about words and their usage as much as anything else. Language is a prison for us when it comes to new ideas. We are forced to use the language we have and to try to overcome the difficulty that presents to us when we think we understand something in a new way. Therefore, it will be necessary to develop a vocabulary that puts new meaning to old words and to develop a history of the new ideas for their novelty is not in their chronological age, but in their failure to be thoroughly understood over a considerably long period of time. In some perverse way, the moment of history in which we were called upon to try to shed light on the use of cybernetics and systems theory in management theory has made the job considerably easier than it would have been even a relatively short time ago. The reason for this is the context of our current political, commercial and economic status world-wide and, in particular, here in the United States. A good summary of the "crisis" is given by Soros (2008). More will be said about these contextual influences as the ideas are developed.

Let us begin by reintroducing some of the words with which we will be dealing and their commonly accepted meanings. Then we will begin to put those definitions into the context of this narrative, which will be a substantially difficult task due to the many inherent contradictions with which we will be forced to grapple.

No word could be better chosen to illustrate the points just made than "cybernetics". Cybernetics is a term that refers to a collection of ideas relating machines to human beings. We need not delve too deeply into its varied meanings and its history for this has been done quite well by N. Katherine Hayles (1999) in her very thorough narrative about information and its relationship to the human beings who generate it. It would be good if one were to read her book before tackling the ideas in this chapter for the idea of applying cybernetics to management theory will be very dependent on how one answers questions she raises. The chapter will provide sufficient detail from Hayles and others to make that digression unnecessary. The same will be true with the other authors whose work will be heavily relied upon as this approach to management theory is developed. The same will also be true for the application of systems science, since it will be the theory of complex systems that dominates all others. Most of what is said here about systems science will be built upon the writings of the late Robert Rosen, who was a great friend, colleague and mentor. We will cite his many works as they are drawn upon in the development of our narrative. One of his latest works deals with the issue of cybernetics in the spirit of criticism he has refined over fifty years in the area of systems theory as well. In his discussion of psychomimesis, Rosen puts our problem into perspective from the onset.

Weiner provided the ultimate in mimetics with his idea of reproducing every behavior of an organism by, in effect, setting coefficients in a function generator. He thus proposed a biological version of the Ptolemaic epicycles as his solution to the problems of life and of mind- another version of the perfect actor, whose scripts were now coefficient arrays or parameter vectors. (Rosen, 2000, pp 119.)

This concept of mimesis exists in the context of Cartesian reductionist systems theory. When we discuss the way we make models of the complex real world, the notion of mimesis will join a number of others as representatives of the surrogate formal world we consistently use to replace the complex real world. The justification traditionally given for this is the legacy of various forms of positivist philosophy and their relatives. The refutations by Kant (Rosen 1986a) have gone unheeded to this day. This is one major reason why we must try again to put these matters into perspective so that we can make progress.

What Rosen is objecting to is also echoed throughout Hayles's book. The origins of this mode of thinking are easily traced back to Descartes and his predecessors. From the beginning, the relationship of cybernetics to the machine metaphor of Descartes will be a central theme. In many ways, the originator of the cybernetic idea was really Descartes, but that is a difficult claim to justify since he did not know what a machine was. People like Norbert Weiner and so many others gave the skeleton designed by Descartes its flesh in our modern conception of the matter.

Our task is to bring new insights to the theory of management. This entails a critique of present ideas and, in particular, the values and premises upon which they rest. This is, of course, no small task and will require careful development. It is Rosen, more than anyone else, who has provided a rich basis for this critique.

A theory of management has to deal with the notion of what is meant by "management" in general, and any theory about this function must necessarily spell out the underlying values and premises upon which it rests. It has to be clear from the beginning of this discussion that the meanings of the word "management" have to come from a context. Any attempt to provide a context independent theory would be so general as to be useless. As we will see, this is in perfect harmony with Rosen's approach to complex systems, and we will establish that what is being managed, or what we are attempting to manage, are indeed complex systems. Let us be perfectly clear about this. Complex systems exist in a context and must be discussed in that context. It makes a difference if we are talking about managing a small business, a government agency, a large corporation, an ecosystem or part of one, or an economic system, to give but a few examples.

The word "theory" also brings up problems. We are familiar with theories in the physical sciences and all too often try to use physical or "hard" science as a model of how things should be done in the so-called "soft" sciences. Even this way of expressing the two endeavors is replete with prejudice and subjective underpinnings. It is one of the ironies that arises from the study of complex reality that, in fact, the "arrow" of condescension is pointing the wrong way here. It is the approach of hard science that is open to severe criticism for its failure to escape the self-imposed limits of mechanistic Cartesian reductionism.

Having recognized this, our task becomes clearer. It is not to approach management as a hard science that can be given a theoretical basis as physics has, but rather to learn from the shortcomings of that approach and to present the people who "manage" as clear a picture of the real world complex systems they are trying to understand and help function optimally. They must be dissuaded from the belief that they are at the controls of a machine and that complex reality is misleadingly represented by this model.

Complex systems, as defined by Rosen and those who practice his relational approach to systems, are distinguished from their counterparts in the Cartesian world by a very definitive criterion, namely their non-computability. This aspect of complex systems theory, more than any other, is what sets it apart and makes it especially compatible with the human aspects of management theory that are usually, by necessity, discarded from a Cartesian reductionist approach. Much has been written to justify this foundation concept of what makes the real world system complex, and we will not repeat it here. The arguments are available in detail elsewhere. (Rosen, 1991 & 2000; Louie, 2007). To a great extent, the reason for this lack of computability is the fact that real world complex systems are replete with closed loops of causality. (Rosen, 1991, 1993 & 2000; Kercel 2007).

There is a certain irony in the fact that Rosen uses the highest form of mathematics, Category Theory, to basically prove the uselessness of the traditional analytical mathematical approach to nature, as exemplified in non-linear dynamics. His reason has many bases. One is that he wants to reach those who demand that mathematics is the only way to go. More importantly, he, as his mentor Rashevsky (1954), sees the difference in nature between two distinct branches of mathematics. One branch is typified by the analytical mathematics taught to engineers, scientists, and other practitioners of the Cartesian reductionist/mechanist approach. The other includes topology and category theory. As I make clear in my book on Network Thermodynamics (Mikulecky, 1993), often the same result can be obtained by both, but the semantics that accompany the syntax are very different. It is this semantic difference that will be at the core of what makes complex systems theory so very fundamentally different from Cartesian reductionist methods.

With this introduction to set the stage, let us proceed to the task at hand. We will next ground our ideas in an historical progression that goes back quite far. Then we will tackle the problem directly, showing what we can and cannot expect a theory of management to do. There will be no attempt to create such a theory, for one of the lessons we will learn is that the issue of "managing" complex systems is an oxymoron. Rather, we will provide an approach to complex systems that will get us as close as possible to being able to interact with them in ways that bring about outcomes as close to our desires as is possible.

BACKGROUND

This narrative begins with an unusual happening in the United States and, for that matter, the world. In 1929, at the age of 30, Robert Maynard Hutchins became the youngest person to preside over a university. He took that post after being Dean of Yale Law School for two years. He remained as president until 1945 and then was Chancellor until 1951. In the 1930's, Nicholas Rashevsky, known to many of us as "The father of Mathematical Biology", joined the faculty at Chicago and started a program in Mathematical Biology. He also started a journal and published a book on the use of mathematical models in biology. His work during this period focused on the development of a theoretical approach to both biology and the social sciences that would parallel the role of mathematical theory in the physical sciences. So, indeed, he began to sow the seeds of a reductionist approach to social science. Nevertheless, Rashevsky was extremely productive in the realm of "hard" science and published models for reaction-diffusion systems that could lead to pattern generation and his neural networks were far ahead of their return in a popular setting many years later. Ironically, he did a complete turn around and gave birth to the new relational approach that jumps outside the bounds of reductionist science.

The intellectual history of this period at the University of Chicago is of particular interest to us because of the way Rashevsky, Hutchins and others were coming to a similar conclusion about our scientific and philosophical development. Let us first see how Hutchins approached it as told by Robert Rosen in the introduction to his book on anticipatory systems (Rosen, 1985). Rosen developed the ideas for this book while a visiting Fellow at the Center for the Study of Democratic Institutions which was founded by Hutchins after he left the University of Chicago.

Rosen describes the holistic worldview that Hutchins made famous. He was so aware of the huge intellectual losses we suffered by reducing knowledge to "disciplines" that could exist and do their stunted version of scholarship in isolation from the rest of the body of knowledge. He recognized the complex interconnected network of ideas that was disjointed into disciplinary containers to be censored by the guardians of those academic political fiefdoms. This was especially true when it came to the interaction between hard and soft science. Rosen quotes a 1931 presentation by Hutchins:

Science is not the collection of facts or the accumulation of data. A discipline does not become scientific merely because its professors have acquired a great deal of information. Facts do not arrange themselves. Facts do not solve problems. I do not wish to be understood. We must get the facts. WE must get them all...But at the same time we must raise the question whether facts alone will settle our difficulties for us. And we must raise the question whether...the accumulation and distribution of facts is likely to lead us through the mazes of a world whose complications have been produced by the facts we have discovered. ...The gadgeteers and data collectors masquerading as scientists have threatened to become the chieftains of the scholarly world.

As the renaissance could accuse the Middle ages of being rich in principles and poor in facts, we are now entitled to enquire whether we are not rich in facts and poor in principles.

Rational thought is the only basis of education and research. Whether we know it or not, it has been responsible for our bewilderment...Facts are the core of an anti-intellectual curriculum.

The scholars in a university which is trying to grapple with fundamentals will, I suggest, devote themselves first of all to a rational analysis of the principles of each subject matter. They will seek to establish general propositions under which the facts they gather may be subsumed. I repeat, they would not cease to gather facts, but they would know what facts to look for, what they wanted them for, and what to do with them after they got them. (Rosen, 1985, pp. 3)

This was the atmosphere in which Rashevsky lived as he pursued his detailed mathematical approach to biology and the social sciences. Clearly, when Rosen came to Rashevsky to do his doctorate in the late 1950's, something had changed. That change is documented in the now classical paper by Rashevsky (1954): Topology and Life: In search of general mathematical principles in biology and sociology. He never did things in a small way.

This paper was the outcome of an internal struggle Rashevsky was having. On one hand he believed that he had demonstrated (and he certainly had) to the world that there was a fruitful mathematical approach to these problems. On the other hand, the answers were not satisfying. Something was wrong. The problem, it turns out, is at the root of all modern science and its use of analytical mathematics to create models of things that are complex and whose complexity eludes these methods. Today we have the artificial life and intelligence studies that refuse to acknowledge this demonstrable truth.

Rashevsky came to the following conclusion:

As we have seen, a direct application of the physical principles, used in the mathematical models of biological phenomena, for the purpose of building a theory of life as an aggregate of individual cells is not likely to be fruitful. We must look for a principle which connects the different physical phenomena involved and expresses the biological unity of the organism and the organic world as a whole. (Rashevsky, 1954, pp 321)

This was the birth of what we can now call the "relational" approach to systems. The principles Rashevsky sought were to come from his student, Robert Rosen. Over a period of almost 40 years, Rosen synthesized Hutchins' call for a science that gave a framework for the organization of facts in terms of principles with Rashevsky's recognition that the principles needed were those that allowed the suppression of certain detail in order to achieve the general principles sought after. In 1958, Rosen published "A relational theory of biological systems" and the new approach was born.

It is worth pausing to answer the obvious question about the relationship of biological theory to management theory at this point. That relationship is in the distinction between the classical reductionist approach to complex systems and the relational approach. Just as there is a very profound limit to what we can learn about living organisms using classical reductionist methods, even though we can amass facts in astronomical numbers, there is a limit to what we can learn about living organizations using these limited methods. Notice that there is no call to throw the baby out with the bathwater here. There is much data to be gained by classical methods. What we seek is a framework for dealing with those data.

THE NATURE OF COMPLEX SYSTEMS

Complex systems are what make up the real world. Yet if one accepts the machine metaphor and the accompanying reductionist baggage, this class of systems is ignored in favor of a surrogate world made up of simple systems. This distinction will be the subject of this section. Please note that the distinction being made has everything to do with the essential components for any successful theory of management.

The ideas underlying the development of the theory of anticipatory systems came from Rosen's experiences at the Center for the Study of Democratic Institutions. It quickly became clear that a group of well-educated scholars, economists, urban planners, political scientists and other professionals and leaders could discuss a problem and have deep questions about the decision-making process. Rosen described their problem like this:

However different the contexts in which these questions were posed, they were all alike in their fundamental concern with the making of policy, the associated notions of forecasting the future and planning for it. [Emphasis his] (Rosen, 1985, pp 6)

Thus, the basic ingredient of any theory of management, the ability to foresee outcomes, is what was at stake then and is our concern now. The same conditions prevail as did then, there are myriad theories that build on the assumptions inherent in the simple systems world and essentially none that confront the difficulties of real world complexity. Even the vast majority of people using the word "complexity" are still bound up in the world of simple systems having merely put old wine into new bottles.

First of all, how does a situation like this come about so that most of the users of these words see their meaning in a totally different way? The answer lies in the way we perceive the world around us. Rosen was careful when he described in detail what it meant for a real world system to be "anticipatory". (Rosen, 1975 & 1985). His examples ranged from biochemical systems involving chains of metabolic steps arranged so that the level of a toxic intermediate was kept low by

Figure 1. The modeling relation is a model of our perceptive process.

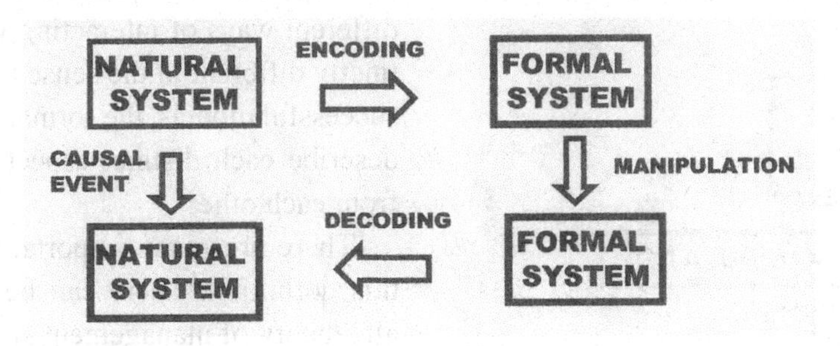

increasing the activity of the enzyme that turned it into its benign product whenever the level of a precursor many steps up the line was high, to obvious examples of animal and human behavior. In all these examples, the common thread was the existence of a "model" of the world that was used to compare with sensory or other detectable forms of input so that behavior could be modified to achieve the desired result. We are interested solely in human versions of this process here, and the "modeling relation" becomes a model of how we actually make models. The diagram in figure 1 depicts this relation.

The left side of the figure represents the sensory image of an event in the real world. The perception of this event involves the "natural system" in two states, one before and one after an observed change. We seek meaning in our world so that we assign cause to such a change. We will have much more to say about this cause later. How do we arrive at having a cause or explanation for what happens around us? We encode the natural system into a surrogate, a formal system in our mind that we have learned to manipulate. We perform a manipulation in our mind using the rules of the formal system and we obtain a result. We then "decode" or compare the two results. By some subjective criteria, we determine whether or not the formal system did a good job of "explaining" what we observed. If it did, we say that we have a good "model". Clearly, we should not expect such a model to be universal. Yet, classical science has consistently tried to provide a universal model believing that the reductionist paradigm could answer all questions about the real world. This idea has severely restricted the scope of what is to be recognized as science as Rosen has pointed out repeatedly. (Rosen 1985, 1986 a & b, 1991, 1993, 2000). The failure of Cartesian reductionism to deal with systems is now well known and should need no further elaboration here. However it is worth noting that the creation of University Centers for the study of complex systems is the direct result of the acknowledgement of so many scientists and administrators that we need to go beyond those self-imposed limits if we are to answer many of the important questions that have eluded us. The modeling relation is therefore our model of how we think and it reminds us that traditional science is dependent on a subjective choice of a particular formal system. That system is what Rosen calls "The Newtonian Paradigm" and it includes all of the physics that has been developed including quantum mechanics. If that seems strange it is because it is not always made clear that quantum mechanics is basically a new mathematical formalism created to fill in a missing aspect of the paradigm that began with Newton and his contemporaries using the Cartesian mechanistic largest model as its basis. Rosen has pointed out clearly that the problem is a deep one and that it is the reason for the failure of the formalist school Russell and others tried to create. It is also interesting that it was in the branch of mathematics called Number Theory that the whole thing collapsed even before it was tried on the

Figure 2. What traditional science did to the modeling relation.

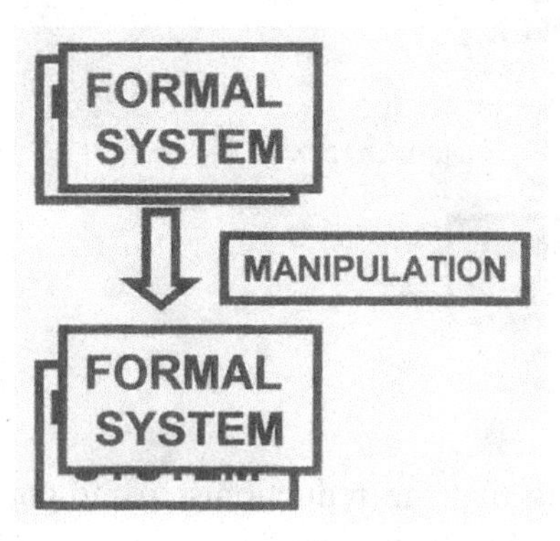

world of material things. It was Kurt Gödel who liberated us with his famous uncertainty theorem as Rosen's work reminds us.

In fact, the world of simple systems has been manipulated to look like figure 2.

There are a number of things that Figure 2 represents:

1. The encoding and decoding have been left out. In fact, they have been forgotten. The map has become the territory.
2. There is but one formal system possible. The absence of an acknowledgement of the surrogate nature of the formal system has given it the status of reality.
3. The formal system is a "largest model". It encompasses all that science is able to deal with in the spirit of the positivist philosophy.
4. We need to add that the notion of causality, direct cause, used in this paradigm is a distortion of the causal relations in the complex real world. We shall see how complex causality involves networks of interacting causes.

Real world complexity cannot be captured this way. One working definition of real world complexity is:

Complexity is the property of a real world system that is manifest in the inability of any one formalism being adequate to capture all its properties. It requires that we find distinctly different ways of interacting with systems. Distinctly different in the sense that when we make successful models, the formal systems needed to describe each distinct aspect are *not* derivable from each other

There are many important consequences to this definition. There can be no "one size fits all" theory of management simply because such a theory has to be based on a model that cannot be universal. The desire to see the world as a collection of simple, machine-like systems is rooted in this fact. If we were able to have such a world, its management would be no problem. In fact, the real world of human organizations, ecosystems and other complex systems is not one that lends itself to formalization. One might wonder why if this is true for number theory it should not be true for this subject.

Our answer to this is a pragmatic one. We set out to use the attributes of complex systems in ways that we are able to deal with. This means that any theory that is aimed at the management of such systems will be both incomplete and many faceted. It will include the need for constant observation and adaptation. It will sacrifice detail for the ability to make predictions and judgments.

An example of what we can do is in the realm of biology. We will use a biological example to show a more general approach to relational systems modeling.

A Short Introduction to Relational Systems

Relational systems theory is an extension of systems theory to include the real world complex systems. That inclusion is based on the major difference between relational theories and classical theories, namely, that relational theories are not formulated in terms of reductionist analysis in terms of the constituent parts of a system, but rather they focus on the system as defined by what it does, its function. The basis for a relational depiction of a system is a block diagram much like those used in classical systems theory, yet fundamentally different. That difference needs to be made clear, for it is the way the complexity of a real world system can be far more closely captured. Notice that relational models can be made for classical systems in terms of their parts. Syntactically, they will look the same. It is the semantics that makes the very significant difference.

The origins of this difference are in classical physics and have been discussed in various ways, none of which ever really homed in on the major difference. It is thermodynamics that really tells us that there is an alternative to the classical approach and that its claim to being the only "largest model" of the real world is false. As well as it has served us, there is more.

The whole is more than and different from the sum of its parts.

That statement has become a mantra in complexity science. (Mikulecky, 2007 a & b). It is used much more than it is understood. It has deep meaning, and that meaning is the foundation concept for relational systems theory. What does it mean for a whole, made up of material parts, atoms and molecules, to be more than its mere sum? It means a number of interrelated things:

1. It means that if the system is reduced to its parts, or even to subsystems, something real about it is lost. That "something" that is lost can only be identified in the whole system and is related intimately to what we observe when we see the system in action. In other words, we are talking about function. We can call the thing we observe that is lost when the system is reduced a *functional component.*
2. If the functional component in the whole system is lost even though in the collection of parts we have all the material elements that we had to start with, then the functional component has an existence, an ontology, at least as real as the material parts.
3. The whole system defines a context for the functional component, and that component has no meaning outside the context of the whole system.
4. The functional component in turn gives meaning to the system in terms of its observed actions. Hence, we have a closed causal loop in every whole system. The whole gives the defining context to its functional components, and those functional components define the system of interest.

Simple Machines vs. Complex Systems

We have been very successful using the reductionist world view. We have machines and technology that make its utility clear. We have unsuccessfully attempted to capitalize on the world view that led to these successes to solve problems it cannot solve. We construct a machine and it seems to be what we decided that particular combination of parts would be. It provides us with a desired function. That is, it does most of the time and for a limited period of time. We replace worn parts and do other things to extend this period. Nevertheless, our real machine is a complex system that differs fundamentally from the simple machine our theories created. Sooner or later, the inability to control and predict the behavior of the complex system will catch up with us. They do not always wear out or break down in the same manner. Hence, we need a back-up of spare parts or replacement machines to cover this gap between reality and our picture of it.

Let us consider how much more these obvious truths about the real world become when we leave the world of man-made machines and want to manage human and other natural systems. The diversity of essential information needed to predict the behavior of and control such systems is no longer something that we wish to approach with the techniques we used so successfully to produce our technological wonderland. Hence, a theory of management that relies on classical systems theory is going to be severely limited in its value at best.

The Use of Relational Systems Theory to Answer Schrödinger's Question: "What is Life?

Schrödinger (1944) grappled with a definition of life and expressed his frustration in his book by that title. Robert Rosen's creation of Relational Biology was motivated by Schrödinger's puzzlement. "What is life?" remains an ill-posed question to this day (Mikulecky, 2000). Rosen (1958) adapted the area of mathematics known as category theory to formulate relational systems theory in order to approach this famous question in an entirely different manner. Why category theory? Category theory is a very powerful form of mathematics. The most useful aspect of category theory from Rosen's point of view was its adaptability to add a semantic component involving causality. This allowed a direct way of codifying the observed functional components in any real world complex system. Now that we realize that the models we create of real world events hinge on a successful assignment of cause to changes in the real world, we have to be able to incorporate that causal reasoning in a rational, systematic way into our formal description in order to have a complete model. Here is where classical science fails us completely and its largest model is essentially bankrupt.

Rosen (1972, 1986a, 1991, 2000) showed that a category theory analysis of any simple machine produced by classical science's largest model, the Newtonian Paradigm, was causally incomplete. In fact, the analysis *always* leads to an infinite regression of causes. This is a very serious shortcoming and should not be dismissed as a flaw that can be rectified.

The Four Aristotelian Causes: Answers to the Question "Why?" Information Theory Extended to Complex Reality

Once again we see that the self-imposed boundaries of classical science fail to give us any clue about dealing with causal reasoning because of the dogmatic insistence that science can only deal with questions about "how?" and never questions about "why?" The fertile ideas of Aristotle in this area were, therefore, taboo. In fact, the information theory used in classical science is restricted to a very formal and sterile syntactic notion of this rich semantic area. The idea of asking "how?" fits the limited scope of the machine metaphor completely. We ask how machines work and our answer defines the machine. Had we included the asking of why the machine exists, we would have been led naturally to the issue of function.

Aristotle proposed that there are four distinct ways to answer the question "why?" For example, "why the house?" The house exists because:

1. **Material Cause:** The bricks, mortar, wood, nails, etc., of which the house is made.
2. **Efficient Cause:** The materials were put into the form we recognize as the house by an agent, the builder.
3. **Formal Cause:** The form the house took came from some plan, a blueprint. The builder followed it when he constructed the house.
4. **Final Cause:** There was a reason or purpose for the house. Someone needed a dwelling place.

Clearly these answers furnish us far more information about the house than the usual notion of information theory ever could.

The Metabolism, Repair [M, R] System

Rosen applied his causal version of category theory to a relational model of the living organism to repose Schrödinger's question in the following way:

How does an organism differ from a machine?

Given that the machine metaphor dominated biology since Descartes and was certainly the underlying motivation for Schrödinger's question, this was a revolutionary way to approach the issue. It is worth understanding Rosen's strategy here in detail for it is a key addition to our ability to understand complex systems when classical methods are exhausted.

The [M, R] system focused on the functions that define an organism. The central one is that myriad biochemistry, physiology and anatomy we use to describe the organism in detail. That the organism is not a machine should have been obvious by noting one crucial fact. In all the years of study, even with our most modern methods, we have not even come close to reverse engineering the simplest of organisms. If we are so good at dealing with machines in this manner, why does this object defy our methods? We understand the answer to "how?" in so many ways at so many levels, and yet we cannot produce an organism. Something is radically different about it, and that difference puts it into a category different from machines with no real overlap when viewed from this perspective.

The representation of metabolism via category theory is, at first, disappointingly simple:

f: A ---> B

or alternatively

f - - -> A ---> B.

The causal entailment is due to a category of agents, f, that map the pool of materials, A, into a new pool of materials, B. This includes chemical transformation, but also movement from one location to another.

There is something else we know about an organism that is as vital a function as metabolism and that is that they are constantly "repairing" themselves. Actually, this feature is central to distinguishing them from machines. We design machines to last. We repair them when we are forced to because of the limits of what we can do. Not so in the organism. It is almost misleading to call what they do "repair". They are building themselves continually and have distinct biochemistry that tears down components along controlled pathways. This is also a part of the general concept of repair. Growth, adaptation, wound healing, etc., would all be impossible were this not the way they are.

We represent this "repair" function by the mapping: Φ: B---> f. Thus, Φ is the efficient cause of this function that takes things that result from metabolism and replace the agents that carry out that metabolism. Now we have the following diagram, figure 3.

The process could go on indefinitely were this the representation of a machine. However, it is possible to use category theory and certain known properties of the organism to prove that ß is the inverse mapping of b: f --->. B so that the diagram now becomes closed as shown in figure 5. (Rosen, 1972).

This is a result that is only possible in the relational description of the system. It would be inconceivable that any consideration of material parts could have given a clue about this profound attribute of the organism. The organism, distinct from a machine, is closed to efficient cause.

Figure 3. The solid arrows represent efficient cause and the dotted arrows material cause. Metabolism is being carried out by the agent f which is being replaced by Φ in the constant turnover of the organism's constituents. The diagram could easily represent a machine at this point for we still lack causal entailment for Φ. Let ß, ß: f ---> Φ, be the efficient cause of Φ and f be the material cause of Φ . Then we have entailment for Φ as shown in figure 4.

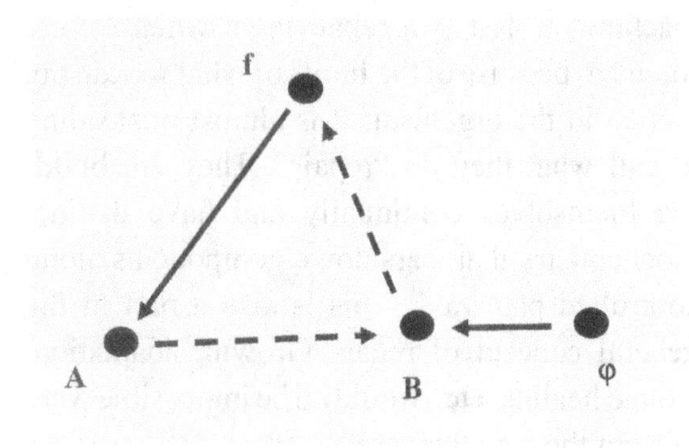

An Application: Is Gaia (the Earth System) an Organism?

One might legitimately ask what this has to do with management theory. One of the most controversial management issues in our day has to do with notions of "managing" the environment, ecosystems, etc. If the answer to the question asked is "yes" we have established some very hard conditions on any theory that purports to tell us how to manage this system.

We will proceed by making some simple assumptions about the earth system in order to compare its relational model with Rosen's organism. Let us assume that the metabolism, m, of the earth consists of certain ongoing cycles including ecosystems, the water cycle, and others, C that are made from resources, R, which include sunlight, the atmosphere, and the planet. As a relational diagram, this is, m: R --->C. As in the case of the organism, we require that m is entailed. Therefore, some set of natural processes must renew these metabolic processes from existing cycles when they are disrupted, n: ---> m. As in the case of the organism, n is unentailed. Another process, g, by analogy with the example above by Rosen is obtained. In fact, the diagrams are the same with the correspondences (A, R), (B, C), (f, m), (Φ, n), and (ß, G). Using causal reasoning, the earth system, or Gaia, is indeed closed to efficient cause and fits Rosen's definition of an organism. It is clearly not a machine, and we should not expect to be able to manage the environment as if it were. This opens up entirely new questions about environmental programs. The problem of managing a complex system now becomes clearer. The closed loop of causality that is characteristic of complex systems presents a whole set of problems that mechanistic theories are unable to deal with. Let us consider a few of them.

1. A complex system is impossible to model on a computer. The impredicativities or closed loops make this inescapable (Louie, 2007: Kercel, 2007).
2. The understanding of how the systems works gives no clue about constructing the system. Reverse engineering is impossible. The functional components used to model these systems have a context dependence that makes it impossible to find 1:1 mappings to the system's material parts.
3. The existence of closed loops of causality is a bigger problem than this example suggests because we have isolated the organism from its environment and modeled them separately. In the complex real world, there are clearly other closed causal loops involving the effect of organisms on the system they are in and influences from that system on the organism. Had we tried to deal with a single cell in a multicellular organism, the issue of homeostasis would have come up immediately. Cells make the homeostatic environment that allows their survival.

Figure 4. The entailment of Φ is accomplished by using the pool of agents f.

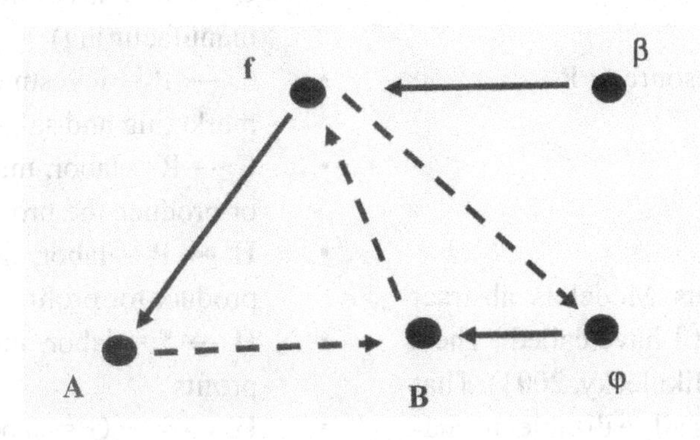

Figure 5. The final diagram is closed and no longer has the attributes of a machine.

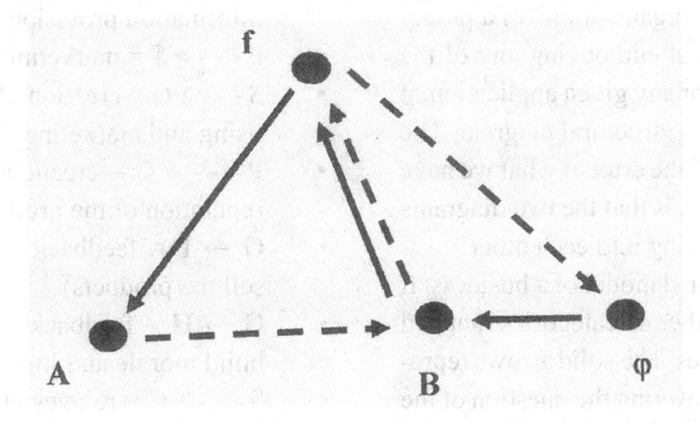

4. In today's world, management issues have parallel closed loops of causality networked in national and global economies, commerce, environmental effects, etc. Isolating an organization from these other aspects of the system of which it is an integral part can only lead to trouble.

In the next section we present a crude relational model of a business to exemplify what has been presented. This is not an attempt to produce a definitive model but merely an exercise aimed at putting ideas to work.

A RELATIONAL SYSTEMS MODEL OF A BUSINESS

Semantics of the symbols used:

- Dotted arrows (- - - >): Material Causes (Agents or materials, money, or "good will" to transform them. The material being transformed is the material cause of the product of the transformation)
- Solid arrows (→): Efficient Causes (Agents which actually make the transformation happen)

The various members of the system (Here we define "system" boundaries in a porous way to include the clients, consumers, consultants, etc.):

- People: **H**
- Capital: C
- Raw materials and resources: R
- Products: P
- Profit: $
- Good will: G

The Relational Systems Model is abstract and is an example of what I have called "Thermodynamic reasoning" (Mikulecky, 2001). That is, since it is abstract, it fits all realizable mechanistic models but, therefore, it cannot be used to distinguish between alternative mechanistic models. It retains the "organization" in a purely functional sense without embodying any of the structure. Therefore, for any given application, it needs an accompanying structural diagram. The most difficult idea, and the crux of what we have been saying throughout, is that the two diagrams do not have a 1:1 mapping into each other!

Figure 6 is a relational model of a business. It is composed of a number of categories mapped according to causal rules. The solid arrows represent material cause answering the question of the entailment of each item at the point of an arrow. The dotted arrows are efficient cause and these are the agents are responsible for the entailments represented by the solid arrows.

Interpretation of the mappings (organizational functions):

- C → R = investment (efficient cause for manufacturing)
- C → P = investment (efficient cause for marketing and sales)
- C → R = labor, management manufacture or produce the product
- **H** → P = labor, management market the product for profit
- **H** → $ = labor, management manage the profits
- **H** - - - > G = labor, management create good will
- R - - - > P = manufacturing and service/ information provision
- P - - - > $ = marketing and sales
- $ - - - > G = creation of good will by advertising and marketing
- P - - - > G = creation of good will due to reputation of the product
- G → P = feedback (good will helping to sell the products)
- G → **H** = feedback (good will helping to build morale and loyalty)
- $ - - - > C = reinvestment
- $ - - - > **H** = rewards

Clearly, this is not an organizational chart. Nor is it able to be mapped onto an organizational chart. This is important because this diagram is therefore information that can not be obtained by any ma-

Figure 6. The relational model of a business.

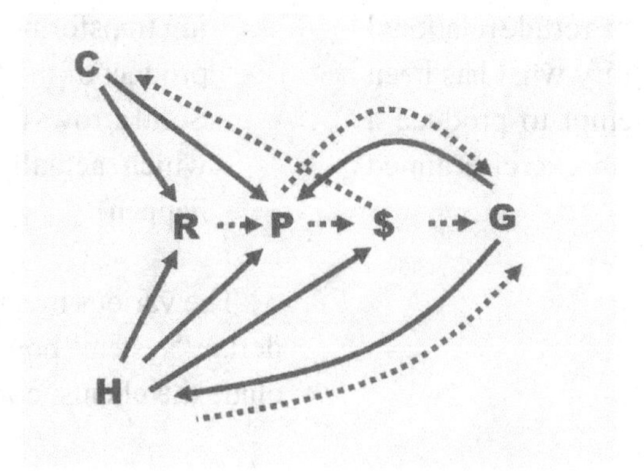

nipulation of the organizational chart. It refers to process not structure. With an organizational chart, function can only be inferred and incompletely at best. Notice that what is tracked in this diagram is a set of functions. These are dynamic and are not mapped onto the organizational chart in any way. The use of structural information, by means of organizational charts, protocols, etc., cannot duplicate the functional relationships illustrated in this diagram. The detailed structure of the diagram is open to modification and is in no way meant to be the only way such a model could be created. It is meant only to illustrate the distinctly different view of what an organization like a business might look like in relational terms.

The meaning of this is at the heart of why the relational model is so vital to management theory. When a function is lost or less than optimally performed in the organization, the first impulse is to go to the organizational chart and to pin down responsibility for that function. It is nowhere to be found in that diagram except by inference. When the relational diagram is used along with the rich theoretical base Rosen provides, the organization can be understood.

There is more. Rosen (1972) also showed that such diagrams had the ability to focus on those aspects of the system that were crucial for function to remain operative even when damage occurs. Hence, we can understand why functions can go on even when positions on the organizational chart might be vacant. We can also understand why incompetence might exist without detection. As long as the functional relations are maintained, the actions of individuals may or may not be as important as position titles and salaries suggest.

Self repair is a component of the organism diagramed earlier. If the organization is like an organism, many problems can be solved internally with little intervention from outside. This feature alone needs further study in this context and can lead to very important properties being a part of a really viable organization.

At this beginning stage, the lessons to be learned are open to investigation. Clearly, we can explore relationships this way that are invisible in any structural analysis of the organization.

CONCLUSION

Our classical approach to formulating theories of management has been too heavily influenced by the methodology of reductionism, especially as it exists in hard science. The social sciences have suffered from this "physics envy" and even though much has been written about the problem, a new approach is still wanting. In this spirit, we offer relational systems theory as another body of ideas about how complex real systems can be better understood and thereby controlled and utilized more effectively.

The essential difference here lies in the role of structure relative to function and the nature of their relationship. Contrary to the simple mechanistic systems utilized as models of real world systems by the reductionists, we acknowledge from the start that real world complex systems do not have a largest model. They require distinctly different models for each distinctly different way of interacting with them. In particular, systems operating in nature are much more poorly characterized by taking them apart and studying their component parts. The systems nature of these complex entities is captured by observing them in action and characterizing them by what they actually do.

Relational systems theory focuses on this functional identification of a complex system and builds a causal network to describe the relationships. The result is always divorced from a structural schematic of the system.

The implications of this for the construction of theories of management are profound. The manager is not the controller of a machine. The manager is a part of a system that is defined in a context and that has no real meaning outside that context. There is no necessary relationship between organizational charts, job titles, job descriptions, and what actually happens in the functioning organization.

This is a new view of organizations and little has been done to exploit it. It is open to the creator of a theory of management to use what we have learned up to now and to forge ahead.

ACKNOWLEDGMENT

My sincere thanks go to Helen Keitz for proofreading most of the manuscript. Any remaining errors are mine.

REFERENCES

Hayles, N. K. (1999). *How we became posthuman: Virtual bodies in cybernetics, literature, and Informatics.* Chicago: The University of Chicago Press.

Kercel, S. W. (2007). Entailment of ambiguity. *Chemistry & Biodiversity, 4*(10), 2369–2385. doi:10.1002/cbdv.200790193

Lakoff, G. (2008). *The political mind: Why you can't understand 21st- century American politics with an 18th- century brain.* New York, NY: Viking.

Lakoff, G., & Johnson, B. B. (1999). *Philosophy in the flesh: The embodied mind and its challenge to western thought.* New York, NY: Basic Books.

Louie, A. H. (2007). A Rosen etymology. *Chemistry & Biodiversity, 4*(10), 2296–2314. doi:10.1002/cbdv.200790188

Mikulecky, D. C. (1993) *Applications of network thermodynamics to problems in biomedical engineering.* New York: New York University Press.

Mikulecky, D. C. (2000). Robert Rosen: The well-posed question and its answer – Why are organisms different from machines? *Systems Research and Behavioral Science, 17*(5), 419–432. doi:10.1002/1099-1743(200009/10)17:5<419::AID-SRES367>3.0.CO;2-D

Mikulecky, D. C. (2001). Network thermodynamics and complexity: A transition to relational systems theory. *Computers & Chemistry, 25,* 369–391. doi:10.1016/S0097-8485(01)00072-9

Mikulecky, D. C. (2007a). Complexity science as an aspect of the complexity of science. In C. Gershonen, D. Aerts, & B. Edmonds (Eds.), *Worldviews science and us: Philosophy and complexity. (pp. 30-52).* Hackensack, NJ: World Scientific.

Mikulecky, D. C. (2007b). Causality and complexity: The myth of objectivity in science. *Chemistry & Biodiversity, 4*(10), 2480–2490. doi:10.1002/cbdv.200790202

Rashevsky, N. (1954). Topology and life: In search of general mathematical principles in biology and sociology. *The Bulletin of Mathematical Biophysics, 16,* 317–348. doi:10.1007/BF02484495

Rosen, R. (1958). The Representation of biological systems from the standpoint of the theory of categories. *The Bulletin of Mathematical Biophysics, 20,* 317–341. doi:10.1007/BF02477890

Rosen, R. (1972). Some relational cell models: The metabolism – repair system. In *Foundations of mathematical biology* (pp. 217-253). New York: Academic Press.

Rosen, R. (1973). On the relation between structural and functional descriptions of biological systems. In M. Conrad & M.E. Magar (Eds.) *The physical principles of neuronal and organismic behavior.* New York: Gordon and Breach.

Rosen, R. (1975). Biological systems as paradigms for adaptation. In R. H. Day & T. Groves, (Eds) *Adaptive economic models*. New York: Academic Press.

Rosen, R. (1985). *Anticipatory systems*. New York: Pergamon Press

Rosen, R. (1986a). Causal structures in brains and machines. *International Journal of General Systems*, *12*, 107–126. doi:10.1080/03081078608934929

Rosen, R. (1986b). Some comments on systems and system theory. *International Journal of General Systems*, *13*, 1–3. doi:10.1080/03081078608934949

Rosen, R. (1991). *Life itself*. New York: Columbia University Press.

Rosen, R. (1993). Drawing the boundary between subject and object: Comments on the mind-brain problem. *Theoretical Medicine*, *14*, 89–100. doi:10.1007/BF00997269

Rosen, R. (2000). *Essays on life itself*. New York: Columbia University Press.

Schrödinger, E. (1944). *What is life?* Cambridge, UK: Cambridge University Press.

Soros, G. (2006). *The Age of fallibility: Consequences of the war on terror*. New York: Public Affairs.

Soros, G. (2008). The crisis & what to do about it. *The New York Review of Books*, *60*(19), 63–65.

Strauss, L. (1964). *The city and man*. Chicago: The University of Chicago Press.

Section 2
Research, Theory, and Metatheory

Chapter 6
Consortial Benchmarking:
Applying an Innovative Industry-Academic Collaborative Case Study Approach in Systemic Management Research

Holger Schiele
Universiteit Twente, The Netherlands

Stefan Krummaker
Leibniz Universität Hannover, Germany

ABSTRACT

Case study research has its virtues in theory refinement and theory building. At the same time, this research method is criticized for low validity, poor generalizability and theory-induced bias that may reduce managerial relevance. Consortial benchmarking, where practitioners and researchers jointly benchmark "best practice" firms on a particular research question, is a new form of multi-case research that maximizes rigor, innovativeness and relevance as well as allowing researchers to take a systemic viewpoint when building theories in management. This chapter describes the concept and the application of consortial benchmarking. Consortial benchmarking contributes to unearth phenomena buried under traditional theories; it enhances existing approaches and contributes to building innovative theories. Due to the method's multi-case nature results are sufficiently generalizable. Since the consortiums comprise academics and practitioners, researcher bias is minimized and relevance and validity are maximized.

INTRODUCTION: BRIDGING THE PRACTITIONER-ACADEMIC DIVIDE THROUGH A PARTICULAR FORM OF CASE STUDY RESEARCH, CONSORTIAL BENCHMARKING

Although case study research has supposedly been in a crisis for decades (Yin, 1981), Eisenhardt and Graebner suggest that "...papers that build theory from cases are often regarded as the 'most interesting' research..." (Eisenhardt & Graebner, 2007, p. 25). Researchers agree that case study research can provide a powerful research strategy for theory-building in management research (Stake, 2006; Eisenhardt, 1989; Larsson, 1993; Weick, 2007; see Halinen & Tornroos, 2005; Wilson & Vlosky, 1997 and Weick, 1993 for examples of theory-building from cases). However, to fully utilize the potentials

DOI: 10.4018/978-1-61520-668-1.ch006

of the case study methodology researchers need to develop methods that improve rigor, innovativeness and relevance of case study research.

We propose consortial benchmarking as a novel research tool that can contribute to the revitalization of case study research. Its particular strength lies in bridging the practitioner-academic divide regularly discussed e.g. in special issues of top tier journals like the Academy of Management Journal (2007 and 2001) or the British Journal of Management (2002). This is particularly – but not exclusively – true with research settled in a complex environment.

From a background in systems theory it may actually be self-defeating to rely on a single theory for analysis, only (Wallis, 2008). Systems theory challenges this reductionist approach and asks to (re-) contextualize observations and embed them in the system they are a part of (Capra, 1996). Consortial benchmarking, by including academics and practitioners in the discourse, can prevent an analysis from being based on a single theory, which is often to be found in purely academic inquires.

Consortial benchmarking is a research-oriented partnership between industry and academia that meets a growing need in management research (Hatchuel, 2001, Tranfield, Denyer, Marcos, Burr, 2004, Trim & Lee, 2004). It brings together a group of investigators (the consortium) who are interested in finding an answer to a specific research question. The team is composed of practitioners from several firms and academics who add theoretical knowledge and enhance methodological rigor. The consortium visits advanced firms (different from those of the sponsoring firms) and collects data about the research topic. It analyses the data jointly and discusses the emerging constructs and possible relationships between different constructs and/or variables. As opposed to a classical multi-case study research, with consortial benchmarking not only the academic researcher is asking questions, but also the practitioners who are in the role of co-researchers. In practice, this means that a team of a dozen persons is visiting several firms. The research team agrees on a common set of questions. Researchers originating from different organizations and having different backgrounds as well as many different perspectives come together. In this setting, many different angles are applied to understanding the phenomenon. This is a chance to get a more holistic perspective on a research topic.

This chapter's contribution is to introduce a four-step approach to conducting a consortial benchmarking study. We focus on how to organize a consortial benchmarking project, but also embed this method in the methods discussion. In this way, we aim to enhance case study methodology and offer a blueprint for researchers who want to apply consortial benchmarking. Furthermore, since consortial benchmarking produces rich data that embeds different perspectives it allows to analyze a question from different angles, is open for surprising results and thus supports researchers in capturing the complexity of a non-linear managerial phenomenon, a precondition of systemic research. Thus, our chapter also contributes to systemic thinking and theory building in management.

This chapter is organized as follows: while illustrating the strength of consortial benchmarking in theory-building, we first take a closer look at the limitations of "classical" case study research methods and then discuss how consortial benchmarking can reduce or even overcome the objections discussed. Then consortial benchmarking is introduced in detail and we show how a consortial benchmarking study can be conducted.

REQUIREMENT OF CASE STUDY RESEARCH: INNOVATIVE ENQUIRIES AND THEORY-BUILDING FROM CASES

Generally, case study research is a preferred strategy when "how" or "why" questions arise

(Yin, 2003; Woodside & Wilson, 2003). Case study research is particularly appropriate when little is known about a phenomenon, when current understanding seems inadequate or when a fresh perspective on a phenomenon– typically from an application-oriented point of view – is needed (Eisenhardt, 1989). Case study research based on a systemic theory in the sense of the most cited expert perspective (Wallis, 2008) should be open for multi-agent and unpredictable approaches. Closely linked to this concept is the idea of reconsidering the context of knowledge creation (Bennet & Bennet, 2007). Case studies analyze an issue in its systemic context – as opposed to theory driven research. In other words: Cases can put a theory back into its cultural, organization, social context – and, (only!) if it does not accommodate the observation – expand the theory. Case study research is a fruitful approach for sharpening existing theory by identifying gaps and starting to fill them (Siggelkow, 2007). Glaser and Strauss point out that the intimate connection with empirical reality provides the possibility of developing a relevant, valid and testable theory (Glaser & Strauss, 1967). These are essential criteria for a "good theory" (Bacharach, 1989).

Even though a wealth of potential benefits of case study research are under discussion, building theories from single cases can be particularly subject to limitations, such as a lack of validity (Yin, 2003; Schofield, 2006) and generalizability (Leonard-Barton, 1990; Lincoln & Guba, 2006). Poorly executed case studies that apply only one source of evidence can result in a narrow or strongly biased theory (Yin, 2003; Eisenhardt, 1989; Eisenhardt, 1991). Analogously, with case studies rooted in a single theoretical paradigm and single method, there is a danger of overlooking real phenomena (Trim & Lee, 2004, Jick, 1979). Ultimately, such research may have not only low validity but also limited relevance. This is a serious concern, particularly with management-oriented topics.

In management-oriented domains such as business-to-business research, the "search for relevance" has been an ongoing concern (Hatchuel, 2001, Tranfield et al., 2004, Trim & Lee, 2004). For instance, 93% of participants surveyed during an industrial marketing and purchasing group (IMP) conference claimed that their own current research had a substantial value to managers. At the same time, respondents made the same claim about only 41% of their colleagues. Cross-checking these data with practitioners' claims revealed an even larger gap (Brennan & Ankers, 2004). Case study research is especially suited to filling this "relevance gap" because, unlike quantitative, survey-based research, it is built on bilateral communication. Case study research has the potential to identify and explore relevant topics and can capitalize on this unique potential.

Our proposition is that powerful next-generation case study work in management research will be of maximum benefit if it fulfills the following three requirements of good case study research:

1. It shows a high level of rigor in terms of validity and generalization and
2. contributes to innovative theory-building or enhances existing theories, which at the same time are
3. relevant because they address managerial issues of practical interest.

This is not to say that research should exclusively follow these lines, but case study research may come into its own here. The question arising from this proposition is how to build a case study research method which – by its very nature – ensures compliance with the requirements of rigor, innovativeness and relevance. We suggest consortial benchmarking as an innovative approach for such case study research.

OVERCOMING LIMITS OF CASES STUDY RESEARCH THROUGH CONSORTIAL BENCHMARKING

Limitations of Classical Case Study Research and Improvements Provided by Consortial Benchmarking: Rigor, Innovativeness and Relevance

The reasons for trying a new methodological approach to case study research can be found in the many criticisms aimed at case studies. One criticism of case study reseach is intrinsic lack of rigor, leading to limited validity of findings. Multi-case approaches can increase validity (Miles & Huberman, 1994; Schofield, 2006) because they utilize a replication logic to compare the findings from one case with those of other cases (Yin, 2003). This makes possible an independent corroboration of propositions (Eisenhardt, 1991).

Consortial benchmarking can be seen as a multi-case study research approach. The research team visits different firms and compares and cross-validates the findings of each case with those of other cases. While replications are a sign of robust findings, contrary results indicate the need for further research and a closer examination of anomalies (Miles & Huberman, 1994). Thus, by using a multi-case replication logic, consortial benchmarking helps to increase both the validity and the generalizability of the findings and, as a result, contributes to the development of "better theories" (Eisenhardt & Graebner, 2007).

Closely linked to the single-multiple case debate is another criticism of case study research: its generalizability (Punch, 2005). The key question is whether analyzing a case aims at generalization at all, or whether it tends toward understanding and describing that particular case in depth. This is what Stake calls an intrinsic case (Stake, 1995). Intrinsic case study research is not carried out because the selected case is representative of other cases. Thus, the purpose is not to build a generalizable theory. Instead, theory-building utilizes instrumental cases (Stake, 2005). Here, the cases themselves are of secondary interest. They play a supportive role in understanding the phenomena in question. Instrumental case study research aims at analytical generalization (Yin, 2003).

By its very nature, consortial benchmarking is a form of instrumental case study. The cases to be analyzed are not known in advance. They are chosen in the first phase of the project, only after the research questions have been agreed upon. Their sole purpose is to aid understanding of the phenomena being studied.

Another limitation of building theory from cases is the often isolated use of sources of evidence (e.g. exclusively relying on interviews), which can result in a narrow or strongly biased theory (Yin, 2003; Eisenhardt, 1989; Eisenhardt, 1991). The resulting theories have low or even no validity and tend not to be generalizable.

Consortial benchmarking uses different data sources and methods for theory-building to achieve a deeper and richer understanding of the studied phenomena. The research team combines interviews and presentations from the visited firms with documentary analysis or participant observations. Comparing diverse firms is a way to unveil patterns across organizations. In addition, since the team comprises members with different kinds of expertise and experience, the research topic is analyzed from multiple perspectives. As a result, a single investigator's individual preconceptions are less likely to bias the findings. Using such a team of researchers can be regarded as a multiple source of evidence strategy (Yin, 2003; Shank, 2002). Hence, triangulation is an inherent characteristic of consortial benchmarking. Patton argues that, "...by triangulating with multiple data sources, observers, methods and/or theories, researchers can make substantial strides in overcoming the skepticism that greets singular methods, lone analysts, and single perspective interpretations" (Patton, 2002, p. 556).

With regard to quantitative research, when hypotheses deduced from existing theories are tested, there is a danger of ignoring important phenomena that were overlooked in the context that led to that particular theory or that were irrelevant in the past (Rößl, 1990; Siggelkow, 2007). As an example, consider the discussion of why innovation networks have probably existed for a long time, but have largely been neglected in business research until recently. "Has a century of methodological individualism made us blind to the importance of these interactions?" (DeBresson & Amesse, 1991, p. 369). According to this interpretation, predominant models were not very conducive to the multi-player perspective at the heart of the network phenomenon. From an integral research background, such "white spots" are exactly what should be avoided.

According to systemic thinking, an organization such as a firm exists because it is able to bridge a gap in complexity between its in-system and the outside-system, i. e. the environment (Steinle, 2005). For instance, a firm may concentrate only on a particular market segment and apply particular tools to run the business. However, being part of the environment as a system obviously means that the reduction of complexity in the in-system does not prevent it from being exposed to developments in the outside-system. In other words, the reduction of complexity means that there is a risk created. In this process of complexity-reduction (which is needed for operative reasons) some important influences may have been overlooked, for instance particular market developments or new tools available for the competitors. To prevent such white spots from becoming dangerous, firms may need to be open to challenge their assumptions reducing white spots.

Complex methods from psychology have been suggested for identifying white spots (Goffin, Lemke, Szwejczewski, 2006). The collaborative form of agenda-setting in consortial benchmarking is another relatively simple form of reducing theory-induced biases (as well as practice-induced biases). The peculiarity of this approach – allowing consortium members who are practitioners to discuss the topic and ask questions – prevents the academic researcher from being too myopic on the research issue. This feature of consortial benchmarking significantly increases the relevance of the research.

A final but serious criticism, which actually transcends case study research, is the lack of relevance of academic enquiries. In their seminal work on research relevance, Gibbons and his colleagues distinguish between mode 1 knowledge and mode 2 knowledge (Gibbons, Limoges, Nowotny, Schartzmann, Scott, & Trow, 1994). Mode 1 is knowledge creation that is disciplinarily confined, primarily cognitive and concerned with theory rather than practice. Gibbons et al. diagnose a trend toward mode 2, a transdisciplinary type of research carried out in the context of its application and aimed at practical relevance, thus overcoming the "academic-practitioner divide" (Brennan & Ankers, 2004). Wallis, for instance, showed that even in the process of the development of a theory, in that case the complex adaptive systems theory, the more scholarly oriented authors focused on a different sets of attributes than the more practically oriented authors (Wallis, 2008).

The UK "Industry-Academic Links Report" analyzes reasons for the still acute academic-practitioner divide. It finds that "…users believe that research can benefit them but do not regard many research topics as focusing upon key issues of relevance" (Starkey & Madan, 2001, p. S3). To overcome this problem and to focus research on relevant topics, it has been argued that mode 2 research is best carried out in some form of industry-academic collaboration (Starkey & Madan, 2001; Hatchuel, 2001; Tranfield et al., 2004; Trim & Lee, 2004).

Consortial benchmarking, one such form of industry-academic collaboration, is inclined to mode 2 form of research or, more precisely, is what Huff has called "mode 1.5 form of research", combining rigor and relevance (Huff, 2000). Visiting best practice firms seeing their installations and talking to the people working on the subject of enquiry is research carried out in the application context. The presence of practitioners in the research team and their inclusion in collective agenda-setting structurally ensures that relevant topics are studied.

Summing up the strengths of consortial benchmarking in case study research and examining it in terms of the three exigencies outlined in the introduction, it becomes apparent that:

1. Consortial benchmarking, as a genuinely instrumental form of case study research, is a powerful means of reducing limitations concerning the validity and generalizability of theory-building from cases, identifying transferrable patterns.
2. Since it utilizes multiple cases, different sources of data and multiple analysts to examine the data and to review the findings, the theory developed has the potential to be more holistic and innovative and rests on a strong empirical basis and multi-faceted and multi-perspective data analysis.
3. Involving practitioners in the agenda-setting of a research project is a viable method of ensuring the relevance of research right from the beginning.

Based on this proposition it may be worth exploring the consortial benchmarking method and its application more in detail.

Consortial Benchmarking in its Research Context: An Application-Oriented Enquiry

Benchmarking is a methodology developed for comparing firms with the objective of identifying and transferring best practices. Benchmarking is rooted in the work of Camp, who pioneered this approach in the 1980s while working with Xerox (Camp, 1989). Consortial benchmarking is a special type of benchmarking and can be characterized as a form of collective case study that analyzes the research topic in several firms (cases) (Punch, 2005). Reflecting an application-oriented understanding of management research (Schmalenbach, 1911), consortial benchmarking has received particular attention in German-speaking countries (Schweikert, 2000; Fahrni, Völker, & Bodmer, 2002; Felde, 2004; Puschmann & Alt, 2005).

In consortial benchmarking, a consortium of interested firms and researchers organizing the study visits best practice sites – or, more precisely, "best pattern sites" since practices are strongly bound to their context while patterns could better be used to adopt to other situations and stretch the frontier even further – to compare their approaches and find "how" and "why" answers to the research questions. The aim is to derive results with a sufficient degree of transferability from this comparison. The consortium defines the research questions, selects the firms to be visited and discusses the benchmarking results. In contrast to traditional individualistic forms of benchmarking, several firms conduct the benchmarking exercise simultaneously, resulting in a cross-industry benchmarking study (Fahrni et al., 2002).

Inspired by the process benchmarking work of the American Productivity & Quality Center (Schweikert, 2000; Brueck, Riddle, & Paralez, 2003), consortial benchmarking should be distinguished from the consortium survey (Morris & LoVerde, 1993). In a consortium survey, the objects and subjects of analysis are identical; that is, the firms belonging to the consortium analyze their own organizations and compare the results with each other. In consortial benchmarking projects, the consortium members visit third parties.

The Four Phases of a Consortial Benchmarking Study

The procedure for a consortial benchmarking study can be divided into four distinct phases:

Figure 1. The four steps of a consortial benchmarking project

I. Preparation
- develop reference framework
- form industry-academic research consortium

II. Kick-off workshop
- refine reference framework
- develop questionnaire
- select best-practice firms

III. Benchmarking visits
- visit best-practice firms
- wrap-up: lessons learned in consortium
- provide feedback

IV. Final meeting
- collate and discuss results from individual visits
- prepare final report

the *preparation of the research issue* and consortium formation, a refining *kick-off workshop*, *benchmarking visits to best pattern firms* and a final *lessons-learned meeting* (see figure 1). Why exactly these four steps, one may ask? The preparation phase is necessary for the initiators to gain an overview on the existing knowledge in the field. Once the consortium members are defined, a workshop has proven to be the best way how to include their additional insights and interests into the research agenda. This is a particular feature of consortial benchmarking. Before conducting the first visit, every member needs to be sure that his particular issues will be addressed. After the visits to the best pattern firms a lessons-learned meeting is very helpful to reflect all visits, but from a distance. This reflection cannot be done after visiting the last benchmarking firm, because then the researchers may still be too much influenced by this particular firm. Therefore a final lessons-learned meeting of its own has its virtues here.

- *Preparation*: the initial phase of a consortial benchmarking study has two main steps: (1) developing a reference framework for the planned research and (2) forming a research consortium.
  1. Since the research question is typically scoped within the context of existing theory (Eisenhardt & Graebner, 2007), a reference framework is generated by the researcher organizing the consortial benchmarking study. Siggelkow advises researchers to start with a frame of reference and not to ignore existing knowledge in order to justify engaging in case study research (Siggelkow, 2007). Such a framework can be regarded as what Eisenhardt calls *apriori* specification of constructs, which helps researchers "...to shape the initial design of theory-building research" (Eisenhardt, 1989, p. 536). The reference framework contains basic terms and assumed relationships between them, thereby offering a structure for hosting observations. Since consortial benchmarking aims at identifying new theories and theory enhancements, the framework is not a strict analytic grid, but rather is subject to adaptations during a study as new areas of interest emerge from the data. It is important for the researchers to avoid becoming hostages of their frame of reference, rather, allowing observations to challenge it. Following the standards of applied science, the research framework

reflects theoretical as well as practical perspectives, so as to derive models and rules that help solve practical problems (Kubicek, 1975). One challenge at this point is not to develop a reference framework which is too complicated. Experience shows that there is a diminishing marginal return to complexity with reference frameworks.

2. Further, during the preparation phase, the members of the sponsoring consortium are identified and their participation assured. In addition to academic or consultant organizers, consortium members are firms, usually represented by one or two delegates, who are interested in the research topic and want to obtain first-hand information on best patterns. Identifying a sufficient amount of sponsoring firms is the prime challenge at this phase. There is a trade-off between the size of the individual monetary contribution per firm and the number of sponsoring firms. However, because too many participants are not feasible during the benchmarking visits, the participation fee has to be established by dividing the estimated costs through 6 to 8, which would be the ideal number of firms, in our experience. Topics suited for a consortial benchmarking project may not need to be too narrow (the topic will narrow down during the research). Typical examples of projects we organized included "e-procurement," "supplier relationship management" or "how to get innovations from suppliers." In the end of phase I the organizers have gathered a sufficient amount of firms joining the consortium so that the project becomes economically feasible.

- *Kick-off workshop*: the aim of the initial workshop is to incorporate the consortium members' input into the research framework for analysis. The best pattern firms to be visited are also selected at this time. The reference framework proposed by the researchers is discussed by the practitioners and, if necessary, enhanced or modified. This is a "relevance check" of the *a priori* construct the researchers have chosen. The framework is further operationalized in a questionnaire to structure the benchmarking visits. This questionnaire should not be too long, because otherwise it becomes difficult to ensure that all questions are tracked during all visits. Ensuring that similar questions are asked at each visit is a task for the organizers. While there needs to be time for exploring the particular contributions of each visited firm, the main structure of the enquiry should be kept intact in order to compare findings.

1. The selection of the firms to be visited requires careful planning. Two complementary approaches can be used. One option is to use the know-how of the consortium members by employing some kind of voting mechanism to identify the firms to be visited. This method is comparable to selection mechanisms for identifying best-practice cases described in the literature (Petersen, Handfield, Ragatz, 2005). Another option is to send potential firms a questionnaire, the results of which could then be used to further refine selection (Boutellier et al., 1999; Puschmann & Alt, 2005). In both cases a short-list of potential firms to be visited has to be produced. This list can comprise some 30 to 40 firms, for which an outside-in analysis has to be prepared and which will be ranked. The list of candidates must be sufficiently long, because not all firms will agree to be visited. What has been very helpful to identify best

pattern firms are prizes which are being awarded by different institutions, as well as mentions in the literature. The second phase in the process of consortial benchmarking results in the compilation of a list of best pattern firms to be visited and formulation of interview and research guidelines agreed by the consortium members.

- *Benchmarking visits*: the core element of consortial benchmarking is the visits to the selected best pattern firms. Initially, the number of visits is not specified. Following the idea of theoretical sampling, selection and analysis of cases continue until theoretical saturation is achieved (Strauss & Corbin, 1998; Locke, 2005). The visiting phase is concluded once no further new or contrasting results are drawn from the collected data. In our experience of five consortial benchmarking projects, theoretical saturation is generally achieved after half a dozen visits.
  1. In a typical consortial benchmarking process, the visits are organized by the researchers, who contact the best pattern firms, develop an agenda with them and set up the practical structure of the visits. An important task of the organizers is to manage the structure of the visits, in order to prevent the discussion from focusing on marginal topics.
  2. Each visit takes one and a half days. The first day usually includes briefing consortium team members with a detailed inside-out analysis of the firm to be visited and possibly a visit to the production facilities or a first informal dinner meeting with members of the visited firm. The second day is taken up with presentations by the best pattern firms and a discussion of the research questions. Normally, there are about three to four different presentations by the visited firms. In order to stress the interactive character of consortial benchmarking and the mutual learning experience, it can also be proposed that, in addition to the research agenda, the visited firm raises an issue of their particular interest which is then been discussed with the visitors. This offer can substantially increase the willingness of firms to accept hosting the benchmarking team. In our experience, these firms often tend to have issues they would like to discuss with a set of experts, even though generally they are considered to be best practice (maybe this characteristic of asking questions has contributed for these firms to become known as best practice…).
  3. Immediately after each visit, the members of the benchmarking team meet to summarize the findings and compare them against the framework. Thus, like other inductive analytic techniques, data analysis in consortial benchmarking is characterized by an iterative process of data collection and abstracting and comparing findings. From an organizational point of view it has to be made sure that the visit to the best pattern firm does not take too long because then all members of the consortium have to hurry to get back home. It is no viable option to compare and summarize the observations from the visit at a later stage. It is also important to have this meeting in order to promote a discussion between the members of the consortium. Therefore it is not an option, either, for the organizers to collect the feedback from the participants individually. In practice,

then, the consortium still meets at the site of the best pattern firm to compile the results.

- *Final meeting*: after the visits are completed, the results of the individual benchmarks are collated and discussed in the consortium, and a conclusion on generalizable best patterns is produced in the form of a final report.
  1. A consortial benchmarking project may take as long as two years, one year being the time reserved for the visits to the best pattern firms. This period may seem to be long, but – from a pragmatic point of view – practitioners may require more time, considering their tough schedule. They may ideally have two days available every two month, but most likely not two days every single month. Also, breaks due to holiday seasons have to be taken into consideration. Sure, considering the clock-speed some industries are in currently, it may seem desirable to cut-down the time needed for a study. However, in our experience the limiting factor is the availability of the practitioners in the research consortium.

Once the consortial benchmarking study has been concluded, in each sponsoring firm at least two change agents are generated. While surveying participants in several consortial benchmarking projects, Schweikert found that a particular benefit seems to be consortial benchmarking's influence on change processes that subsequently occur within the consortium member firms themselves (Schweikert, 2000). At the same time, the academic participants can introduce their findings into their respective academic communities, so that the final report of the visits is not the last document arising from the venture.

CONCLUSION: SUITABILITY AND LIMITATIONS OF CONSORTIAL BENCHMARKING CASE STUDY RESEARCH

Building new or extending existing theories is a core activity of management research, enabling researchers to identify novel constructs, variables and relationships that were formerly ignored and to unveil possible answers to phenomena that were unknown and unaccounted for in the past. Advances in management research frequently emerge when researchers cherish richness (Weick, 2007), e.g. by adopting a systemic viewpoint (Davis, Eisenhardt, & Bingham, 2007). Purely theoretical deductive research is frequently confronted with the problem that "...if theory talks only to theory, the collective research exercise runs the danger of becoming entirely self-referential and out-of-touch with reality, of coming to be considered irrelevant" (Siggelkow, 2007, p. 23). Tacit knowledge hosted by practitioners is most likely not made explicit in this way (Bennet & Bennet, 2007). Conducting a joint practitioner-academic research process such as proposed by consortial benchmarking can prevent academic researchers from being caught in the "irrelevance trap."

However, consortial benchmarking is not only a promising approach for doing relevant research, but since it uses multiple source of evidence and utilizes different analysis techniques it is also a way to conduct rigorous management research. Thus, consortial benchmarking combines the three requirements for good case study research, namely ensuring that it (1) exhibits a high level of rigor in terms of validity and generalizability and (2) contributes to innovative theory-building or the enhancement of existing theories, which at the same time are (3) relevant, in that they cover managerial issues of practical interest. By joining rigor and relevance, consortial benchmarking provides bridging infrastructure to fill the frequently cited gap between academia and practice in management research.

In addition, consortial benchmarking first supports building and refining theories from a systems theory and management cybernetic viewpoint. By using multiple cases, different sources of evidence and data triangulation consortial benchmarking cherishes richness and allows capturing the complexity of a phenomenon. For example, since academics and practitioners with different backgrounds analyze the collected data together and discuss the emerging findings, single-perspective biases are reduced. Moreover, working with a heterogeneous research team avoids building narrow and reductionist theories in terms of "trivial machines" (von Foerster, 1984). In our experience, more often than the practitioners – who want to solve a practical problem and often are intuitively open to a holistic approach – academic members in a research consortium have to take care not to become the agents of reductionism, if they stick too much to a single theory, only.

Second, from a cybernetic viewpoint consortial benchmarking supports increasing variety (Law of Requisite Variety) (Ashby, 1956). Visiting different firms and comparing data enables the research team not only to discover different relevant states of a system, but also to learn about different relevant ways of reacting to those states. Thus, consortial benchmarking builds knowledge about alternatives for "controlling" a system which broadens the behavioral repertoire of managers. Having the capacity to react in a broad variety to different states of a system allows managers to "control" a system more effectively. Moreover, it shows managers that controlling a system is a holistic and complex cybernetic challenge and not a simple and precise intervention.

From a practitioner perspective, joining a consortial benchmarking project can avoid a core problem with sponsoring purely academic research, namely that the practitioner cannot always be sure that results fit to the particular purpose and that the implications are directly applicable. Being an integral part of the research team in a consortial benchmarking project is the key advantageous feature here. Further, consortial benchmarking is a unique form of accessing both, updated scientific know-how (from the academic members of the research consortium) and updated best practice know-how from leading firms (through the benchmarking visits). Eventually, while it would be somewhat exaggerated to call a single benchmarking project a "pocket MBA," consortial benchmarking definitively comprises a personal skills development component. Apart from being a technique of creating change agents, the skills and knowledge enhancing element also makes consortial benchmarking attractive from a human resource development perspective.

However, consortial benchmarking also has its limitations. A collaborative research project requires a more active participation from the practitioners than in the case of commissioning a research institute or a consultancy with a study. From an academic perspective it has to be noted that first, given the staggering volume of rich data from multiple sources of evidence "...there is a temptation to build theory which tries to capture everything. The results can be a theory which is rich in detail but which may lack the simplicity of overall perspective (Eisenhardt, 1989). Here, a particular challenge at the industry-academic interface arises: Reality may present itself to practitioners as a complex system. They may search for answers to each of its elements, which lead to inflated approaches. At the same time, academic theory – and closely linked – publication processes overwhelmingly still follow a Cartesian-reductionist approach (Capra, 1996), i. e. requiring a pure and single-theory based approach. Also, since one criterion of good theory is testability (Bacharach, 1989), complex "multi-theories" frequently face the problem of transferring comprehensive findings into a manageable number of simple hypotheses that can serve to test the emergent theory using quantitative research techniques.

As a second limitation, employing a research team can lead to collective issues, such as team cohesion or team identity, as well as group phenomena, such as group think, that may influence the research process and bias findings (Janis & Mann, 1977). Further research on consortial benchmarking should take these limitations into consideration.

The challenge in good case study research is not just to select the right questions to ask – and the right people to ask them to – in order to generate a large amount of rich data and to analyze the data thoroughly, but also to draw valid, generalizable, innovative and relevant conclusions. Consortial benchmarking offers a promising method of increasing the value of next-generation case study research and thus of reducing the skepticism some scholars, paper reviewers and practitioners may still have about this kind of research.

REFERENCES

Ashby, W. R. (1956). *An introduction into cybernetics*. New York: Wiley.

Bacharach, S. B. (1989). Organizational theories: Some criteria for evaluation. *Academy of Management Review*, *14*(4), 496–515. doi:10.2307/258555

Bennet, A., & Bennet, D. (2007). *Knowledge mobilization in the social sciences and humanities*. Marlinton, WV: MQI Press.

Boutellier, R., Baumbach, M. & Bodmer, C. (1999). Successful-practices in after-sales-management. *io Management, 68*(1/2), 23-27.

Brennan, R., & Ankers, P. (2004). In search of relevance: Is there an academic-practitioner divide in business-to-business marketing? *Marketing Intelligence & Planning*, *22*(5), 511–519. doi:10.1108/02634500410551897

Brueck, T., Riddle, R., & Paralez, L. (2003). *Consortium benchmarking methodology guide*. Denver, CO: AWWA Research Foundation.

Camp, R. C. (1989). *Benchmarking: The search for industry best practices that lead to superior performance*. Milwaukee, WI: Quality Press.

Capra, F. (1996). *The web of life: A new scientific understanding of living systems*. New York: Anchor Books Doubleday.

Davis, J. P., Eisenhardt, K. M., & Bingham, C. B. (2007). Developing theory through simulation methods. *Academy of Management Review*, *32*(2), 480–499.

DeBresson, C., & Amesse, F. (1991). Networks of innovators: A review and introduction to the issue. *Research Policy*, *20*, 363–379. doi:10.1016/0048-7333(91)90063-V

Eisenhardt, K. M. (1989). Building theories from case study research. *Academy of Management Review*, *14*(4), 532–550. doi:10.2307/258557

Eisenhardt, K. M. (1991). Better stories and better constructs: The case for rigor and comparative logic. *Academy of Management Review*, *16*(3), 620–627. doi:10.2307/258921

Eisenhardt, K. M., & Graebner, M. E. (2007). Theory building from cases: Opportunities and challenges. *Academy of Management Journal*, *50*(1), 25–32.

Fahrni, F., Völker, R., & Bodmer, C. (2002). *Erfolgreiches Benchmarking in Forschung und Entwicklung, Beschaffung und Logistik* [Successful benchmarking in research and development, purchasing and logistics]. München, Germany: Hanser.

Felde, J. (2004). *Supplier collaboration: An empirical analysis of Swiss OEM-supplier relationships*. Bamberg, Germany: Difo-Druck.

Gibbons, M., Limoges, C., Nowotny, H., Schartzmann, S., Scott, P., & Trow, M. (1994). *The new production of knowledge: The dynamics of science and research in contemporary societies*. London: Sage.

Glaser, B. G., & Strauss, A. L. (1967). *The discovery of grounded theory: strategies for qualitative research*. New York: DeGruyter.

Goffin, K., Lemke, F., & Szwejczewski, M. (2006). An exploratory study of 'close' supplier-manufacturer relationships. *Journal of Operations Management, 24*(2), 189–209. doi:10.1016/j.jom.2005.05.003

Halinen, A. & Tornroos, J. (2005). Using case methods in the study of contemporary business networks. *Journal of Business Research, 58*(9 - Special Issue), 1285-1297.

Hatchuel, A. (2001). The two pillars of new management research. *British Journal of Management, 12*(Special Issue), S33–S39. doi:10.1111/1467-8551.12.s1.4

Huff, A. S. (2000). Presidential Address: "Changes in Organizational Knowledge Production. *Academy of Management Review, 25*(2), 288–293. doi:10.2307/259014

Janis, I. L., & Mann, L. (1977). *Decision making: A psychological analysis of conflict, choice, and commitment*. New York: Free Press.

Jick, T. D. (1979). Mixing qualitative and quantitative methods: Triangulation in action. *Administrative Science Quarterly, 24*(4), 602–611. doi:10.2307/2392366

Kubicek, H. (1975). *Empirische Organisationsforschung: Konzeption und Methodik* [Empiric organisational research: Conception and methodology]. Stuttgart, Germany: Poeschel.

Larsson, R. (1993). Case survey methodology: Quantitative analysis of patterns across case studies. *Academy of Management Journal, 36*(6), 1515–1546. doi:10.2307/256820

Leonard-Barton, D. (1990). A dual methodology for case studies: Synergistic use of a longitudinal single site with replicated multiple sites. *Organization Science, 1*(3 - special issue), 248-266.

Lincoln, Y. S., & Guba, E. G. (2006). The only generalization is: There is no generalization. In R. Gomm, M. Hammersley & P. Foster (Eds.), *Case study method: Key issues, key texts* (pp. 27-44). London: Sage.

Locke, K. D. (2005). *Grounded theory in management research*. Thousand Oaks, CA: Sage.

Miles, M. B., & Huberman, A. M. (1994). *Qualitative data analysis: An expanded sourcebook*. Thousand Oaks, CA: Sage.

Morris, G. W., & LoVerde, M. A. (1993). Consortium surveys. *The American Behavioral Scientist, 36*(4), 531–550. doi:10.1177/0002764293036004008

Patton, M. Q. (2002). *Qualitative research evaluation methods*. Thousand Oaks, CA: Sage.

Petersen, K. J., Handfield, R. B., & Ragatz, G. L. (2005). Supplier integration into new product development: Coordinating product, process and supply chain design. *Journal of Operations Management, 23*(3/4), 371–388. doi:10.1016/j.jom.2004.07.009

Punch, K. (2005). *Introduction to social research: Quantitative and qualitative approaches*. Thousand Oaks, CA: Sage.

Puschmann, T., & Alt, R. (2005). Successful use of e-procurement in supply chains. *Supply Chain Management: An International Journal, 10*(2), 122–133. doi:10.1108/13598540510589197

Rößl, D. (1990). Die Entwicklung eines Bezugsrahmens und seine Stellung im Forschungsprozess [Development of a reference framework and its position in the research process]. *Journal für Betriebswirtschaft, 40*(2), 99–110.

Schmalenbach, E. (1911). Die Privatwirtschaftslehre als Kunstlehre [The subject of private economy as craft = Business administration as applied science]. *Zeitschrift für handelswissenschaftliche . Forschung, 6*, 304–316.

Schofield, J. W. (2006). Increasing the generalizability of qualitative research. In R. Gomm, M. Hammersley & P. Foster (Eds.), *Case study method: Key issues, key texts* (pp. 69-97). London: Sage.

Schweikert, S. (2000). *Konsortialbenchmarking-projekte: Untersuchung und Erweiterung der Benchmarking-methodik im Hinblick auf ihre Eignung, Wandel und Lernen in Organisationen zu unterstützen* [Consortial benchmarking projects: Analysis and amplification of this benchmarking method what concerns the suitability to support change and learning in organisations]. Flein, Germany: Verlag Werner Schweikert.

Shank, G. D. (2002). *Qualitative research: A personal skills approach*. Upper Saddle River, NJ: Merrill/Prentice Hall.

Siggelkow, N. (2007). Persuasion with case studies. *Academy of Management Journal, 50*(1), 20–24.

Stake, R. E. (1995). *The art of case study research*. Thousand Oaks, CA: Sage.

Stake, R. E. (2005). Qualitative case studies. In N. K. Denzin & Y. S. Lincoln (Eds.), *The Sage handbook of qualitative research* (pp. 443-466). Thousand Oaks, CA: Sage.

Stake, R. E. (2006). The case study method in social inquiry. In R. Gomm, M. Hammersley & P. Foster (Eds.), *Case study method: Key issues, key texts* (pp. 19-26). London: Sage.

Starkey, K., & Madan, P. (2001). Bridging the relevance gap: Aligning stakeholders in the future of management research. *British Journal of Management, 12*(Special Issue), S3–S26. doi:10.1111/1467-8551.12.s1.2

Steinle, C. (2005). *Ganzheitliches Management: Eine mehrdimensionale Sichtweise integrierter Unternehmungsführung* [Integral Management. A multi-dimensional view of holistic business administration]. Wiesbaden, Germany: Gabler.

Strauss, A. L., & Corbin, J. (1998). *Basics of qualitative research: Techniques and procedures for developing grounded theory*. Thousand Oaks, CA: Sage.

Tranfield, D., Denyer, D., Marcos, J., & Burr, M. (2004). Co-producing management knowledge. *Management Decision, 42*(3/4), 375–386. doi:10.1108/00251740410518895

Trim, P. R. J., & Lee, Y. (2004). A reflection on theory building and the development of management knowledge. *Management Decision, 42*(3/4), 473–480. doi:10.1108/00251740410518930

von Foerster, H. (1984). Principles of self-organization in a socio-managerial context. In H. Ulrich & G. J. B. Probst (Eds.), *Self-organization and management of social systems* (pp. 2-22). Berlin: Springer.

Wallis, S. E. (2008). Emerging order in CAS theory: Mapping some perspectives. *Kybernetes, 37*(7), 1016–1029. doi:10.1108/03684920810884388

Weick, K. E. (1993). The collapse of sensemaking in organizations: The Mann Gulch disaster. *Administrative Science Quarterly, 38*(4), 628–652. doi:10.2307/2393339

Weick, K. E. (2007). The generative properties of richness. *Academy of Management Journal, 50*(2), 14–19.

Wilson, E. J., & Vlosky, R. P. (1997). Partnering relationship activities: Building theory from case study research. *Journal of Business Research, 39*(1), 59–70. doi:10.1016/S0148-2963(96)00149-X

Woodside, A. G., & Wilson, E. J. (2003). Case study research for theory-building. *Journal of Business and Industrial Marketing*, *18*(6/7), 493–508. doi:10.1108/08858620310492374

Yin, R. K. (1981). The case study crisis: Some answers. *Administrative Science Quarterly*, *26*, 58–65. doi:10.2307/2392599

Yin, R. K. (2003). *Case study research: Design and methods*. Thousand Oaks, CA: Sage.

Chapter 7
Systemic Paradoxes of Organizational Change:
Implementing Advanced Manufacturing Technology

Marianne W. Lewis
University of Cincinnati, USA

ABSTRACT

This chapter explores systemic challenges surrounding a highly disruptive type of organizational change—the implementation of advanced manufacturing technology (AMT). To unpack the intricate, multi-layered systems surroundings AMT implementation, the author applies an inductive method that relies on multiple paradigm lenses to highlight varied elements and contrasting understandings of the change process. Using Burrell & Morgan's (1979) typology, she constructs four accounts of AMT implementation. These accounts share a theme of paradox, yet each also accentuate different tensions and vicious cycles. To accommodate disparate paradigm insights, the proposed metaframework offers a more holistic, systemic view, depicting change as a multidimensional cycle swirling around cognitive, action and institutional paradoxes. The concluding discussion addresses implications of the metaframework for managing change paradoxes and future research.

INTRODUCTION

Plus ça change, plus c'est la même chose. (The more things change, the more they stay the same)

This succinct French proverb expresses the paradoxical relationship between stability and change. Organizational scholars increasingly stress the need to explore such paradoxes, encouraging theories of organizational change to address tensions between order, efficiency and control, and disorder, innovation and flexibility (e.g., Lewis, 2000; Luscher & Lewis, 2008). Systems theory may enable rich depictions of such intricacy and its dynamics. Masuch (1985), for instance, called for studies of vicious cycles accompanying organizational change. He defined vicious cycles as reinforcing patterns that foster counter-productive results, such as organizational development attempts that reproduce the status quo. According to Davis, Maranville & Obloj

DOI: 10.4018/978-1-61520-668-1.ch007

(1997), studies increasingly note paradoxes of change, but few delve deeper into these organizational struggles.

Rapid technological changes have proven particularly challenging. Advanced manufacturing technology (AMT)—flexible manufacturing systems and programmable machinery—provides a case in point. The period from the late 1970s through mid-1980s saw an intense influx of efforts to integrate AMT within innovative social and technical configurations. Yet organizations rarely achieved the acclaimed benefits of AMT, including greater efficiency and quality, employee empowerment and production flexibility (Gupta, Lewis, & Boyer, 2007). Computerization typically marked a drastic shift from previous mechanized machinery, requiring new understandings of technology, work and organizational roles. Rather than foster dramatic changes, implementation efforts often intensified the use of extant mindsets and routines, triggering tensions and vicious cycles (Pichault, 1995).

To comprehend challenges of AMT implementation and other disruptive changes, researchers have veered increasingly from the functionalist mainstream, applying more critical and interpretive paradigms. Paradigms denote cohesive sets of assumptions (Kuhn, 1970) that help orient researchers relative to varied theoretical views and construct distinct explanations of phenomena. As paradigms multiply, studies may contribute diverse insights, which extend understandings of organizational change paradoxes. Yet the pervasive "paradigm mentality" stresses incommensurability, resulting in interwoven systems of theory often deemed tenuous and paradoxical themselves.

According to Van de Ven & Poole (1995), the rising disparity of organizational change theories fueled a compartmentalization of perspectives—isolated modes of inquiry incapable of enriching each other. Similarly, Quinn et al. (1994, p. 109) criticized extant theories as oversimplified and narrow: "Researchers tend to seek new knowledge more often through differentiation within perspectives than they do by integrating across perspectives." They propose that paradox and plurality become central to change theories. Similar calls are heard in technology literature as studies conducted within the confines of a single paradigm may mask the intricacy of AMT implementation (e.g., Scarbrough & Corbett, 1992; Thomas, 1994). Comprehending this disruptive change may require cultivating diverse paradigm insights.

This study examines paradoxes of organizational change from multiple perspectives. The result enables insights into the systems influencing AMT implementation and the systems affecting the development of related theory. I first discuss paradoxes and the theory-building strategy that aided my exploration. The strategy—metatriangulation (Lewis & Grimes, 1999)—entailed using paradigm lenses to construct alternative accounts of AMT implementation. The second section summarizes these accounts, which highlight varied vicious cycles during the change process. Third, I use paradox literature to build a metaframework, depicting change as a multidimensional cycle, swirling around cognitive, action and institutional paradoxes. Paradigm lenses detail each paradox, revealing complex, systemic tensions between stability and change. The conclusion addresses implications for managing change paradoxes and future research.

SYSTEMIC PARADOXES: THE ROLE OF MULTIPLE PARADIGMS

In more recent years, organizational scholars have pondered the systemic nature of paradox and related tensions and vicious cycles (e.g., Argyris, 1993; Luscher, Lewis & Ingram, 2006; Sundaramurthy & Lewis, 2003; Westenholz, 1993). According to Lewis (2000), paradox denotes contradictory elements that are interwoven and present simultaneously. Yet paradoxes are perceptual, arising from the human tendency to polarize phenomena into concepts that mask complex interrelationships. Polarities such as stability/change, consensus/conflict, trust/mistrust are prime examples. Defined as opposites, when existing side-by-side they seem puzzling and absurd.

Tensions and vicious cycles arise through actors' reactions to paradox. Vince & Broussine (1996) explained that conflicting feelings, perspectives or practices foster tensions that raise actors' defenses. In a desire to support extant understandings and protect their egos, actors attempt to pull polarities apart. Yet emphasizing one side of a polarity (e.g., change) intensifies pressure from the other (stability) in a vicious cycle (Masuch, 1985). Defensive reactions initially product positive effects (e.g., formal signs or pretenses of change), but eventually exacerbate the underlying tension (e.g., rising fear of uncertainty, attempts to retain the status quo).

Due to their perceptual and intricate nature, researching paradoxes poses a considerable challenge. Teunnissen (1996) warned that traditional theory-building strategies based on linear rationality and internal consistency are inadequate. Rather, he suggested that plurality play a critical role in paradox studies. In particular, theoretical triangulation may help researchers use diverse perspectives to expose multiple layers of paradox—to bring varied facets into relief and construct rich images of systemic tensions and vicious cycles. Opposing paradigms are paradoxical themselves, potentially providing contrary, but interwoven insights into organizational systems of paradoxes.

Metatriangulation

Following these suggestions, I applied a relatively novel theory-building strategy termed *metatriangulation*. According to Gioia & Pitre (1990), metatriangulation entails using multiple paradigms to construct varied representations of a phenomenon. Theorists then seek to link the disparate perspectives within an accommodating understanding. In this context, accommodation means retaining paradigm distinctions to avoid synthesizing their insights within a new, yet bland and still oversimplified view. Ideally, the result is a metaframework, providing a parsimonious depiction of the phenomena, which may be complicated using diverse lenses to detail its features.

I used metatriangulation for two primary reasons. First, I sought to explore challenges of AMT implementation by cultivating different perspectives. My second goal was to move beyond incommensurability, examining how paradigm interplay may extend theoretical understandings. Lewis & Grimes (1999) detailed the metatriangulation process, and Lewis & Keleman (2002) examined its role in exploring plurality and paradox. To avoid repetition, I briefly outline three key steps in the process—focusing paradigm lenses, constructing paradigm accounts, and metatheorizing—and specify their use in this study.

Focusing paradigm lenses. Paradigms help focus researchers on certain facets of complex phenomena. Paradigm assumptions delimit what is and is not relevant, constraining researchers to a limited and manageable field of vision. Numerous scholars have mapped paradigms of organization studies, providing varied categorizations (see Lewis & Grimes, 1999). I chose Burrell & Morgan's (1979) typology, because their four paradigms offer opposing views of technology (Grint, 1991) and paradox (Teunnisen, 1996). Figure 1 illustrates the opposing paradigm assumptions distinguished by the typology.

The objective-subjective axis polarizes epistemological and ontological assumptions of social science. Objectivist paradigms (functionalist, radical structuralist) assume an external, concrete reality of law-like relationships. Through these lenses, technology appears stable and generalizable, highlighting impacts of specific task and machinery designs. Similarly, paradoxes are considered observable and predictable, evident in contradictory organizational demands or structures. In contrast, subjectivist paradigms (interpretivist, radical humanist) view reality as

Figure 1. Opposing paradigm assumptions

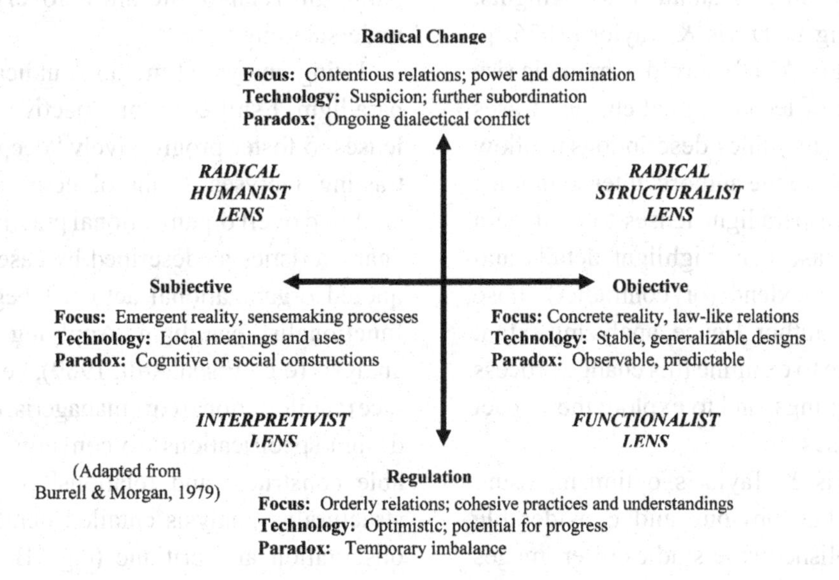

emergent; produced continuously through actors' sensemaking processes. Using these lenses, researchers examine influences of language and symbols on local meanings and uses of technology. Paradoxes appear cognitively or socially constructed as actors attempt to cope with conflicting emotions or behaviors.

The regulation-radical change dimension differentiates assumptions regarding the nature of society. Regulation paradigms (functionalist, interpretivist) assume social relations are orderly, even harmonious, focusing researchers on cohesive practices and understandings within organizations. These lenses provide a relatively optimistic view of technology, highlighting the potential for advances to enhance productivity or empower users. Paradoxes arise from temporary imbalances between opposing, but complementary elements, such as divergent understandings between work groups. On the other hand, radical change lenses (radical structuralist and humanist) view social relations as inherently contentious, highlighting power and domination in organizations. Technology is viewed with suspicion, as a potential means of subordinating labor to management. Radical notions of paradox stem from the Hegelian assumption that competing forces (thesis and antithesis) are in dialectical conflict. The more powerful force shapes the resulting synthesis, spurring a new antithesis in a never-ending struggle (Van de Ven & Poole, 1995).

Constructing paradigm accounts. In metatriangulation, researchers apply their focused lenses to analyze data and construct accounts that elaborate paradigm differences. Such accounts respond to Morgan's (1983) call for multiple representations grounded in conflicting assumptions. Using divergent lenses to analyze data helps loosen researchers' own assumptions and deepen their understandings of alternative paradigms. Researchers "learn *experientially* the observational focus, analytical methods, and writing styles of each paradigm" (Lewis & Grimes, 1999, p. 681).

Burrell & Morgan's (1979) paradigm lenses helped detail varied depictions of AMT implementation. Rather than analyze data from a single source, I followed Lewis & Grimes' (1999) approach, examining numerous, existing case studies. Case studies are the predominant means of investigating AMT implementation across paradigms, providing an abundant, rarely tapped source of data (Dean, Yoon & Susman, 1992; Knights, 1995). According to Davis & Taylor (1976, p. 391), the advent of AMT spurred a dramatic rise in case research of technological change. Cases also offer sufficiently thick descriptions to allow readers to reanalyze the authors' interpretations. Using alternative paradigm lenses to analyze a richly detailed case may highlight details and explanations that extend (or contradict) those presented by the author. Hence, analyzing extant cases enabled me to examine this change process across varied settings, and to explore the impact of paradigm lenses.

Despite Davis & Taylor's optimism, using existing cases has obvious and considerable drawbacks. Published case studies offer images that have been filtered through the perceptions of local actors, case authors, and journal or book reviewers. What remains is often a muted version of the experience, stripped of subtleties and imbued with biases. To manage this limitation, I identified twenty cases that maximized case details and diversity (sources noted in References section of this chapter). Regardless, results of this study should be considered highly exploratory, offering a basis for future research to test, elaborate and/or refute.

After collecting the sample, I used the paradigm lenses to analyze the cases and construct alternative accounts of AMT implementation. In metatriangulation, data analysis occurs in two parts. Researchers become familiar with the data, then reexamine the data through each lens in turn (Lewis & Grimes, 1999). I first read through the cases. Taking extensive notes aided my awareness of case distinctions, as well as broad patterns across the studies. I then applied each lens in turn, reanalyzing the cases and my own notes to extend my initial understandings. I began each analysis with cases written from that paradigm perspective, helping me find my paradigm "voice" as exemplified by the case authors' language, imagery and methods. As few cases described all aspects of an emerging account, I also reviewed paradigm-related literature to crystallize my understandings.

Using analytical methods indicative of each paradigm, I shifted from objective to subjective lenses to foster progressively "deeper" and contrasting analyses. In the objective paradigms, I explored overt organizational practices and AMT characteristics as described by case authors and quoted organizational actors. I began with the functionalist paradigm. Applying comparative analysis (e.g., Eisenhardt, 1989), I examined surface manifestations (e.g., managerial explanations, design specifications) to converge on recognizable constructs and relationships. The radical structuralist analysis entailed iterating between observation and critique (e.g., Benson, 1977), exposing labor control capabilities of AMT and the influence of power on implementation. Subjective lenses aided analysis of more latent case details. I viewed descriptions of organizational characteristics and actors' behaviors as "entry points" into underlying cognitive and social processes. Interpretivist analysis required coding language and symbols (e.g., Guba & Lincoln, 1989), helping reveal actors' sensemaking processes and shared meanings of AMT and work-related roles. Lastly, I approached radical humanism using critical theory (e.g., Steffy & Grimes, 1986) to question the legitimacy of emergent meanings. Reinterpreting cases and my accumulated notes, I coded deterministic, masculine and managerially sympathetic rhetoric to reveal biases expressed by organizational actors, case authors and myself.

Metatheorizing. While analyzing data aids construction of distinct paradigm accounts, metatheorizing entails exploring themes across accounts in search of contrasting and complementary insights. According to Gioia & Pitre (1990), the goal of metatheorizing is to accommodate diverse paradigm explanations within a metaframework. By operating at a higher abstraction level than typical theoretical models, a metaframework acts as a *point of contact* between paradigms. Ideally, the result corresponds to Rothenberg's description of paradoxical thinking as researchers reframe paradigm disparity at a meta-level: "What emerges is not mere combination or blending of elements; the conception does not only contain different elements, it contains opposing and antagonistic elements, which are understood as coexistent" (1979, p. 55).

In this study, the concept of paradox aided my metatheorizing. Paradigm accounts shared themes of paradox, yet revealed different tensions and vicious cycles during AMT implementation. To comprehend this disparity, I reviewed theories of organizational change paradoxes (e.g., Bartunek, 1988; Lewis, 2000; Westenholz, 1993). Paradox theories facilitated a meta-view, grounded on assumptions that paradigms are partial, conflicting and interwoven and that change is more complicated than either/or thinking can manage. Using these theories as a guide, I reexamined my case analyses and paradigm accounts, juxtaposing paradigm insights, then linking their varied depictions. The metaframework section details my metatheorizing process and results.

VICIOUS CYCLES OF AMT IMPLEMENTATION: PARADIGM ACCOUNTS

In metatriangulation, paradigm accounts cultivate diversity and systemic insights. As Martin (1992, p. 5) explained, the goal of developing multiple representations is to explore each paradigm *from within*, preserving the integrity of their divergent insights. In isolation, resulting accounts are not necessarily surprising. Rather accounts elaborate the disparity of paradigm assumptions, demonstrating the impact of a researcher's choice of lens as "we see what we expect to see." When juxtaposed, however, account differences may suggest more complicated, puzzling phenomena.

During my initial read of the case studies, I became aware of a cyclical trend underlying AMT implementation. Cycles broadly appeared as follows: assessment of the organizational and environmental context, AMT adoption, initial design of AMT machinery and operator tasks, unintended consequences, reassessment and redesign. In most cases, cycles turned vicious. Redesign efforts intensified actors' frustrations, group conflicts and poor production performance. Some organizations grappled continuously with resistance and technical problems, while others scrapped AMT altogether. Results rarely lived up to AMT's billing as an opportunity to dramatically enhance productivity and operator work, tending to be more computerized (and troublesome) versions of the technologies they had replaced. Each paradigm account, abbreviated here to retain ample space for discussing the metaframework, offers a different explanation of this cyclical trend (see Lewis, 1996, for complete accounts). The accounts move beyond general assumptions of technology and paradox (Figure 1), elaborating paradigm foci on AMT and related paradoxical tensions and vicious cycles (see Figure 2).

Functionalist Account

The functionalist lens focused on systemic relationships between AMT design and organizational practices that impact production performance. AMT appeared as task and machinery design specifications that may enable process control and flexibility. To attain this potential, organizations often supported AMT with practices aimed at enhancing efficiency (e.g., total quality management [TQM], just-in-time [JIT] inventory) and fostering continuous improvements (e.g., problem-solving teams). Yet tensions between the desire for order and the uncertainty of change triggered vicious cycles. Inertia and bounded rationality often perpetuated existing practices rather than fostering innovation as actors clung to their routines.

During implementation, organizational routines both enabled *and* inhibited change. Actors' routines provided guidance and a knowledge base, but were often inappropriate for new computeriza-

Figure 2. Paradigm accounts of AMT implementation

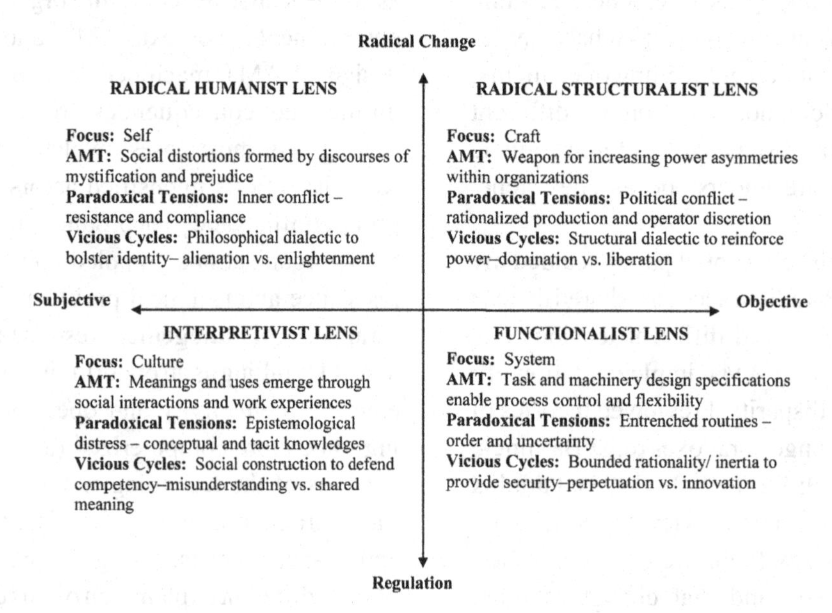

tion. Managers typically viewed AMT as a chance to cut costs and raise productivity, standardizing operators' work methods. Similarly, most engineers applied entrenched technical logic, building sophisticated designs by mathematically modeling production activities within AMT machinery. Formal controls served as designers' (managers, engineers) defensive reactions to uncertainty, providing a sense of order. Yet computer models and standardization were incapable of capturing less salient aspects of production. Highly computerized systems with minimal operator intervention were unwieldy and rigid, particularly compared to those in which operators programmed the machinery.

Routines also appeared nested, requiring concurrent development of new routines via experimentation *across* managers, engineers and operators. Yet frequently experimentation was impeded by problem-solving routines that followed hierarchical boundaries, separating initial design (e.g., occurring in engineering labs) from operations (e.g., designs "debugged" on the workfloor). Paradoxically, as production problems and pressures escalated during implementation, actors often relied more heavily on, rather than alter, their routines. One case author explained the paradox as follows: "solving problems that arise from a new (technological) process frequently requires assumptions that differ radically from traditional approaches to managing production ... Yet, on-going operations require applying routines predictably, efficiency, and accurately. Too often routine wins the battle" (Tyre, 1991, p. 228).

This account echoes functionalist technology literature, which stresses conflicting demands for system flexibility and control (e.g., Gupta et al., 2007; Upton & McAfee, 1998). Excessive uncertainty may spark chaos, while extreme order may foster stagnation. As routines evolve through pressures for reliability, stagnation is much more likely. Developing more balanced systems that fit a technological change becomes problematic. Bounded rationality and inertia may induce vicious cycles as actors apply existing routines for security (Mirvis, 1988). Work and communication patterns often perpetuate outmoded routines rather than aid innovation during a technological change (Fairhurst, et al., 1995; Pichault, 1995).

Radical Structuralist Account

The radical structuralist paradigm provided a craft focus, revealing how AMT impacts operators' control over their skills and work. Through this lens, AMT appeared as a "weapon that would strike at the heart of craft power" by increasing power asymmetries (Cockburn, 1983, p. 60). Although AMT may support operators' expertise and discretion, it also may be used to transfer their problem-solving and manual responsibilities to computerization. In most cases, political conflicts erupted as operators fought to protect their craft, while designers intensified labor controls. Tensions fueled a structural dialectic as the groups battled over whether to employ the liberating or dominating capabilities of AMT. Because designers controlled the implementation process, the result was typically the latter. Designers' desires to reinforce their power overshadowed their needs for operator cooperation, as they used AMT to further rationalize production.

Such rationalization was exemplified by standardized operator work involving basic machine loading and monitoring activities and by polarized technical skills that separated planning (AMT design and machine programming) from execution (daily operation of machinery). Designers often sought normative (e.g., problem-solving teams) and stress (e.g., JIT) controls over production. Yet highly rationalized implementations paradoxically frustrated designers' goals. Over time, operators became increasingly dependent on computers as their skills deteriorated, reducing their ability to effectively respond to production problems. In addition, the slightest error, passive resistance or sabotage could prove devastating, rippling throughout a tightly integrated, computerized process. While some operators accentuated such problems to reassert the value of their craft, designers often used crises as excuses to further rationalize production.

Radical structuralists claim that conflicting political interests are inherent in capitalist organizations (e.g., Braverman, 1974). According to Benson (1977), a structural dialectic drives vicious cycles during organizational change as those in power attempt to reinforce power asymmetries and labor-management distinctions. In the case of AMT, although designers need operator commitment and creativity, rationalizing production may reduce their dependence on labor. Burris (1993) described the typical result as a technocracy—an organizational form that links AMT within a web of subtle control mechanisms. Matthews (1996) found that in technocracies quality and JIT practices increase the visibility of AMT production, intensifying operator surveillance and pressures for speed and accuracy. Yet technocracies are fragile due to their structural contradictions. Using AMT to deskill and divide work raises the costs and likelihood of production breakdowns and fuels operator resistance. Although structural contradictions may trigger liberating changes, research finds that designers more often extend rationalization in a continuing dialectical cycle (e.g., Colclough & Tolbert, 1992).

Interpretivist Account

The interpretivist lens highlighted influences of culture on organizational change. Meanings and uses of AMT appeared to emerge through daily work interactions. Occupational subcultures struggled with "epistemological distress" (Zuboff, 1988, p. 82), unsure of how to make sense of their more computerized and ambiguous work. For operators, the previous, mechanized processes demanded considerable tacit knowledge. Operators played a hands-on role in production, using their senses (e.g., taste, sight, smell) to intuitively manipulate materials and identify problems, then relaying information to designers. AMT, however, required more conceptual knowledge. Computerized machinery produced data that could be transferred across the organization. Actors then interpreted computerized cues to determine sources of production problems and make adjustments. By interacting with those in their occupation—who share their work norms and capabilities—actors attempted to construct shared meanings of AMT. Yet as actors sought to defend their existing competencies, they often blamed problems on other occupational groups, limiting interactions and fostering misunderstandings between subcultures.

Operator and designer competencies revolved around varied knowledge bases. Operators felt most effective applying their tacit knowledge of production materials and physical activities. Designers were more at ease using conceptual knowledge of how production tasks interrelate within the overall process. During implementation, each knowledge base proved vital, yet insufficient. When problems arose, operators often used manual overrides or rushed to the scene, feeling helpless behind a computer screen. In contrast, designers would engage in highly technical debates distanced from the process, relying on computers for information. Operators needed greater conceptual knowledge to effectively use AMT and monitor production, while designers required more tacit knowledge to augment finite computer data. Rather than expand their knowledge base, subcultures often interpreted problems and others' responses in ways that supported their views of production and their respective competencies. For example, rising frustrations of operators reinforced designers' beliefs that operators are irrational and intensified their efforts to computerize production, exacerbating operators' anxieties in a vicious cycle.

Interpretivist literature emphasizes the ambiguity of computer-mediated work. Weick (1990) described AMT as equivoque, admitting varied meanings across subcultures as actors use their existing interpretive schemes to comprehend complex, computerized cues. Such schemes, typically shared by occupational subcultures, promote self-serving interpretations of the value of their work and knowledge (Van de Maanen & Barley, 1984). However, AMT may render existing knowledge bases inadequate. Researchers suggest that operators need a conceptual understanding not just of computer data, but of how to work around computerized machinery to anticipate problems and respond appropriately (e.g., Howard & Schneider, 1988). Likewise, designers need an appreciation of operators' tacit knowledge to recognize subtleties of production and limits of computerization. Yet subcultures often view work through divergent interpretive schemes, influencing actors' perceptions and social interactions in directions that frustrate mutual understandings (Davis & Taylor, 1979; Scarbrough & Corbett, 1992).

Radical Humanist Account

The radical humanist account counters the functionalist starting point by focusing on actors' sense of self—their egos and social identities. This lens exposed how discourses of mystification and prejudice distort meanings of AMT. Case analyses revealed actors' exaggerating the sophistication of computers and differences between white- and blue-collar work. AMT implementation seemed to provoke inner conflicts as actors grappled with resistance and compliance. On the one hand, actors viewed AMT as an opportunity to alter existing social relations. By requiring more homogeneous skills across subcultures, computerization may blur distinctions between designers and operators of technology. Yet actors often stressed their exclusive expertise. The result was a philosophical dialectic. Rather than foster enlightenment, actors' attempts to bolster their identities fueled feelings of alienation.

Across cases, AMT implementation exposed the fiction of mutually exclusive organizational identities. Yet as actors engaged in more similar, computer-mediated work, identity crises often sparked turf wars. Many managers tried to reinforce their authority, degrading operators relative to the "power of technology" and hoarding "ownership" of information and design decisions. Engineers stressed their technical prowess by accenting the complexity of computerization, particularly during debates over whether operators or engineers would program computers. Lastly, as operator identities often derived from the masculinity of manual skills, operators often compared computerized work to feminine secretarial duties and emphasized the need for their physical presence on the line. Social distortions intensified as actors reproduced notions of superiority, reverting to past prejudices based on class or gender. Instead of using implementation as a chance to negotiate more democratic roles and identities, actors further mystified technology, authority and skills, reinforcing extant social biases.

Radical humanist researchers question the legitimacy of AMT meanings and work-related roles. Knights (1995) explained that tensions surround new technologies as actors find themselves in an increasingly insecure world. Actors' ideologies, or beliefs in the value of technology and their own abilities, foster discourses that bolster their identities and degrade others. Vallas & Beck (1996) found that operators often stress tacit skills to devalue, and thereby avoid, more conceptual work. Likewise, designers characterize operators' use of intuition as superstitious and ignorant compared to their technical acumen. Such discursive practices "define *the way subjects see the world and themselves* and thereby discipline those subjects" (Bloomfield & Combs, 1992, p. 467). To attain the enlightenment potential of AMT, actors must critically examine their language and underlying ideologies, and negotiate more legitimate identities and democratic work roles. According to Collinson, without such negotiations, actors' "strategies of resistance, compliance, and consent often have the effect, paradoxically, of perpetuating and even strengthening the very organizational conditions that dominate them" (Collinson, 1992, p.18).

PARADOXES OF ORGANIZATIONAL CHANGE: A METAFRAMEWORK

Despite varied assumptions and foci, the accounts share themes of paradox. Tensions appeared to spark vicious cycles that inhibited change, intensifying actors' frustrations, group conflicts and production problems during AMT implementation. In the final phase of metatriangulation, I sought a metaframework capable of depicting this pattern, yet preserving distinct paradigm insights. To consider the accounts simultaneously, I explored the growing literature on organization paradoxes. According to Quinn et al. (1994, p. 115), paradox operates at a meta-level, helping researchers examine tensions from opposing theoretical viewpoints.

Researchers propose that paradoxes may exist in three realms: cognitive, action, institutional (see Davis et al., 1995). Vicious cycles emanate from each realm as actors respond defensively to tensions, seeking to protect their egos and entrenched practices. Cognitive paradoxes refer to the self-referential nature of cognition. According to Westenholz (1993), actors use extant frames of reference to make sense of change. Bounded rationality and selective perception help actors stress certain aspects, and disregard those that contradict expectations. Action paradoxes occur in a more behavioral and social realm. Mixed messages—inconsistencies between what is said and done or between actors' views of social encounters—may trigger vicious cycles (Argyris, 1993). Lastly, institutional paradoxes arise as mixed messages become embedded within organizations. Putnam (1986) described such conflicting institutional properties as practices for employee empowerment and surveillance.

Using a paradox lens, I juxtaposed paradigm accounts in search of tensions operating in cognitive, action and institutional realms. I began asking broad questions, such as: what is the crux of vicious cycles? Are anomolies neglected by one paradigm explained by another? Paradigms appeared to highlight varied and interwoven dimensions of change paradoxes. Objective and subjective assumptions exposed different temporal dimensions. Objectivist lenses accentuated relatively observable and stable artifacts (e.g., routines, power asymmetries, AMT designs), while subjectivist lenses offered insights into their ongoing social construction (e.g., latent processes through which actors' perceptions and uses of AMT emerge). Regulation and radical change assumptions helped reveal varied spatial dimensions, providing insights from different levels in the organization. Regulation paradigms exposed the overarching effects of AMT on production performance and shared subcultural understandings. In contrast, radical change lenses accentuated the work floor and impacts on actors' skills, power and identities.

Linking insights from paradox theories and paradigm accounts, the resulting metaframework depicts change as a multidimensional cycle revolving around cognitive, action and institutional paradoxes (see figure 3). Its value lies in its simplicity *and* complexity. While offering a parsimonious view of change, paradigm lenses unravel each paradox. For clarity, I discuss the metaframework in stages, interpreting each paradox through the four lenses.

Cognitive Paradox

In figure 3, context denotes the ongoing accumulation of past cycles, situating change within current and historical conditions. According to the *cognitive paradox*, context continuously influences actors' beliefs and perceptions. Yet actors filter experiences through their cognitive frames, choosing interpretations and memories that support existing frames in a self-referential cycle (Weick, 1990). Cognitions are highly resistant to change for four reasons: (1) it takes more effort to develop new mindsets than to alter existing ones; (2) existing frames provide a sense of security; (3) adopting new understandings implies that the old ones were wrong; and (4) rationalizing why past frames are appropriate defends the ego (Davis et al., 1997).

Paradigm lenses revealed different facets of the cognitive paradox and its influence on how actors' viewed AMT. From a functionalist perspective, computerization offered a tool for coping with fluctuating pressures by enhancing process flexibility and control. Designers often approached implementation with problem-solving logics overemphasizing control. Managers viewed technology as a cost-cutting tool, while engineers saw opportunities to automate and integrate production. The radical structuralist lens exposed how cognition reflects political interests. For designers the control capabilities of AMT offered means of reducing their dependence on labor. Meanwhile,

Figure 3. Organizational change cycle: A metaframework

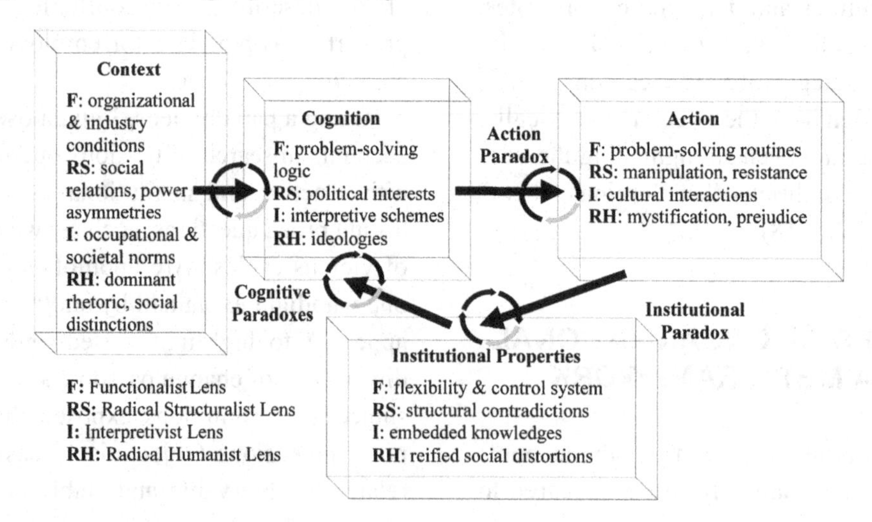

operators grew wary of technological change, seeking to retain discretion over their work and skills. Conflicting interests often blinded actors to the possibility that AMT may offer mutual benefits, particularly in sites marked by antagonistic labor-management relations.

Subjectivist lenses addressed how actors socially construct their cognitive frames. From an interpretivist viewpoint, actors formed interpretive schemes that supported norms and competencies of their occupational subculture. Such schemes limited actors' willingness to expand their knowledge base. Designers, for instance, often viewed AMT as a chance to demonstrate their conceptual knowledge and receive peer recognition, striving to design highly sophisticated systems. The radical humanist lens questioned how ideologies distort actors' perceptions in ways that bolster distinct identities. Designers' beliefs in the power of computerization relative to human abilities reinforced the superiority of technical expertise, while operators' beliefs in craftsmanship emphasized more sensual, masculine skills.

Action Paradox

The action paradox denotes the tenuous relationship between cognition and action. According to Argyris (1993), mixed messages arise as actors interpret social encounters through varied cognitive frames. Yet rather than engaging in a "meta-level discourse" to examine perceptual differences, actors follow ingrained communication and behavioral patterns (Mirvis, 1988, p. 281). Extant patterns offer the semblance of order, temporarily reducing actors' anxiety, but inhibiting development of new behaviors and shared understandings. The result is a vicious cycle: change-related decision making or negotiations perpetuate misperceptions and reproduce past actions.

The functionalist lens highlighted how traditional problem-solving routines, which separate technology design and use, inhibit experimentation. Managers and engineers, steeped in control-oriented logics, developed initial AMT designs, limiting consideration of alternatives to a narrow range of highly computerized systems. Operators then "debugged" designs in daily production, relying on inadequate routines formed through their work with previous, mechanized systems. Radical structuralism helped critique this pattern. Designers excluded operators from decision making, offering "participation" late in the process as a means of co-optation. Meanwhile, operators used past practices and avoided interacting with designs as a form of passive resistance.

Subjectivist lenses examined discourse; the means by which actors attempt to collectively make sense of organizational change. From an interpretivist perspective, subcultures used social interactions to promote their competencies. Occupational subcultures often developed means of coping with AMT problems that applied their existing conceptual or tacit knowledge. Designers analyzed computer data and mathematical models, while operators examined machinery and materials to identify the sources of problems. Yet as each knowledge base proved insufficient, actors avoided sharing their frustrations for fear of appearing incompetent. The radical humanist lens further exposed how actors apply discourse to bolster their identities. Designers degraded operators to reinforce their superiority, while operators devalued computerized work to buoy their masculinity. In conjunction, mystification and prejudices intensified actors' frustrations, reinforced class and gender biases, and limited negotiation of more socially legitimate identities.

Institutional Paradox

In the metaframework, institutional properties denote the products of patterned actions, reified over time. Paradox lies in the conflict between intentions of change-oriented actions and the relative stability of institutions. Actions produce institutional properties, yet are channeled through extant properties, constraining change efforts (Davis et al., 1997).

Objectivist lenses viewed institutional properties as static and distinct, providing powerful guides for actors. From a functionalist standpoint, designers supported AMT with institutional properties (e.g., operational infrastructure of inventory, cost, quality practices) that balance flexibility and control. Yet most systems were control-heavy as designers employed existing practices geared toward efficiency and predictability. Often sophisticated computerization was coupled with standardized tasks and minimal operator training, and placed within a hierarchical structure limiting operator-designer coordination. The radical humanist lens helped critique such systems for structural contradictions. Although designers needed operator skills and creativity to attain flexibility, they often used AMT to further rationalize production. Linked with problem-solving teams, JIT and other practices, computerization intensified work pressures and labor monitoring.

From subjectivist perspectives, institutional properties appeared more ambiguous and fluid. The interpretivist lens viewed institutional properties as knowledge embedded within organizational structures and practices. AMT enabled actors to further formalize physical and intellective knowledges of production. Yet computer programs and standardized work methods contain only explicit (and partial) knowledge—understandings capable of being expressed and modeled. Hence, using AMT also required an implicit or intuitive knowledge of how the technology and production process work. Radical humanism helped criticize institutional properties as reified distortions. While actors often praised change, their rhetoric and behaviors reinforced the notion that extant competencies, social distinctions and work practices are fixed, inhibiting attempts at reconstruction.

Cognitive Paradox Revisited

The metaframework depicts institutional properties influencing cognition, as actors evaluate AMT designs and institutional properties in use. Actors filter outcomes through their existing cognitive frames, often perceiving outcomes as supporting their initial expectations and beliefs. Hence, the cognitive paradox returns. Cognition may inhibit actors from making perceptual adjustments and perpetuate vicious cycles.

From a functionalist perspective, actors used their existing assumptions to assess the effectiveness of AMT. Without a flexibility-control balance, computerized systems proved sensitive to breakdowns. Although designers made numerous adjustments, most changes fixed symptoms, not root causes. For example, when dealing with poor machine reliability, designers often tried to increase centralized computer control, rather than reduce technical complexity or allow operators to adjust computer programs. The radical structuralist lens exposed political interests influencing AMT assessments. Cases depicted how even minor production problems or sabotage can cripple tightly integrated systems. Yet most designers used crises as chances to further rationalize production.

From an interpretivist perspective, formalized computer programs and work methods produced a mismatch between knowledge embedded within an AMT design and the complexity of production reality. Actors filtered resulting problems through their extant interpretive schemes. Designers frequently saw operators' frustrations as examples of irrational human behavior and needs for greater computerization. The radical humanist lens extended interpretivist insights by revealing how ideologies perpetuate distortions, rather than enlightening actors to changes in work and social relations. As computerization increasingly blurred differences between tacit and conceptual work, operators and designers reiterated respective beliefs in the value of craft and technical expertise.

MANAGING PARADOXES OF ORGANIZATIONAL CHANGE

Organizational change paradoxes mark a tremendous challenge for two primary reasons. First, as paradigm lenses revealed, each paradox operates across multiple, systemic dimensions. Breaking out of vicious cycles requires managing subjectivity (e.g., emotions, meanings, identities) and objectivity (e.g., design specifications, routines) across organizational levels. "Managing" becomes the shared responsibility of managers, engineers and operators. Second, cognitive, action and institutional paradoxes are interwoven. The change cycle spirals continuously, blurring impacts of each paradox as tensions in one locale reinforce tensions in another. The following discussion presents approaches for managing each paradox, but these approaches proved most effective in combination. Case organizations applying only one or two approaches realized short-lived change, later regressing to past practices or thinking.

Paradigm accounts suggested four approaches to managing change paradoxes: paradoxical thinking, open communications, dynamic and humanized designs, and shock treatment. Managing cognitive paradoxes requires paradoxical thinking to critique existing frames based on either/or distinctions. Paradoxical thinking signifies the capacity to reframe contradictions and comprehend their simultaneous existence (Argyris, 1993; Luscher & Lewis, 2008). During AMT implementation, self-reflection helped actors question conflicting political interests, occupational skills and social identities. Whether paradoxical thinking led to change, however, depended upon subsequent actions, in particular whether paradoxical thinkers were able to voice their views and influence decisions. Power asymmetries and the action paradox remained potential barriers to collective reframing.

Inclusive and open communications, beginning early in the change process, often helped manage action paradoxes. Heated debates, paradoxical leadership and change forums facilitated cross-group interactions. Thomas (1994) described contentious debates helping designers and operators recognize common AMT concerns. Such conflicts were energizing, exposing misunderstandings and motivating greater collaboration. Paradoxical leadership also may promote openness. Leaders helped others consider opposing perspectives and new practices. In another case, an experienced operator championed AMT, envisioning a "whole new philosophy, or new mentality, of production" (Tyre, 1991, p. 229). By fostering similar thinking in others, he encouraged consideration of radical technology designs. Forums for change aided discussions among actors with differing ideologies and fostered experimentation. Change forums provided a context for action physically separate from day-to-day responsibilities, reducing anxieties.

Avoiding the pull toward excessive rigidity and control requires redesigning institutional properties in more dynamic and humanistic directions. Such designs aid emergence of new work methods and knowledges, helping manage institutional paradoxes. Dynamic and humanistic AMT designs provided operators' discretion over computerized production, and fostered frequent and informal interactions between operators, engineers and managers. This finding supports a growing consensus in AMT research: the more computerized the production process, the more vital human intervention becomes (Upton & McAfee, 1998). By programming the machinery, operators were better able to translate their previous, tacit understandings into computer-mediated work. Operator programming also increased process flexibility, speeding responses to changing production materials and demands. However, for actors to experiment with diverse designs, they must recognize institutional properties as socially constructed and malleable. Although past investments (e.g., expensive, fixed machinery) may reduce choice, opportunities to alter existing social relations, work methods and organizational practices remain.

Furthermore, AMT enables considerably more task and machine design variations and in-use development than mechanized technologies.

As new meanings and technologies are put into practice, outcomes may provide means of managing the cognitive paradox. Crises offer shock treatment, accentuating simultaneous contradictions and the opportunity for paradoxical thinking. Such cues signify the need to search for inaccurate assumptions and artificial distinctions, widening the range of design alternatives considered. Yet actors' often interpreted surprising behaviors of others' and system outcomes as illogical and/or isolated occurrences, rather than explore deeper causes. To manage this paradox, Argyris (1993) prescribed looking for rationality in apparently irrational situations. Shockingly unanticipated system problems and seemingly illogical human reactions may mark misunderstandings that require more than adjustments within existing cognitive frames. Assessing experiences within a more critical and self-reflective mindset may aid understanding of interconnections between complex social, political and technical elements.

FUTURE RESEARCH DIRECTIONS

Maruyama (1976) claimed that most organizational change theories rest on notions of internal consistency and linearity. Yet the complexity of change requires an appreciation of tensions and vicious cycles. Such criticisms appear increasingly as organizations struggle to adapt in highly turbulent environments (e.g., Davis, et al., 1997; Lewis, 2000; Teunnisen, 1996). In response, I sought to complicate existing understandings by exploring plurality and paradox.

The paradigm accounts and metaframework depict intricate paradoxes. Paradigm lenses exposed vicious cycles operating across multiple dimensions, intensifying stability/change tensions. AMT offered an incredible breadth of possibilities, including rigidity, rationalization and domination, as well as innovation, liberation and enlightenment. While organizations appeared drawn toward the former, the latter remained not only possible, but a more socially legitimate and organizationally beneficial direction. To attain AMT benefits, however, required managing objectivity and subjectivity. Without collaboration, suspicion between designers and operators led to cultural misunderstandings, political conflicts and artificial social distinctions that perpetuated vicious cycles.

In multiparadigm inquiry, such endings ideally leave a project unfinished, open to alternative perspectives and subsequent research (Martin, 1992). Future inquiries may elaborate (or refute) these insights by contributing more detailed studies of AMT implementation. In addition, researchers may use the paradigm accounts and metaframework as guides for examining other disruptive changes—changes that fuel paradoxes by threatening actors' understandings of themselves (their roles, skills, identities) and the world (the way technology and organizations work).

This study illustrates the merit of using divergent lenses. Paradigm accounts highlighted varied facets of an intricate phenomenon, while the metaframework illustrated paradigm interplay. Pulling me in opposing directions, metatriangulation accentuated diverse and neglected views and highlighted organizational change paradoxes. This theory-building process also exposed research tensions, as paradigms and academic practices dramatically impact on what is seen and published. I became acutely aware of vicious cycles within my work and the limits of my selective focus. Exploring insights of alternative paradigms may help theorists critically reflect on their methods, question incommensurability and construct more accommodating, provocative understandings.

For too long social scientists have hung back from the fray, concerned with rituals of decontamination, with controlling their anxiety by rigorous method and defending their "dogma of

Immaculate Perception." Any paradigm must be partially self-fulfilling. If nothing else we inflict our lassitude. The question, then, is not whether our values influence our research, but how? (Hampden-Turner, 1981, p. 130)

REFERENCES

Argyris, C. (1993). *Knowledge for action: A guide to overcoming barriers to organizational change*. San Francisco: Jossey-Bass.

Bartunek, J. M. (1988). The dynamics of personal and organizational reframing. In R. E. Quinn & K. S. Cameron (Eds.), *Paradox and transformation* (pp. 137-162). Cambridge, MA: Ballinger.

Benson, J. K. (1977). Organizations: A dialectical view. *Administrative Science Quarterly, 22*(1), 1–21. doi:10.2307/2391741

*Berggren, C. (1992). *Alternatives to lean production: Work organization in the Swedish automobile industry*. Ithaca, NY: ILR Press. [Cases: TC and Udevalla]

Bloomfield, B. P., & Coombs, R. (1992). Information technology, control, and power: The centralization debate revisited. *Journal of Management Studies, 29*, 459–484. doi:10.1111/j.1467-6486.1992.tb00674.x

Braverman, H. (1974). *Labor and monopoly capital: The degradation of work in the twentieth century*. New York: Monthly Review Press.

Burrell, G., & Morgan, G. (1979). *Sociological paradigms and organizational analysis*. Portsmouth, NH: Heinemann.

*Ciborra, C. C., Patriotta, G., & Erlicher, L. (1995). Disassembling frames on the assembly line. In W.J. Orlinkowski, G. Walsham, M. R. Jones, J. I. DeGross (Eds.) *Information Technology and Changes in Work* (pp. 397-418). New York: Chapman and Hall.

*Cockburn, C. (1983). *Brothers*. London: Pluto Press. [Case: British Printers]

Colclough, C., & Tolbert, C. M., III. (1992). *Work in the fast lane: Flexibility, divisions of labor, and inequality in high-tech industries*. Albany, NY: State University of New York Press.

Collinson, D. L. (1992). *Managing the shopfloor: Subjectivity, masculinity and workplace culture*. New York: de Gruyter.

Davis, A. S., Maranville, S. J., & Obloj, K. (1997). The paradoxical process of organizational transformation. *Research in Organizational Change and Development, 10*, 275–314.

Davis, L. E., & Taylor, J. C. (1976). Technology, organization and job structure. In R. Dubin (Ed.), *Handbook of work, organization, and society* (pp. 379-419). Chicago: Rand McNally.

Dean, J. W. Jr, Yoon, S. J., & Susman, G. I. (1992). Advanced manufacturing technology and organization structure: Empowerment or subordination? *Organization Science, 3*(2), 203–229. doi:10.1287/orsc.3.2.203

Eisenhardt, K. M. (1989). Building theories from case study research. *Academy of Management Review, 14*, 535–550.

Fairhurst, G. T., Green, S., & Courtright, J. (1995). Inertia forces and the implementation of a sociotechnical systems approach: A communication study. *Organization Science, 6*(2), 168–180. doi:10.1287/orsc.6.2.168

Gioia, D. A., & Pitre, E. (1990). Multiparadigm perspectives on theory building. *Academy of Management Review, 15*(4), 584–602. doi:10.2307/258683

*Giordano, L. (1992). *Beyond Taylorism: Computerization and the new industrial relations*. New York: St. Martin's Press. [Case: Pine Hill]

*Graham, M. B. W. (1986). A tale of two FMSs. In C. A. Voss (Ed.), *Managing advanced manufacturing technology* (pp. 353-366). London: Croon Helm. [Cases: FMSa and FMSb]

Grint, K. (1991). *The sociology of work: An introduction*. London: Polity Press.

Guba, E. G., & Lincoln, Y. S. (1989). *Fourth generation evaluation*. Newbury Park, CA: Sage.

Gupta, S., Lewis, M. W., & Boyer, K. (2007). Innovation-supportive culture: The case of advanced manufacturing technology. *Journal of Operations Management*, *25*(4), 871–884. doi:10.1016/j.jom.2006.08.003

Hampden-Turner, C. (1981). *Maps of the mind*. New York: MacMillan.

*Hirschhorn, L., & Mokray, J. (1992). Automation and competency requirements in manufacturing. In P. S. Adler (Ed.), *Technology and the future of work* (pp.15-45). New York: Oxford University Press. [Case: DEC]

Howard, R., & Schneider, L. (1988). Technological change as a social process: A case study of office automation in a manufacturing plant. *Central Issues in Anthropology*, *7*(2), 79–84. doi:10.1525/cia.1988.7.2.79

*Jones, B., & Scott, R. (1986). 'Working the system': A comparison of the management of work roles in American and British flexible manufacturing systems. In C.A. Voss (Ed.), *Managing advanced manufacturing technology* (pp. 353-366). London: Croon Helm. [Cases: Alpha and Turnco]

*Kestleloot, R. (1989). Introduction of computerised numerical control and the rationalisation of production. In A. Francis & P. Grootings (Eds.), *New technologies and work: Capitalist and socialist perspectives* (pp. 165-186). London: Routledge. [Case: VM]

Knights, D. (1995). Refocusing the case study. *Technology Studies*, *2*(2), 230–254.

Kuhn, T. S. (1970). *The structure of scientific revolutions*. Chicago: University of Chicago Press.

Lewis, M. W. (1996). *Advanced manufacturing technology design: A multiparadigm study*. Unpublished dissertation, University of Kentucky, KY.

Lewis, M. W. (2000). Exploring paradox: Toward a more comprehensive guide. *Academy of Management Review*, *25*(4), 760–776. doi:10.2307/259204

Lewis, M. W., & Grimes, A. J. (1999). Metatriangulation: Building theory from multiple paradigms. *Academy of Management Review*, *24*(4), 672–690. doi:10.2307/259348

Lewis, M. W., & Kelemen, M. (2002). Multiparadigm inquiry: Exploring organizational pluralism and paradox. *Human Relations*, *55*(2), 251–275. doi:10.1177/0018726702055002185

Luscher, L., & Lewis, M. W. (2008). Organizational change and managerial sensemaking: Working through paradox. *Academy of Management Journal*, *51*(2), 221–240.

Luscher, L., Lewis, M. W., & Ingram, A. (2006). The social construction of organizational change paradoxes. *Journal of Organizational Change Management*, *19*(4), 491–502. doi:10.1108/09534810610676680

Martin, J. (1992). *Cultures in Organization*. Oxford, UK: Oxford University Press.

Masuch, M. (1985). Vicious circles in organizations. *Administrative Science Quarterly*, *30*(1), 14–33. doi:10.2307/2392809

Matthews, R. A. (1996). *Fordism, flexibility and regional productivity growth*. New York: Garland.

*Milkman, R., & Pullman, C. (1991). Technological change in an auto assembly plant. [Case: GM]. *Work and Occupations*, *18*(2), 123–147. doi:10.1177/0730888491018002001

Mirvis, P. H. (1988). On the crafting of a theory. In R. E. Quinn & K. S. Cameron (Eds.), *Paradox and transformation* (pp. 279-288). Cambridge, MA: Ballinger Publishing Co.

Morgan, G. (Ed.). (1983). *Beyond method.* Newbury Park, CA: Sage.

Pichault, F. (1995). The management of politics in technically related organizational change. *Organization Studies*, *16*(3), 449–476. doi:10.1177/017084069501600304

Poole, M. S., & Van de Ven, A. H. (1989). Using paradox to build management and organization theories. *Academy of Management Review*, *14*(4), 562–578. doi:10.2307/258559

Quinn, R. E., Kahn, J. A., & Mandl, M. J. (1994). Perspectives on organizational change: Exploring movement at the interface. In J. Greenberg (Ed.), *Organizational behavior: The state of science* (pp. 109-133). Hillsdale, NJ: Lawrence Erlbaum Associates.

*Rosenbrock, H. H. (1990). *Machines with purpose*. New York: Oxford University Press. [Case: Esprit]

Rothenberg, A. (1979). *The emerging goddess*. Chicago: University of Chicago Press.

Scarbrough, H., & Corbett, J. M. (1992). *Technology and organization: Power, meaning and design*. New York: Routledge.

*Shaiken, H. (1986). *Work transformed: Automation and labor in the computer age*. New York: Holt, Rinehart, and Winston. [Case: Ford]

*Staehle, W. H. (1984). Job design and automation in the Federal Republic of Germany. In F. Butera & J. E. Thurman (Eds.), *Automation and work design* (pp. 208-232). New York: Elsevier. [Case: PCB Co.]

Steffy, B. D., & Grimes, A. J. (1986). A critical theory of organization science. *Academy of Management Review*, *11*, 322–336. doi:10.2307/258463

Sundaramurthy, C., & Lewis, M. W. (2003). Paradoxes of governance: Managing control and collaboration. *Academy of Management Review*, *28*(3), 397–415.

Teunissen, J. (1996). Paradoxes in social science and research. In W. Koot, I. Sabelis, & S. Ybema (Eds.), *Contradictions in context* (pp. 17-38). Amsterdam: VU University Press.

*Thomas, R. J. (1994). *What machines can't do*. Berkeley, CA: University of California Press. [Case: AutoParts]

*Tyre, M. (1991). Managing innovation on the factory floor. [Case: Italian Finishing]. *Technology Review*, (October): 59–65.

*Upton, D. (1990). *John Crane UK Limited: The CAD-CAM link*. Boston, MA: HBS Case Services. [Cases: JC Reading and JC Slough]

Upton, D., & McAffee, J. (1998). Computer integration and catastrophic process failure in flexible production: An empirical investigation. *Production and Operations Management*, *7*(3), 265–281.

Vallas, S. P., & Beck, J. P. (1996). The transformation of work revisited: The limits of flexibility in American manufacturing. *Social Problems*, *42*(3), 339–362. doi:10.1525/sp.1996.43.3.03x01421

Van de Ven, A. H., & Poole, M. S. (1995). Explaining development and change in organizations. *Academy of Management Review*, *20*(3), 510–540. doi:10.2307/258786

Van Maanen, J., & Barley, S. R. (1984). Occupational communities. *Research in Organizational Behavior, 6*, 287–365.

Vince, R., & Broussine, M. (1996). Paradox, defense and attachment: Accessing and working with emotions and relations underlying organizational change. *Organization Studies, 17*(1), 1–21. doi:10.1177/017084069601700101

Weick, K. E. (1990). Technology as equivoque: Sensemaking in new technologies. In P. S. Goodman & L. S. Sproull (Eds.), *Technology and organizations* (pp. 1-44). San Francisco: Jossey-Bass.

Westenholz, A. (1993). Paradoxical thinking and change in frames of reference. *Organization Studies, 14*(1), 37–58. doi:10.1177/017084069301400104

*Wilkinson, B. (1983). *The shopfloor politics of new technology*. London: Heinemann. [Case: Plating Company]

*Zuboff, S. (1988). *In the age of the smart machine*. New York: Basic books. [Case: Piney Wood]

ENDNOTE

* Case studies analyzed.

Chapter 8
Metatheorising Transformational Management: A Relational Approach

Mark G. Edwards
University of Western Australia, Australia

ABSTRACT

Corporate management is facing a world full of transformational challenges. How might theory development contribute to a more transformative vision of management? While there have been attempts by theorists to move beyond conventional conceptualizations, more innovative and, in particular, more integrative theoretical frameworks are still needed. Conventional and new paradigm management theories take contending sides in the change debate and often define their approaches in terms of dichotomous oppositions. Using an integrative approach to metatheory building, this article proposes that the application of a relational lens overcomes many common polarities and oppositions present within current theorisings. The relational qualities that emerge from this metatheoretical approach are presented as useful guides for developing innovative theories that address the operational and transformational challenges of 21st century management. The metatheoretical analysis not only provides an integrative framework for exploring more visionary conceptualisations of management it also shows that metatheorising has powerful critical capacities for assessing scientific theories in the social sciences.

1. THE TRANSFORMATION IMPERATIVE FOR CORPORATE MANAGEMENT

This paper argues for the development of overarching and transformative understandings of management in the 21st century. Contemporary organizations and corporations and their systems of management are not providing a viable intergenerational future for the planet. And the lack of adequate theory is contributing to this failure. Management theory is in the paradoxical situation of being both conceptually fragmented and yet also dominated by conventional forms of theorising management that seem to ignore the global challenges that currently confront corporations, governments and their host communities.

DOI: 10.4018/978-1-61520-668-1.ch008

In a recent paper entitled "The State of Affairs for Management Education and Social Responsibility), management ethicists Mary Gentile and Judith Samuelson write that they had:

. . . come to realize, like many activists, and a growing number of investors and consumers, that it is business - not government, and not what we like to call "Civil Society," but competitive, profit-hungry, talent-rich, problem-solving business—that will have the greatest impact, for good or for ill, on the institutions and resources that are critical to our survival as a planet and wellbeing as a civilization. (2005, p. 497)

At this moment in the world of critical theorising about organisations there is no more urgent project than the articulation, development and implementation of fundamentally transformative forms of business management. While this transformation imperative has been growing for some decades, and while many innovative and radical kinds of management approaches have emerged in the last 30 years, the need for a coherent and substantive response from the corporate world to planetary crises is becoming more apparent and more urgent.

One avenue for meeting that challenge is through the development and institutionalisation of, what are currently regarded as, innovative forms of management. How do we identify those innovative forms and what might be their qualities? Many theorists have referred to the wave of innovative theories of management as the "new management paradigm" (Burnes, Cooper, & West, 2003; Huse, 2003; Lichtenstein, 2000) and have suggested that these ideas herald a new movement for transformation in organisational life. However, the promises of the new paradigm have not been fulfilled and, although new paradigm approaches have contributed to critical theorising on management, they have not had a significant impact on the world of corporate management (Lichtenstein, 2000).

On every front, the complex work of managing and guiding corporations is being contested and new levels of accountability and social responsibility are being demanded. And these demands are arising from many directions – economic, environmental, communal, social, and political. However, given such situations as the role of management in global financial crisis and the track record of executive remuneration scandals over several decades, it is evident that these valid demands for transformation in corporate management systems are not being met. The financial crisis and ensuing economic implications is the culmination in a long line of company failures and market weaknesses that have their genesis at many different levels of society – government oversight, market regulation, the lack of investigative journalism, poor corporate governance, amoral management systems and personal greed and corruption (Avgouleas, 2009; Epstein & Hanson, 2006). The Enron, Worldcom, Tyco and Arthur Anderson collapses in the U.S. and the HIH Insurance, One.Tel, and Ansett Airlines debacles in Australia were, in very significant ways, precursors to these global failures and they each highlight the crucial role of management in the creation of irresponsible business practices. These failures of conventional management require some big picture rethinking. As well as a practical and operational response to these issues, there needs to be an academic contribution that provides a conceptual revisioning of management. The building of theory complements and, in some ways, drives the more pragmatic establishment and routinisation of better management systems and practices in the world of corporate business. The development and teaching of theory feeds into and influences social and business practices in fundamental and far-reaching ways. And the requisite transformation in management systems will not occur without a commensurate revision of management theory. As Sandra Waddock notes,

If business schools do not teach future managers and accountants about the integral relationships that exist between corporations and societies, we cannot expect top CEOs to understand them. Business educators must focus on integrity at the individual, company, and societal levels - and they need to work toward an attendant transformation in the curriculum that covers business in society, not just business in economy. (Waddock, 2005, p. 146)

"Integral relationships" can only be developed and explored when they have been named and identified and integrative theory and metatheory is needed for that to occur. How, for example, might we better integrate extended stakeholder theory (Zsolnai, 2006) with economic models of wealth creation? To even consider such questions, a more expansive appreciation of the range of extant theories and metatheories is vital. Waddock makes a salient point on how a limited theoretical base can impact on the level of ethical and social awareness in the business professions. She states that:

Because most management theory focuses predominantly on maximizing shareholder wealth, it considers only some stakeholders and fails to educate managers and accounting professionals about all of the consequences of their decisions. (Waddock, 2005, p. 146)

There is a serious lack of metatheoretical reflection occurring within business schools that is feeding into the narrow preoccupations of the world of corporate business. As Samantra Ghoshal succinctly put it "Bad Management Theories Are Destroying Good Management Practices" (Ghoshal, 2005). From a metatheorising perspective, this calls for an evaluation of how the new management paradigms might contribute to a more sustaining and sustainable organisational life. We need to work towards developing good metatheory in order to critically examine bad management theory (Hambrick, 2005; Pfeffer, 2005). Towards this end, I present a metatheoretical overview of theories of postconventional management and offer some explanations for why more integrative approaches to corporate management have not had a more widespread uptake or impact. I will also consider what conditions might be required to support the emergence of management systems that are relevant to a contemporary global and interconnected society.

2. CORPORATE RESPONSIVENESS AND THE CHANGE DILEMMA

Organizations are powerful and influential social entities. They contribute enormously to what changes and what doesn't in our world. Governments, commercial corporations, NGOs and cultural institutions all play their role in shaping what happens at multiple levels in both natural and social systems. This shaping occurs at the level of personal views and behaviours, interpersonal interactions, neighbourhood and communal life all the way to the worlds of international politics, economics and social and global social, biological and environmental changes. This is increasingly true of large national and multinational corporations. The majority of the world's top 100 economies are corporations and this economic power means that there is a commensurate level of responsibility for these organisations to contribute to the sustainable welfare of the planet and its inhabitants. While corporate business activities have contributed to the economic welfare of many millions of people across many countries, these same developments seem to be threatening the sustainability of many global environmental systems. As economic growth proceeds, so do the global challenges for ensuring the health of natural environments. John Cavanagh and Jerry Mander are among many commentators who recognise the global responsibilities that multinational corporations need to meet. In their view:

The global corporations of today stand as the dominant institutional force at the center of human activity. Through their market power, billions of dollars in campaign contributions, public relations and advertising, and the sheer scale of their operations, corporations create the visions and institutions we live by and exert enormous influence over most of the political processes that rule us. (Cavanagh & Mander, 2002, p. 22)

This power gives rise to a dilemma. Organisations need to learn and transform in order to cope with the changes that surround them. However, the immense influence of corporations on social life, through such means as those mentioned by Cavanagh and Mander, has resulted in a situation where stability can be artificially maintained through a kind of disassociation with the natural and social environments. The very success of corporate life to create material wealth among select nations and privileged populations means that radical change is less likely to be embarked on. In place of a transformation that is requisite to the challenges that confront them, large businesses and global corporations have moved their focus to influencing the social perceptions of change, to implementing incremental "reforms" and to projecting a sense of economic stability that supports the status quo of unsustainable cycles of production and consumption. This double bind – of needing to transform but doing everything to avoid deep change - has been called the "change paradox" (Quinn & Cameron, 1988) and is a well known phenomenon among change theorists (Lewis, 2000; Tsoukas & Chia, 2002).

Many feel that corporate and institutional leadership is not up to the transformational task that is being asked of large corporations. Mander and his colleagues sum up this dilemma:

It is imperative to rethink human priorities and institutions. Yet the institutions with the power to provide such leadership are neither inclined nor suited to doing so. Nor is there realistic cause for hope that leaders who are lavishly rewarded by the status quo will experience a sudden epiphany. (Mander, Cavanagh, Anderson, & Barker, 2003, p. 39)

The authors go on to propose that citizen-lead activism might provide a new source for creating the conditions by which corporate transformation can occur. It is evident that the source of that change will not come solely from the arena of corporate practice itself. To respond adequately to global issues large corporations and business organisations will need to implement some kind of large-scale integrative transformation. However, while there are many local innovations occurring, there has been little evidence of any significant transformational shift in organisational activities at the national, international or global levels. The success rates of even conventional change efforts has been notably small (Forster, 2005). When we look at transformational change in response to global crises it seems that things are even less promising. Recent research focusing on the FTSE 350 (the largest companies listed on the London stock exchange) has shown that corporate response to global critical issues has been anything but transformational (Cumming, Bettridge, & Toyne, 2005). Researchers reviewed how large companies responded to 14 "social, ethical and environmental business-critical global issues such as climate change, governance and technology" (Cumming et al. 2005, p. 42). Companies were rated in terms of their transformational response to these 14 global issues. It was found that most corporate responses to these challenges were "characterized by a wide-ranging series of incremental changes, with no convincing examples yet existing of transformation implemented across the entirety of the company's operations" (Cumming et al. 2005, p. 42).

It should not be surprising that true organisational transformation is a rare thing. There is a considerable body of research that demonstrates the difficulties with undertaking radical change and with making it stick (see, for example, Elrod & Tippett, 2002; Sarker & Lee, 1999; Zell, 2003). It is unlikely that organisations by themselves have the capacity to meet the need for global change and that the stimulus for requisite levels of transformation will need to come from many directions other than self-regulated corporate codes, voluntary charters or from individual corporate initiatives.

In the following pages, I will suggest that the momentum for real corporate reform might also be supported from the world of business schools and higher education through the development of new (meta)theoretical visions. Research and education institutions have a privileged position in which to construct and explore more visionary ideas of what organisational management can be. All significant and lasting change requires both interior vision and exterior action; the embedding of more integrative and embracing systems of social functioning as well as the freedom and agency of groups and individuals to give life to those systems. All of the global challenges that we currently face, whether they be environmental, socio-cultural or economic in origin, require some level of "big picture", or metatheoretical, response. Metatheories have been extremely influential in the development of modern economies, systems of governance and educational systems and yet metatheory development has been virtually ignored as a topic for research. Metatheoretical research can enrich our capacity to develop scientific responses to global challenges. To bring about the emergence of forms of management that are adequate to our times, both metatheoretical vision and applied action will be required. Before mapping out a framework for contextualising these ideas, I will make some comments on the links between integrative metatheory and the idea of a postconventional management.

3. METATHEORISING, TRANSFORMATION AND POST/CONVENTIONAL MANAGEMENT

3.1 Metatheorising

Metatheorising is the development of conceptual frameworks whose subject matter is other theory (Ritzer, 2006). This is a highly abstract activity and it might justly be asked, what use such activity has for addressing the failures of corporate management? Why might it be important to develop abstract conceptual systems when we face concrete problems such as corruption, environmental degradation, natural resource depletion, global warming and social inequality? One response is that global problems of this scale need the involvement of a big picture form of scientific research that can connect very disparate fields of human inquiry and scientific research. The development of metatheoretical frameworks for corporate management provides one crucial aspect for such a science. Developing new understandings of management will be crucial in any process of addressing these massive challenges.

Metatheory is the science of the big picture. The influence of metatheorists of the past, such as Adam Smith, Georg Hegel and Karl Marx, can hardly be overestimated and their impact on social development, economics, trade and the cultural life of nations across the world is undeniable. The power of metatheory can be appreciated more clearly when the relationship between ideas and actions is regarded as a complementary process. Our internal ideas do not merely represent external objects and, similarly, metatheories are not simply abstractions of pre-existing social theories. Thoughts and things are involved in a mutual process of co-creation and metatheory produces social realities as much as it analysis it. This is the "double hermeneutic" of Anthony Giddens (1984), the constitutive process of Stanley Deetz (1996) and the self-fulfilling prophecy of Robert Merton (1968). A conceptual lens does not merely interpret organisational structures, processes, objects and powers it is core to the process of constituting them. So the question is not whether metatheory has relevance to global issues, but how we might develop metatheory that is more scientifically based, more integrative and more conscious of its own assumptions and cultural strengths and weaknesses.

Metatheorising is the review and analysis of research paradigms, theories, models and cultural traditions of thought. The four basic aims of metatheorising are (Colomy, 1991; Ritzer, 2001):

i. to become more familiar with the range of extant theories within a domain (M_R);
ii. to prepare for the development of a particular theory or model of greater refinement (M_P);
iii. to construct more encompassing overarching frameworks (metatheories) (M_O);
iv. to use overarching metatheories for the adjudicative evaluation of extant theories and metatheories (M_A).

Metatheorising is a rigorous scientific activity when these four aims are based on a methodical analysis of extant theories within a specified domain of relevance. It is sometimes claimed that metatheory does not provide useful information because it is so abstract and cannot, therefore, be tested by empirical research. I have addressed these and other critiques of metatheorising in greater detail elsewhere (Edwards, 2010) but a few points might be raised here. The claims of irrelevance and untestability misunderstand the place of metatheory in research and the valid contributions that it can make. Metatheorising is not directly concerned with making empirical claims nor can it be evaluated through empirical forms of hypothesis testing. Metatheory is chiefly about other middle-range theory and can only be appraised through reference to those theories (Edwards, 2008). Ritzer argues:

... we need to stop using the standard applied to works in sociological theory in assessing metatheoretical works. Material produced in the latter need to be evaluated, and some of it rejected, but by standards indigenous to metatheorising. (Ritzer, 1991, p. 310)

It is at the level of situating, connecting, critiquing and developing other middle-range theory or primary research that metatheorising makes its contributions. In a time when mainstream organisational and economic theory has been spectacularly unsuccessful in accounting for, or explaining, the mechanisms of corporate failure, metatheory offers a means for researching our basic conceptualisations of organisational and management issues. Many theorists have pointed out the inadequacies of the dominant agency theory approaches to governance and economic growth (Fontrodona & Sison, 2006; Wright, Mukherji, & Kroll, 2001) and they point to the need for widening the conceptual base for the study of corporate economics. Thomas Clarke states that "multiple theoretical lenses are appropriate" for a rejuvenated study of corporate governance (2005, p. 605). The collapse of Enron and many other large corporations in the USA in 2001 sparked a particularly intense review of the inherent weaknesses of dominant theories of management, governance and corporate ethics. In his analysis of the relationship between established economic theories of corporate governance and the Enron collapse, Clarke concludes:

A multi-theoretic approach to corporate governance is essential for recognising the many mechanisms and structures that might reasonably enhance organisational functioning. For example, the board of directors is perhaps the most central internal governance mechanism. Whereas agency theory is appropriate for conceptualising the con-

trol/monitoring role of directors, additional (and perhaps contrasting) theoretical perspectives are needed to explain director's resource, service and strategy roles. (Clarke, 2005, p. 605)

Metatheorising is ideally suited to this task of reconceptualising organisational life through the application of "multiple theoretical lenses". This is a profoundly transformative kind of research. Pursued as a way of developing knowledge, metatheorising requires reflection and an expansion of awareness about the landscape of ideas that are present within a relevant domain. Metatheoretical frameworks also provide directions for seeing how a field of study can grow and develop. It is largely metatheoretical activity that creates the impetus for theory to shift from one stage in its historical unfolding to some more encompassing stage. The movement from modern to postmodern theorising was encouraged through metatheoretical processes of analysis and such transformations are supported by the reflective multiparadigm review of the state of a field of inquiry (Lewis & Grimes, 1999; Lewis & Kelemen, 2002). This type of research can give direction to the development of knowledge by identifying the means by which disparate theoretical viewpoints can be connected. Accordingly, metatheorising enhances the transformational potentials that remain largely untapped within mainstream conceptualisations of management. Before developing the metatheoretical sections of this chapter further, a few comments will be made on the connections between metatheory and cybernetics.

3.2 Metatheory and the Cybernetics of Management

Cybernetics has been defined as the interdisciplinary study of effective organisation (Beer, 2004). In particular, cybernetics has focused on organisation through communicative processes and the "analytic study of the isomorphisms of communication structure in mechanisms, organisms and societies" (Macrae, 1951, p. 135). Because organised communication is a characteristic of many features of the physical, biological and social worlds, cybernetics is inherently interdisciplinary. Bernard Scott (2001) has even described cybernetics as "metadisciplinary":

Cybernetics was formulated by its founders as a meta-discipline with the aim not only of fostering collaboration between disciplines (interdisciplinarity), but also of sharing knowledge across disciplines (transdisciplinarity). As a metadiscipline, cybernetics comments on forms of knowing (the cognitive processes and communicative practices of observers) and also on forms of knowledge (for example, similarities and differences between different discipline areas). (Scott, 2001, p. 411)

Like metatheorising, cybernetics is about the identification of patterns across different domains of scientific inquiry. Scott also describes other aspects of cybernetics shares with metatheoretical research:

The power of cybernetics as a transdiscipline is that it abstracts, from the many domains it adumbrates, models of great generality. Such models serve several purposes: they bring order to the complex relations between disciplines; they provide useful tools for ordering a complexity within disciplines; they provide a 'lingua franca' for interdisciplinary communication; they may also served as powerful pedagogic and cultural tool for the transmission of key insights and understandings to succeeding generations. (Scott, 2001, p. 412)

From the beginning cybernetics has been applied to management issues (Espejo, 1996; Schwaninger, 2001; Stephens & Haslett, 2005) and topics such as strategic management continue to be a focus of cybernetic research (Winter & Thurm, 2005). Where the metatheory and cybernetics differ is in the scope of their generalising interests.

While cybernetics is interested in specific fields such as self-organisation, communication and decision making, metatheory has a broader agenda of considering the second-order conceptual patterns that can evinced across any group of theories and models. Cybernetics might usefully be regarded as one particular kind of integrative research in ways similar to general systems theory or chaos and complexity theory, whereas metatheoretical research will take all these as its subject matter. Whatever the precise details of their relationship to each other, all of these metatheory building forms of research can be used to generate new insights and to encourage a "cross fertilization between areas of thought too long separated" (Macrae, 1951, p. 149).

3.3 Transformational Management

Notions of transformation are frequently used in the context of the new management paradigm. There are two aspects to transformative management that are of special interest here. First, transformation refers to some extra-ordinary level of whole-of-system change. It is a type of qualitative shift that heralds the emergence of ground-breaking forms of management. This is not the kind of transformation that is concerned merely with innovative product development, technological change or any conventional notion of generating change within any conventional management paradigm. Authentic transformation is radical, whole-of-system change that presents a fundamentally new organisational landscape (Chapman, 2002). Second, I do not mean transformative in the sense of substitutive revolution. Transformation is not a kind of "neophilia" (Bubna-Litic, 2008) where the latest management fad replaces the status quo. This "out with the old, in with the new" view replaces one form of coercive control or management enforced change programme with another. There is no integrative inclusion here. Revolutionary approaches do present transformational visions but they are more about indiscriminate replacement than an integrative transformation of existing structures. Such revolutions do not value what precedes them and ultimately result in regressive collapse or, at least, in a retreat to some more simplistic state of governing, managing and organising.

3.4 Post/Conventional Management Theories

Idealised forms of management can be viewed as a spectrum of approaches ranging from preconventional to conventional and postconventional theories. Such a scale has been developed by Bill Torbert and his colleagues to characterise levels of organisational and leadership (Fisher, Rooke, & Torbert, 2003; Torbert, 1994). Theories that assume that management is essentially concerned with one or other of these "developmental action logics" (Rooke & Torbert, 2005) might also be categorised according to this typology.

Adopting Torbert's model, we can propose that preconventional management theories assume that management is about opportunism. It involves the exercising of corporate power to achieve material gain for ego-centric or ethnocentric purposes. Clearly the preconventional layer of management theories and guiding assumptions is no longer acceptable as a conceptual base for corporate viability, let alone global and intergenerational sustainability into and beyond the 21st century. Conventional management theories assume that management is about the exercising of norm-focused diplomacy, technical expertise and goal-centred achievement to attain organisational goals. Theories in this layer are concerned with management hierarchies, transactional stability and economic growth. Postconventional theories recognise the shortcomings in conventional models and describe contrasting theories where management is heterarchical (delayered), reflexive, communally-aware and critical of management systems. Where postconventional theories provide a contrasting perspective to conventional

Table 1. The spectrum of management theories

	Management Theories	Assumptions
Pre-conventional	"organisation as weapon", "dark side" of management, pathological management	top-down, material growth, "greed is good", instrumentalism, opportunistic, ego-centric
Conventional	functionalist theories of management, agency theory of management	top-down, transactional stability, economic growth, hierarchy, organisation-centric
Postconventional	CSR/TBL, postmodern and feminist theories of management	bottom-up, transformational, critical, pluralistic growth, heterarchical, community-centric
Integrative	Torbert's developmental action inquiry, relational management	reciprocating, transformational, holarchical, developmental growth, glocal-centric

approaches, integrative theories attempt to develop models that can accommodate both orientations. In practice this means proposing theories that can account for both transactional/stable and transformational/change imperatives, both top-down and bottom-up management styles and both economic and developmental understandings of growth. Table 1 shows these layers of theory and some of their contrasting assumptions.

The distinguishing feature of postconventional and integrative theories of management is that they are all concerned with transformational change to one degree or another (Nutt & Backoff, 1997). In contrast, conventional management theories are primarily concerned with greater effectiveness and efficiency within the current economic paradigm (Mitroff, 1998). In addition to this more transformational focus, the postconventional can be distinguished from the conventional on a number of other dimensions. Conventional theories of management are those that: i) are based on a positivist management tradition which sees the world as predictable and controllable (Berkes, 2003); ii) assume a functionalist perspective towards the use of human and natural "resources" for the pursuit of organisational goals (Donaldson, 2001); iii) take a top-down approach to decision-making, governance and general organising (Conger, 2000); iv) have a provisional approach to organisational communication and information dissemination (Atwater & Wright, 1996); v) take a more conservative view towards stakeholders and their priorities (Key, 1999); and vi) view issues such as sustainability, CSR and corporate ethics as peripheral to the main concern of running a business (Friedman, 2007). Conventional theories of management uncritically assume or explore these characteristics to discover ways of increasing the effectiveness and efficiency of managers and management systems.

Postconventional theories emphasise the other side of these qualities in that they adopt: i) a social constructivism approach towards causality (Barker, Nancarrow, & Spackman, 2001); ii) an interpretive perspective towards organisation and organising as processes of meaning-making (Chia, 1995); iii) a bottom-up, participative view towards decision-making, governance and general organising (Bennis, 2000); iv) an interactive approach towards organisational communication (Cheng, Sculli, & Chan, 2001; Plummer & Fennell, 2007); v) the importance of an expanded inclusion of stakeholders (Zsolnai, 2006); vi) a deeper understanding of the connections between organisations and the social, environmental, political and cultural communities that support them (Senge, Lichtenstein, Kaeufer, Bradbury, & Carroll, 2007). We have here the juxtaposition of a mainstream conventionalism with an emerging post-conventionalism. In many ways the new paradigm theories of management describe the polar opposite of the old functionalist paradigm. While postconventional management theory identifies the weaknesses within mainstream theory, it does not integrate the valid goals and assumptions for stability, structure and efficiency that are its chief concern.

The dichotomies and oppositions created by both conventional (e.g. functionalist) and post-conventional (e.g. interpretivist) management paradigms have become reified into concrete categories that are impeding our capacity to cope with crucial organisational issues (Chia, 1999). A more integrative lens is required to overcome this impasse. Consequently, the issue for a metatheoretical and integrative approach to these contrasting management paradigms is not which one is better or more scientifically valid, but how both might they be integrated within a more encompassing framework for management theory; one that retains the best elements of both conventionalism and postconventionalism. In other words, how might we develop metatheories and theories that progress their transformational goals while also conserving what is worthwhile within conventional views?

4. RELATIONALITY AND THE INTEGRATION OF THE "OLD" AND "NEW" MANAGEMENT THEORIES

One metatheoretical tool that is well suited to helping in the integration of contending paradigms is the lens of relationality (Bradbury & Lichtenstein, 2000; Cooper, 2005; Letiche, 2006). Relationality is an approach to research that attempts to capture the "interrelated, interdependent and intersubjective nature of social-organizational phenomena" (Bradbury & Lichtenstein, 2000, p. 551). Relationality breaks down pre-existing categorical boundaries by identifying the interstitial "space between" (Buber, 1958). As Robert Cooper says, "Relationality makes us see the world as a complex network of active connections rather than visibly independent and identifiable forms and objects" (Cooper, 2005, p. 1704).

The relational perspective can also be applied to categories of conceptualising. In which case it can be used to transcend the simple either/or dichotomies that conventional ("old) and post-conventional ("new") theories of management set up. The relationality lens is metatheoretical because it reflexively questions the distinctions we create within any conceptual framework. As a metatheorising process, relationality "invites us to see the world as the movement of relationships between things rather than the things themselves as static or quasi-static structures"(Cooper, 2005, p. 1708). It is this 'movement" that creates a transformational potential in the application of the relationality lens. For example, Stuart Clegg and his colleagues have suggested that finding relationships between contradictory or oppositional elements can act to stimulate the development of new synthesising potentials (Clegg, Cunha, & Cunha, 2002). The synthesising position does not eradicate the contending poles that created the tension, but rather the new integrative synthesis comes from the ongoing "bi-directional relationship between poles" and it emerges "without replacing or attenuating any of those tensions" (Clegg et al., 2002, p. 489).

Clegg and his colleagues provide the example of the need to plan and act to demonstrate this capacity of relationality to accommodate and transcend structural ambiguities (see figure 1). The necessity to plan and to act set up inherent tensions between such things as design and implementation and between structure and process. These polarities are often seen in the tensions between planning departments and works departments and in the contrast between conventional management theory's focus on control and planning and postconventional theory's focus on process and operations. In considering these opposed positions, relationality focuses on the contextual realities that give rise to these categories. Clegg points out that both can be seen within the context of improvising and the mutualising process that creates both planning and action.

The relationality lens permits a metatheoretical reframing to occur that can replace either/or

Figure 1. A relational approach to the plan-implement dichotomy (after Clegg, et al., 2002)

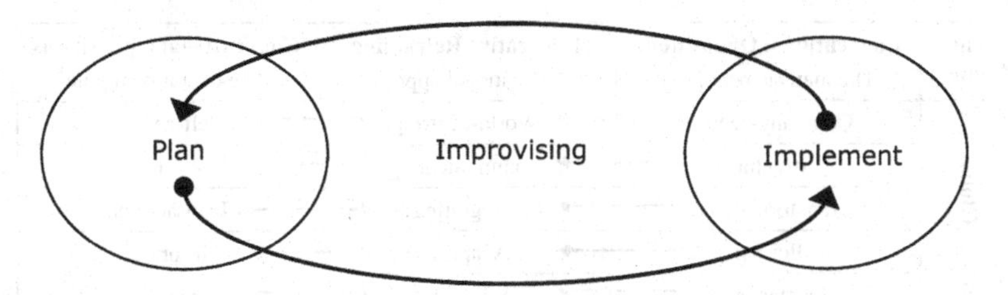

understandings of change when one pole in a conflicting position s chosen over and above another. In their study of organisational change and paradox Lotte Lüscher and Marianne Lewis found that "a paradox lens and paradoxical inquiry may offer means for new and more enabling understandings of contradictory managerial demands and ubiquitous tensions" (Lüscher & Lewis, 2008, p. 239). Metatheoretical reframing, through the application of such lenses as relationality, can create potentials for transformation that were not formerly apparent.

Organizational change spurs reframing, as actors seek to make sense of disparities between their expectations and new experiences (Balogun & Johnson, 2004). According to Bartunek (1984), frames provide a structure of assumptions, rules, and boundaries that guide sensemaking and over time become embedded and taken-for-granted. Shocks and surprises signal that existing frames may no longer apply. Reframing, therefore, enables actors to alter meanings attributed to changing situations. (Lüscher & Lewis, 2008, p. 222)

Relational approaches assist in working towards transformational change because they help to discover a position in which oppositions, dilemmas and even paradoxes are integrated within a social process of sense-making. Using the method of Luscher and Lewis (2008) this process can be briefly described as follows: problems are formulated out of the "mess" of managing, from problems arise oppositional dilemmas, within dilemmas we encounter fundamental paradoxes, these paradoxes can be resolved through relational transformations that create new systems of acting that transcend and integrate the oppositional poles. Paradoxes emerge in situations of confusion and complexity and their resolution can "yield a transcending new configuration" (Clarke-Hill, Li, & Davies, 2003, p. 5).

Metatheorising on management paradoxes can therefore generate "new configurations" and "guides for sense-making" that transcend some of the tired old oppositions that have constricted management theories and practices. The following two tables (Figure 2 and Table 2) list a number of simultaneous oppositions that have been identified in the extensive literature on organisational paradox (see, for example, Clarke-Hill et al., 2003; Clegg et al., 2002; Fiol, 2002; Lewis & Kelemen, 2002; Lüscher & Lewis, 2008; Quinn & Cameron, 1988; Stacey, 2005). It needs to be pointed out that some of these polarities are real paradoxical oppositions that are present in all social settings, while others are more contrived or polemical oppositions that have been identified in the critical literature on management theory. For example, the individual-collective polarity has been regarded as inherent dimension to all social activity (Ritzer, 1992), while the open-to-change and resistant-to-change (Humphreys & Brown, 2002) and rational-emotional (Martin, 2000) oppositions have been identified in the postmodern, feminist theory and critical theory critiques of management theory.

Figure 2. Relational transformations for some conventional dichotomies

The Context	Conventional Oppositions The management pole		Integrative Reframing The relational approach		Conventional Oppositions The operational pole
Global	Company-centric	→	World-centring	←	Self-centric
	Structure	→	Communicating	←	Agency
	Transformational	→	Integrating	←	Transactional
Social	Formal	→	Adapting	←	Informal
	Set standards	→	Achieving	←	Meet standards
	Management	→	Organising	←	Labour
Organisational	Knowledge	→	Learning	←	Ignorance
	Profit growth	→	Developing	←	Wage growth
	Directive	→	Deciding	←	Submissive
	Leader	→	Serving	←	Follower
	Boss	→	Tasking	←	Worker
Interpersonal	Individualist	→	Teaming	←	Collectivist
	Employer	→	Contracting	←	Employee
	Initiate/Proactive	→	Co-creating	←	Resist/Reactive
	Indispensable	→	Conserving	←	Dispensable
Personal	Expert	→	Discovering	←	Novice
	Fixers	→	Solving	←	Problems
	Rational	→	Feeling	←	Emotional
	Motivates	→	Motivating	←	Needs motivation
	Goal-driven	→	Interesting	←	Pay-driven

5. THE INTEGRATIVE THIRD WAY

5.1 Integrating Oppositions of the Conventional Management Paradigm

Applying the metatheoretical lens of relationality to both these conventional and postconventional dichotomies opens up a contextualising third way for the development of theory. This third way has the potential to reframe the management-operational oppositional dichotomies that are created in both conventional and postconventional theory. This integrative alternative describes a movement towards transformational theory that retains oppositional tensions while also unlocking the possibility for new visions of management and organisation. The relational approach described above can be applied to any of the contradictions, dichotomies and oppositions associated with, on the one hand, conventional, modernist and functionalist theories of management and, on the other hand, postconventional, postmodernist and interpretive theories. Figure 2 sets out several integrative reframings for oppositions that exist within conventional theories of management. Contending oppositions are mapped out according to a micro-meso-macro scale of focus ranging from the individual and interpersonal (micro) through to the team and organisational levels (meso) through to the social and global levels (macro).

Conventional theories often assume dichotomies that are structural in nature. For example, they juxtapose the influence of organising systems against the capacity of individuals to act independently. In terms of knowledge management, they oppose subjective and objective forms of knowing and learning. In the context of industrial relations they contrast the executive management

Table 2. Relational transformations of some postconventional dichotomies

The Context	Postconventional Dichotomies The management pole	Integrative Reframing The relational approach	Postconventional Dichotomies The operational pole
	Globalisation	Glocalising	Localisation
	Oppressing	Liberating	Oppressed
	Production	Living	Consumption
	Source of power	Empowering	Object of power
	Financial stakeholders	Including	Extended stakeholders
	Autocratic	Sociocratic	Democratic
	Hierarchy	Wholing (Holarchy)	Heterarchy
	Control	Networking	Freedom
	Anti-environmental	Sustaining	Pro-environmental
	Top-down	Reciprocating	Bottom-Up
	Agentic	Acting-Listening	Communal
	Competitive	Collaborating	Co-operative
	Dominating	Negotiating	Dominated
	Objective measurement	Pragmatic relating	Subjective experience
	Mental	Educating/Skilling	Manual
	Male	Humanising	Female

levels with operational levels or company profits with labour costs. In the area of leadership they take a top-down view of decision-making and governance. Conventional theories see change as initiated by executive levels of management and as either implemented or resisted by operational levels within the organisation. At the psychological and interpersonal levels conventional theories of management tend to oppose the rational with the emotion, the expertise and "know how" of the manager with the lack of knowledge and/or skills of other employees and the self-directed motivation of mangers with extrinsic rewards of operational employees. Applying the relational lens to these oppositions results in a reframing of the context of theory building. For example, it is not just a matter of choosing between objective structures and subjective agency in explaining social phenomena within organisations. Communicating can be regarded as "the site and surface" (Taylor & Every, 2000) of organising processes and as a more dynamic way of theorising about social causation.

In Table 1 the integrative positions are expressed in continuous verb forms wherever possible because of the processual nature of organising (Bakken & Hernes, 2006; Tsoukas & Chia, 2002; Weick, 1995). An organisation is an ongoing process of creating relationships and the integrative position, expressed as a continuous verb (Weick, 1995), is a way of dealing with the fallacy of the concreteness of the dualistic oppositions that both conventional and postconventional theories are prone to. As Bakken and Hernes have pointed out, "A problem in working with dichotomous notions is that they cannot be seen to interact relationally" (2006, p. 1611). That relational truth of a situation is better captured through language that conveys images of becoming *and* movement. Together, the integrative terms are meant to describe a transformational vision of organising that retains the contributions of both conventional and postconventional theories of management. The following describes how the integrative terms reframe existing dichotomies.

World-centring: Reframing our focus of responsibility from the organisation and/or oneself to the larger social and global sphere which, while including personal and organisational responsibility, connects globalisation with a personal world-centric perspective.

Communicating: Overcoming the separation of structure/systems and agency/acts with a mediating view of communicating so that all staff members are seen as creating structure and systems and all have responsibility for their actions.

Integrating: Moving beyond the trap of choosing between revolutionary change, which seeks transformation, and incremental change, which seeks efficiency and increase.

Adapting: Providing a balance between formal structures and informal dynamism.

Achieving: Attaining meaningful goals rather than a contest between those who set standards and those who are expected to meet them.

Organising: Reframing the division between management and labour, which is based on a mechanistic view, into a context of co-operative organising.

Learning: Moving beyond the assumption that learning and knowledge is more a managerial function that an operational function.

Improvising: Bringing out the extemporaneous nature of planning and implementing.

Developing: Reframing the management concern with profit/economic growth and the labour concern with wage growth into a concern for human development.

Deciding: Seeing the process of performing as not reducible to giving and following directions.

Serving: Reframing leadership as existing across all parts of the organisation and as each employee as a servant or leader-follower in all their work.

Collaborating: Moving the organising focus onto appreciative relationships and collaborative tasks rather than bosses and workers.

Teaming: Rather than assuming the division between the organisation and the individual, teaming reframes the group as a central social reality in organisational life.

Enabling: Overcoming the assumption that labour resists and management initiates by recognising the different roles that are enabling of some valued outcome.

Conserving: Reframing the relationship between managers and staff as conservers of organisational resources rather than as disposable or non-disposable assets.

Discovering: Integrating the division between assumed management expertise and manual labour within a context of discovering solutions and innovations.

Feeling: Bringing into awareness assumptions regarding the rationality of management and to issues of emotion, feeling and aesthetic appreciation.

Motivating: Seeing all work as needing to be intrinsically interesting, motivating, rewarding irrespective of its place in the organisation or its level of remuneration.

Contracting: Rather than basing theories of management on the traditional manager-employee dyad, a more integrative view will be more open to contractual arrangements as defining managerial relationships.

Bringing these relational reframings together describes a vision of management that is much more distributed and flexible to the demands of contemporary work relationships and tasks. There is a focus on work development and interdependence across all aspects of the organisation. There is a direct connection between the personal, the team, the organisational, the social and the global in the implications of managerial work. There is an integrative treatment of innovation that also retains what is of value. Consequently, learning becomes a core organisational ability that is needed at all levels. Finally, there is the idea of effectiveness and efficiency as a contracting relationship between management and contracted staff rather than a command relationship between bosses and employees.

5.2 Integrating Oppositions of the Postconventional Management Paradigm

Postconventional theories also tend to express their positions with reference to contrasting dichotomies. Where conventional theories base these dichotomies on rational paradoxes and ambiguities, postconventional dichotomies are described as a result of the deconstruction of political, ideological and cultural assumptions (Hassard & Kelemen, 2002).

Glocalising: Integrating the move towards globalisation with the need for localisation of cultural opportunities, sensitivities and diversities.

Liberating: Recognising the oppressive power of organisations and management systems and taking steps to turn that power toward emancipatory goals.

Living: Reframing the cycle of production and consumption to one of creating opportunities for working to live rather than living to produce or to consume.

Empowering: Seeing management as a system of empowering stakeholders rather than as the exercising of power of some over others.

Including: Rather than seeing stakeholders as either finance-based or community-based, the integrative position finds a place for many groups within an inclusive, yet differentiated, model of relationships.

Sociocratic: Enabling governance across all organisational levels rather than solely at the board or executive levels, while recognising the limitations of democratic and autocratic systems.

Wholing (Holarchy): Integrating multilevel realities (across level structures and processes) with heterarchical realities (within levels structures and processes).

Networking: Managing becomes a system for enabling networking and creating when it stops being a system of imposing control and granting freedom.

Sustaining: Reframing management as a process for sustaining the organisation and its host environments and communities.

Reciprocating: Management is reframed as a multilevel decision-making process that is embedded at all levels with managing, informing and communicating moving from the top down and from the bottom up. Management is based on reciprocation rather than control.

Acting-Listening: Moving beyond the assumption that management acts and operational levels listen and improvising a relationship of mutual acting-listening.

Negotiating: Recognising the reality of conflict, negotiating assumes the value of opposing positions and develops procedures for resolving conflicting goals.

Pragmatic partnership: Recognising the importance of both objective data and subjective experience and reframing both into the pragmatics of working within appreciative partnerships.

Educating/Skilling: Both management and operations require mental, emotional and manual skills and the skilling and educating of all employees needs to replace more limited assumptions.

Humanising: Humanising the workplace reframes the gender debate to one of making all workplaces more humane, flexible and contributing to family life.

This set of relational reframings of postconventional assumptions describes a transformative vision for theorising management. There is a focus on the transformation of organisational relationships and structures to facilitate reciprocating forms of decision-making and governance. These integrative reformulations also extend traditional managerial roles across the organisation and lead to theories of extended stakeholder representation and power. They require a transformation in the sense of identity and perspective that we assume in managing organisational power and the reverberations that emanate out from those decisions. No longer is organisational loyalty to be held as more important than the sense of responsibility to the local community or the global environment. The implications of these transformations are immense and, when considered across a broad communal and societal base, they suggest a potential for organisational change of great significance. These guiding qualities of glocalising, liberating, living, empowering, including, sociocratic, wholing, sustaining, reciprocating, acting-listening, negotiating, pragmatic relating, educating and humanising provide a vision of management that is about the full-spectrum development of individuals and communities than the exclusive pursuit of efficiency, market dominance or financial profit. It is not that the economics is forgotten but that it is contextualised with a more integrative and sustaining picture of the role of management in societal and global development.

6. TOWARDS SUSTAINING MANAGEMENT THEORIES FOR THE 21ST CENTURY

The relationality lens has been used here to identify qualities important for theories of 21st century management. The types of changes that these qualities point to are so broad and so radical in their implications that their appearance on a global scale seems hardly likely. However, true transformation is never something that seems possible before it happens. The scale of impact that climate change, peak oil, global warming refugees, water and food shortages, growing population and economic dislocation will have on local communities, nations and the corporate world will be immense. However, the detail in how these changes will unfold at the regional and local levels will be unpredictable and so will be the variety of responses that they evoke. Business corporations, being among the most powerful of all organisations, will have a particular responsibility to respond adaptively, that is, with integrative and visionary transformations, to these challenges. "New metaphysical foundations" (Steingard, 2005) will be required to underpin that change. Nowhere is this seen more clearly than in the connection between sustainability and management. The economic preoccupations of conventional management and organisation theory are out of step with the need for long-term sustainable development. Dexter Dunphy and his colleagues argue that forms of "cosmocentric consciousness, or spiritual intelligence" will be required to develop viable forms of sustainable organising (Dunphy, Griffiths, & Ben, 2003). Our theories of management will need to also incorporate these new metaphysical foundations if they are to be sources for describing management styles and systems that promote local, regional and global sustainability.

The depth of the scale of this change has led some theorists to talk about the connections between spirituality and management (Calas & Smircich, 2003; Mitroff, 2003; Steingard & Fitzgibbons, 2004). Spirituality is seen in this management context as "a holistic infusion of experience and wisdom into the management disciplines" (Steingard, 2005, p. 227). Ian Mitroff has gone so far as to suggest that, "Spirituality may in fact be the most important component of all managerial systems" (Mitroff, 1996, p. 68). The relationship between spirituality and management theory will necessitate "inquiry into new ontological, epistemological and teleological dimensions of research and practice" (Steingard, 2005, p. 228).

The integrative terms listed above provide some direction for theory development that reflects the urgent need for transformational yet also sustaining forms of management. In Table 3 these terms are applied to the conventional concerns for organising structure and the production process and to the postconventional concerns for power and relational issues. The integrative terms give direction for developing ideas about the multi-level nature of sustainability and organisational life. For example, at the personal level the principle of "humanising" points to a workplace that promotes human dignity and the opportunities for furthering human potential rather than as a place for producing economic wealth. At the interpersonal level, the principle of "discovering" supports the idea of a sustaining workplace as a place of innovation irrespective of its formal function. At the organisational level, we have the principle of "learning" embedded within all the processes of the corporation and consequently supporting the transformative possibilities that ensue. At the global level we have the principle of glocalising which captures the postconventional concern for finding interdependencies between local and global sustainability. Many other examples for how these integrative principles can stimulate transformational theories are presented in Table 3.

The integrative principles set out in the foregoing sections are not prescriptive of the structures or processes that managers might employ to achieve their business objectives. There will be numerous innovative approaches that could apply these principles in some form. However, the changes required for these transformations to take hold and shape new management systems will be significant and in many cases radically different to the current status quo. These transformations will not begin at any one level and then trickle on to other levels. They will arise at multiple sites, in many forms and across various streams of corporate activity. For example, without change in the realities of interpersonal relationships more systemic and societal change will not be taken up. Without transformation in organisational policies, goals and behaviours, the task of personal learning will not be adequately supported.

If management theorists are to develop more integrative approaches that have relevance to personal ethical dilemmas, to corporate responsibility, to globalisation and to climate change then they will need to be aware of the grounding assumptions and conceptual architectonics that structure their ideas. Awareness of this kind entails familiarity with the role of meta-level research and metatheories but it also leads to a shift in how theorists consciously position and reflect upon their own work. There are powerful connections between researchers' awareness of their own role in transforming social life, the types of management and change theories they produce and the impact of those ideas in the marketplace and in communities more generally. Steingard, drawing on the observation of other theorists, makes a clear connection between personal transformation and the larger domain of economics and management.

Recent ethics scandals, rapid globalization, fundamental corporate exploitation of person and planet (Mandel, 1992) all require transcending the small self of the ego so that managers can engage in a more 'enlightened economics and management' (Maslow et al., 1998, p. 20). (Steingard, 2005, p. 237)

Steingard's use of words such as transformation, self, transcendence and enlightenment are not mystical daydreams in this context. They are apt terms for describing the level of change that is urgently required of our organisations, man-

Table 3. Integrative principles for theories of sustaining management

Level of focus for sustaining management	Integrative principles for conventional process/ structural concerns	Integrative principles for postconventional power/relationship concerns
Sustaining at the personal level	• Feeling: supporting long-term emotional health and interpersonal relations • Motivating: providing sustaining incentives • Interesting: ensuring engaging work • Achieving: enabling achievement throughout the working life	• Living: work as sustaining of personal life • Educating/Skilling: supporting life-long learning • Humanising: the workplace as an opportunity for deepening human potential and dignity
Sustaining at the interpersonal level	• Discovering: innovation and novelty • Solving: work that engages problem-solving and invention • Communicating: supporting the creation of social identity and interaction • Learning: embedding learning at all levels	• Collaborating: forming sustaining partnerships with colleagues • Negotiating: resolving meaningful issues through embedded negotiation processes • Relating: achieving sustainable growth through partnerships
Sustaining at the group level	• Tasking: seeing the work task as sustaining leader-follower relationships • Teaming: seeing teams as sustaining group identity, creativity and social belongingness • Deciding: consultative and group-based approaches to decision-making	• Reciprocating: work as sustaining leadership at all levels • Acting-Listening: recognising the value & difficulties of both leader & follower roles • Including: supporting a sustainable level of diversity
Sustaining at the organisational level	• Organising: sustainability as core to organisational mission and vision • Integrating: enabling both transformational and transactional goals and processes • Adapting: change as a sustaining feature of the organisation	• Wholing (Holarchy): allowing both hierarchy and heterarchy to sustain the organisational identity • Empowering: sustaining the decision-making relationships through empowering all levels
Sustaining at the industry level	• Conserving: industry networks are sustaining natural & community resources • Contracting: more flexible and sustaining forms of work relationships	• Networking: creating sustainable industries through peer support and trans-organisational incentives.
Sustaining at the societal level	• Serving: industries & organisations as contributing to environmental and socio-cultural health • Developing: sustainable development as a societal responsibility	• Sociocratic: Organisations as sustaining of social democracy • Liberating: industries and organisations as sustaining emancipator social goals
Sustaining at the global level	• World-centring: industries & organisations as supporting corporate global responsibility	• Glocalising: industries and corporations as sustaining local, regional, global and intergenerational health

agement systems and metatheories and theories of management.

7. SUMMARY AND CONCLUSION

This paper has argued that corporate management is failing to meet the global challenges that now confront it and that academic theorising is complicit in this failure. An important part of the difficulties in building transformational theories of management is the propensity for both conventional and postconventional approaches to set up conceptual dichotomies and oppositions that stymie further theoretical development. Theories of management that are based on these oppositions will not be capable of developing the guiding models, the insightful ideas or the practical interventions that businesses will need to implement to meet the global challenges of 21st century. The application of the relationality lens offers a way out of this impasse. The relationality view sees opposing dichotomies as occasions for taking an integrative perspective. Such a perspective recognises the veracity of the defining poles but also transcends the contradictions and limitations inherent within those contending positions. In this chapter the relationality lens was focused on a number of dichotomies present within conventional and postconventional theory and a large number of integrative principles were developed. Together, these principles (expressed as continuous verbs to highlight their dynamic quality) provide a scaffolding guide for the construction of transformational management theories.

The metatheoretical nature of the arguments and analytical processes presented here has been highly abstract but it would be an error to assume that abstraction necessarily detracts from the practical implications of this kind of research. Of course, high levels of abstraction are needed for any reappraisal of theory. More importantly however, the issue of relevance and practical application does not lie with whether ideas come from the middle-range of theory construction or the meta-level of grand theory. Metatheories have had and continue to have a powerful impact of social systems of all kinds. What is important is that metatheory be grounded on the analysis of its "data" of extant middle-range theory. And it is on these grounds that the value of meta-level research needs to be judged. It is not the abstract nature of metatheoretical frameworks that needs to be questioned but why organisational theorists do not employ more sophisticated methods for developing, testing, and exploring their potentials. In this chapter I have explored the capacity of metatheorising to generate new conceptual possibilities through the analysis and integration of diverse middle-range theories in the field of transformative corporate management. This kind of exploration is not possible without an overarching perspective that respects and includes the contributions of the plurality of views in this field. Metatheory and the world of practice are intimately connected. Social metatheorising creates as much as it interprets social realities. The strong connections between the realities of management and the academic world of ideas and research are described well in this quote from Sandra Waddock

The majority of top executives and accountants are decent people who possess integrity and live by personal standards. But some have been led astray by a lack of self-examination, by the fact that no one in their organizations offers them alternatives to a profit-based style of management, and by the fact that they learned no different course of action during their business school education. (Waddock, 2005, p. 147)

The need for envisaging "a different course of action" through the development of transformational metatheory and theory and to offer and apply these alternatives within our research, teaching and theory building is urgent. Without developing and implementing more transformative approaches to change, business managers and the institutions that educate them will continue to fall short of their community and global responsibilities. Integrative metatheoretical research has an important role to play in redressing this situation.

REFERENCES

Atwater, L. E., & Wright, W. J. (1996). Power and transformational and transactional leadership in public and private organizations. [Article]. *International Journal of Public Administration, 19*(6), 963–989. doi:10.1080/01900699608525127

Avgouleas, E. (2009). (forthcoming). The Global Credit Crisis, Behavioural Finance, and Financial Regulation, In Search of a New Orthodoxy. *Journal of Corporate Law Studies, 9*(1).

Bakken, T., & Hernes, T. (2006). Organizing is Both a Verb and a Noun: Weick Meets Whitehead. *Organization Studies, 27*(11), 1599–1616. doi:10.1177/0170840606068335

Barker, A., Nancarrow, C., & Spackman, N. (2001). Informed eclecticism: A research paradigm for the twenty-first century. *International Journal of Market Research, 43*(1), 3.

Bennis, W. (2000). Leadership of change. In M. Beer & N. Nohria (Eds.), *Breaking the Code of Change* (pp. 113-121). Boston, Mass.: Harvard Business School Press.

Berkes, F. (2003). Alternatives to conventional management: Lessons from small-scale fisheries . *Environments, 3*(1).

Bradbury, H., & Lichtenstein, B. M. B. (2000). Relationality in organizational research: Exploring The Space Between. *Organization Science, 11*(5), 551. doi:10.1287/orsc.11.5.551.15203

Buber, M. (1958). *I and Thou* (2d ed.). New York: Scribner.

Bubna-Litic, D. (2008). *Neophilia: A Consuming Passion Or Fabrication.* Paper presented at the ACSCOS 2008: The 3rd Australasian Caucus of the Standing Conference on Organizational Symbolism, Sydney.

Burnes, B., Cooper, C., & West, P. (2003). Organisational learning: The new management paradigm? *Management Decision, 41*(5/6), 452. doi:10.1108/00251740310479304

Calas, M., & Smircich, L. (2003). Introduction: Spirituality, management and organization. *Organization, 10*(2), 327. doi:10.1177/1350508403010002008

Cavanagh, J., & Mander, J. (2002). Fixing the Rotten Corporate Barrel. *Nation,* pp. 22-24, from http://search.ebscohost.com/login.aspx?direct=true&db=aph&AN=8649666&site=ehost-live

Chapman, J. A. (2002). A framework for transformational change in organisations. *Leadership and Organization Development Journal, 23*(1/2), 16–25. doi:10.1108/01437730210414535

Cheng, T., Sculli, D., & Chan, F. (2001). Relationship dominance - Rethinking management theories from the perspective of methodological relationalism. *Journal of Managerial Psychology, 16*(2), 97. doi:10.1108/02683940110380933

Chia, R. (1995). From modern to postmodern organizational analysis. *Organization Studies, 16*(4), 580. doi:10.1177/017084069501600406

Chia, R. (1999). A “Rhizomic” model of organizational change and transformation: Perspectives from a metaphysics of change. *British Journal of Management, 10*(3), 209. doi:10.1111/1467-8551.00128

Clarke, T. (2005). Accounting for Enron: shareholder value and stakeholder interests. *Corporate Governance: An International Review, 13*(5), 598–612. doi:10.1111/j.1467-8683.2005.00454.x

Clarke-Hill, C., Li, H., & Davies, B. (2003). The paradox of co-operation and competition in strategic alliances: Towards a multi-paradigm approach. *Management Research News, 26*(1), 1. doi:10.1108/01409170310783376

Clegg, S. R., Cunha, J. V. d., & Cunha, M. P. e. (2002). Management paradoxes: A relational view. *Human Relations, 55*(5), 483.

Colomy, P. (1991). Metatheorizing in a Post-positivist Frame. *Sociological Perspectives, 34*(3), 269–286.

Conger, J. A. (2000). Effective change begins at the top. In M. Beer & N. Nohria (Eds.), *Breaking the Code of Change* (pp. 99-112). Boston, Mass.: Harvard Business School Press.

Cooper, R. (2005). Peripheral Vision: Relationality. *Organization Studies, 26*(11), 1689–1710. doi:10.1177/0170840605056398

Cumming, J. F., Bettridge, N., & Toyne, P. (2005). Responding to global business critical issues: A source of innovation and transformation for FTSE 350 companies? *Corporate Governance*, *5*(3), 42. doi:10.1108/14720700510604689

Deetz, S. (1996). Describing differences in approaches to organization science: Rethinking Burrell and Morgan and their legacy. *Organization Science*, *7*(2), 191–207. doi:10.1287/orsc.7.2.191

Donaldson, L. (2001). *The contingency theory of organizations*. Thousand Oaks, CA: Sage.

Dunphy, D., Griffiths, A., & Ben, S. (2003). *Organisational Change for Corporate Sustainability: A Guide for Leaders and Change Agents of the Future*. London: Routledge.

Edwards, M. G. (2008). Where's the Method to Our Integral Madness? An Outline of an Integral Meta-Studies. *Journal of Integral Theory and Practice*, *3*(2), 165–194.

Edwards, M. G. (2010). *Organizational Transformation for Sustainability: An Integral Metatheory*. New York: Routledge.

Elrod, P. D., & Tippett, D. D. (2002). The "death valley" of change. *Journal of Organizational Change Management*, *15*(3), 273. doi:10.1108/09534810210429309

Epstein, M. J., & Hanson, K. O. (2006). *The Accountable Corporation*: Westport, Conn.: Praeger Publishers.

Espejo, R. (1996). *Organizational transformation and learning: A cybernetic approach to management*. Chichester, UK: Wiley.

Fiol, C. M. (2002). Capitalizing on paradox: The role of language in transforming organizational identities. *Organization Science*, *13*(6), 653. doi:10.1287/orsc.13.6.653.502

Fisher, D., Rooke, D., & Torbert, B. (2003). *Personal and Organizational Transformations: Through Action Inquiry* (4th ed.). Boston: Edge\Work Press.

Fontrodona, J., & Sison, A. J. G. (2006). The Nature of the Firm, Agency Theory and Shareholder Theory: A Critique from Philosophical Anthropology. *Journal of Business Ethics*, *66*(1), 33. doi:10.1007/s10551-006-9052-2

Forster, N. (2005). *Maximum Performance: A Practical Guide to Leading and Managing People at Work*. Cheltenham, UK: Edward Elgar.

Friedman, M. (2007). The Social Responsibility of Business Is to Increase Its Profits. In W. C. Zimmerli, M. Holzinger & K. Richter (Eds.), *Corporate Ethics and Corporate Governance* (pp. 173-178). Berlin: Springer.

Gentile, M. C., & Samuelson, J. F. (2005). The State of Affairs for Management Education and Social Responsibility. *Academy of Management Learning & Education*, *4*(4), 496–505.

Ghoshal, S. (2005). Bad management theories are destroying good management practices. *Academy of Management Learning & Education*, *4*(1), 75–91.

Giddens, A. (1984). *The Constitution of Society*. Cambridge: Polity Press.

Hambrick, D. C. (2005). Just How Bad Are Our Theories? A Response to Ghoshal. *Academy of Management Learning & Education*, *4*(1), 104–107.

Hassard, J., & Kelemen, M. (2002). Production and Consumption in Organizational Knowledge: The Case of the 'Paradigms Debate'. *Organization*, *9*(2), 331–355. doi:10.1177/1350508402009002911

Humphreys, M., & Brown, A. D. (2002). Narratives of organizational identity and identification: A case study of hegemony and resistance. *Organization Studies, 23*(3), 421. doi:10.1177/0170840602233005

Huse, M. (2003). Renewing Management and Governance: New Paradigms of Governance? *Journal of Management & Governance, 7*(3), 211. doi:10.1023/A:1025004111314

Key, S. (1999). Toward a new theory of the firm: a critique of stakeholder "theory". *Management Decision, 37*(4), 317. doi:10.1108/00251749910269366

Letiche, H. (2006). Relationality and Phenomenological Organizational Studies. *Tamara: Journal of Critical Postmodern Organization Science, 5*(3), 7–18.

Lewis, M. W. (2000). Exploring paradox: Toward a more comprehensive guide. *Academy of Management Review, 25*(4), 760. doi:10.2307/259204

Lewis, M. W., & Grimes, A. J. (1999). Metatriangulation: Building theory from multiple paradigms. *Academy of Management Review, 24*(4), 672–690. doi:10.2307/259348

Lewis, M. W., & Kelemen, M. L. (2002). Multiparadigm inquiry: Exploring organizational pluralism and paradox. *Human Relations, 55*(2), 251–275. doi:10.1177/0018726702055002185

Lichtenstein, B. B. (2000). Valid or vacuous? A definition and assessment of new paradigm research in management. *The American Behavioral Scientist, 43*(8), 1334. doi:10.1177/00027640021955892

Lüscher, L. S., & Lewis, M. W. (2008). Organisational change and managerial sensemaking: Working through paradox. *Academy of Management Journal, 51*(2), 221–240.

Macrae, D. G. (1951). Cybernetics and Social Science. *The British Journal of Sociology, 2*(2), 135–149. doi:10.2307/587385

Mander, J., Cavanagh, J., Anderson, S., & Barker, D. (2003). Alternatives to economic globalization. *Tikkun, 18*(1), 39–41.

Martin, J. (2000). Hidden gendered assumptions in mainstream organizational theory and research. *Journal of Management Inquiry, 9*(2), 207–216. doi:10.1177/105649260092017

Merton, R. K. (1968). *Social Theory and Social Structure*. New York: Free Press.

Mitroff, I. I. (1996). On the fundamental importance of ethical management: Why management is the most important of all human activities. *Journal of Management Inquiry, 7*(1), 68–79. doi:10.1177/105649269871011

Mitroff, I. I. (1998). On the fundamental importance of ethical management: Why management is the most important of all human activities. *Journal of Management Inquiry, 7*(1), 68–79. doi:10.1177/105649269871011

Mitroff, I. I. (2003). Spiritual I.Q: The farthest reaches of human development. *World Futures, 59*(7), 485–494. doi:10.1080/713747072

Nutt, P. C., & Backoff, R. W. (1997). Facilitating transformational change. *The Journal of Applied Behavioral Science, 33*(4), 490. doi:10.1177/0021886397334005

Pfeffer, J. (2005). Why Do Bad Management Theories Persist? A Comment on Ghoshal. *Academy of Management Learning & Education, 4*(1), 96–100.

Plummer, R., & Fennell, D. (2007). Exploring co-management theory: Prospects for sociobiology and reciprocal altruism. *Journal of Environmental Management, 85*(4), 944–955. doi:10.1016/j.jenvman.2006.11.003

Quinn, R. E., & Cameron, K. S. (1988). *Paradox and Transformation: Toward a Theory of Change in Organization and Management.* Cambridge, Mass.: Ballinger.

Ritzer, G. (1991). *Metatheorizing in Sociology*. Toronto: Lexington.

Ritzer, G. (1992). *Metatheorizing*. Newbury Park, California: Sage.

Ritzer, G. (2001). *Explorations in Social Theory: From Metatheorizing to Rationalisation*. London: Sage.

Ritzer, G. (2006). Metatheory. In G. Ritzer (Ed.), *Blackwell Encyclopedia of Sociology*. New York: Wiley.

Rooke, D., & Torbert, W. R. (2005). 7 Transformations of Leadership. *Harvard Business Review*, *83*(4), 66.

Sarker, S., & Lee, A. S. (1999). IT-enabled organizational transformation: a case study of BPR failure at TELECO. *The Journal of Strategic Information Systems*, *8*(1), 83–103. doi:10.1016/S0963-8687(99)00015-3

Schwaninger, M. (2001). System theory and cybernetics: A solid basis for transdisciplinarity in management education and research. *Kybernetes*, *30*(9/10), 1209. doi:10.1108/EUM0000000006551

Scott, B. (2001). Cybernetics and the social sciences. *Systems Research and Behavioral Science*, *18*(5), 411. doi:10.1002/sres.445

Senge, P. M., Lichtenstein, B. B., Kaeufer, K., Bradbury, H., & Carroll, J. S. (2007). Collaborating for Systemic Change. *MIT Sloan Management Review*, *48*(2), 44–53.

Stacey, R. (2005). Organisational identity: The paradox of continuity and potential transformation at the same time. *Group Analysis*, *38*(4), 477–494. doi:10.1177/0533316405058540

Steingard, D. (2005). Spiritually-Informed Management Theory: Toward Profound Possibilities for Inquiry and Transformation. *Journal of Management Inquiry*, *14*(3), 227–241. doi:10.1177/1056492605276841

Steingard, D., & Fitzgibbons, D. E. (2004). Towards a spiritually integral theory of management. *Journal of Management. Spirtuality and Religion*, *1*(2), 145–175.

Stephens, J. R., & Haslett, T. (2005). From Cybernetics and VSD to Management and Action. *Systemic Practice and Action Research*, *18*(4), 395. doi:10.1007/s11213-005-7170-x

Taylor, J., & Every, E. (2000). *The Emergent Organisation: Communication as its Site and Surface*. Mahwah, New Jersey: Lawrence Erlbaum Associates.

Torbert, W. R. (1994). Cultivating postformal adult development: Higher stages and contrasting interventions. In M. E. Miller & S. R. Cook-Greuter (Eds.), *Transcendence and mature thought in adulthood: The further reaches of adult development* (pp. 181-203). London: Rowman & Littlefield.

Tsoukas, H., & Chia, R. (2002). On organizational becoming: Rethinking organizational change. *Organization Science*, *13*(5), 567. doi:10.1287/orsc.13.5.567.7810

Waddock, S. (2005). Hollow Men and Women at the Helm... Hollow Accounting Ethics? *Issues in Accounting Education*, *20*(2), 145–150. doi:10.2308/iace.2005.20.2.145

Weick, K. E. (1995). *Sensemaking in organizations*. Thousand Oaks, CA: Sage.

Winter, W., & Thurm, M. (2005). Second-order cybernetics! In systemic management thinking? *Kybernetes*, *34*(3/4), 419. doi:10.1108/03684920510581602

Wright, P., Mukherji, A., & Kroll, M. J. (2001). A reexamination of agency theory assumptions: Extensions and extrapolations. *Journal of Socio-Economics*, *30*(5), 413. doi:10.1016/S1053-5357(01)00102-0

Zell, D. (2003). Organizational Change as a Process of Death, Dying, and Rebirth. *The Journal of Applied Behavioral Science*, *39*(1), 73–96. doi:10.1177/0021886303039001004

Zsolnai, L. (2006). Extended stakeholder theory. *Society and Business Review*, *1*(1), 37–44. doi:10.1108/17465680610643337

Chapter 9
The Structure of Theory and the Structure of Scientific Revolutions:
What Constitutes an Advance in Theory?

Steven E. Wallis
Institute for Social Innovation, USA; Foundation for the Advancement of Social Theory, USA

ABSTRACT

From a Kuhnian perspective, a paradigmatic revolution in management science will significantly improve our understanding of the business world and show practitioners (including managers and consultants) how to become much more effective. Without an objective measure of revolution, however, the door is open for spurious claims of revolutionary advance. Such claims cause confusion among scholars and practitioners and reduce the legitimacy of university management programs. Metatheoretical methods, based on insights from systems theory, provide new tools for analyzing the structure of theory. Propositional analysis is one such method that may be applied to objectively quantify the formal robustness of management theory. In this chapter, I use propositional analysis to analyze different versions of a theory as it evolves across 1,500 years of history. This analysis shows how the increasing robustness of theory anticipates the arrival of revolution and suggests an innovative and effective way for scholars and practitioners to develop and evaluate theories of management.

INTRODUCTION

As scholars, we seek to improve our understanding of management practices. An important part of this process is how we advance our theories. While an advance in understanding might be understood as relating to individual perception, advances in theory relate to the development of formal structures that are communicable, testable, and useable across our discipline. The question of what actually constitutes an advance in theory is still open, and new answers to that question are only now emerging. For example, it has been claimed that a theory of greater complexity should be considered as one that is more advanced (Ross & Glock-Grueneich, 2008). Another approach claims that improved theories are those that combine multiple theoretical lenses (Edwards & Volkmann, 2008). Still another approach

DOI: 10.4018/978-1-61520-668-1.ch009

suggests that theories of greater structure may be considered more advanced (Wallis, 2008b).

For scholars outside this growing metatheoretical conversation, the standard method for advancing a theory is to determine if that theory works in practice. However, each theorist seems to claim that his or her theory is best, so this is not a very useful measure. Investigating the Faust-Meehl Strong Hypothesis for Cliometric Metatheoretical investigations, Meehl notes that many authors claim their theories are good because they are parsimonious. However, Meehl (2002, p. 345) notes, this claim is misused, and represents a weak claim for successful theory.

Popper (2002) suggests that the best theories are those that are falsified. Yet, this level of testing seems to represent too high a hurdle for social scientists (Wallis, 2008d). Few theorists even attempt to falsify their own theories, or encourage others to do so. Some authors, in claiming that they have developed an advanced theory, invoke the spirit of Thomas Kuhn and his description and discussion of paradigmatic revolution.

Drawing on centuries of hindsight, Kuhn (1970) developed the idea of scientific paradigms; each of which includes laws, theories, application and instruments which combine to support "coherent traditions of scientific research" (Kuhn, 1970, p. 10). A paradigmatic revolution is said to occur when the traditions of a science change in significant ways. For example, moving from the Ptolemaic view of the solar system (where the Earth is at the center, surrounded by nested crystal spheres on which are embedded stars, planets, etc.) to a Copernican view where the sun is at the center. Revolutions also result in major improvements to the effectiveness of practitioners. With modern physics, it is possible to have communication satellites, while under the Ptolemaic paradigm, no such achievement would be possible.

Some authors in the field of management claim that their theories are not only effective and useful, but have achieved the status of paradigmatic revolution – ushering in a new age of management, presumably as great as the shift in thinking between Ptolemy and Copernicus. For example, after the development of Total Quality Management (TQM) by Ishikawa, a Kuhnian revolution was claimed. It was argued of TQM that, "All of these characteristics and underlying philosophies point to fundamental changes in the rules of business--a paradigm shift" (Amsden, Ferratt, & Amsden, 1996). While some authors claim revolution, others lend legitimacy to such claims. For example, Clarke & Clegg (2000, p. 45) refer to a proliferation of paradigms and describe over twenty publications that claim significant paradigmatic changes. They closely investigate some claims of paradigmatic revolution including, "*Transition From Industrial To Information Age Organization*." On the other hand, some authors are content to strongly imply a revolution, as would be found in a shift toward more spiritual management practices (Steingard, 2005). Still others do not make such claims, but explicitly seek revolution in their field (e.g. Stapleton & Murphy, 2003).

The nature of these claims seems to suggest that management science, as with the broader social sciences, does not have a shared understanding of what constitutes a Kuhnian revolution, or even the advance in theory needed for such a revolution. This lack of advance is reflected in management studies where the field is disparaged as being fragmented (Donaldson, 1995) by academics and where practitioners have little interest in the theories of academia (Pfeffer, 2007). In short, these "paradigm wars" lead to a loss of legitimacy from philosophers and practitioners (McKelvey, 2002).

The responsibility for these spurious claims may rest upon Kuhn's shoulders. While he wrote convincingly his focus, "leaves largely intact the mystery of how science works" (Nickles, 2009). In a sense, Kuhn described that houses of theory were built, but did not describe the method of construction. We can say that Kuhn's approach missed the mark in two important and closely related ways. The first was his focus on empirical data as a tool for advancing revolution. That focus, we will briefly explore in this section. Second, in looking at data, Kuhn missed the opportunity to focus on theory. That focus we will investigate (and remedy) in the remainder of this chapter.

For the first focus, Kuhn (1970) highlighted the idea that collecting facts is critical to the advancement of science. For example, he suggests that Coulomb's success in developing a revolutionary theory of electrostatic attraction (EA) depended on the construction of a special apparatus to measure the force of electric charge (Kuhn, 1970, p. 28). Kuhn provides this kind of specific example for the development of empirical data, but does not provide close descriptions of how scientists used that data to develop their theories. This pursuit of the empirical is exemplified by Popper (2002, p. 113) who suggests that scientists should begin with relatively arbitrary propositions. Then, they should move to the more serious work of deductive testing and falsification. In his view, it seems that the development of theory is relegated to a secondary status, while objective analysis reigns supreme. This empirical approach has colored the social sciences from the outset – and for good reason.

Social scientists of the early 19th century might have experienced an appreciable envy of their counterparts in physics, who were then reveling in the newfound success of their science. It was as if social scientists had looked up one day to see their counterparts living in comfortable homes of brick – safe behind solid walls of useful theory – while the social scientists languished outside in the cold. Those early social theorists recognized the benefit of having solid walls, but were unsure about the process of building a house of theory. It must have seemed to them that the house of physics was built using factual bricks of empirical analysis. Comte, for example, is said to have developed theories using a positivist, or empirical approach (Ritzer, 2001). However, in the words of Poincaré, "...a collection of facts is no more a science than a heap of stones is a house" (Bartlett, 1992). When social scientists used that empirical approach, however, the results were disappointing. Instead of solid walls, they had only piles of bricks.

By the middle of the twentieth century, it was becoming clear that social theory was not very useful in practice (Appelbaum, 1970; Boudon, 1986). As a result, three general remedies emerged. One remedy was for scientists to focus on smaller scale systems (Lachmann, 1991, p. 285). This approach led to the development of organizational studies and management science, as found in the writings of Lewin, McGregor, and others (Weisbord, 1987). Another remedy focused on investigations that were essentially a-theoretical. These "epistemologies of practice" (Schön, 1991) suggested the need for investigation, reflection, and action instead of the act of creating formal theories (Burrell, 1997; Shotter, 2004). Finally, the failure of a social science based on empirical investigation prompted the call for still more empirical investigation – a call that continues today (e.g. Argyris, 2005).

Unfortunately, the results generated by those alternatives do not seem to be any more useful than their predecessors. For example, despite the popularity of these approaches, studies have shown that Total Quality Management (TQM) fails at least 70 percent of the time (MacIntosh & MacLean, 1999), organization development culture change efforts seem to fail about the same rate (M. E. Smith, 2003) and Business Process Engineering (BPR) should not be considered a viable approach (Dekkers, 2008). Other authors echo this concern. For example, Ghoshal (2005) suggests that management theory as taught in MBA programs is a contributing factor to serious issues such as the Enron collapse which leads to concerns about the viability of management science in academia (Shareef, 2007). **The essential idea, that social scientists could engage in empirical observation and use the resulting data to create useful theories, appears to have been flawed.**

Kuhn reported that houses of theory were built, and that they were built from empirical bricks, but he did not explain the process by which the bricks were assembled. If we are to understand how to build solid houses of theory, it seems that our focus should be directed toward understanding theory. Only by looking between the bricks can we learn how they are put together. Only by investigating how these houses of theory are assembled, regardless of what empirical building blocks are used, can we find how they are built, and how we may advance management theory.

In this chapter I will investigate one method for objectively measuring theory to ascertain if this method may be used as a path for the advancement of management theory. In a metaphorical sense, I will identify the previously unknown techniques of bricklayers responsible for the well-built house of physics and, from that perspective, suggest how management scientists might build solid houses of useful theory. In this, we will seek to answer Kuhn's question, "Why should the enterprise sketched above move steadily ahead in ways that, say, art, political theory, or philosophy, does not?" (Kuhn, 1970, p. 160). Several perspectives may prove useful in this investigation. The first comes from developments in systems theory and the closely related field of complexity theory, specifically mutual causality – the idea that everything is interrelated. When applied with academic rigor, this idea of interrelatedness allows the objective analysis of the structure of theory.

Moving forward, we first review background information that identifies important similarities between theories of physics and theories of the social sciences. These similarities allow us to conduct analyses on one form of theory and draw inferences to another. Next, as part of understanding both forms of theory, we will look at the broader context of the growing conversation on metatheory, with a focus on the structure of theory, which may be analyzed in an objective way described in terms of formal robustness. That understanding of theory leads into the main thrust of the chapter where EA (electrostatic attraction) theory is analyzed in various forms as it evolved over time – moving from antiquity (where the theory merely described curiosities), into modernity (where robust theories supported paradigmatic revolution). By comparing the developmental path of EA theory with the present structure of some theories of management, inferences about the present state of management theory can be made along with suggestions for accelerating the advancement of management theory toward more effective application in practice.

BACKGROUND

The Common Ground Between Physical and Social Theories

The contrast between the physical sciences and the social sciences may framed in terms of complexity. In classical physics it is generally considered possible to develop predictive theories or laws to explain and forecast the workings of the natural universe because the physical universe is relatively stable and predictable. In contrast, complexity theory suggests that social systems exhibit inherent complexities, understood as non-linear dynamics (Olson & Eoyang, 2001; Wheatley, 1992). Therefore, in the social world, prediction (and the creation of predictive theory) is considered problematic or impossible. This point of view is not a strong one, however, because a statement such as, "It is not possible to create useful theories in social systems" is itself a theory that makes a prediction about a social system. The self-contradictory nature of that position renders it questionable. Therefore, we cannot rule out the possibility of predictive theories within the social sciences (Fiske & Shweder, 1986).

Moreover, the present chapter is not about theory creation, so many of these concerns may be set aside. The goal here is to measure the similarities between existing theories. This is an important distinction because the a-theoretical camp has not shown that theories of management *cannot exist* because, indeed, they do. They have only shown that within the current paradigm of management science we don't have the ability to create *effective* theory, which is reasonable since the evidence shows we don't. The validity of the analysis in this chapter rests on the similarity between theories of physics and management, leading us to ask: How might the two be compared?

The essential commonality between theories explored in the present chapter is found in the **structure** of the theory as seen in the interrelated nature of the propositions contained within the theory. Theories of physics and theories of management both contain interrelated propositions. For an example, physicist Georg Ohm developed the proposition (for a simple electrical circuit) that an increase in resistance and an increase in current would result in an increase in voltage. As an example from management theory, Bennet & Bennet (2004) suggest that (in an organization) more individuals and more interactions will result in more uncertainty. This similarity between propositional structures in theories of physics and theories of management provides a basis for comparison. Thus, structural inferences from one set of theories may be applied to another set of theories with some level of reliability.

Of course, other aspects are not held in common between theories of physics and theories of management – specifically where theories from each discipline are used to describe relationships among different things. For example, Newton's laws describe the motion of planetary bodies in the context of our solar system, while management theory describes some relationships between humans in the context of the workplace. In this chapter we are focusing on the theories themselves, not the things described by those theories. Therefore, as demonstrated above, the comparison between structures of theories should hold true. **Metaphorically, we are not trying to differentiate between the bricks of physics and the rough stones of management; we are looking at the mortar that can serve equally well to hold them all together.**

Further, we are not testing the process by which the theories were created, such as the formal process of grounded theory (Glaser, 2002) or more intuitive methods (Mintzberg, 2005). Neither will we consider the falsifiability (Popper, 2002) of those theories per se, although this analysis does suggest some insights and opportunities for further investigations along those lines. Because this is essentially a metatheoretical investigation, we begin with a brief explication of metatheory.

Metatheory

In previous decades, the term metatheory meant the speculative construction of one theory from two or more theories (Ritzer, 2001). This understanding of metatheory is being superceded by scholars who use the term to describe investigations into the structure, function, and construction of theory (Wallis, 2008b, 2008d) as well as the more carefully considered construction of overarching theory (Edwards & Volkmann, 2008) and investigations into the validity of theory as related to the complexity of theory (Ross & Glock-Grueneich, 2008), as well as the investigations of other authors in the present volume.

The "theory of theory" or metatheoretical conversation draws on insights from Kuhn (1970), Popper (2002), and Ritzer (2001), as well as methodologies from Stinchcombe (1987), Dubin (1978), and Kaplan (1964). More recently, notable scholars such as Weick (2005), Van de Ven (2007), Starbuck (2003) and others have summarized our present understanding of theory development and called for a new look at theory. The goal of this conversation is to develop a better understanding of theory – including how theory is created, structured, tested, and applied – in order to engender better theories and support the development of improved applications.

Theory may be understood as, "an ordered set of assertions about a generic behavior of structure assumed to hold throughout a significantly broad range of specific instances" (Southerland, 1975, p. 9). Theory is of key importance to practitioners as, "practice is *never* theory-free" (Morgan, 1996, p. 377) and to scholars because "there are *no* facts independent of our theories" (Skinner, 1985, p. 10) (emphasis, theirs). While Burrell (1997) suggests that theory has failed, others call for better theory (e.g. Sutton & Staw, 1995). This investigation falls into the later camp. This topic is of critical importance to our field because, "What constitutes good, useful, or worthy theory in our field remains up in the air and cannot be resolved through empirical validation alone." (Maanen, Sørensen, & Mitchell, 2007, p. 1153). This echoes Nonaka's (2005) argument that the creation of theory requires more than the traditional, positivist approach of seeking objective facts.

While there has been a great deal of conversations around the creation of theory (e.g., K. G. Smith & Hitt, 2005) and the testing of theory (Lewis & Grimes, 1999; Popper, 2002), these conversations have not shown efficacy in advancing theory. Although, some academicians seem to imply that the creation of more theory is taken as a reasonable measure of success. For example, one web page notes that an accomplished professor emeritus, "...is the sole author of six books. He is author or co-author of over 100 papers" (GMU, 2009). While these are certainly impressive numbers, there was no mention of the value of the work or its application in the world – the value sits upon a shelf. Another popular method for determining accomplishment is counting citations. These methods (and others) might indicate some sort of popularity (Wallis, 2008a), but do not seem to indicate any way to advance a theory. Indeed, in a recent HERA study, the author admits that there does not seem to be any reliable method for evaluation (Dolan, 2007). Another approach is called for.

Structure of Theory

Kaplan (1964, pp. 259-262) suggests six forms of structure for theoretical models. His forms of structure include a literary style (with an unfolding plot), academic style (exhibiting some attempt to be precise), eristic style (specific propositions and proofs), symbolic style (mathematical), postulational style (chains of logical derivation), and the formal style. The formal style avoids "reference to any specific empirical content" to focus instead on "the pattern of relationships."

Dubin's (1978) approach is similar, in that he suggests how theories of the highest "efficiency" are those that express "the rate of change in the values of one variable and the associated rate of change in the values of another variable" (Dubin, 1978, p. 110). Such relationships might be understood as structural in the sense that they represent causal and co-causal relationships between events. Because those relationships are well explained, we might expect such a theory to be more useful in practice, allowing the practitioner to use the theory to understand or predict those changes. In short, we might expect that theories with a higher level of structure to be more effective in practice.

Because theory indicates changes between multiple interrelated events, the structure of theory might be understood as a system. Briefly, the history of systems theory might be best seen in Hammond (2003) while the breadth of the theory might be best seen from the systemic perspective of Daneke (1999). The application of systems theory to management is provided in Stacey, Griffin, & Shaw (2000) while Steier (1991) draws on an understanding of cybernetics to explore reflexive research and social construction. More relevant to the present study, advances in complexity theory, systems theory, and cybernetics suggest that a systemic perspective might provide a useful lens for viewing management theory (e.g. Yolles, 2006).

The systems perspective may be applied to a conceptual system. In this case, the present methodology focuses on the systemic relationship between propositions in a body of theory measured in terms of "robustness" (Wallis, 2008b). It should be noted, by way of clarification, that the understanding and use of robustness as used here is different from a more common understanding, where robustness might be understood as strong, resistant to change, longevity, or widely distributed. Rather, **robustness refers to the specific and objective measure of the relationship between propositions in a theory**.

The idea of a robust theory comes from physics and mathematics, and represents a theory with complete internal integrity. For example, Ohm's law of electricity (E=IR) is considered to be a robust theory because it is amenable to algebraic manipulation – that is to say, this formula is equally valid if written as I=E/R, which means it is equally valid whether it is used to find volts (E), amps (I), or resistance (R). When I undertook to understand the structure of theory, I drew on insights from dimensional analysis, systems theory, Hegelian dialectic, and Nietzsche's insights into the co-definitional relationships between the dimensions of those dialectics. These, and other ideas, I combined to develop the process of Reflexive Dimensional Analysis (Wallis, 2006a, 2006b). That methodology was further refined (Wallis, 2008b) to develop a method of propositional analysis that could be used to objectively determine the robustness of a theory.

By way of background, a causal proposition describes a relationship between aspects – where each aspect relates to some observable or conceptual phenomena. For an abstract example, a proposition might be represented as, "A causes B" (or, "changes in A cause changes in B"). A co-causal proposition might be, "Changes in A and B cause changes in C." Such co-causal propositions are described as concatenated (Kaplan, 1964; Van de Ven, 2007).

Van de Ven suggests that concatenated concepts may be difficult to justify and suggests, instead, that the more commonly used chain of logic is the better way to construct a theory. A chain of logic might be understood as explaining how changes in A are caused (or explained) by changes in B that are caused by changes in C. Conversely, Stinchcombe (1987), suggests that such a chain is less effective because any intermediary terms (B, in this abstract example) are redundant and so do not represent a useful addition to the theory. Further, any such chain must ultimately rest on some unspoken assumption. Extending the abstract example, the chain of steps (A, B, C, etc.) continues until the argument reaches a point where everyone agrees that some foundational claim is "true" (perhaps Z, in this case). However, insights developed from Argyris' "ladder of inference" suggest that those underlying assumptions are not necessarily reliable guides (Senge, Kleiner, Roberts, Ross, & Smith, 1994, p. 242-243). In short, relying on unspoken assumptions may lead to folly as easily as wisdom.

The robustness of a theory may be objectively determined in a straightforward manner (for an in-depth example, see Wallis, 2008b). First, the body of theory is investigated to identify all clear propositions. Those propositions are then compared with one another to identify overlaps and redundant aspects are dropped. Second, the propositions are investigated for conceptual relatedness between the aspects described in the propositions. Those propositions that are causal in nature are conceptually linked with aspects of the theory that are resultant (each aspect may then be understood as a dimension representing a greater or lesser quantity of some aspect or phenomena). Those resultant aspects that are described by two or more causal aspects are understood to be concatenated and are considered to be more complex, more complete, and more useful than aspects that are not as complex, or as well structured.

Third, the number of concatenated aspects in the theory are divided by the total number of aspects in the theory to provide a ratio – a number between zero and one. This ratio is the robustness of the theory and represents the degree to which the theory is structured. A value of zero represents a theory with no robustness, as might be found in a bullet point list of concepts with no interrelationship between them. A theory with a value of one suggests a fully robust theory; an example is Ohm's E=IR. Because of the successful application of robust theories in math and physics, it may be expected that **a robust theory of the social science can be reliably applied in practice, and will be more easily falsifiable in the Popperian sense** (Wallis, 2008b). Metaphorically, bricks that are directly mortared to other bricks would be highly robust (as found in a structured wall or home), while bricks that are scattered about would not be robust at all. A pile of bricks would be somewhere in the middle (as a pile might have slightly more structure than scattered bricks, though far less structure than a home).

For an abstract example of determining robustness, consider a theory of five aspects (A, B, C, D, and E), each representing differentiable concepts or phenomena. The causal relationships between these aspects are suggested by two propositions: (1) A causes B; and (2) More C and more D results in more E. Of these, only E is concatenated because there are two aspects of the theory that are causal to E. Therefore, the robustness of this theory is 0.20 (the result of one concatenated aspect divided by five total aspects).

This method of propositional analysis allows us to examine a theory and assign a relatively objective measure of that theory's structure. With this method of measurement in hand, we can apply the yardstick of robustness to theories across time. And, importantly, we can determine if the robustness of the theory is increasing, decreasing, or merely wandering.

FORWARD TO REVOLUTION

According to Kuhn, a paradigmatic revolution is a situation where, "the older paradigm is replaced in whole or part by an incompatible new one" (Kuhn, 1970, p. 92). Kuhn also suggests that a scientific revolution occurs when a new paradigm emerges, one that provides a better explanation, answers more questions, and leaves fewer anomalies. Such a revolution in management is expected to bring more effective theories and practices to managers. However, Kuhn's description of revolution is problematic because it does not describe how much better the explanation must be. Nor does it describe exactly what reduction in anomalies must occur for a paradigmatic change to be considered revolutionary. There is no method of measurement. This issue was highlighted recently when Sheard (2007) framed the conversation as a contrast between superficial and profound revolution and asked, "Who decides what is 'profound'?" Yet, in his reflections, Sheard shied away from establishing a metric for delineating revolution stating that revolutions, "may be qualitatively sensed, but are not amenable to any ratio of distinction" (Sheard, 2007, p. 136).

This lack of distinction between superficiality and profundity may lead to spurious and conflicting claims for the existence of revolutionary change. Taking an example from social entrepreneurship theory, many authors agree that the act of social entrepreneurship is an important part of that theory (e.g. Austin, Stevenson, & Wei-Skillern, 2006; Bernier & Hafsi, 2007; de Leeuw, 1999; Guo, 2007; Mort, Weerawardena, & Carnegie, 2003). Yet, Fowler (2000) suggests that the focus is not so much the act of social entrepreneurship as it is the social value proposition created by that act. Is this difference between Fowler and others revolutionary? Following Kuhn's example of historical evaluation, it is impossible to know without centuries of perspective; which, in turn, renders the concept of paradigmatic revolution useless for any conversation around contemporary issues. So scholars and practitioners continue to claim revolutionary improvement without any measure of what that means. In short, claims of revolutionary theory are unsupportable because there is no clear understanding of what constitutes a revolution.

While scholars earn their pay by arguing points such as these, managers are rewarded for effectively applying those theories in practice. Academia does not seem to be producing any useful tools for today's managers; indeed, "Management research produced by academics does not fare particularly well in the marketplace of ideas that might be adopted by managers" (Pfeffer, 2007, p. 1336). Pfeffer goes on to cite the work of Mol & Bikenshaw (forthcoming) who suggest that of the 50 most important innovations in management, none of them originated in academia. He also cites Davenport & Prusak (2003) as noting that business schools "have not been very effective in the creation of *useful* business ideas" (emphasis theirs). Obviously, this does not bode well for the social sciences in general or business schools, in particular.

In short, the current paradigm of social sciences in the social sciences (in general) and management science (in particular) has not produced anything that managers can reliably apply for great effectiveness, let alone anything that might be considered revolutionary. Meanwhile, business students must wonder about the value of their tuition and managers must spend their lives without knowing what, if any, theory to apply for successful practice. This leads us to consider a challenging possibility: If we can identify a quantifiable link between management theory and paradigmatic revolution, we may be able to evaluate the usefulness of theory in terms of its potential for revolutionary implementation. That, in turn, would allow us to predict, and or instigate, a revolution in management theory.

A Working Hypothesis

An important part of a systemic perspective is to avoid looking at "things" because an improved understanding may be gained by looking at the relationships between them (Ashby, 2004; Harder, Robertson, & Woodward, 2004). The present chapter follows that suggestion by investigating the co-causal relationships between aspects within a theory in terms of that theory's robustness. Instead of looking to our empirical bricks of data, we will focus on the theoretical mortar that binds them together. The present hypothesis suggests that **revolution is enabled by the structure of the theory rather than some notion of objective data.** To investigate this idea, I will revisit Kuhn's work – investigating it from a metatheoretical perspective.

Within his descriptions of paradigm revolution, Kuhn provides several examples of revolutionary theorists and their fields of study. Among others, he mentions Coulomb (and his work in advancing electrical theory), Newton (mechanical motion), and Einstein (relativity). Each of those scientists developed the final theory – advancing his field to paradigmatic revolution. The theories developed by these exemplars of scientific revolution are similar in at least one important way. Each has a robustness of 1.0 (on a scale of zero to one). For example, Newton's F=ma has three aspects; each one concatenated from the other two. Therefore the robustness of Newton's formula is 1 (the result of three concatenated aspects divided by three total aspects).

Is it only coincidence that all these revolutionary theories have perfect robustness? If so, it seems an odd sort of combination, especially given the great differences between some areas of study. For example, who would imagine, a priori, that a theory involving electricity and a theory involving planets would have the same structure? Yet, the robustness of both theories is the same (Robustness = 1.0) as are many effective theories in physics. Such a relationship between structure and efficacy should not be too surprising because (as noted above) theories with a higher level of structure have long been expected to be more advanced. The problem, in physics and management, has been the lack of a standardized method for measuring the structure of a theory. Therefore, instead of seeking steadily higher levels of structure, management theorists were content to reach a level of logical structure deemed acceptable by the editorial/review process; there was no incentive to advance beyond that mark.

So, rather than dismiss this relationship out of hand, the following analysis suggests that there is some sort of connection between the structure of a theory and the usefulness of that theory in practice. Simply put, it is suggested that **the robustness of a theory may be understood as a key indicator of a scientific revolution**. The implication of this insight is very significant. If there is an objective approach to identifying revolutionary theory when it emerges, the development of that theory can be accelerated, thus enabling a revolution in management theory within decades instead of centuries, and, importantly, providing the attendant benefits to humanity and our understanding of our social world.

If the robustness of theory were, as hypothesized, a valid indicator of paradigmatic revolution, we would expect to see the development of a theory from low robustness to high robustness over some length of time. This expectation raises a question: How does the robustness of those theories change over time?

In choosing a body of theory to study, it should be stated here that no paradigmatic revolution has occurred in management theory. Perhaps this lack is why managers express frustration in their need for usable knowledge (Czarniawska, 2001) of the sort that would be provided by useful theories. Because of this lack, we cannot draw upon management theory for the present analysis. Therefore, we must investigate the history of some other body of theory. Because Kuhn used the example of electrical theory as part of a revolutionary paradigm, that area of theory appears to offer a reasonable area of study. And, as noted above, because the analysis is limited to the structure of the theory, the inferences drawn from EA (electrostatic attraction) theory may be transferred to the structure of management theory. Thus, for this analysis, I will investigate the evolution of EA theory and determine the level of robustness during different stages of the development of this theory. Mimicking Kuhn, for data I will draw on "The Development of the Concept of Electric Charge: Electricity from the Greeks to Coulomb" (Roller & Roller, 1954).

Analysis

In the present section, the method of propositional analysis will be applied to differing versions of the theory of electrostatic attraction as found in Roller & Roller, as that theory was understood at different points through history. The present history begins with a revolution in thinking that occurred when ancient Greeks began to explain, rather than simply describe, phenomena they encountered.

Roller & Roller present Plutarch as an example of thinking about this time. Following the example of Roller & Roller, this particular analysis includes magnetism, because, in ancient times, both magnetism and what we now understand as electrostatic attraction were believed to represent the same phenomena.

Around the year 100 CE, Plutarch wrote that lodestones (naturally occurring magnets) exhale, thus pushing the air, which would then push objects of iron (Figure 1). Amber behaved the same, except that amber needed rubbing to encourage it to exhale. The exhalations of amber would then push the air, which then would effect small objects (such as hair) instead of iron (Roller & Roller, 1954, p. 3).

Deconstructing Plutarch's theory into its essential propositions, it may be said that rubbing (amber) creates exhalations; exhalations push air;

Figure 1. Plutarchean electrostatic attraction theory

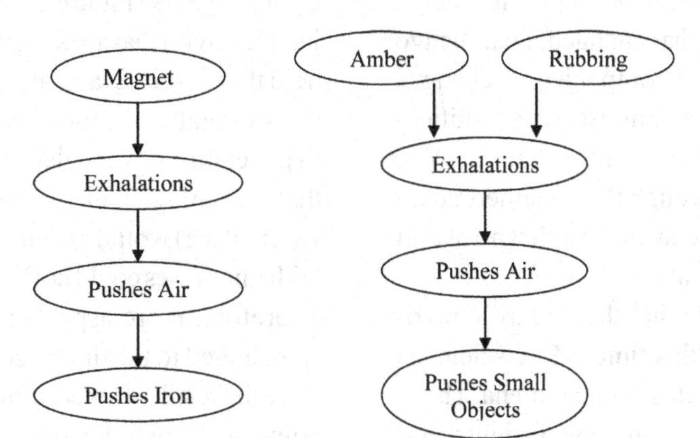

and air pushes small objects. Magnets exhale, exhalations push air, air pushes iron. In this, it may be seen that there are seven aspects of the theory (Rubbing, Amber, Magnet, Air, Iron, Push, Small objects). Magnets are causal to Push, which is causal to the movement of Air and moving Air causes Push, which is causal to the movement of Iron. In this sequence, there are four aspects and each one is the result of only one other aspect. None of them are concatenated. Indeed, Exhalations are synonymous with Push, as both appear to be a general representation of some form of force.

Instead of concatenation, the relationship between these aspects may be understood as linear (Stinchcombe, 1987, p. 132). Where, for an abstract example, it may be said that A changes B, which changes C. In such a relationship, Stinchcombe notes, the concept of B is redundant. Therefore, it may be seen that Plutarch's theory contained a redundant term by including the concept of air in the model. Redundant terms detract from the robustness of the model. Similarly, Occam's razor suggests the need for parsimony in theory construction. In these older versions of the theory, the linear relationships between multiple aspects of the theory are examples of a lack of parsimony and therefore a weakness in the structure of the theory.

In contrast to linear relationships between some aspects of the model, Rubbing and Amber, together, cause Exhalations (Push); that Push is causal to the movement of Air, which is causal to the movement of Small objects. Here, the Push may be understood as a concatenated aspect of the theory because it is caused by a combination of Rubbing and Amber.

In determining the level of robustness of this version of theory by propositional analysis, it should be noted there are seven aspects – only one of which is concatenated. The others have simple, linear, causal relationships. Therefore, the robustness of Plutarch's theory may be set at 0.14 (the result of one concatenated aspect divided by seven total aspects).

The next clear demarcation of theory surfaces in 1550. Jerome Cardan theorized that the rubbing of amber produced a liquid. And, that dry objects (such as chaff) would move toward the amber as they absorbed the liquid (Roller & Roller, 1954, p. 4, 5). Here, there are six aspects (Rubbing, Amber, Liquid, Movement, Absorption, and Dry objects). And, as with Plutarch's model, only one is concatenated (Rubbing and Amber together produce Liquid). Therefore, the robustness of Cardan's theory is 0.17 (the result of one divided by six).

Although Cardan suggests a liquid instead of Plutarch's exhalations of air, the theories are similar in their structure and level of robustness. The relationship between these theories stands as an example of how theories may appear to change because the terminology has changed. That change in terminology may be accompanied by changes in underlying assumptions, philosophical justifications, or even simple changes in speculation. Yet, looking at the theory through the metatheoretical lens of robustness, it becomes clear that no useful change has occurred at all.

Roller & Roller note that the scientific revolution took hold about this time. More scientists began to investigate electrical phenomena. Those scientists began to develop new insights and a new vocabulary to relate the results of their experiments. About this time, every important experimenter had his own theory (Kuhn, 1970, p. 13). Continued experimentation led to the discovery that objects besides amber would exhibit what is now called electrostatic attraction when they were rubbed. About 1600, Gilbert called this class of objects, "electrics."

According to Roller & Roller (1954, p. 10, 11) Gilbert's version of theory adds heat to the theory and suggests that rubbing and heat (but only heat from rubbing), and electrics, causes the release of an invisible liquid which then causes the attraction of dry objects (Figure 2). A moist barrier would interfere with that attraction. Additionally, Gilbert held that amber, glass, and gems all belonged to a class of material called "wet." So, he concluded, that wet things were electric things. Yet, he found that wet things that softened or melted (such as wax and ice) would not attract. Similarly, electrics with impurities could not be rubbed to develop EA. Therefore, more aspects and more propositions were added to the theory suggesting that electrics were the result of "wet" things with higher melting points and lower levels of impurities.

Gilbert's theory of magnetism suggested that each magnet possesses a "form" and that form would awaken a similar form in particles of iron that was near to the magnet. Indeed, he noted that the nearer the iron was to the magnet, the more mutual attraction would occur. Here, attraction may be understood as a synonym for movement.

In total, Gilbert's theory included 14 aspects (Rubbing, Heat, Electrics (objects that exhibit EA), Impurities, Melting point, Attraction, Liquid, Dry objects, Moist barriers, Magnets, Form, Awakening, Iron, Proximity). Of these, Electrics may be said to be concatenated because they

Figure 2. Gilbertian version of electrostatic attraction theory

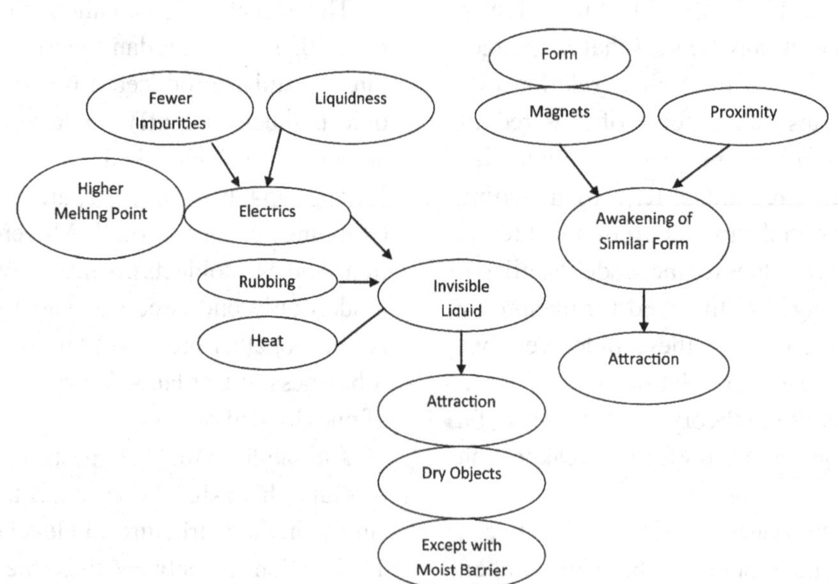

are formed with more Liquidness and fewer Impurities. Similarly, Attraction is concatenated because it is generated by more Electrics, more Rubbing, and more Heat. Additionally, it may be said that Magnets and greater Proximity results in more Awakening. Therefore, Gilbert's version of electrical theory has a robustness of 0.21 (the result of three concatenated aspects divided by 14 total aspects).

In his time, Gilbert might have claimed that his own theory of attraction explained more than Plutarch's theory. The moist barrier, for example, was not a part of Plutarch's theory. Because Gilbert's theory explains more than previous theories, today's management theorist might be tempted to claim that it represents a scientific revolution. Yet, Kuhn does not suggest that a revolution occurred until much later. This example suggests how today's general academic understanding of what constitutes a revolution is unclear, and how that lack of clarity opens the door for false claims of revolutionary advancement.

With continued experimentation, scientists generated more innovative terminology. By the mid 18th century, the "two-fluid theory" had emerged (Roller & Roller, 1954, p. 47, 48); described as:

- There are two kinds of electric fluids (vitreous & resinous).
- Unelectrified objects contain equal amounts of the two fluids.
- Rubbing an object removes one of the two electric fluids.
- More imbalance results in greater strength of electrification.
- Touching objects will cause fluid to flow from one object to another, and so de-electrify the objects as the levels of electric fluid come into balance.
- Objects with similar fluids repel one another when they are near.
- Objects with differing fluids attract one another when they are near.

In this theory, there are eleven aspects (Vitreous fluid, Resinous fluid, Objects, Rubbing, Balance, Electrification, Repulsion of objects, Attraction of objects, Flow of fluid, Touching, and Nearness). The relationships leading to concatenated aspects may be summarized as:

- Rubbing and objects decreases balance thus increasing electrification.
- Touching and electrification and objects cause flow which then increases balance and so decreases electrification.
- Objects and nearness and balance cause attraction.
- Objects and nearness and lack of balance cause repulsion.

Note that many aspects are described in terms of linear relationships. For example, Flow increases Balance which decreases Electrification. It may be seen that the four aspects of Balance, Flow, Attraction, and Repulsion are concatenated by their relationship to the other aspects. Therefore, the robustness of this theory is 0.36 (the result of four concatenated aspects divided by eleven total aspects).

The existence of many theories, and many aspects, meant that more new theories were called for thus creating, "a synthesis that serves not only to reconcile the contradictory features, but to provide explanations of a wider range of phenomena" (Roller & Roller, 1954, p. 81).

In what may be considered the final stage of development of this theory, from the perspective of Roller & Roller, Charles Coulomb developed his theory about 1785. Coulomb focused on only three aspects. Force, Electric charge, and Distance (Figure 3). He determined that the Force was equal to the Distance (squared) divided by the Charge. He also found that the Distance (squared) is equal to the Force multiplied by the Charge. And, the Charge is equal to the distance (squared) divided by the Force.

Therefore, it may be understood that each of the three aspects of Coulomb's theory is

Figure 3. Coulomb's theory of electrostatic attraction

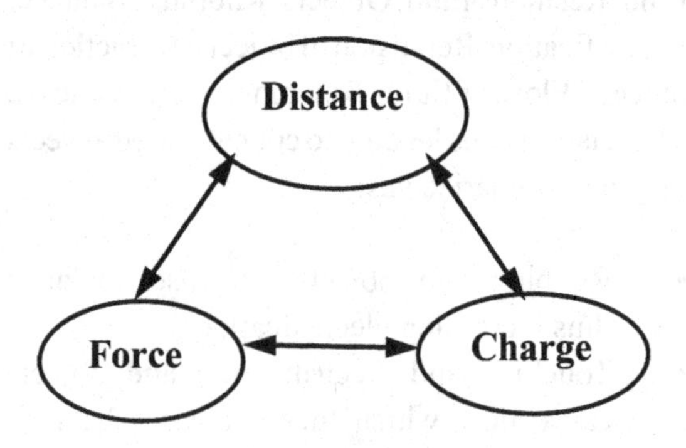

concatenated from the other two. Therefore, the robustness of Coulomb's theory is 1.0 (the result of three concatenated aspects divided by three total aspects). One benefit of developing a theory with a robustness of 1.0 was that mathematical techniques could now be used in conjunction with the experimental process. The result of this combination was revolutionary.

Discussion

The above investigation used information from Roller & Roller (1954) to benchmark the development of EA theory at five points across hundreds of years. This objective analysis used the total number of aspects for each theory, and the concatenated aspects of those theories to identify the formal robustness of each of the five theories. That information is summarized in Table 1.

The graph in figure 4 shows the variation in the total number of aspects and the number of concatenated aspects over time. Note the pre-revolutionary surge during the scientific revolution. This period of increased experimentation led scientists to suggest more aspects and to identify more relationships between those aspects. This may be understood as the time when the "scientist in crisis" is generating "speculative theories" (Kuhn, 1970, p. 87). Those theories may lead to a "critical mass" of ideas (Geisler & Ritter, 2003) and generate communities of practice (Campbell, 1983, p. 127). This peak lends validity to the idea that theory which is more complex may be considered more advanced (Ross & Glock-Grueneich, 2008).

Also, note the change in focus over time (Figure 4). Early on, the body of theory included magnetics and electrostatics because both were thought to represent the same essential effect. As time and experimentation progressed, the field of study narrowed to the study of electrostatic attraction, only. Yet, despite the narrowed focus, the number of aspects that may be said to define theory continued to increase.

The same phenomenon appears to be occurring within the social sciences. In the field of management theory, the fragmentation of the field has been reported as problematic (Donaldson, 1995); yet, that fragmentation might also be understood as a narrowing of the focus – with each fragment representing a more focused sub-field.

In Figure 5, the robustness of theories is plotted over time. Note the rapid increase in robustness on the right hand of the chart. This rise corresponds

Table 1. Summary of Aspects and Robustness of Theories

Year	Total Number of Aspects	Number of Concatenated Aspects	Robustness	Name of theorist or theory
100	7	1	0.14	Plutarch
1550	6	1	0.17	Cardan
1600	14	3	0.21	Gilbert
1750	11	4	0.36	Two Fluid theory
1785	3	3	1.0	Coulomb

with Kuhn's description of scientific revolution culminating in paradigmatic change. The asymptotic change suggests an "event horizon" or a "phase shift" beyond which a theory may be considered a law. After this point in paradigm change, the focus would not be on developing new forms of theory, rather the focus would be on conducting empirical analysis to verify and/or falsify the theory. Once verified, the focus would shift to the application of theory in practice as a useful tool. This kind of change has not been found in management theory.

The asymptote at the right-hand side of figure 5 is also suggestive of a "power curve," a vertical (or nearly so) line that stands as a diagrammatic indicator that something significant has occurred, such as a quantum increase in the capacity of a system (Kauffman, 1995). In this case, the system under consideration is the structure of a theory. The theory at the top of the curve has significant capacity for enabling action, where theories at the bottom of the curve have very limited capacity. In short, theory with higher robustness has greater capacity to support paradigmatic revolution than theories of lower robustness.

The relationship between robustness and paradigmatic revolution suggests that the robustness of a theory may be used as a milestone for marking the objective development of a theory and progress toward revolution. Similarly, the robustness of a theory may also be considered something of a predictor for such a revolution.

In addition to the relatively passive approach of tracking changes in theories developed by others, a more activist approach may also be inferred. That is to say, if a theorist works toward the purposeful creation of robust theory, she may be able to purposefully spark a paradigmatic revolution. With that opportunity, there are also limitations. For example, we should probably disregard a speculative theory that seems to represent a robust relationship if it has no basis in reality.

To conclude this section, the advancement toward robustness appears to be a useful indicator and potential instigator of paradigmatic revolution. The test of robustness might be understood as a validation of theory in the Popperian sense, although it is validation with considerably more rigor than Popper appears to have considered in his time. While validation is useful and necessary, there still remains the need to falsify those theories, as suggested by Popper (2002). In the following two sub-sections, I will investigate the implications of advancing management theory toward robustness. The first will relate more to academicians, who might be more interested in advancing management theory. The second will relate more to practitioners, who might be more interested in the application of robust theory.

Figure 4. Change in aspects over time

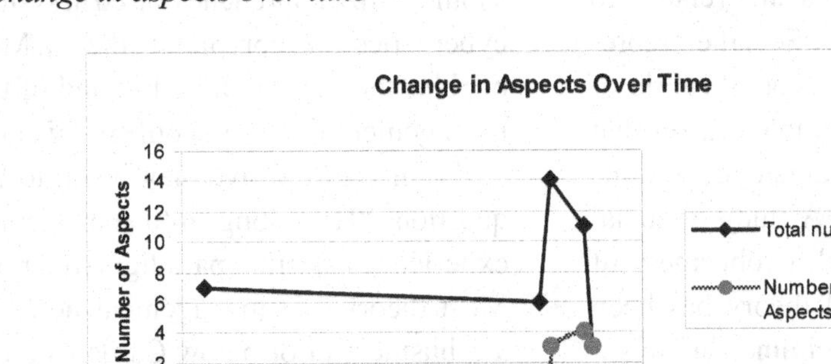

Figure 5. Robustness over time

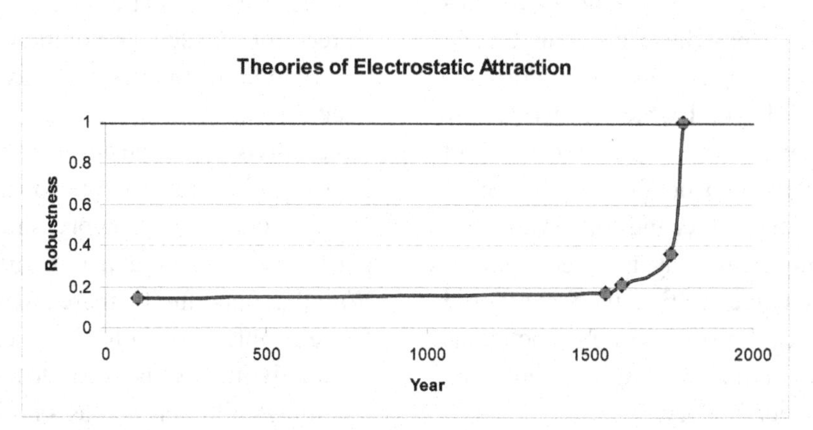

Whither Management Theory?

To date, no comprehensive test of robustness has been conducted of the field of management theory. However, some indicator of the field may be inferred from tests of robustness performed on bodies of theory from related sub-fields. In figure 6, the robustness of each of eight theories are indicated on the curve from figure 5 – the development of EA theory. By showing those theories in relation to the time required to develop EA theory to robustness, we may infer how much time might be required for each body of theory to reach a useful level of robustness. This is, of course, working under the assumption that the current paradigm of management science might follow the same trajectory as the EA theory – a question that is very much open for consideration.

Briefly, those eight studies are related to management theory as follows. Social entrepreneurship theory is part of the general rubric of management theory for the simple reason that management is sometimes understood in terms of an entrepreneurial activity. A study of social entrepreneurship theory found a robustness of 0.13 (Wallis, 2009d). Integral theory has been applied to a wide range of disciplines in the social sciences (including management). A study of integral theory found a robustness of 0.10 (Wallis, 2008c). A study of a structure of ethics found a robustness of 0.15 (Wallis, 2009f). Organizational learning theory, has been found to have a robustness of 0.16 (Wallis, 2009c). Peak performance theory has a robustness of 0.17 (Wallis, 2009e). Institutional theory is a little better with a robustness of 0.31 (Wallis, 2009b). Higher levels of robustness are found in studies related to systems theory. A study of complexity theory, as it has been applied to organizations, finds a robustness of 0.56 (Wallis, 2009a). And, a study of Complex Adaptive Systems (CAS) theory as it relates to management and organizations finds a robustness of 0.63 (Wallis, 2008b).

It should be noted that the areas of theory with the highest levels of robustness are those that are more closely related to systems theory (i.e. complexity theory and CAS theory). Therefore, it may be suggested that future studies of management should utilize approaches based in systems theory, cybernetics, and complexity theory. More studies of robustness are required in and of the field of management theory to confirm this idea.

From figure 6, we may begin to answer the question, "How long until management theory experiences a true paradigmatic revolution?" Most theories of management noted here have a robustness at or below Cardan's theory of EA (Robustness = 0.17). When Cardan presented his theory in 1550, Coulomb's revolutionary theory was a distant 235 years away. When the two-fluid

Figure 6. Robustness of some management theories

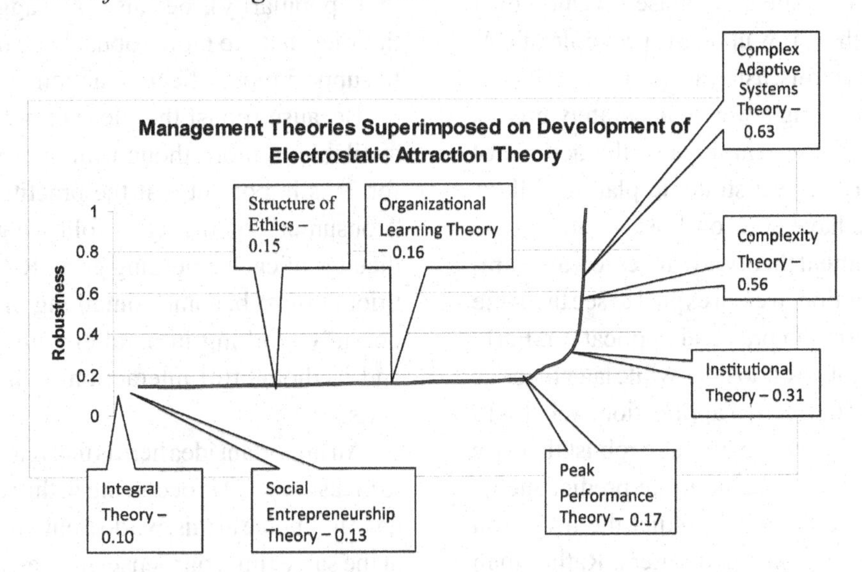

theory of electricity emerged in 1750 (R = 0.36), Coulomb's discovery was a relatively modest 35 years in the future. Some management theories today, specifically in CAS theory and complexity theory, have levels of robustness that exceed the two fluid theory, suggesting those theories might achieve revolutionary status much sooner. **Accelerating management theories toward robustness (and related revolution in improved efficacy) is important because of the depth and breadth of problems faced by practitioners.**

Linking Theory and Practice

Managers, consultants, CEOs, and all kinds of practitioners might read this chapter and ask, "What's in it for me?" In brief, then, this study suggests that theories of higher robustness are expected to be more effective in application. Further, we may now purposefully advance a theory toward robustness and so enable a paradigmatic revolution. With a paradigm revolution, improvements in theory are associated with highly effective improvements in practice.

To encapsulate an example from history, the low robust theories of EA were associated with explaining mere curiosities, such as the way that hair is attracted to amber because of exhalations. In management practice, this is like a performance management guru claiming that a stitch in time saves nine. Perhaps it is true in some metaphorical sense, but making it work in practice is entirely in the hands of the employee. Worse, there is no way to tell if these kinds of claims are actually true. This means that managers are likely relying on false information. In short, managers might be better off with no theory at all.

The EA theories of medium robustness, developed during the scientific revolution, were associated with public displays of new scientific insights – creating controlled shocks and showing how electrostatics might work under varying conditions; interesting, but of uncertain value. In management, this might be conceptually similar to conflict resolution or a facilitated organizational change process. There are successes and failures. The successes are widely touted while the failures are quietly ignored. Either way, the credit or blame might be applied to the consultant, the theory, both, or some other factor (such as a sudden change in the economy).

At the end of the scientific revolution, when the understanding of EA reached a robustness of one, it had become a very useful theory. A recent search of the US patent database revealed over 7,000 patents that draw upon the principle of EA. In management terms, using a highly robust theory would be like having a way to accurately predict the behavior of your employees, the actions of the market, or the best strategic plan to follow. Obviously, we have none of those – yet.

As management theory advances toward paradigmatic revolution, we can expect to see the same kinds of evolution in practical application. Early theories will explain curiosities while later theories may be used for effective application. What will the future look like when we have robust theories of management? We can no more predict such a future than Plutarch could predict the invention of cell phones or laptop computers. Rather than attempting to predict an incomprehensible future, this section will serve to suggest what practitioners might do in the near term to improve their use of theory and to support more effective practice.

As we know too well, the emergence of a new management guru is accompanied by the arrival of thick hardback books gracing the bookstore shelves, their covers proclaiming some "new way" to work. Their pages are packed with wisdom-filled anecdotes and careful explanations detailing exactly why the reader should adopt this new point of view. Essentially, each new book represents a new theory, a new lens that provides the thoughtful reader with a new way to see the world. Along with that new view comes the implication and/or description of new actions, policies, and behaviors the practitioner should enact to achieve success. However, implementing a new system is a difficult and expensive process. Because, as the limited success of TQM and other methods have shown, past benefits are no indicator of future success. The difficulty here is that practitioners really have no certain way of determining if that guru's approach is likely to be successful, or not. The present chapter provides some remedy, suggesting that practitioners should choose the theory with the highest level of robustness (avoiding choosing theories based only on their popularity), because, as suggested above, theories that are more robust have more capacity to support more effective action.

Because robust theories are not immediately available, a more thoughtful approach is called for. It is important that the practitioner not be a "consumer" of theory – following the faddish dictates of each emerging guru. Rather, the practitioner must become something of a researcher, possibly working in parallel with academicians and in thoughtful interaction with management texts.

An important idea here is that practitioners need to measure what is occurring in the workplace (we have no choice in this, we do it automatically) while at the same time, our sense of measurement (what we measure and how we measure it) must change. We must learn to understand the invisible things, such as morale (Dubin, 1978; van Eijnatten, van Galen, & Fitzgerald, 2003). In the development of the physical sciences, Kuhn suggests that the emergence of a new paradigm with its robust theory is accompanied by the development of new instruments for measurement (Kuhn, 1970, p. 28). However, in the study of management, no instruments currently exist for a CEO to measure (for example) the morale of her corporation. Indeed, the only instruments available to practitioners are the practitioners themselves. This "self as instrument" (McCormick & White, 2000) includes the self-identification of phenomenological reactions. **An important consideration here is how to calibrate ourselves as an instrument for effective measurement.**

Bateson (1979) suggests that the process of calibration is enhanced by the use of "double description" where multiple streams of information are combined to suggest a new, third form of information that is more useful than the previous two. Other examples of double description include binocular vision (where the extra sense of depth is added), and synaptic summation (where neuron A and neuron B must both fire to trigger neuron C). In example after example, Bateson shows how these double descriptions create an extra dimension of understanding. Importantly, this is an understanding that is of a different (and higher) logical type.

A parallel may be drawn between the structure of Bateson's approach and the structure of theory. As described above, the idea of a concatenated aspect of theory may be found in a proposition describing how aspect A and aspect B combine to understand aspect C. This understanding of aspect C through the understanding of aspects A and B suggests a greater level of understanding – a higher logical type. The parallel between the idea of double description and the idea of concatenated theory suggests that applying the two ideas in parallel might provide more benefits than either one of them alone. In short, this similarity suggests the practitioner might improve the process of self-calibration using robust theory as a guide. The validation of this idea will require additional studies.

LIMITATIONS AND OPPORTUNITIES FOR FUTURE RESEARCH

This study is limited because it examines the development of theory in only a single field – electrostatic attraction. Future studies of this type might investigate other forms of theory. For example, studies might be conducted on the evolving robustness of theories of motion, thermodynamics, and relativity. Such studies will provide additional insight into the advancement of management theory.

The present study is also limited because it presents the insights of a single researcher. Future studies may investigate the validity of the present methodology by engaging multiple researchers in parallel studies of the same body of data. It is anticipated that, procedural errors aside, the results of multiple researchers will be similar to those presented here. This kind of study would add greatly to the validity of the metatheoretical conversation and so support the advancement of theory in a useful direction.

Future research involving the testing or development of theory should include propositional analysis as an objective test for the formal robustness of theory. That way, scholars and practitioners will have a method of effectively evaluating the theory and its potential for advancement, calibration, and application. This "R" level should be indicated in the abstract of each publication.

Future studies might also investigate the robustness of management theories over time and investigate the link between robust theory and calibration. These studies will be critical to supporting paradigmatic revolutions in management. More generally, managerial scholars may best be served by abandoning (at least temporarily) the tight focus on empirical research. Rather than employ methods based on empirical perception and so-called facts, scholarship should instead focus on metatheoretical efforts to identify robust relationships between concatenated aspects of theory. Only after we have developed highly robust theories will it make sense to engage in empirical research.

Of course, such an approach is more easily said than done. As with the development of electrical theory, we might expect many arguments to emerge around the specific meaning of each aspect of the theory. However, as long as we keep in mind that each aspect should be understood only in terms of two or more other aspects of the theory, we will have a compass indicating the direction toward success in the field of management theory.

CONCLUSION

Although management science does not have theories that are highly effective in practice, we do have a boom in theory creation. In some sense, the increase in theory creation parallels the global information boom. While the business world is well acquainted with the difficulties (and opportunities) of that vast amount of information (Wytenburg, 2001), we academicians can readily retreat to our disciplinary niches (or create new ones), and so insulate ourselves from information overload. Instead of retreating, I suggest that we advance; and, in so doing, I suggest that we recalibrate our views of the world.

When we look at the vast number of management theories, we should not see a fragmented and chaotic field. Instead, from a metatheoretical vantage point, we should see a field that is rich in resources from which we can build more robust theories. Rather than focus on empirical data from direct observation, **we should use existing theories as data** to investigate and advance management theory using rigorous metatheoretical methodologies. Given that we have the pursuit of robustness as a viable direction for positive and objective advancement and that we have a huge field of theory to draw from, **my hope is that we can advance effective theories into practice on the order of years, rather than centuries.**

In the present chapter, I used propositional analysis (a metatheoretical methodology founded on principles of systems theory) to objectively investigate the development of theory over time in terms of its formal robustness. In this, I expanded our understanding of paradigmatic revolutions by developing a more detailed understanding of the role played by the structure of theory in advancing a science toward revolution. Specifically, by explicating how the achievement of fully robust theory appears to be an integral aspect of paradigmatic revolution. Importantly, with this new understanding of formal robustness, we have the opportunity to measure, and purposefully advance management theory toward paradigmatic revolution and improved efficacy.

What does it take to be an Einstein? What does it take to be a stonemason who can take a pile of bricks and turn it into a well-built house? What does it take to create a revolutionary theory that, in turn, radically alters the fabric of management life? The study presented in this chapter suggests how scholars and practitioners in the field of management may anticipate great professional success by developing and applying management theory of appropriate robustness. Without purposeful advancement, management theory can expect to remain moribund for decades or centuries – with dire implications for practitioners and management programs in universities.

REFERENCE LIST

Amsden, R. T., Ferratt, T. W., & Amsden, D. M. (1996). TQM: Core paradigm changes. *Business Horizons*, *39*(6), 6–14. doi:10.1016/S0007-6813(96)90031-2

Appelbaum, R. P. (1970). *Theories of Social Change*. Chicago: Markham.

Argyris, C. (2005). Double-loop learning in organizations: A theory of action perspective. In K. G. Smith & M. A. Hitt (Eds.), *Great Minds in Management: The Process of Theory Development* (pp. 261-279). New York: Oxford University Press.

Ashby, W. R. (2004). Principles of the self-organizing system. *Emergence: Complexity and Organization*, *6*(1-2), 103–126.

Austin, J., Stevenson, H., & Wei-Skillern, J. (2006). Social and commercial entrepreneurship: Same, different, or both? *Entrepreneurship Theory and Practice*, *30*(1), 1–22. doi:10.1111/j.1540-6520.2006.00107.x

Bartlett, J. (1992). *Familiar Quotations: A Collection of Passages, Phrases, and Proverbs Traced to their Sources in Ancient and Modern Literature* (16 ed.). Toronto: Little, Brown.

Bateson, G. (1979). *Mind in Nature: A Necessary Unity*. New York: Dutton.

Bennet, A., & Bennet, D. (2004). *Organizational Survival in the New World: The Intelligent Complex Adaptive System*. Burlington, MA: Elsevier.

Bernier, L., & Hafsi, T. (2007). The changing nature of public entrepreneurship. *Public Administration Review*, *67*(3), 488–503. doi:10.1111/j.1540-6210.2007.00731.x

Boudon, R. (1986). *Theories of Social Change* (J. C. Whitehouse, Trans.). Cambridge, UK: Polity Press.

Burrell, G. (1997). *Pandemonium: Towards a Retro-Organizational Theory*. Thousand Oaks, CA: Sage.

Campbell, D. T. (1983). Science's social system and the problems of the social sciences. In D. W. Fiske & R. A. Shweder (Eds.), *Metatheory in Social Science: Pluralism and Subjectivities* (pp. 108-135). Chicago: University of Chicago Press.

Clarke, T., & Clegg, S. (2000). Management Paradigms for the New Millennium. *International Journal of Management Reviews*, *2*(1), 45–64. doi:10.1111/1468-2370.00030

Czarniawska, B. (2001). Is it possible to be a constructionist consultant? *Management Learning*, *32*(2), 353–266. doi:10.1177/1350507601322006

Daneke, G. A. (1999). *Systemic Choices: Nonlinear Dynamics and Practical Management*. Ann Arbor, MI: The University of Michigan Press.

de Leeuw, E. (1999). Healthy cities: Urban social entrepreneurship for health. *Health Promotion International*, *14*(3), 261–269. doi:10.1093/heapro/14.3.261

Dekkers. (2008). Adapting organizations: The instance of Business process re-engineering. *Systems Research and Behavioral Science, 25*(1).

Dolan, C. (2007). *Feasability Study: The Evaluation and Benchmarking of Humanities Research in Europe*. Arts and Humanities research Council.

Donaldson, L. (1995). *American Anti-Management Theories of Organization: A Critique of Paradigm Proliferation*. New York: Cambridge University Press.

Dubin, R. (1978). *Theory Building* (Rev. Ed.). New York: The Free Press.

Edwards, M., & Volkmann, R. (2008). *Integral Theory into Integral Action: Part 8*. Retrieved 11/03/08, 2008, from http://www.integralleadershipreview.com/archives/2008-01/2008-01-edwards-volckmann-part8.html

Fiske, D. W., & Shweder, R. A. (Eds.). (1986). *Metatheory in Social Science: Pluralisms and Subjectivities*. Chicago: University of Chicago Press.

Fowler, A. (2000). NGDOS as a moment in history: Beyond aid to social entrepreneurship or civic innovation? *Third World Quarterly*, *21*(4), 637–654. doi:10.1080/713701063

Geisler, E., & Ritter, B. (2003). Differences in additive complexity between biological evolution and the progress of human knowledge. *Emergence*, *5*(2), 42–55. doi:10.1207/S15327000EM050206

Ghoshal, S. (2005). Bad management theories are destroying good management practices. *Academy of Management Learning & Education*, *4*(1), 75–91.

Glaser, B. G. (2002). Conceptualization: On theory and theorizing using grounded theory. *International Journal of Qualitative Methods*, *1*(2).

GMU. (2009). *John Nelson Warfield*. Retrieved from http://policy.gmu.edu/tabid/86/default.aspx?uid=87

Guo, K. L. (2007). The entrepreneurial health care manager: Managing innovation and change. *The Business Review, Cambridge*, *7*(2), 175–178.

Hammond, D. (2003). *The Science of Synthesis: Exploring the Social Implications of General Systems Theory*. Boulder, CO: University Press.

Harder, J., Robertson, P. J., & Woodward, H. (2004). The spirit of the new workplace: Breathing life into organizations. *Organization Development Journal*, *22*(2), 79–103.

Kaplan, A. (1964). *The Conduct of Inquiry: Methodology for Behavioral Science*. San Francisco: Chandler Publishing Company.

Kauffman, S. (1995). *At Home in the Universe: The Search for Laws of Self-Organization and Complexity*. New York: Oxford University Press.

Kuhn, T. (1970). *The Structure of Scientific Revolutions* (2nd ed.). Chicago: The University of Chicago Press.

Lachmann, R. (Ed.). (1991). *The Encyclopedic Dictionary of Sociology* (4 ed.). The Dushkin Publishing Group.

Lewis, M. W., & Grimes, A. J. (1999). Metatriangulation: Building theory from multiple paradigms. *Academy of Management Review*, *24*(4), 627–690. doi:10.2307/259348

Maanen, J. V., Sørensen, J. B., & Mitchell, T. R. (2007). The interplay between theory and method. *Academy of Management Review*, *32*(4), 1145–1154.

MacIntosh, R., & MacLean, D. (1999). Conditioned emergence: A dissipative structures approach to transformation. *Strategic Management Journal*, *20*(4), 297. doi:10.1002/(SICI)1097-0266(199904)20:4<297::AID-SMJ25>3.0.CO;2-Q

McCormick, D. W., & White, J. (2000). Using One's Self as an Instrument for Organizational Diagnosis. *Organization Development Journal*, *18*(3), 49–63.

McKelvey, B. (2002). Model-centered organization science epistemology. In J. A. C. Baum (Ed.), *Blackwell's Companion to Organizations* (pp. 752-780). Thousand Oaks, CA: Sage.

Meehl, P. E. (2002). Cliometric metatheory: II. Criteria scientists use in theory appraisal and why it is rational to do so. *Psychological Reports*, *91*, 339–404. doi:10.2466/PR0.91.6.339-404

Mintzberg, H. (2005). Developing theory about the development of theory. In K. G. Smith & M. A. Hitt (Eds.), *Great Minds in Management: The Process of Theory Development* (pp. 355-372). Oxford, UK: Oxford University Press.

Morgan, G. (1996). *Images of Organizations*. Thousand Oaks, CA: Sage.

Mort, G. S., Weerawardena, J., & Carnegie, K. (2003). Social entrepreneurship: Towards conceptualisation. *International Journal of Nonprofit and Voluntary Sector Marketing*, *8*(1), 76–88. doi:10.1002/nvsm.202

Nickles, T. (2009). *Scientific Revolutions*. Retrieved 04/23/2009, 2009, from http://plato.stanford.edu/entries/scientific-revolutions/

Nonaka, I. (2005). Managing organizational knowledge: Theoretical and methodological foundations. In K. G. Smith & M. A. Hitt (Eds.), *Great Minds in Management: The Process of Theory Development* (pp. 373-393). New York: Oxford University Press.

Olson, E. E., & Eoyang, G. H. (2001). *Facilitating Organizational Change: Lessons From Complexity Science*. San Francisco: Jossey-Bass/Pfeiffer.

Pfeffer, J. (2007). A modest proposal: How we might change the process and product of managerial research. *Academy of Management Journal, 50*(6), 1334–1345.

Popper, K. (2002). *The Logic of Scientific Discovery* (J. F. Karl Popper, L. Freed, Trans.). New York: Routledge Classics.

Ritzer, G. (2001). *Explorations in Social Theory: From Metatheorizing to Rationalization*. London: Sage.

Roller, D., & Roller, D. H. D. (1954). *The Development of the Concept of Electric Charge: Electricity from the Greeks to Coulomb* (Vol. 8). Cambridge, MA: Harvard University Press.

Ross, S. N., & Glock-Grueneich, N. (2008). Growing the field: The institutional, theoretical, and conceptual maturation of "public participation," part 3: Theoretical maturation. *International Journal of Public Participation, 2*(1), 14–25.

Schön, D. A. (1991). *The Reflective Turn: Case Studies In and On Educational Practice*. New York: Teachers Press.

Senge, P., Kleiner, K., Roberts, S., Ross, R. B., & Smith, B. J. (1994). *The Fifth Discipline Fieldbook: Strategies and Tools for Building a Learning Organization*. New York: Currency Doubleday.

Shareef, R. (2007). Want better business theories? Maybe Karl Popper has the answer. *Academy of Management Learning & Education, 6*(2), 272–280.

Sheard, S. (2007). Devourer of our convictions: Populist and academic organizational theory and the scope and significant of the metaphor of 'revolution'. *Management and Organizational history, 2*(2), 135-152.

Shotter, J. (2004). *Dialogical Dynamics: Inside the Moment of Speaking*. Retrieved June 18, 2004, from http://pubpages.unh.edu/~jds/thibault1.htm

Skinner, Q. (1985). Introduction. In Q. Skinner (Ed.), *The Return of Grand Theory in the Human Sciences* (pp. 1-20). New York: Cambridge University Press.

Smith, K. G., & Hitt, M. A. (Eds.). (2005). *Great Minds in Management: The Process of Theory Development*. Oxford, UK: Oxford University Press.

Smith, M. E. (2003). Changing an organisation's culture: correlates of success and failure. *Leadership and Organization Development Journal, 24*(5), 249–261. doi:10.1108/01437730310485752

Southerland, J. W. (1975). *Systems: Analysis, administration, and archetectura*. New York: Van Nostrand.

Stacey, R. D., Griffin, D., & Shaw, P. (2000). *Complexity and Management: Fad or Radical Challenge to Systems Thinking*. New York: Routledge.

Stapleton, I., & Murphy, C. (2003). Revisiting the Nature of Information Systems: The Urgent Need for a Crisis in IS Theoretical Discourse. *Transactions of International Information Systems, 1*(4).

Starbuck, W. H. (2003). Shouldn't organization theory emerge from adolescence? *Organization, 10*(3), 439–452. doi:10.1177/13505084030103005

Steier, F. (1991). *Research and Reflexivity*. London: Sage Publications.

Steingard, D. S. (2005). Spiritually-Informed Management Theory: Toward Profound Possibilities for Inquiry and Transformation. *Journal of Management Inquiry, 14*(3), 227–241. doi:10.1177/1056492605276841

Stinchcombe, A. L. (1987). *Constructing Social Theories*. Chicago: University of Chicago Press.

Sutton, R. I., & Staw, B. M. (1995). What theory is not. *Administrative Science Quarterly, 40*(3), 371–384. doi:10.2307/2393788

Van de Ven, A. H. (2007). *Engaged Scholarship: A Guide for Organizational and Social Research*. Oxford, UK: Oxford University Press.

van Eijnatten, F. M., van Galen, M. C., & Fitzgerald, L. A. (2003). Learning dialogically: The art of chaos-informed transformation. *The Learning Organization, 10*(6), 361–367. doi:10.1108/09696470310497203

Wallis, S. E. (2006a, July 13, 2006). *A sideways look at systems: Identifying sub-systemic dimensions as a technique for avoiding an hierarchical perspective.* Paper presented at the International Society for the Systems Sciences, Rohnert Park, CA.

Wallis, S. E. (2006b). *A Study of Complex Adaptive Systems as Defined by Organizational Scholar-Practitioners.* Unpublished Theoretical Dissertation, Fielding Graduate University, Santa Barbara.

Wallis, S. E. (2008a). Emerging order in CAS theory: Mapping some perspectives. *Kybernetes, 38*(7).

Wallis, S. E. (2008b). From Reductive to Robust: Seeking the Core of Complex Adaptive Systems Theory. In A. Yang & Y. Shan (Eds.), *Intelligent Complex Adaptive Systems*. Hershey, PA: IGI Publishing.

Wallis, S. E. (2008c). *The integral puzzle: Determining the integrality of integral theory.* Retrieved 07/14, 2008, from http://www.integralworld.net/wallis.html

Wallis, S. E. (2008d). Validation of theory: Exploring and reframing Popper's worlds. *Integral Review, 4*(2), 71–91.

Wallis, S. E. (2009a). The Complexity of Complexity Theory: An Innovative Analysis. *Emergence: Complexity and Organization, 11*(4).

Wallis, S. E. (2009b). *From reductive to robust: Seeking the core of institutional theory.* Under submission - available upon request.

Wallis, S. E. (2009c). Seeking the robust core of organizational learning theory. *International Journal of Collaborative Enterprise, 1*(2). doi:10.1504/IJCENT.2009.029288

Wallis, S. E. (2009d). Seeking the Robust Core of Social Entrepreneurship Theory. In J. A. Goldstein, J. K. Hazy & J. Silberstang (Eds.), *Social Entrepreneurship & Complexity*. Litchfield Park, AZ: ISCE Publishing.

Wallis, S. E. (2009e). *Theory of peak performance theory.* Under submission - available upon request.

Wallis, S. E. (2009f). *Towards a robust systemization of Gandhian ethics*. Under submission - available upon request.

Weick, K. E. (2005). The experience of theorizing: Sensemaking as topic and resource. In K. G. Smith & M. A. Hitt (Eds.), *Great Minds in Management: The Process of Theory Development* (pp. 394-413). New York: Oxford University Press.

Weisbord, M. R. (1987). *Productive Workplaces: Organizing and Managing for Dignity, Meaning, and Community*: Jossey-Bass.

Wheatley, M. J. (1992). *Leadership and the New Science*. San Francisco: Barrett-Koehler.

Wytenburg, A. J. (2001). Bracing for the future: Complexity and computational ability in the knowledge era. *Emergence, 3*(2), 113–126. doi:10.1207/S15327000EM0302_08

Yolles, M. (2006). Knowledge cybernetics: A new metaphor for social collectives. *Organizational Transformation and Social Change, 3*(1), 19–49. doi:10.1386/jots.3.1.19/1

Section 3
Cybernetics and Organizational Evaluation

Chapter 10
The Dynamic Usage of Models (DYSAM) as a Theoretically-Based Phenomenological Tool for Managing Complexity and as a Research Framework

Gianfranco Minati
Italian Systems Socety, Polytechnic University of Milan, Italy

ABSTRACT

In this paper, after recalling some fundamental concepts used in the science of complexity, we focus on theoretical and applicative cases of interest for the science of management of complex systems, where processes of emergence occur with the acquisition of new properties. The tool proposed is the DYnamical uSAge of Models (DYSAM). Within this framework we then focus upon a) the theoretical difference between growth and development; b) the sustainability of development rather than of growth as originally introduced in the literature; c) the concept of long tail (when, after initial large volume sales, low-revenue and infrequent buying may become a very important percentage of the entire business) as in telecommunications and management of long-tailed systems; d) non-reductionist management of complexity not reduced to solutions, and e) a future line of research to model processes of emergence.

INTRODUCTION

The Science of complexity or *Nonlinear Science* introduced a variety of approaches providing a conceptual framework for modeling and studying complexity in Management.

In the first section we introduce the concepts of the constructivist role of the observer, the theory of *logical openness,* the concept of *coherence,* Multiple Systems and Collective Beings, and DYnamical uSAge of Models (DYSAM). Those concepts allow one to introduce the reader, in the second section, to discussions of new, possible and concrete approaches such as the Dynamic Usage of Models (DYSAM) dealing with the difference between growth and development, and the concept of *Long Tail* in business. Third and fourth sections refer specifically to sustainability and the peculiari-

DOI: 10.4018/978-1-61520-668-1.ch010

ties in the management of complexity. Fifth and sixth sections present distinctions between the management of complex and non-complex phenomena. Seventh section presents a possible line of future research as introduced in the literature. The Appendix introduces precise definitions of Linear, Linearization and Approximation for the reader. This paper focuses upon new theoretical approaches for dealing with and modeling complex systems as well as processes of the acquisition of new properties.

BACKGROUND

Various approaches have been introduced in the literature for dealing with *complex systems* intended as systems where processes of self-organization or, better, emergence occur leading to the acquisition of new properties.

Indeed, systems do not only *possess* properties, but are also able to *acquire*, i.e., make emergent, new ones. Examples of the emergence of systemic properties in complex systems are a) the acquisition of properties such as collective learning abilities in social systems such as flocks, swarms, markets, firms, industrial districts and, in physics, superconductivity and lasers; b) behavior in natural and artificial systems; and c) functionalities in networks of computers (e.g., the Internet). We focus upon some crucial aspects to be necessarily considered in modeling such phenomena and the importance of *managing social complex systems*. The aspects considered are:

The Constructivistic Role of the Observer

In the scientific literature systems are traditionally described as entities established by interacting elements able to *acquire* in an *objectivist way*, i.e. observer independent, properties which their component elements do not possess. The *necessary and sufficient conditions* for establishing this phenomenon is assumed to be that elements as *designed* (for artificial systems) or *represented* (for natural systems) by the observer, interact in a suitable way, for instance when an electronic device acquires properties, i.e., functionalities, when *powered on* allowing individual electronic components to interact.

Moreover, two conceptually different cases may be considered (Guberman & Minati, 2007):

a) Systems are considered *as given* in an *objectivist* way when they are artificially designed, i.e., the component parts and how they interact are known in advance because they are designed in a certain way.
b) Systems considered in a *constructivist* way include natural systems, i.e., which have not been artificially designed. In this case the observer decides upon a suitable level of description to be applied (i.e., by considering what should be considered as components and interactions) to the systems, *as if they had been designed as such*. Observers constructively model phenomena *as systems* (Butts & Brown, 1989; von Glasersfeld, 1995).

In this view, the observer becomes generator of *cognitive existence*, i.e., the observer does not distinguish between model and *real* system. In this case, the system *is* the model and is a cognitive strategy. The question is *how is it more effective to think that something is* (the model), rather than to try to find out *what it really is* (the latter case is a particular case of the former).

The observer is theoretically part of the phenomenon itself as for a) *uncertainty principles* based on the model and the level of description adopted; b) cognitive science when science studies itself; and c) *second order cybernetics* when the system is not only able to *regulate* itself by using rules, but also by *producing* new rules, for instance, through learning.

Table 1. Example of a hierarchy of logically open models

Level of openness	Example of a hierarchy of logically open models when considering systems able to send and receive information.
1	It corresponds to the classic thermodynamic level where matter and energy are able to cross system's border. This may be the case where systems are able to send and receive signals, but not to attribute or process meaning. An example is given when two or more people may physically exchange words with no common understanding because they speak different languages. In the same ways computers may physically exchange messages between each other but have not the software able to process them.
2	At this level the meaning of messages is assumed to be identical and constant between sender and receiver. The process of interacting is assumed to be context-independent. This is the classical approach based on objectivism. Examples are rules, instructions, and formal language for programming.
3	At this level the process of interacting is assumed to be context-sensitive with reference to the sending/receiving systems. Each system generates a model of the other having *learning capabilities* and the communication process is activated between models. Examples are the interactions between teacher and student, seller and buyer, physician and patient, user and information systems able to process users' profiles. It is also what usually goes on between corresponding agents via electronic mail in the Internet whom never met in person.
4	At this level during the communication process the systems exchange not only messages, but also information about their context: the process of interacting is assumed to be context-sensitive with reference to the sending/receiving agents and to their environment. Messages are semantically processed with continuous reciprocal modeling of systems and of their context. A typical example occurs when two agents are negotiating in different times, having the possibility of influencing their contexts.
5	At this level the system may *decide* which of the previous level of openness to adopt depending on a strategy and on contextual evaluation. The possibility to dynamically *decide* which level of openness to adopt may be realized as the highest level of openness. Each level of openness includes the *possibility* to assume the previous one.

The Theory of Logical Openness

Logical Openness is conceptually different from classical *thermodynamic openness* (Minati *et al.*, 1998; Minati & Pessa, 2006) dealing with the exchange of matter and energy. *Logical Openness* relates to the constructivist role of the observer generating *n-levels* of models (meta-modeling) by:

- adopting *n* different *levels of description*, i.e., disciplinary knowledge used, scalarity, nature of variables and interaction considered, micro, macro or mesoscopic level.
- simultaneously *representing* one level through another allowing *decisions*, for instance, through correspondences and simulations;
- Simultaneously *considering* more than one level as in the Dynamic Usage of Models (DYSAM).

Logical openness relates to the theoretically active role of the observer self-generating and simultaneously using several levels of description rather than selecting a single one considered as the best among available choices.

It is possible to introduce a hierarchy of logically open models based on suitable *openness levels*. Examples of a hierarchy of this kind, within the context of social systems and with reference, for instance, to education and to cognitive processing of information, may be the following in table 1.

Other examples are also given when interaction among people takes place by using different kinds of technologies are listed in table 2.

The hierarchy of the levels of openness before illustrated and the related possibilities of closeness are synthesized within the following table 3.

We just mention the relationships with *emergence* and the *Dynamic Usage of Models (DYSAM)*, introduced in (Minati and Pessa, 2006). Common to all the subjects is the crucial role of

Table 2. Example of a hierarchy of logically open models when interacting agent use different technologies

Levels of Openness	Example of a hierarchy of logically open models when interaction among people takes place by using different kinds of technologies, by allowing:
1	One way interaction with no model of the receiver or real time feedback; for instance a book writer.
2	One way interaction with no model of the receiver but with real time feedback; for instance a theater actor.
3	Two ways interaction with no model of the receiver; for instance selling by telephone/TV or Internet.
4	Two ways interaction with a model of the receiver; for instance private direct selling.
5	Two ways interaction with a model of the receiver and of its context; for instance business marketing through sales managers, etc.

the *observer producing and using models*. We may figure out a complete theory of emergence as one able to model processes and observer as a unique entity. In the same way a complete theory of openness and of dynamical usage of models may be supposed as a theorization of processes, models and user in an integrated way. *The very first step should be the definition and assumption of a language able to* ***only*** *express such integration.* We still use descriptions and languages based on dividing, on considering as separated the process and the observer.

The Concept of Coherence

Coherence is a concept used within various disciplines: a) in physics the coherence of two waves relates to how well they are correlated as quantified by the cross-correlation function allowing prediction of the value of the second wave from the value of the first; b) in philosophy by considering consistency, non-contradictoriness and robustness of concepts; c) in cognitive science by considering systems of cognitive processes allowing the emergence of properties such as vision, learning and making cognitive inferences; d) in linguistics with reference to semantics; and e) for *long-range correlations* in different disciplinary fields. In our case, coherence, as for the *binding problem* and *collective behavior*, is considered as the dynamic establishment of and maintaining a property *continuously* established by interacting components (see, for instance, Mikhailov & Calenbuhr, 2002 for an overview of models of

Table 3. Levels of openness/closeness

Levels of openness	Related levels of closeness
1. Thermodynamic level: crossing of matter-energy borders of the system	No crossing of matter/energy borders of the system
2. Meaning assumed identical between sender and receiver	Crossing of matter/energy borders of the system, but no common meaning between sender and receiver
3. Interacting systems produce mutual context-sensitive models: systems have learning capabilities	Meaning assumed identical between sender and receiver, but the systems do not produce mutual context-sensitive models and have not learning capabilities
4. Interactive systems produce dynamic mutual context-sensitive models: systems have learning capabilities	Interacting systems produce mutual, but not dynamic context-sensitive models: systems have learning capabilities
5. The system may continuously decide which level to use in interacting	Interactive systems produce dynamic mutual context-sensitive models, systems have learning capabilities, but they cannot decide which level to use in interacting

complex coherent actions related to processes of self-organization).

Coherence is the *identity*, the *property of properties* of collective phenomena as modeled by the observer. Non-systemic properties, such as weight, age and geometrical values may be considered *observer independent*. Systemic properties such as adaptability, autopoiesis, chaoticity and openness are considered as being continuously acquired by phenomena modeled as a system by the observer, i.e., as coherent phenomena (*how can one realize, or detect coherence?*).

Multiple Systems and Collective Beings

A Multiple System (MS) is a set of systems established, or modeled as such, by the *same* components interacting in *different* ways, i.e., having multiple simultaneous or dynamical roles (Minati, 2006a; Minati & Pessa, 2006).

The same interacting components may establish different systems at different times (i.e., simultaneously or dynamically).

Examples of MSs are a) virtual corporations, i.e., networked corporations establishing systems activated on demand; b) networked interacting computer systems performing cooperative tasks as on the Internet; and c) electricity networks in *systems engineering* (an unfortunate emergent property is the black-out) where different systems play different roles in continuously new, emerging usages. Collective Beings (CBs) are particular cases of MSs established by agents possessing a (natural or artificial) cognitive system. In this case, the multiple roles are *active*, i.e., *decided* by the composing autonomous agents. Agents are considered to interact by simultaneously or dynamically using the *same* or *different* cognitive models in the model constructivistically designed by the observer. Examples are *Human Social Systems* when:

(a) agents *simultaneously generate* and *belong to* different systems (e.g., behave as buyers in a market *and* components of communities such as mobile telephone networks *and* families *and* traffic systems *and* workplaces);
(b) agents may *dynamically* give rise to different systems, such as temporary communities (e.g., an audience, passengers on trains or in queues), at different times and without considering multiple belonging.

MSs and CBs should be not confused with sub-systems having specific roles. Concepts of MSs and CBs allow one to realize how managing one has no functional *consequences* on the other, as for subsystems, but rather *influences* elements and interactions *while* establishing another system. This calls for *multiple management* allowing, for instance, the possibility of manipulation (Minati, 2004; 2006b).

The DYnamical uSAge of Models (DYSAM)

DYSAM (Minati & Brahms, 2002; Minati & Pessa, 2006) as meta-modeling, i.e., modeling models, is based on strategies to select, invent and use models for decision making. DYSAM is based on strategies using *independent* and *irreducible* models as in well-established approaches such as the Bayesian method, Ensemble Learning, Evolutionary Game Theory, Machine Learning and Pierce's abduction (Minati, 2007). Models may be corporate models, theories of management, approaches and methodologies used, for instance, with industrial districts when business relationships are *simultaneously* competitive *and* cooperative (Axelrod, 1997; Dei Ottati, 1994) as in the notion of "co-opetition" (Brandenburger & Nalebuff, 1997), and soft-systems methodologies (Checkland & Scholes, 1990) with their specific level of description. While pragmatism is *event-driven*, DYSAM is *theoretically observer-driven*. The conceptual difference lies in the effectiveness

Figure 1. Conceptual schema of DYSAM

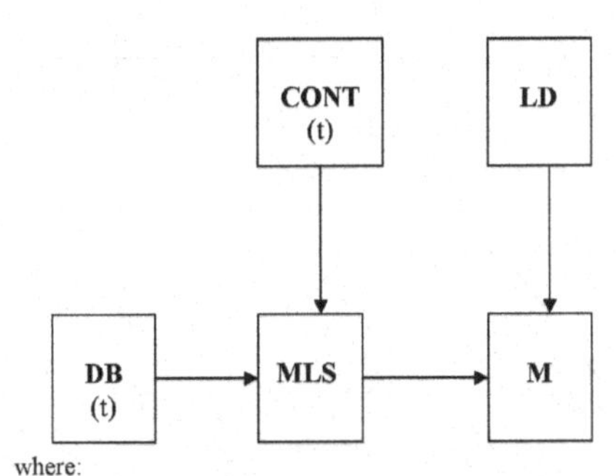

where:

- DB(t) - evolving data base of interconnected models mutually represented by a meta-language, a trained Neural Networks, etc.
- CONT (t) – dynamic context information
- MLS- model proposed for the current activity
- LD - Levels of description considered over time
- M - Dynamic Usage of Models

of *coherence between models*, i.e., systems of models. Approaches DYSAM-like are used, for instance:

a. in generic medicine when testing multiple pharmacological treatments to cope with an illness not exactly diagnosed or dealing with unexpected side effects and simultaneously considering the psychological, biological and chemical levels of description;
b. when modeling biological systems, like the brain, as quantistic or not;
c. for the use of surviving resources in damaged systems (i.e., in case of disabilities managing balancing and compensation);
d. for learning the use of the five sensory modalities in the evolutionary age for children not having the purpose to choose the *best* one, but to use all of them together;
e. when modeling the multiple disciplinary knowledge used by the observer dealing with a phenomenon.

For instance, the crying of a human being may be represented as physical *or* chemical *or* biological *or* psychological process. The problem is not to select *the best* approach once for all, but all of them simultaneously by using the meta-knowledge related to the mutual representations of levels of knowledge, e.g., chemical effects of psychological phenomena, psychological effects of physical phenomena, biological effects of chemical phenomena, etc. The approach is based on using and rather than or.

A general, conceptual schema of DYSAM is presented in figure 1.

DYSAM may be intended as a methodology to use available resources in *new ways* as discussed later.

An introductory model and simulation of DYSAM based on Neural Networks is available (Minati & Pessa, 2006, pp. 75-88).

Complex systems cannot be suitably represented by linear (see Appendix) combinations of systems. Complex systems cannot be managed as linear systems or as their linear combination because linearity excludes processes of emergence, i.e., the acquisition of new properties to be managed.

DYSAM FROM GROWTH TO DEVELOPMENT

Growth

The concept of growth (Minati & Pessa, 2006) relates to the *quantitative increase* in the values of variables with time.

Figure 2. The logistic curve for population growth

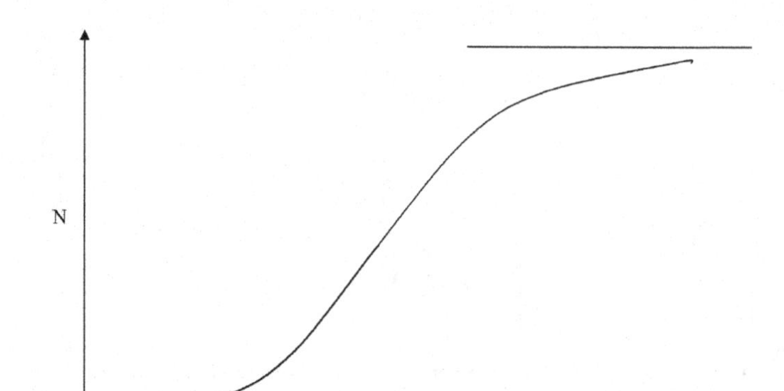

This process may occur in various ways, such as, in the case of a variable x, exponential, x^k, factorial $x!$, or kx. Between processes having *continuous positive* quantitative increases, we can consider processes having *decreasing but always positive* quantitative increases. This is the case for so-called logistic growth or a logistic curve or logistic function as introduced by the Belgian mathematician P. Verhulst (1804-1849) in the study of population growth with limited resources (Bradley, 2007). Taking P as the number of elements of a population having limited resources to reproduce, its growth over time t is described in general by the equation $P(t) = 1 / 1 + e^{-t}$. A graphical example showing the dependence upon boundary conditions such as reproduction rates for the population and resources is given in figure 2.

In the first stage there is an *increasing* process of growth whereas in the second case there is a *decreasing* processes of increasing. It describes a typical process of the saturation of markets. The logistic function is applied to model processes of growth in various disciplinary fields such as biology and economics.

Development

The process of development is conceptually very different from that of growth even though they are often considered as being coincident. Within the framework of this conceptual misunderstanding, development may be considered, for instance, as a *sequence* of processes of growth, successive ones starting from the decreasing increase of the previous one as shown in figure 3.

The process of development relates to the *evolution* of a system over time. In particular, it relates to the acquisition of subsequent emergent properties over time. Such a process is considered positively and as a development by the observer when it fits a suitable model, otherwise it may be considered negatively, for instance, as degenerative, deviant, unstable and chaotic. Systemically, development relates to the maintaining of properties such as a) suitable relations between processes, such as proportions and respecting limits, b) sustainable, consumption of resources, c) avoidance of contradictions, d) coherence, e) autopoiesis, f) ability to self-regulate, and g) ability to react against negative actions trying to destroy the process of development itself.

Figure 3. Development as a sequence of processes of growth

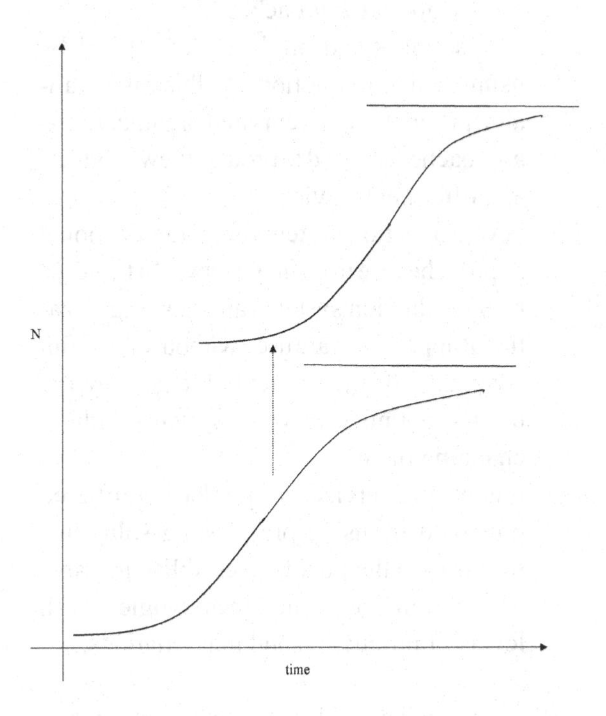

This definition applies, for instance, to biological, economical and social systems. *A common misunderstanding is to assume that processes enabling the system considered to develop must* continuously *grow*.

Development may be intended as a series of coherent processes maintaining evolutionary activity.

Examples are given by considering development as a property adopted by biological systems through evolutionary ages, as in childhood, and by economic systems such as corporations when acquiring increasing profitability is considered as a systemic emergent property of various departments such as production, delivery, financial, marketing, R&D, and human resource management. In this case processes establishing the system acquiring developmental properties may not all be quantitatively increasing.

Moreover, some processes may quantitatively decrease to sustain coherence.

The challenge is to *transform* processes and not only to increase them. Transformation may occur, for instance, through technological and organizational innovation, and emergence in such a way as to keep and improve the acquisition of evolutionary properties in spite of having reached quantitative limits.

Development relates to the quantitative and structural growth of acquired evolutionary properties often confused, through the adoption of a reductionistic approach, with the quantitative increases in the necessary composing processes.

DYSAM for Development

Development requires coherence acquired, for instance, through a Dynamic Usage of Models rather than an unlimited growth of each *process*. Traditional approaches focusing on identifying the *best* approach may be considered as *particular cases*.

This conceptual framework is suitable for further theoretical developments dealing with coherence between models; processes of dynamic selection amongst models; relation with the level of description adopted; structuring available models, i.e., their interdependence; constructivistic invention and validation (not reducible to simulation as in Agent-Based Models - ABMs). Our proposal is that theories of management should consider this dynamic framework as not being reducible to single or static combinations of approaches insufficient by definition for dealing with complexity, i.e., the continuous acquisition of new properties through processes of emergence. Management of non-complex systems is a particular case when dynamic models may be reduced to a single one, as when dealing with the optimization and design of linear systems.

DYSAM relates to networked *simultaneous* multi-modeling. While multiple-modeling may be intended as considering the same problem from different points of view, for instance legal,

Figure 4. logistic curve and related evolutionary events

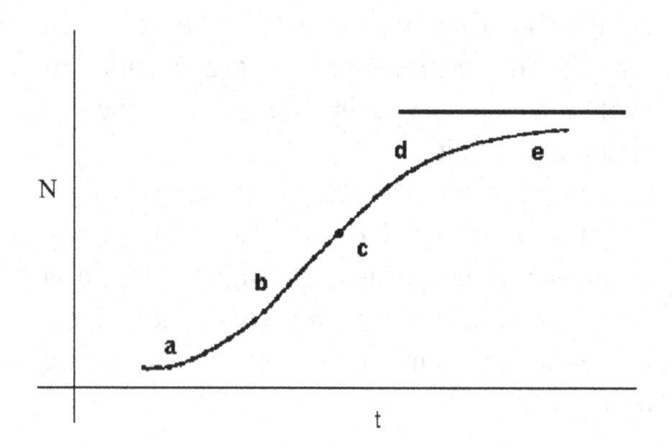

economic or organizational, DYSAM relates to considering:

- The inter-relations between different models used for the same problem;
- The multiple, simultaneous and inter-related modeling of the subsequent, continuous process of acquisition of emergent properties.

This is the case for *development* as a systemic, emergent, acquired property to be continuously multi-modeled through DYSAM to be managed, i.e., sustained, continuously redefined, and evolutionarily oriented.

We may consider processes of growth as *life-cycles*, as in figure 4.

We may consider a logistic curve as the place where the following kinds of events occur with sequential continuity:

a. *pre-existing services and products are offered by using new solutions:* In this case the goal is to produce or offer new services more efficiently by using more advanced technologies and organizational approaches;
b. *new services and products are offered by using new solutions:* In this case the goal is to produce new products or offer new services by using new advanced technologies and organizational approaches;
c. new services and products are offered by using available solutions: In this case available production systems and organizational approaches are used to produce new products and offer new services;
d. new production systems and organizational approaches are used in old ways: In this case new production systems and new organizational approaches are used without taking full advantage of their potential, e.g., they are used to optimize previous systems without changing them;
e. pre-existing services and products are offered produced by using pre-existing solutions: In this case the goal is to establish massive use of well-established technologies, high levels of production and mass markets.

We may consider the case when point ***e*** is reached. One non-systemic solution is to try to *move the asymptote up the more as possible.* This is the case for mass markets when trying to *artificially* improve consumption. *This is a very expensive strategy subtracting resources to the establishment of new markets.*

Besides it is not strategic at all. *The reductionistic idea is to improve consumption to sustain corporations rather having corporations to serve social needs materialized in acquired emergent properties such as markets.*

DYSAM is a methodology, a way of thinking to be used to adopt another conceptual framework where a development different from a perpetuation of the existing one be possible.

Dealing with crisis and paraphrasing Foerster, if a given phenomenon looks strange, or unexpected or difficult to be managed this means that the theoretical framework used to model this phenomenon is inappropriate. We need to find a more general one containing the crisis as obvious and new possible scenarios.

This approach is the one of the second-order cybernetics no more focused on self-regulating, but on the process of inventing new rules such as in cognitive systems when learning and making logical inferences like abductions.

DYSAM allows to move far from the classic *if you have a hammer, everything is a nail* when inventing new configurations, like assembling by using the glue, tying, whole pieces, making pieces assembled for other reasons, and self-assembling of materials. We consider different usages, different configurations –cases a), and b)- rather than new tools to do the same –cases c), d), and e)-.

Ford invented to increase remunerations of his workers to allow them to buy cars: we still use the same approaches. War is another source of business during crisis.

Can we invent something more intelligent like making *ethics as quality* (Minati, 2002), education, green technologies, and peace, all economically *more profitable*? We may try to *effectively*, i.e. not for political or ideological reasons but because of profitability, apply ideas such as ones in (Daly, 1996; Georgescu-Roegen, 1971; 1976; 1977a; 1977b; 1979).

We conclude this section with some practical examples of applications of DYSAM to management of some markets. This relates *to make or maintain development as emergent property acquired by a system*. We will consider markets like tourism, fashion and building activity of architecture.

In the first case the property to be tourist for a place is a complex emergent property. Process of growth cannot be effectively considered for tourism without considering it emerging from a variety of independent processes like natural resources, cultural heritages, accommodation, transportation system, linguistic barriers, social safety, information system, how expensive is life for tourists, and collateral interests. Tourism is not the sum of all these different businesses. Only managing them in an integrated and dynamic model may allow the emergent property to be sustained.

In the second case the property to be *fashion products* is a complex emergent property. The property emerges from a variety of independent processes like quality of cloth, colors, model dress, price, duration, and homogeneity with different aspects related, for instance, to functionality –work, cars, dancing-, suitability with social values and religion, stereotypes of beauty, and climatic conditions. Fashion is complex transformation of such aspects in products and, conversely, a way to induce new aspects. Fashion is a dynamical use of all those aspects.

In the third case we may consider how dynamical usages of models establish new markets for architecture like *reusing* old building and changing preferences, for instance, from the preference to inhabit new building to inhabit historic, restructured ones.

SUSTAINABILITY OF WHAT?

The concept of sustainability is a particularly fitting one for describing processes occurring over time with reference to available resources and their reproduction rate. This was the conceptual content of the message from the Club of Rome in 1972, when the book "Limits to Growth" was published as the first report of the Club of Rome (Meadows *et al.*, 1972). Focus was placed upon the process of growth with reference to population, use of resources and pollution as a consequence. The concept of sustainability should be suitably reformulated with reference to *development.* How can one sustain the emergence of a property acquired by a complex system, such as profitability, competitiveness, ability to innovate and regenerate?

The approach to quantitatively sustain *current* processes establishing a system able to acquire a developmental property is based upon the ineffective assumption that properties acquired by the current configuration of processes should be valid after any *quantitative* changes. The current configuration of processes should be not intended as *iterative* and generating the same processes of the acquisition of properties.

A typical example is given by the recent financial crisis based on the idea that the iteration of debts could produce value. In this case sustainability relates to the system of processes and not to individual systems.

WHEN LONG TAILS BECOME A SYSTEM

The Long Tail

In an article entitled *The Long Tail* published in the Magazine *Wired*, October 2004, Chris Anderson introduced the idea that business of the future would relate to *selling less of more* (Anderson, 2008). This is the case of important niche strategies of businesses, such as Amazon, Barnes & Noble and Netflix selling a large number of unique items, each of them in small quantities. This concept was introduced in Statistics several years ago (see, for instance, Zipf, Power laws and Pareto distributions). In the case considered by Anderson, low-revenue and infrequent buying may sum up as becoming the more important or a very important percentage of the entire business as in figure 5.

Niche products (Part 1) rapidly become low request ones and may then collectively establish a market share (Part 2) comparable or even superior to the initial one if the distribution channel is sufficiently large and constant. This is the case related to broadband access in telecommunication.

Systems of Long Tails

The concept of *Long Tail* applies especially to *virtual goods* as for digital services and products on the Internet. In this case virtual goods may easily combine into Multiple Systems, acquiring emergent functionalities and value thanks to the availability of broadband access in telecommunications. Examples are meta-services such as networks of networks, multiple usages of nodes such as servers, data base integration and cross, multiple accesses.

This *corresponds* to Multiple Systems for software products based on re-using core functionalities and adapting through suitable human-machine interfaces thanks to the larger computing power available in personal computers and portable electronic devices able to deal with data, image and voice.

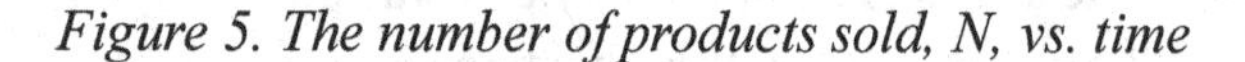

Figure 5. The number of products sold, N, vs. time

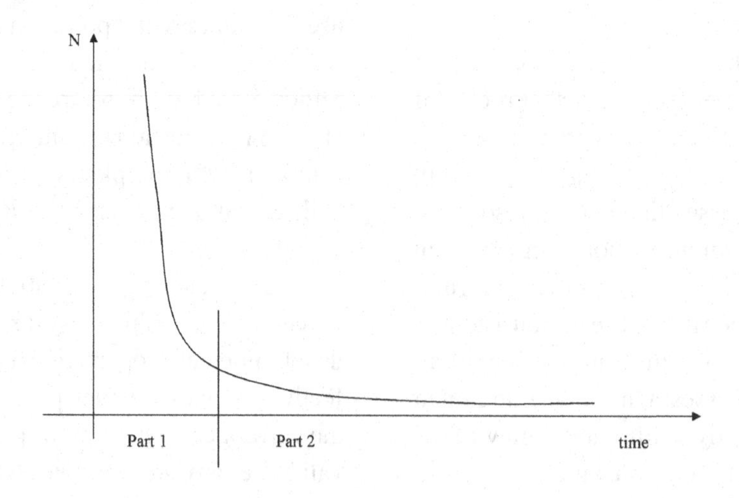

DYSAM deals with related emergent problems and properties such as market regulation, processes of added value, sociological aspects, security and privacy.

MANAGING THROUGH NECESSARY CONDITIONS?

Reductionism is based upon managing systems by acting upon what are assumed as *necessary conditions* for the emergence of the system and its related acquisition of properties.

First of all, the necessary conditions considered may be *temporary*. Temporality is due, for instance, to innovation. Different businesses require different properties of the same resources over time. The necessary properties of human resources changed over time from worker supply to knowledge and information processor supply, corresponding to the shift from industrial to post-industrial society. Regulation of necessary conditions may make the establishment of the system possible, but not regulate, i.e., manage, its acquired properties.

Management of the acquisition of properties relates to dynamic *sufficient* conditions, as in DYSAM. Crucial variability in complex systems no longer relates only to changes in the values taken by variables over time, but with the changing of models and their inter-relations.

FROM SOLUTIONS TO THE MANAGEMENT OF COMPLEXITY

Complexity cannot be *solved*, i.e., *simplified* or *reduced* to non-complexity, such as through a) linearization or b) combination of simpler components as in mathematics (see Appendix).

Complexity should be suitably modeled and dealt with by using effective approaches. Complexity in social systems such as corporations is not dealt with by using traditional approaches based, for instance, *only* upon optimizing and planning. Various approaches have been proposed in the management science literature (Emery, 1969; Flood & Carson, 1988; Flood & Jackson, 1991; Jackson, 2000). We propose innovative approaches by focusing upon *some* aspects used by scientists to model phenomenological emergence using different approaches.

Future Research Directions

Current research issues relate to the development of models of several kinds of disciplinary phenomena to allow *simulation*. Moreover, such an approach is unable to deal with dynamic, emergent global scenarios as highlighted by the recent financial crisis. We think research should deal with modeling global processes such as the acquisition of properties by complex systems rather than focusing upon simulating the dynamics of single properties over time. More specifically, we think to model processes of emergence by identifying suitable meso- and macro-state variables and searching for meta-structures and carrying out meta-structural analysis (Minati, 2008).

CONCLUSION

We believe that management theory should be a system of context-sensitive, adaptive, learning, emergent approaches, as for DYSAM, allowing for *coherent multiple, simultaneous or dynamic management of complex systems* intended as Collective Beings at multiple levels of description, as for logical openness. This concept of management may be extended from dealing with institutions and corporate complex organizations to other specific disciplines such as medicine or teaching.

REFERENCES

Anderson, C. (2008). *Long Tail, The, Revised and Updated Edition: Why the Future of Business is Selling Less of More*. New York: Hyperion.

Axelrod, R. (1997). *The Complexity of Cooperation. Agent-Based Models of Competition and Cooperation*. Princeton, NJ: Princeton University Press.

Bradley, D. M. (2007). Verhulst's logistic curve. In *Proceedings of the National Academy of Sciences (PNAS),* (pp. 1-5). Retrieved October 22, 2008, from http://arxiv.org/PS_cache/arxiv/pdf/0706/0706.3163v1.pdf

Brandenburger, A. M., & Nalebuff, B. J. (1997). *Co-Opetition. 1. A revolutionary mindset that combines competition and cooperation. 2. The Game Theory strategy that's changing the game of business*. New York: Doubleday.

Butts, R., & Brown, J. (Eds.). (1989). *Constructivism and Science.* Dordrecht, Holland: Kluwer.

Checkland, P., & Scholes, J. (1990). *Soft Systems Methodology in Action.* New York: Wiley.

Daly, H. E. (1996). *Beyond Growth: The Economics of Sustainable Development*. Boston: Beacon Press.

Dei Ottati, G. (1994). Co-operation and Competition in the Industrial Districts as an Organizational Model. *European Planning Studies, 4*(3), 463–483. doi:10.1080/09654319408720281

Emery, F. E. (Ed.). (1969). *Systems Thinking: Selected Readings.* New York: Penguin.

Flood, R. L., & Carson, E. (1988). *Dealing with Complexity: An Introduction to the Theory and Application of Systems Science*. New York: Kluwer.

Flood, R. L., & Jackson, M. C. (Eds.). (1991). *Critical Systems Thinking: Directed readings*. Chichester, UK: Wiley.

Georgescu-Roegen, N. (1971). *The Entropy Law and the Economic Process*. Cambridge, MA: Harvard University Press.

Georgescu-Roegen, N. (1976). *Energy and Economic Myths: Institutional and Analytical Economic Essays*. New York: Pergamon Press.

Georgescu-Roegen, N. (1977a). Bioeconomics: A new look at the nature of the economic activity. In L. Junker (Ed.), *The Political Economy of Food and Energy* (pp. 105-134). Ann Arbor, MI: University of Michigan.

Georgescu-Roegen, N. (1977b). Matter matters, too. In K. D. Wilson (Ed.), *Prospects for Growth: Changing Expectations for the Future* (pp. 293-313). New York: Praeger.

Georgescu-Roegen, N. (1979). The Role of Matter in the Substitution of Energies. In A. Ayoub (Ed.), *Energy: International Cooperation on Crisis* (pp. 95-105). Québec: Press de l'Université Laval.

Guberman, S., & Minati, G. (2007). *Dialogue about systems*. Milan, Italy: Polimetrica.

Jackson, M. C. (2000). *Systems approaches to management*. NewYork: Kluwer.

Meadows, D. H., Meadows, D. L., Randers, J., & Behrens, W. W., III. (1972). *The limits to growth: a report for The Club of Rome's project on the predicament of mankind.* New York: Universe Books.

Mikhailov, A. S., & Calenbuhr, V. (2002). *From Cells to Societies. Models of Complex Coherent Action*. Berlin: Springer.

Minati, G. (2004). Buying consensus in "free markets" . *World Futures, 60*(1-2), 29–37. doi:10.1080/725289194

Minati, G. (2006a). Multiple Systems, Collective Beings, and the Dynamic Usage of Models. *Systemist, 28*(2), 200–211.

Minati, G. (2006b). Some Comments on Democracy and Manipulating Consent in Western Post-Democratic Societies. In G. Minati, E. Pessa & M. Abram (Eds.), *Systemics of Emergence: Research and Applications* (pp.569-584). New York: Springer.

Minati, G. (2007). Some new theoretical issues in Systems Thinking relevant for modelling corporate learning. [TLO]. *The Learning Organization, 14*(6), 480–488. doi:10.1108/09696470710825097

Minati, G. (2008). *New Approaches for Modelling Emergence of Collective Phenomena-The Meta-structures project.* Milan, Italy: Polimetrica.

Minati, G. (20020. Ethics as emergent property of the behaviour of living systems. In Parra-Luna F. (Ed.), *Encyclopaedia of Life Support Systems (EOLSS)*, (Vol. 1, Physical Sciences Engineering and Technology Resources, Systems Science and Cybernetics: The Long Road to World Socio-systemicity). Oxford, UK: EOLSS Publishers. Retrieved from http://www.eolss.net

Minati, G., & Brahms, S. (2002). The Dynamic Usage of Models (DYSAM). In G. Minati & E. Pessa (Eds.), *Emergence in Complex Cognitive, Social and Biological Systems* (pp. 41-52), New York: Kluwer.

Minati, G., Penna, M. P., & Pessa, E. (1998). Thermodynamic and Logical Openness in General Systems. *Systems Research and Behavioral Science, 15*(3), 131–145. doi:10.1002/(SICI)1099-1743(199803/04)15:2<131::AID-SRES127>3.0.CO;2-O

Minati, G., & Pessa, E. (2006). *Collective Beings.* New York: Springer.

von Glasersfeld, E. (1995). *Radical constructivism: a way of knowing and learning.* London: Falmer Press.

APPENDIX - LINEAR, LINEARIZATION AND APPROXIMATION IN MATHEMATICS

1. Linear Function

A linear function $f(x)$ satisfies the following two properties:

- *Additivity*: $f(x + y) = f(x) + f(y)$.
- *Homogeneity*: $f(\alpha x) = \alpha f(x)$ for every α.

Systems that satisfy both homogeneity and additivity properties with reference to their components are linear systems.

2. Linearization

A function $f(\overline{x})$, for instance, in the vicinity of a point $\overline{x}$, may be linearized as $f(\overline{x} + y) = f(\overline{x}) + d / dx\, f(\overline{x})y$, see the graph in figure 6.

3. Approximation

A function $f(x)$ passing through a point x_0 where it is provided with all necessary derivatives, may be *approximated* as a point x_0, i.e., in the vicinity of its neighbors $(x- x_0)$ through the Taylor polynomial defined as: $P_k(x) = f(x_0) + f'(x_0)(x- x_0) / 1! + f''(x_0)(x- x_0) / 2! + \ldots f^n(x_0)(x- x_0) / n!$. The error of this approximation is smaller than the value of the first ignored derivative.

Figure 6. Linearization

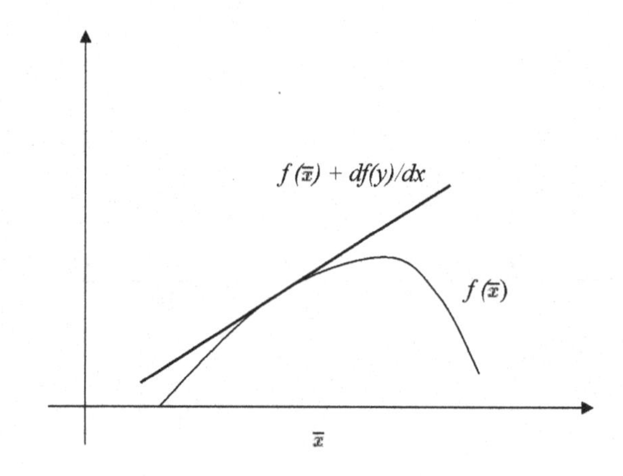

Chapter 11
Knowledge Cybernetics: A Metaphor for Post-Normal Science

Maurice I. Yolles
Liverpool John Moores University, UK

ABSTRACT

Knowledge cybernetics is part of complex systems, and a post-normal science approach principally concerned with the development of agents like autonomous social collectives that survive through knowledge and knowledge processes. Deriving from epistemological antecedents created by Stafford Beer and explored through notions of ontology by Eric Schwarz, a new form of knowledge management arises that is connected with the notions of Marshall and her new radical classifications for knowledge. These ideas can be closely associated with concepts of lifeworld and the ideas of communicative action by Habermas, and leads to a useful knowledge cybernetic framework. This has the capacity to relate to and develop a variety of what might be thought of as otherwise disparate theories that can ultimately be expressed in terms of knowledge.

INTRODUCTION

Systems theory has been developed to allow us to model what we see about us so that we can increase our understanding of the problem-solving and decision-making processes that allow us to create improvement. It is not important whether the systems are regarded as a metaphor or as real, since they provide us with templates of ideal relationships and modes of being that can be applied to the complex human activity situations that we see around us. Where complex situations are represented as systems that, over time, represent characteristics of durability, notions of viable systems using cybernetic principles have developed. These enable us to explain how and why such durability continues, and gives us a better understanding about the nature of the complexity. There are very few theoretical formulations for autonomous viable systems, the most well known being that of managerial cybernetics as developed by Stafford Beer (1959, 1985). However, a different approach was developed by Eric

DOI: 10.4018/978-1-61520-668-1.ch011

Schwarz (1994, 1997), who recognises that viable systems can pass through processes of emergence and evolution towards complexity and autonomy. This occurs through the development of patterns: patterns of self-organisation that accommodate phenomenal change through morphogenesis and new forms of complexity; patterns for long term evolution towards autonomy; and patterns that lead to systems functioning viably through their capacity to create variety. One of the problems with Schwarz's theory is that it is does not engage with theory that relate to human activity systems, for instance from social or psychological sciences. While it provides templates for creating structures and mechanisms of viability, it has no human related content. Knowledge Cybernetics is a development of Schwarz's approach to modelling viable systems, drawing on a variety of other works to fill this epistemological gap.

Like the promise of Schwarz's modelling approach, Knowledge Cybernetics has developed as part of post-normal[1] science. Since its formal inception in 2006, it has had a number of empirical developments. These include, for instance: Guo's (2006) study of Organisational Patterning that empirically explores the pathology and coherence of a number of State banking corporations in China in relation to their capacity to successfully undertake transformational change; Jirapornkul's (2009) empirical examination of Thai corporate cultural coherence that derives from a study by Yolles (2007) exploring cultural mapping; Fink's (2008) exploration of culture shock and culture stretch in multicultural environments, in particular within and processes of hybridisation; Choudhury et al. (2007) have developed a new mathematical area of knowledge processes from ideas asserted within KC; and Achakul is currently in the process of empirically exploring the relationship between knowledge profiling (Yolles, 2006) and motivation.

The purpose of this chapter is to illustrate some of the modelling utilities of Knowledge Cybernetics. Cybernetics is concerned with the control and communication features of coherently controlled (systemic) structures and their regulation that are essential to all social (and other) contexts. It is in particular concerned with "circular causality", for instance by the action of a system in an environment that causes change. That change is manifested in the system through feedback (often in the form of information), can in turn affect the way it behaves. The feedback systems adopted in Knowledge Cybernetics arise originally from Schwarz, expressed here in terms of Social Viable Systems theory, and are constituted within a metamodel of cybernetics processes of autogenesis and autopoiesis[2].

Knowledge Cybernetics can be classified as part of the Maruyama's *relevantial universe*[3], in contrast to his relatively simple *relational* or very simple *classificational* universes. Each of the three universes have different degrees of complex potential to provide information. If Knowledge Cybernetics were classificational, then, attempting to *migrate* a relevantial theory into its frame of reference would be of little use since it would involve the reduction of information, and all information filtering processes are notoriously problematic. In contrast, migrating theory from a classificational universe to relevantial universe enriches the former, but how it is enriched is a serious matter to question. This process of migration can only occur through the use of a set of principles that guide how it can be done. While it should be possible to use any appropriate relevantial theory for this, this paper uses Knowledge Cybernetics, and it is shown that the migration process is capable of adding theoretical bones to any appropriate theory of interest. For instance in Yolles (2006) the theory was used to explore Myers-Briggs Type Inventory (MBTI), showing how a classificational type theory could be developed within a relevantial universe, and in so doing providing for greater potential to the theory to explain more complex personality processes.

Knowledge Cybernetics is metaphorical in that it: explores knowledge formation and its relationship to information; provides a critical view of individual and social knowledge, and their processes of communication and associated meanings; and seeks to create an understanding of the relationship between people and their social communities for the improvement of social collective viability, and an appreciation of the role of knowledge in this. In a coherent autonomous human activity system knowledge occurs in structured patterns. This provides the structure that enables the system to recognise its existence, maintain itself, and change, and its manifestations constitute systemic content. While the notion of system (attributed to Bertalanffy, 1951 through his notion of the "general system") is used to explain behavioural phenomena, its cybernetic exploration derives from the work of Rosenblueth, Wiener and Bigelow (1943) who were interested in its teleogical properties that relate to its identity, degree of autonomy and coherence.

Autonomous system theory was a particular interest of Beer (1979). He recognised the practical utility of the idea of the metasystem explored by Whitehead and Russell (1910) in their logical study of formal systems, and used it as way of exploring the viability of complex social systems through processes of self-regulation, self-organisation and control. A consequence has been the emergence of a new paradigm with its own new frame of reference that transforms the way in which organisations can be examined. It takes us away from the simple input-output model of a system, in which the system components behave such a way that they transform the inputs into the outputs, to a model that explains how such behaviour is controlled.

Beer's paradigm of managerial cybernetics effectively has two dimensions: one was ontological and the other epistemological, though his explicit interest only ever lay in the latter. While epistemological approaches enable the nature of knowledge to be explored, ontological[4] approaches define types of being in a way that enable complex cybernetic relationships to be expressed simply.

As part of his paradigm Beer developed his Viable System theory that adopted an implicit ontology (Yolles, 2004) in that it analytically distinguishes between two types of behaviour, metasystemic that is connected with worldview and knowledge, and systemic that is to do with phenomenal energetic behaviour. Its epistemology was explicit, used to analyse and diagnose complex problem situations (Beer, 1979; Yolles, 1999). Within this he also created his ontologically conforming Viable System Model.

Making the implicit explicit enhances the capacity to develop the analytical exploration of social situations, and if adequately established, can offer access to social geometry that is able to richly explore social situations in a way that often otherwise requires dense narrative. One such ontological construction has been proposed by Eric Schwarz (see Schwarz, 1994, 1997, 2001; Yolles, 1999). Schwarz's approach explains how persistent viable systems are able to maintain themselves, change, and die. The approach was developed, according to Schwarz (2005), as a general theory of viable autonomous systems, and its creation was stimulated during the preparation for a course of lectures on the "Introduction to Systems Thinking" at the University of Neuchâtel, in particular by Prigogine's dissipative structures theory, Erich Jantsch's (1980) Self-Organizing Universe, Maturana and Varela's (1979) autopoietic approach and of course embedding cybernetic concepts. Schwarz tried to extract the basic common features of these different approaches and produce a unique metamodel that constitutes a transdisciplinary epistemo-ontological framework, from which other phenomenological models could be constructed through a combination of logical deduction and intuition. The metamodel itself has some internal dynamics, coherence and self-referential character, and it also had resonances with philosophia perennis. While many (phenomenological) models show that the evolution of systems go through the successive stages of emergence, growth, stability, and decay, the interest of this metamodel is its global coherence and its questioning of the foundations of the usual materialistic, dualistic, realistic, reductionist, mechanistic approach that, for Schwarz, provides the basis for a language for a new holistic paradigm.

The form of the metamodel is defined analytically by its ontology, while its content is epistemological. This content derives from a variety of works that include contributions from Beer's cybernetic approach, Habermas's (1971), Knowledge Constitutive Interests, Marshall's (1975) knowledge schema that links with the ideas on generic forms of knowledge by Schutz and Luckmann (1974). Knowledge Cybernetics has developed a rich and extending epistemological nature, with its core general model (based on that of Schwarz, but with recursive elements that engage with transitive contexts) referred to as Social Viable Systems (SVS). In developing SVS as a social metamodel, it also needed to take into consideration communications processes. In doing this it has taken heed of the ideas of Beer (1979), ideas on lifeworld by Schutz and Luckmann (1974), by Habermas (1987) in his theory of Communicative Action, with some incidental reference to Luhmann's (1986) social communication. Overall, the SVS metamodel is intended as a way of creating social geometries for autonomous systems that can explore and explain complex situations.

It is probably useful at this stage to provide a map of this paper. In the next section Social Viable Systems theory will be introduced. Following this some discussion of the rise of Knowledge Cybernetics as an approach is considered as well as the evolution of its frame of reference. Finally, a few illustrations of how Knowledge Cybernetics has been used are provided.

SOCIAL VIABLE SYSTEMS THEORY

The basis of SVS, the ontology of which is shown in Figure 1, was developed from Yolles (1999), and with its current formulation is available in Yolles (2005). The three domains constitute distinct modes of being: measurable energetic phenomenal behaviour, information rich images or systems of thought, and knowledge related existence that is expressed through patterns of meaning. The term existential is taken directly from Schwarz's usage; the term noumenal is taken from the positivist work of Kant (e.g., see Weed, 2002), and though we also refer to the sphere of mind and thinking as did he, our approach is

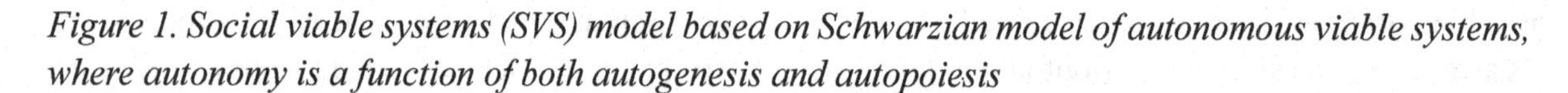

Figure 1. Social viable systems (SVS) model based on Schwarzian model of autonomous viable systems, where autonomy is a function of both autogenesis and autopoiesis

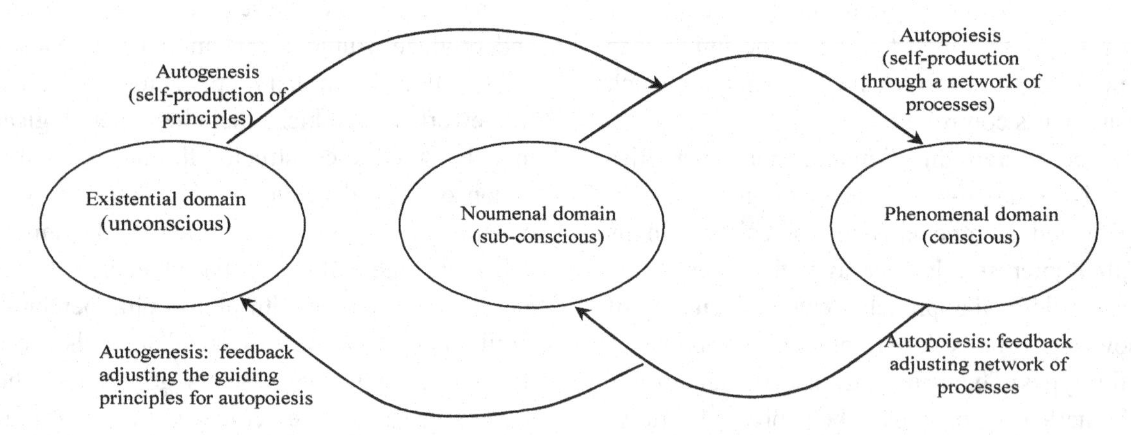

constructivist; and the term phenomenal has been adopted because of intended consistency with the principles of phenomenology as founded by Husserl (1950) (also see Osborn, 1934) and after him Heidegger (1927).

The three domains of SVS are analytically distinct classifications of being, and they each have properties that are manifestations of knowledge. The phenomenal domain has social interests adapted from Habermas's (1971) in a way explained in Yolles and Guo (2003). As well as the phenomenal domain there are the noumenal and existential domains. These have properties that arise as an extension of Habermas's notions, as listed in Table 1, and draw on both systemic and cybernetic notions. There is a connection here to Schutz and Luckmann (1974) in that the epistemological content of each of the 3 domains can be defined in terms of relevancies. The existential domain has thematic relevance that determines the constituents of an experience; the noumenal or virtual domain has interpretative relevance that creates direction through the selection of relevant aspects of a stock of knowledge to formulate ideate

Table 1. Domain cognitive properties that determine social orientation (sociality) developed from Habermas's knowledge constitutive interests

	Sociality		
Cognitive Properties	**Kinematics** (through social motion)	**Direction** (determining social trajectory)	**Possibilities/potential** (through variety development)
Cognitive interests	**Technical**	**Practical**	**Critical Deconstraining**
Phenomenal (conscious) domain Activities Energy	Work. This enables people to achieve goals and generate material well-being. It involves technical ability to undertake action in the environment, and the ability to make prediction and establish control.	Interaction. This requires that people as individuals and groups in a social system to gain and develop the possibilities of an understanding of each others' subjective views. It is consistent with a practical interest in mutual understanding that can address disagreements, which can be a threat to the social form of life.	Degree of emancipation. For organisational viability, the realising of individual potential is most effective when people: (i) liberate themselves from the constraints imposed by power structures (ii) learn through precipitation in social and political processes to control their own destinies.
Cognitive purposes	**Cybernetical**	**Rational/Appreciative**	**Ideological/Moral**
Noumenal or virtual (subconscious) domain Organising Information	Intention. Within the governance of social communities this occurs through the creation and pursuit of goals and aims that may change over time, and enables people through control and communications processes to redirect their futures.	Formative organising. Within governance enables missions, goals, and aims to be defined and approached through planning. It may involve logical, and/or relational abilities to organise thought and action and thus to define sets of possible systematic, systemic and behaviour possibilities. It can also involve the (appreciative) use of tacit standards by which experience can be ordered and valued, and may involve reflection.	Manner of thinking. Within governance of social communities an intellectual framework occurs through which policy makers observe and interpret reality. This has an aesthetical or politically correct ethical positioning. It provides an image of the future that enables action through politically correct strategic policy. It gives a politically correct view of stages of historical development, in respect of interaction with the external environment.
Cognitive influences	**Socio**	**Base**	**Political**
creating cultural disposition Exustential (unconscious) domain Worldviews Knowledge	Formation. Enables individuals/groups in a social community to be influenced by knowledge that relates to its social environment. It affects social structures and processes that define the social forms that are related to community intentions and behaviours.	Belief. Influences occur from knowledge that derives from the cognitive organisation (the set of beliefs, attitudes, values) of other worldviews. It ultimately determines how those in social communities interact, and it influences their understanding of formative organising. Its consequences impact of the formation of social norms.	Freedom. Influences occur from knowledge that affect social community polity, determined in part, by how participants think about the constraints on group and individual freedoms; and in connection with this, to organise and behave. It ultimately has impact on unitary and plural ideology and morality, and the degree of organisational emancipation.

structures or a system of thought; and the phenomenal domain is associated with motivational relevance that causes a local conclusion through *action*. The notions of conscious, subconscious and unconscious derive from Freudian psychology, are connected to the ideas of Wollheim's (1999), and also related to the ideas of organisational psychology as promoted, for instance, by Kets de Vries (1991).

The nature of autopoiesis and autogenesis is or particular interest in SVS. Here autopoiesis is constituted simply as a network of processes that enables noumenal activity to become manifested phenomenally, conditioned by autogenesis – a network of principles that create a second order form of autopoiesis that guides autopoietic processes. After Schwaninger (2001), autopoiesis may be thought in terms of processes of operative management, and autogenesis as process of strategic management.

In another investigation, Marshall (1995) was interested in exploring the way military personal

Table 2. Types of knowledge in Marshall's (1995) knowledge schema, related to the view of Paris et al (1998)

Knowledge type and use	Nature of Knowledge According to Marshall et al	Nature of Knowledge According to Paris et al
Identification *Used in the creation of pattern recognition*	In complex situations people respond to a large number of events that sometimes unfold rapidly and often unexpectedly. Time constraints may be tight, and there may be a need to identify almost instantaneously which aspects of the situation demand their immediate attention and which do not. Identification knowledge relates to situation awareness. Essentially, this schema is needed as an overall control mechanism and is used repeatedly in tactical settings. It is the knowledge required to recognise the nature of situations.	Effective identification involves recognising a situation by focusing on the particular configuration of features that are present in it. Such configurations, which tap into an individual's knowledge, allow operators to identify specific tracks of possible action, project future actions of those tracks, and ultimately assign threat potential to them. Effective identification further requires the timely and accurate reporting of the ongoing state of those features to fellow team members, within and beyond ownership.
Planning *Used to connect a goal state to a set of possible actions to realize that state.*	A full response by an individual in a tactical setting often requires that a series of response actions be developed and carried through. This activity requires a third type of knowledge, namely the ability to create, organize, and prioritise plans for each contact of interest on the display. This knowledge involves additional specific details about how events may unfold in real time and about steps needed to ready various response mechanisms. It involves the application of rules and strategies to the current situation, and enables us to connect a goal state to a set of possible actions to realize that state.	Effective planning arises from: (1) a solid body of experience/ knowledge which addresses the appropriateness and optimal timing of specific responses to potential threats, and (2) rules of engagement that define the current situational constraints and provide the specific framework within which that knowledge must be implemented.
Elaboration *Used in the creation a mental model about the current problem situation*	After the initial identification has been made, individuals need to elaborate their understanding and interpretation of a target. To do so, they call on their already-existing knowledge of similar situations and use them to develop a better understanding of the current situation. Some of this elaboration is similar to the critical thinking skills outlined by Cohen, Freeman, & Thompson (1997), and some is analogous to case-based reasoning (Kolodner, 1993). It is the knowledge needed to determine what tasks have high priority.	Elaboration taps the background store of information that summarizes what has been learned previously about similar situations. It enables operators to create mental models of particular situations. Effective elaboration involves applying previous knowledge (e.g., of mission profiles) to the current situation, such that the most reliable and acceptable hypothesis may be formulated with regard to the intent of a specific track.
Execution *Used to guide implementation & determines who should perform required actions.*	Centres on how to carry out the plans that have been developed. This knowledge includes knowing who should be informed about current plans, who has responsibility for various operations and activities required in the plans, and when to issue the appropriate commands.	Effective execution requires sufficient follow-through by all team members to accomplish stated objectives.

made decisions in the field. To progress her work she abandoned the traditional way of defining knowledge as procedural and declarative (Davis and Olson, 1984), and instead defined a new set of classifications the essence of which is provided in Table 2. Marshall's notions were not entirely new. Schutz and Luckmann (1974) had identified three types of generic knowledge: thematic, interpretive and motivational. Relating the two allows Marshall's 4 types of knowledge to be reduced to 3, conveniently connecting her notions with SVS (Figure 2). Interestingly, Marshall's planning type knowledge can decomposed into identifier conceptual planning knowledge and elaborator critical planning knowledge.

DEVELOPING A SOCIAL FRAME OF REFERENCE

In developing the ontological principles to be used and its epistemological trappings, SVS was applied to a number of areas, all of which contributed towards the development of a frame of reference the epistemological dimensions of which constitute knowledge cybernetics. The first development towards this came by exploring Sorokin's (1939-42) theory of socio-cultural dynamics.

Yolles and Frieden (2005) explored Sorokin's ideas on change in large scale cultures, and formulated an enantiomer[5] theory of cultural change. Frieden's new rational constructivist information theory, which derives from Fisher Information, provided a useful means by which epistemological considerations can be conditioned according to rigorous rules embedded in its mathematics and the social geography of SVS. In applying both approaches to Sorokin's work certain demands were made on his theory that many might consider provided for its development. Sorokin was concerned with macroscopic cultural change, and postulated that the internal dynamics of all cultures could be tracked by exploring the interaction between two enantiomer forces that he called ideational and sensate. In order to set-up these forces within SVS and therefore enable them to be introduced into Frieden's information theory, it was necessary to explore them in terms of recursions of SVS.

Figure 2. Ontology of knowledge types

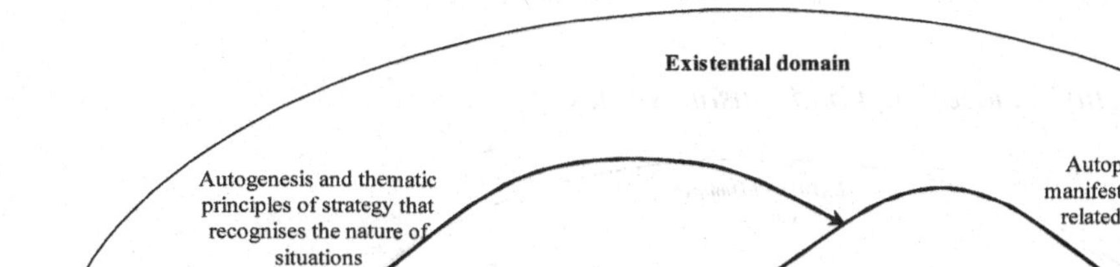

When recursions do occur the meaning of each domain changes, and it becomes a sub-context of the context defined by the domain in which it is embedded. The distinction between sensate and ideationality is illustrated in Figure 3.

As this work developed, the notions of Shotwell et al (1980) were also included. Their interest lay in exploring how children imagine and play, and they created an enantiomic theory to explain this. Their empirically validated classifications of dramatists and patterners provide a useful elaborator dimension for SVS, and as with the identifier attribute taken from Sorokin in Figure 3.

Finally, the executor attribute was distinguished into the attributes of fundamentalism and pragmatism. The celebration of pragmatism arises from the ideas of James (1907). Like pragmatism, fundamentalism defines an agent's behavioural direction, and can be defined as practises based on a rigid adherence to some traditional doctrine[6], or an adherence to a prescriptive idea or set of principles, and being motivated by theory to which it adheres strictly. For Graham (2004, 2005) the fundamentalist's direction (which he refers to as *proper aim*) is called *intuitionism* – a condition in which there is conformity to a priori knowledge that enables truth to emerge when engaged with epistemic principles. The relationship between the two enantiomers is illustrated graphically in Figure 4.

The resulting representation accumulated from these ideas is given in Figure 5 and listed with meanings in Table 3. The figure illustrates the enantiomic interactions that are possible in any autonomous human activity system. Fundamentally, this schema provides the generic frame of reference from which the exploration of a whole variety of complex human and social situations can occur, and which can enable the possibility of relational connections between varieties of apparently disparate models. In the next section we shall briefly outline some of the applications of this SVS metamodel. In particular, it should be recalled that each of the domains maintain their cognitive properties at the social level of interaction, for which Table 1 was constructed. While the basic epistemological domain properties are always maintained, when the SVS model is recursively applied (as for instance in Figure 5) the content nature of the domains must be re-interpreted to provide adjusted meanings. The nature of this re-interpretation occurs because the domains are now seen as sub-contexts of the (supra-domain) context in which it resides. The basic theory that outlines this is provided in Yolles (2005).

Figure 3. Basis that distinguishes ideational and sensate values

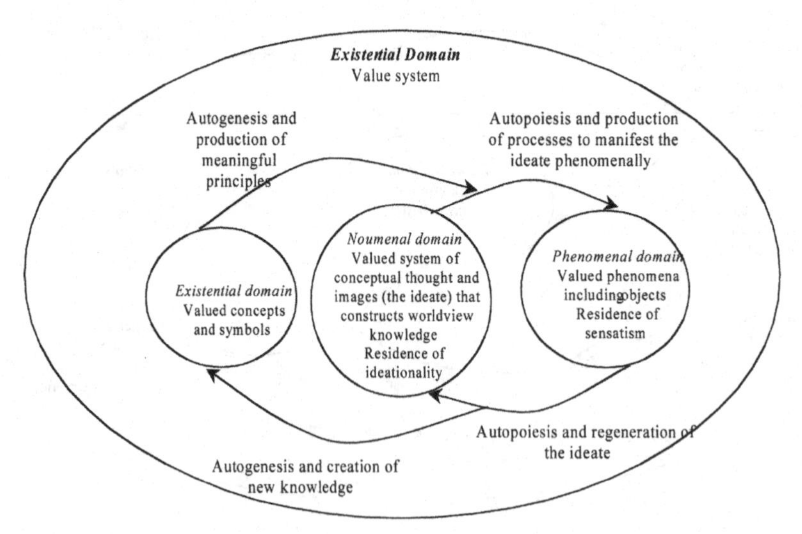

Figure 4. Basis that distinguishes executor enantiomers

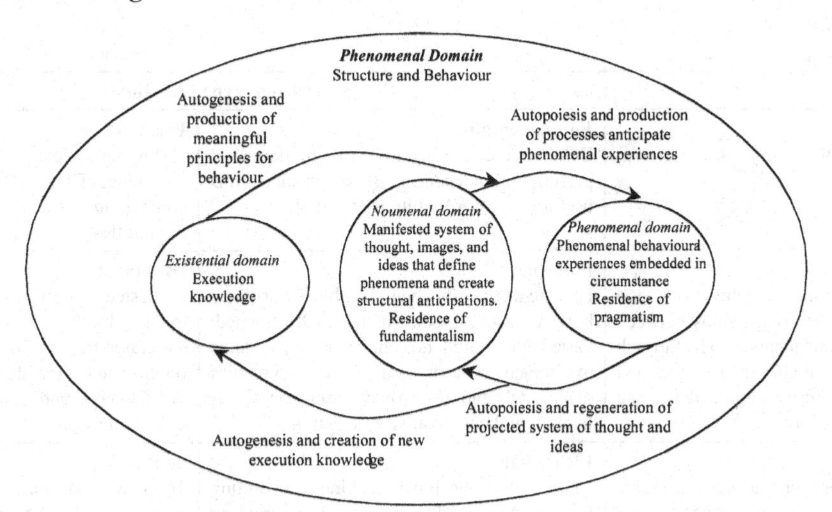

The dynamic changes that the system passes through is due to either impulses from the external environment, and/or through emergent changes from its internal enantiomer dynamic (as explained in some depth by Sorokin) so that the autonomous (complex) system maintains its viability and sustainability, as explored by Schwarz (1994) and Yolles (1999, chapter 8).

SOME APPLICATIONS OF SVS KNOWLEDGE

In this section we shall briefly illustrate three instances of the application of Knowledge Cybernetics to some of the application areas (Organisational Patterning, Personality Type, and Knowledge Profiling) and finish with an indication of how it could act as a vehicle for Beer's Viable Systems Model (VSM). The utility of incorporating VSM into this frame of reference is that it operates in a potentially more extensive way than it does in Managerial Cybernetics, with the possibility of drawing on work from authors like Schutz and Luckmann, Piaget, Habermas, Schwarz, which have been used to establish its theoretical knowledge base domain. In addition it operates with in a more context sensitive way since its enables recursive processes that are not permitted in VSM.

Figure 5. Ontological distribution of the distinct knowledge types with their enantiomic opposites using SVS

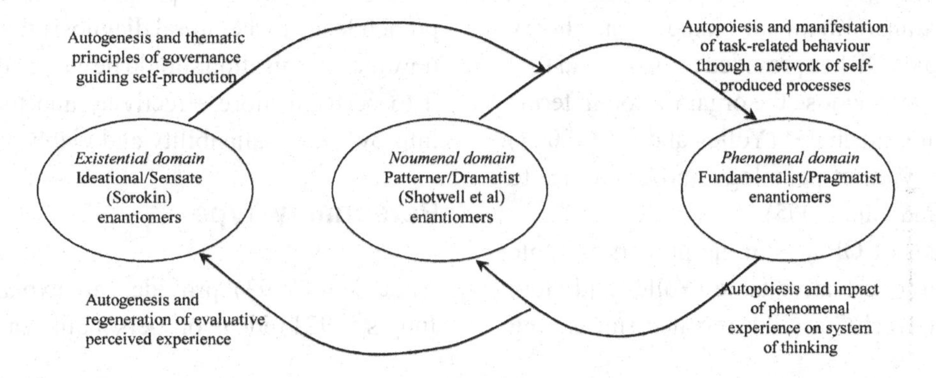

Table 3. Adaptation of the theories of Sorokin (1939-42) and Shotwell et al (1980), defining generic domains for SVS

Knowledge type	Knowledge Type Enantiomer	
Executors Supports the ability to carry out or perform activities.	**Fundamentalism** Behaviour conforms to some fundamental prescription independent of circumstance. It is useful where conformity is essential.	**Pragmatism** Behaviour reflects the demands of circumstance. They create meaning through context, to the detriment of rules and regularities.
Elaborators Supports both elaborators (who understand how to deal with the relationships between cultural attributes) and planners (who through their understanding of cultural attributes and its patterns of knowledge are able to determine possible trajectories for action).	**Patterner** Persistent curiosity about the object world and how it works, is constructed, and is named, varied or explored. It is connected to problems of symmetry, pattern, balance, and the dynamics of physical relationships between entities, and is likely to indicate relative connection.	**Dramatist** Interested in sequences of interpersonal events, having dramatic or narrative structures that are likely to involve distinction (e.g., the distinction of scenes or chapters), and undertaking effective communications.
Identifiers Supports the creation or translation of ideas and concepts; its members are able to accommodate the knowledge.	**Ideationalist** Centres on conceptual imaging constituting knowledge. Good at acquiring or creating knowledge. No know-how to develop them for material implementation.	**Sensatist** To do with the senses. Able to develop or engineer existing ideas for material implementation. Good concept translator. Cannot generate new ideas or concepts.

Organisational Patterning

While a methodology that adopts VSM is useful to explore structural faults there are other methodologies that are also capable to dealing with problem situations in organisations that are seen as complex systems. One of these is Organisational Development (OD), an approach that has a history of more than half a century, and which can be usefully used to make interventions into the difficult area of cultural change.

However, there has been some criticism of OD (Yolles, 1999), and Yolles (2000) proposed a related approach that draws on cybernetic principles that derive from SVS, and it has been called Organisational Patterning (OP). One of the problems that were highlighted for OD was its inability to deal with transformational change. The theory that underpins OP has provided an analytical tool that is able to diagnose the organisation in terms of its cultural attributes (Yolles and Guo, 2004) and assign types of pathology and coherence to it (Yolles and Guo, 2005).

The basis of OP lays in the properties Table 1 results in a derivative table (Yolles and Guo, 2004) from which Guo (2006) created a measuring instrument. This instrument was constituted as a questionnaire in which the properties of each of the domains were expressed as questions. There were in excess of 500 respondents across four Chinese State Commercial Banks that were situated in different geographical regions. The instrument was analysed statistically using variance analysis that enabled the variations in the responses to be explored within banks and across banks, and correlation analysis that enabled respondents within banks but across departments. The inference from the variance analysis was taken as an indicator of pathology for a bank, or across the set of branches of a given bank an indicator of pathology that has a cultural derivative. The inference from the correlation analysis was taken as an indicator of coherence across the departments. The overall approach leads to a cultural diagnosis that suggests how the organisation should be changed to enable it to perform more effectively and to therefore improve its sustainability and viably.

Personality Type

Anderson (1993) provides an explanation of Jung's (1921) ideas on personality in which he argues that a personality typology rests on two elements, attitudes and functions. These are often presented through the three dimensions of human psyche: (1) attitudes - extrovert and introvert; (2) perception functions - sensing and intuition; and (2) judgement functions - thinking and feeling. This idea was developed further by Myers-Briggs, who produced a measuring instrument for personality type and its relationship to decision making behaviour.

For Aveleira (2004) the work of Jung is concerned with creating a set of classifications about the nature of rationality and its connection with thinking, feeling, perception and intuition. Jung's exploration of the theory of personality is contained in Jung (1957-1979). The attributes of the model have been simply represented by Briggs Myers (2000, p.9) and explored by Higgs (2001). The enantiomer attributes can easily also be graphically through the SVS model (Yolles, 2006). To do this we shall were required to formulate a metaphoric system an autonomous personality agent in which the connection between the Jung's dimensions of personality type is expressed. There is also a link between the virtual and phenomenal domains that needs at brief explanation. Individuals tend to exhibit behavioral patterns in what they say and do, how they relate to people, and how they perform tasks or process information (McKenna et al (2002). Notions of personality Extroversion and Introversion have been related to the notions adapted by Yolles (2005) from Schwaninger (2001) of behaviour that is intrinsic (where a social collective can reconfigure itself in relation to its environment) and extrinsic (where the collective can effectively influence and shape its environment, and this implies the ability of market organisations to perform well in competitive environments).

The attribute of personality orientation can also be represented as a social geometry. To do this the relationship between extravert and introvert can be expressed in terms of the phenomenal domain in a similar way to that of fundamentalism and pragmatism earlier. However, this time the phenomenal domain occurs as part of the social collective in the suprasystem.

This connects directly to decision making behavior and more generally behavioral style, though it should be seen to be conditioned by context and circumstance. McKenna et al (2002) note that in the literature a connection is often taken between personality type and behavioral style, and there is a tendency in the management literature to adopt the premise that consistent behavioral patterns are synonymous with personality. Thus for instance, George and Jones (2002, p. 43) define personality as the pattern of relatively enduring ways in which a person feels, thinks and behaves, while Robbins (2001, p. 92) discusses personality in terms of the sum total of ways in which an individual reacts to and interacts with others, and is most often described in terms of measurable traits that a person exhibits. Taking personality type and behavioral style to be related therefore enables us to connect agent personality attributes to behavioral potential in an environment. Unlike the propositions of Myers-Briggs, the ontological nature of personality type demands that we take behavioral style as being determined by the primary enantiomers, with orientation conditioning the behavior that occurs within the social context. Hence while personality style is represented at one focus of examination, orientation is represented at another.

Earlier we said that we would represent the metaphor of personality type as an autonomous personality system graphically through SVS. This is composed of three sub-systems (the personality system, the virtual system and personality metasystem). The personality system is created through judging/perceiving and is constituted as an image of, or system of thought about the current phenomenal experience interpreted by the personality and taken to be representative of phenomenal reality. It ultimately acts as a basis for the creation of decision making behavior in the social collective. The other two sub-systems are representative of what the Myer-Briggs model calls the functions: the virtual system provides contextual form for that image through feeling/thinking, while the metasystem establishes it within a base of existent knowledge and conception through sensing/intuition.

This development has also been argued to represent a Jungian/Myers-Briggs sociocognitive theory of personality temperament. An illustration of the possible explanatory power of the model can be provided. Consider the connection between the virtual agentic personality and the system of the agentic personality. This operates as an operative couple (Yolles, 2006) in which feeling/thinking informs perceiving/judging while the latter affects the former in a feedback process. Break the ontological couple, and neither feeling nor thinking can in any way inform perceiving or judging. Similarly there is a higher order couple between the personality metasystem of sensing/intuition and the operative couple. This operates to enable sensing and/or intuiting to impact on the interaction between feeling/thinking and perceiving/judging. In this case perceiving/judging is influenced either through sensing and/or intuiting (see for instance Cole Wright, 2005), or through the external environment. In the case where a pathological break occurs in both the higher order couple and the operative couple, then personality is only influenced by external influences. In this case for instance, an individual may develop what may be called an automata personality that changes according to the environment in which s/he is hosted, resulting in a highly programmable individual. This leads to non-repetitive behaviours, whose evolution is not foreseeable (Chittaro and Serra, 2004).

Knowledge Profiling

Following Yolles (2002), we can formulate Table 3 to represent the knowledge profile possibilities of an agent. To do this two propositions are needed. The first proposition is that any agent may have a style for one type of knowledge, and therefore is particularly good at working in a given type of knowledge. Thus, those agents that are particularly good technology translators (Iles and Yolles, 2000 and 2002) or creators of knowledge have a style for knowledge identification. In unitary styles an individual will have a bent towards only one of the three types of knowledge: identification, elaboration, or execution. If they are plural they will have more than one of the three styles to some degree of simultaneously. A knowledge type may also be associated with the local generation of knowledge, which is simply a learning process. If it is possible to evaluate the learning capabilities of a person in a type of knowledge, then it can be referred to as a learning index.

The second proposition is not interested in the relative knowledge type of an agent, but rather to the nature of the knowledge type itself that we refer to as orientation. Rather like the Honey and Mumford (1986) inventory tests for learning style, knowledge orientation distinguishes each type of knowledge into two enantiomers in continual interaction. Some pilot studies have been undertaken for this successfully. In this table the term idealistic represents a balanced position between the ideational and sensate enantiomers. Landmark values are quantitative measures of qualitative values (Yolles, 2001).

Knowledge profiling can also be related to Kolb's (1974) ideas, linked with those for instance of Honey and Momford (1986) on learning effectively deal with cognitive aspects, and thus reside in the existential domain with identifiers. Hence, the sensate and ideational poles of identifiers can be related to the Kolb dimensions of convergers/divergers and assimilators/accommodators. Indeed, ideational personalities may be related to Honey and Momford's "activist" that links to Kolb's "Concrete Experience" through being described as having the innovative traits of divergers and accommodators, while sensate personalities relate to Honey and Momford's "theorist" that connects to Kolb's "abstract conceptualisation" in that they are practical transformers of convergers and assimilators.

Kolb's work was originally intended to propose a cycle of learning which has been severely criticised (e.g., Cunningham, 1990; Laurillard, 1987). However, the cyclic model is hardly referred to today let alone used. Where Kolb's work is popular is in its demonstration that, in a constructivist world, the learning ability of people differs. It is this aspect of the model that was developed further by Honey and Mumford (1986), when they formulated their Learning Styles Inventory (LSI).

The principles for this work centre on learning preferences. Activists operate through concrete experience, Theorists prefer Abstract Conceptualisation, Pragmatists prefer to operate through active experimentation and Reflectors prefer reflective observation. Honey and Mumford suggested that Kolb's four learning styles could be paired resulting in new classifications.

It is of interest to those who may seek synergy that there seem to be broad relationships between LSI and knowledge profiling. There is a superficial comparison of Kuhn's Theorist and Pragmatist are relatable to our Fundamentalist and Pragmatist, but this would seem to be invalid when one explores them further. More appropriately, Kohn's vertical axes are also seen to be expressions of Thinking and Feeling, which are also Jung's (1921) enantiomers for personality type, and which therefore offers immediate correspondence, extending to a relationship with Patterning and Dramatist enantiomers. The explanation would be that noumenal domain with be recursively defined to create a mental model that determines (through autopoiesis) learning behaviour.

Kolb's Pragmatists and Reflectors are also associated with doing and watching, and these are also likely to be noumenal expressions of what Jung has called extraversion and introversion. Indeed, this track seem to be a rich vein when one takes Honey and Mumford's development into consideration, and recognises the connection between these classifications and Jung's notion of personality type. The further development of these connections, however, requires more space that is available here. Accepting that there is an immediate linear relationship between Kuhn's pragmatists (doers) and reflectors (watchers) and Jung's extraversion and introversion, we are drawn towards considering an extension of our own profiling approach to include the additional enantiomers extraversion (or extrinsic orientation to behaviour) and introversion (intrinsic orientation to behaviour). Further, changing the context from personality to learning, the approach defined by Jung and developed by Myer and Briggs may well provide the basis for an improved Learning Style Inventory. There has been some movement toward supporting this as a possible research approach through the empirical work of Huitt (1988, 1997).

Beer's Viable Systems Model

The Viable System Model (VSM) is a model that many have used within a methodology (e.g., Jackson, 1992; Yolles, 1999) with the intended purpose of finding and correcting structural faults in an organisation. It is therefore an important approach. Here, however, our interest is simply to consider the ontological nature of VSM. It can be represented in SVS as is illustrated in Figure 6. Here, in the existential domain sit Policy (system 5) and Futures (system 4). As long as it is possible to express these individually as autonomous systems, then they have each have a local phenomenal domain that can be structurally coupled together. This explains how policy and futures intimately affect each other in the existential environment of the social community, each contributing to the evolutionary systemic future of the other. The same relationships are possible in the noumenal domain between integration (system 3), coordination (system 2) and operational audit (system 3*), with undeclared structural coupling between them where each of these local systems may be consid-

Figure 6. Formulation of VSM in SVS

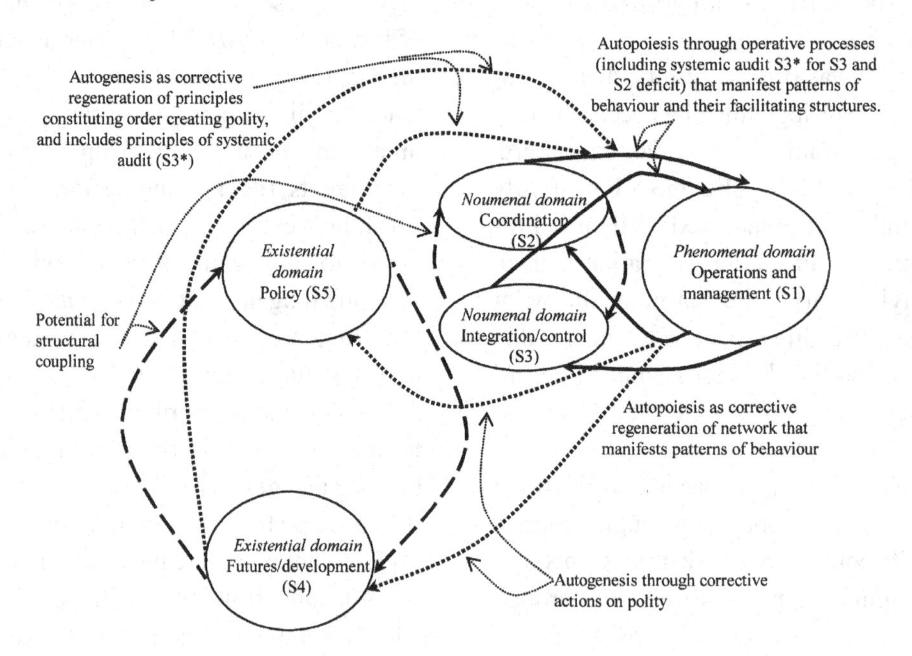

ered to be autonomous. Finally, in the phenomenal domain only one system of operations (system 1) is shown, but there could be a multiplicity of them all structurally coupled.

For Beer recursion of the model could occur in each system 1 that is itself a viable system. However, there is an argument that there is more to this model that has been elaborated on by Beer, and it is that each of the systemic functions (1-5) can also be seen as a set of distributed parts that interact with each other richly, and they may in this case be regarded as subsystems of the overall system at a given focus of examination. Hence, recursion can be applied to them individually *where it is found* that they can be regarded as autonomous in their own right, noting that autonomy is the precondition of viability. We refer to this as a lateral form of recursion which occurs within a given domain or focus of examination. An instance of this occurs when S4 and/or S5 can be regarded as operating as an autonomous system in their own right. Paul Stokes (2006) indicates that if this is true, then it constitutes an emergent property to the VSM, though he remains to be convinced. So at this juncture it is necessary to at least briefly explore how the claim of this emergent property can be made.

To do this we first need to reconsider the definition of a system. A system is composed of a set of interacting parts that each operate within it according to some innate or constructed purpose. It maintains a boundary that enables us to distinguish between parts that are richly interacting (and inside the system) and parts that are poorly interacting (and outside the system). The assembly of richly interacting parts together defines structure and contributes to process. Whenever structure is identified composed of a set of richly interacting parts then it is possible to identify a system. This principle can be referred to as one of lateral ontology. This is because a system is a contextual domain that maintains within it a set of lateral sub-contextual domains that are often referred to as sub-systems. Each lateral domain is a core or being that is differentiated in some way from its structural companions, and its sub-context is epistemologically defined. The principle of systems is that each of these lateral sub-contextual domains may itself be seen as a system with its own sub-sub-contextual domains. This *recursive* drilling down to different lateral systemic foci is sometimes referred to as the systemic hierarchy.

The introduction of the metasystem by Beer into social systems defined a new type of ontology which Beer did not recognise since his whole interest lay in epistemology (Yolles, 2004). This is called a transverse ontology since it introduces to self-organising systems the notion of a higher order controller of the system. The transverse nature of the system is that the domains of Being of the system and metasystem are quite distinct, as are their contextual natures. While the system has phenomenal structures, processes and phenomenal (e.g., behavioural) influences on an immediate environment, the metasystem is fundamentally paradigmatic in nature. However, the notion of the transverse ontology brings not only a new way of seeing what Beer has done, but effectively redefines his paradigm to introduce a new conceptualisation that permits new ways of exploring situations that are posited.

It is now possible to extend the notion of recursion from the lateral to the transverse ontology that was intimated by Yolles (1999). In this case whenever a metasystem can be defined that satisfies the principles of a system, which includes having structure, then the metasystem can itself be defined systemically. As an example, consider a social system composed of structures like divisions that themselves have departments. The global metasystem of the social system is composed of a collective paradigm that is itself composed of a set of paradigms in interaction that result in phenomenal influences on the system. It is quite possible to create a model of the metasystem in which these paradigms together interact richly to create an operational knowledge structure such that it can also be classified as a system in its own right. If we were then to ask the thorny question of what it is that constitutes the meta-metasystem, then perhaps we should point to the worldviews of the people who make up the social systems and sub-systems, but likely we are then talking about a complexity of metasystems that is beyond the argument we wish to pursue here.

So metasystems, if composed of a set of parts that is richly interactive and which together create structure and phenomenal responses, can be regarded as a system in its own right. This transverse form of recursion is not anything that Beer was concerned with. However, it leads to some important modelling possibilities. Thus for instance it is possible to identify the parts to a metasystem as being composed, for instance, of S3-S5 functions[7]. These functions can be distributed when their phenomenal responses are at least implicitly richly interactive. Thus for instance most complex organisations have policy functions that are quite distributed, and their interactivity is pathological since policies arising from different departments are not related and may even contradict, thereby impacting on systemic cohesiveness.

One of the questions that this now begs is how does this sit with the notion of pathological autopoiesis? Following Yolles (1999) we note that the autopoietic nature of an organisation should relate to system focuses and the organisation as a whole. It should not apply to only the metasystem. An example of when this might occur is when the metasystem attempts to control for the sake of control. Seeing control as a product of the organisation destroys the viability and autonomy of the broader system. In Beer's terms, a system in this condition can be described as pathologically autopoietic (Beer, 1979, pp. 408-412). Ultimately, the pathology of a viable system concerns the failure of its cohesiveness. This manifestation of pathological autopoiesis does not impact on the capacity of S5, say, to operate in a cohesive way within the organisation as a whole. There is a need here to discuss further the autonomous nature of the distinct systemic functions of the VSM, but discussing the nature of autonomy would require more space than is available here. Rather the reader is directed to Yolles (1999).

Formulating Beer's Viable Systems Model within a frame of reference created by knowledge cybernetics requires a modification to Beer's model. This concerns the effective regulation of the dynamic internal to the organization. It is in charge of the functional units of the system and controls and monitors what is going on. It is responsible for the implementation of policies, resource allocation, and the control and monitoring of the implementation activities, and

Figure 7. Alternative representation of Beer's viable system model

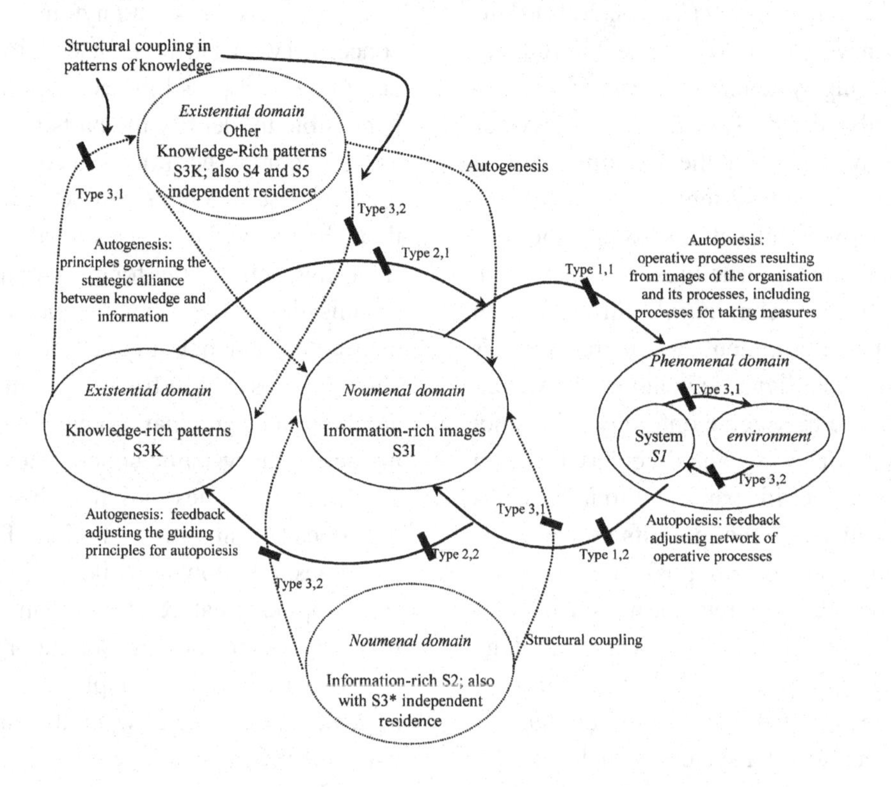

Figure 8. Type pathologies

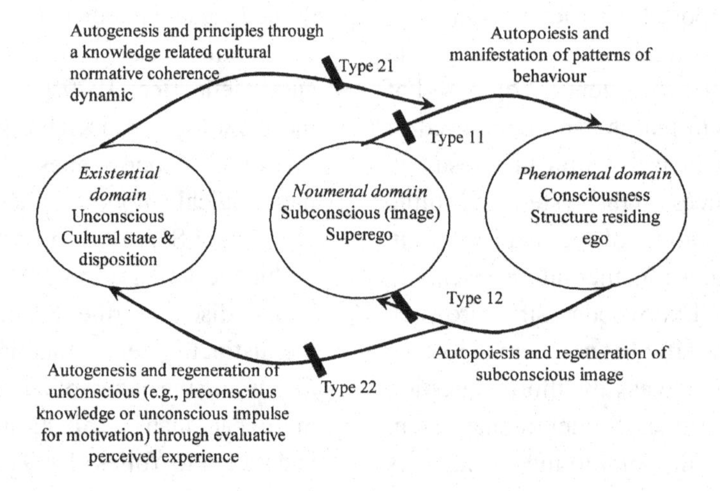

determines information needs. It is involved in synergy related tasks. S3 is therefore very much information rich. However, if it can be argued that S3 also has a knowledge component so that it becomes split into S3a (knowledge rich) and S3b (information rich), then S3a would become part of the existential domain. The representation of this is given in Figure 7, indicating the new set of interactions that are possible. The epistemology of this model requires development through empirical processes.

While there is no space here to explore this representation of Beer's model further, it does provide a detailed way of exploring ontologically a variety of pathological occurrences. Thus wherever an ontological couple can be shown to exist there is the possibility of pathologies to emerge through the breaking of an ontological channel. This includes the notion of pathological autopoiesis, a term that Beer (1979, pp. 408-412) has taken some lengths to explain. We can explain it as occurring when the autopoietic link between the noumenal and phenomenal domains is broken, so that no images or system of thought can be manifested phenomenally, or where no feedback from the phenomenal domain can enable images or systems of thought to develop…thereby, for instance, inhibiting the process of adaptation. An elaboration of notions of pathology in SVS is provided in Figure 8 and Table 4, in which type pathologies are identified. While not essential, the representation of this is expressed in terms of psychological metaphor for organisational consciousness, sub-consciousness, and unconsciousness.

OVERVIEW

We have defined the basis of the frame of reference that entertains knowledge cybernetics, and have provided some illustrations of the variety of applications it can take, including VSM and organisational pathology, Organisational Patterning, personality type, political temperament, and

Table 4. Nature of ontological pathologies

Pathology Type	Nature		
1 (11 and 12)	Can result in disassociative behaviour that has little reference to subconscious images. When this occurs, behaviour may be influenced directly by the unconscious. Type 11 relates to phenomenal image projection, while type 12 to an ability to have a feedback affect.		
2 (21 and 22)	No changes in the normative coherence can develop within the cultural fabric of the plural actor. In type 21 existing knowledge cannot have an impact on the autopoietic loop, while in type 22 learning is not possible. This has major implication for the way in which patterns of behaviour become manifested. An example of the type of pathology might be when patterns of behaviour occur independently of subconscious constraint, but responsive to the instinctive unconscious.		
	Associative Type Combinations		
	T11	**T12**	**T21**
T12	No phenomenal image projection or feedback resulting in direct link to existential domain		
T21	No knowledge development/ learning and no phenomenal image projection. Feedback cannot be responded to.	No feedback resulting in regeneration of subconscious image, and no learning process development.	
T22	No phenomenal image projection, and no possibility of coherence through learning capacity.	No regeneration of subconscious image through experience, and no evaluative process deriving from experience.	No influence of knowledge or knowledge development (i.e., no learning or reflection). Image and phenomenal image projection cannot develop.

knowledge profiling. There are other applications that exist but have not been considered in this paper, and these include Joint Alliance Theory (e.g., Yolles, 2000b; Iles and Yolles, 2003a) intended to provide a social geometry and graphic illustration of the needs for the development of joint alliances, Boundary Critique (Yolles, 2001 the interests of which are to explore ways by which conflict processes and social improvement can be achieved), Knowledge Migration (Iles et al, 2004) that define the great inhibitor for mutual understanding in social communities, and this work links closely to principles that underpin action research and processes of social communication, and Taoism (Yolles and Ye, 2005) that is intended to explore the synergy between western science and provide some explanation for the Tao based treatments using Chinese metaphors..

Overall, the frame of reference has demonstrated a great deal of potential in creating ways of analysing complex situations, and more than this, bringing what many might consider as disparate models of complex issues together. It has also demonstrated a possibility to be used to diagnose complex situations in social collectives and, ultimately using additional tools like VSM, to be used as a means by which improvements can be engineered.

In particular we have shown that (within a learning context) there is a close connection between Jung's ideas on personality style (and Myers-Briggs development of this), Kolb's notions of learning style (and Honey and Momford's development of this) and our knowledge profiling extended to include extroversion and introversion.

Having defined the metaphorical nature of knowledge cybernetics, there is a question of whether any of the metaphorical models provided have any practical value. Whether they do depends on how one sees the nature of metaphors. They are not simple comparitors, and for Brown (2003) they provide a very important way of creating a basis for new knowledge. We do not say that the models given here are true; indeed we cannot say this because of their constructivist nature. They are simply representations that will have to be evaluated and believed if there is evidence that they are practically useful to explain and perhaps to diagnose and intervene in situations that we see. Two areas have been explored in this way, to produce tentative empirical evidence. One is knowledge profiling, and the other is Organisational Patterning, and the outcome of the latter would seem to be valuable. Similar empirical explorations need to be undertaken for other areas of exploration, in particular that of personality type and learning style, since both are popular and important areas of consideration. The ability of the knowledge cybernetic framework to link such apparently disparate approaches as personality type and learning style such that specific connections and relationships can be made does provide at least this role for our approach.

REFERENCES

Anderson, J. R. (1993). *Rules of the mind.* Hillsdale, NJ: Erlbaum.

Aveleira, A. (2004, Oct). Consciousness and reality: A stable-dynamic model based on Jungian psychology. *Metareligion*. Retrieved December, 2005 from http://www.meta-religion.com/Psychiatry/Analytical_psychology/consciousness_and_reality.htm

Beer, S. (1959). *Cybernetics and management.* London: English University Press.

Beer, S. (1979). *The heart of enterprise*. Chichester, UK: Wiley.

Beer, S. (1985). *Diagnosing the system*. Chichester, UK: Wiley.

Bertalanffy, L. V. (1951). General systems theory: A new approach to the unity of Science. *Human Biology*, *23*(Dec), 302–361.

Briggs Myers, I. (2000). *Introduction to types: A guide to understanding your results on the Myers-Briggs Type Indicator*. Oxford, UK: CPP Ltd.

Brown, T. L. (2003). *Making truth: Metaphor in science*. Chicago, IL: University of Illinois Press.

Chittaro, L., & Serra, M. (2004). Behavioral programming of autonomous characters based on probabilistic automata and personality. *Journal of Computer Animation and Virtual Worlds, 15*(3/4), 319–326. doi:10.1002/cav.35

Choudhury, M. L., Zaman, S. I., & Nasar, Y. (2007). A knowledge-induced operator model,. *The Journal of Science, 12*(part 1, December).

Cocchiarella, N. (1991). Formal ontology, handbook of metaphysics and ontology. In B. Smith, H. Burkhardt, (Eds.), *Philosophia.* Munich, Germany: Verlag.

Cohen, J., & Stewart, I. (1994). *The collapse of chaos: Discovering simplicity in a complex world.* London: Viking.

Cole Wright, J. L. (2005). *The Role of reasoning and intuition in moral judgment: A Review*. Paper submitted as part of the doctoral studies comprehensive exam, Department of Psychology, University of Wyoming. Retrieved July 2008 from http://uwstudentfpweb.uwyo.edu/n/narvik/psychology/The%20Role%20of%20Reasoning%20and%20Intuition%20in%20Moral%20Judgments,%20Submitted%20Draft.doc

Cunningham, I. (1990). Openness and learning to learn. In O. Boyd-Barret, E. Scanlon, (Eds.) *Computers and learning*. London: Addison Wesley.

Davis, G. B., & Olson, M. H. (1984). *Management information systems: Conceptual foundations, structure, and development*. New York: McGraw-Hill.

Demetriou, A., Doise, W., & Van Lieshout, C. F. M. (1998). *Life-span developmental psychology*. New York: John Wiley & Son.

Duverger, M. (1972). *The Study of Politics*. London: Nelson.

Eysenck, H. J. (1957). *Fact and fiction in psychology.* Middlesex, UK: Pelican.

Fink, G. (2008, June). *Collective cultural shock, cultural stretch and hybridization*. Paper presented at IACCM conference, Management of Meaning in Organizations, Poznań, Poland.

George, J. M., & Jones, G. R. (2002). *Organizational behaviour*. Upper Saddle River, NJ: Prentice-Hall.

Graham, P. J. (2004). Theorizing justification. In M. M. O'Rourke, J. Campbell, H. Silverstein (Eds.) *Contemporary topics in philosophy 5: Knowledge and skeptics.* Cambridge, MA: MIT Press. Also see, http://www.csun.edu/~philos33/Theorizing_Just_Graham.pdf

Graham, P. J. (2005). Liberal fundamentalism and its rivals. In J. Lackey, E. Sosa (Eds) *The Epistemology of Testimony*. Oxford, UK: UP. Also see http://www.philosophy.ucr.edu/people/graham/Liberal_Fundamentalism.pdf.

Guo, K. J. (2006). *Strategy for Organisational Change in State Owned Commercial Banks in China*. Unpublished doctoral thesis, under submission at John Moores University, Liverpool, UK.

Habermas, J. (1971). *Knowledge and human interests*. Boston: Beacon Press.

Habermas, J. (1987). *The theory of communicative action,* (Vol. 2). Cambridge, UK: Polity Press.

Heidegger, M. (1927). *Sein und Zeit*, also published as Heidegger, M., Stanbaugh, J., *Sight and Time*, 1996, New York: State University of New York Press.

Higgs, M. (2001). Is there a relationship between the Myers-Briggs type indicator and emotional intelligence? *Journal of Managerial Psychology, 16*(7), 509–533. doi:10.1108/EUM0000000006165

Honey, P., & Mumford, A. (1986). *The manual of learning styles*. Berkshire, UK: Maidenhead. See also http://www.fae.plym.ac.uk/tele/course/cognition3.html

Huitt, W. (1988). Personality differences between Navajo and non-Indian college students: Implications for instruction. [Retrieved]. *Equity & Excellence, 24*(1), 71–74. doi:10.1080/1066568880240110

Huitt, W. (1997). Individual differences. *Educational Psychology Interactive*. Retrieved May, 2005 from http://chiron.valdosta.edu/whuitt/col/intro/research.html

Husserl, E. (1911). Philosophie als strenge Wissenschaft. *Logos* 1, 289-341. English translation by Quentin Lauer in Husserl, 1965, Philosophy as rigorous science. In *Phenomenology and the crisis of philosophy* (pp. 71-147). New York: Harper Collins.

Iles, P., & Yolles, M. (2002). International joint ventures, HRM and viable knowledge migration. *International Journal of Human Resource Management, 13*(4), 624–641. doi:10.1080/09585190210125633

Iles, P., & Yolles, M. (2003a). International HRD alliances in viable knowledge migration and development: The Czech Academic Link Project. *Human Resource Development International, 6*(3), 301–324. doi:10.1080/13678860210122652

Iles, P., & Yolles, M. I. (2003). Knowledge migration and the transfer of HRM knowledge in international joint ventures and HRD alliances in the Czech Republic and Bulgaria. *Estonian Business Review, 17*, 82–97.

Iles, P. A., Ramgutty-Wong, A., & Yolles, M. I. (2004). HRM and knowledge migration across cultures: Issues, limitations, and Mauritian specificities. *Employee Relations: International Journal of Human Resource Management, 26*(6), 643–662. doi:10.1108/01425450410562227

Iles, P. A., & Yolles, M. (2001). Across the great divide: HRD, technology translation and knowledge migration in bridging the knowledge gap between SMEs and Universities. *Human Resource Development International, 4*(1), 1–35. doi:10.1080/13678860122995

Ionescu, G. (1975). *Centripetal politics*. London: Hart-Davis, MacGibbon.

Jackson, M. C. (1992). *Systems methodology for the management sciences*. New York: Plenum.

James, W. (1907). *Pragmatism*. New York: Meridian Books.

Jantsch, E. (1980). *The self-organising universe: Scientific and human implications of the emerging paradigm of evolution*. New York: Pergamen Press.

Jirapornkul, S. (2009). *Changing values of Thai managers and employees and its implications for Thai organizations*. Unpublished doctoral thesis, Institute of International Studies, Ranmkhamheng University, Bangkok.

Jung, C. G. (1921). *Psychological types*. Princeton, NJ: Princeton University Press.

Jung, C. G. (1957-1979). *Collected Works*, Bollinger Series (vols. 1-20). New York: Pantheon.

Kets de Vries, M. F. R. (1991). *Organisations on the couch: Clinical perspectives on organisational behaviour and change*. San Francisco: Jossey-Bass.

Kolb, D. A. (1974). *Organisational psychology: An experiential approach*. Englewood Cliffs, NJ: Prentice-Hall.

Laurillard, D. (1987). Computers and the emancipation of students. In O. Boyd-Barret & E. Scanlon (Eds.), *Computers and learning*. Workingham, UK: Addison Wesley.

Luhmann, N. (1986). The autopoiesis of social systems. In G. Hofstede, & M. Sami Kassem, (Eds.) *Sociocybernetic paradoxes*. London: Sage.

Marshall, S. P. (1995). *Schemes in problem solving*. Cambridge, UK: Cambridge University Press.

Maruyama, M. (1965). Metaorganization of information: Information in a classificational universe, relational universe, and relevantial universe. *Cybernetica, 8*(4), 224–236.

Maruyama, M. (1972). Non-classificational information and non-informational communication. *Dialectica, 26*(1), 51. doi:10.1111/j.1746-8361.1972.tb01227.x

Maruyama, M. (1980). Mindscapes and science theories. *Current Anthropology, 21*, 589–599. doi:10.1086/202539

Maturana, H., & Varela, F. J. (1979). *Autopoiesis and cognition.* Boston: Boston Studies in the Philosophy of Science.

May 2005, from http://chiron.valdosta.edu/whuitt/papers/mbtinav.html

McKenna, M. K., Shelton, C. D., & Darling, J. R. (2002). The impact of behavioral style assessment on organizational effectiveness: A call for action. *Leadership and Organization Development Journal, 23*(6), 314–322. doi:10.1108/01437730210441274

Nicolis, G., & Prigogine, I. (1989). *Exploring complexity: An introduction.* New York: W. H. Feeman and Co.

Osborn, A. D. (1934). The philosophy of Edmund Husserl: In its development from his mathematical interests to his first conception of phenomenology. In *Logical Investigations*, New York: International Press.

Paris, C., Johnston, J. H., & Reeves, D. (1998). *A theoretical framework and measurement strategy for training team tactical decision making.* Paper presented at Proceedings of the Command and Control Research and Technology Symposium, Naval Postgraduate School, Monterey, CA.

Piaget, J. (1950). *The psychology of intelligence.* New York: Harcourt and Brace.

Poli, R. (2001). The basic problem of the theory of levels of reality. *Axiomathes, 12*(3-4), 261–283. doi:10.1023/A:1015845217681

Poli, R. (2005). Personal communication.

Robbins, S. P. (2001). *Organizational behaviour.* Upper Saddle River, NJ: Prentice-Hall.

Rosenblueth, A., Wierner, N., & Bigelow, J. (1943). Behaviour, purpose and teology. *Philosophy of Science, 10*(S), 18-24.

Schutz, A., & Luckmann, T. (1974). *The structures of the lifeworld.* London: Heinamann.

Schwaninger, M. (2001). Intelligent organisations: An integrative framework. *Systems Research and Behavioral Science, 18*, 137–158. doi:10.1002/sres.408

Schwarz, E. (1994, April). A metamodel to interpret the emergence, evolution and functioning of viable natural systems. In R. Trappl (Ed.), *Cybernetics and systems '94*, (pp.1579-1586). Singapore: World Scientific.

Schwarz, E. (1994, September). *A trandisciplinary model for the emergence, self-organisation and evolution of viable systems*. Paper presented at the International Information, Systems Architecture and Technology, Technical University of Wroclaw, Szklaska Poreba, Poland.

Schwarz, E. (1997). Towards a holistic cybernetics: From science through epistemology to being. *Cybernetics & Human Knowing*, *4*(1), 17–50.

Schwarz, E. (2001, August). *Anticipating systems: An application to the possible futures of contemporary society*. Invited paper presented at CAYS'2001, Fifth International Conference on Computing Anticipatory Systems, Liege, Belgium.

Schwarz, E. (2005). Personal communication.

Shotwell, J. M., Wolf, D., & Gardner, H. (1980). Styles of achievement in early symbol use. In F. Brandes (Ed.), *Language, thought, and culture* (pp.175, 199). New York: Academic Press.

Sorokin, P. A. (1937-1942). *Social and cultural dynamics*, (Vols. 1-4). New York: American. Book Co.

Sternberg, R. J. (1996). *Cognitive psychology.* New York: Harcourt Brace College Publishers.

Stokes, P. (2006). Personal communication.

Weber, M. (2003). Personal Communication.

Weed, L. (2002). Kant's noumenon and sunyata. *Asian Philosophy*, *12*(2), 77–95. doi:10.1080/0955236022000043838

Whitehead, A. N., & Russell, B. (1910). *Principia mathematica*. Cambridge, MA: Cambridge University Press.

Wollheim, R. (1999). *On the emotions*. New Haven, CT: Yale University Press.

Yolles, M. (2007). Exploring cultures through knowledge cybernetics. [JCCM]. *Journal of Cross-Cultural Competence and Management*, *5*, 19–74.

Yolles, M., & Guo, K. (2004, July). *Cybernetic organisational development*. Presented at the International Society of Systems Science Conference, Pacific Grove, Monterey, CA.

Yolles, M., & Guo, K. (2005, July). *Understanding coherence and pathology in Chinese state owned commercial banks.* Presented at the International Society of Systems Science Conference, Cancun, Mexico.

Yolles, M. I. (1999). Management systems: A viable approach. *Financial Times*. London: Pitman.

Yolles, M. I. (2000). From viable systems to surfing the organisation. *Journal of Applied Systems*, *1*(1), 127–142.

Yolles, M. I. (2000b). The theory of viable joint ventures. *Cybernetics and Systems*, *31*(4), 371–396. doi:10.1080/019697200124757

Yolles, M. I. (2001). Viable boundary critique. *The Journal of the Operational Research Society*, *51*(January), 1–12.

Yolles, M. I. (2002). Introduction to knowledge profiling. In G. Ragsdell, D. West, & J. Wilby, (Eds.), *Systems Theory and Practice in the Knowledge Age*. New York: Klewer Academic/ Plenum Publishers.

Yolles, M. I. (2002). Introduction to knowledge profiling, In G. Ragsdell, D. West, & J. Wilby (Eds.), *Systems theory and practice in the knowledge age*. New York: Kluwer Academic/Plenum Publishers.

Yolles, M. I. (2003). The political cybernetics of organisations. *Kybernetes*, *23*(9/10), 1253–1282. doi:10.1108/03684920310493242

Yolles, M. I. (2004). Implications for Beer's ontological system/metasystem dichotomy. *Kybernetes*, *33*(3), 726–764. doi:10.1108/03684920410523670

Yolles, M. I. (2005). Revisiting the political cybernetics of organisations. *Kybernetes*, *34*(5/6), 617–636. doi:10.1108/03684920510595328

Yolles, M. I. (2006). *Organisations as complex systems: An introduction to knowledge Cybernetics*. Greenwich, CT: Information Age Publishing.

Yolles, M. I. (2007a). The dynamics of narrative and antenarrative and their relation to story. *Journal of Organizational Change Management*, *20*(1), 74–94. doi:10.1108/09534810710715298

Yolles, M. I. (2009). (in press). Migrating personality theories Part 1: Creating agentic trait psychology? *Kybernetes*, *36*(6).

Yolles, M. I., & Frieden, R. (2005). A metahistorical information theory of social change: The theory. *Organisational Transformation and Social Change*, *2*(2), 103–136. doi:10.1386/jots.2.2.103/1

Yolles, M. I., & Guo, K. (2003). Paradigmatic metamorphosis and organisational development. *Systems Research and Behavioral Science*, *20*, 177–199. doi:10.1002/sres.533

Yolles, M. I., & Ye, Z. (2005, July). *Taoist viable systems*. Presented at the International Society for Systems Science Conference, Cancun, Mexico.

ENDNOTES

1 Research in multidisciplinary areas with a plurality of paradigms needs more than a *normal* science approach in which single narratives create story lines. In contrast *post-normal science* is concerned with complexity and has interests that relate to uncertainty, value loading, and a plurality of legitimate perspectives. It is within complexity and uncertainty that antenarratives (Yolles, 2007a) can be assembled and coordinated given the right frame of reference that enables a plural collective co-construction of multiple voices to develop, each with a narrative fragment and none with an overarching conception of the story that is becoming. *Normal science* is likely to be inadequate for the social sciences (Manuel-Navarrete, 2001), in particular when there is a plurality of knowledge based narratives that will be unable to account for the whole of *Reality*. Knowledge Cybernetics has shown that it can provide an entry into *post-normal science*, with cybernetic metarules that can seek and manifest any implicit orchestration in pluralities of knowledge.

2 The concepts of autopoiesis and autogenesis can be more simply represented in "living systems" like the social (Yolles, 2009) in which intelligence may be assigned. While Maturana & Varela (1979) were responsible for the idea of autopoiesis, Piaget (1950) developed the idea of operative intelligence for is research into child development and which appears to adopt equivalent principles. He saw reality is a dynamic system of continuous change defined in reference to dynamic change through transformation, and states (Demetriou, Doise & Van Lieshout, 1998). Transformations refer to any kind of change, while states refer to the condition in which a thing or person can be found between transformations. Operative intelligence is the active part of intelligence that is responsible for the representation and manipulation of the transformational aspects of reality, and it involves all actions that are undertaken so as to anticipate, follow or recover these transformations. It frames how the world is understood, and it is contextually adaptive. It operates through two functions: assimilation and accommodation. Assimilation refers to the active transformation of information

that can be integrated into existing mental schemes, and accommodation refers to active transformation of mental schemes, enabling referencing of individual interactions (Sternberg, 1996). Piaget also has the notion of figurative intelligence which is the static part of intelligence that derives contextual meaning from experiences involving operative intelligence. It involves any means of representation that may be used to maintain mental states that intervene between transformations. Now Piaget's notion of figurative intelligence can be adapted to become dynamic if one sees figurative intelligence as the creator of a figurative base that develops noumenally in any personality. Now this occurs through a dynamic process of sedimentation of cultural and epistemic beliefs that result in the figurative base, and so figurative intelligence can be elevated into a dynamic process equivalent autogenesis that develops from a higher order set of principles by which operative intelligence is guided.

3 Maruyama (1965, 1972, 1980) was interested in creating a way of exploring personality that is not as limited as the grounded theory approaches, illustrations of which are Myers-Briggs Type Inventory and the Five Factor Model. In order to distinguish his own more sophisticated approach (called Mindscapes) from these, he developed the idea of his *Universes*. He embedded the distinctions across his universes in the notion of complexity, and his interest appear to take him to distinguishing between theories that have differing potential to generate information of various theories. Relevantial universe approaches have greater potential to generate information than do relativistic or classificational universe approaches. In a world where the notion of complexity is becoming more important, the Maruyama universes are likely to also become important, particularly in the area of comparative theory, which is an interest of this paper. Sadly, the science of comparative theory seems to be of little interest to academics, even though there is a general recognition that the processes of theory convergence can generate new insights into important areas of science. The idea of the Maruyama universes has yet to be widely known, and its importance has yet to be broadly recognised.

4 Ontology is the study of Being or existence that according to Michel Weber (2003) (who appears to be referring to Cocchiarella (1991)) may also be defined as a matter of *argumented systematisation* about the nature of reality. Such *systemisation* can define distinctions in Being through the use of concepts, entities and even events, their properties and relations constructed according to some predefined set of categories that conforms to the distinction in their natures. Following a notion intimated by Roberto Poli (2001, 2005), ontology can be seen as a form of social geometry. To understand why, consider firstly that geometry is defined as a formulation of spatial relationships that have symbolic expression. A function of ontology is to define a frame of reference that topologically distinguishes between arbitrarily defined distinct modes of Being through the creation of a referencing system. In a coherent system these modes necessarily will define symbolic social relationships.

5 The term enantiomer (also enantiomorph that in particular relates to form or structure) means a mirror image of something, an opposite reflection. The term derives from the Greek *enantios* or "opposite," is used in a number of contexts, including architecture, molecular physics, political theory, and computer system design. The related word enantiodromia has also been used as a key Jungian concept used in his notions about consciousness (e.g., http://

www.endless-knot.us/feature.html), and (from the OED Online) it is the process by which something becomes its opposite, and the subsequent interaction of the two: applied esp. to the adoption by an individual or by a community, etc., of a set of beliefs, etc., opposite to those held at an earlier stage. For Jung the word enantiodromia represents the superabundance of any force that inevitably produces its opposite. Consequently the word enantiodromia often implies a dynamic process which is not necessarily implied by the word enantiomer. Jung used it particularly to refer to the unconscious acting against the wishes of the conscious mind, that which is responsible for one's thoughts and feelings, and the seat of the faculty of reason (as indicated in www.absoluteastronomy.com/encyclopedia/E/En/Enantiodromia.htm, see Jung's book *Aspects of the Masculine*, chapter 7, paragraph 294). By using the simpler word enantiomer we shall not exclude the possibility of any dynamic action that may have been implied by the term enantiodromia and its connection to the idea of yin-yang interaction.

[6] See http://dictionary.laborlawtalk.com/fundamentalism

[7] Beer's VSM model involves concepts that may be defined as follows. It has the following distinct systemic functions: S1 is *operations* that may be constituted as a single or multiple system; S2 is *coordination* that can provide effective control, and has interests in a limited synergy across divisions of an organisation, trying to harmonise the culture and structure of the enterprise whilst also trying to reduce chaos and introduce order while trying to amplify the capability for control for the induction of self-regulatory operational behaviour. S3 is *Integration* (and *control*), concerned with effective regulation of the dynamic internal to the organisation; S4 is *futures* is important to the identity of the organisation, and involves issues of development and strategic planning; S5 is *policy* and is concerned with the establishment and maintenance of a coherent context for the processes of the organisation, and relates to what the organisation sets out to do and defines.

Section 4
Multiple Levels and New Perspectives

Chapter 12

The Arrival of the Fittest:
Evolution of Novelty from a Cybernetic Perspective

Alexander Riegler
Katholieke Universiteit Leuven, Belgium; Vrije Universiteit Brussel, Belgium

ABSTRACT

Organizations and organisms are both complex systems exposed to evolutionary changes. The authors challenge the perspective of mainstream evolutionary theory, according to which evolutionary progress is accomplished in terms of blind variation and external selection. Instead, they present a perspective that complies with Bateson's emphasis on the "negative" character of cybernetic explanation, which offers explanations in terms of constraints rather than causes or forces. His concept of "pathways of viability" is aligned with the work of evolutionary theorists such as Waddington, von Bertalanffy, Riedl, and Kauffman, who reject external physical causation in favor of internally-driven "stimulus-and-response" and therefore move the focus from external selection to epigenetic mechanisms. Such a cybernetic evolutionary theory responds to various open questions in biology and management theory, including the dispute between homogenists and heterogenists as well as "path-dependence" in companies. The authors conclude that the strongest players are not those who adapt to the economic environment but those who emerge from it by co-creating it.

It would be disastrous for a company [...] to have to rely only upon its customers to find out whether the engine was properly put into a car or whether the cylinders are equal in size. (Riedl, 1977, p. 362)

DOI: 10.4018/978-1-61520-668-1.ch012

INTRODUCTION

Organizations, like organisms, are complex systems. From the perspective of the observer they need to adapt to their environment: their managers need to react to fluctuations in the environment with appropriate organizational change because, as in nature, the fittest will allegedly survive. In this paper

I point out that if we take the analogy between management and nature seriously, certain reservations have to be taken into account. They cast doubts on the common sense idea that evolution takes place in terms of natural selection and that it consequently amounts to progress (Riegler, 2001, 2008). The arguments presented here are based on the cybernetic insight that it is not external selection that determines the evolution of novelty in a complex system but the interdependences of elements within the complex system itself.

In his 1967 paper *Cybernetic Explanation*, Gregory Bateson stresses the peculiar "negative" character of cybernetic explanation. That is, in cybernetics phenomena are accounted for in terms of constraints rather than causes or forces. What Bateson referred to as "pathways of viability" must be considered a key concept in accounting for evolutionary phenomena that cannot be explained by the "positive" mainstream evolutionary theory, which adheres to a causal – and in the sense of Bateson – non-cybernetic explanation. Based on the work of evolutionary theorists such as Waddington, von Bertalanffy, Riedl, and Kauffman, whose results provide support for the present systemic account, I shall outline a genuinely "Batesonian" account for evolution, which, due to its cybernetic character, is applicable to both nature and management organizations.

The paper first reviews the basics of current mainstream evolutionary theory and discusses its shortcomings. Bateson's rejection of external physical causation and acceptance of internally-driven "stimulus-and-response" justifies moving the focus from external selection to epigenetic mechanisms proposed by Waddington and von Bertalanffy. They are identified as the driving force for evolutionary progress as they implement canalization based on the hierarchical interdependencies among genetic components. The paper continues with the formulation of the cybernetic theory, which receives support from Kauffman's observation that in complex systems order arises "for free" in the absence of external influences. Finally, the implications for management theory are discussed.

CURRENT EVOLUTIONARY THEORY

The current synthetic theory of evolution features two main factors in evolution: variance in terms of *genetic* mutation (in order to generate "blind" variation) and elimination of *phenotypic*[1] variants in terms of environmental selection. This paradigm has been shaped over several decades. First, by merging Darwin's original theory with Mendelian genetics resulting in "Neo-Darwinism", and later, with population genetics and ecology resulting in mainstream synthetic evolutionary theory.

The inclusion of genetics shifted the attention from the macroscopic level down to the level of genes, thus providing a new basis of explanation that was at the time not available to Darwin himself. One of the main achievements was the formulation of the "Weismann-Doctrine" or "central dogma" of molecular biology, according to which nucleic acids act as templates for the synthesis of proteins, but never the reverse. This makes it impossible that characteristics acquired during the development of an individual organism (*ontogenesis*) can be passed on to the next generation (as Lamarckism claims). Therefore, the dogma lays down the flow direction of genetic information during gene expression, i.e., the process by which the genetic sequence is converted into the structures and functions of a cell: deoxyribonucleic acid (DNA) → ribonucleic acid (RNA) → proteins → organism.[2] Evolutionary changes only occur due to mutations that modify the structure of DNA or errors in the transcription process. Mutations are saltatory and non-directional and they can be artificially triggered, e.g., through chemical or thermic stimuli. However, this only increases the *probability* of their occurrence but does not bias the *direction* of their impact.

PROBLEMS WITH MAINSTREAM EVOLUTIONARY THEORY

It is no accident that the mainstream account of evolution as portrayed in the previous section is attacked by both science and religion, because it does not reveal anything about how meaningful complex structures occur. All it says is that once they have emerged, their respective fitness will be judged by selection; it remains silent with regard to how complex novelties are created.

So it is doubtful whether variation created by random mutations is a sufficient account for the apparently designed order we meet in nature. As the cybernetician Gregory Bateson (1967) wrote, "If we find a monkey striking a typewriter apparently at random but in fact writing meaningful prose, we shall look for *restraints*, either inside the monkey or inside the typewriter." (p. 31, my emphasis). This analogy makes clear the problem that evolutionary theory faces: how can the "book of nature" be written by haphazard processes alone?

This is the hard core of the creationists' argument against evolutionary theory, i.e., the improbability of creating complex structures from random mutation and selection. Michael Behe (1996) referred to it as "irreducible complexity," which can allegedly be found in certain properties of an organism. These properties are so intricate and complex that they cannot possibly be generated by blind natural causes and therefore need to be accounted for in terms of intelligent design.

It is clear that, due to Weismann's doctrine, the creation of complexity cannot occur in a *positive* fashion as there is no way for the phenotype to inform the genotype which adaptive changes would be most favorable. Like Bateson's monkey analogy suggests, evolution is a blind process, albeit no random one. Donald Campbell (1960) called it "blind variation and selective retention." He wrote: "An essential connotation of blind is that the variations emitted be *independent* of the environmental conditions of the occasion of their occurrence" (p. 381, my emphasis), i.e., the organism itself is in charge of creating variations. Moreover, from many phenomena showing that evolution is not concerned with optimization (e.g., Gould, 2002) we know that these variations must be due to system-internal factors.

Another criticism applies to equating evolution with progress towards optimal solutions. How "optimal" are phenomena such as neck bones in mammals and atavisms such as the Darwin hump at the outer human ear conch? Giraffes are not particularly elegant when they bend to drink water from the ground because, despite their long neck, they only have seven cervical vertebrae – like almost all mammals. In this awkward position, giraffes are easy prey for predators. On the other hand, dolphins no longer need a neck but, being mammals too, they still have seven, although tightly compressed, vertebrae. Less spectacular, but nevertheless questioning the optimizing character of evolution, is the still slightly pointed end of the human ear, "Darwin's hump." Like many other atavisms, i.e., bygone conditions taken from phylogeny[3] that are re-established in the phenotype, it is a remnant of our mammal ancestors that had fully pointed ears, as cats and dogs still have.

In the face of these and other phenomena (cf. Riedl, 1978, for more examples), Ernst Haeckel claimed that the ontogenesis of individuals is the shortened recapitulation of phylogeny (Richardson & Keuck, 2002). His "law" describes the phenomenon that, during the very early development of individuals, phylogenetically old patterns are repeated. For example, in their early embryological period, mammals develop a complete gill circulation even though gills are completely useless for land-borne animals. There are mutations of horses with three toes instead of two. Three is the number of toes the fossil Eohippus, an ancestor of recent horses, had. Apparently the information for setting up a leg of the fossil Eohippus is still in the genotype of horses. Such examples demonstrate that old phylogenetic phases and states have to be passed through in the individual development of organisms even though these phenotypes do not have any selective advantage. In the case of the giraffe they are even counter-productive. From these examples it is obvious that external selection does not create optimal creatures. Rather, internal genetic processes make them what they are.

In the following, I will show that these observations, together with Bateson's cybernetic insights, can be used to formulate a cybernetic evolutionary theory. It builds on two cornerstones, i.e., on a different understanding of "causation" in biological and social systems, and on an "epigenetic" understanding of individual development.

PHYSICAL AND CYBERNETIC CAUSATION

As the above examples suggest, in the perspective of mainstream synthetic theory of evolution, organisms are described as physical entities that are at the mercy of external physical forces. This does not square with Bateson's idea that within the interaction between organism and environment the organism supplies its response from "its own energy sources." He stresses the difference between cause-and-effect relationships and stimulus-and-response ones. The former belongs to the traditional physical science while the latter is typical of cybernetic approaches.

Cause-and-effect is motivated by the observation that physical systems transfer their energy, which is summarized in the Law of Conservation of Momentum and Energy. For example, when a moving ball hits a resting one the former will transfer its energy onto the latter thereby causing it to move. Since the components of the system are passive, the behavior of the system can be described easily in mathematical and technical terms.

Biological and social systems, which are at the focus of cybernetics, however, are far from being passive; nor can they be described easily in terms of mathematics. (For example, what would be, the psychological equivalent of momentum and energy?) Classical theories of economics and management theory, too, have been criticized for their lack of more human aspects as opposed to technical aspects. After all, human nature is not passive, inert and immutable like a ball. Even in miniscule systems such as nervous cells, the transfer of signals cannot be compared to the balls in example above: "If we consider the passage of an impulse along an axon… [w]e deal with event sequences which do not necessarily imply a passing on of the same energy…" (Bateson, 1967, p. 32). In neural activity the signal transfer changes from electrical to chemical; energy is accumulated and compared with thresholds that determine whether or not a cell releases its energy largely independently of the amount of incoming energy.

In larger biological systems, the independence of each element increases even more, resulting in a stimulus-and-response relationship. "If I kick a dog, his immediately sequential behavior is energized by his metabolism, not by my kick" because "the energy of the response is usually provided by the respondent" (Bateson, 1967, p. 30). In other words, external factors may influence the internal dynamics of a complex entity such as an organism but they do not determine it.

EPIGENETICS

In the early 20th century, in experiments on sea urchins it was observed that a normal individual can develop from spatially well separated halves of a divided ovum, or from the fusion product of two whole ova. According to Ludwig von Bertalanffy this "miracle" was a case of "equifinality." He defined equifinality as "the fact that the same final state can be reached from different initial conditions and in different ways" (Bertalanffy, 1950, p. 160), and this accounts for the apparent canalized nature of development.

Figure 1. Waddington's epigenetic landscape (Adapted from Waddington, 1957)

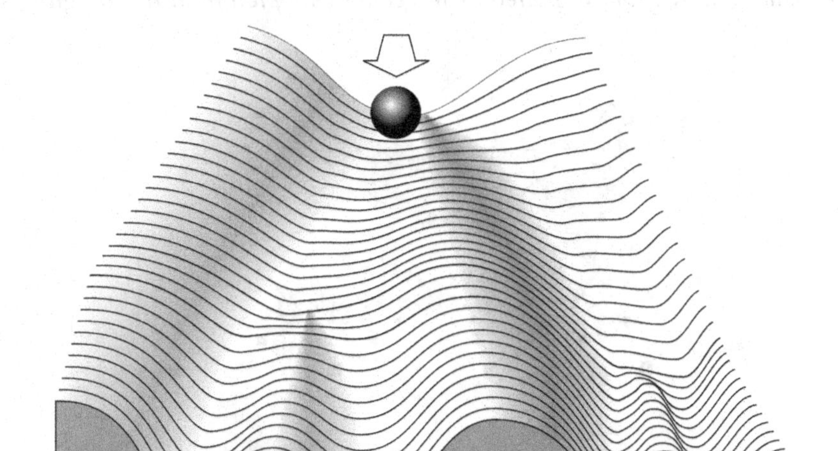

Another experimental insight was the discovery of the "Spemann organizer," a genetic region that directs the development of certain parts of the embryo. Manipulation of the region resulted in an amphibian embryo with two heads and two spinal cords. This so-called "induction" refers to the interaction between two cell groups such that one group influences the developmental fate of the other (Gilbert, 1991).

While most researchers tried to track down possible chemical substances that give rise to the organizer phenomenon, Conrad Waddington focused on the developmental action of genes to understand the Spemann's organizer. As a result of his research, he introduced the concept of the "epigenetic landscape" in which the actions and effects of genes are illustrated through the downward rolling of a ball in an inclined landscape (Waddington, 1957). The ball, representing the stage of development at a given time step, follows a certain path through a continuously ramifying system of valleys or pathways (Figure 1). This *is* a negative cybernetic explanation in the sense of Bateson: "In cybernetic language, the course of events is said to be subject to restraints, and it is assumed that, apart from such restraints, the pathways of change would be governed only by equality of probability." (Bateson, 1967, p. 29).

Such pathways are synonymous with the potential developmental paths of organisms.[4] Thus, development is canalized to certain attractors, i.e., genetic predispositions and interaction among genes (such as polygeny, where development depends on the collaboration of several genes) that determine the course of the development of an organism (Figure 2). As long as the ball does not transcend the ridge to the neighboring valley it will roll back downhill to the bottom. In other words, genetic heritage does not straightforwardly determine what the final phenotype will look like. Rather, gene expression follows the complex contextual dynamics of overlapping activities of genes and their mutual interdependencies, which is referred to as the epigenetic system (for a recent overview, cf. Ferguson-Smith, Greally & Martienssen, 2009). Given the intrinsic complexity of this highly dynamic system, how can evolution ever congruently improve the epigenetic landscape if it can only randomly change single genes?

Figure 2. Underneath the epigenetic landscape; its shape results from the interactions among genes (black squares), visualized by "ropes" pulled by the genes (Adapted from Waddington, 1957)

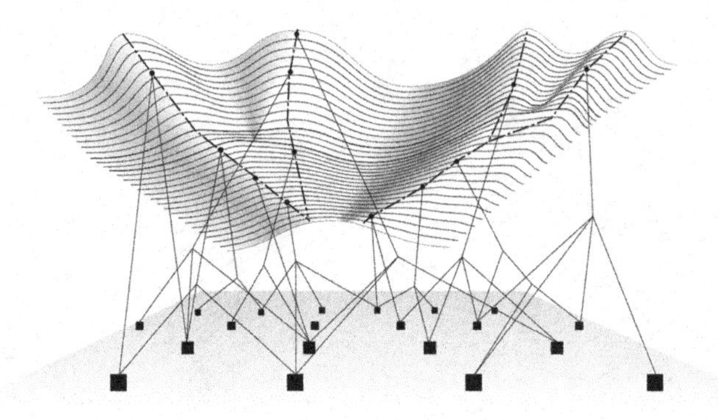

EVOLUTIONARY PROGRESS AND SLOWDOWN

To illustrate the effect of epigenetic structures, one can refer to a jigsaw puzzle. As Bateson put it,

the selection of a piece for a given position in a jigsaw puzzle is 'restrained' by many factors. Its shape must conform to that of its several neighbors and possibly that of the boundary of the puzzle; its color must conform to the color pattern of its region; the orientation of its edges must obey the topological regularities set by the cutting machine in which the puzzle was made; and so on. (Bateson, 1967, p. 29)

In such a jigsaw puzzle, removing parts seems to be easier than adding parts as the latter entails the effort of searching for the proper place. For evolution, however, the situation seems to be reversed. The more complex a system becomes, the more organization it needs to survive. Consequently, it is, in general, much easier to add a component, which is not likely to do much harm, than to take away a component, which is likely to disturb the complex network of interdependencies (Saunders & Ho, 1976). However, "random addition may *interfere* with any well connected function, making it non-operational" (Castrodeza, 1978, p. 470).

In management theory, too, this is a central problem when it comes to assessing the impact of greater diversity in organizations. Will the addition of new elements to the organization disturb its equilibrium to a greater extent than the organization can benefit from having a richer pool of expertise? In a sense homogenists share the concerns of Castrodeza and fear that cultural diversity in a company may lead to problems of incommensurability such as communication failures.

One should expect that, as the probability of interference increases, changes in evolution will decline as increasingly less random mutations can improve the epigenesis of ontogenetic development in a congruent way. Such a slowdown of evolutionary processes can be observed in the fossil record. They take place in two phases: at the beginning, phenotypic distances quickly increase; while later there are only a few changes to ancestors, i.e., evolutionary development converges. The transition between the two phases denotes the cessation of all changes within evolutionary development as only those organisms survive that embody the old structures and carry them as a burden irrespective of external influences (Riedl, 1978). Consequently, it becomes necessary, in the individual development of organisms, to pass through various developmental stages of their respective ancestors before they can finally develop the phenotypic characteristic for their species (cf. Haeckel's Law). What can be concluded from this is that certain characters become more important because increasingly more new characters are functionally or developmentally dependent on them. In some cases such morphological patterns, which have become fixed in their phylogenetic development, receive new freedom again. But this new freedom only consists of features that are based on those old patterns. Any removal or other modifications of the old features will be lethal as other features have become dependent on them, thereby *canalizing* evolutionary developments.

EVOLUTIONARY CANALIZATIONS

Bateson stated that "choices are not all at the same level" (Bateson, 1967, p. 31). Consequently, it may become unnecessary to decide between certain pathways as they are no longer available because at some higher level a "switch gene" acts as a regulator that sets a different course that excludes some, if not a major part of, the epigenetic landscape. In other words, the genetic makeup of an organism forms a hierarchy in which higher genes orchestrate lower ones.

This is compatible with Bateson, who indicated that the components of the hierarchy are the genes themselves:

If, in the communicational and organizational processes of biological evolution, there be something like levels – items, patterns, and possibly patterns of patterns – then it is logically possible for the evolutionary system to make something like positive choices. Such levels and patterning might conceivably be in or among genes or elsewhere. (Bateson, 1967, p. 31)

A "positive choice" is nothing other than an early decision of a higher, "regulatory gene," pruning the later branches of the pathway.

In this perspective, the evolutionary and ontogenetic development of an organism is a sequence of decisions that have to orchestrate a huge number of details such as the structural compositions of body parts. Consequently, if at the highest levels of this organizational hierarchy an error occurs, the phenotype of the organism may suffer spectacular deviations. An example is the two-headed amphibian mentioned above. Another example is the *antennapedia* mutation of *Drosophila*, which can be artificially triggered through a mutation of a distinctive gene so that the whole complex subsystem of its legs is developed where its antennae usually are. It seems a likely supposition that various *structural* gene locations correspond with each other on a *higher functional* level. These are regulatory genes, which connect all the corresponding structural genes and which are able to retrieve all the information necessary for building entire parts of the organism.

In evolution, compounds of structural genes, e.g., the genes necessary to build the antennae of a drosophila, that have been approved by their evolutionary success are treated as elementary components by elements at higher levels, i.e., regulator genes. The earlier such a compound appears in the history of the system the more likely it is that many other structures become dependent on it. Ultimately, such historically grown systems arrive at a point where it is impossible to remove an older layer. Here, as when removing a fundamental card from a card-house, the entire system would collapse.

Rupert Riedl (1978) pointed out that such *system-internal canalization* is to be interpreted as the result of interdependencies. Canalization refers to restriction of freedom when choosing a future state. In a non-canalized system, a state can at any given moment change to any other state; while a highly canalized system will eventually end up in one of several attractor states, such as a fixed state or cyclic sequence of states.

While in the traditional evolutionary perspective it is argued that systems are canalized due to external constraints – i.e., selection – cybernetic evolutionary theory maintains that, due to inner canalization imposed by the interdependencies and the hierarchical structures among genes, the freedom of variability is enormously restricted. Evolution takes advantage of these "positive choices." In Bateson's words, if hierarchical canalization is used, the development of the organism will "not necessarily be faced with alternatives at the lower level" (p. 31) anymore. Therefore, by applying canalization to structural parts evolution can ignore large portions of the "search space". This improves evolutionary speed and progress by magnitudes and makes, in fact, evolution of non-simple life forms possible in the first place.

CYBERNETIC EVOLUTION

Applying Bateson's paradigm of negative cybernetic explanations to evolution means that novel structures can only appear in congruence with the present structure since mutations and other genetic changes must preserve the framework of constructional and functional conditions within the organism. Phenotypic variations are so heavily constrained by the *context* of the structure of the organism that it does not make sense to consider selection on them an independent factor in evolution. In other words, the central aspect of evolutionary processes is the organism's structural constraints, which provide the context within which evolutionary change occurs.

To consider the epigenetic system as a complex self-regulating and self-organizing and therefore cybernetic system leads to the main insight that internal selection generated by the functional-systemic conditions in the organization of organisms is crucial for evolutionary progress and novelty. This renders external selection as the determining factor superfluous: "natural selection [...] is merely a filter for unsuccessful morphologies generated by development" (Gilbert, Opitz & Raff, 1996, p. 368). Imagine, as an extreme case, an extraterrestrial spaceship burning down planet Earth. This is clearly an external selectionist force but can hardly be called a contribution to evolutionary progress.

The superfluousness of external selection was also demonstrated by Stuart Kauffman's (1993) network model. Kauffman investigated the question of what would happen in a complex system without selection by external forces. He demonstrated that a network of binary nodes displays the tendency to move into a few typical recurrent cycles of activity. The dynamics are even so stable that external forces cannot seriously perturb these systems. As described by von Bertalanffy's concept of equifinality and Waddington's epigenetic landscape, they cannot move them out of those stable cycles since they have only a narrow space of possibilities in which to select from complexes of mutually linked subsets and therefore they become rigorously canalized. For example, if in a network of n nodes each node has two inputs and outputs, the number of states that can be occupied by the network is 2^n but the number of stable cycles it eventually arrives at is only $\sqrt{n}$. Again, no external force needs to be assumed to arrive at this high degree of order, there is "order for free" (Kauffman, 1995).

WHAT ARE THE CONSEQUENCES FOR MANAGEMENT THEORY?

According to the cybernetic perspective, the development of organisms is guided by the internal constraints that emanate from the reciprocal and hierarchical dependencies of the genetic material. These dependencies drastically reduce degrees of freedom and randomness in evolution. At the same time, however, the resulting canalizations drive the generation of evolutionary novelty because they drastically reduce the improbability of the creation of complex structures. Canalizations are the constraints, the "negative" elements of cybernetics, with which natural evolution has to cope in order to "simply get things working at all" (Dembski & Ruse, 2004, p. 8). Does this also apply to evolution in economics in general and to management theory in particular?

Ever since Darwin created evolutionary theory based on economic ideas of his time, there has been a close relationship between both fields. Since cybernetic evolutionary theory is able to account for more phenomena than mainstream evolutionary theory, there are reasons to favor its inclusion in any evolutionary management theory.[5] There are at least two issues that are of interest here. These issues are the advantage or disadvantage that canalized evolution has, and what role the environment plays.

Mary Uhl-Bien and Russ Marion (2008) argue that canalization (or "path-dependence," as they call it) is treacherous for organizations that focus on innovation as it occurs in complex systems that go through the same series of actions practically independently of the environment. The authors suggest that companies become "path-creative" to avoid getting stuck in such a counter-innovative routine. However, is this a good idea? As pointed out in the paper, the creation of highly complex organisms was possible only through developmental canalizations that, on the one hand, created burdens and excluded a variety of phenotypic variations from coming into existence but, on the other hand, enabled the evolution of genuinely novel structures. Without canalization, the issue of irreducible complexity would be unavoidable and the inclusion of an "intelligent designer" a necessity.

How does canalization enable the emergence of genuine complexity and novelty in *any* complex system, including economic ones? To answer this question it is necessary to recall the core of the creationist's argument, i.e., that the sheer number of components in a complex organism and their interaction makes it entirely improbable that by random combination of these elements anything useful can naturally evolve over even millions of years. This can be easily debunked with Herbert Simon's (1969) analogy of the watchmakers who have to build clocks consisting of n parts. Whenever they are interrupted in their work at random moments with a probability of p (i.e., corresponding to random mutations) this causes an unfinished clock to fall apart. For the watchmaker who tries to assemble each watch in one go, the probability of actually finishing one is $p_F = (1 - p)^n$. However, a watchmaker who, like a regulatory gene, divides the design of a watch into subassemblies of k parts each, so that, in the worst case, only k components fall apart yields a tremendous advantage with regard to the number of completed watches. For each watch he needs to put together 111 partial assemblies. His probability of completing a watch is $p_F = (1 - p)^k$. If we assume $n = 1000$ parts, an interruption probability of $p = 10^{-2}$ and subassemblies of $k = 10$ parts, the "regulatory" watchmaker, by assembling hierarchically, will produce watches 3775 times faster than his colleague. As Simon (1969, p. 195) put it, "hierarchic systems will evolve far more quickly than nonhierarchical systems of comparable size." Furthermore, the evolution follows clearly a direction that "is provided [...] by the stability of the complex forms, once these come into existence." (p. 203) These aspects, stability and acceleration, must therefore be considered a great advantage that outweighs the disadvantage of burdening organisms with "outdated" genetic material.

This means that strong control in a complex system such as a business organization may be impossible as in highly interdependent systems change is not easy. Furthermore, the environment certainly cannot impose changes upon the system. It is the system that dictates which changes are possible and how to react to changes from the environment. In this sense, Alan Kay's "The best way to predict the future is to invent it" is appropriate. Or in the words of Thomas Hout (1999), "The best management models don't adapt to the new economy; they emerge from it. It's no longer the survival of the fittest; it's the arrival of the fittest."

DIRECTIONS FOR FUTURE RESEARCH

Only over the last few years, the epigenetic perspective has caught the interest of mainstream evolutionary theory. As much as biologists are still trying to determine the viable pathways of future research, management theory, too, needs to lay out future directions for including the cybernetic perspective. In particular, finding answers to the following issues may prove useful.

1. In biology the equation "one gene = one protein" had to be abandoned. Likewise it seems appropriate to consider the direct mapping "single cause → single problem" unfeasible. Instead, problems may be the result of a series of constraints. Hence there is the necessity to devise tools that trace backwards the polygenetic interaction of elements acting as constraints and that disentangle them.
2. While in the biological context the core building blocks are genes, it is not clear what the "rope-pulling" entities (cf. Figure 2) are in the context of management theory.
3. The development of a complex biological organism follows, as in a relay race, a sequence of decisions that orchestrate a huge number of structural details. Future research will have to identify these decision points in the context of management theory and identify how the "relay race" can be divided into the most appropriate number of segments.
4. Since the removal of a component becomes gradually more difficult later on, there is a need to design ways to anticipate the importance of a component in advance such that its inclusion can be avoided while its removal is still possible.
5. In the economic context, companies are perpetually challenged, which puts pressure on their ability to explore new areas as fast as possible and before competitors move in. The race may be triggered by the economic environment but the direction depends solely on the company's cybernetic-epigenetic processes. So its speed is determined by the polygenetic synergies that can be formed in the company. Future research needs to find out which polygenetic synergies are most useful to form in order to take maximal advantage of the canalization they bring about.

REFERENCES

Arthur, W. (2002). The emerging conceptual framework of evolutionary developmental biology. *Nature*, *415*, 757–764.

Bateson, G. (1967). Cybernetic explanation. *The American Behavioral Scientist*, *10*(8), 29–32.

Behe, M. (1996). *Darwin's black box*. New York: The Free Press.

Campbell, D. T. (1960). Blind variation and selective retention in creative thought as in other knowledge processes. *Psychological Review*, *67*(6), 380–400. doi:10.1037/h0040373

Castrodeza, C. (1978). Evolution, complexity, and fitness. *Journal of Theoretical Biology*, *71*, 469–471. doi:10.1016/0022-5193(78)90174-1

Dembski, W. A., & Ruse, M. (Eds.). (2004). *Debating design. From Darwin to DNA*. Cambridge: Cambridge University Press.

Ferguson-Smith, A. C., Greally, J. M., & Martienssen, R. A. (Eds.). (2009). *Epigenomics*. New York: Springer.

Gilbert, S. F. (1991). Induction and the origins of developmental genetics. In S. F. Gilbert (Ed.), *A conceptual history of modern embryology* (pp. 181–206). New York: Plenum Press.

Gilbert, S. F., Opitz, J. M., & Raff, R. A. (1996). Resynthesizing evolutionary and developmental biology. *Developmental Biology*, *173*, 357–372. doi:10.1006/dbio.1996.0032

Gould, S. J. (2002). *The structure of evolutionary theory*. Cambridge, MA: Harvard University Press.

Hout, T. M. (1999). Books in review: Are managers obsolete? *Harvard Business Review*, *77*(2), 161–168.

Kauffman, S. A. (1993). *The origins of order.* New York: Oxford University Press.

Kauffman, S. A. (1995). *At home in the universe*. London: Viking.

Raff, R. A. (2000). Evo-devo: The evolution of a new discipline. *Nature Reviews. Genetics*, *1*(1), 74–79. doi:10.1038/35049594

Richardson, M. K., & Keuck, G. (2002). Haeckel's ABC of evolution and development. *Biological Reviews of the Cambridge Philosophical Society (London)*, *77*, 495–528. doi:10.1017/S1464793102005948

Riedl, R. (1977). A systems analytical approach to macro-evolutionary phenomena. *The Quarterly Review of Biology*, *52*, 351–370. doi:10.1086/410123

Riedl, R. (1978). *Order in living systems*. New York: Wiley.

Riegler, A. (2001). The cognitive ratchet. The ratchet effect as a fundamental principle in evolution and cognition. *Cybernetics and Systems*, *32*(3/4), 411–427. doi:10.1080/01969720151033571

Riegler, A. (2008). Natural or internal selection? *Artificial Life*, *14*(3), 345–362. doi:10.1162/artl.2008.14.3.14308

Saunders, P. T., & Ho, M.-W. (1976). On the increase in complexity in evolution. *Journal of Theoretical Biology*, *63*, 375–384. doi:10.1016/0022-5193(76)90040-0

Simon, H. A. (1969). *The sciences of the artificial*. Cambridge, MA: MIT Press.

Uhl-Bien, M., & Marion, R. (2008). *Complexity leadership*. Charlotte, NC: Information Age Publishing.

von Bertalanffy, L. (1950). An outline of general system theory. *The British Journal for the Philosophy of Science*, *1*(2), 134–165. doi:10.1093/bjps/I.2.134

Waddington, C. H. (1957). *The strategy of the genes*. London: Allen and Unwin.

KEY TERMS AND DEFINITIONS

Atavism: Bygone condition taken from the evolutionary development and history of a species and that is re-established in the phenotype.

Canalization: Effect caused by constraining the development of a system. A canalized system will eventually end up in one of several attractor states, such as a fixed state or cyclic sequence of states.

Conrad Waddington: A developmental biologist and philosopher (1905–1975) who invented the notion of "epigenetic landscape", thereby laying the foundations of systems biology.

Constraints: Restriction on the degree of freedom when choosing among potential future states.

Epigenetic Landscape: Visualization of the actions and effects of genes in an epigenetic system. Its stage of development at a given time step is represented by a downward-rolling ball that follows a certain path through a continuously ramifying system of valleys or pathways.

Epigenetic System: The complex contextual dynamics of overlapping activities of genes and their mutual interdependencies that implements the expression of genes.

Equifinality: A term coined by Ludwig von Bertalanffy. It refers to the fact that the same final state can be reached from different initial conditions and in different ways.

Gregory Bateson: An anthropologist (1904–1980) who had a major influence on cybernetics and second-order cybernetics.

Herbert A. Simon: An economist and psychologist (1916–2001) and author of the influential paper, "The architecture of complexity".

Homogenists: In management theory, those who have concerns about cultural diversity in a company as it may lead to problems of incommensurability such as communication failures.

Irreducible complexity: A term coined by Michael Behe to refer to the notion that an organism's properties are so intricate and complex that they cannot possibly be generated by blind natural causes and therefore need to be accounted for in terms of intelligent design.

Negative Explanation: According to Gregory Bateson, in cybernetics, phenomena are accounted for in terms of constraints rather than causes or forces.

Organizational Hierarchy: In evolution theory, referring to the fact that certain types of genes regulate the working of other, structural genes.

Path-Dependence: In management theory, the notion that complex systems go through the same series of actions practically independently of the environment.

Polygeny: In genetics, referring to fact that the unfolding of a phenotypic trait depends on the collaboration of several genes. The effect of a single gene upon several traits is called pleiotropy.

Rupert Riedl: A zoologist (1925–2005) who developed an early version of systems biology based on morphological-genetic observations.

Stuart A. Kauffman: A biologist (1939–) who investigated formal aspects of complex genetic and metabolic networks.

System-Internal Canalization: The fact that in organisms canalization arises from the (hierarchical) interaction between and interdependencies among genes rather than from environmental conditions.

ENDNOTES

1. The "phenotype" is the physical manifestation of the organism.
2. This is a slightly simplified representation because it seems possible to go back from RNA to DNA, and because the RNA can also make copies of itself.
3. Phylogeny is the evolutionary development and history of species.
4. The epigenetic landscape, however, should not be confused with "fitness landscapes" in which external factors select for "optimal" organisms.
5. The cybernetic evolutionary theory also connects to the modern "evo-devo" movement, i.e., the fusion of genetically based evolutionary theory and developmental theory in biology (Gilbert, Opitz & Raff, 1996; Raff, 2000; Arthur, 2002).

Chapter 13
Co-Construction of Learning Objects:
Management and Structure

Thomas Hansson
Blekinge Institute of Technology, Sweden

ABSTRACT

It is an unsettled issue between research traditions how we should negotiate the implied rather than acknowledged dispute between individual agency, i.e. the ability/need/urge of a manager to act on/in the world on the one hand and the functioning of a structured social system where management and employee initiatives, relations and reactions are crucial for the main activity. This chapter resolves parts of the debate by drawing on general activity theory and a digital tool for facilitating job-related group interaction.

INTRODUCTION

Kaptelinin & Nardi (2006, p. 235) suggest research should "theorize transformations between individual and collective levels." Regardless of methods, however, there seems to be creative dynamics at work between approaches. The reason is that there is transaction of situated and de-contextualized meanings going on. Furthermore, human interactions form (Wells, 2007, p. 165) an "occurrence of a joint activity in which multiple employees are collaboratively involved." And so, it is intriguing to learn how management, staff and employees deal with recurring contradictions between agency and systems thinking.

Garrison (2001, p. 276) argues against Western thinking based on a list of dualisms in Dewey (1952/1989, p. 408): "The material and spiritual, the physical and the mental or psychological; body and mind; experience and reason; sense and intellect, appetitive desire and will; subjective and objective, individual and social; inner and outer;" In responding to the Deweyan philosophical approach, Roth (2007, p. 40) acknowledges the *dialectical* as opposed to *dualistic* relation between managerial agency and collective employment. Kaptelinin & Nardi (2006, p. 11) outlines agency versus structure for ICT environments, saying: "activity theory has

DOI: 10.4018/978-1-61520-668-1.ch013

always had a strong notion of the individual, while at the same time understanding and emphasizing the importance of a socio-cultural matrix within which individuals develop." So, emphasis is on management, structure and a combination of the two deployed as a way of describing and explaining team learning in a digital setting.

Lev Vygotsky (1987) is a renowned proponent of a combined view on agency and systems thinking. He emphasizes the crucial impact of "structured situatedness" for development of human activity systems, suggesting that facilitating agency, today categorized as 'scaffolding' (Wood, Bruner & Ross, 1976) as a way of enhancing sought processes and outcomes of contextualized learning. Scaffolding is a pedagogic strategy which a facilitator employs to support the learner. Peter Senge (1990), a contemporary promoter of organizational theory, likewise outlines the significance of personal mastery in learning organizations, emphasizing the crucial impact of management to help employees think about the company and themselves in terms of relation building processes in a social system.

By agency we understand that individuals are ready, willing and able to act on impressions, take action, support activities and adapt to people and objects. A preparedness to act on personal needs, motives and goals so as to control other people's actions is a specific human ability, be it informed, planned or spontaneous. Furthermore the general idea for exercising agency, leadership or management is to produce an effect according to an original plan or to follow an adjusted intention. People seem to continuously contribute to the functioning of social systems where they listen to, calculate, process and respond to what is happening in physical, virtual and social worlds. Thus, any such system – a football team, an army, an orchestra or a staff meeting – is made up of people relating to each other with a shared understanding of the borders of the system, what the consequences would be if they crossed them, what keeps the community going and what separates the insiders from members of a neighboring system.

This article provides a conceptual account and empirical analysis of how strategic IT management and collective input to focus group sessions between managers and employees are classified differently, depending if the employees act from a self-managed and self-conscious level of awareness, attention and intention or from a high level of professional thinking. In contemporary organizational theory, researchers mistakenly (Hansson, 2002) try to explain the development of higher managerial functions like memorizing, rationalizing or decision-making as a result of agency executed through individual "push" obtained through the pursuit of personal needs, motives or goals. I advocate a theory that accounts for organizational development defined by the balancing effect of collective "pull" obtained through employees who deal properly with systemic factors like objective, instrument and contexts of production, distribution and consumption respectively. The deployed theory (Engeström, 1999) covers psychological subject-instrument-object relations and organizational objective-other people-rules and regulations-division of labor-relations. The combination encompasses individual and social influences on workplace learning. By deploying the suggested approach it is possible to improve on theory, for example by discovering and verifying the impact of individual agency in an ICT context where a digital tool mediates professional management and employee intentions.

PROBLEM DESCRIPTION

Nardi (1996, p. 69) introduced the problem of balancing agency with structure in a computing milieu by asking: "What are the relations between artifacts, individuals, and the social groups to which they belong?" Until now personal chemistry, compatibility of goals, interests or ambitions have mystified what goes on when people cooperate and form rewarding activities. Concepts like luck, magic or fortune, however, have failed to provide an explanatory basis for the theory and method needed to explore the formation of human activity. It is however useful to put into perspective how modern focus group activities start off, change and develop in a modern medium. So far, such phenomena have been explored as group dynamics, functioning teams or virtual communities. Expressed differently, the problem is to find the variables that inspire and/or sustain productive communications between employees, more specifically the relation-building mechanisms that inspire individuals and social systems to communicate through a boundary object (Van Oers, 1998) or a designed space for interaction (Winograd, 1996). Depending on perspective of change management, the medium for the study is a "transformative artifact", learning management system (LMS) or soft- and hardware system called *Zing*. The platform provides an interactive context for the users to share physical, social, emotional and cognitive experiences. Following Van Oers (1998, p. 137), mediating software communications sometimes come as: "a result of a personal (mental) or social act of interpretation of an activity setting (contextualizing), trying to bring the determining factors under control." In deciding if the deployed platform is a process, an elaborate context or a simple tool, Ducheneaut & Bellotti (2001), emphasize the potential of an effective tool to promote relation building processes.

It is also relevant to study general activity theory (GAT) and describe the catalyst mechanisms that inspire and sustain an emerging professional culture during focus group sessions between managers and employees. On this note, Nardi (2007, p. 6) says Raeithel (1996) explained co-construction of a shared object to mean "re-definition of the object of collective activity." Kaptelinin & Miettinen's (2005) definition of "object of activity" covers both the actual (collective) activity and the objective of shared work. Even today, Engeström's (1987) original concept of co-construction of an object, like in our case *Zing* software sessions, has been modified. Kaptelinin & Nardi (2006) say co-construction equals the traditional process of finding out what managers expect of employees (object construction) and also how the employees should go about realizing (object instantiation) the manager's expectations.

PURPOSE OF RESEARCH

The purpose of this study is to explore the potential of GAT to explain what happens to employees during a workplace session, when verbal exchanges are mediated by modern technology. The digital platform enables for a study into group processes defined as a vehicle for higher order thinking. By engaging in verbal co-construction, i.e. communication, co-operation and co-ordination of first several knowledge objects and eventually and in the lucky cases one learning object, employees seem to be able to either explore the object or remain at a low level of thinking, merely supplying requested data. The result of their interactions depends on how the group communicates during a 45 minute session. It seems as if employees who struggle with relational issues contribute by self-conscious and self management (SC/SM) input of menial information at a basic level of *object construction*. They dutifully complete the steps of a boring process. Other employees contribute to inspiring and productive group interactions, generating professional employee thinking (PET) as they *instantiate the object* of inquiry and act out a specific discourse for raising the group's level of knowledge of the given theme, which is computer sales. By changing from merely supplying data to transforming the object, there seems to be a delicate balancing going on between individual and group needs.

The purpose of studying a manager and five employees during such a session is to back track shifts in a situated activity of object construction that eventually brings higher order thinking into place. Data on the process makes it possible to analyze an advanced conception of the discoursed context as object instantiation. Vygotsky (1998) elaborates on a theory of agency and structure. Here it is contingent on how individual employees express (a) SC/SM in a context of supplying factual information and deploy (b) PET for expanding their knowledge about the topic of the discussion.

STRUCTURING OF CONCEPTS

People seem to think in a strange way when they explain how they learn. Their descriptions of a learning object are based on the contention that learning involves acquisition of an "outer" quality, something "external" that existed before learning happened to them and became the learner's property. A definition (http://en.wikipedia.org/wiki/Learning_object) of *learning object* describes "a digital or non-digital entity that may be used and re-used for learning, education or training". However, the semantic field is made up of object *plus* learning. And, even though learning objects are a human construction, a cultural artifact created to some purpose, they primarily materialize as human goals.

The first and second columns (Table 1) contain categorizations at a basic and naïve level of human becoming. This study focuses on columns three and four. The last column covers scientific thinking about communications, learning, knowledge and behavior. The first horizontal line of Table 1 applies for Vygotsky's (1998) definition of discernible stages of human development. The second line helps identify Wartofsky's (1979) and Bereiter's (2003) interpretations of how people perceive and conceive of objects. In the third line Popper and Eccles (1977) define abstractions as "worlds" with an added dimension of human behavior. The fourth line explicates kinds of agency. In the fifth line of the third column (bold) things begin to get complicated. Several inspirations compete about how to conceptually categorize how humans work together, divide labor and reach a shared objective. The sixth line displays how individual operations frame mental operations on a learning object. Here Engeström (2007) defines development of collective and productive learning activities as an "expansive space". But (co-)configuration and instantiation of an object are hard to separate and assign a proper position. It is reasonable to categorize an object (of activity) as either a transparent affordance or as the creative result of a shared effort. Table 1 clarifies the relations and the overall structure of a semantic field for exploring relations between learning objects, individuals and the social world. There are several approaches for describing what happens when self-controlled subjects and collective team players deal with social, material and cultural artifacts. The fourfold categorization is a display of artifacts, individuals, social systems and activities.

Table 1 first covers a situation where the agent is able to recognize/indentify an object through internalization and individual "push". Then there is an agent who searches/establishes object relations through externalizing individual "push". During the next stage employees present/contextualize an object through externalizing collective "pull". Finally the trajectory describes an ideal situation where employees co-construct a learning object through individual internalizing "push" and externalizing collective "pull".

BACKGROUND

Managerial Control

Facilitation, management and leadership by means of agency and intentionality describe near synonymous behaviors. On agency, Vygotsky (1986) outlines the characteristics of a stepwise process which implies the advancement of intentionality.

Table 1. Conceptual matrix over "learning object" processes

Unconscious reflexes	Consciousness of objects	Self-consciousness/Self-management	Scientific thinking
Primary artifact (material)	Primary artifact (tool)	Secondary transformative artifact (sensory)	Tertiary artifact (functional theory)
World 1: User operations	World 1: User operations	World 2: Logical structure of interaction	World 3: Hidden and visible cognitions
Need-based agency	Need-based agency	Delegated agency	Conditional agency
Discovery	Co-ordination	**Co-operation**	Co-construction
Positioning obj.	Define object	Report factual data	Instantiate learning object
Object identification	Object relations	Object transformation	Co-configuration work/Learning by experiencing

By referring to an example of how children become aware of their intentions when they sketch a drawing, Vygotsky observed that at an early age the child simply draws, then the child labels the picture after drawing it and at a mature stage the child makes up a plan before drawing the picture. So, planning is a significant part of agency and a prerequisite for successful management.

In the West, the propositional antithesis to "collective culture" is individual leadership. Kaptelinin & Nardi (2006, p. 247-248) enrich the analytic potential of the latter concept by suggesting there is (a) need-based agency as in biological and social needs; (b) delegated agency as in acting on someone's behalf; and (c) conditional agency as when actions produce (un)intended effects. But long before it became necessary to fine-tune the operational meaning of agency, people realized that any notion of humanity carries with it an idea of fostering, dedication, purposefulness or will-power. It is equally true that a single-minded materialistic approach to how the human mind works have disconnected research from real life experiences. For some time, also, general activity theorists were under the stigmatizing influence of Marxist writings. Surprisingly enough, Hegelian (1904, p. 269) conceptions of modern man, the industry worker or the employee, reveal a self-centered view on agency: "If man saw [...] that whatever happens to him is only an outcome of himself, and that he only bears his own guilt, he would stand free." Marx (1990, p. 177) complements Hegel's comprehension of Modern Man as an outcome of his own labor, describing him as "the architect of his own future" (ibid, p. 271) equipped with an ability to master the laws of his own formation. Also, but from a perspective of the general laws that govern man's historical development, the general opinion was that employees had to become agents of a new line of development. This inspiration originated from Engels (1966, p. 302) bold prognosis. "The objective, external forces which have hitherto dominated history will pass under the control of men themselves. It is only from this point that men, with full consciousness, will fashion their own history."

By emphasizing the proper object of research as *individual within a group*, Bruner (1987, p. 15) says Vygotsky confronted concepts like freedom, necessity, agency and causality, arguing this was so "because he [Vygotsky] was so dedicated to the concept of self-regulation." Vygotsky himself (1997, p. 166) say: "[individual] Thought plays the part of an advance guide of our behavior." On intentionality related to mediation, Kaptelinin & Nardi (2006, p. 10) say "*people* act *with* technology, [...] People act as *subjects* in the world." The authors (ibid, p. 33) also argue that individual agency is "an ability to act in the sense of *producing effects* and an [...] *ability and need to act.*

There is, as indicated, a risk that people confuse current trends and tendencies in ICT like individual self-control, ownership and private projects with collective practices, peripheral participation and Internet communities.

Organizational Development

One objective of this text is to promote systems thinking about relations, i.e. second order cybernetics. But what is the position of current organization theory? Rigg (2008, p. 105) argues for a 'both-and' understanding of relations between 'I' and 'we', criticizing the latter because "organizational or systemic capacity rarely goes beyond the notion of peers". Instead, Rigg (ibid, p. 106) introduces the concept "multi-agency partnerships", but without clarifying the relations of such networks. A more rewarding contribution to organization theory is Vince (2004), defining organizational learning as a contextualized collective process of inquiry into established practices. For the mentioned examples, the counter argument to agency is organization. However, the concept "organization" denotes patterns of social interaction and some researchers verify to the argument that organization theory as void of theory by claiming that an organization is a framework of discoursed and "interactively shared meanings". The analytical power of such a statement is questionable as it lacks reference to the impact of a contextualized activity.

Action network theory (ANT), a late follower of the Vygotskian original, purports an extreme view of relational agency in objects and people. The main advocate of the theory, Latour (1994), says people and tools are placed in an all-encompassing network without boundaries, or social relations, between objects and the individual. Miettinen (1999, p. 177) echoes Vygotsky's example of intentionality, saying that if adults only broke their direct and spontaneous instrumental relation to objects, they would be able to imagine, plan and visualize a different future. It is far from clear, however, how the shift from one object relation to another would come about. In short, ANT is an extreme form of integrating/integrated subjects and contextualized objects for meeting the purpose of this study.

Traditional General activity theory (GAT) on the other hand, stresses (Lee 1985, p. 68) that Vygotsky and Marx (1990) had several things in common, e.g. balanced relations between objects and people plus emphasis on situated activity rather than individual acts. From a social cybernetic perspective, their primary idea lay in "showing what role or effect an item has in some system of which it is part." In another statement about society defined as a political unit, Vygotsky (2004, p. 343) says that "We cannot master the truth about personality and personality itself so long as mankind has not mastered the truth about society and society itself." Vygotsky (1998) held that description and analysis of social structures should start with systems thinking because the object of research is the social organization first and the individual psyche second. He also outlined the relationship between man and the world as an impetus for generalization, abstraction and learning, opting for influences of external activity systems, or in present day terms "learning organizations".

At first every higher form of behavior is assimilated by the child exclusively from the external aspect. [...] It is only due to the fact that other people fill the natural form of behavior with a certain social content, for others rather than for the child himself, that it acquires the significance of a higher function. Finally, in the process of a long development, the child becomes conscious of the structure of this function and begins to control his own internal operations and to direct them. (Vygotsky, 1998, p. 171)

Just like Yrjö Engeström (1987), Scribner (1985, p. 123) positions Vygotsky's ideas in the realm of systems thinking by referring to expanding and growing cultures combined with people's need to "search for specifically human behavior in history." From a perspective of fragmented contemporary human histories, ethno-methodologists like Garfinkel (1967) study everyday activity and structured social behavior in great detail but with little success. Participatory learning theory (Lave & Wenger, 1991) likewise emphasizes context, collaboration, inter-subjectivity and discourse. Such research on human relations is usually conducted among members of a narrowly defined group of people in delimited and contingent learning contexts. In clarifying the relations between human developing, contextual learning, systems thinking and agency, Bronfenbrenner (1970) provides a holistic approach. Carefully defined micro-, meso-, exo- and macro-levels of analysis forms a basis for investigation. Each level covers expansive activities in social systems. In a similar line of research, Engeström (1999) defines contextualized phenomena where people work together towards a shared goal, thus forming an: "object-oriented, collective and culturally mediated activity, or activity system. The minimum elements of this system include the object, subject, mediating artifacts (signs and tools) rules, community, and division of labor." Likewise Nardi (1996) defines "collective activity" as an analytical tool for understanding emerging contradictions during cooperative work. Today such definitions refer to intranet employees, virtual teams, web-based communities or net-cultures.

Synthesizing Individual Agency and Collective Teamwork

This section covers a synthesis between managerial agency and social structure. Many approaches to understanding systems thinking, systemic practices or collective behavior reflect a dualism between materialistic and intentionalist Psychology, the former emphasizing collective systems and the latter stressing individual needs, motives and goals. However, some misconceptions prevail. In commenting on the relation between man and environment, Hodkinson, Biesta & James (2008, p. 33) say: "Any place where people act and interact has a learning culture, where learning of some type takes place." Next the authors (ibid, p. 34) present a circular argument about activity systems, suggesting: "Cultures are (re) produced by individuals, just as individuals are (re)produced by cultures." However, they (ibid, p. 30) confuse relations between "individual" and "social" by aggregating to their theoretical basis neighboring, but fundamentally different, approaches to workplace learning, representations or Philosophy. Their confusion is based on a lack of interest in separating transaction by/of an artifact from interaction with another human being. Furthermore, their (ibid, p. 30) attempt at explaining learning culture characteristics vs. providing a GAT account of learning "from a broadly situated socio-cultural perspective" turns into abstract conceptual analysis without a proper definition of the difference between mediated and mediating influences or the "object of activity" (Foot, 2002). For example, they (ibid p. 34) confuse expectations with needs, motives and goals. Also, missing from the account is a clarification of how they understand theoretical development as the result of emerging relations between behavior, context, process, objective or outcome. Moreover, but without actually doing so, the authors (ibid, p. 37) claim they build on analysis of empirical data, quoting Lave (1996, p. 162) saying "Researchers would have to explore each practice to understand what is being learned and how." Finally, they corrupt an explicit mission to integrate individual agency and collective systems thinking because of a missing link between items in a diverse list of distantly related theories.

Contrary to the presented attempt, Vygotsky (1987) provides and empirically verified statement about the operational relation between individual thought and shared action within one comprehensive theoretical frame.

In subjecting to his will the process of his own reactions, man enters in this way into a substantially new relation with the environment, comes to a new functional exploitation of elements in the environment as stimuli-signs which he uses, depending on external means, and directs and controls his own behavior, controls himself from outside, compelling stimuli-signs to affect him, and elicits reactions he desires. (Vygotsky, 1987, p. 63)

In following the GAT-tradition, Yaroshevsky (1989, p. 80) compliments Vygotsky's ambition to integrate individual life with the development of mankind perceived as a social system. In order to do so, the researcher must weave "the individual's brief life into the great age-long history of social being [combining] the macroscale of the life of the people down the ages and [...] the microscale of the individual's routine contacts with his brethren." The quote provides a synthesizing approach to the old-school dichotomization between management and staff, between Self and Other plus between agency and social structure.

One would think that consciousness is a purely individual quality, but in another synthesizing approach Vygotsky (1999) argues that consciousness is contextualized in the social moment, on time and in place. Leontev (1978) is also clear on the issue, stating that there is only activity defined as a relation between an agent and the object towards which the action is directed. Leontev's major concern is to explain relations between trajectories of needs-motive-objective and activity-awareness-personality. Sure enough, subjects and objects acquire properties/characteristics when activities are enacted on/with/by individual agents. Research in Kaptelinin & Nardi (2006, p. 31) adopt a similar transformational view of relations between man and the world, saying the purpose of GAT is to "understand individual human beings, as well as the social entities they compose." The authors (ibid, p. 37) conclude "A key factor of an individual's success is the success or failure of the social entity [...] to which the individual belongs." Such social entities would be pairs, groups, families, organizations, communities, nations or cultures. For the researched context, Koschman (1996) and Gifford & Enyedi (1999) say a shift is underway turning towards models of working which include collaborative learning, for example among focus group employees in corporate settings.

In finding a solution to the separation between individual and/or collective co-construction of a learning object, Moll (1990, p. 1) says there is a "cognitive gap" between dichotomized approaches. Unfortunately research so far has been reluctant to clarify how individual input contributes to collective co-construction in digital environments. In spite of this lack of interest, Rydberg & Christiansen (2008, p. 209) argue that during processes of meaningful exchanges, the interlocutors gradually feel "invited to mimic" each other's behavior, "spread the knowledge" or "formulate new rules". This contention, however, lies far from what is implied by co-construction of a learning object. From a different perspective, Levin & Wadsmanly (2008, p. 234) say co-construction of an object equals "cognitive transformation", a definition which likewise confuses the concept, as co-construction is a far more situated and interactive process than the authors' black-box theory suggests.

In a final reference, Wertsch (1998) offers "mediated action" as a synthesis to the split between individual and collective approaches. According to Wertsch, a special dynamics is set in motion when an agent acts with culturally developed tools. The analytic concept – mediated action – inspires the researcher to go beyond comparing, abstracting and generalizing the individual agent. Provided the researcher has got an intention to develop theory, he can understand the forces that shape human action, more specifically understanding the studied object of activity, which in our case is to collect data among employees on a digital platform.

Table 2. Dichotomization of influences on co-construction of learning objects

Transaction (by/of)	Transformation	Interaction (with)
Agency	O	Structure
Personal mastery	B	Systems thinking
Subjective	J	Objective
Internal	E	External
Symbolic	C	Material
Mental action	T	Material action
Intention	S	Communication

THE OBJECT OF ACTIVITY

In exploring the explanatory power of GAT, it is necessary to introduce human-human and human object relations plus the concept of "object of activity". With an eye to individual consciousness about the existence of Self, Vygotsky (1994, p. 19) emphasized interaction between environment and person, citing Marx: "My relationship to my environment [...] is my consciousness". An additional note would be that agency relates to systems thinking, an idea similar to how individual relates to collective and how internal relates to external.

Preceding quotes and references emphasize the importance of agency in human development. But one would rather have an informed contemporary explanation focusing on a transformational move from agency towards structured activity or vice-versa. Galperin argues in Arievitch (2003, p. 279) that it is important to analyze the "culturally constructed nature of mind without losing the aspect of individual psychological functioning." It is however an unsolved problem and a matter of debate (ibid, p. 281) how "mental, psychological emerges out of material, nonpsychological." Another suggestion points to the need to envision a move between physical and metaphysical conceptualizations. This is so because according to Galperin (ibid., p. 284) people "understand individual mental development as the gradual internalization and transformation of socially constructed shared activities." By pointing to the object-relatedness of human activity, Galperin (ibid., p. 286) sees a way to "eliminate the dualism of mental and material, external and internal processes." A synthesizing solution would be Garrison's (2001, p. 288) response to Engeström & Miettinen's (1999) exploration of John Dewey's conception of relations between objects and objectives because "objects never lose their event quality". Table 2 contains some of the dualisms which would be potentially relevant for analyzing management of focus group interactions in a digital medium.

Rather than building on the neighboring differences in Table 2, Kaptelinin & Nardi (2006, p. 143) synthesize "object of activity" by contrasting Vygotsky's (1997) individual-psychological and Engeström's (1999) activity-oriented and organizational points of view. They say the *form of activity* is for Vygotsky individual and collective but for Engeström it is collective alone. The *object owners* are for Vygotsky the individual but for Engeström they are communities. *Salient and related phenomena* are for Vygotsky motivation and need. For Engeström they are the transforming routines for production in human activity systems. The next section follows Engeström's focus on activity systems.

LEARNING WITH TECHNOLOGY

The *Zing* platform and the business context of management, agenda, employees, focus group and has a significant impact on how the subjects perceive and conceive of the task at hand, the world and themselves operating the system. Nardi (1996, p. 70) asks of researchers who wish to clarify the impact of context on the form and contents of human interactions: "How can we confront the blooming, buzzing confusion that is 'context' and still produce generalizable results?" Later on Nardi (ibid.) motivates the question, saying "It is especially difficult to isolate and emphasize critical properties of artifacts (*Zing*, this author) and situations (*focus group*, this author) in studies that consider a full context (*data collection and co-construction*, this author)."

This study explores situated group interaction and an emerging activity which motivates the employees to commit themselves to a shared learning object, an objective or an "objectified motive" (Christiansen 1996). Activities may overlap and objects may be contradictory or in open conflict. Rueda, Gallego & Moll (2000, p. 71) note that by deploying a "boundary crossing object" (Rogoff, 2003) like a *Zing* session (characterized as medium plus activity), analysis of mediation between employees is an opportunity, because "The sociocultural perspective focuses on features of the basic social organization and the underlying assumptions of a given social context, and considers the effects these might have on *participation and competence* (emphasis by this author) as well as how the individual transforms the context." In drawing on Tuomi-Gröhn, Engeström and Young (2003), Walker & Nocon (2007, p. 180) say the transformative nature of interactions makes it necessary to define the employees' competence and ability to elicit higher mental functions in the given context. The outcome depends on how they - through participation and competence - "(a) understand and negotiate the meanings, through the use of material and symbolic artifacts and (b) understand and negotiate the meanings, through engagement with others, of the practices of a group and of the roles of individuals therein." Both processes are likely to come true during the studied focus group session.

The major contribution in Engeström (2007, p. 34) and Bødker & Andersen (2005) lies in the way the authors supply a framework for separating mediating processes for collaborative co-construction of a learning object from technological tool usage to produce pre-empted results. The configuration of the studied technology provides a unique context which enables for several ways of mediating between objects, processes, texts and people. In the lucky cases the flexibility of an interface enables for "multi-mediation of activities", a term introduced by Bødker & Andersen (2005). More specifically, *Zing* sessions mediate by several means: facilitator, speech, writing, keyboards, screen, peers etc. For the researched context, Engeström's (2007, p. 34) bipolar process-result scheme (Table 3) encompasses software flexibility with the specifics of a business context.

Table 3 suggests that "transformative learning" (Engeström, 2007, p. 36) would be a process encompassing one type of discourse related to co-configuration work for protecting self consciousness/self-management (SC/SM) and another type of discourse related to co-configuration work, safeguarding professional employee thinking (PET). So the researcher wishes to bridge the gap between tools, applications and procedures so as to trace co-configuration of a learning object during a successful focus group session in a business environment. The employees' are salespeople and their needs, motives and goals provide the necessary input to transformations between creative, social, self-centered and material levels of thinking. Also, and contrary to Engeström's (ibid, p. 36) prognosis, the studied employees experience a harmonious relation between design and implementation. Finally, Engeström's argument that pressures for self control versus collective consensus accompanied by past, present and future

Table 3. Mediating means for analyzing a sales course

Epistemology	Process vs. Results
Where to?	Higher mental functions vs. Company survey
Why?	Collect and categorize data vs. Learn about customer needs
The order of things?	*Zing* session logics vs. Service and sales strategy
Location?	Work sites vs. Open market
Who, What, When?	Employees, Managers, Text log, Continuous observation
Instrument?	Keyboard, screen, etc. vs. Interpretation, categorizing, etc.

demands on profitable productivity (ibid, p. 36) are left behind, because the employees operate from a development rather than a production rationale. Thus, saying and writing at different levels of transformative learning becomes the main objective for the employees. Engeström's (2007, p. 38) account of such learning by creative, reflected and strategic co-construction applies when:

- *Transformative learning* broadens the use of shared objects, e.g. the deployed platform
- Learning by *experiencing* puts the employees into real-life situations that require personal engagement in actions with material objects, artifacts and human beings, e.g. learning teams
- *Horizontal* and dialogical learning transform the *activity* by crossing boundaries and tying knots between activity systems, e.g. references to Aussie football

The first statement is true about *expansive learning* for reasons of developmental group dynamics between peers. The next statement is adequate for *experiential learning* because the employees foresee future company applications for themselves in a new role as facilitators. The last statement is appropriate for *democracy* because the employees bring their experience to situations, settings and contexts where teamwork is a prerequisite for development.

METHODOLOGY

It is a mystery how the contents of an argument, the genius, uniqueness or creativity of an utterance, the embedded value of a statement, social relations, perceptions or expectations, trigger responses among peers and enable for communities of practice to share experiences and co-construct learning objects. It matters a lot if we consider the individual agent by reputation, strategy, previous contact, familiarity, antagonism or persistence, endowing on him/her the ability to inspire collectives of individuals to commit themselves to a shared activity. And it could well be the other way around: the decoding of individual intentions by input-process-feedback enables for analysis of the social system rather than individual learning processes for discovering (understanding the formation of) a learning object.

There are implications of using GAT for studying agency and structure in an ICT setting. Focus is on patterns of continuous activity rather than fragmented episodes; a data collection technique involving direct observation and log data. Still, the methodology for exploring how employees and management interact during a *Zing* session needs specifying. Nardi (1996, p. 95) summarizes the main objective for laboratory-like studies of contextualized man-machine interaction such as the reported case. Research for producing and collecting data should establish (i) a point of time when a first instantiation of the phenomenon under study, i.e. community feeling, acquired its

Table 4. Analytical scope for understanding ICT mediated learning

Transparency (in objects)	Affordance (by objects)	Creativity (people)
Primary artifact	*Secondary artifact*	Tertiary artifact
User operations	*Logical structure of interaction*	Cognitions
Conditional agency	*Delegated agency*	Need-based agency
Coordination	*Cooperation*	Co-construction

characteristics. Research should also (ii) identify the main contradictions at each phase of the employees' development. Finally, (iii) research should trace the development of the social system – an emerging result of how the employees solve natural contradictions as defined by the setting, the software and the ongoing activity. Here I follow a line of research for studying (iii) the hidden processes of a focus group session through the instantiation of a learning object.

As to the practical implications about *Zing*, Wartofsky (1979) outlines a typology of artifacts for understanding human behavior. It is deployed for demonstrating soft- and hardware plus organization as a means for creating cognitions related to data collection. This is the general outline for analyzing focus group sessions between a facilitator and several employees: The primary artifact is the equipment (keyboards, lap tops, video-camera and router). The secondary artifact is the functioning of the equipment (plus working routines surrounding it) for transmitting the skills that the employees demonstrate in producing the sought survey data orally and in writing. The tertiary artifact transcends the practical processes and realities of the physical world and enables for the researcher to trace emerging learning objects. Interestingly enough, Bødker (1991), Wartofsky (1979) and Kaptelinin & Nardi (2006) all take onboard a similar perspective based on transparency, affordance, agency and creativity. Table 4 describes sought qualities where the first layer represents mediation, the second usage, the third agency and the final layer mental processes related to organization of work. A transitional creep between columns from transparency to affordances is obvious. But a move from affordance to creativity seems hard to accomplish.

Table 4 indicates that mediating interactions cover goals that are hard to define from the inside for the subjects as well as from the outside for the analyst. Therefore it is reasonable to assume that during *construction of the object*, the subjects pay attention to the task at hand in a self-conscious and self-controlled (SC/SM) way. During *instantiation of the object*, on the other hand, the subjects devote their attention to arguments, statements and/or questions whilst applying professional employee thinking (PET) about prospects, applications, solutions and results. It seems equally reasonable to assume that during instantiation of a learning object the employees apply "discursive mediation" to help them share and improve on their beliefs, values and intentions. Finally, while discoursing (Foucault 1993) between the employees is the mediating means for SC/SM- and PET-ambitions, factual information is the goal for the facilitating manager. Table 5 indicates some additional influences, foci and cognitions that act on the corporate discourse during a qualified process of relation building, team-working and discovery.

The implications of Vygotsky's (1998, p. 169) renowned quotation (below) are rarely acknowledged, for example as regards individual versus social construction of meaning. In fact, it demonstrates an expansive context for providing a general law for how higher mental functions (PET) emerge. "Every function in the cultural development of the child appears on the stage twice, in two forms – at first as social, then as psychological;

Table 5. Means, processes and objectives

Define the theme	Construct the object	Instantiate the object
Ritual	Group dynamics	Personal motive
Learn about the theme	Stick to the theme	Expand the theme
Intuitive	SC/SM	PET
Tradition/culture	Social relations	Individual

at first as a form of cooperation between people, as a group, an *intermental* category, then as a means of individual behavior, as an *intramental* category." (italics by this author) When Vygotsky (1997, p. 106) framed the "general genetic law of cultural development" he defined discernible stages of human becoming. His (ibid., p. 165) fourfold categorization builds on concepts like time, contexts and history. First there are basic reactions like (i) unconscious reflexes and (ii) consciousness of objects which fall outside the current purpose. The studied focus group operates at significantly higher levels of either (iii) self-consciousness/self-management (SC/SM) or (iv) professional employee thinking (PET). Consequently, if contextual learning in focus groups were supported by "individual subject" the outcome would remain at a SC/SM level. But if learning were supported by "collective subject" the outcome would be PET. Pedler, Burgoyne & Brook (2005, p. 10) define items (iii) and (iv) as key principles for successful social activities. For SC/SM operations applies that work is directed towards problems without any right answers and problem solving activities aim at personal development. For PET to appear there is a need for deliberate work between peers who search for solutions to puzzles that require expert knowledge and result in organizational development.

Software and Context

The software offers several enabling characteristics. It is a ready-made tool without need for additional affordances. The technology is easy to appropriate for the employees. Basically any situation where spoken (direct) and written (reflected) queries are produced (negotiated) and collected (saved) provides an opportunity. Fitzgerald & Findlay (2004) say the platform scaffolds complex thinking, sense making and decision making processes through self-controlled interaction. *Zing* is a pre-packaged "interaction design" (Winograd 1996), i.e. a space for human communication and action. The software transforms the users' way of thinking, action and understanding, but the process will take off only if a competent manager-facilitator, or 'cultural broker' (Van Oers, 1998) supports activities. After successful sessions the employees become technologically empowered and socially contextualized agents. Still, the efficiency of the technology is dependent on the manager-facilitator's leadership, communication and social skills, all aiming at the development of a work related experiences where employees learn about each other and customer sales.

Developing a "domain object" like *Zing* is an overall concern whenever people meet as strangers in an unfamiliar situation. In operating such "user interfaces", Beaudouin-Lafon (2000) say we must learn to separate between domain objects in a process of *object construction* obtained through another process of *object instantiation*. For the studied case, properly managed employee input turns individual initiatives into a rewarding and productive session on sales strategy. Interaction between the manager-facilitator and the employees is the actual component which – if properly managed – transforms the employees' thinking through subtle commands for qualifying and expanding the domain object, i.e. visual text in frames on the screen and a hidden text log inside the manager's computer.

This study builds on data produced during a session among employees and a manager at a small-middle sized (SME) enterprise. The traditional power structure of any organizational culture supports enabling socio-cultural artifacts like agenda, materials, language, tools, titles and software. This is a hierarchical context where situational, transactional and transformational leadership resides on top without much "social butterflying" going on with the staff. The manager's behavior enables for growth of relations through structured talking. Discursive practices enabled by the technology, on the other hand, are the means and the medium for staff. In the lucky cases, learning with technologies complements the manager's job by facilitating interactive Web 2.0 experiences. However, the manager's practices also impose restrictions on interactive construction of meaning. Taken together, the shared context is a "social space" for relation building and decision making. Hirst & Vadeboncoeur (2006, p. 206) say such spaces are "most easily defined by conversation, speech and intention." As long as the social Web 2.0 space covers a participatory and collective approach to the discourse, i.e. a development rationale, any arrangement offers transformation of the employees' objectives, relations and identities. But equally important is that the session forms a situated practice; a one-off opportunity. As to the importance of situatedness, Gieryn (2000, p. 471) suggests that a shared physical context, for example during a workplace meeting "stabilizes and gives durability to social structural categories, differences and hierarchies; arranges patterns of face-to-face interaction that constitute network formation and collective action; ["Place"] embodies and secures otherwise intangible cultural norms, identities, memories." The reported focus group session is situated in time and place but still a one-off opportunity, hardly forming a sustainable community of practice.

So, the interface meets several criteria for qualifying as good methodology even if there were no previous computing culture among the employees. For the given context, the software (i) facilitates externalization of focus group ideas; (ii) enables for the employees to engage in productive discourse and act in/as a social system; (iii) generates spontaneous talk and reflective writing; and (iv) enables for the manager to lead the discussion, collect necessary data and analyze staff experiences. By controlling software as well as interactions, the manager keeps the group to the agenda, asking the employees to comment orally and on their keyboards throughout the session. The setting enables for the manager to visualize employee input on a screen and communicate, ask, explain, clarify and mediate with the group. These are the manager's themes as they appear on the screen during a 45-minute session on October 10, 2008: *Using the software* (5 min); *Customer sales experiences* (5 min); *On the job ICT–experiences* (7 min); *Ideal uses of ICT* (15 min); *Your own uses of media* (5 min); *Other* (8 min).

The described totality of affordances (competence, software, motivation, rank, history) helps the manager-facilitator identify and lead the group towards supplying data – and eventually co-constructing a learning object. The proper running of focus group sessions constitutes a specific environment which generates data as well as communication, interaction and ultimately a learning object. Contrary to Engeström's (2007, p. 35) statement: "that many of the technologies introduced to facilitate learning are themselves poorly analyzed and understood in terms of their epistemic qualities and potentials." focus groups on *Zing* provide an activity and a context; a straightforward and self-explaining artifact. Also contrary to Engeström's (2007, p. 36) ideal of "overarching concepts and visions ("where to" artifacts) are typically not considered as part of the technology." Because such a quality would lead to control by objectives – an ideal much too close to classic conditioning to be valid for the studied context. However, the software enables for the manager to calculate the semantics of saved text logs and extract business- related "concepts and visions" from individual employee entries.

On the idea of management by discoursing, Wells (2007, p. 164) says "the discourse ensures that all participants are working toward the same goal and are coordinating their individual actions and their use of mediating artifacts to use it." Vygotsky and Engeström argue that interaction is a "mediated and mediating activity". Also human development – emerging as a result of interaction – is based on GAT concepts like appropriation and internalization of physical and symbolic tools, cultural artifacts. Put differently, the software is an affordance for management and employees equally to appropriate the tool and engage in "object-related meaningful activity" (Arievitch, 2003, p. 280). Furthermore, activities ensure that every component of the interactions carry a human quality in their objects, objectives and meanings. There is a direct communication process for collecting data called "information exchange" (ibid., p. 280) to construct a learning object. There is also "material transformation" of the situation to help instantiate the object. Thus, the participants transcend - by means of the evolutionary conditions of social interaction - the most apparent objective; which is to collect corporate data. A good session is all about employees enabling for others to follow their line of thinking. Properly managed sessions acknowledge the role of social interaction in the cognitive development of employees by boosting collective exchange of meanings.

RESULTS

Roth (2004) argues that GAT is becoming popular in studies of human interaction and communication. In order to be able to understand how people operate and process language, it is necessary to attend to the cognitive semantic language-as-product side of interactions as well as to the social interactive, conversational language-as-action tradition, typically employed in discourse analysis (Wells, 2007) and pragmatics (Clark, 1992). In order to clarify the operational difference (i.e. effect on individuals in a community of practice) between agency defined by individual input in a focus group session and systems thinking defined by the way individuals inspire and react to peer input, focus is on *context* and *group activity*. The manager plays a crucial role during sessions as he is the facilitating socio-instrumental leader following a pre-set agenda. He is busy talking, typing, reading and reviewing the employees' input. The manager's most frequent comment is "type it; use your keyboards; write it down; let's see what we have got here".

Text Log Notes

The manager's computer automatically saves a log file over all text log entries. This data complements what the observer-researcher has jotted down during the session. The data enables for further analysis, either manually of by means of a digital tool like *Leximancer*™ suited to categorizing large corpuses of data. The manager's entries and one employee's (020; talkative socio-emotional male) entries are given in chronological order just as they appear in the log file. I have excluded the first item on the manager-facilitator's list, i.e. the technical handling of the system plus all other employee entries.

2.1 *What were the positive experiences in your practical sales course?* (1) Good resources- projectors and Internet made all kinds of sales easy; (7) A small enterprise; (10) Good liaisons officer feedback

2.2 *What were some negative experiences in your sales course?* (1) Unsupportive supervisor, minimal feedback given on everyday sales experience from supporting staff; (3)

no assistance with programming; (10) NO release time at all over the duration of the course

3.0 *ICT experiences on the course*; N/A

3.1 *Was ICT sales encouraged or discouraged during the course, please explain your answers;* (4)encouraged- laptops available, good sales network setup, ICT used for all customers on 'laptop day' (once a week). Projectors in all customer service rooms

3.2 *What activities with ICT were you able to undertake while on the course?* (2) Photoshop, movie maker, used projector for sales lessons (I cant do cursive) with a Netwok of computers.

3.3 *Could you describe the types of ICT skills the apprentices with whom you worked were able to use?* (3) Minimal, some colleagues still have handwritten programs, most staff had basic skills, struggled with programs other than internet and word processors. One 25 year old instructed rest of staff when necessary. (10) You can see how the importance of support when our instructor stands infront of the dias and don't even know how to turn the lights on, or with customers when you do not know how to work the Smart Board & computer System (or be able to identify why it is not working).

4.0 *Ideal uses of ICT;* N/A

4.1 *What is the most intriguing use of technologies in sales that you have ever heard about?* (1)zing!; (2) smart boards, video conferencing

4.2 *How would you like to include ICT into sales?* (1) every customer to have a laptop drilled to their desk

4.3 *Do you think there is a place in sales for customers to use simulated spaces such as Second Life? If so why?* (1) (I dont know what it is) but NO

5.0 *Your own uses of technologies;* N/A

5.1 *Could you describe in what ways you use technologies to assist in your sales?* (1) Basic, word processing and internet (email etc)

5.2 *Do you have an avatar and if so could you describe how you 'live' with it?* (4) no?

6.0 *Anything else?* (3)Not enough sales via ICT, should be evident through all campains; (8) ICT is starting to valued- as it makes sales jobs easier and customers' learning more engaged and open-ended

Direct Observation by the Researcher

Observation data complements the text log. During the studied session all employees have a choice to make and the observer first notes individual behavior as it appears to him, and later on categorizes their input as SC/SM= self-conscious self management or verbal action directed towards creating confidence in self or PET= actions reflecting professional employee thinking. The average distribution of SC/SM vs. PET input for the reported focus group session is balanced compared to other sessions.

The manager introduces the theme, the background to the meeting and the software. Already from the beginning, there is one male employee (020), nodding, talking loudly and typing on the wireless keyboard. Another less talkative male employee is sitting next to him. Then there is a female employee who is cautious at the beginning, eventually supplying reflected input. Another slightly older woman remains silent throughout the session. A young female employee supports the talkative man, smiling, laughing and providing sparse comments. Another female employee provides a few contributions to the discussion during the last minutes of the meeting. A fourth female employee is really into it with creative questioning, at times resisting the pace that the manager is setting up.

A primary hypothesis suggests that because the facilitator is a good instrumental leader, the employees try to make an impression by becoming good team workers and supporting their peers. Both roles are necessary for a functioning process, and besides, it would be foolish to challenge company leadership. The employees use their communicative competence for solving the contextualized task by balancing SC/SM with PET-entries and thus creating positive group dynamics.

The Facilitator-Manager's Entries

The facilitator-manager's immediate comments look like a summary of the oral discussion. They are continuously noted under separate headings and for a certain position. The themes cover: 2(14) customers' enthusiasm for learning; 2(15) small business-would get to know all the customers; 2(16) good liaison support important; 3(11) Lack of support; 3(12) Aggravation between customers; 3(13) lack of resources; 3(14) priority in the sales instructions re ICT; 3(17) release time for planning of campaigns; 3(18) Lack of expertise re specific pieces of software being used; 3.1(10) Encouraged; 3.1(11) important to have a good intranet; 3.1(12) Using ICT to intro to topics because customers find it interesting; 3.1(13) using 3D ICT and getting customers to manipulate objects; 3.1(14) Able to personalise learning - with a difficult customer; 3.2(9) 6 people - one Mac and the rest on Windows; 3.3(8) IT is not a key learning area and therefore not a priority.

ANALYSING THE DATA

Any form of or mediated activity operates as a means for achieving the goal of individual actions. However in the lucky here-and-now cases when employees interact effectively, their goals tend to go beyond the original target. In the unfortunate there-and-then cases, shared goals become a secondary objective. In most cases the failure of a group to reach consensus is due to an inability in the individual subjects to take on challenges, i.e. to manage contradictions and help positive dynamics emerge.

Mediation by means of a shared discourse differs from instrumental ICT tool mediation, which so far has been a frequently studied theme. This fact carries some implications on how we conceive of the trajectory of object construction, object transformation (= discoursing) and object instantiation (= co-construction). Very little research has focused on verbal activities from a perspective of how agents process learning objects. The question is whether it matters if we understand discoursing between people as a decisive context or an activity for obtaining a projected objective. A tentative answer is that interaction between focus group employees defines transactions between the subjects rather than transformation of commodities, artifacts or management objectives. Activities in the observed focus group appear as social language between employees. Their operations on the keyboard and oral workplace rhetoric are socially intuitive rather than deliberately planned. The employees realize that their interpretation of the situation as well as their speaking and writing influence the birth, transformation and contents of a uniquely appropriated learning object. And this development is contrary to the stereotypical model of how employees achieve a pre-empted knowledge object.

It is usually easy to see why a certain behavior is rational for the individual, e.g. to supply boring data during a session. Also, it is difficult to see how one kind of input comes naturally as SC/SM and another kind comes out as elaborated PET. One reason is that the contextual framing of the session merely inspires provision of raw data. But if every employee stopped at providing factual information, very little group dynamics, motivation or creativity would emerge. So why do employees find it rational take on the extra "burden" of supplying PET when all that the manager expects of them is that they retell their experiences of a customer sales course? It remains a mystery by what inter- or intrapersonal means employees manage to "balance" their verbal input so that co-construction of a learning object becomes a rational thing to do.

SOLUTIONS AND RECOMMENDATIONS

One lesson learnt is the difficulty of sticking to a systemic perspective in corporate initiatives at facilitating co-construction of learning objects. However, an obvious solution to avoiding this barrier is to combine a digital system with an explicit and shared view on how to manage a social system of employees. It is necessary that the manager clarifies the primary objective, which is to collect data. It is a bonus objective to be able to make the most of the opportunity to co-construct a learning object. The first objective meets the company's production rationale and the bonus objective supports a development rationale. As expected, management should interact with staff in a flexible, communicative and entrepreneurial way on a platform which promotes balancing of the instrumental, professional and social aspects of workplace learning.

FUTURE RESEARCH

A relevant focus for research would be to investigate how the mediating software promotes a collective sense of professional employee thinking, in spite of primary contradictions between objectives. More specifically, research needs to identify the relevant criteria for identifying shifts between conditional, delegated and need-based agency.

CONCLUSION

In choosing between individual rationality and collective consensus, it is usually a wise choice to act from a systems-systematic perspective. Neither the individual employee nor the collective team of focus group employees influence to the same extent the quality of learning during sessions where the job to be done is co-construction of a learning object. It is rather a pro-active individual within the group who controls the collective development of higher mental functions for all focus group members, the manager-facilitator included.

The contents of this text cover differences between collective and individual perspectives on human activity systems. It seems as if people rather intuitively construct transform and instantiate a learning object, regardless if they were instructed to do so or if they were merely asked to supply answers on their experiences of ICT in sales. The outcome is a shared discourse which follows the same "rules" as people do in the process of collectively co-constructing shared objects. So paradoxically, the process and the product are near-identical. In GAT, on the one hand, the individual agent engages in object-oriented activity, deliberately fulfilling his needs, motives and goals. In systems thinking on the other hand, individual employees dutifully supply data and apply simplistic rules according to the manager's pre-set blueprint. Thus far everything is clear. But outlining the actual mechanisms of how the employee's inter-mental world is transformed by sub-optimized SC/SM input and how their peers' intra-mental world is influenced by valuable PET-entries remains a mystery.

This study started off with an objective to separate between individual and collective influences on human behavior. In talking about collectively co-constructed and shared "togetherness" it would seem foolish to refer to sole employees. It would be equally foolish to refer to the actions of a collective of employees who follow management instructions. But it would be wise to refer to pro-active employees in a responsive group of peers. The mediating tool and the actions of the focus group define the corporate setting as a comprehensive activity system with a shared object of activity.

REFERENCES

Arievitch, I. (2003). A potential for an integrated view of development and learning: Galperin's contribution to sociocultural psychology. *Mind, Culture, and Activity . International Journal (Toronto, Ont.)*, *10*(4), 178–288.

Beaudouin-Lafon, M. (2000). Instrumental interaction: An interaction model for designing post-WIMP user interfaces. In *Proceedings of the 2000 ACM Conference on Human Factors in Computing Systems,* The Hague, Netherlands, (pp. 446-453).

Bereiter, C. (2003). Artifacts, canons, and the progress of pedagogy: A response to contributors. In B. Smith (Ed.), *Liberal education in a knowledge society,* (pp. 223-244). Chicago: Open Court.

Bødker, S. (1991). *Through the Interface: A Human Activity Approach to User Interface Design.* Hillsdale, NJ: Lawrence Erlbaum.

Bødker, S., & Andersen, P. B. (2005). Complex mediation. *Human-Computer Interaction, 20,* 353–452. doi:10.1207/s15327051hci2004_1

Bronfenbrenner, U. (1970). *Two Worlds of Childhood: U.S. and U.S.S.R.* Russell Sage Foundation.

Bruner, J. (1987). Prologue in R. W. Rieber & A. S. Carton (Eds.), *The Collected Works of L.S. Vygotsky,* (Vol. 1, Problems of general psychology, pp. 1-16). New York: Plenum.

Christiansen, E. (1996). Tamed by a rose: Computers as tools in human interaction. In B. Nardi (Ed.), *Context and Consciousness: Activity Theory and Human-Computer Interaction,* (pp. 175-198). Cambridge, MA: MIT Press.

Clark, H. H. (1992). *Arenas of Language Use.* Chicago: University of Chicago Press.

Dewey, J. (1952/1989). Modern Philosophy. In J. A. Boydston (Ed.). *John Dewey: The Later Works,* (Vol. 16, pp. 407-419). Carbondale: Southern Illinois University Press.

Ducheneaut, N., & Bellotti, V. (2001). E-mail as habitat: An exploration of embedded personal information management. *Interaction, 8,* 30–38. doi:10.1145/382899.383305

Engeström, Y. (1987). *Learning by Expanding: An Activity-Theoretical Approach to Developmental Research.* Helsinki, Finland: Orienta-Consultit.

Engeström, Y. (1999). Introduction. In Y. Engeström, R. Miettinen, & R-L. Punamäki (Eds.), *Perspectives on Activity Theory,* (pp. 1-16). Cambridge, UK: Cambridge University Press.

Engeström, Y. (2007). Enriching the theory of expansive learning: Lessons from journeys towards coconfiguration. *Mind, Culture, and Activity . International Journal (Toronto, Ont.)*, *14*(1), 23–39.

Fitzgerald, R., & Findlay, J. (2004). A computer-based research tool for rapid knowledge-creation. In L. Cantoni & C. McLoughlin (Eds.), *Proceedings of World Conference on Educational Multimedia Hypermedia and Telecommunications,* (EDMEDIA) in Lugano, Switzerland. Chesapeake, VA: AACE.

Foot, K. (2002). Pursuing an evolving object: a case study in object formation and identification. *Mind, Culture, and Activity, 9*(2), 132–149. doi:10.1207/S15327884MCA0902_04

Foucault, M. (1993). *Diskursens ordning*. (L'ordre de discourse). Stockholm/Steghag: Symposion.

Garfinkel, H. (1967). *Studies in Ethnomethodology*. New York: Prentice Hall.

Garrison, J. (2001). An introduction to Dewey's theory of functional "trans-action": An alternative paradigm for activity theory. *Mind, Culture, and Activity . International Journal (Toronto, Ont.)*, *8*(4), 275–296.

Gieryn, T. (2000). A place for space in sociology. *Annual Review of Sociology*, *26*, 463–496. doi:10.1146/annurev.soc.26.1.463

Gifford, B., & Enyedi, N. (1999). Activity centered design: Towards a theoretical framework for CSCL. In *Proceedings of the 1999 Conference on Computer Support for Collaborative Learning,* (pp. 189-196). Stanford, California.

Hansson, T. (2002). Leadership by activity theory and professional development by social construction. *Systemic Practice and Action Research*, *15*(5), 411–436. doi:10.1023/A:1020129327695

Hegel, G. W. F. (1904). *The Phenomenology of Mind,* (transl. J. B. Baillie). New York: Harper Row.

Hirst, E., & Vadeboncoeur, J. (2006). Patrolling the borders of otherness: Dis/placed identity positions for teachers and students in schooled spaces. *Mind, Culture, and Activity . International Journal (Toronto, Ont.)*, *13*(3), 205–227.

Hodkinson, P., Biesta, G., & James, D. (2008). Understanding learning culturally: Overcoming the dualism between social and individual views of learning. *Vocations and Learning*, *1*, 27–47. doi:10.1007/s12186-007-9001-y

Kaptelinin, V., & Miettinen, R. (2005). Perspectives on the object of activity. *Mind, Culture, and Activity*, *12*(1), 1–3. doi:10.1207/s15327884mca1201_1

Kaptelinin, V., & Nardi, B. (2006). *Acting with Technology: Activity Theory and Interaction Design*. Cambridge MA:The MIT Press.

Koschman, T. (1996). Paradigm shifts in instructional technology. In T. Koschman (Ed.), *CSCL Theory and Practice of an Emerging Paradigm* (pp. 1-23). Mahwah, NJ: Lawrence Erlbaum.

Latour, B. (1994). On technical mediation: Philosophy, genealogy and sociology. *Common Knowledge*, *3*, 29–64.

Lave, J. (1996). Teaching as learning, in practice. *Mind, Culture, and Society*, *3*(3), 149–164. doi:10.1207/s15327884mca0303_2

Lave, J., & Wenger, E. (1991). *Situated Learning: Legitimate Peripheral Participation*. Cambridge, UK: Cambridge University Press.

Lee, B. (1985). Intellectual origins of Vygotsky's semiotic analysis. In J.V. Wertsch (Ed.), *Culture, Communication, and Cognition: Vygotskian perspectives* (pp. 66-93). Cambridge, UK: Cambridge University Press.

Leontev, A. (1978). *Activity, Consciousness and Personality*. Englewood Cliffs, NJ: Prentice Hall.

Levin, T., & Wadsmanly, R. (2008). Teachers' views on factors affecting effective integration of information technology in the classroom: Developmental scenery. *Journal of Technology and Teacher Education*, *16*(2), 233–263.

Marx, K. (1990). *Capital: A Critique of Political Economy,* (Vol. 1). London: Penguin.

Miettinen, R. (1999). The riddle of things: Activity theory and actor-network theory as approaches to studying innovation. *Mind, Culture, and Activity . International Journal (Toronto, Ont.)*, *6*(3), 170–195.

Moll, L. (1990). Introduction. In L. Moll (Ed.), *Vygotsky and Education. Instructional Implications and Applications of Sociohistorical Psychology*. Cambridge, UK: Cambridge University Press.

Nardi, B. (1996). Studying context: A comparison of activity theory, situated action models and distributed cognition. In B. Nardi (Ed.), *Context and Consciousness: Activity Theory and Human-Computer Interaction* (pp. 69-102). Cambridge, MA: MIT Press.

Nardi, B. (2007). Placeless organizations: Collaborating for transformation. *Mind, Culture, and Activity . International Journal (Toronto, Ont.)*, *14*(1/2), 5–22.

Pedler, M., Burgoyne, J., & Brook, C. (2005). What has action learning learned to become? *Action Learning Research and Practice*, *2*(1), 49–68.

Popper, K., & Eccles, J. (1977). *The Self and its Brain*. Berlin: Springer-Verlag.

Raeithel, A. (1996). *From coordinatedness to coordination via cooperation and co-construction*. Paper presented at the Workshop on Work and Learning in Transition, San Diego, CA.

Rigg, C. (2008). Action learning for organizational and systemic development: Towards a 'both-and' understanding of 'I' and 'we'. *Action Learning Research and Practice*, *5*(2), 105–116. doi:10.1080/14767330802185616

Rogoff, B. (2003). *The Cultural Nature of Human Development*. New York: Oxford University Press.

Roth, W.-M. (2004). Activity theory and education: An introduction. *Mind, Culture, and Activity . International Journal (Toronto, Ont.)*, *11*(1), 1–8.

Roth, W.-M. (2007). Emotion at work: A contribution to third-generation cultural-historical activity theory. *Mind, Culture, and Activity . International Journal (Toronto, Ont.)*, *14*(1/2), 40–63.

Rueda, R., Gallego, M., & Moll, L. (2000). The last restrictive environment: A place or a context? *Remedial and Special Education*, *21*(2), 70–87. doi:10.1177/074193250002100202

Rydberg, T., & Christiansen, E. (2008). Community and network sites as technology enhanced learning environments. *Technology, Pedagogy and Education*, *17*(3), 207–219. doi:10.1080/14759390802383801

Scribner, S. (1985). Vygotsky's uses of history. In J.V. Wertsch (Ed.). *Culture, Communication, and Cognition: Vygotskian Perspectives* (pp. 119-145). Cambridge, UK: Cambridge University Press.

Senge, P. (1990). *The Fifth Discipline: The art and Practice of the Learning Organization*. New York: Doubleday.

Tuomi-Gröhn, T., Engeström, Y., & Young, M. (2003). From transfer to boundary-crossing between school and work as a tool for developing vocational education: An introduction. In T. Tuomi-Gröhn & Y. Engeström, (Eds.), *Between School and Work: New Perspectives on Transfer and Boundary-crossing,* (pp. 1-15). Kidlington, UK: Elsevier Science.

Van Oers, B. (1998). The fallacy of decontextualization. *Mind, Culture, and Activity . International Journal (Toronto, Ont.)*, *5*(2), 135–142.

Vince, R. (2004). Action learning and organizational learning: Power, politics and emotions in organizations. *Action Learning*, *1*(1), 63–78. doi:10.1080/1476733042000187628

Vygotsky, L. (1986). *Thought and Language*. Cambridge, MA: MIT Press.

Vygotsky, L. (1987). Thinking and speech. In R. W. Rieber & A. S. Carton (Eds.), *The Collected Works of L. S. Vygotsky,* (Vol. 2, The fundamentals of defectology, pp. 122-138). New York: Plenum.

Vygotsky, L. (1994). The socialist alteration of man. In R. van der Veer & J. Valsiner (Eds.), *The Vygotsky Reader*. Oxford, UK: Blackwell.

Vygotsky, L. (1997). *Educational Psychology,* (transl. R. Silverman). Boca Raton, FL: St Lucie Press.

Vygotsky, L. (1998). Pedagogy of the adolescent. In R. Rieber (Ed.), *The Collected Works of L. S. Vygotsky,* (Vol. 5, Child psychology, pp. 31-184) (transl. M. J. Hall). New York: Plenum

Vygotsky, L. (1999). Consciousness as a problem in the psychology of behavior. *Undiscovered Vygotsky: Etudes on the pre-history of cultural-historical psychology,* (Vol 8, pp. 251-281). New York: Peter Lang.

Vygotsky, L. (2004). The historical meaning of the crisis in psychology: A methodological investigation. In R.W. Rieber & D.K Robinson (Eds.), *The Essential Vygotsky* (pp. 227-357). New York: Kluwer Academic.

Walker, D., & Nocon, H. (2007). Boundary-crossing competence: Theoretical considerations and educational design. *Mind, Culture, and Activity . International Journal (Toronto, Ont.), 14*(3), 178–195.

Wartofsky, M. (1979). *Models*. Dordrecht: Riedel.

Wells, G. (2007). The mediating role of discoursing in activity. *Mind, Culture, and Activity . International Journal (Toronto, Ont.), 14*(3), 160–177.

Wertsch, J. (1998). *Mind as Action*. New York: Oxford University Press.

Winograd, T. (Ed.). (1996). *Bringing Design to Software*. New York: Addison Wesley.

Wood, D., Bruner, J.S., & Ross, G. (1976). The role of tutoring in problem solving. *Journal of Psychology and Psychiatry, 17*.

Yaroshevsky, M. (1989). *Lev Vygotsky,* (transl. S. Syrovatkin). Moscow: Progress.

ADDITIONAL READINGS

Billet, S. (2008). Relational Interdependence Between Social and Individual Agency in Work and Working Life. *Mind, Culture, and Activity, 13*(1), 53–69. doi:10.1207/s15327884mca1301_5

Keller, C. M., & Keller, J. D. (1996). *Cognition and Tool Use: The Blacksmith at Work*. Cambridge England: Cambridge University Press.

Leontev, A. N. (1981). *Problems of the Development of Mind*. Moscow: Progress.

Rogoff, B. (2003). Firsthand Learning Through Intent Participation. *Annual Review of Psychology, 54*, 175–203. doi:10.1146/annurev.psych.54.101601.145118

Stahl, G. (2006). *Group Cognition: Computer Support for Building Collaborative Knowledge*. Cambridge: MIT Press.

KEY TERMS AND DEFINITIONS

Activity Theory: General activity theory (GAT) is a meta-theoretical paradigm – or a psychological framework – for analyzing human activities as complex, socially situated phenomena beyond paradigms of psychoanalysis or behaviorism.

Agency: This is a human ability to make choices and impose them on the world. Agency is normally contrasted to natural forces or deterministic processes which operate by physical laws.

Artifact: A human construction created to some purpose.

Change Management: The term defines a planned approach to transforming established routines in the direction of a desired future state, including organizational and individual change models and processes, basically by human resource management.

Focus Group: Interviewing in a group of peers is a form of data collection in which an interactive group of people are asked about their attitude towards a phenomenon. The interviewees are free to talk with other group members and initiate their own themes.

ICT: Information and communication technology.

Knowledge Object: The externalized result of a communication, instantiation and co-construction process based on a shared objective in a functioning activity system.

Leadership: There is little evidence that innate characteristics, personality, private inclination or personal traits could explain the types of behavior people associate with effective leadership.

Learning Object: The concept defines an abstraction deployed for describing discoursed cognitive contents between interlocutors at the stage of becoming rather than completion.

Managerial Control: Control by planning, organizing, decision making, staffing and directing helps employee procedures stick to company standards and achieve goals in the desired manner.

Mediation: The concept refers to transfer of input from one force to another within a given cultural, material or social realm by a mediating object. In modern media the mediating object is the medium of communication itself, e.g. ICT.

Organizational development: (OD) is – however different from action research – an interventionist strategy for changing the values, beliefs, attitudes, routines and structures of people and organizations. It is a pre-planned management effort or change process, based on behavioral science to increase the organization's effectiveness.

Organizational Learning: Is a characteristic of an organization that is able to sense changes in signals from its contingent internal and external environment and adapt accordingly by changing established routines and procedures.

Relation Building: A process between people including a first step of identifying another human being and another step for establishing contact with that person.

Task: A task is part of a set of actions. Task performance is a measure of how sb accomplishes a job, solves a problem or takes on an assignment. *Task* is a near-synonym for a chore, an assignment or an activity of longer duration.

Section 5
Metamodelling and Mathematics

Chapter 14
A System Approach to Describing, Analysing and Control of the Behaviour of Agents in MAS

František Čapkovič
Slovak Academy of Sciences, Slovak Republic

ABSTRACT

The Petri nets (PN)-based analytical approach to describing both the single agent behaviour as well as the cooperation of several agents in MAS (multi agent systems) is presented. PN yield the possibility to express the agent behaviour and cooperation by means of the vector state equation in the form of linear discrete system. Hence, the modular approach to the creation of the MAS model can be successfully used too. Three different interconnections of modules (agents, interfaces, environment) expressed by PN subnets are introduced. The approach makes possible to use methods of linear algebra. Moreover, it can be successfully used at the system analysis (e.g. the reachability of states), at testing the system properties, and even at the system control synthesis.

INTRODUCTION

If it is possible to believe in different encyclopaedias, Aristotle (384-322 B.C.E.) is considered to be the author of the sentence: "The whole is more than the sum of its parts". Indeed, usually it is true that people working together often can accomplish tasks that could not be done working separately. Nowadays, this idea is evolved in science especially in modelling, analysing, management and control of complex systems as well as in the theory of multi agent systems (MAS). Especially, the synergy of subsystems in complex systems (as well as agents in MAS) and the emergent behaviour of the complex system and/or MAS in the whole are in the centre of interest at present research in different branches of science. To realize these ideas, actual methods of cybernetics along with those of system theory (Takahara and Mesarovic, 2004) are utilized arm in arm. System theory represents (Bale, 1995) a framework at description and analysing any group of objects that work in concert to produce some result. It studies complex systems in nature, society, and science. With respect to the fact that system

DOI: 10.4018/978-1-61520-668-1.ch014

theory is interdisciplinary field of science, the system approach can be used also for modelling and analyzing MAS of different kinds – software agents, social agents, different kinds of material agents e.g. robots, devices in manufacturing systems (like machine tools, automatically guided vehicles), etc. Inventing or contriving the idea of management, or explanation and formulating it mentally have its origin in system theory. Namely, the nature of management may be conceptualised (Charlton and Andras, 2003) from a perspective of systems theory as the process by which an organisation generates a global representation of its own processes. In other words, management depends upon modelling. Modelling allows management to perform its distinctive information-processing activities such as monitoring, evaluation, prediction and control. The purposes to which these activities are directed, define the function of management. This function is a product of the interaction between a management system and its environment. This is a consequence of the simple fact that management systems will tend to adapt in order to survive and grow (in whatever specific context in environments). For a human organization (such as a company or enterprise, hotel, hospital and so on) the environment can include different aspects – e.g. physical (like climate, location, etc.), organisational (depending on law, politics, etc.) and others. Here, management systems are a form of social organizational system. To manage and/or control complex systems and MAS in general, the cybernetics aspect is very important too. Namely, cybernetics study feedback and derived concepts such as communication and control in living organisms, machines and organizations. Hence, methods of cybernetics can be widely utilized in order to study cooperative interactions among subsystems of complex systems as well as among agents in MAS. In this chapter the principles of both system theory and cybernetics are put to use. The abstract systems based on Petri nets (PN) and digraphs are used at mathematical modelling the subsystems and/or elementary agents and groups of them as well as at analysing their behaviour. The methods of cybernetics are used here at control synthesis by means of simultaneous utilizing the straight-lined and backward development of system dynamics. The strong connection between system theory and cybernetics is illustrated on several examples from technical area. The agent based approach can also model (to a certain extent) environment as one of the cooperating agents. This can be exploited especially in management systems. The management aspect of the system theory is illustrated by an example of the negotiation process of two companies.

Agents are (Fonseca *et al.*, 2001) persistent (software, but not only software) entities that can perceive, reason, and act in their environment and communicate with other agents. MAS are usually apprehended as a composition of collaborative agents working in shared environment. In such a way the agents together perform a more complex functionality. Communication among the agent in MAS enables the agents to exchange information. Consequently, the agents can coordinate their actions and cooperate with each other. The agent behaviour has a character of discrete event system (the system driven by occurrence of discrete events). Namely, such a system persists in a given state (e.g. a kind of activity) till then when an occurrence of a discrete event forced it to change the state into another one (e.g. to finish or abort the previous activity and to start another one). The agent behaviour involves both internal and external attributes. While the external attributes are (Demazeau, 2003) that the agent (i) evolves in an environment; (ii) is able to perceive this environment; (iii) is able to act in this environment; (iv) is able to communicate with other agents; (v) exhibits an autonomous behaviour, the internal attributes of the agent are that it encompasses some local control in some of its perception, communication, knowledge acquisition, reasoning, decision, execution, and action processes. The internal attributes characterize rather the agent inherent abilities. The external attributes of agents are manifested themselves in different measures in a rather wide spectrum of MAS applications - like e.g. computer-aided design, decision support, manufacturing systems, robotics and control, traffic management, network monitoring, telecommunications, e-commerce, enterprise modelling, society simulation, office and home automation, etc. It is necessary to distinguish two groups of agents and/or agent societies, namely, human and artificial. The principle difference between agents (as to behaviour) consists especially in the different internal abilities. These abilities are studied by many branches of science including those finding themselves out of the technical branches - e.g. economy, sociology, psychology, etc. MAS are also used in intelligent control, especially for a cooperative problem solving (Yen *et al.*, 2001).

In order to describe the behaviour of discrete event systems (DES), Petri nets (Peterson, 1981; Murata, 1989) are widely used - in flexible manufacturing systems, communication systems of different kinds, transport systems, etc. Agents and MAS can be understood (observing their behaviour) to be a kind of DES. PN yields both the graphical model and the mathematical one, and they have a formal semantics too. The so called place/transition PN (P/T PN), sometimes also named as ordinary PN, will be used in this chapter. For simplicity, below we will use the abbreviation PN. There are many techniques for proving the PN basic properties (Peterson, 1981; Murata, 1989) like reachability, liveness, boundedness, conservativeness, reversibility, coverability, persistence, fairness, etc. Consequently, PN represent the enough general means to be able to model a wide class of systems. These arguments are the same like those used in DES modelling in general in order to prefer PN to other approaches. In addition, there were developed many methods in PN theory that are very useful at model checking - e.g. like the methods of the deadlocks avoidance, methods for computing P (place)-invariants and T (transition)-invariants, etc. Moreover, PN-based models dispose of the possibility to express not only the event causality, but also of the possibility to express analytically the current states expressing the system dynamics development. Even, linear algebra and matrix calculus can be utilized on this way. This is very important especially at the DES control synthesis. The fact that most PN properties can be tested by means of methods based on the reachability tree (RT) and invariants is indispensable too. Thus, the RT and invariants are very important in PN-based modelling DES. In sum, the modelling power of PN consists especially in the facts that (i) PN have formal semantics. Thus, the execution and simulation of PN models are unambiguous; (ii) notation of modelling a system is event-based. PN can model both states and events. (iii) there are many analysis techniques associated with PN. Especially, the approach based on P/T PN enables us to use linear algebra and matrix calculus - exact and in practice verified approaches. This makes possible the MAS analysis in analytical terms, especially, by computing RT, invariants, testing properties, model checking, even, the efficient model-based control synthesis. Moreover, the fact that PN can be used not only for handling software agents but also for material agents - like robots and other technical devices, social agents, etc. – is very important. PN are suitable also at modelling, analysing and control of any modular DES and they are able to deal with any problem on that way. Mutual interactions of agents are considered within the framework of the global model. Such an approach is sufficiently general in order to allow us to create the model that yields the possibility to analyse any situation. Even, the environment behaviour can be modelled as an agent of the agent system too. Thus, the model can acquire arbitrary structure and generate different situations.

THE PETRI NET-BASED MODEL

Let us use the analogy between the DES atomic activities $a_i \in \{a_1, \cdots, a_n\}$ and the PN places $p_i \in \{p_1, \cdots, p_n\}$ as well as between the discrete events $e_j \in \{e_1, \cdots, e_m\}$ occurring in DES and the PN transitions $t_j \in \{t_1, \cdots, t_m\}$. Then, DES behaviour can be modelled by means of P/T PN. The analytical model has the form of the linear discrete system as follows

$$\mathbf{x}_{k+1} = \mathbf{x}_k + \mathbf{B}.\mathbf{u}_k, k = 0, \cdots, K$$

$$\mathbf{B} = \mathbf{G}^T - \mathbf{F}$$

restricted by the constraint in the form of the inequality

$$\mathbf{F}.\mathbf{u}_k \leq \mathbf{x}_k$$

Here, k is the discrete step of the dynamics development; $\mathbf{x}_k = (\sigma_{p_1}^k, \cdots, \sigma_{p_n}^k)^T$ is the n-dimensional state vector in the step k; $\sigma_{p_i}^k \in \{0, 1, \cdots, c_{p_i}\}$, i=1,...,n, express the states of the DES atomic activities, namely the passivity is expressed by $\sigma_{p_i}^k = 0$ and the activity is expressed by $0 \leq \sigma_{p_i}^k \leq c_{p_i}$; c_{p_i} is the capacity as to the activities - e.g. the passivity of a buffer means the empty buffer, the activity means a number of parts stored in the buffer and the capacity is understood to be the maximal number of parts which can be put into the buffer; $\mathbf{u}_k = (\gamma_{t_1}^k, \cdots, \gamma_{t_m}^k)^T$ is the m-dimensional control vector of the system in the step k; its components $\gamma_{t_j}^k \in \{0, 1\}$, j=1,...,m, represent occurring of the DES discrete events (e.g. starting or ending the atomic activities, occurrence of failures, etc.) - when the j-th discrete event is enabled $\gamma_{t_j}^k = 1$, when the event is disabled $\gamma_{t_j}^k = 0$; **B**, **F**, **G** are structural matrices of constant elements; $\mathbf{F} = \{f_{ij}\}$, $f_{ij} \in \{0, M_{f_{ij}}\}$, i=1,...,n, j=1,...,m, express the causal relations between the states of the DES (in the role of causes) and the discrete events occurring during the DES operation (in the role of consequences) - nonexistence of the corresponding relation is expressed by $M_{f_{ij}} = 0$, existence and multiplicity of the relation are expressed by $M_{f_{ij}} > 0$; $G = \{g_{ij}\}$, $g_{ij} \in \{0, M_{g_{ij}}\}$, i=1,...,m, j=1,...,n, express very analogically the causal relations between the discrete events (as the causes) and the DES states (as the consequences); the structural matrix **B** is given by means of the arcs incidence matrices **F** and **G** according to the above introduced relation; $(.)^T$ symbolizes the matrix or vector transposition. The PN marking which in PN theory is usually denoted by $\boldsymbol{\mu}$ was denoted here by the letter **x** usually denoting the state in system theory. The expressive power of the PN-based approach consists in the ability to describe in details (by states and events) how agents behave and/or how agents collaborate. The deeper is the model abstraction level the greater is the model dimensionality (n, m). It is a limitation, so a compromise between the model grain and its dimensionality has to be done. However, such a 'curse' occurs in any kind of systems. There are many papers interested in PN-based modelling of agents and MAS from different reasons – (Hung and Mao, 2002;Nowostawski *et al.*, 2001) and a copious amount of other papers. However, no systematic modular approach in analytical terms occurs there. An attempt at forming of such an approach is presented in this paper. It arises from the author's previous results (Čapkovič, 2005; 2007;2007a;2008).

MODULAR APPROACHES TO MODELLING

The modular approach makes possible to model and analyse each module separately as well as the global composition of modules. In general, three different kinds of the model creation can be distinguished according to the form of the interface connecting the modules (PN subnets), namely (i) the interface consisting exclusively of PN transitions; (ii) the interface consisting exclusively of PN places; (iii) the interface in the form of a PN subnet with an arbitrary structure containing both positions and transitions. Let us introduced the structure of the PN model of MAS with agents A_i, i= 1, 2, ..., N_A, for these three different forms of the interface among agents.

The Transition-Based Interface

When the interface contains only m_c additional PN transitions, the structure of the actual contact interface among the agents A_i, i = 1, 2, ..., N_A, is given by the $(n \times m_c)$-dimensional matrix $\mathbf{F}_c$ and $(m_c \times n)$-dimensional matrix $\mathbf{G}_c$ as follows

$$\mathbf{F} = \begin{pmatrix} \mathbf{F}_1 & \mathbf{0} & \cdots & \mathbf{0} & \mathbf{0} & \mathbf{F}_{c_1} \\ \mathbf{0} & \mathbf{F}_2 & \cdots & \mathbf{0} & \mathbf{0} & \mathbf{F}_{c_2} \\ \vdots & \vdots & \ddots & \vdots & \vdots & \vdots \\ \mathbf{0} & \mathbf{0} & \cdots & \mathbf{F}_{N_A-1} & \mathbf{0} & \mathbf{F}_{c_{N_A-1}} \\ \mathbf{0} & \mathbf{0} & \cdots & \mathbf{0} & \mathbf{F}_{N_A} & \mathbf{F}_{c_{N_A}} \end{pmatrix} = \left(blockdiag(\mathbf{F}_i)_{i=1,\cdots,N_A} \mid \mathbf{F}_c \right)$$

$$\mathbf{G} = \begin{pmatrix} \mathbf{G}_1 & \mathbf{0} & \cdots & \mathbf{0} & \mathbf{0} \\ \mathbf{0} & \mathbf{G}_2 & \cdots & \mathbf{0} & \mathbf{0} \\ \vdots & \vdots & \ddots & \vdots & \vdots \\ \mathbf{0} & \mathbf{0} & \cdots & \mathbf{G}_{N_A-1} & \mathbf{0} \\ \mathbf{0} & \mathbf{0} & \cdots & \mathbf{0} & \mathbf{G}_{N_A} \\ \mathbf{G}_{c_1} & \mathbf{G}_{c_2} & \cdots & \mathbf{G}_{c_{N_A-1}} & \mathbf{G}_{c_{N_A}} \end{pmatrix} = \begin{pmatrix} blockdiag(\mathbf{G}_i)_{i=1,\cdots,N_A} \\ \mathbf{G}_c \end{pmatrix}$$

$$\mathbf{B} = \begin{pmatrix} \mathbf{B}_1 & \mathbf{0} & \cdots & \mathbf{0} & \mathbf{0} & \mathbf{B}_{c_1} \\ \mathbf{0} & \mathbf{B}_2 & \cdots & \mathbf{0} & \mathbf{0} & \mathbf{B}_{c_2} \\ \vdots & \vdots & \ddots & \vdots & \vdots & \vdots \\ \mathbf{0} & \mathbf{0} & \cdots & \mathbf{B}_{N_A-1} & \mathbf{0} & \mathbf{B}_{c_{N_A-1}} \\ \mathbf{0} & \mathbf{0} & \cdots & \mathbf{0} & \mathbf{B}_{N_A} & \mathbf{B}_{c_{N_A}} \end{pmatrix} = \left(blockdiag(\mathbf{B}_i)_{i=1,\cdots,N_A} \mid \mathbf{B}_c \right)$$

where $\mathbf{B}_i = \mathbf{G}_i^T - \mathbf{F}_i$; $\mathbf{B}_{c_i} = \mathbf{G}_{c_i}^T - \mathbf{F}_{c_i}$; i=1,..., N_A; $\mathbf{F}_c = \left(\mathbf{F}_{c_1}^T, \cdots, \mathbf{F}_{c_{N_A}}^T\right)^T$; $\mathbf{G}_c = \left(\mathbf{G}_{c_1}, \cdots, \mathbf{G}_{c_{N_A}}\right)$; $\mathbf{B}_c = \left(\mathbf{B}_{c_1}^T, \cdots, \mathbf{B}_{c_{N_A}}^T\right)^T$ with $\mathbf{F}_i, \mathbf{G}_i, \mathbf{B}_i$, i=1,... N_A, representing the parameters of the PN-based model of the agent A_i and with $\mathbf{F}_c, \mathbf{G}_c, \mathbf{B}_c$ representing the structure of the interface between the agents cooperating in MAS.

The Place-Based Interface

When the interface contains only n_d additional PN places the structure of the actual contact interface among the agents A_i, i=1,..., N_A, is given by the $(n_d \times m)$-dimensional matrix $\mathbf{F}_d$ and $(m \times n_d)$-dimensional matrix $\mathbf{G}_d$ as follows

$$\mathbf{F} = \begin{pmatrix} \mathbf{F}_1 & \mathbf{0} & \cdots & \mathbf{0} & \mathbf{0} \\ \mathbf{0} & \mathbf{F}_2 & \cdots & \mathbf{0} & \mathbf{0} \\ \vdots & \vdots & \ddots & \vdots & \vdots \\ \mathbf{0} & \mathbf{0} & \cdots & \mathbf{F}_{N_A-1} & \mathbf{0} \\ \mathbf{0} & \mathbf{0} & \cdots & \mathbf{0} & \mathbf{F}_{N_A} \\ \mathbf{F}_{d_1} & \mathbf{F}_{d_2} & \cdots & \mathbf{F}_{d_{N_A-1}} & \mathbf{F}_{d_{N_A}} \end{pmatrix} = \begin{pmatrix} blockdiag(\mathbf{F}_i)_{i=1,\cdots,N_A} \\ \mathbf{F}_d \end{pmatrix}$$

$$\mathbf{G} = \begin{pmatrix} \mathbf{G}_1 & \mathbf{0} & \cdots & \mathbf{0} & \mathbf{0} & \mathbf{G}_{d_1} \\ \mathbf{0} & \mathbf{G}_2 & \cdots & \mathbf{0} & \mathbf{0} & \mathbf{G}_{d_2} \\ \vdots & \vdots & \ddots & \vdots & \vdots & \vdots \\ \mathbf{0} & \mathbf{0} & \cdots & \mathbf{G}_{N_A-1} & \mathbf{0} & \mathbf{G}_{d_{N_A-1}} \\ \mathbf{0} & \mathbf{0} & \cdots & \mathbf{0} & \mathbf{G}_{N_A} & \mathbf{G}_{d_{N_A}} \end{pmatrix} = \left(blockdiag(\mathbf{G}_i)_{i=1,\cdots,N_A} \mid \mathbf{G}_d \right)$$

$$\mathbf{B} = \begin{pmatrix} \mathbf{B}_1 & \mathbf{0} & \cdots & \mathbf{0} & \mathbf{0} \\ \mathbf{0} & \mathbf{B}_2 & \cdots & \mathbf{0} & \mathbf{0} \\ \vdots & \vdots & \ddots & \vdots & \vdots \\ \mathbf{0} & \mathbf{0} & \cdots & \mathbf{B}_{N_A-1} & \mathbf{0} \\ \mathbf{0} & \mathbf{0} & \cdots & \mathbf{0} & \mathbf{B}_{N_A} \\ \mathbf{B}_{d_1} & \mathbf{B}_{d_2} & \cdots & \mathbf{B}_{d_{N_A-1}} & \mathbf{B}_{d_{N_A}} \end{pmatrix} = \begin{pmatrix} blockdiag(\mathbf{B}_i)_{i=1,\cdots,N_A} \\ \mathbf{B}_d \end{pmatrix}$$

where $\mathbf{B}_i = \mathbf{G}_i^T - \mathbf{F}_i$; $\mathbf{B}_{d_i} = \mathbf{G}_{d_i}^T - \mathbf{F}_{d_i}$; i=1,..., N_A; $\mathbf{F}_d = \left(\mathbf{F}_{d_1}, \cdots, \mathbf{F}_{d_{N_A}}\right)$; $\mathbf{G}_d = \left(\mathbf{G}_{d_1}^T, \cdots, \mathbf{G}_{d_{N_A}}^T\right)^T$; $\mathbf{B}_d = \left(\mathbf{B}_{d_1}, \cdots, \mathbf{B}_{d_{N_A}}\right)$ with $\mathbf{F}_i, \mathbf{G}_i, \mathbf{B}_i$, i=1,... N_A, representing the parameters of the PN-based model of the agent A_i and with $\mathbf{F}_d, \mathbf{G}_d, \mathbf{B}_d$ representing the structure of the interface between the agents cooperating in MAS.

The Interface in the Form of a PN Subnet

When the interface among the agents A_i, $i=1,\ldots,N_A$, has a form of the PN subnet containing n_d additional places and m_c additional transitions its structure is given by the $(n_d \times m_c)$-dimensional matrix $\mathbf{F}_{d\leftrightarrow c}$ and $(m_c \times n_d)$-dimensional matrix $\mathbf{G}_{c\leftrightarrow d}$. However, it is only the structure of the PN subnet. Moreover, the row and the column consisting of corresponding blocks have to be added in order to model the contacts of the interface with the elementary agents. Hence, we have the following structural (incidence) matrices

$$\mathbf{F} = \begin{pmatrix} \mathbf{F}_1 & \mathbf{0} & \cdots & \mathbf{0} & \mathbf{0} & | & \mathbf{F}_{c_1} \\ \mathbf{0} & \mathbf{F}_2 & \cdots & \mathbf{0} & \mathbf{0} & | & \mathbf{F}_{c_2} \\ \vdots & \vdots & \ddots & \vdots & \vdots & | & \vdots \\ \mathbf{0} & \mathbf{0} & \cdots & \mathbf{F}_{N_A-1} & \mathbf{0} & | & \mathbf{F}_{c_{N_A-1}} \\ \mathbf{0} & \mathbf{0} & \cdots & 0 & \mathbf{F}_{N_A} & | & \mathbf{F}_{c_{N_A}} \\ \mathbf{F}_{d_1} & \mathbf{F}_{d_2} & \cdots & \mathbf{F}_{d_{N_A-1}} & \mathbf{F}_{d_{N_A}} & | & \mathbf{F}_{d\leftrightarrow c} \end{pmatrix} = \begin{pmatrix} blockdiag(\mathbf{F}_i)_{i=1,\ldots,N_A} & | & \mathbf{F}_c \\ \mathbf{F}_d & | & \mathbf{F}_{d\leftrightarrow c} \end{pmatrix}$$

$$\mathbf{G} = \begin{pmatrix} \mathbf{G}_1 & \mathbf{0} & \cdots & \mathbf{0} & \mathbf{0} & | & \mathbf{G}_{d_1} \\ \mathbf{0} & \mathbf{G}_2 & \cdots & \mathbf{0} & \mathbf{0} & | & \mathbf{G}_{d_2} \\ \vdots & \vdots & \ddots & \vdots & \vdots & | & \vdots \\ \mathbf{0} & \mathbf{0} & \cdots & \mathbf{G}_{N_A-1} & \mathbf{0} & | & \mathbf{G}_{d_{N_A-1}} \\ \mathbf{0} & \mathbf{0} & \cdots & \mathbf{0} & \mathbf{G}_{N_A} & | & \mathbf{G}_{d_{N_A}} \\ \mathbf{G}_{c_1} & \mathbf{G}_{c_2} & \cdots & \mathbf{G}_{c_{N_A-1}} & \mathbf{G}_{c_{N_A}} & | & \mathbf{G}_{c\leftrightarrow d} \end{pmatrix} = \begin{pmatrix} blockdiag(\mathbf{G}_i)_{i=1,\ldots,N_A} & | & \mathbf{G}_d \\ \mathbf{G}_c & | & \mathbf{G}_{c\leftrightarrow d} \end{pmatrix}$$

$$\mathbf{B} = \begin{pmatrix} \mathbf{B}_1 & \mathbf{0} & \cdots & \mathbf{0} & \mathbf{0} & | & \mathbf{B}_{c_1} \\ \mathbf{0} & \mathbf{B}_2 & \cdots & \mathbf{0} & \mathbf{0} & | & \mathbf{B}_{c_2} \\ \vdots & \vdots & \ddots & \vdots & \vdots & | & \vdots \\ \mathbf{0} & \mathbf{0} & \cdots & \mathbf{B}_{N_A-1} & \mathbf{0} & | & \mathbf{B}_{c_{N_A-1}} \\ \mathbf{0} & \mathbf{0} & \cdots & \mathbf{0} & \mathbf{B}_{N_A} & | & \mathbf{B}_{c_{N_A}} \\ \mathbf{B}_{d_1} & \mathbf{B}_{d_2} & \cdots & \mathbf{B}_{d_{N_A-1}} & \mathbf{B}_{d_{N_A}} & | & \mathbf{B}_{d\leftrightarrow c} \end{pmatrix} = \begin{pmatrix} blockdiag(\mathbf{B}_i)_{i=1,\ldots,N_A} & | & \mathbf{B}_c \\ \mathbf{B}_d & | & \mathbf{B}_{d\leftrightarrow c} \end{pmatrix}$$

where $\mathbf{B}_i = \mathbf{G}_i^T - \mathbf{F}_i$; $\mathbf{B}_{d_i} = \mathbf{G}_{d_i}^T - \mathbf{F}_{d_i}$ $\mathbf{B}_{c_i} = \mathbf{G}_{c_i}^T - \mathbf{F}_{c_i}$; $i = 1, \ldots, N_A$; $\mathbf{B}_{d\leftrightarrow c} = \mathbf{G}_{c\leftrightarrow d}^T - \mathbf{F}_{d\leftrightarrow c}$. It can be seen that the matrices **F**, **G**, **B** acquire a special structure. Each of them has the big diagonal block with the smaller blocks in its diagonal describing the structure of the elementary agents A_i, $i=1,\ldots,N_A$, and the part in the form of a special structure of the matrix (like the capitol letter L turned over to the left for 180°) containing the small blocks representing interconnections among the agents. In these matrices the smaller blocks $\mathbf{F}_{d\leftrightarrow c}$, $\mathbf{G}_{c\leftrightarrow d}$, $\mathbf{B}_{d\leftrightarrow c}$ are situated in their diagonals just in the breakage of the turned L, but outwards.

The Reason of the Modular Models

The modular models described above are suitable for modelling the very wide spectrum of the agent cooperation in MAS. The elementary agents can have either the same structure or the mutually different one. The modules can represent not only agents but also different additional entities including the environment behaviour. Three examples will be presented below (in the section titled "Illustrative Examples") in order to illustrate the usage of the proposed models.

ANALYSING THE AGENT BEHAVIOUR

The agent behaviour can be analysed by means of testing the model properties. This can be done by using the graphical tool and/or analytically. The graphical tool was developed in order to draw the PN model of the system to be analysed, to simulate its dynamics development for a chosen initial state (PN marking), to compute its P-invariants and T-invariants, to compute and draw its RT, etc. The RT is the most important instrument for analysing the dynamic behaviour of agents and MAS. Because the same leaves can occur in the RT repeatedly, it is suitable to connect them in such a case into one node. Consequently, the reachability graph (RG) is obtained from RT. Both RT and RG have the same adjacency matrix. RG is very useful not only at the system analysis (model checking), but also at the control synthesis. However, the RG-based control synthesis is not handled in this paper. It was presented in (Čapkovič, 2005; 2007; 2007a; 2008).

ILLUSTRATIVE EXAMPLES

The advantage of the modular approach to modelling MAS is that different kinds of the agent communication can be analysed in different evoking dynamic situations occurring at the agent cooperation, negotiation, etc. The models can be created flexibly by means of arbitrary aggregating or clustering elementary agents into MAS. To illustrate using the modular models of MAS, let us introduce three examples as follows. In spite of their simplicity they give us the basic conception of the utility of such models.

Example 1

Consider the simple MAS with two agents A_1, A_2 f the same structure. Its PN-based model is in Figure 1. The system parameters are the following

$$\mathbf{F} = \begin{pmatrix} \mathbf{F}_1 & \mathbf{0} & \mathbf{F}_{c_1} \\ \mathbf{0} & \mathbf{F}_2 & \mathbf{F}_{c_2} \end{pmatrix} ; \quad \mathbf{F} = \begin{pmatrix} \mathbf{F}_1 & \mathbf{0} & \mathbf{F}_{c_1} \\ \mathbf{0} & \mathbf{F}_2 & \mathbf{F}_{c_2} \end{pmatrix}$$

$$\mathbf{G} = \begin{pmatrix} \mathbf{G}_1 & \mathbf{0} \\ \mathbf{0} & \mathbf{G}_2 \\ \mathbf{G}_{c_1} & \mathbf{G}_{c_2} \end{pmatrix} ; \quad \mathbf{G} = \begin{pmatrix} \mathbf{G}_1 & \mathbf{0} \\ \mathbf{0} & \mathbf{G}_2 \\ \mathbf{G}_{c_1} & \mathbf{G}_{c_2} \end{pmatrix}$$

Where the structural matrices of the elementary agents are the following

$$\mathbf{F}_1 = \mathbf{F}_2 = \begin{pmatrix} 1 & 1 & 1 & 1 & 0 & 0 & 0 \\ 1 & 1 & 0 & 0 & 0 & 0 & 0 \\ 1 & 0 & 0 & 0 & 0 & 0 & 0 \\ 0 & 1 & 0 & 0 & 0 & 0 & 0 \\ 0 & 0 & 0 & 0 & 0 & 0 & 0 \\ 0 & 0 & 0 & 0 & 0 & 0 & 1 \\ 0 & 0 & 0 & 0 & 0 & 0 & 0 \\ 0 & 0 & 1 & 1 & 0 & 0 & 0 \\ 0 & 0 & 0 & 0 & 0 & 0 & 0 \\ 0 & 0 & 0 & 0 & 1 & 1 & 0 \\ 0 & 0 & 0 & 0 & 0 & 0 & 0 \\ 0 & 0 & 0 & 0 & 0 & 0 & 0 \end{pmatrix}$$

$$\mathbf{G}_1^T = \mathbf{G}_2^T = \begin{pmatrix} 0 & 0 & 0 & 0 & 0 & 0 & 0 \\ 0 & 0 & 0 & 0 & 0 & 0 & 0 \\ 0 & 0 & 0 & 0 & 0 & 0 & 0 \\ 0 & 0 & 0 & 0 & 0 & 0 & 0 \\ 1 & 0 & 0 & 0 & 0 & 0 & 0 \\ 0 & 1 & 0 & 0 & 0 & 0 & 0 \\ 0 & 0 & 0 & 0 & 0 & 0 & 1 \\ 0 & 0 & 0 & 0 & 0 & 0 & 0 \\ 0 & 0 & 0 & 1 & 0 & 0 & 0 \\ 0 & 0 & 1 & 0 & 0 & 0 & 0 \\ 0 & 0 & 0 & 0 & 1 & 0 & 0 \\ 0 & 0 & 0 & 0 & 0 & 1 & 0 \end{pmatrix}$$

Figure 1. The PN-based model of the two agents cooperation

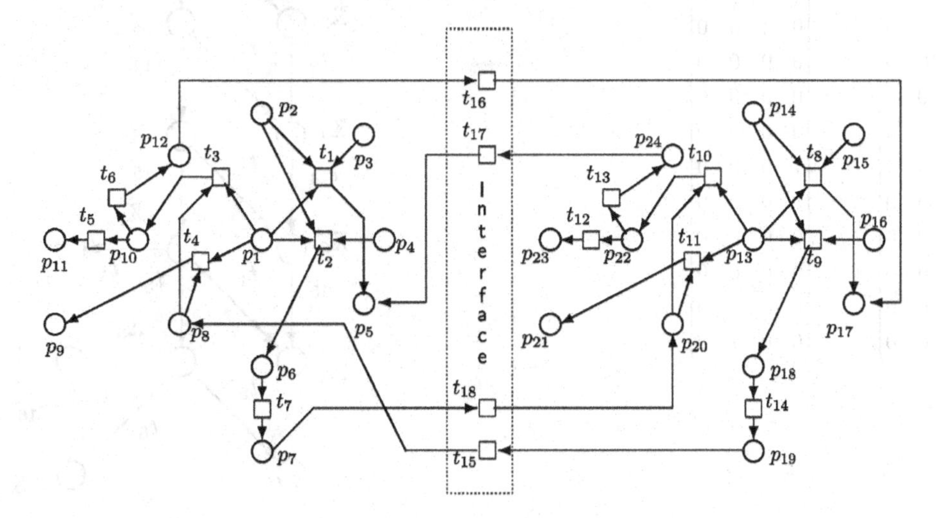

The interpretation of the PN places is the following: p_1 = the agent (A_1) is free; p_2 = a problem has to be solved by A_1; $p_3 = A_1$ is able to solve the problem (P_{A1}); $p_4 = A_1$ is not able to solve P_{A1}; $p_5 = P_{A1}$ is solved; $p_6 = P_{A1}$ cannot be solved by A_1 and another agent(s) should be contacted; $p_7 = A_1$ asks another agent(s) to help him to solve P_{A1}; $p_8 = A_1$ is asked by another agent(s) to solve a problem P_B; $p_9 = A_1$ refuses the help; $p_{10} = A_1$ accepts the request of another agent(s) for help; $p_{11} = A_1$ is not able to solve P_B; $p_{12} = A_1$ is able to solve P_B. In case of the agent A_2 the interpretation is the same only the indices of the places are shifted for 12 in the MAS in order to distinguish A_2 from A_1. The same is valid also for the agents transition, only the shifting is for 8 (because the number of transitions in the model of A_1 is 7). The transitions represent the starting or ending the atomic activities. The interface between the agents is realized by the additional transitions t_{15}-t_{18}. The number of the transitions follows from the situation to be modelled and analysed. Namely, the situation, when A_2 is not able to solve its own problem P_{A2} and A_2 asks A_1 for help to solve it, is modelled. Because A_1 accept the request and it is able to solve the problem P_{A2}, finally the P_{A2} is resolved by the agent A_1. Consequently, the interface can be described by the structural matrices

$$\mathbf{F}_{c_1} = \begin{pmatrix} 0&0&0&0\\0&0&0&0\\0&0&0&0\\0&0&0&0\\0&0&0&0\\0&0&0&0\\0&0&0&1\\0&0&0&0\\0&0&0&0\\0&0&0&0\\0&0&0&0\\0&1&0&0 \end{pmatrix} \quad \mathbf{F}_{c_2} = \begin{pmatrix} 0&0&0&0\\0&0&0&0\\0&0&0&0\\0&0&0&0\\0&0&0&0\\0&0&0&0\\1&0&0&0\\0&0&0&0\\0&0&0&0\\0&0&0&0\\0&0&0&0\\0&0&1&0 \end{pmatrix}$$

$$\mathbf{G}^T_{c_1} = \begin{pmatrix} 0&0&0&0\\0&0&0&0\\0&0&0&0\\0&0&0&0\\0&0&1&0\\0&0&0&0\\0&0&0&0\\1&0&0&0\\0&0&0&0\\0&0&0&0\\0&0&0&0\\0&0&0&0 \end{pmatrix} \mathbf{G}^T_{c_2} = \begin{pmatrix} 0&0&0&0\\0&0&0&0\\0&0&0&0\\0&0&0&0\\0&1&0&0\\0&0&0&0\\0&0&0&0\\0&0&0&1\\0&0&0&0\\0&0&0&0\\0&0&0&0\\0&0&0&0 \end{pmatrix}$$

In general, we can analyse arbitrary situations. In our case, for the initial state e.g. in the form $\mathbf{x}_0 = \left({}^{A_1}\mathbf{x}_0^T, {}^{A_2}\mathbf{x}_0^T\right)^T$ where ${}^{A_1}\mathbf{x}_0^T = (1,1,1,0,0,0,0,0,0,0,0,0)^T$ and ${}^{A_2}\mathbf{x}_0^T = (1,1,0,1,0,0,0,0,0,0,0,0)^T$, we can compute (by means of the procedure in Matlab (Čapkovič, 2003)) the parameters of the RT/RG, i.e. the adjacency matrix and the feasible state vectors being the nodes of the RT/RG. The feasible state vectors are given in the form of the

Figure 2. The reachability graph of the PN-based model of the two agents cooperation

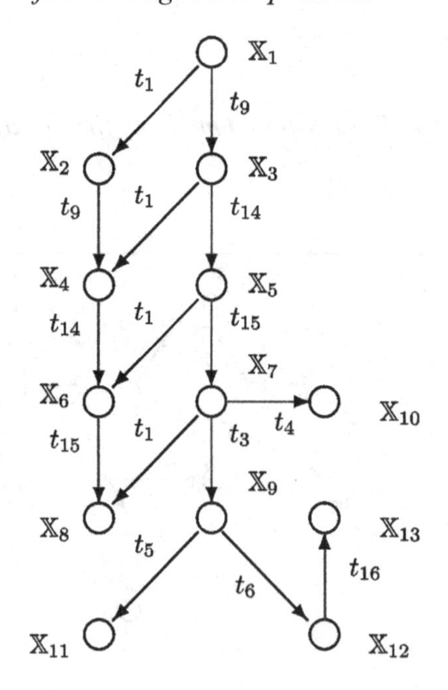

columns of the matrix $\mathbf{X}_{reach}$. In our case, the RG for the modelled situation is displayed in Figure 2. There, the RG nodes are the feasible state vectors $X_1, ..., X_{13}$. They are expressed by the columns of the matrix $\mathbf{X}_{reach} = \left({}^1\mathbf{X}^T_{reach}, {}^2\mathbf{X}^T_{reach}\right)^T$ as follows, where

$$
{}^1\mathbf{X}_{reach} = \begin{pmatrix}
1 & 0 & 1 & 0 & 1 & 0 & 1 & 0 & 0 & 0 & 0 & 0 & 0 \\
1 & 0 & 1 & 0 & 1 & 0 & 1 & 0 & 1 & 1 & 1 & 1 & 1 \\
1 & 0 & 1 & 0 & 1 & 0 & 1 & 0 & 1 & 1 & 1 & 1 & 1 \\
0 & 0 & 0 & 0 & 0 & 0 & 0 & 0 & 0 & 0 & 0 & 0 & 0 \\
0 & 1 & 0 & 1 & 0 & 1 & 0 & 1 & 0 & 0 & 0 & 0 & 0 \\
0 & 0 & 0 & 0 & 0 & 0 & 0 & 0 & 0 & 0 & 0 & 0 & 0 \\
0 & 0 & 0 & 0 & 0 & 0 & 0 & 0 & 0 & 0 & 0 & 0 & 0 \\
0 & 0 & 0 & 0 & 0 & 0 & 1 & 1 & 0 & 0 & 0 & 0 & 0 \\
0 & 0 & 0 & 0 & 0 & 0 & 0 & 0 & 0 & 1 & 0 & 0 & 0 \\
0 & 0 & 0 & 0 & 0 & 0 & 0 & 0 & 1 & 0 & 0 & 0 & 0 \\
0 & 0 & 0 & 0 & 0 & 0 & 0 & 0 & 0 & 0 & 1 & 0 & 0 \\
0 & 0 & 0 & 0 & 0 & 0 & 0 & 0 & 0 & 0 & 0 & 1 & 0
\end{pmatrix}
$$

$$
{}^2\mathbf{X}_{reach} = \begin{pmatrix}
1 & 1 & 0 & 0 & 0 & 0 & 0 & 0 & 0 & 0 & 0 & 0 & 0 \\
1 & 1 & 0 & 0 & 0 & 0 & 0 & 0 & 0 & 0 & 0 & 0 & 0 \\
0 & 0 & 0 & 0 & 0 & 0 & 0 & 0 & 0 & 0 & 0 & 0 & 0 \\
1 & 1 & 0 & 0 & 0 & 0 & 0 & 0 & 0 & 0 & 0 & 0 & 0 \\
0 & 0 & 0 & 0 & 0 & 0 & 0 & 0 & 0 & 0 & 0 & 0 & 1 \\
0 & 0 & 1 & 1 & 0 & 0 & 0 & 0 & 0 & 0 & 0 & 0 & 0 \\
0 & 0 & 0 & 0 & 1 & 1 & 0 & 0 & 0 & 0 & 0 & 0 & 0 \\
0 & 0 & 0 & 0 & 0 & 0 & 0 & 0 & 0 & 0 & 0 & 0 & 0 \\
0 & 0 & 0 & 0 & 0 & 0 & 0 & 0 & 0 & 0 & 0 & 0 & 0 \\
0 & 0 & 0 & 0 & 0 & 0 & 0 & 0 & 0 & 0 & 0 & 0 & 0 \\
0 & 0 & 0 & 0 & 0 & 0 & 0 & 0 & 0 & 0 & 0 & 0 & 0 \\
0 & 0 & 0 & 0 & 0 & 0 & 0 & 0 & 0 & 0 & 0 & 0 & 0
\end{pmatrix}
$$

The cooperation of three agents of the same kind can be modelled analogically – see Figure 3 or its simplified form given in Figure 4 where the numbers between the agents and interfaces express the indices of the PN places. For simplicity, no shifting of indices of PN places and transitions in case of agents A_2 and A_3 are made.

Figure 3. The example of the PN-based model of the three agents cooperation. It documents that the number of agents can increase

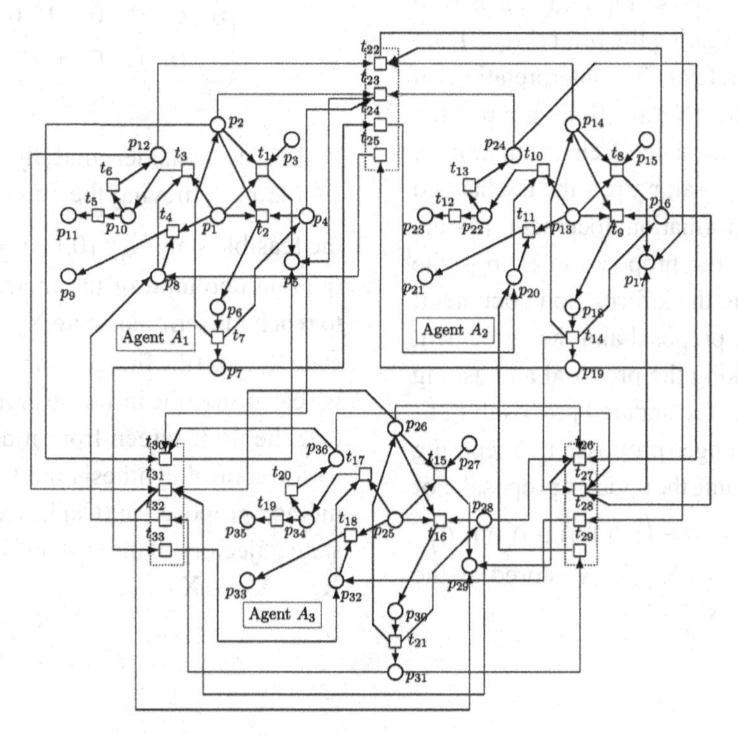

Figure 4. The simplified figure of the PN-based model of the three agents cooperation. The numbers between the elementary blocks represent the indices of the PN places inside of the PN models of agents, while in the interfaces the PN transitions executing the cooperation are hidden

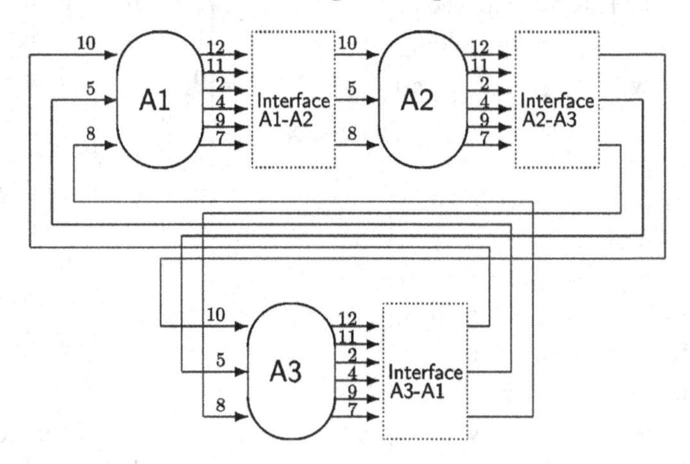

Example 2

Consider two virtual companies A, B (Lenz *et al.*, 2001). In the negotiation process the company A creates an information document containing the issues of the project (e.g. which the mutual software agents already agreed on) and those that are still unclear. The PN-based model and the corresponding RG are displayed in Figure 5 as well as in Figure 6 (representing the print screen from the graphical PN simulator). The interpretations of the PN places and the PN transitions are: p_1 – the start depending on the state of environment; p_2, p_4 - the updated proposal; p_3, p_5 - the unchanged proposal; p_6 - the information document; p_7 - the proposal to A; p_8 - the proposal to B; p_9 - the contract; t_1 - creating the information document; t_2, t_9 – checking the proposal and the agreement with it; t_3, t_8 - checking the proposal and asking changes; t_4 - sending the updated proposal; t_5, t_{10} - accepting the unchanged proposal; t_6 - preparing the proposal; t_7 - sending the updated proposal. For the initial state $\mathbf{x}_0 \equiv X_1 = (1,0,0,0,0,0,0,0,0)^T$ we have the RG nodes X_1, ..., X_9 stored as the columns of the matrix

$$\mathbf{X}_{reach} = \begin{pmatrix} 1 & 0 & 0 & 0 & 0 & 0 & 0 & 0 & 0 \\ 0 & 0 & 0 & 0 & 1 & 0 & 0 & 0 & 0 \\ 0 & 0 & 0 & 1 & 0 & 0 & 0 & 0 & 0 \\ 0 & 0 & 0 & 0 & 0 & 0 & 0 & 1 & 0 \\ 0 & 0 & 0 & 0 & 0 & 0 & 0 & 0 & 1 \\ 0 & 1 & 0 & 0 & 0 & 0 & 0 & 0 & 0 \\ 0 & 0 & 1 & 0 & 0 & 0 & 0 & 0 & 0 \\ 0 & 0 & 0 & 0 & 0 & 0 & 1 & 0 & 0 \\ 0 & 0 & 0 & 0 & 0 & 1 & 0 & 0 & 0 \end{pmatrix}$$

Let us consider that the terminal state $\mathbf{x}_t$ should be achieving the contract represented by the feasible state $X_9 = (0,0,0,0,1,0,0,0,0)^T$ – i.e. the ninth column of the matrix $\mathbf{X}_{reach}$. In order to reach the terminal state $X_9 \equiv \mathbf{x}_t$ from the initial state $X_1 \equiv \mathbf{x}_0$ (the first column of the matrix $\mathbf{X}_{reach}$) we can utilize the in-house graphical tool GraSim (see the print screen from it displayed in Figure 7) for control synthesis built on the base of the method proposed in (Čapkovič, 2005). Then, the state trajectory of the system is $X_1 \rightarrow X_2 \rightarrow X_3 \rightarrow X_5 \rightarrow X_7 \rightarrow X_9$.

Figure 5. The cooperation of two virtual companies: (a) the PN-based model; (b) the RG

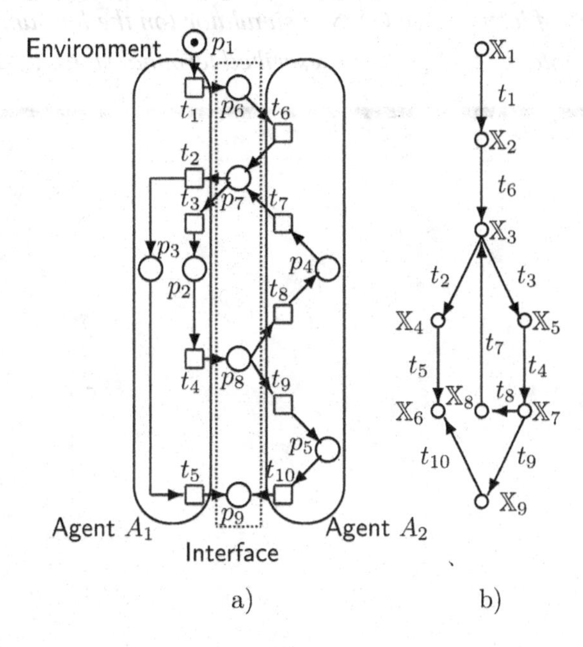

Figure 6. The PN-based model of the system drawn by means of the PN simulator. (The print screen from the own (in-house) PN simulator)

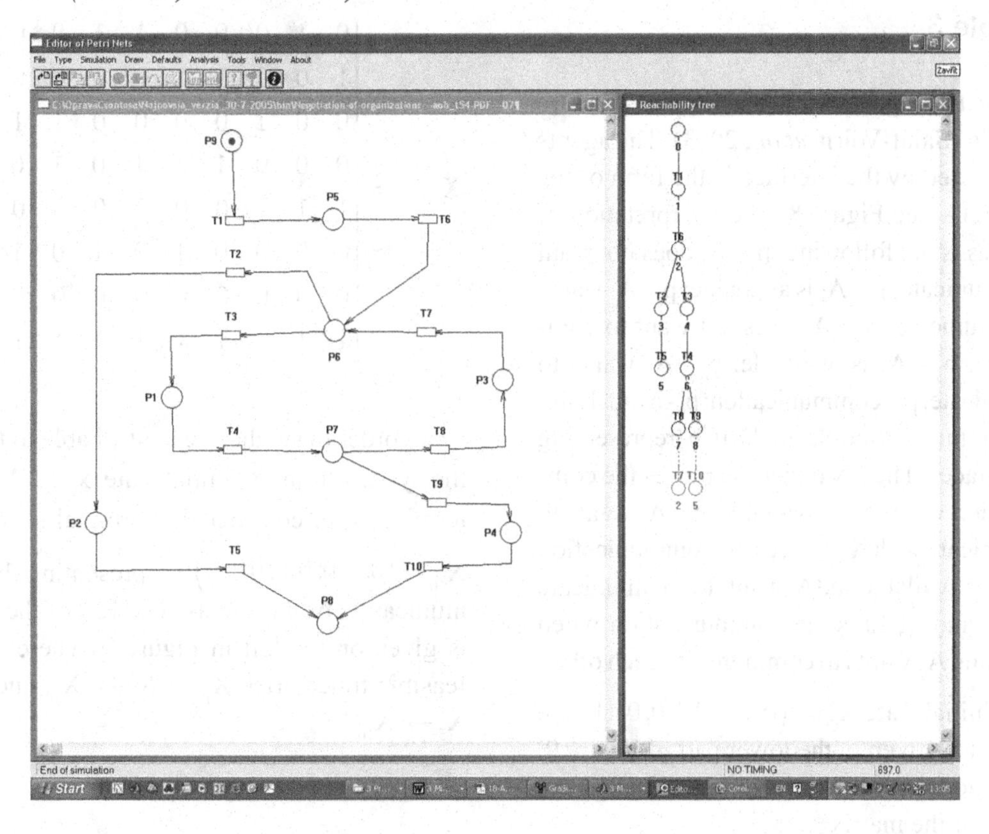

Figure 7. The print screen from the graphical tool GraSim. The reachability graph of the PN model of the system drawn by means of icons in the GraSim simulator (on the left) and the example of the state trajectory from the initial state $\mathbf{x}_0 \equiv X_1$ *to the prescribed terminal state* $\mathbf{x}_t \equiv X_9$ *(on the right)*

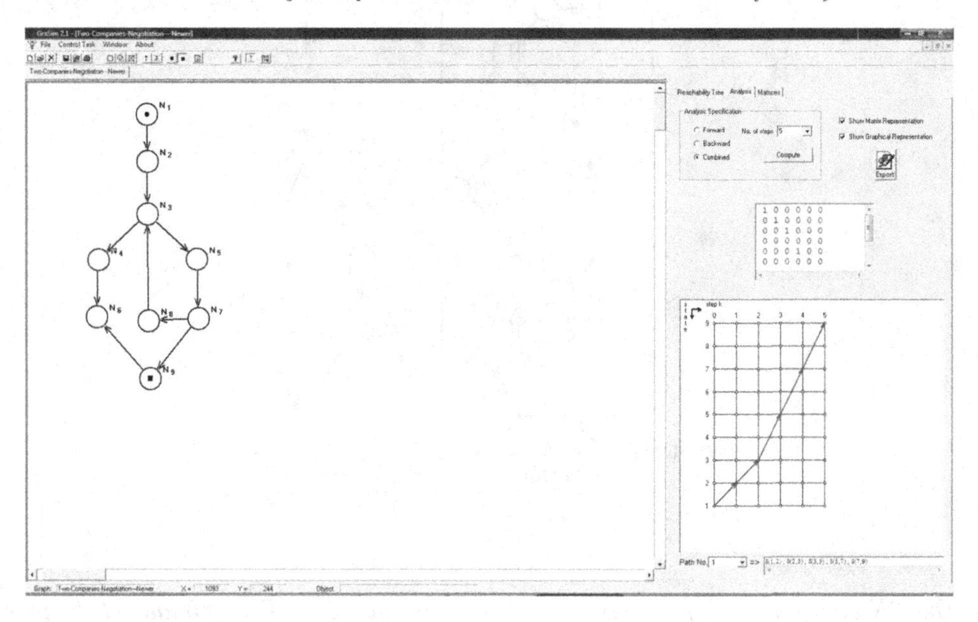

Example 3

Consider two agents with the simple structure defined in (Saint-Voirin *et al.*, 2003). The agents are connected by the interface in the form of the PN subnet – see Figure 8. The interpretation of the places is the following: p_1 - A_1 does not want to communicate; p_2 - A_1 is available; p_3 - A_1 wants to communicate; p_4 - A_2 does not want to communicate; p_5 - A_2 is available; p_6 - A_2 wants to communicate; p_7 - communication; p_8 - availability of the communication channel(s) Ch (representing the interface). The PN transition t_9 fires the communication when A_1 is available and A_2 wants to communicate with A_1, t_{10} fires the communication when A_2 is available and A_1 wants to communicate with A_2, and t_{12} fires the communication when both A_1 and A_2 wants to communicate each other. For the initial state $\mathbf{x}_0^T = (0,1,0,0,1,0,0,1)^T$ we have the RG given in the lower part of Figure 9. The RG nodes are the state vectors stored as the columns of the matrix

$$\mathbf{X}_{reach} = \begin{pmatrix} 0 & 1 & 0 & 0 & 0 & 1 & 1 & 0 & 0 & 0 \\ 1 & 0 & 0 & 1 & 1 & 0 & 0 & 0 & 0 & 0 \\ 0 & 0 & 1 & 0 & 0 & 0 & 0 & 1 & 1 & 0 \\ 0 & 0 & 0 & 1 & 0 & 1 & 0 & 1 & 0 & 0 \\ 1 & 1 & 1 & 0 & 0 & 0 & 0 & 0 & 0 & 0 \\ 0 & 0 & 0 & 0 & 1 & 0 & 1 & 0 & 1 & 0 \\ 0 & 0 & 0 & 0 & 0 & 0 & 0 & 0 & 0 & 1 \\ 1 & 1 & 1 & 1 & 1 & 1 & 1 & 1 & 1 & 0 \end{pmatrix}$$

In order to synthesize control able to transfer the system from the initial state $\mathbf{x}_0 \equiv X_1$ to the terminal one, consider the terminal state $\mathbf{x}_t \equiv X_{10} = (0,0,0,0,0,0,1,0)^T$ representing the communication of the agents. The RG of the system is given on the left in Figure 9. There are two feasible trajectories $X_1 \rightarrow X_3 \rightarrow X_{10}$ and $X_1 \rightarrow X_5 \rightarrow X_{10}$.

Figure 8. The PN based model of two agents cooperation by means of the interface in the form of the PN subnet

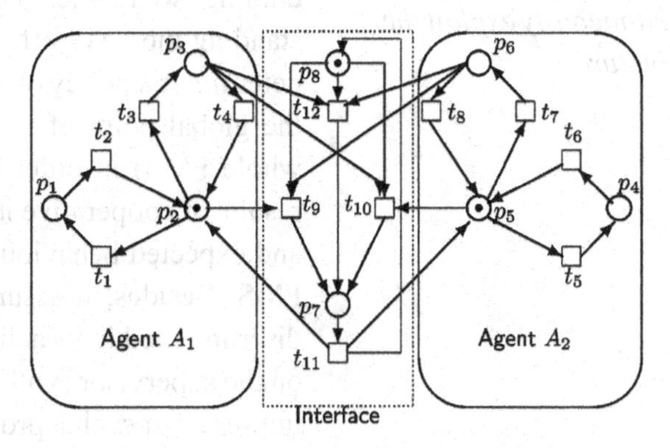

Figure 9. The RG two agents cooperation (on the left) and two trajectories from the initial state to the terminal one

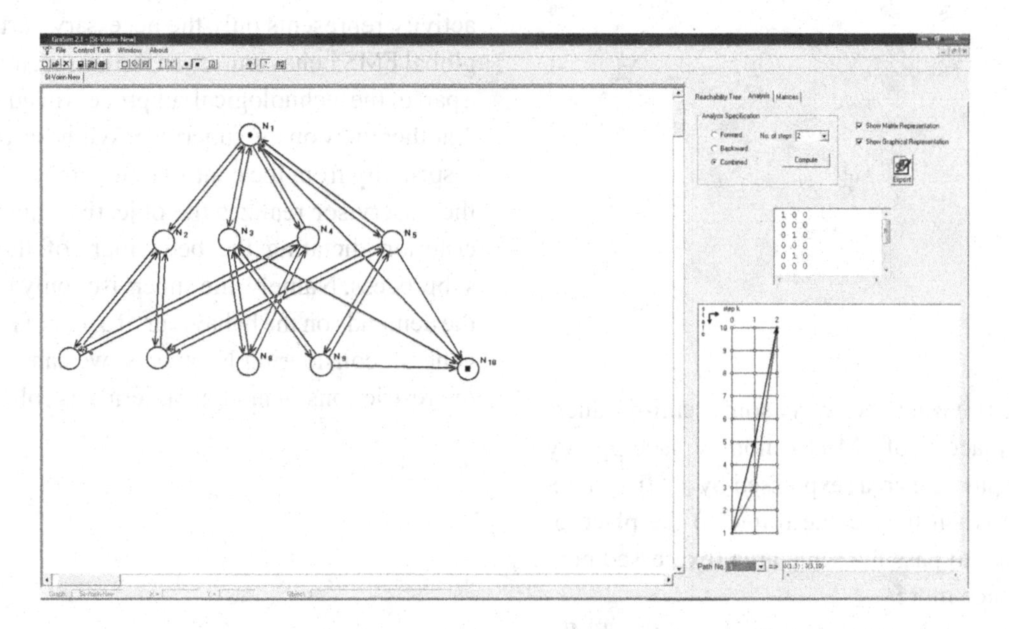

SUPERVISORY CONTROL OF AGENTS IN MAS

Many times the agents working in a common space - e.g. the tracks for AGVs (automatically guided vehicles) in a flexible manufacturing system (FMS), or tracks for trains in a railway network, etc. - have to be supervised in order to avoid a crash. To illustrate this, consider N_t tracks of AGVs in FMS. Denote them as agents A_i, i=1,...,N_t. The AGVs (in any track A_i there exist $n_j \geq 1$ AGVs) carry semi-products from a place of FMS to another place and then they (empty or with another load) come round. Consider the tracks with AGVs to be the autonomous agents. The PN model of the single agent A_1 is given by the upper picture in Figure 10. During its activities n_1 AGVs (represented by means of tokens) have to pass this track as well as an area (common for all agents), even two times. Namely, in case of the AGVs of the

Figure 10. The PN-based model of one of the agents (the upper picture) and supervising four such agents in order to simultaneously exploit the restricted area (the lower picture)

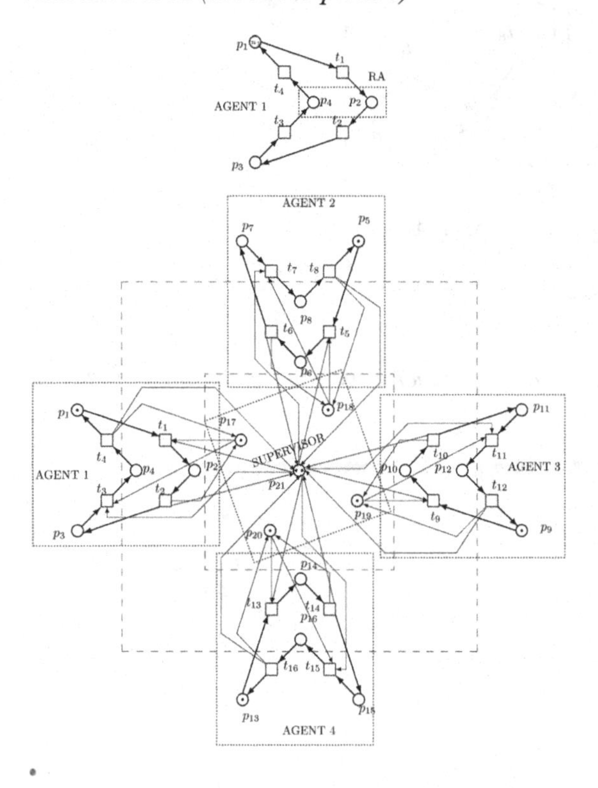

agent A_1: (i) when they carry some semi-products from a place p_1 of FMS to another place p_3 they have to pass the area (expressed by p_2) first time, and (ii) when they come round to the place p_1 they have to pass the same area (expressed now by p_4) once more.

However, because the space of the FMS, where the agents operate, is limited, there exists the restriction that only certain limited number of different AGVs, namely $N < \sum_{i=1}^{N_t} n_i$ or often $N << \sum_{i=1}^{N_t} n_i$, can operate in the restricted area simultaneously, the agents A_i have to be limited in their autonomous activities by a supervisor. The reason is that the agents themselves are not able to coalesce on a procedure satisfying all of them because the autonomous agents are usually egoistic (selfish). A violent driving of individual agents in the limited space (restricted area) might tend to wrecks with exterminatory effects, including some mechanical devastations, even standing the FMS off. Therefore, the supervisor determines a policy of the agents behaviour from the global point of view (i.e. conducive to the whole FMS) in order to achieve the satisfying results of cooperative interaction among devices and expected behaviour (function) of the global FMS. Besides, it assures that no agent will be discriminated in its activities. The opposite view on the supervisor synthesis process can evoke an impress that such a process expresses the agents negotiation (although unwilling). Such a view is not so fantastic, because the supervisor does not drive its own selfish will or interest but its activity represents only the necessary part of the global FMS behaviour, even the correct model of a part of the technological subprocess inside FMS. Another view on the supervisor synthesis process (especially from the control point of view) is that the supervisor realizes the objective function (a criterion dictating the behaviour) of the FMS subprocess. Namely, the supervisor only realizes the demands on the behaviour of a part of FMS. In general, considering N_A agents, we can describe the restrictions in analytical terms as follows

$$\begin{array}{ccccccccccccc}
\sigma_{p_2} & + & \sigma_{p_4} & & & & & & & & & \leq & n_1 \\
 & & & & \sigma_{p_6} & + & \sigma_{p_8} & & & & & \leq & n_2 \\
\ldots & & \ldots & & \ldots & & \ldots & & \ldots & & \ldots & \ldots & \ldots \\
 & & & & & & & & \sigma_{p_{N_A-2}} & + & \sigma_{p_{N_A}} & \leq & n_{N_A} \\
\sigma_{p_2} & + & \sigma_{p_4} & + & \sigma_{p_6} & + & \sigma_{p_8} & + \cdots + & \sigma_{p_{N_A-2}} & + & \sigma_{p_{N_A}} & \leq & N
\end{array}$$

For illustration, consider $N_A = 4$, $N = 2$, $n_1 = n_2 = n_3 = n_4 = 1$. Consequently, we have

$$\begin{array}{l}
\sigma_{p_2} + \sigma_{p_4} \leq 1 \\
\sigma_{p_6} + \sigma_{p_8} \leq 1 \\
\sigma_{p_{10}} + \sigma_{p_{12}} \leq 1 \\
\sigma_{p_{14}} + \sigma_{p_{16}} \leq 1 \\
\sigma_{p_2} + \sigma_{p_4} + \sigma_{p_6} + \sigma_{p_8} + \sigma_{p_{10}} + \sigma_{p_{12}} + \sigma_{p_{14}} + \sigma_{p_{16}} \leq 2
\end{array}$$

To synthesize the supervisor we can utilize the method (Iordache and Antsaklis, 2006) based on P-invariants of P/T PN. P-invariants are vectors,

v, with the property that multiplication of these vectors with any state vector **x** reachable from a given initial state vector $\mathbf{x}_0$ yields the same result (the relation of the state conservation)

$$\mathbf{v}^T.\mathbf{x} = \mathbf{v}^T.\mathbf{x}_0$$

Taking into account the consecutive states (that are obtained by firing of only one transition), it results that

$$\mathbf{v}^T.col_t\left(\mathbf{B}\right) = 0$$

for each transition t. Here, $col_t\left(\mathbf{B}\right)$ is the column of **B** corresponding to the transition t.

It means that, algebraically, these vectors are solutions of the following equation

$$\mathbf{B}^T.\mathbf{v} = \mathbf{0}$$

with **v** being n-dimensional vector and **0** being the m-dimensional zero vector, which is usually introduced - see e.g. (Murata, 1989) - as the definition of the P-invariant of PN. However, usually there are several P-invariants in PN models. Hence, the set of the P-invariants of PN is created by the columns of the $\left(n \times n_x\right)$-dimensional ($n_x$ expresses the number of invariants) matrix **V** being the solution of the equation as follows

$$\mathbf{V}^T.\mathbf{B} = \mathbf{0}$$

The main idea of the approach to the supervisor synthesis consists in imbedding of additional PN places (slacks) and finding the structural interconnections between them and the original PN places. Consequently, a new PN subnet representing the supervisor and its interface with the original system are found and added to the PN model. Thus, the desired behaviour of agents is forced. In PN with the slacks we have to use the following structure with augmented matrices. Consequently, the previous equation has to be written into the form

$$\begin{bmatrix}\mathbf{L} & \mathbf{I}_s\end{bmatrix}.\begin{bmatrix}\mathbf{B}\\ \mathbf{B}_s\end{bmatrix} = \mathbf{0}$$

where $\mathbf{I}_s$ is $\left(n_x \times n_x\right)$-dimensional identity matrix and **L** describes conditions (as to marking of some places in the PN models of agents) of the desired MAS behaviour. In other words, by means of n_x different slacks (one of them into each unequality) we transform the unequalities describing the marking conditions into the following vector equation

$$\begin{bmatrix}\mathbf{L} & \mathbf{I}_s\end{bmatrix}.\begin{bmatrix}\mathbf{x}\\ \mathbf{x}_s\end{bmatrix} = \mathbf{b}$$

This relation is very important especially for computing the initial state of the supervisor at a given initial state of the original system. Thus, the initial state is the following

$$\mathbf{x}_s^0 = \mathbf{b} - \mathbf{L}.\mathbf{x}_0$$

While **B** is the known structural matrix of the agents (without the supervisor), $\mathbf{B}_s$ is the supervisor structure which is searched by the synthesis process. Thus, after multiplying the matrices $\begin{bmatrix}\mathbf{L} & \mathbf{I}_s\end{bmatrix}$ and $\begin{bmatrix}\mathbf{B} & \mathbf{B}_s\end{bmatrix}^T$ we have

$$\mathbf{L}.\mathbf{B} + \mathbf{B}_s = \mathbf{0}$$

Consequently,

$$\mathbf{B}_s = -\mathbf{L}.\mathbf{B}$$

Here, $\mathbf{B}_s$ can be decomposed (factorized) into the matrices $\mathbf{G}_s^T$ and $\mathbf{F}_s$ - i.e. $\mathbf{B}_s = \mathbf{G}_s^T - \mathbf{F}_s$. These matrices represent the supervisor structure, more precisely the interconnections of the incorporated slacks with the original PN structure. The augmented state vector and the augmented structural matrices (of the original system together with the supervisor) are the following

$$\mathbf{x}_a = \begin{bmatrix} \mathbf{x} \\ \mathbf{x}_s \end{bmatrix}; \quad \mathbf{F}_a = \begin{bmatrix} \mathbf{F} \\ \mathbf{F}_s \end{bmatrix}; \quad \mathbf{G}_a^T = \begin{bmatrix} \mathbf{G}^T \\ \mathbf{G}_s^T \end{bmatrix}$$

In our case (example) of the agents (the tracks with AGVs) we have $n_x = 5$, and

$$\mathbf{L} = \begin{pmatrix} 0&1&0&1&0&0&0&0&0&0&0&0&0&0&0&0 \\ 0&0&0&0&0&1&0&1&0&0&0&0&0&0&0&0 \\ 0&0&0&0&0&0&0&0&0&1&0&1&0&0&0&0 \\ 0&0&0&0&0&0&0&0&0&0&0&0&0&1&0&1 \\ 0&1&0&1&0&1&0&1&0&1&0&1&0&1&0&1 \end{pmatrix}$$

$$\mathbf{b} = \begin{pmatrix} 1 & 1 & 1 & 1 & 2 \end{pmatrix}^T$$

$$\mathbf{B}_s = -\mathbf{L}.\mathbf{B} = \begin{pmatrix} -1&1&-1&1&0&0&0&0&0&0&0&0&0&0&0&0 \\ 0&0&0&0&-1&1&-1&1&0&0&0&0&0&0&0&0 \\ 0&0&0&0&0&0&0&0&-1&1&-1&1&0&0&0&0 \\ 0&0&0&0&0&0&0&0&0&0&0&0&-1&1&-1&1 \\ -1&1&-1&1&-1&1&-1&1&-1&1&-1&1&-1&1&-1&1 \end{pmatrix}$$

$$\mathbf{F}_s = \begin{pmatrix} 1&0&1&0&0&0&0&0&0&0&0&0&0&0&0&0 \\ 0&0&0&0&1&0&1&0&0&0&0&0&0&0&0&0 \\ 0&0&0&0&0&0&0&0&1&0&1&0&0&0&0&0 \\ 0&0&0&0&0&0&0&0&0&0&0&0&1&0&1&0 \\ 1&0&1&0&1&0&1&0&1&0&1&0&1&0&1&0 \end{pmatrix}$$

$$\mathbf{G}_s^T = \begin{pmatrix} 0&1&0&1&0&0&0&0&0&0&0&0&0&0&0&0 \\ 0&0&0&0&0&1&0&1&0&0&0&0&0&0&0&0 \\ 0&0&0&0&0&0&0&0&0&1&0&1&0&0&0&0 \\ 0&0&0&0&0&0&0&0&0&0&0&0&0&1&0&1 \\ 0&1&0&1&0&1&0&1&0&1&0&1&0&1&0&1 \end{pmatrix}$$

When the initial state of the non-supervised agents is

$$\mathbf{x}_0 = \begin{pmatrix} 1&0&0&0&1&0&0&0&1&0&0&0&1&0&0&0 \end{pmatrix}^T$$

$$\mathbf{x}_s^0 = \mathbf{b} - \mathbf{L}.\mathbf{x}_0 = \begin{pmatrix} 1 & 1 & 1 & 1 & 2 \end{pmatrix}^T$$

Having these parameters we can realize the supervisor structure. The structure of the supervised system is displayed in the lower picture in Figure 10. Although the number of AGVs in any elementary agent A_i (track) is only $n_i = 1$ and the number of AGVs permissible simultaneously share the restricted area is only $N_A = 2$, the RG of the supervised system has 176 nodes and 512 edges. For more AGVs in any agent (track) as well as for more AGVs permissible simultaneously share the restricted area more complicated RG can occur. Namely, the supervisor guarantees only fulfilling the prescribed restrictions, however, it does not guarantee that there exists only a single state trajectory from an initial state to a terminal one. Consequently, the approach presented above, yielding the space of feasible trajectories can help to analyse the supervised plant as to the selection of the most suitable trajectories. In such a supervisor structure only the presence of N AGVs in the restricted area simultaneously is assured without designation which agents (in our example which N = 2 agents from four existing ones) have the priority to enter by their AGV into the area. To resolve this problem it is necessary e.g. to introduce something like semaphore lights for any track (agent) in order to avoid a collision (crash). Of course, in case of AGVs the classical semaphores are an illusion from the technical point of view because AGVs themselves are not able to recognize the light colours. Especially, in the given initial state, when all of the agents compete for entering the area, it is necessary to choice N agents from the N_t existing ones. During the global system (FMS) dynamics development it is probable that not all of the agents will compete for entering. However, in general, also in such a case more than N agents can compete. Consequently, to be equitable, it is necessary to give them the same chance to be chosen for entering. Thus, e.g. a likelihood-based approach can be used on that way. But such an approach is out of the topic of this paper. Another way can be based on a set of rules (e.g. IF-THEN rules) predefined with respect to the global FMS demands. In such a case there exist external interferences into the PN transitions enabling and/or firing. In our case, into the transitions $t_i \in \{t_1, t_2, t_5, t_6, t_9, t_{10}, t_{13}, t_{14}\}$.

However, we can synthesize another supervisor for the system being already supervised (by the existing supervisor synthesized above). For example, when we want to enter priorities (as to the agents or groups of agents) into the system (this can be actual in case of AGVs inside of FMS performing an assembly of parts in a strictly predefined order), the new supervisor has to take into account the priorities e.g. the priority π_{A_i} of agents A_i descends with the increasing agent number - i.e. $\pi_{A_1} > \pi_{A_2} > \pi_{A_3} > \pi_{A_4}$.

Another Example

Consider another example, more simple, concerning the so called *mutex* (mutual exclusion) of two agents. It is given in Figure 11 (see e.g. (Badouel, 2002)). The main aim of this example is to point out that the numerical method of the synthesis described above can be utilized also in such a case. Namely, the mutex is very important especially in the case of limited sources (e.g. of energy, material, space, etc.), where it prevents a selfish behaviour of agents. It can be synthesized by means of agent-based approach as follows.

Consider the left subnet in Figure 11 consisting of $P_1 = \{p_1, \cdots, p_4\}$ and $T_1 = \{t_1, \cdots, t_4\}$ to be the PN model of an agent A_1 and the right subnet consisting of $P_2 = \{p_5, \cdots, p_8\}$ and $T_2 = \{t_5, \cdots, t_8\}$ to be the PN model of an agent A_2. When both agents (e.g. robots) depend on a limited common source of a material, it is necessary to supervised their access to the source. In general, without any interest what kind of activities the places p_i, i=1,...,8, mean, we can be interested in eliminating the simultaneous executing of the activities representing by the places p_1, p_4, p_5, p_8. To synthetize the mutex in this example, we have to set the condition

$$\sigma_{p_1} + \sigma_{p_4} + \sigma_{p_5} + \sigma_{p_8} \leq 1$$

i.e. $\mathbf{L} = \begin{pmatrix} 1 & 0 & 0 & 1 & 1 & 0 & 0 & 1 \end{pmatrix}^T$

Because the structural matrices of the agents are

$$\mathbf{F}_1 = \mathbf{F}_2 = \begin{pmatrix} 0 & 1 & 0 & 0 \\ 0 & 0 & 1 & 0 \\ 0 & 0 & 0 & 1 \\ 1 & 0 & 0 & 0 \end{pmatrix};$$

Figure 11. The PN-based model of the mutual exclusion

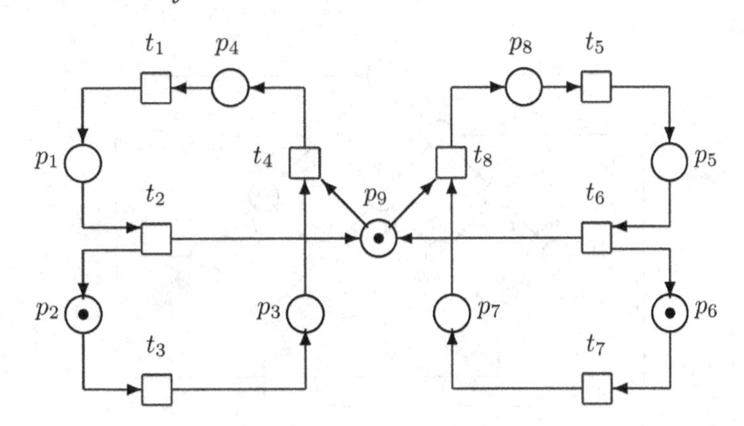

$$\mathbf{G}_1 = \mathbf{G}_2 = \begin{pmatrix} 1 & 0 & 0 & 0 \\ 0 & 1 & 0 & 0 \\ 0 & 0 & 1 & 0 \\ 0 & 0 & 0 & 1 \end{pmatrix}$$

we have

$$\mathbf{B}_1 = \mathbf{B}_2 = \begin{pmatrix} 1 & -1 & 0 & 0 \\ 0 & 1 & -1 & 0 \\ 0 & 0 & 1 & -1 \\ -1 & 0 & 0 & 1 \end{pmatrix}$$

$$\mathbf{B} = \begin{pmatrix} \mathbf{B}_1 & \mathbf{0} \\ \mathbf{0} & \mathbf{B}_2 \end{pmatrix}$$

$$\mathbf{B}_s = -\mathbf{L}.\mathbf{B} = \begin{pmatrix} 0 & 1 & 0 & -1 & 0 & 1 & 0 & -1 \end{pmatrix}^T$$

$$\mathbf{F}_s = \begin{pmatrix} 0 & 0 & 0 & 1 & 0 & 0 & 0 & 1 \end{pmatrix}^T;$$

$$\mathbf{G}_s = \begin{pmatrix} 0 & 1 & 0 & 0 & 0 & 1 & 0 & 0 \end{pmatrix}^T$$

In such a way we can realize the supervisor ensuring the mutex. It has one PN place p_9 and its connection with two autonomous agents A_1, A_2 is expressed by $\mathbf{F}_s$, $\mathbf{G}_s$. When the initial states of the autonomous agents are ${}^0\mathbf{x}_1 = {}^0\mathbf{x}_2 = (0,1,0,0)^T$, the initial state of the supervisor is

$$\mathbf{x}_s^0 = \mathbf{b} - \mathbf{L}.\mathbf{x}_0 = 1 - \mathbf{L}.\left({}^0\mathbf{x}_1^T \quad {}^0\mathbf{x}_2^T\right)^T = 1 - 0 = 1$$

It means, that the initial state of the supervised agents is

$$\mathbf{x}_0 = (0,1,0,0,0,1,0,0,1)^T$$

Thus we have the same structure as those given in Figure 11. The RG of this structure is given in Figure 12. The nodes of the RG are represented by the state vector given by the column of

$$\mathbf{X}_{reach} = \begin{pmatrix} 0 & 0 & 0 & 0 & 0 & 0 & 1 & 0 & 0 & 0 & 1 & 0 \\ 1 & 0 & 1 & 0 & 0 & 1 & 0 & 0 & 0 & 1 & 0 & 0 \\ 0 & 1 & 0 & 0 & 1 & 0 & 0 & 0 & 1 & 0 & 0 & 1 \\ 0 & 0 & 0 & 1 & 0 & 0 & 0 & 1 & 0 & 0 & 0 & 0 \\ 0 & 0 & 0 & 0 & 0 & 0 & 0 & 0 & 0 & 1 & 0 & 1 \\ 1 & 1 & 0 & 1 & 0 & 0 & 1 & 0 & 0 & 0 & 0 & 0 \\ 0 & 0 & 1 & 0 & 1 & 0 & 0 & 1 & 0 & 0 & 1 & 0 \\ 0 & 0 & 0 & 0 & 0 & 1 & 0 & 0 & 1 & 0 & 0 & 0 \\ 1 & 1 & 1 & 0 & 1 & 0 & 0 & 0 & 0 & 0 & 0 & 0 \end{pmatrix}$$

The columns of this matrix represent the feasible states $X_1, \ldots, X_{12}$ of the supervised system.

It is necessary to say that the supervisor itself ensures only that the system will behave so that the prescribed condition – the mutex – will be satisfied. However, it does not give us the complete

Figure 12. The RG of the supervised agents

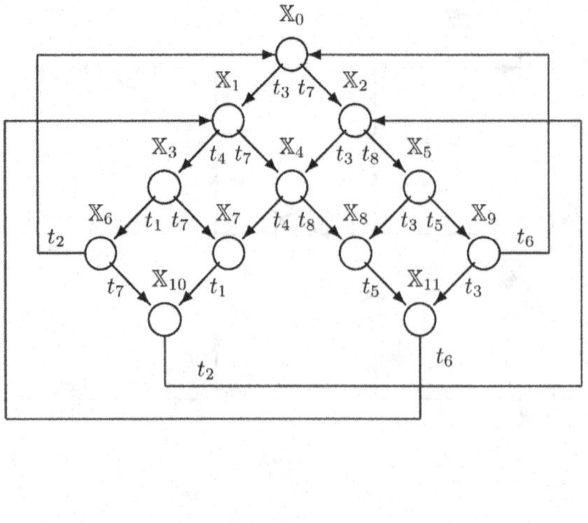

information of the supervised system behaviour. In order to analyse the system behaviour in the whole as well as to synthesize control from a given initial state $\mathbf{x}_0 \equiv X_1$ to a desired terminal state $\mathbf{x}_t$ we have to use the developed graphical tool GraSim again. In Figure 13 the print screen of the GraSim is displayed. On the left side the RG drawn by means of icons is placed. In the modelled situation when the initial state $\mathbf{x}_0$ of the system (denoted by the small token in the form of the filling circle) and the terminal state $\mathbf{x}_t$ (denoted by the small token in the form of the filling square) are the same – i.e. the RG node $N_1 = X_1 = \mathbf{x}_0 = \mathbf{x}_t$ – we have two possible trajectories (on the right side). The first of them (the lower one) is the trajectory $X_1 \rightarrow X_2 \rightarrow X_4 \rightarrow X_7 \rightarrow X_1$ while the second one (the upper one) is $X_1 \rightarrow X_3 \rightarrow X_6 \rightarrow X_{10} \rightarrow X_1$. No other trajectory exists in this situation. Of course, at both trajectories the mutex property is assured by the supervisor.

CONCLUSION

The PN-based modular approach was utilized in order to model the agent cooperation in MAS in the form of the vector linear discrete dynamic system. Such a system approach is based on the analogy with DES. It is applicable for both the wide class of agents and the wide class of forms of agent cooperation in MAS. Three possible forms of the module representing the interface among agents were proposed, described and illustrated - namely, the interface: (i) based on additional PN transitions; (ii) based on additional PN places; (iii) in the form of the additional PN-subnet. The dynamic behaviour of the systems were tested for arbitrarily chosen initial states by means of corresponding RG. Using the PN-based approach enable us to find feasible states in analytical terms and to insight into their causality. This allows to observe the system dynamics and to find fit control strategies. Moreover, the approach to supervising the agents was introduced. By means of the supervisor synthesized by virtue of desired conditions for the MAS behaviour, some real complicated situations (like limited common sources – e.g. small common working space of agents, limited amount of energy or material, etc.) can be successfully avoided and the prescribed aim of the MAS can be successfully accomplished.

Figure 13. The print screen from the control synthesis tool GraSim

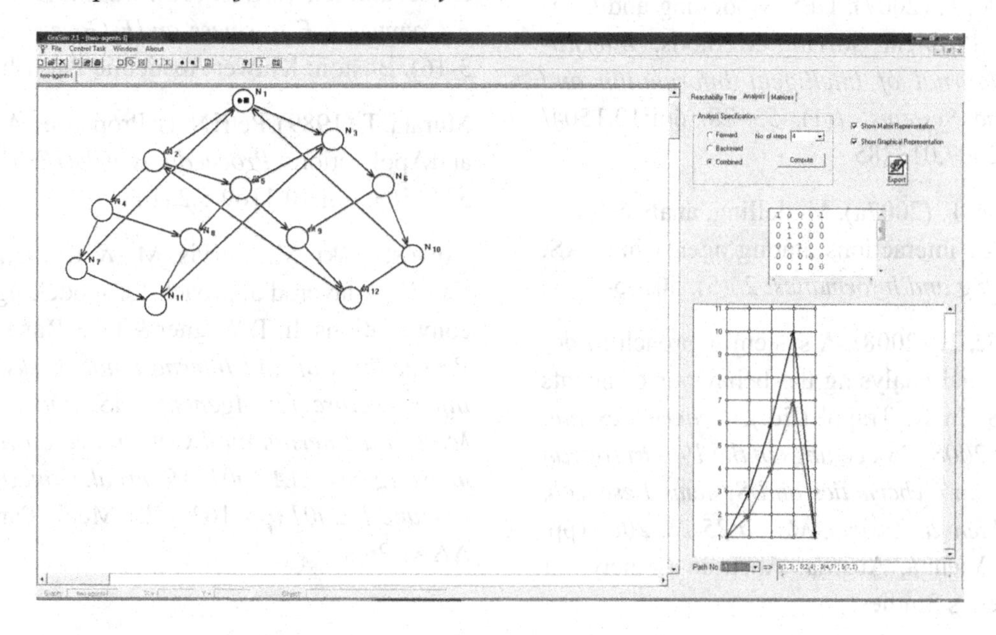

ACKNOWLEDGMENT

The research was partially supported by the Slovak Grant Agency for Science VEGA under grant # 2/0075/09. The author thanks VEGA for this support.

REFERENCES

Badouel, E., Caillaud, B., & Darondeau, P. (2002). Distributing Finite Automata Through Petri Net Synthesis. *Formal Aspects of Computing, 13*, 447–470. doi:10.1007/s001650200022

Bale, L. S. (1995). Gregory Bateson, Cybernetics, and the Social/Behavioral Sciences. *Cybernetics & Human Knowing, 3*(1), 27–455.

Čapkovič, F. (2003). The generalised method for solving problems of DEDS control synthesis. In P. W. H. Chung, C. Hinde & M. Ali (Eds.), *Developments in Applied Artificial Intelligence, Lecture Notes in Artificial Intelligence*, (Vol. 2718, pp. 702-711). Berlin: Springer.

Čapkovič, F. (2005). An Application of the DEDS Control Synthesis Method. *Journal of Universal Computer Science, 11*(2), 303–326.

Čapkovič, F. (2007). DES Modelling and Control vs. Problem Solving Methods. *International Journal of Intelligent Information and Database Systems, 1*(1), 53–78. doi:10.1504/IJIIDS.2007.013285

Čapkovič, F. (2007a). Modelling, analysing and control of interactions among agents in MAS. *Computing and Informatics, 26*(5), 507–541.

Čapkovič, F. (2008). A system approach to describing and analysing the behaviour of agents in MAS. In R. Trappl (Ed.), *Cybernetics and Systems 2008, Proceedings of the 19th European Meeting on Cybernetics and Systems Research, Vol. 1, Vienna, Austria, March 25-28, 2008* (pp. 70-75). Vienna, Austria: Austrian Society for Cybernetics Studies.

Charlton, B. G., & Andras, P. (2003). What is management and what do managers do? A systems theory account. *Philosophy of Management, 3*, 1–15.

Demazeau, Y. (2003) Y. MAS methodology. *Tutorial at the 2nd French-Mexican School of the Repartee Cooperative Systems - ESRC 2003*, Sept. 29-Oct. 4, 2003. Rennes, France: IRISA.

Fonseca, S., Griss, M., & Letsinger, R. (2001). *Agent Behavior Architectures - A MAS Framework Comparison* (HP Labs Technical Report HPL-2001-332). Palo Alto, CA: HP.

Hung, P. C. K., & Mao, J. Y. (2002). Modeling e-negotiation activities with Petri nets. In R. H. Spraguer, Jr. (Ed.), *Proceedings of 35th Hawaii International Conference on System Sciences HICSS 2002, Big Island, Hawaii,* (Vol. 1, pp. 26). Piscataway, NJ: IEEE Computer Society Press.

Iordache, M. V., & Antsaklis, P. J. (2006). *Supervisory Control of Concurrent Systems: A Petri Net Structural Approach.* Boston: Birkhauser.

Lenz, K., Oberweis, A., & Schneider, S. (2001). Trust based contracting in virtual organizations: A concept based on contract workflow management systems. In Schmid, B., Stanoevska-Slabeva, K., & Tschammer, V. (Eds.), *Towards the E-Society – E-Commerce, E-Business, and E-Government* (pp. 3-16). Boston: Kluwer Academic Publishers.

Murata, T. (1989). Petri Nets: Properties, Analysis and Applications. *Proceedings of the IEEE, 77*(4), 541–588. doi:10.1109/5.24143

Nowostawski, M., Purvis, M., & Cranefield, S. (2001). A layered approach for modelling agent conversations. In T. Wagner & O. F. Rana (Eds.), *Proceedings of 2nd International Workshop on Infrastructure for Agents, MAS, and Scalable MAS, 5th International Conference on Autonomous Agents - AA 2001, Montreal, Canada, May 28-June 1, 2001* (pp. 163-170). Menlo Park, CA: AAAI Press.

Peterson, J. L. (1981). *Petri Net Theory and Modeling the Systems*. New York: Prentice Hall Inc.

Saint-Voirin, D., Lang, C., & Zerhouni, N. (2003). Distributed cooperation modelling for maintenance using Petri nets and multi-agents systems. In *Proceedings of 5th IEEE Int. Symp. on Computational Intelligence in Robotics and Automation, CIRA'03, Kobe, Japan, July 16-20,* (Vol. 1, pp. 366-371). Piscataway, NJ: IEEE Press.

Takahara, Y., & Mesarovic, M. D. (2004). *Organization Structure: Cybernetic Systems Foundation*, (IFSR International Series on Systems Science and Engineering, Vol.22). New York: Springer.

Yen, J., Yin, J., Ioerger, T. R., Miller, M. S., Xu, E., & Volz, R. A. (2001). CAST: Collaborative agents for simulating teamwork. In B. Nebel (Ed.), *Proceedings of 17th International Joint Conference on Artificial Intelligence - IJCAI' 2001, Seattle, WA* (Vol. 2, pp. 1135-1142). San Francisco, CA: Morgan Kaufmann Publishers.

KEY TERMS AND DEFINITIONS

Agent: The entity that can perceive, reason, and act in their environment and communicate with other agents in multi agent system.

Control Synthesis: Finding suitable control interferences able to transfer a system from a given initial state into a prescribed terminal state.

Digraph (DG): The directed graph. It is the discrete structure consisting of nodes and directed arcs among them. It is the term from Graph Theory, where it is defined in details by means of the mathematical terminology.

Discrete Event Systems (DES): Systems driven by discrete events. Their behaviour depends on the occurrence of discrete events.

Model: An abstract representation of the real system. The mathematical model based on Petri nets is used for modelling discrete event systems and multi agent systems.

Module: A specific part of a whole (or an aggregate) - e.g. a subsystem, an agent, etc.

Multi Agent Systems (MAS): The composition of collaborative agents working in shared environment. The agents together perform a more complex functionality.

Petri Nets: The special kind of bipartite directed graphs. The bipartite directed graph is a kind of directed graphs. It is defined in Graph Theory.

Reachability Graph (RG): The digraph expressing the relations among feasible states of Petri net. It comprehensively expresses the causality of the Petri net-based mathematical model.

Reachability Tree (RT): The tree (the term from Graph Theory) expressing the causal development of the Petri net-based model from a given initial state. It yields successive branching of paths towards the states reachable form the initial state. In such a way it expresses the causality of the Petri net-based mathematical model.

Chapter 15
Identification and Response Prediction of Switching Dynamic Systems Using Interval Analysis

Kyarash Shahriari
Centre de Recherch Industrielle du Quebec (CRIQ), Canada

ABSTRACT

A novel method based on interval analysis is proposed in this work for modeling and response prediction of SISO uncertain switching dynamic systems. To describe the system's dynamic in any operating mode, a local linear model is used. The validity domain of any local model is determined in system's input-output space. To take into account the modeling error, adjustable parameters of local models are considered time-varying and characterized by intervals of real numbers. A model whose parameters are characterized by intervals is called an interval model. A procedure is also developed to perform n-step prediction of system's response using the multi-mode interval model. Since the model parameters are intervals, the predicted response at any instant is not a real number anymore but an interval of real numbers. The set of predicted intervals at different instances generates a tube through time called wrapping envelope. However, the identification/characterization procedure proposed in the early stage of this work guarantees that the wrapping envelope includes the system's response taking into account possible modeling error and perturbations. This envelope can be used in diagnosis to supervise healthy operation of the system as well as in process safety analysis to guarantee that the physical variables of the system never enter in forbidden operating zones and the system remains in safe operating conditions.

INTRODUCTION

Modeling, parameter identification/characterization and response prediction of uncertain switching dynamic systems is of the most challenging problems in control engineering especially in diagnosis and process safety analysis in which one wishes to calculate accurately system's response to determine whether the system is in healthy operational state/condition or to guarantee that it never enters in forbidden operating zones. This is classically performed with the aide of a mathematical model

DOI: 10.4018/978-1-61520-668-1.ch015

of the system whilst the latter usually describes the system's behavior in a simplified manner. This leads to a difference between the system's response and the predicted value called *modeling error*. There exist three major approaches to deal with this problem that are the deterministic, probabilistic, and set-membership approaches. In the deterministic approach, the model parameters are constant scalars and are adjusted in such way that a certain optimization criterion e.g. the power of the error is minimized. However, this approach does not provide any information on modeling error in prediction phase. An alternative is to use the probabilistic approach in which the modeling error is characterized by a probability density function (PDF). In this case, the PDF is used to calculate a probabilistic interval for the system's response at any instant. Though, it suffers from three major shortcomings:

- It is not always an easy task to characterize modeling error by a certain PDF,
- The properties of the PDF may be modified during iterative algorithms, and
- The existence of the system's response in the probabilistic interval at any instant is not guaranteed.

In the third approach, the model parameters are considered time-varying but bounded variables which are characterized by an interval of real numbers. Since the model parameters are intervals, the predicted system's response at any instant is not anymore a real number but an interval of real numbers. The set of predicted intervals at different instances generates a tube through time called *wrapping envelope*. If the model parameters are characterized properly, it is guaranteed by the inclusion property of interval analysis that the wrapping envelope includes the system's response (Neumaier, 2001). This fundamental property is the main motivation of exploring this approach in modeling, identification and response prediction of uncertain dynamic systems.

On the other hand, switching dynamic systems can always be described by single-mode interval models. However, wrapping envelope generated by single-mode interval model for the system's response is not generally precise enough to perform an adequate diagnosis or process safety analysis. One eventually can use multiple-mode strategy to improve the precision of the envelope; a multi-mode model consists of a set of local models in such way that any of them describes the system's behavior in an operating mode. Many research projects have already been carried out on multiple modeling among which (Takagi, 1985) is one of the early ones in control engineering. In this work, the input space has been partitioned in fuzzy sets and every partition has been described by a local model. The output of the multi-mode model has then be the fuzzy interpolation of the outputs of local models. Following the original work and in adaptive control, Tagaki-Sugeno-Kang and Quasi-Linear-Fuzzy models have been proposed in (Sugeno, 1988) and (Yager, 1993) respectively. T.A. Johansen and B.A. Foss also suggested a heuristic algorithm in which splitting the system's operating regime, structural and parametric identification are carried out in parallel and the validity of every local model is determined in input space (Johansen, 1995). The output of the multi-mode model is the weighted-sum of the outputs of local models. Another method has been proposed in (Venkat, 2003) in which system's input space is split into local zones to describe the non-linear dynamic of a chemical system. System's output is the fuzzy interpolation of the local models' outputs. A hybrid observer has been proposed in (Balluchi, 2001). The remarkable point in this work is that the observer consists of two blocks. The first block determines the active local model with respect to the system's inputs and outputs and the second block uses the information of the first block to estimate the system's state variables. This work has been followed by (Balluchi, 2002), (Ragot, 2003), (Babaali, 2005) and (Domlan, 2006). Other works which can be cited in multiple model approach are (Gasso, 2000),(Gugaliya, 2005) and (Ling, 1997). A review of the works on this subject can be found in (Murray-Smith, 1997).

Although many works have already been carried out on parameter characterization of mathematical models using interval analysis to take into account the modeling error and on multiple model approach to improve the precision of the model, few have treated them together. The number of works is still less on n-step response prediction.

INTERVAL ANALYSIS

Interval analysis against real analysis that operates on real-valued numbers, acts on sets of real numbers. Archimedes was of the early pioneers who used bounded numbers in his work to calculate π (Heath, 1853). In new age and in the beginning of the 20th century, the concept of the bounded value functions was discussed in (Young, 1908). A formal algebra of multi-value numbers was developed in (Young, 1931) and interval analysis as we know it today in (Warmus, 1956), (Sunaga, 1958) and (Moore, 1962) (Moore, 1966). Reference (Neumaier, 2001) can be cited as a new textbook on this subject. Interval analysis also found its place in engineering through the work presented in (Kolev, 1993), control engineering, and system identification (Milanese, 1996), (Walter, 1997), and (Jaulin, 2001).

Definition

Interval $[x] = [\underline{x}, \overline{x}]$ is a closed set of convex and continuous real numbers defined by lower bound $\underline{x} \in \Re$ and upper bound $\overline{x} \in \Re$. In which follows, x (respect. X) is a real variable (respect. a real vector) and interval $\left[x\right]$ (respect. interval vector $\left[X\right]$) is the support of variable x (respect. vector $\left[X\right]$). An interval can be chosen as the support of an uncertain variable $x \in \Re$ whose true value is not known. In this case, the upper and lower bounds are chosen so that to guarantee that for any possible value of x, the inequality $\underline{x} \leq x \leq \overline{x}$ is true.

Interval Arithmetic

The operations of interval arithmetic are defined in such way that the resulting interval always contains the true result that would be obtained by using exact inputs and exact calculations.

Theorem 1 (Interval arithmetic operations): (Neumaier, 2001) In interval arithmetic:

1. For all intervals,

$$-[x] = [-\overline{x}, -\underline{x}]$$

2. For $\circ \in \left\{+, -, \times, \div\right\}$, if $(x \circ y)$ is defined for all $x \in [x]$ and $y \in [y]$, we have:

$$[x] \circ [y] = [\min(\overline{x} \circ \overline{y}, \overline{x} \circ \underline{y}, \underline{x} \circ \overline{y}, \underline{x} \circ \underline{y}),$$
$$\max(\overline{x} \circ \overline{y}, \overline{x} \circ \underline{y}, \underline{x} \circ \overline{y}, \underline{x} \circ \underline{y})]$$

3. For monotonic function ζ,

$$\zeta([x]) = [\min(\zeta(\underline{x}), \zeta(\overline{x})), \max(\zeta(\underline{x}), \zeta(\overline{x}))]$$

where

$$\zeta([x]) = \{\zeta(x) \mid \forall x \in [x]\}$$

Interval Evaluation of Expressions

In arithmetic expressions and in real functions, one can replace the variables with intervals and evaluate the resulting expressions using interval arithmetic. $[f]([x])$ is defined as interval extension of real function $f(x)$ by replacing real argument x by interval $[x]$ and real arithmetic operations by their interval counterparts. It should be noticed that different expressions for the same function may produce different interval results.

Theorem 2 (Inclusion property): (Neumaier, 2001) Suppose that the arithmetic expression $f(z_1, z_2,...,z_n)$ can be evaluated at $z_1, z_2,..., z_n \in \Re$, and let $[x_1] \subset [z_1],...,[x_n] \subset [z_n]$
Then

1. f can be evaluated at $[x_1],[x_2],...,[x_n]$ and $[f]([x_1],...,[x_n]) \subseteq [f]([z_1],...,[z_n])$
2. $f([z_1],...,[z_n]) \subseteq [f]([z_1],...,[z_n])$

The former is called the *inclusion isotonicity* property and the latter, the *range inclusion* property.

Normalized Form of Intervals

Intervals can also be determined in the normalized form:

$$[x] = [\underline{x}, \overline{x}] = x_c + \lambda_x \times [-1,1]$$

$$x_c = \text{mid}([x]) = \frac{\underline{x} + \overline{x}}{2}, \qquad \lambda_x = \text{rad}([x]) = \frac{\overline{x} - \underline{x}}{2} \geq 0$$

where x_c is called the *midpoint* and λ_x is called the *radius* of interval $[x]$. If the normalized form is substituted in the original interval form, one can determine the resulting interval for interval operations only in terms of the midpoints and the radiuses of $[x]$ and $[y]$ and can eliminate $\min(\cdot)$ and $\max(\cdot)$ functions from the expressions. This simplifies calculation in many cases.

Interval Vector

Interval vector $[X]$ is the counterpart of vector X whose entries are intervals; that is:

$$[X]^T = [[x_1],[x_2],...[x_n]]^T$$

An interval vector can also be described in the normalized form. In this case, X_c is the vector of midpoints and λ_X is the vector of radiuses of the entries of the interval vector:

$$[X] = X_c + \lambda_X \cdot \times [v]$$

where

$$X_c = \begin{bmatrix} x_{c,1} \\ \vdots \\ x_{c,n} \end{bmatrix}_{n\times 1}, \quad \lambda_X = \begin{bmatrix} \lambda_{x1} \\ \vdots \\ \lambda_{xn} \end{bmatrix}_{n\times 1}, \quad [v] = \begin{bmatrix} [-1,1] \\ \vdots \\ [-1,1] \end{bmatrix}$$

and the symbol $\cdot\times$ represents the entry-by-entry product of two vectors.

Remark 1: A vector with scalar entries determines a point in space $\Re^n$ whilst an interval vector represents a hypercube in this space.

Product of a Pair of Interval Vectors

In many cases, the normalized form facilitates arithmetic operations on intervals. In this paper to optimize the adjustable parameters of the model, one needs to calculate the resulting interval of multiplying two interval vectors. If the normalized form is not used, as we will see in the next section, functions $\min(\cdot)$ and $\max(\cdot)$ intervene in the optimization criterion expression and make it non-linear with respect to the parameters. To eliminate them, the resulting interval is described in terms of the midpoints and the radiuses of interval vectors $[X]$ and $[Y]$; that is:

$$[z] = [\underline{z}, \overline{z}] = [X]^T \times [Y] = (X_c + \lambda_X \cdot \times [v])^T \times (Y_c + \lambda_Y \cdot \times [v])$$

where

$$\underline{z} = X_c^T Y_c - | X_c^T | \lambda_Y - \lambda_X^T | Y_c | - \lambda_X^T \lambda_Y \quad \text{(1-a)}$$

$$\overline{z} = X_c^T Y_c + | X_c^T | \lambda_Y + \lambda_X^T | Y_c | + \lambda_X^T \lambda_Y \quad \text{(1-b)}$$

Wrapping Effect

The image of an interval vector with respect to a mathematical transformation is not always a hypercube and approximating it by an interval vector leads to a source of pessimism in resulting domain. While using iterative algorithms, this pessimism can be accumulated during iterations and may cause the explosion of the domain. The phenomenon of pessimism accumulation during iterations is called the *wrapping effect* (Milanese, 1996), (Shahriari, 2007). For instance, the image of interval vector $[X]=[[x_1],[x_2]]^T=[[-1,1],[-1,1]]^T$ with respect to transformation:

$$Y=[x_1^2, x_1^2+x_1x_2]^T \quad (2)$$

is a non-linear shape whereas if it is evaluated using interval tools, the resulting domain is:

$$[Y_1]=[[x_1]^2,[x_1]^2+[x_1][x_2]]^T=[[0,1],[-1,2]]^T$$

The wrapping effect can also be due to the way that mathematical transformation is evaluated using interval analysis. For instance, Eq. (2) can also be evaluated as follows:

$$[Y_2]=[[x_1][x_1],[x_1][x_1]+[x_1][x_2]]^T=[[-1,1],[-2,2]]^T$$

which contains more pessimism compare to the former calculation. The accumulation of pessimism at every stage of calculation, especially in iterative algorithms, may provide great resulting domains or even may cause the explosion of them. To mitigate the wrapping effect and overestimation of resulting domain, one should try to avoid iterative algorithms to evaluate mathematical expressions using interval analysis. This is especially the case for n-step prediction of system's response using input-output models which is discussed in more detail in System Simulation section.

SINGLE-MODE MODELING

System identification and parameter characterization using interval models has already been studied for Finite Impulse Response (FIR), Input/Output (IO) and state-space models in many works among which (Adrot, 2004), (Armengol, 1999), (Shahriari, 2007), (Milanese, 1996), and (Ploix, 1999) can be cited. In this paper, the problem is treated for both FIR and IO model structures while the system's inputs and responses in training data set are uncertain variables characterized by intervals. A solution is also suggested for the problem of non-validity of dynamic models due to the memory effect (Shahriari, 2006a).

To follow a systemic procedure, the flowchart proposed by L. Ljung for black-box systems identification is adopted in this work (Ljung, 1999). This flowchart shown in Figure 1 originally consists of six steps from designing an experience to acquiring training data and validation of the model. Nevertheless, another step is added to the original version in the context of this work in which one defines the identification semantic. This semantic which is studied in more detail in which follows, determines the properties of the model parameters.

Model Structure

In this section, we start with a general description of a linear time-invariant system through which we derive the discrete-time FIR and IO structures used in this work. It is well-known that a linear time-invariant causal system can be modeled by its impulse response as follows (Ljung, 1999):

$$y(t)=\int_{\tau=0}^{\infty} g(\tau)u(t-\tau)d\tau \quad (3)$$

If $g(\tau)$ and $u(s)$ for $s \leq t$ are known, the corresponding output $y(s), s \leq t$ of the system can be computed for any input. The impulse

Figure 1. System identification flowchart

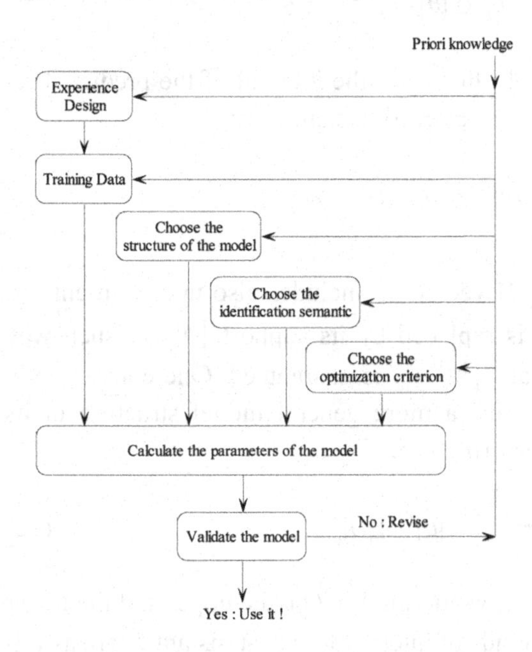

response is thus a complete characterization of the system.

1. **Sampling:** Since in engineering, one deals in most of the cases with observed inputs and outputs in discrete time, it is assumed that $y(t)$ is observed at the sampling instances $t_k = kT, k = 1, 2, \ldots$. Therefore:

$$y_{kT} = \int_{\tau=0}^{\infty} g(\tau)u(kT - \tau)d\tau \quad (4)$$

where T is called the *sampling rate*. It is supposed that the input signal u_k is kept constant between the sampling instances which is often the case in computer control applications:

$$u(t) = u_{kT} \qquad kT \leq t < (k+1)T \quad (5)$$

Inserting Eq. (5) into (4) gives:

$$y_{kT} = \int_{\tau=0}^{\infty} g(\tau)u(kT - \tau)d\tau = \sum_{l=1}^{\infty}\left[\int_{\tau=(l-1)T}^{lT} g(\tau)d\tau\right]u_{kT-l} = \sum_{l=1}^{\infty} g_l u_{kT-l} \quad (6)$$

where

$$g_l = \int_{\tau=(l-1)T}^{lT} g(\tau)d\tau \quad (7)$$

The value of T is an important factor in every system identification procedure. However, for ease of notation, variable kT will be replaced by k and Eq. (6) will be rewritten as follows:

$$y_k = \sum_{l=1}^{\infty} g_l u_{k-l} \quad (8)$$

2. **Finite impulse response:** It is practically difficult to handle Eq. (8) since to estimate the output at any instant, one needs to calculate an infinite series. Therefore, the Finite Impulse Response of the system is often used instead of Eq. (8) to describe the system by truncating the infinite series after N terms. Additive error e_k is then used to compensate the modeling error due to truncating of Eq. (8). Mathematically stated:

$$y_k = \sum_{l=1}^{N} g_l u_{k-l} + e_k \quad (9)$$

The FIR is then written in the vectorial form as follows:

$$y_k = \theta_k^T \times \phi_k$$

where

$$\theta_k^T = [g_1, \ldots, g_k, e_k]$$

$$\phi_k^T = [u_{k-1}, \ldots, u_{k-N}, 1]$$

Vector θ_k is called the *parameters vector* and ϕ_k *regression vector* of the model at instant *k*.

3. **Input/Output model:** An alternative for FIR is IO model. Probably, the simplest relationship between the system's inputs and outputs in discrete time is obtained by describing it as a linear difference equation (Ljung, 1999):

$$y_k + a_1 y_{k-1} + \dots + a_{na} y_{k-na} = b_1 u_{k-1} + \dots + b_{nb} u_{k-nb} + e_k \tag{10}$$

where additive term e_k is used to compensate the modeling error at instant k. Hence, Eq. (10) is also called an *equation error model.* In (10), if one fixes $na = nb = N$, the model is called IO whereas if he/she fixes $na = 0$ and $nb = N$, it becomes FIR. na and nb are chosen considering the order (in IO case) and the settling time as well as the sampling rate (in FIR case) of the system. In both cases, N is called the *moving horizon* of the model. Relationship (10) can also be written in the vectorial form as follows:

$$y_k = \theta_k^T \times \phi_k \tag{11}$$

where

$$\theta_k^T = [a_1, \dots, a_{na}, b_1, \dots, b_{nb}, e_k]$$

$$\phi_k^T = [-y_{k-1}, \dots, -y_{k-na}, u_{k-1}, \dots, u_{k-nb}, 1]$$

for θ_k and ϕ_k as the parameters and regression vectors at instant *k*.

4. **Time-variant system and interval model:** If the system is time-variant or uncertain, model parameters vary in time. Therefore, they are not constant scalars anymore and carry index k noted $g_{l,k}$, $a_{l,k}$ and $b_{l,k}$. To obtain a time-invariant model which is true at every instant, one can characterize time-variant parameters vector θ_k by time-invariant interval vector $[\theta]$ such that:

$$\forall k, \theta_k \in [\theta]$$

In this case, the interval of the predicted response at every instant k is:

$$[env]_k = [\theta]^T \times \phi_k$$

If vector ϕ_k includes also uncertain entries, it is replaced by its support $[\phi]_k$ in such way that $\phi_k \in [\phi]_k$ is guaranteed. One consequently obtains a more general model structure in its vectorial form:

$$[env]_k = [\theta]^T \times [\phi]_k \tag{12}$$

Considering Eq. (1), the upper and the lower bounds of interval $[env]_k$ at instant k are as follows:

$$\underline{env} = \theta_c^T \phi_{k,c} - | \theta_c^T | \lambda_{\phi k} - \lambda_\theta^T | \phi_{k,c} | - \lambda_\theta^T \lambda_{\phi k} \tag{13-a}$$

$$\overline{env} = \theta_c^T \phi_{k,c} + | \theta_c^T | \lambda_{\phi k} + \lambda_\theta^T | \phi_{k,c} | + \lambda_\theta^T \lambda_{\phi k} \tag{13-b}$$

where

$$\theta_c = \text{mid}([\theta]) \in \Re^{N+1} \qquad \phi_{k,c} = \text{mid}([\phi]_k) \in \Re^{N+1}$$

$$\lambda_\theta = \text{rad}([\theta]) \in \Re^{N+1} \qquad \lambda_{\phi k} = \text{rad}([\phi]_k) \in \Re^{N+1}$$

The set of predicted response intervals at different instances determines the wrapping envelope of the system's response:

$$\{[env]_k\} = \{[env]_1, [env]_2, \dots\}$$

The model of Eq. (12) in which the adjustable parameters are characterized by intervals is called the *interval model.* In Eq. (13), θ_c and λ_θ should be optimized to minimize the width of the wrapping envelope which is explained in detail in the following sections.

Training Data Set

In any systems identification procedure, one needs a set of training data to tune model parameters. We assume in this work that Training Data Set $TDS = \{[u]_k, [y]_k\}$ is already available. In TDS, u_k (respect. y_k) represents the system's input (respect. response) at instant k. The uncertainty is introduced from this stage to the problem; it is supposed that the true values of u_k and y_k -because of technical reasons such as the measuring error and noise- are not known precisely and at any instant *k*, only their upper and lower bounds can be determined with precision. Uncertain variables u_k and y_k are then characterized by intervals in such way that:

$$\forall k, u_k \in [u]_k, y_k \in [y]_k$$

TDS should be richly informative and represent almost all the dynamics of the system.

Semantic of Identification

In the case that system's response in TDS is an uncertain variable characterized by intervals, the identification semantic defines the properties of interval model and consequently, the specifications of the generated wrapping envelope. This semantic can be extracted from the modeling objective and is described in the form of a mathematical (logical) expression made up of quantifiers $\forall$, $\exists$ and $\neg$, model parameters and system's inputs/response. For instance, if an interval model is identified using the following semantic:

$$\forall k, \exists y_k \in [y]_k, \exists \theta_k \in [\theta] \mid y_k = \theta_k^T \times \phi_k \qquad (14)$$

at any instant k, system's response $[y]_k$ and predicted interval $[env]_k$ have at least one common point; mathematically stated:

$$\forall k, [y]_k \cap [env]_k \neq \varphi$$

whereas if the semantic is defined as follows:

$$\forall k, \forall y_k \in [y]_k, \exists \theta_k \in [\theta] \mid y_k = \theta_k^T \times \phi_k \qquad (15)$$

the wrapping envelope includes at any instance, the system's response; that is:

$$\forall k, [y]_k \subseteq [env]_k$$

The system's response and the wrapping envelope for the identification semantics of Eq. (14) and (15) are shown in Figure 2a and 2b respectively. However, it is the latter which corresponds to the objective of this paper. Different identification semantics have been presented in (Calm, 2006) in more details. The semantic of Eq. (15) can also be described by a pair of inequalities at any instant k as follows:

$$\forall k, \begin{cases} \overline{y_k} \leq \overline{env_k} \\ \underline{env_k} \leq \underline{y_k} \end{cases} \qquad (16)$$

indicating that system's response must be included in the generated wrapping envelope.

Optimization Criterion

The system's response can be wrapped by different tubes with different sizes. Smaller the radius of the wrapping envelope, more precise the tube of the system's response. Thus, the radius of the wrapping envelope is considered in a natural manner as the optimization criterion to adjust model parameters.

Figure 2. System response and generated wrapping envelope for stated identification semantics in Eq. (14) and (15) respectively

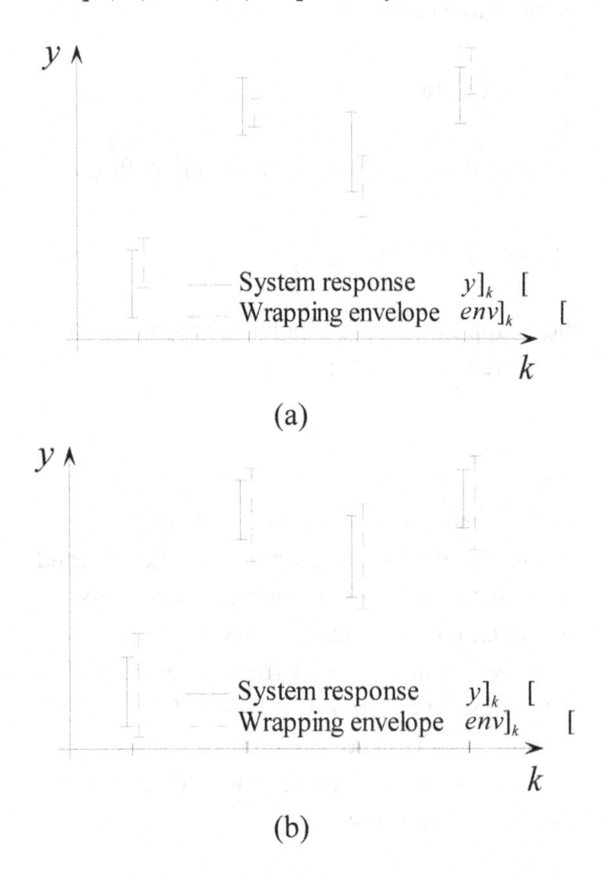

Definition 1: The width of the wrapping envelope in time interval from $k = i$ until $k = j$ is the mean-value of its radius at different instants. Mathematically stated:

$$OC_{i,j} = \frac{1}{j-i+1}\sum_{k=1}^{j} r_k \tag{17}$$

where (from Eq. (13))

$$r_k = \frac{\overline{env} - \underline{env}}{2} = |\theta_c^T|\lambda_{\phi k} + \lambda_\theta^T|\phi_{k,c}| + \lambda_\theta^T\lambda_{\phi k} \tag{18}$$

Definition 2: The precision of the wrapping envelope in time interval from $k = i$ until $k = j$ is the exponential function-value of $(-OC_{i,j})$; that is:

$$P_{i,j} = \exp(-OC_{i,j}) \tag{19}$$

Tuning Model Parameters

Regarding to the identification semantic, there exist different numerical methods to tune parameters of an interval model. Among them numerical optimization method (Adrot, 2004) and the method based on modal interval (Armengol, 1999) can be cited. Parameters tuning using the semantic of Eq. (15) which corresponds to the objective of this paper can easily be reformulated in the form of an optimization problem subject to a set of constraints. To do that, one initially needs to calculate the upper and the lower bounds of the wrapping envelope in terms of the model parameters which has already been performed in Eq. (13). Considering Eq. (17) and (18) and inserting (13) into (16), we have:

$$\min_{\theta_c,\lambda_\theta}(OC_{i,j}) = \min_{\theta_c,\lambda_\theta}\left(\frac{1}{j-i+1}\sum_{k=1}^{j} r_k\right) =$$

$$\min_{\theta_c,\lambda_\theta}\left(\frac{1}{j-i+1}\sum_{k=1}^{j}|\theta_c^T|\lambda_{\phi k} + \lambda_\theta^T|\phi_{k,c}| + \lambda_\theta^T\lambda_{\phi k}\right)$$

subject to

$$\forall k, \begin{cases}\overline{y}_k - \theta_c^T\phi_{k,c} - |\theta_c^T|\lambda_{\phi k} - \lambda_\theta^T|\phi_{k,c}| - \lambda_\theta^T\lambda_{\phi k} \le 0\\ \theta_c^T\phi_{k,c} - |\theta_c^T|\lambda_{\phi k} - \lambda_\theta^T|\phi_{k,c}| - \lambda_\theta^T\lambda_{\phi k} - \underline{y}_k \le 0\end{cases} \tag{20}$$

By finding the minimizer of objective function $OC_{i,j}$, one can obtain an interval model which generates the thinnest wrapping envelope for TDS. A local (respect. global) minimizer is a set of parameters that minimizes locally (respect.

globally) the value of the objective function. Because of non-linear term $\left|\theta_c^T\right|$ in the objective function and in the constraints, problem of (20) is a non-linear optimization problem subject to non-linear constraints with respect to the parameters. However, if the true values of system inputs in TDS are known, $\lambda_{\phi k}$ is void and consequently, $\left|\theta_c^T\right|\lambda_{\phi k} = 0$. Therefore, Eq. (20) turns into a linear optimization problem subject to linear constraints. Both problems can be solved using any local or global solver.

Memory Effect in Dynamic Models

One of the properties of dynamic models is the *memory effect* (Shahriari, 2006a). In identification procedure, parameters can not be tuned before instant $k < N$ as the regression vector of the model can not be built before this instant. This problem also appears in simulating the system where the model's output can not be calculated before instant $k \leq N$. In other words, the model is not valid in modeling and in simulation from $k = 1$ until $k = N$. To diminish the non-validity of the model due to the memory effect, one may reduce its moving horizon. However, this solution causes the loss of precision since the system is described by a model whose structure does not correspond to the system's dynamic. Even with the least moving horizon $N = 1$, this problem remains at instant $k = 1$. As a preliminary to present the proposed solution, we recall the definition of a static model.

1. **Static model:** A static model is a model in which at any instant, the output is estimated from the state of the input(s) at that instant. In other words, the model has no memory and it is valid at every instant. Considering Eq. (12), the static interval model of a SISO system is in the following form:
2. $[env]_k = [\theta]^T \times [\phi]_k = [[g_0],[e]] \times \begin{bmatrix} [u]_k \\ 1 \end{bmatrix}$
3. **Proposed solution:** The proposed solution to overcome the non-validity of dynamic models in the very first instances of identification and simulation procedures consist of using one static and a set of dynamic models whose moving horizons vary between $MH = 1$ to $MH = N$ (Shahriari, 2006a). These are called *auxiliary* models and the set of them is called *F model* shown in Figure 3.

Figure 3. Structure of F model

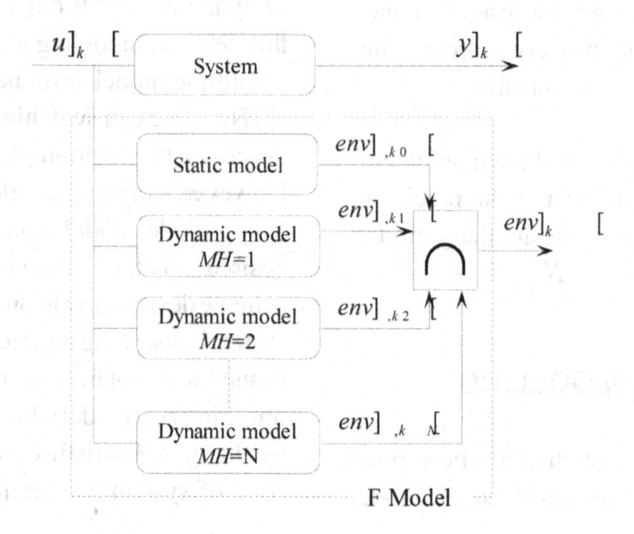

Model parameters for any auxiliary model are calculated as it has been explained in previous section. The resulting generated interval of auxiliary model i at instant k is noted $[env]_{i,k}$. Since the system response at any instant is always included in the wrapping envelope of valid auxiliary models, it is also included in the intersection of the wrapping envelopes generated by the latter. Mathematically stated:

$$[y]_k \subseteq [env]_k = \bigcap_{i=0}^{\min(k,N)} [env]_{i,k} \tag{21}$$

since for $k < N$, only k first and for $k \geq N$, all N auxiliary models are valid. The proposed solution is not ideal, since from $k = 1$ until $k = N$, the wrapping envelope is generated by auxiliary models with reduced moving horizons which leads to an imprecise envelope (see Figure 4). However, this structure provides the possibility to partially overcome the problem.

The problem of non-validity of dynamic models due to the memory effect may not appear critical/vital at first glance since once the moving horizon is passed, the model is valid for all coming instances. Nevertheless, it is not the case for multi-mode models. In the latter, one loses the trace of the wrapping envelope after every switching from an operating mode to another one. Moreover, the simulation may event provide no result if switching happens frequently.

Definition 3: The precision of the wrapping envelope of a F model is defined as the precision of the wrapping envelope of the auxiliary model with moving horizon $MH = N$.

MULTIPLE MODEL MODELING

In the previous section, a method has been proposed to characterize parameters of a single mode linear interval model. Interval tools have been used to deal with modeling error whereas F model has been proposed for the problem of non-validity of dynamic models due to the memory effect. In this section, modeling a switching system using a multiple model is studied.

Figure 4. Wrapping envelopes by FIR (a) and proposed F model (b)

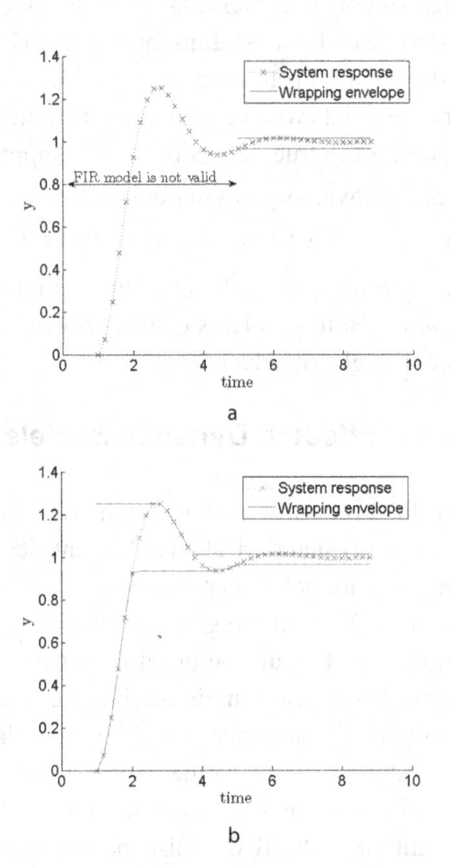

Non-linear or switching systems can always be described by single-mode linear interval models. However, wrapping envelopes produced by linear single-mode models may not be as precise as desired. To obtain more precise envelopes and to achieve desired precisions, one solution is to split system's operating regime into several local zones in such way that every zone can be described by a linear interval model while the envelope generated by the model satisfies modeling precision. Any zone of system's operating regime is called an *operating mode* and the corresponding model is called a *local model*. The set of local models is the *multi-mode model*. For a non-linear system, this approach is very likely to linearizing the system around different operating points. In which follows, multiple model modeling will be considered for switching systems in two different cases.

The first is the case in which the instant of switching from a mode to another one is determined by an external signal. Systems in this case can be assumed as it is shown in Figure 5a. Since the switching instant is determined by the *switching signal*, the TDS which corresponds to every operating mode can be isolated. It is then used to optimize parameters of the corresponding local model. Therefore, multiple model modeling is reduced to repeating the modeling procedure explained in the previous section as many times as the number of the operating modes of the system.

The second is the case in which the switching instance is not determined a priori and should be detected. In this case, it is supposed that switching take place under certain conditions on system's state variables. Such systems can be presumed as it is shown in Figure 5b and for multiple model modeling, one should perform following four main steps.

Determining the Characteristic Variables

Characteristic variables are the variables by which switching from one mode to another can be determined. Since in black-box identification approach chosen in this paper, characteristic variables are not known a priori, the entries of the regression vector are considered as the characteristic variables. Hence, regression space $\mathcal{X}_\phi$ and the space of the characteristic variables are identical and at every instant k, ϕ_k (respect. $[\phi]_k$) represents a point (respect. a hypercube) in this space. As for a F model, characteristic variables are the entries of the regression vector of its auxiliary model with moving horizon $MH = N$.

Detecting the Switching Instances

In this step, the objective is to detect the instance of switching from a mode to another in TDS in order to isolate subset $TDS_i \subseteq TDS$ which corresponds to the data of operating mode i and then, to tune the model parameters of local F_i models. A strategy based on the precision of the wrapping envelope is proposed herein. Since the precision of F model is defined as the precision of the auxiliary model with moving horizon $MH = N$, one may use only this auxiliary model during this step.

Suppose that the desired precision is predefined value *pre* and that the last switching has been detected at instant *begin*. Before instant *begin*, *i-1* switching have been detected and therefore,

Figure 5. Switching system while switching is determined (a) and undetermined (b)

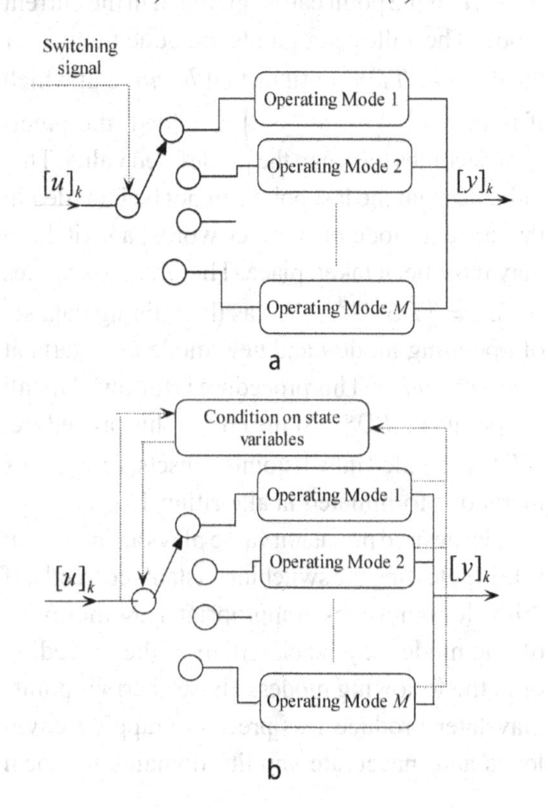

at instant *begin*, the system enters in the ith operating mode. At the beginning, the initial training data set for the current mode is supposed to include only a minimum number of points to tune the parameters of the current local model that is $TDS^{begin,begin+N} = \{([u]_k,[y]_k) \mid begin \le k \le begin+N\}$. Since this is a minimum number of necessary points to tune the adjustable parameters, the generated wrapping envelope for these points is the best in terms of the precision. If the true value of the system's inputs/response are known, then $P_{begin,begin+N} = 1$; otherwise, $P_{begin,begin+N} = \exp(-\text{rad}([y]_N))$. If precision P is less than the desired value, then the latter should be modified since even for a least number of points, it can not be achieved.

In the next step, following point $([u]_{begin+N+1},[y]_{begin+N+1})$ is added to TDS_i and the model parameters are re-tuned using $TDS^{begin,begin+N+1}$. If the precision of the wrapping envelope is still superior to the desired one, it shows that the point can be included in the current mode. The following points are added one after the other to TDS_i until instant *begin+s* at which if point $([u]_{begin+s},[y]_{begin+s})$ is added, the precision becomes less than the predefined value. This indicates that the last point can not be included in the current mode or in other words, a switching may have been taken place. Therefore, one takes $TDS_i = TDS^{begin,begin+s-1}$ as the training data set of operating mode *i* and new mode *i+1* starts at instant *begin+s*. This procedure is followed for all the points in TDS. At the end of this procedure, TDS is divided into disjoints subsets TDS_i. This method is formulated in algorithm 1.

The desired precision value plays an important role in detecting the switching instants correctly. If this value is not chosen appropriately, some points of one mode may be classified in the preceding or in the following modes. These aberrant points may later produce less precise wrapping envelopes and inaccurate validity domains for local models. One may precede a preliminary analysis to observe the evolution of precision $P_{i,j}$ with respect to *j* and then to chose the value of *pre*. As for aberrant points, one solution is to eliminate *N* first and last points from any TDS_i so that we are sure that remaining points correspond to only one operating mode.

An alternative strategy for detecting switching instances based on the consistency of system's response with generated wrapping envelope and a heuristic algorithm for optimizing the value of *pre* have been suggested in (Shahriari, 2006b).

Algorithm 1

pre: Desired modeling precision. It is a user-defined value.
TDS: Initial training data set
N: Moving horizon of the model

Start
$begin \leftarrow 1$, $end \leftarrow N$, $i \leftarrow 1$
While *end<(the number of* TDS_i entries)
Tune the parameters of model using $TDS^{begin,end}$
If *(the precision of the envelope)<pre*
Get $TDS^{begin,end-1}$ as the data of ith mode
Tune the parameters of F model using $TDS^{begin,end-1}$
$i \leftarrow i+1$
$begin \leftarrow end$
$end \leftarrow begin + N$
Go to 3
Else
$end \leftarrow end + 1$
Go to 3
End

Validity Domains of Local Models

Every mathematical model can be considered as a function from regression vector space $\mathcal{X}_\phi$ into the system's output space. Mathematically stated:

$$f : \phi \to y$$

where f represents the function of the model. Consequently, the validity domain of every local model can be determined as a subset of space $\mathcal{X}_\phi$. Every subset TDS_i determines a set of points/hypercubes in this space. The region filed up with these points/hypercubes is an approximation of the validity domain of operating mode *i*.

Definition 4: The validity domain of local interval model *i* is the convex hull CH_ϕ^i of the points/hypercubes determined by the entries of TDS_i in regression vector space $\mathcal{X}_\phi$ of the model.

Definition 5: Consequently, local model *i* is valid at instant *k* iff the regression vector of the model is in convex hull CH_ϕ^i (when its entries are real values) or has at least one common point with it (when its entries are uncertain variables characterized by intervals). Mathematically stated:

$$\phi_k \in CH_\phi^i \vee [\phi]_k \cap CH_\phi^i \neq \varphi$$

The difference between CH_ϕ^i and its true domain depends on the quality of TDS_i. More TDS_i is informative, more CH_ϕ^i approaches the true domain. If calculating convex hull CH_ϕ^i is time-consuming (because of the dimensions of $\mathcal{X}_\phi$ or a great number of points in TDS_i) or its form is complex (because of the high number of vertexes and sides), for simplicity reasons, the validity domain of every mode *i* can be approximated by the smallest outer hypercube of convex hull CH_ϕ^i noted as $\lozenge CH_\phi^i$. Consequently:

$$CH_\phi^i \subseteq \lozenge CH_\phi^i$$

In some cases, convex hulls intersect. The most important reason for this phenomenon is uncertainty on TDS entries (Shahriari, 2008). If the entries are real values, regression vector ϕ_k determines a single point in space $\mathcal{X}_\phi$ whereas if they are uncertain characterized by intervals, interval vector $[\phi]_k$ determines a hypercube in this space. Consequently, convex hulls are more voluminous and may overlap. Another reason for intersecting the validity domains is aberrant points classified in a wrong operating mode which is principally due to the wrong chose of desired modeling precision *pre* used to detect switching instances (Shahriari, 2007).

Generally, the dimension of the regression vector space of an IO model is lower than the dimension of the space of a FIR for the same system. For instance, in a second order system, the IO model has four parameters (and therefore, space $\mathcal{X}_\phi$ has four dimensions) whilst the same system may be described by a FIR of order $N = 10$ with 10 parameters (hence, space $\mathcal{X}_\phi$ has 10 dimensions). Calculating the former is less time and resource consuming than the latter. This is a good justification to explore the possibility of determining the validity domains of a FIR in input-output space.

Theorem 3 (Validity domain of a FIR model): Suppose that one knows a priori the order of the system under study, i.e. of nth order, and suppose that the validity domain of every system's operating mode is a convex hull in observable state space. Then, for a FIR model, its validity domain can be determined in input-output space $\mathcal{X}_{\{u_{k-1},\ldots,u_{k-n},y_{k-1},\ldots,y_{k-n}\}}$ with $2 \times n$ or reduced input-output space $\mathcal{X}_{\{u_{k-1},\ldots,u_{k-n+1},y_k,y_{k-1},\ldots,y_{k-n+1}\}}$ with $2 \times n - 1$ instead of its original regression vector space $\mathcal{X}_{\{u_{k-1},\ldots,u_{k-nb}\}}$ with $nb + 1$ dimensions.

In which follows, ζ_k is a vector with the same dimensions as the validity domain that determines a point in this space; that is:

$$\zeta_k = [u_{k-1}, \ldots, u_{k-nb}]^T$$

$$\zeta_k = [u_{k-1}, \ldots, u_{k-n}, y_{k-1}, \ldots, y_{k-n}]^T$$

$$\zeta_k = [u_{k-1}, \ldots, u_{k-n+1}, y_k, y_{k-1}, \ldots, y_{k-n+1}]^T$$

In the above, the validity domains are determined in input space, in input-output space or in reduced input-output space respectively. ζ_k is an interval vector if its entries are intervals.

Aggregating Similar Local Models

During data acquisition, system may enter several times in an identical operating mode. In this case, the data corresponds to that local mode may be found in disjoint time intervals in TDS. Since the detecting method proposed dose not verify whether the following operating mode is a new mode or is a mode which has already been identified, several F models may be assigned to one operating mode. Principally, this makes no problem. However, to diminish the number of local models and to simplify the structure of the multi-mode model, one tries to aggregate identical local models. The following proposed solution is based on the validity domains of local models. For two different convex hulls CH^i and CH^j, three cases may happen:

- The former is the subset of the latter:

$$CH^i \subseteq CH^j$$

In this case regarding to definition (5), local model F_j is valid as soon as F_i is. Therefore, the former is considered as a subset of the latter. Model F_i is eliminated and training data set TDS_i is added to TDS_j. The parameters of F_j are then re-tuned using $TDS_i \cup TDS_j$ while the validity domain of new local model F_j is convex hull CH^j.

- They intersect, but neither does include the other one:

$$\left(CH^i \cap CH^j \neq \varphi\right) \wedge$$
$$\left(CH^i \cap CH^j \neq CH^i \wedge CH^i \cap CH^j \neq CH^j\right)$$

In this case, both F_i and F_j are valid for some instances. However, none of them includes completely the other one. Therefore, no act is performed since one may aggregate two different operating modes. The possible reasons for intersecting validity domains have already been explained previously.

- They are two disjoint convex hulls:

$$CH^i \cap CH^j = \varphi$$

which means that F_i and model F_j describe two different operating modes. Consequently, no aggregation is made.

The above rules should be applied to every pair of $\left(CH^i, CH^j\right)$ to eliminate as many repeated F models as possible and to simplify the structure of the multi-mode model. To make the aggregation procedure easier, one may also use outer hypercube approximations $\left(\Diamond CH^i, \Diamond CH^j\right)$ rather than convex hulls $\left(CH^i, CH^j\right)$.

Aggregating similar local models that describe identical operating modes is the last step in multiple-model modeling procedure. At the end of this stage, one obtains a set of local F models and the corresponding convex hulls which determine the validity of every local model. This interval multi-mode model can then be used to carry out the n-step prediction of the system's response which will be described in the next section.

SYSTEM SIMULATION

After identifying the multi-mode interval model of the system, this model can be used to generate the wrapping envelope in order to compare it with the actual system's response to assure the healthy operating of the system (diagnosis and fault detection) or in order to perform one-step/n-step prediction of the system's response to guarantee that it never enter into forbidden operating zones (process safety). To do that, one should also determine the simulation semantic, the counterpart of the identification semantic, and develop a strategy to detect active operating mode at any instant.

Semantic of Simulation

The semantic of simulation as its counterpart in identification which defines the properties of model parameters, determines the properties of the wrapping envelope. It is extracted from the objective of simulation and likewise to the identification one, is described in the form of a mathematical expression. It should be remember that the identification and the simulation semantics dependent on each other. In other words, one is not permitted to identify an interval model using an identification semantic and then, to simulate the system using a simulation semantic which is not consistent with the former. Considering the objective of this paper and the identification semantic used to characterize model parameters, the wrapping envelope at every instant must include system's response; that is:

$$[P.env]_k = \left\{\theta^T \times \phi \mid \forall\theta \in [\theta], \forall\phi \in [\phi]_k\right\} \quad (22)$$

To distinguish between the wrapping envelope for TDS and the one generated during prediction, the former is noted as $\left[env\right]_k$ and the latter $\left[P.env\right]_k$. Regarding to Eq. (22), $[P.env]_k$ at instant k is calculated directly through interval evaluation of the model's expression:

$$[P.env]_k = [\theta]^T \times [\phi]_k$$

One also notes that the simulation semantic in Eq. (22) is consistent with and the complementary of the identification semantic in Eq. (15).

Predicting System Response

In this section, the problem of generating the wrapping envelope is treated in two different cases: one-step or n-step prediction of the system's response. In each case, the prediction is carried out by means of the simulator of the model shown in Figure 6a. This simulator consists of one F model and one ACK block for every operating mode; the latter determines whether the respective model is active or not. It should be mentioned that local models and corresponding ACK blocks operate independently. Considering the possible intersection of validity domains and uncertainty on the entries of the regression vector, more than one local model may be valid at a given instant *k*. In this case, the simulator's output is:

$$[P.env]_k = \bigcup_i [P.env]_{i,k} \qquad i \in V$$

where V is the set of valid local models. The wrapping envelope is then generated by the set of $[P.env]_k$ at different instances; that is:

$$\left\{[P.env]\right\} = \left\{[P.env]_1, [P.env]_2, \ldots\right\} \quad (23)$$

The operation of ACK locks is represented by a two-state automaton as shown in Figure 6b. ACK_i is in *active* state if the local F_i model is valid and is in *transitory* state otherwise. However, regarding to whether one wishes to carry out one-step or n-step prediction and whether the validity domains of the local models are determined in

Figure 6. Simulator (a) and ACK blocks (b)

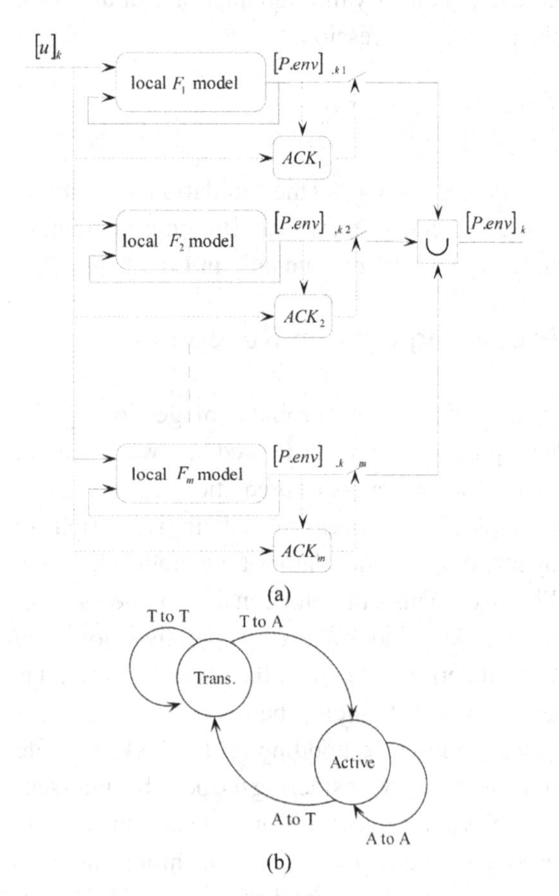

input space $\{u_{k-1},\ldots,u_{k-N}\}$, input-output space $\{u_{k-1},\ldots,u_{k-N},y_{k-1},\ldots,y_{k-N}\}$ or reduced input-output space $\{u_{k-1},\ldots,u_{k-N-1},y_k,y_{k-1},\ldots,y_{k-N-1}\}$, different transition conditions are defined to determine the switching from active to transitory state or vice-versa. Before starting to deal with this problem, the following theory is presented for an interval IO model.

Theorem 4 (Wrapping envelope of an IO model): Suppose that at instant *k* in an IO model, one or several system's responses $[y]_{k-p}$ in regression vector $[\phi]_k$ are replaced with their respective predicted intervals $[P.env]_{k-p}$. The new vector is noted as $[\phi]_k^{'}$. If

$$\forall k, [y]_{k-p} \subseteq [P.env]_{k-p}$$

then

$$[y]_k \subseteq [P.env]_k = [\theta]^T \times [\phi]_k^{'}$$

One-Step Prediction

By one-step prediction, one means to calculate interval $[P.env]_k$ at instant *k* while all system's inputs $[u]_s$ and responses $[y]_s$ are known for $\forall s > 0, s < k$. In this case, the following strategy is proposed for transitions in ACK blocks.

At the beginning, all ACK blocks are initialized in transitory state. For *N* first instants and due to the lack of data, the validity of local models can not be checked. Therefore, ACK blocks remain in transitory state and no prediction is carried out. After $k > N$, vector ξ_k can be built. Considering definition 5, the transition conditions are defined as follows:

- **Switch to active state:** At instant *k*, ACK_i switches to active state (or stays in active state if it has already been) if one the following conditions are satisfied:
  $$\xi_k \in CH^i \tag{24-a}$$
  $$[\xi]_k \cap CH^i \neq \varphi \tag{24-b}$$
- **Switch to transitory state:** Otherwise, it switches to transitory state (or stays in transitory state if it has already been).

Regarding to Eq. (21), the output of local model F_i at instant *k* whose ACK_i block is in active state is calculated as follows:

$$[P.env]_{i,k} = \bigcap_{au=0}^{\min(k,N)} [P.env]_{i,au,k} \tag{25}$$

and if it is in transient state as:

$$[P.env]_{i,k} = \varphi$$

n-Step Prediction

By n-step prediction one means to calculate the interval $[P.env]_k$ from $k = 1$ until $k = ph$ while the only system's inputs are known. *ph* is called the *prediction horizon*. Considering the space in which the validity domain of local models are determined, two different cases are considered. In both cases, *ACK* blocks are initialized in transitory state.

1. **Validity domains are determined in input space:** Since system's inputs $[u]_k$ are known for $\forall k \leq ph$, one proceeds as follow:
   - **Transitory to active state:** For every instant $k > 0$, vector ξ_{k+N} is built. If one of the conditions of Eq. (24) is satisfied, ACK_i switches at instant $k+1$ to active state. The satisfaction of one of these conditions is interpreted as the system's inputs over *N* following instances brings the system to operating mode *i*. An ACK_i which is activated will stay at least *N* instants in this state before possible switching to transitory state.
   - **Transitory to transitory state:** Otherwise, ACK_i stays in the transitory state.
   - **Active to transitory state:** As mentioned before, the minimum staying time in active mode is *N* instances. Afterward at any instant $k > N$, ξ_k is built. If the conditions of Eq. (24) are not satisfied anymore, it means that the system has already left operating mode *i* and ACK_i switches at instant $k+1$ to transitory state.
   - **Active to active state:** Otherwise, ACK_i stays in active state.
2. **Validity domains are determined in input-output space:** If the validity domains of local models are determined in input-output space while only the system's inputs are known, vector ξ_{k+N} can not be built directly. Therefore, the previous strategy is not applicable anymore and one should concern the new following plan.
   - **Transitory to active state:** To determine whether the local model is potentially active at instant $k+1$ or not, one needs vector ξ_{k+N} to verify conditions of Eq. (24) while only the system's inputs are available. To build the vector, system's response is predicted. At instant *k*, only the static model of F_i model is valid which generates interval:

$$[P.env]_{i,au=0,k} = [\theta]_{i,0}^T \times \begin{bmatrix} [u]_k \\ 1 \end{bmatrix}$$

At instant $k+1$, it replaces interval $[y]_k$ in the regression vector of auxiliary model $au = 1$:

$$[P.env]_{i,au=1,k+1} = [\theta]_{i,1}^T \times \begin{bmatrix} -[P.env]_{i,0,k} \\ [u]_k \\ 1 \end{bmatrix}$$

The static model calculates interval $[P.env]_{i,0,k+1}$ as well and considering Eq. (25), the output of F_i model is:

$$[P.env]_{i,k+1} = [P.env]_{i,au=0,k+1} \cap [P.env]_{i,au=1,k+1}$$

The procedure of substituting the system's response with the respective predicted intervals is continued till instant $k+N$ at which one can build vector

$$[\xi]_{k+N} = \left[[P.env]_{k+N-1},\ldots,[P.env]_k,[u]_{k+N-1},\ldots,[u]_k\right]^T$$

and verify its intersection with convex hull CH^i. If the condition of Eq. (24) is satisfied, ACK_i switches at instant $k+1$ to active state. As the previous case, a ACK_i which is activated will stay at least N instances in this state before possible switching to transitory state.

- **Transitory to transitory state:** Otherwise, it stays in the transitory state.
- **Active to transitory state:** For active model F_i, the system's inputs and predicted outputs are available for N past instances and $[\xi]_k$ can be build. If the validity conditions are not satisfied anymore, it means that the system has already left operating mode *i* and ACK_i switches at instant $k+1$ to transitory state.
- **Active to active state:** Otherwise, it stays in the active state.

One can note from the proposed strategies that in n-step prediction, one looks at the future of the system to verify whether it switches to an operating mode or not whereas he/she looks at its past to deactivate a local model. This is to guarantee that any possible activation of an operating mode is considered and the simulator calculates all the possible output values of the system.

NUMERICAL EXAMPLE

In this section, characterization and prediction methods are applied on the following academic example.

System

The system under study is a switching system with two operating modes described by the following state space representation:

$$A_1 = \begin{bmatrix} 0.4315 & 0.3158 \\ -0.7105 & -0.1369 \end{bmatrix}, \quad B_1 = \begin{bmatrix} 0.5685 \\ 0.7105 \end{bmatrix}, \quad C_1 = \begin{bmatrix} 1 & 0 \end{bmatrix}$$

$$A_2 = \begin{bmatrix} -0.1275 & 0.3165 \\ -1.2662 & -0.3807 \end{bmatrix}, \quad B_2 = \begin{bmatrix} 1.1275 \\ 1.2662 \end{bmatrix}, \quad C_2 = \begin{bmatrix} 1 & 0 \end{bmatrix}$$

In this system, the switching takes place when the output of the system reaches 3.7; the first mode is active when the output is less that 3.7 and the second when it is more. This system is used to generate training data set $\{(u_k, y_k)\}$.

Training Data Set

We design an experience to obtain training data set for parameter characterization. This data set should be rich and informative to represent the system dynamic in both operating modes one and two. To simulate measuring error, an unknown random error ε_k is added to the system's output y_k at instant *k*. However, we know a priori that it is bounded between -0.1 and 0.1. The output is then characterized by interval

$$[y]_k = y_k + \varepsilon_k + [-0.1 \quad 0.1]$$

which guarantees that

$$\forall k, y_k \in [y]_k$$

The input remains precise. Consequently, the training data set is in the form $TDS = \{(u_k, [y]_k)\}$.

Model Structure

In this example, we chose FIR with moving horizon $N = 10$ to describe the dynamic of the system. F model is used to overcome memory effect and non-validity of FIR model in 10 first instants of identification/simulation.

Detecting the Switching Instances and Splitting TDS

In identification procedure and after having obtained TDS through the experience on the system, the TDS is split into subsets each of which corresponds to one operating mode of the system. Before starting switching detection procedure, we perform a preliminary analysis on TDS to detect the optimal value of *pre*. The result of this preliminary analysis is shown in Figure 7.

To detect the switching, we use Algorithm 1 with *pre=0.8* that results in two subsets TDS_1 form $k=1$ until $k=131$ and TDS_2 from $k=132$ to $k=253$. The system's response for both operating modes is shown in Figure 8. It should be mentioned that model parameters are identified simultaneously while switching detection is performed.

Validity Domains of Local Models

In previous section, TDS has been divided into two parts. We know a priori that the system is of second order. Consequently and regarding to theorem 3, the validity domains of local models

Figure 7. Preliminary analysis on TDS

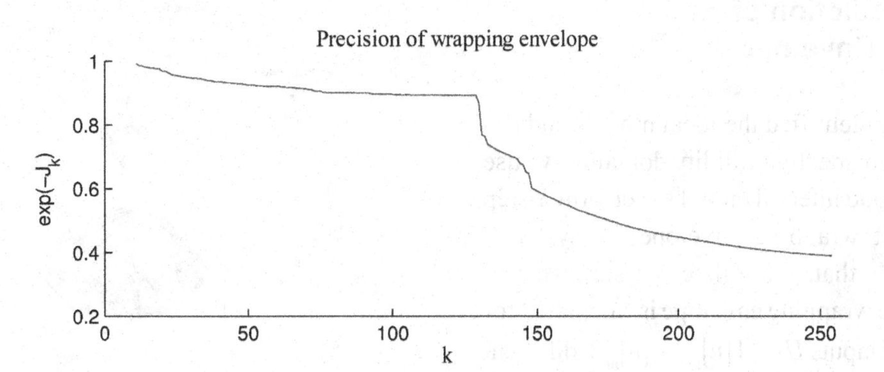

Figure 8. System input/output in TDS

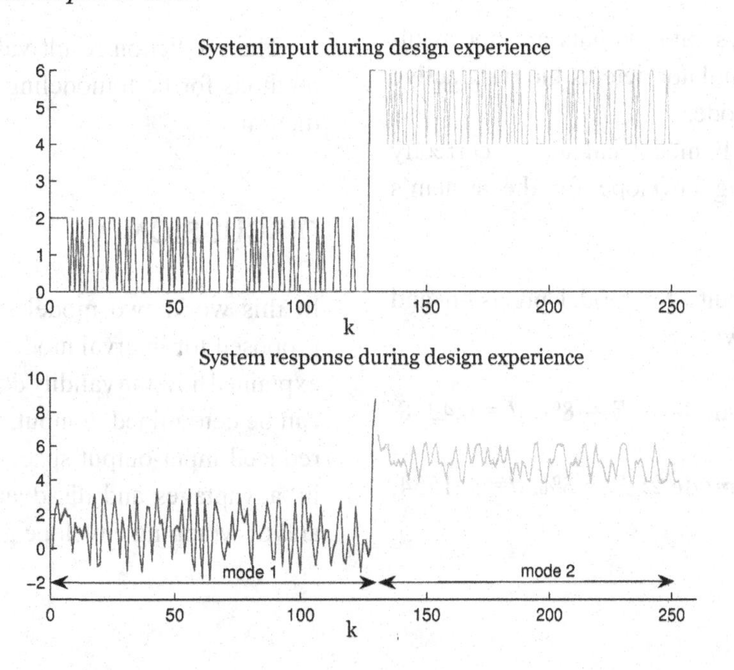

can be determined either in $\{y_{k-1}, y_{k-2}, u_{k-1}, u_{k-2}\}$ or $\{y_k, y_{k-1}, u_{k-1}\}$.

During switching detection procedure and due to the imprecise value of *pre*, a number of input/output couples of the first operating mode are classified in the second one. This can be observed in Figure 8 that corresponds to *k=128*, *129* and *130*. The same phenomenon can also be observed more clearly in Figure 9a, the image of the validity domains in 2D space $\{y_k, y_{k-1}\}$. These aberrant points are removed from the second TDS to eliminate any incorrect activation of local models during prediction phase and the convex hulls are recalculated (see Figure 9b).

n-Step Prediction of Wrapping Envelope

After having identified the local models and determined the respective validity domains, we use this multi-mode interval model to perform n-step prediction of wrapping envelope for system's response. For that, we utilize the simulator of Figure 6. The wrapping envelope is calculated for a sequence of inputs $U = \{[u]_1, ..., [u]_{ph}\}$ different from the one in TDS for *ph=250*. Prediction result is shown in Figure 10. We observe that:

- Although system's outputs are not available, the simulator detects the right active operating mode,
- The active F model calculated correctly the wrapping envelope for the system's response.

Numerical results for model precision and error are as follow:

Operating mode 1: $E = 8\%$, $J = 0.4258$, $P = 0.6533$
Operating mode 2: $E = 8\%$, $J = 0.1554$, $P = 0.8561$

Figure 9. Image of the validity domains of local models in 2D space (a) and recalculated domains after eliminating aberrant points (b)

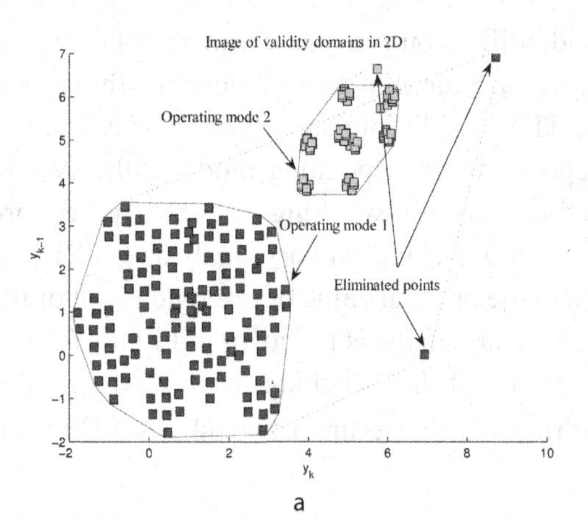

a

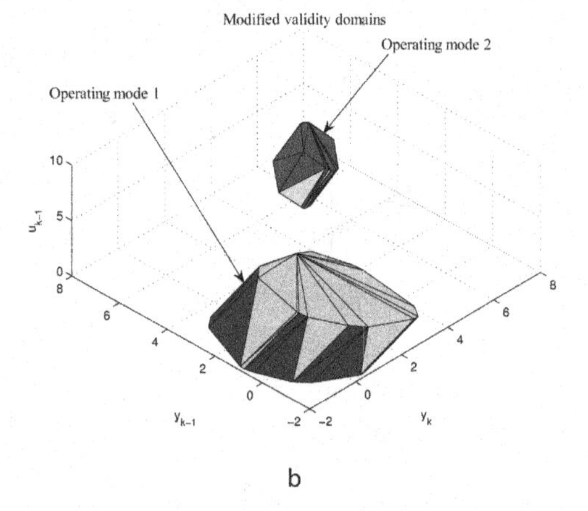

b

The prediction result validates the proposed methods for both modeling and simulation/prediction.

DISCUSSION

In this work, two model structures have been proposed for interval model and it has also been explained how the validity domain of every model can be determined in input, in input-output or in reduced input-output space. However, each has its advantages and disadvantages in prediction and of wrapping envelope generation.

Figure 10. n-step prediction of the wrapping envelope

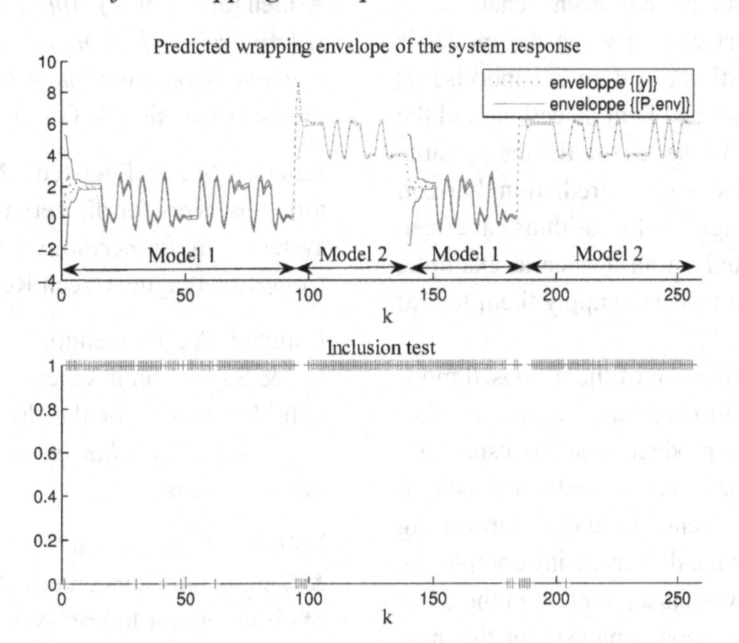

In n-step prediction, replacing system's responses $[y]_k$ by predicted intervals $[P.env]_k$ in an IO model introduces a source of pessimism in the resulting interval at any instant and consequently in the generation of the wrapping envelope. Due to the iterative nature of the IO model and the wrapping effect already explained in section Interval Analysis, we may obtain a very large and consequently, inadequate wrapping envelope. For this reason, IO interval models should be avoided as much as possible especially in n-step prediction procedures.

Another source of pessimism in n-step prediction is when the validity domains are determined in input-output or in reduced input-output space. In this case as mentioned before, replacing the system's responses by the predicted intervals makes the support of vector ξ more voluminous which may activate by error some nearby local models. However, the advantages of determining validity domains in input-output or in reduced input-output space regarding to time and resource consumption can not be neglected.

In one-step prediction, since the system's inputs and outputs are known and no pessimism is introduced in the calculation, either IO or FIR models can be employed and the validity domains can also be determined in input, in input-output or in reduced input-output space. The resulting wrapping envelope in all the cases provides more or less the same precision.

In some processes such as bio-reactors in batch mode in which the input is void, FIR model can not be used. In this case, the best option is an IO model which calculates the trajectory of the physical variables in an iterative manner from the initial state of the system. However, as mentioned, on should always bear in mind the accumulation of the pessimism in iterative calculations using interval tools.

CONCLUSION

In this paper, which consists of two main parts, a method for characterizing model parameters of a switching dynamic system by means of interval analysis and a novel strategy for predicting a guaranteed tube for the response of the system have been suggested. The tube which is called the wrapping envelope, has been generated in two cases; the first case is when the model is used in parallel with the system to supervise its operation (diagnosis and fault detection) and the other is when one wishes to predict the possible system's responses over a prediction horizon (process safety). Suggested algorithms have been tested and validated on an academic example. In future, the author plans to apply them to real processes.

Immediate application of the proposed modeling approach is to perform surety analysis of uncertain dynamic products/systems especially new developed ones can be mentioned. Due to technological advancements, classical modeling approaches can not handle increasing complexity of new products/systems anymore. On the other hand, performing a surety analysis for this new products/systems and prevent any potential harm to people/customers is vital. This work can be considered as an opening to achieve this objective using interval tools. As for future research, using alternative model structure other than FIR and IO employed especially in social/economical/environmental systems and characterizing the parameters of these models by interval analysis is proposed. The main advantage will be keeping the model structure simple while taking into account the complexity of the system.

Although the suggested identification and simulation strategies are generic, due to the diversity of processes and applications, some modification and validation is necessary for any specific problem at hand.

REFERENCES

Adrot, O., Shahriari, K., & Flaus, J. M. (2004). Estimation of bounded model uncertainties. In *11th IFAC Symposium on Automation in Mining and Metal Processing*, Nancy, France.

Armengol, J. (1999). *Application of Modal Interval Analysis to the simulation of the behaviour of dynamic systems with uncertain parameters*, PhD thesis, Universitat de Girona.

Babaali, M., & Egerstedt, M. (2005). Asymptotic observers for discrete-time switched linear systems. In *Proceedings of 16th IFAC World Congress,* Prague, Czech Republic.

Balluchi, A., Benvenuti, L., Di Benedetto, M. D., & Sangiovanni Vincentelli, A. L. (2001). A hybrid observer for the driveline dynamics. In *Proceedings of the European Control Conference*, Porto, Portugal.

Balluchi, A., Benvenuti, L., Di Benedetto, M. D., & Sangiovanni Vincentelli, A. L. (2002). Design of observers for hybrid systems. In *Proceedings of Hybrid Systems: Computation and Control*, (pp. 76–89). Stanford, CA.

Calm, R., Sainz, M. A., Herrero, P., Vehi, J., & Armengol, J. (2006). Parameter identification with quantifiers. In *5th IFAC Symposium on Robust Control Design*, Toulouse, France.

Domlan, E. A. (2006). *Diagnostic des Systmes Chamgement de Regime de Fonctionnement*, PhD thesis, Institut National Polythechnique de Lorraine.

Gasso, K. (2000). *Identification des systmes dynamiques non-linaires: Application Multi Modle*. PhD thesis, Centre de Recherche en Automatique de Nancy.

Gugaliya, J. K., Gudi, R. D., & Lakshminarayanan, S. (2005). Multi mode decomposition of nonlinear dynamics using fuzzy cart approach. *Journal of Process Control*, *15*(4), 417–434. doi:10.1016/j.jprocont.2004.07.004

Heath, T. L. (Ed.). (1853). *The Works of Archimedes*. Cambridge, MA: Cambridge University Press.

Jaulin, L., Kieffer, M., Didrit, O., & Walter, E. (2001). *Applied Interval Analysis*. Berlin: Springer-Verlag.

Johansen, T. A., & Foss, B. A. (1995). Identification of non-linear system structure and parameters using regime decomposition. *Automatica, 31*(2), 321–326. doi:10.1016/0005-1098(94)00096-2

Kolev, L. V. (1993). *Interval Methods for Circuit Analysis*. Hackensack, NJ: World Scientific.

Ling, C., & Edgar, T. F. (1997). Real-time control of a water-gas shift reactor by a model-based fuzzy gain scheduling technique. *Journal of Process Control, 7*(4), 239–253. doi:10.1016/S0959-1524(97)00001-2

Ljung, L. (1999). *System Identification*. Upper Saddle River, NJ: Prentice Hall.

Milanese, M., Norton, J., Piet-Lahanier, H., & Walter, E. (1996). *Bounding Approaches to System Identification*. New York: Plenum Press.

Moore, R. E. (1962). *Interval Arithmatic and Automatic Error Analysis in Digital Computing*. PhD thesis, Applied Mathematics and Statistics Laboratories, Report 25, Standford University.

Moore, R. E. (1966). *Interval Analysis*. Englewood Cliffs, NJ: Prentice Hall.

Murray-Smith, R., & Johansen, T. A. (1977). *Multiple Model Approaches to Modelling and Control*. Danvers, MA: CRC.

Neumaier, A. (2001). *Introduction to Numerical Analysis*. New York: Cambridge University Press.

Ploix, S., Adrot, O., & Ragot, J. (1999). Parameter uncertainty computation in static linear models. *Decision and Control, 1999, Proceedings of the 38th IEEE Conference on, 2*, 1916–1921.

Ragot, J., Maquin, D., & Domlan, E. A. (2003). Switching time estimation of piecewise linear systems. application to diagnosis. In *Proceedings of the 5th IFAC Symposium on Fault Detection, Supervision and Safety of Technical Processes*, (pp. 669–704).

Shahriari, K. (2007). *Analyse de Surete de Procedes Multi Mode par des Modeles a Base d'Intervalles*. PhD thesis, Joseph Fourier University.

Shahriari, K., Adrot, O., & Flaus, J. M. (2006a). Multi mode modeling with linear dynamic models using set-membership tools. *The 11th Information Processing and Management of Uncertainty in Knowledge-Based Systems International Conference*.

Shahriari, K., Flaus, J. M., & Adrot, O. (2006). Linear multi-mode modelling using set-membership approach. In *5th IFAC Symposium on Robust Control Design*.

Shahriari, K., & Tarasiewicz, S. (2008). Linear time-varying systems: Model parameters characterization using intervals analysis . *International Journal of Mathematics and Computer in Simulation, 1*(2), 54–62.

Sugeno, M., & Kang, G. T. (1988). Structure identification of fuzzy model. *Fuzzy Sets and Systems, 28*(1), 15–33. doi:10.1016/0165-0114(88)90113-3

Sunaga, T. (1958). Theory of interval algebra and its application to numerical analysis. *RAAG Memoirs, Ggujutsu Bunken Fukuy-kai,* Tokyo, *2*(29–46), 547–564.

Takagi, T., & Sugeno, M. (1985). Fuzzy identification of systems and its applications to modeling and control. *IEEE Transactions on Systems, Man, and Cybernetics, 15*, 116–132.

Venkat, A. N., Vijaysai, P., & Gudi, R. D. (2003). Identification of complex nonlinear processes based on fuzzy decomposition of the steady state space. *Journal of Process Control*, *13*(6), 473–488. doi:10.1016/S0959-1524(02)00120-8

Walter, E., & Pronzato, L. (1997). *Identification of Parametric Models: From Experimental Data*. Berlin: Springer-Verlag.

Warmus, M. (1956). Calculus of approximations. *Bulletin de l'Academie Polonaise de Sciences*, *4*(5), 253–257.

Yager, R. R., & Filev, D. P. (1993). Unified structure and parameter identification of fuzzy models. *IEEE Transactions on Systems, Man, and Cybernetics*, *23*(4), 1198–1205. doi:10.1109/21.247902

Young, R. C. (1931). The algebra of multi-valued quantities. *Mathematische Annalen*, *104*, 260–290. doi:10.1007/BF01457934

Young, W. H. (1908). Sull due funzioni a piu valori constituite dai limiti d'una funzione di variable reale a destra ed a sinistra di ciascun punto. *Rendiconti Academia di Lincei. Classes di Scienza Fiziche*, *17*(5), 582–587.

KEY TERMS AND DEFINITIONS

Characteristic Variables: The variables by which switching from one mode to another can be determined.

Diagnosis and Fault Detection: The analysis to verify if the process/system is in healthy operational conditions or not. This is generally performed with the aid of a mathematical model by comparing the process/system's response with the one estimated by the model.

Identification: The procedure of calculating the parameters of a mathematical model of a process/system which is generally performed considering an optimization criterion.

Interval Analysis: Interval analysis against real analysis that operates on real-valued numbers, acts on sets of real numbers. The operations of interval arithmetic are defined in such way that the resulting interval always contains the true result that would be obtained by using exact inputs and exact calculations.

Interval Model: A mathematical description of a process/system whose parameters are characterized by intervals.

Memory Effect: The fact that dynamic models are not valid in the very first instances of identification and simulation due to the moving horizon of the model.

Modeling Error: The difference between the process/system's response and the value estimated by the mathematical model.

Multi-Mode Model and Local Models: A mathematical model consisting of several local models each of which describes the process/system's dynamics in a specific operating mode.

Response Prediction: Estimating the response of a process/system using its mathematical model. The prediction can be performed for the next (one-step) or several (n-step) forthcoming instants.

Safety Analysis: By a safety analysis, one means to guarantee that the process/system never enters in forbidden operating zone and stay in safe regions.

Semantic of Identification/Simulation: It defines the properties of the parameters of an interval model and is described in the form of a mathematical (logical) expression made up of quantifiers, model parameters and system's inputs/responses.

Set-Membership Approach: The approach in which variables are characterized -instead of real numbers- as a set of real numbers.

Simulator: A scheme consisting of F models and ACK blocks to perform system's response prediction.

Switching Process/System: A process/system that has several operating modes each of which has a different dynamic. The switching from a mode to another takes place under certain transition conditions.

Switching Signal: The signal by which the switching from an operating mode to another is defined.

Time-Variant Process/System: A process/ system whose dynamic is varying through time.

Uncertain Dynamic Systems: The systems whose dynamics are not well-known or vary through time in a way that can not be determined.

Validity Domain: The domain in which any local model of the multi-mode model is valid.

Wrapping Effect: The accumulation of pessimism in iterative calculations increases the volume of the resulting domain after any iteration. This phenomenon is called the wrapping effect.

Wrapping Envelope: The tube enclosing process/system's response in different time instances. The wrapping envelope is generated by the interval model of the process/system.

APPENDIX A

Proof of the Theorem 3

Proof: The dynamic of a first order SISO system in observable state space can be described by the following equations:

$$x_{k+1} = ax_k + bu_k$$
$$y_k = x_k \qquad (27)$$

where $a, b \in \Re$ are known parameters, $x_k \in \Re$ is the state variable, and $u_k, y_k \in \Re$ are the system's input and output respectively. According the hypothesis of the theorem, the validity domain of operating mode *i* is convex hull $CH^i_{\{x\}}$ in state space $\mathcal{X}_{\{x\}}$ which is determined by a set of linear inequality constraints in the following form:

$$CH^i_{\{x\}} = \{x \mid \forall j, \alpha_{i,j} x + \gamma_{i,j} \leq 0\} \qquad (28)$$

where *j* is the index of the inequality constraint and $\alpha_{i,j}, \gamma_{i,j} \in \Re$ are known values. From Eq. (27) one has:

$$y_k = x_k \qquad (29)$$

Inserting (29) into (28), one obtains:

$$CH^i_{\{y\}} = \{y \mid \forall j, \alpha_{i,j} y + \gamma_{i,j} \leq 0\} \qquad (30)$$

Equations (28) and (30) shows that if the validity domain of operating mode *i* is a convex hull in observable state space, it can also be determined as a convex hull in space $\mathcal{X}_{\{y\}}$ (Input-Output space).

As well as for a first order system, the dynamic of a SISO second order system can be described in observable state space as follows:

$$X_{k+1} = \begin{bmatrix} 0 & a_2 \\ 1 & a_1 \end{bmatrix} X_k + Bu_k$$
$$y_k = \begin{bmatrix} 0 & 1 \end{bmatrix} X_k \qquad (31)$$

where $X_k = \begin{bmatrix} x_{1,k} & x_{2,k} \end{bmatrix}^T$. According to the hypothesis of the theorem, the validity domain of operating mode *i* in the observable space is convex hull $CH^i_{\{x_1,x_2\}}$ where:

$$CH^{i}_{\{x_1,x_2\}} = \{X \mid \begin{bmatrix}\alpha_{i,j} & \beta_{i,j}\end{bmatrix} X + \gamma_{i,j} \le 0\} \tag{32}$$

where $\alpha_{i,j}, \beta_{i,j}, \gamma_{i,j} \in \Re$ are known. Calculating $x_{1,k}$ and $x_{1,k}$ form Eq. (31) with respect to a_1, a_2, b_1, b_2 and y_k and inserting them into (32), one obtains:

$$CH^{i}_{\{UY_1\}} = \{UY_1 \mid \begin{bmatrix}\alpha_{i,j} & \beta_{i,j}\end{bmatrix} \times \begin{bmatrix} a_2 & 0 & b_1 & 0 \\ a_1 & a_2 & b_2 & b_1 \end{bmatrix} UY_1 + \gamma_{i,j} \le 0\} \tag{33}$$

where $UY_1 = [y_{k-1}, y_{k-2}, u_{k-1}, u_{k-2}]^T$ and

$$CH^{i}_{\{UY_{21}\}} = \{UY_2 \mid \begin{bmatrix}\alpha_{i,j} & \beta_{i,j}\end{bmatrix} \times \begin{bmatrix} 0 & a_2 & b_1 \\ 1 & 0 & 0 \end{bmatrix} UY_2 + \gamma_{i,j} \le 0\} \tag{34}$$

where $UY_2 = [y_k, y_{k-1}, u_{k-1}]^T$. Equations (33) and (34) show that if the hypothesis of the theorem is true, the validity domains of the local models of a second order system cab be determined in space $\{UY_1\}$ and space $\{UY_2\}$ as well.

APPENDIX B

Proof of Theorem 4

Proof: At instant *k*, intervals $[P.env]_{k-p}$ have been calculated such that:

$$\forall p < k, [y]_{k-p} \subseteq [P.env]_{k-p}$$

Consequently, regression vector $[\phi]_k$ would be the subset of new vector $[\phi]'_k$ in which one or several system's outputs $[y]_{k-p}$ are replaced by their respective predicted intervals $[P.env]_{k-p}$; that is:

$$[\phi]_k \subseteq [\phi]'_k \tag{35}$$

Considering (35) and from theorem 2, it can be concluded that:

$$[env]_k = [\theta]^T \times [\phi]_k \subseteq [P.env]_k = [\theta]^T \times [\phi]'_k \tag{36}$$

In the other hand, in identification procedure, parameters vector $[\theta]$ is calculated such that:

$$\forall k, [y]_k \subseteq [env]_k \quad (37)$$

Therefore, one can conclude from (36) and (37) that:

$$\forall k, [y]_k \subseteq [P.env]_k \quad (38)$$

Chapter 16
Selection of the Best Subset of Variables in Regression and Time Series Models

Nicholas A. Nechval
University of Latvia, Latvia

Konstantin N. Nechval
Transport and Telecommunication Institute, Latvia

Maris Purgailis
University of Latvia, Latvia

Uldis Rozevskis
University of Latvia, Latvia

ABSTRACT

The problem of variable selection is one of the most pervasive model selection problems in statistical applications. Often referred to as the problem of subset selection, it arises when one wants to model the relationship between a variable of interest and a subset of potential explanatory variables or predictors, but there is uncertainty about which subset to use. Several papers have dealt with various aspects of the problem but it appears that the typical regression user has not benefited appreciably. One reason for the lack of resolution of the problem is the fact that it is has not been well defined. Indeed, it is apparent that there is not a single problem, but rather several problems for which different answers might be appropriate. The intent of this chapter is not to give specific answers but merely to present a new simple multiplicative variable selection criterion based on the parametrically penalized residual sum of squares to address the subset selection problem in multiple linear regression analysis, where the objective is to select a minimal subset of predictor variables without sacrificing any explanatory power. The variables, which optimize this criterion, are chosen to be the best variables. The authors find that the proposed criterion performs consistently well across a wide variety of variable selection problems. Practical utility of this criterion is demonstrated by numerical examples.

DOI: 10.4018/978-1-61520-668-1.ch016

INTRODUCTION

Variable selection refers to the problem of selecting input variables that are most predictive of a given outcome. Variable selection problems are found in all supervised or unsupervised machine learning tasks, classification, regression, time series prediction, pattern recognition.

In the recent years, variable selection has become the focus of considerable research in several areas of application for which datasets with tens or hundreds of thousands of variables are available. These areas include text processing, particularly in application to Internet documents, and genomics, particularly gene expression array data. The objective of variable selection is three-fold: to improve the prediction performance of the predictors, to provide faster and more cost-effective predictors, and to provide a better understanding of the underlying process that generated the data.

A number of studies in the statistical literature discuss the problem of selecting the best subset of predictor variables in regression. Such studies focus on subset selection methodologies, selection criteria, or a combination of both. The traditional selection methodologies can be enumerative (e.g. all subsets and best subsets procedures), sequential (e.g. forward selection, backward elimination, stepwise regression, and stagewise regression procedures), and screening-based (e.g. ridge regression and principal components analysis). Standard texts like Draper and Smith (1981) and Montgomery and Peck (1992) provide clear descriptions of these methodologies.

Some of the reasons for using only a subset of the available predictor variables (given by Miller, 2002) are:

- To estimate or predict at a lower cost by reducing the number of variables on which data are to be collected;
- To predict more accurately by eliminating uninformative variables;
- To describe multivariate data sets parsimoniously; and
- To estimate regression coefficients with smaller standard errors (particularly when some of the predictors are highly correlated).

These objectives are of course not completely compatible. Prediction is probably the most common objective, and here the range of values of the predictor variables for which predictions will be required is important. The subset of variables giving the best predictions in some sense, averaged over the region covered by the calibration data, may be very inferior to other subsets for extrapolation beyond this region. For prediction purposes, the regression coefficients are not the primary objective, and poorly estimated coefficients can sometimes yield acceptable predictions. On the other hand, if process control is the objective then it is of vital importance to know accurately how much change can be expected when one of the predictors changes or is changed.

Suppose that $\mathbf{y}$, a variable of interest, and $\mathbf{x}_1, ..., \mathbf{x}_v$, a set of potential explanatory variables or predictors, are vectors of n observations. The problem of variable selection, or subset selection as it is often called, arises when one wants to model the relationship between $\mathbf{y}$ and a subset of $\mathbf{x}_1, ..., \mathbf{x}_v$, but there is uncertainty about which subset to use. Such a situation is particularly of interest when v is large and $\mathbf{x}_1, ..., \mathbf{x}_v$ is thought to contain many redundant or irrelevant variables.

The variable selection problem is most familiar in the linear regression context, where attention is restricted to normal linear models. Letting w index the subsets of $\mathbf{x}_1, ..., \mathbf{x}_v$ and letting p_w be the number of the parameters of the model based on the wth subset, the problem is to select and fit a model of the form

$$\mathbf{y} = \mathbf{X}_w \mathbf{a}_w + \varepsilon, \qquad (1)$$

where $\mathbf{X}_w$ is an $n \times p_w$ matrix whose columns correspond to the wth subset, $\mathbf{a}_w$ is a $p_w \times 1$ vector of regression coefficients, and $\boldsymbol{\varepsilon} \sim N_n(\mathbf{0},\sigma^2\mathbf{I})$. More generally, the variable selection problem is a special case of the model selection problem where each model under consideration corresponds to a distinct subset of $\mathbf{x}_1, ..., \mathbf{x}_v$. Typically, a single model class is simply applied to all possible subsets.

The fundamental developments in variable selection seem to have occurred directly in the context of the linear model (1). Historically, the focus began with the linear model in the 1960s, when the first wave of important developments occurred and computing was expensive. The focus on the linear model still continues, in part because its analytic tractability greatly facilitates insight, but also because many problems of interest can be posed as linear variable selection problems. For example, for the problem of non-parametric function estimation, $\mathbf{y}$ represents the values of the unknown function, and $\mathbf{x}_1, ..., \mathbf{x}_v$ represent a linear basis, such as a wavelet basis or a spline basis.

One of the fascinating aspects of the variable selection problem has been the wide variety of methods that have been brought to bear on the problem. Because of space limitations, it is of course impossible to even mention them all, and so we focus on only a few to illustrate the general thrust of developments. An excellent and comprehensive treatment of variable selection methods prior to 1999 was provided by Miller (2002). As we discuss, many promising new approaches have appeared over the last decade.

A distinguishing feature of variable selection problems is their enormous size. Even with moderate values of v, computing characteristics for all 2^v models is prohibitively expensive, and some reduction of the model space is needed. Focusing on the linear model (1), early suggestions based such reductions on the residual sum of squares, which provided a partial ordering of the models. Taking advantage of the chain structure of subsets, branch and bound methods such as the algorithm of Furnival and Wilson (1974) were proposed to logically eliminate large numbers of models from consideration. When feasible, attention was often restricted to the "best subsets" of each size. Otherwise, reduction was obtained with variants of stepwise methods that sequentially add or delete variables based on greedy considerations (e.g., Efroymson, 1960). Even with advances in computing technology, these methods continue to be the standard workhorses for reduction.

Once attention was reduced to a manageable set of models, criteria were needed for selecting a subset model. The earliest developments of such selection criteria, again in the linear model context, were based on attempts to minimize the mean squared error of prediction. Different criteria corresponded to different assumptions about which predictor values to use, and whether they were fixed or random (see Hocking, 1976); Thompson, 1978) and the references therein). Perhaps the most familiar of those criteria is the Mallows

$$C_p = \frac{\mathrm{RSS}_w}{\hat{\sigma}^2_{\mathrm{full}}} + 2p_w - n, \tag{2}$$

where RSS_w is the residual sum of squares for the model based on the wth subset and $\hat{\sigma}^2_{\mathrm{full}}$ is the usual unbiased estimate of σ^2 based on the full model. The standard texts, such as Draper and Smith (1981), Montgomery and Peck (1992) and Myers (1992), recommend plotting C_p, against p for all possible regressions and choosing an equation with low C_p or with C_p close to p. If σ^2 is known, any model which provides unbiased estimates of the regression coefficients, i.e. which contains all important regressors, has $E(C_p) = p$.

Two of the other most popular criteria, motivated from very different viewpoints, are the Akaike information criterion (AIC) and the Bayesian information criterion (BIC). Letting $\hat{L}_w$ denote the maximum log-likelihood of the wth model, AIC selects the model that maximizes $(\hat{L}_w - p_w)$, whereas BIC selects the model that maximizes

$(\widehat{L}_w - (\log n)p_w/2)$. Akaike (1973) motivated AIC from an information theoretic standpoint as the minimization of the Kullback-Leibler distance between the distributions of Y under the wth model and under the true model. To lend further support, an asymptotic equivalence of AIC and cross-validation was shown by Stone (1977). In contrast, Schwarz (1978) motivated BIC from a Bayesian standpoint, by showing that it was asymptotically equivalent (as $n \to \infty$) to selection based on Bayes factors. BIC was further justified from a coding theory viewpoint by Rissanen (1978).

Comparisons of the relative merits of AIC and BIC based on asymptotic consistency (as $n \to \infty$) have flourished in the literature. As it turns out, BIC is consistent when the true model is fixed (Haughton, 1988), whereas AIC is consistent if the dimensionality of the true model increases with n (at an appropriate rate) (Shibata, 1981). Stone (1979) provided an illuminating discussion of these two viewpoints.

For the linear model (1), many of the popular selection criteria are special cases of a penalized sum of squares criterion, providing a unified framework for comparisons. Assuming σ^2 known to avoid complications, this general criterion selects the subset model that minimizes

$$\frac{\text{RSS}_w}{\sigma^2} + cp_w, \quad (3)$$

where c is a preset "parametric dimensionality penalty." Intuitively, (3) penalizes RSS_w/σ^2 by c times p_w, the parametric dimension of the wth model. AIC and minimum C_p are essentially equivalent, corresponding to $c = 2$, and BIC is obtained by setting $c = \log n$. By imposing a smaller penalty, AIC and minimum C_p will select larger models than BIC (unless n is very small).

Further insight into the choice of c is obtained when all of the predictors are orthogonal, in which case (3) simply selects all of those predictors with T-statistics t for which $t^2 > c$. When $\mathbf{x}_1, ..., \mathbf{x}_v$ are in fact all unrelated to $\mathbf{y}$ (i.e., the full model regression coefficients are all 0), AIC and minimum C_p are clearly too liberal and tend to include a large proportion of irrelevant variables. A natural conservative choice for c, namely $c = 2\log v$, is suggested by the fact that under this null model, the expected value of the largest squared T-statistic is approximately $2\log v$ when v is large. This choice is the risk inflation criterion (RIC) proposed by Foster and George [1994] and the universal threshold for wavelets proposed by Donoho and Johnstone (1994). Both of these articles motivate $c = 2\log v$ as yielding the smallest possible maximum inflation in predictive risk due to selection (as $v \to \infty$), a minimax decision theory standpoint. Motivated by similar considerations, Tibshirani and Knight (1999) recently proposed the covariance inflation criterion (CIC), a nonparametric method of selection based on adjusting the bias of in-sample performance estimates. Yet another promising adjustment based on a generalized degrees of freedom concept was proposed by Ye (1998).

Many other interesting criteria corresponding to different choices of c in (3) have been proposed in the literature (see, e.g., Hurvitz and Tsai, 1989, 1998; Rao and Wu, 1989; Shao, 1993; Wei, 1992; Zheng and Loh, 1997 and the references therein). One of the drawbacks of using a fixed choice of c is that models of a particular size are favored; small c favors large models, and large c favors small models. Adaptive choices of c to mitigate this problem have been recommended by Benjamini and Hochberg (1995), Clyde and George (1999, 2000), Foster and George (1994), Johnstone and Silverman (1998).

An alternative to explicit criteria of the form (3), is selection based on predictive error estimates obtained by intensive computing methods such as the bootstrap (e.g., Efron, 1983; Gong, 1986) and cross-validation (e.g., Shao, 1997; Zhang, 1992). An interesting variant of these is the little bootstrap (Breiman, 1992), which estimates the predictive error of selected models by mimicking replicate data comparison. The little bootstrap compares favorably to selection based on minimum C_p or the conditional bootstrap, whose performances are seriously denigrated by selection bias.

Another drawback of traditional subset selection methods, which is beginning to receive more attention, is their instability relative to small changes in the data. Two novel alternatives that mitigate some of this instability for linear models are the nonnegative garrotte (Breiman, 1995) and the lasso (Tibshirani, 1996). Both of these procedures replace the full model least squares criterion by constrained optimization criteria. As the constraint is tightened, estimates are zeroed out, and a subset model is identified and estimated. Some interesting criteria taking into account a stability of the regression parameters, the objective of which is to select a minimal subset of predictor variables without sacrificing any explanatory power, have been proposed by Nechval et al. (2008a, 2008b, 2008c, 2009).

The fully Bayesian approach to variable selection is as follows (George, 1999). For a given set of models $M(1), ..., M(2^v)$, where $M(w)$ corresponds to the wth subset of $\mathbf{x}_1, ..., \mathbf{x}_v$, one puts priors $\pi(\mathbf{a}(w)|M(w))$ on the parameters of each $M(w)$ and a prior on the set of models $\pi(M(1)), ..., \pi(M(2^v))$. Selection is then based on the posterior model probabilities $\pi(M(w)|\mathbf{y})$, which are obtained in principle by Bayes's theorem.

Although this Bayesian approach appears to provide a comprehensive solution to the variable selection problem, the difficulties of prior specification and posterior computation are formidable when the set of models is large. Even when v is small and subjective considerations are not out of the question (Garthwaite and Dickey, 1996), prior specification requires considerable effort.

The intent of this paper is to present a new simple multiplicative variable selection criterion based on the parametrically penalized residual sum of squares to address the subset selection problem in multiple linear regression and time series analysis, where the objective is to select a minimal subset of predictor variables without sacrificing any explanatory power as well as to take into account stable subset models. We find that the proposed criterion performs consistently well across a wide variety of variable selection problems.

MULTIPLICATIVE CRITERION OF PARAMETRICALLY PENALIZED RESIDUAL SUM OF SQUARES

This criterion (denoted by $S_{\varphi(p)}$) is given by

$$S_{\phi(p)} = \phi(p_{M(w)})\mathrm{RSS}_{M(w)}, \tag{4}$$

where $\mathrm{RSS}_{M(w)}$ is the residual sum of squares for the wth subset model $M(w)$, which has the number of parameters equal to $p_{M(w)}$; $\phi(p_{M(w)})$ is a specified function of $p_{M(w)}$.

According to (4), the best model (subset of informative variables) denoted by $M^*(w)$ is determined as

$$\begin{aligned} M^*(w) &= \arg \inf_{M(w)\,\in\{M(w)\,:w\,\in\{w\}\}} S_{\phi(p)} \\ &= \arg \inf_{M(w)\,\in\{M(w)\,:w\,\in\{w\}\}} \phi(p_{M(w)})\mathrm{RSS}_{M(w)} \\ &= \arg \inf_{M(w)\,\in\{M(w)\,:w\in\{w\}\}} \phi(p_{M(w)})\frac{\mathrm{RSS}_{M(w)}}{\mathrm{TSS}} \\ &= \arg \inf_{M(w)\,\in\{M(w)\,:w\in\{w\}\}} \phi(p_{M(w)})\left(1 - R^2_{M(w)}\right), \end{aligned} \tag{5}$$

where the coefficient of determination $R^2_{M(w)}$ ($0 \le R^2_{M(w)} \le 1$) for the wth subset model $M(w)$ is computed as

$$R^2_{M(w)} = 1 - \frac{\mathrm{RSS}_{M(w)}}{\mathrm{TSS}}, \tag{6}$$

TSS is the total residual sum of squares. Thus, the $S_{\varphi(p)}$ criterion represents the parametrically penalized data fit indicator. It allows one to select the suitable subset model at a lower cost by reducing the number of variables on which data are to be collected. In this paper we consider the case when $\varphi(p) = p$, i.e. the S_p criterion.

If the $S_{\varphi(p)}$ criterion takes into account only stable subset models, then it (denoted by $S_{\varphi(p);\alpha}$) is given by

$$S_{\phi(p);\alpha} = \left\{ S_{\phi(p)} : \left| \frac{\widehat{a}_i}{s_{\widehat{a}_i}} \right| > t_{k;\alpha}, \forall i = 1(1)p_{M(w)} \right\} =$$

$$\left\{ \phi(p_{M(w)})\left(1 - R^2_{M(w)}\right) : \left| \frac{\widehat{a}_i}{s_{\widehat{a}_i}} \right| > t_{k;\alpha}, \forall i = 1(1)p_{M(w)} \right\}, \quad (7)$$

where $\widehat{a}_i$ is an estimate of the parameter a_i of the model $M(w)$, $s_{\widehat{a}_i}$ represents the estimated standard deviation of $\widehat{a}_i$, $\widehat{a}_i / s_{\widehat{a}_i}$ follows the Student distribution (T-distribution) with $k = n - p_{M(w)}$ degrees of freedom, n is the number of observations, $t_{k;\alpha}$ is an upper-tail value of the T-statistic at the given significance level α, i.e., $\Pr\{T > t_{k;\alpha}\} = \alpha$.

According to (7), the best model (subset of informative variables) denoted by $M^*(w)$ is determined as

$$M^*(w) = \arg \inf_{M(w) \in \{M(w) : w \in \{w\}\}} \phi(p_{M(w)})\left(1 - R^2_{M(w)}\right) \quad (8)$$

subject to

$$\left| \frac{\widehat{a}_i}{s_{\widehat{a}_i}} \right| > t_{k;\alpha}, \forall i = 1(1)p_{M(w)}. \quad (9)$$

Thus, the $S_{\varphi(p);\alpha}$ criterion involves the parametrically penalized data fit indicator and the parameter stability indicator. It reject unstable model at the significance level α and allows one to select the suitable stable subset model minimizing the parametrically penalized residual sum of squares. In this paper we consider the case when $\varphi(p) = 1$, i.e. the $S_{1;\alpha}$ criterion.

EXAMPLES

Example 1: Hald Cement Data

Montgomery and Peck (1992, pp. 256-266) illustrated variable selection techniques on the Hald cement data and gave several references to other analyses. The data are shown in Table 1.

The response variable is the heat evolved y in a cement mix, and the four explanatory variables are ingredients in the mix. When a linear model

$$y = a_0 + a_1x_1 + a_2x_2 + a_3x_3 + a_4x_4 + \varepsilon \quad (10)$$

is fitted, the residuals show no evidence of any problems. But an important feature of these data is that the variables x_1 and x_3 are highly correlated ($r_{13} = -0.824$), as are the variables x_2 and x_4 (with $r_{24} = -0.973$). Thus we would expect any subset w of $\{x_1, x_2, x_3, x_4\}$ that includes one variable from $\{x_1, x_3\}$ and the other variable from $\{x_2, x_4\}$. In fact, S_p and $S_{1;\alpha=0.01}$ choose the model

$$y = a_0 + a_1x_1 + a_2x_2 + \varepsilon. \quad (11)$$

It will be noted that the algorithm of Efroymson (1960) gives the very same result but via more complex way.

Example 2: Simulated Data

The data set (x_i, y_i), $i = 1(1)100$ analyzed here was simulated using the model:

$$y_i = 0.3 + 2x_i - 5x_i^2 + 3x_i^3 + \varepsilon_i, \quad (12)$$

Table 1. The Hald cement data

i	y_i	x_{i1}	x_{i2}	x_{i3}	x_{i4}	i	y_i	x_{i1}	x_{i2}	x_{i3}	x_{i4}
1	78.5	7	26	6	60	8	72.5	1	31	22	44
2	74.3	1	29	15	52	9	93.1	2	54	18	22
3	104.3	11	56	8	20	10	115.9	21	47	4	26
4	87.6	11	31	8	47	11	83.8	1	40	23	34
5	95.9	7	52	6	33	12	113.3	11	66	9	12
6	109.2	11	55	9	22	13	109.4	10	68	8	12
7	102.7	3	71	17	6						

where, for i=1(1)100, x_i=i/100 and ε_i are independent and normal with mean zero and variance 0.15^2. The situation is such that the true model is known to belong to the class of models given by (13). The simulation data are shown, with the true regression curve, in Figure 1.

Assuming that a model of the data belongs to the class of models,

$$y = a_0 + a_1 x + a_2 x^2 + \ \dots \ + a_k x^k + \varepsilon,\ k \geq 1, \tag{13}$$

BIC and $S_{1;\alpha=0.01}$ choose k=3, the true degree. AIC's final choice is k= 8, a clear overfitting.

Example 3: Company Record Data

A company that services copy machines is interested in developing a regression model that will assist in personnel planning (McClave et al., 1998, p. 530). Company records were sampled and the data in Table 2 were obtained.

It needs a model that describes the relationship between the time spent on a preventive maintenance service call to a customer, y (hours), and two independent variables: the number of copy machines to be serviced, x_1, and the service person's experience in preventive maintenance, x_2 (months).

Figure 1. Simulated data set with the true regression curve

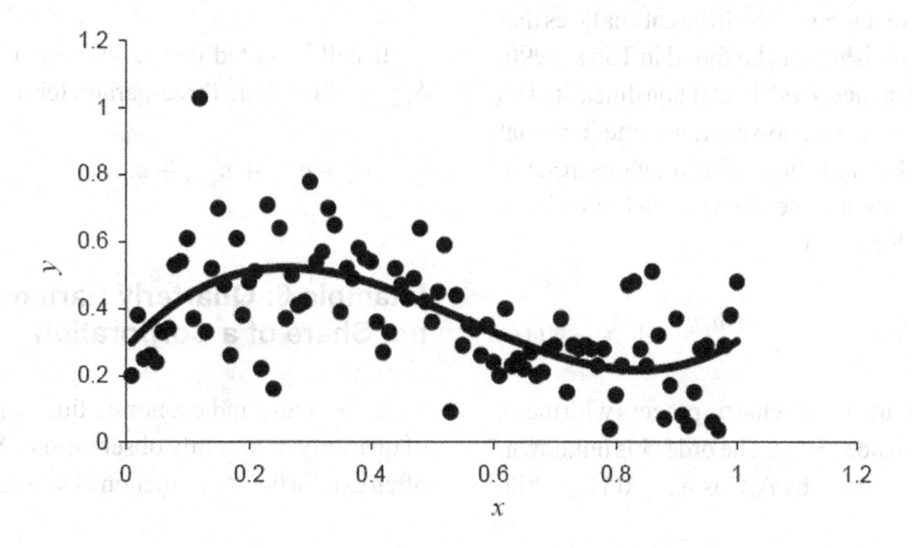

Table 2. The company record data

i	y_i	x_{i1}	x_{i2}	i	y_i	x_{i1}	x_{i2}
1	1.0	1	12	6	1.8	1	1
2	3.1	3	8	7	11.5	10	10
3	17.0	10	5	8	9.3	5	2
4	14.0	8	2	9	6.0	4	6
5	6.0	5	10	10	12.2	10	18

Considering the full model

$$y = a_0 + a_1x_1 + a_2x_2 + a_3x_1x_2 + \varepsilon \qquad (14)$$

to investigate which subset model is more useful for predicting y, we find that S_p and $S_{1;\alpha=0.01}$ choose the subset model

$$y = a_1x_1 + a_3x_1x_2 + \varepsilon. \qquad (15)$$

Example 4: Canadian Lynx Data

The data (Table 3) give the annual number of lynx trappings in the Mackenzie River District of North-West Canada for the period 1821 to 1934, yielding n=114 observations.

The natural logarithm of the series is commonly analyzed. A comprehensive description of the data set as well as a review of the different analyses that have been published can be found in Tong (1990, ch. 7). For instance, evidence of non-linearity has been uncovered. We, however, assume here that the interest lies in fitting a linear autoregression (hence possibly misspecified) model of order k, AR(k), i.e., for t=k+1, …, n,

$$y_t = a_0 + a_1y_{t-1} + \cdots + a_ky_{t-k} + \varepsilon_t, \qquad (16)$$

where $\{\varepsilon_t\}$ is an i.i.d. stochastic process with mean zero and variance $\sigma^2 < \infty$. The order k is unknown. The model selected by AIC is an AR(11), while BIC and S_p choose AR(2). Notice that historically, the AR(2) specification was first advocated by Moran (1953).

The model selected by $S_{1;\alpha=0.05}$ is

$$y_t = a_0 + a_1y_{t-1} + a_2y_{t-2} + a_4y_{t-4} + a_{10}y_{t-10} + a_{11}y_{t-11} + \varepsilon_t \qquad (17)$$

Example 5: House Price Data

A set of 24 observations, given in Table 4, originally published by Narula and Wellington (1977), is used to relate nine variables, x_1, …, x_9, to the sale price, y, of houses.

The final choice of S_p is the two-parameter model

$$y = a_0 + a_1x_1 + \varepsilon. \qquad (18)$$

It will be noted that C_p (Gilmour, 1996) and $S_{1;\alpha=0.05}$ choose the three-parameter model

$$y = a_0 + a_1x_1 + a_2x_2 + \varepsilon. \qquad (19)$$

Example 6: Quarterly Earnings per Share of a Corporation

Many business and economic time series consist of quarterly or monthly observations. Such series often exhibit the phenomenon of seasonality – pat-

Table 3. The Canadian lynx data

Year	Data	Year	Data	Year	Data	Year	Data	Year	Data	Year	Data
1821	269	1840	409	1859	684	1878	299	1897	587	1916	3790
1822	321	1841	151	1860	299	1879	201	1898	105	1917	674
1823	585	1842	45	1861	236	1880	229	1899	153	1918	81
1824	871	1843	68	1862	245	1881	469	1900	387	1919	80
1825	1475	1844	213	1863	552	1882	736	1901	758	1920	108
1826	2821	1845	546	1864	1623	1883	2042	1902	1307	1921	229
1827	3928	1846	1033	1865	3311	1884	2811	1903	3465	1922	399
1828	5943	1847	2129	1866	6721	1885	4431	1904	6991	1923	1132
1829	4950	1848	2536	1867	4245	1886	2511	1905	6313	1924	2432
1830	2577	1849	957	1868	687	1887	389	1906	3794	1925	3574
1831	523	1850	361	1869	255	1888	73	1907	1836	1926	2935
1832	98	1851	377	1870	473	1889	39	1908	345	1927	1537
1833	184	1852	225	1871	358	1890	49	1909	382	1928	529
1834	279	1853	360	1872	784	1891	59	1910	808	1929	485
1835	409	1854	731	1873	1594	1892	188	1911	1388	1930	662
1836	2285	1855	1638	1874	1676	1893	377	1912	2713	1931	1000
1837	2685	1856	2725	1875	2251	1894	1292	1913	3800	1932	1590
1838	3409	1857	2871	1876	1426	1895	4031	1914	3091	1933	2657
1839	1824	1858	2119	1877	756	1896	3495	1915	2985	1934	3396

terns repeated from year to year. Table 5 shows earnings per share of a corporation over a period of 8 years (Newbold, 1995, p. 693).

When a linear autoregression model

$$y_t = a_0 + a_1 y_{t-1} + a_2 y_{t-2} + a_3 y_{t-3} + a_4 y_{t-4} + \varepsilon \quad (20)$$

is fitted to the data to investigate which subset model is more useful for predicting *y* (earnings), S_p and $S_{1;\alpha=0.01}$ choose the subset model

$$y_t = a_4 y_{t-4} + \varepsilon. \quad (21)$$

Example 7: Hudson Data

The data set (x_i, y_i), i=1(1)19, analyzed here was simulated using the model:

$$y_i = 1 + x_i - 0.55x_i^2 + 0.001x_i^3 + \varepsilon_i, \quad (22)$$

where ε_i, i=1(1)19, are independent and normal with mean zero and variance 1. The data taken from (Hudson, 1964) are presented in Table 6. The Hudson data with the best regression curve are shown in Figure 2.

Assuming that a model of the data belongs to the class of models (13), the final choice of S_p and $S_{1;\alpha=0.05}$ of the best model is k=3, true degree, i.e.,

$$y = a_0 + a_1 x + a_2 x^2 + a_3 x^3 + \varepsilon. \quad (23)$$

It will be noted that Hudson obtained the very same result via more complex technique.

Table 4. The house price data

y	x_1	x_2	x_3	x_4	x_5	x_6	x_7	x_8	x_9
25.9	4.9176	1.0	3.4720	0.9980	1.0	7	4	42	0
29.5	5.0208	1.0	3.5310	1.5000	2.0	7	4	62	0
27.9	4.5429	1.0	2.2750	1.1750	1.0	6	3	40	0
25.9	4.5573	1.0	4.0500	1.2320	1.0	6	3	54	0
29.9	5.0597	1.0	4.4550	1.1210	1.0	6	3	42	0
29.9	3.8910	1.0	4.4550	0.9880	1.0	6	3	56	0
30.9	5.8980	1.0	5.8500	1.2400	1.0	7	3	51	1
28.9	5.6039	1.0	9.5200	1.5010	0.0	6	3	32	0
35.9	5.8282	1.0	6.4350	1.2250	2.0	6	3	32	0
31.5	5.3003	1.0	4.9883	1.5520	1.0	6	3	30	0
31.0	6.2712	1.0	5.5200	0.9750	1.0	5	2	30	0
30.9	5.9592	1.0	6.6660	1.1210	2.0	6	3	32	0
30.9	5.0500	1.0	5.0000	1.0200	0.0	5	2	46	1
36.9	8.2464	1.5	5.1500	1.6640	2.0	8	4	50	0
41.9	6.6969	1.5	6.9020	1.4880	1.5	7	3	22	1
40.5	7.7841	1.5	7.1020	1.3760	1.0	6	3	17	0
43.9	9.0384	1.0	7.8000	1.5000	1.5	7	3	23	0
37.5	5.9894	1.0	5.5200	1.2560	2.0	6	3	40	1
37.9	7.5422	1.5	5.0000	1.6900	1.0	6	3	22	0
44.5	8.7951	1.5	9.8900	1.8200	2.0	8	4	50	1
37.9	6.0831	1.5	6.7265	1.6520	1.0	6	3	44	0
38.9	8.3607	1.5	9.1500	1.7770	2.0	8	4	48	1
36.9	8.1400	1.0	8.0000	1.5040	2.0	7	3	3	0
45.8	9.1416	1.5	7.3262	1.8310	1.5	8	4	31	0

y, sale price (\$/1000); x_1, taxes (\$/1000); x_2, number of baths; x_3, lot size (ft²/1000); x_4, living space (ft²/1000); x_5, number of garage stalls; x_6, number of rooms; x_7, number of bedrooms; x_8, age (years); x_9, number of fireplaces.

Example 8: Steam Plant Data

The steam plant data taken from (Draper and Smith, 1981, App. A) are presented in Table 7. The used data code is as follows: x_1 = pounds of real fatty acid in storage per month, x_2 = pounds of crude glycerine made, x_3 = average wind velocity in miles per hour, x_4 = calendar days per month, x_5 = operating days per month, x_6 = days below 32°F, x_7 = average atmospheric temperature, degrees F, x_8 = average wind velocity, x_9 = number of startups; y = pounds of steam used monthly.

Considering the full model

$$y = a_0 + a_1x_1 + a_2x_2 + a_3x_3 + a_4x_4 + a_5x_5 + a_6x_6 + a_7x_7 + a_8x_8 + a_9x_9 + \varepsilon \quad (24)$$

to investigate which subset model is more useful for predicting y, we find that S_p and $S_{1;\alpha=0.01}$ choose the subset model

$$y = a_0 + a_2x_2 + a_3x_3 + a_7x_7 + \varepsilon, \quad (25)$$

Table 5. The data of quarterly earnings per share of a corporation

Year	Quarter x_{i2} x_{i3}			
	1	2	3	4
1	0.300	0.460	0.345	0.910
2	0.330	0.545	0.440	1.040
3	0.495	0.680	0.545	1.285
4	0.550	0.870	0.660	1.580
5	0.590	0.990	0.830	1.730
6	0.610	1.050	0.920	2.040
7	0.700	1.230	1.060	2.320
8	0.820	1.410	1.250	2.730

Table 6. The Hudson data

i	x_i	y_i	i	x_i	y_i	i	x_i	y_i	i	x_i	y_i
1	2	2.84	6	12	7.39	11	22	7.35	16	32	9.99
2	4	5.50	7	14	6.67	12	24	6.11	17	34	10.31
3	6	5.96	8	16	5.72	13	26	6.67	18	36	12.03
4	8	4.50	9	18	7.95	14	28	9.67	19	38	13.51
5	10	6.45	10	20	5.93	15	30	7.35			

Figure 2. The Hudson data with the best regression curve

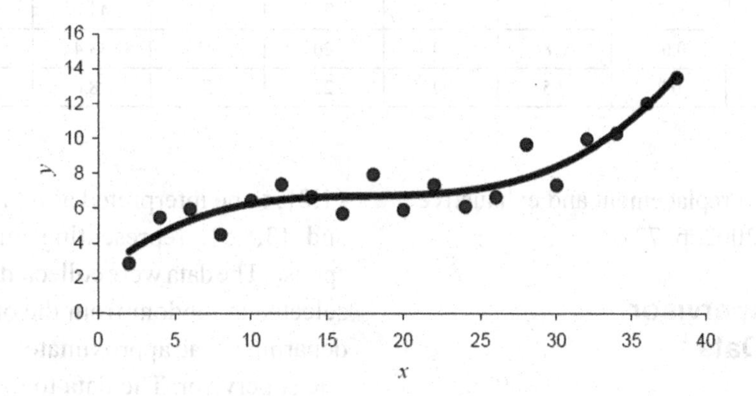

which gives a much better fit than the subset model

$$y = a_0 + a_1 x_1 + a_5 x_5 + a_7 x_7 + \varepsilon \qquad (26)$$

found by forward selection and backward elimination in (Miller, 2002, p. 72), as well as the subset model

$$y = a_0 + a_4 x_4 + a_5 x_5 + a_7 x_7 + \varepsilon \qquad (27)$$

Table 7. The steam plant data

y	x_1	x_2	x_3	x_4	x_5	x_6	x_7	x_8	x_9
10.98	5.2	0.61	7.4	31	20	22	35.3	54.8	4
11.13	5.12	0.64	8	29	20	25	29.7	64	5
12.51	6.19	0.78	7.4	31	23	17	30.8	54.8	4
8.4	3.89	0.49	7.5	30	20	22	58.8	56.3	4
9.27	6.28	0.84	5.5	31	21	0	61.4	30.3	5
8.73	5.76	0.74	8.9	30	22	0	71.3	79.2	4
6.36	3.45	0.42	4.1	31	11	0	74.4	16.8	2
8.5	6.57	0.87	4.1	31	23	0	76.7	16.8	5
7.82	5.69	0.75	4.1	30	21	0	70.7	16.8	4
9.14	6.14	0.76	4.5	31	20	0	57.5	20.3	5
8.24	4.84	0.65	0.3	30	20	11	46.4	106.1	4
12.19	4.88	0.72	6.9	31	21	12	28.9	47.6	4
11.88	6.03	0.79	6.6	31	21	25	28.1	43.6	5
9.57	4.55	0.6	7.3	28	19	18	39.1	53.3	5
10.94	5.71	0.7	8.1	31	23	5	46.8	95.6	4
9.58	5.67	0.74	8.4	30	20	7	48.5	70.6	4
10.09	6.72	0.85	6.1	31	22	0	59.3	37.2	6
8.11	4.95	0.67	4.9	30	22	0	70	21	4
6.83	4.62	0.45	4.6	31	11	0	70	21.2	3
8.88	6.6	0.95	3.7	31	23	0	74.5	13.7	4
7.68	5.01	0.64	4.7	30	20	0	72.1	22.1	4
8.47	5.68	0.75	5.3	31	21	1	58.1	28.1	6
8.86	5.28	0.7	6.2	30	20	14	44.6	38.4	4
10.36	5.36	0.67	6.8	31	20	22	33.4	46.2	4
11.08	5.87	0.7	7.5	31	22	28	28.6	56.3	5

found by sequential replacement and exhaustive search in (Miller, 2002, p. 72).

Example 9: Supervisor Performance Data

The data for the analysis taken from (Chatterjee and Hadi, 2006, p. 56) were generated from the individual employee response to the items on the survey questionnaire. The response on any item ranged from 1 through 5, indicating very satisfactory to very unsatisfactory, respectively. A dichotomous index was created to each item by collapsing the response scale to two categories: {1,2}, to be interpreted as a favorable response, and {3,4,5}, representing an unfavorable response. The data were collected in 30 departments selected at random from the organization. Each department had approximately 35 employees and one supervisor. The data to be used in analysis, given in Table 8, were obtained by aggregating responses for departments to get the proportion of favorable responses for each item for each department.

The resulting data therefore consist of 30 observations on seven variables, one observation for each department. We refer to this data set as the *Supervisor Performance* data. The variable

Table 8. The supervisor performance data

y	x_1	x_2	x_3	x_4	x_5	x_6
43	51	30	39	61	92	45
63	64	51	54	63	73	47
71	70	68	69	76	86	48
61	63	45	47	54	84	35
81	78	56	66	71	83	47
43	55	49	44	54	49	34
58	67	42	56	66	68	35
71	75	50	55	70	66	41
72	82	72	67	71	83	31
67	61	45	47	62	80	41
64	53	53	58	58	67	34
67	60	47	39	59	74	41
69	62	57	42	55	63	25
68	83	83	45	59	77	35
77	77	54	72	79	77	46
81	90	50	72	60	54	36
74	85	64	69	79	79	63
65	60	65	75	55	80	60
65	70	46	57	75	85	46
50	58	68	54	64	78	52
50	40	33	34	43	64	33
64	61	52	62	66	80	41
53	66	52	50	63	80	37
40	37	42	58	50	57	49
63	54	42	48	66	75	33
66	77	66	63	88	76	72
78	75	58	74	80	78	49
48	57	44	45	51	83	38
85	85	71	71	77	74	55
82	82	39	59	64	78	39

description in the Supervisor Performance data is as follows: x_1 = handles employee complaints, x_2 = does not allow special privileges, x_3 = opportunity to learn new things, x_4 = raises based on performance, x_5 = too critical of poor performance, x_6 = rate of advancing to better jobs; y = overall rating of job being done by supervisor.

A linear model of the form

$$y = a_0 + a_1x_1 + a_2x_2 + a_3x_3 + a_4x_4 + a_5x_5 + a_6x_6 + \varepsilon \quad (28)$$

relating y and the six explanatory variables, is assumed. C_p, AIC and BIC choose the subset model

$$y = a_0 + a_1 x_1 + \varepsilon. \quad (29)$$

Notice that S_p and $S_{1;\alpha=0.05}$ give the very same result.

Example 10: Real-Estate Data

A real-estate agent wants to develop a model to predict the selling price of a home. The agent believes that the most important variables in determining the price of a house are its floor space, number of offices, number of entrances, and age of office building. Accordingly, he took a random sample of 11 homes (Table 9) that were recently sold and recorded the selling price (y, in thousands of dollars), the floor space (x_1, in square feet), the number of offices (x_2), the number of entrances (x_3), and the age of office building (x_4, in years).

The proposed multiple regression model is

$$y = a_0 + a_1 x_1 + a_2 x_2 + a_3 x_3 + a_4 x_4 + \varepsilon. \quad (30)$$

It will be noted that S_p and $S_{1;\alpha=0.01}$ choose the above model.

Example 11: Finished Product Quality Data

Many companies manufacture products (e.g., steel, paint, gasoline) that are at least partially chemically produced. In many instances, the quality of the finished product is a function of the temperature and pressure at which the chemical reactions take place. Suppose we want to model the quality y of a product as a function of the temperature x_1 and the pressure x_2 at which it is produced. Four inspectors independently assign a quality score between 0 and 100 to each product, and then the quality y is calculated by averaging the four scores. An experiment is conducted by varying temperature between 80° F and 100° F and pressure between 50 and 60 pounds per square inch (psi). The resulting data taken from (McClave et al., 1998, p. 601) are given in Table 10.

Considering the full model

$$y = a_0 + a_1 x_1 + a_2 x_2 + a_3 x_1 x_2 + \varepsilon \quad (31)$$

to investigate which subset model is more useful for predicting y, we find that S_p and $S_{1;\alpha=0.05}$ choose the subset model

Table 9. The real-estate data

y	x_1	x_2	x_3	x_4
142000	2310	2	2	20
144000	2333	2	2	12
151000	2356	3	1.5	33
150000	2379	3	2	43
139000	2402	2	3	53
169000	2425	4	2	23
126000	2448	2	1.5	99
142900	2471	2	2	34
163000	2494	3	3	23
169000	2517	4	4	55
149000	2540	2	3	22

$$y = a_0 + a_1 x_1 + \varepsilon. \quad (32)$$

CONCLUSION

Subset selection of informative variables in multiple linear regression and time series models is a problem of great practical importance. There are various methods for subset selection and various selection criteria. While there is no clear consensus regarding which method is the best and which criterion is the most appropriate, there is a general agreement an effective method is needed.

It will be noted that the most popular criteria for solving the problem of subset selection of informative variables in multiple linear regression and time series models (such as the Akaike information criterion (AIC) and the Bayesian information criterion (BIC) motivated from very different viewpoints) come from the closely related approach of cybernetics: information, control, feedback, communication. Cybernetics, deriving from the Greek word for steersman (*kybernetes*), was first introduced by the mathematician Wiener, as the science of communication and control in the animal and the machine (to which we now might add: in society and in individual human beings). It grew out of Shannon's information theory, which was designed to optimize the transmission of information through communication channels, and the feedback concept used in engineering control systems. In its present incarnation of "second-order cybernetics", its emphasis is on how observers construct models of the systems with which they interact.

AIC and BIC belong to the class of additive criteria. The criterion, which is proposed in this paper to solve the above problem, belongs to the class of multiplicative criteria. It represents a specific innovative modification of AIC and BIC.

Clearly, this paper does not put to rest the question about which is the best subset selection method. However, the proposed approach has certain advantages. First, it quickly produces a reasonable number of subsets having the desirable quality. Compared to the standard sequential procedures that come up with a single "best" model, the proposed approach provides the analyst with a set of "best" models lying on the efficient frontier. The analyst has the option of comparing these solutions with respect to his or her own experience in the specific context and also with respect to other statistical criteria. Thus, the proposed approach gives the analyst the flexibility to pick the best among the best.

Today, variable selection procedures are an integral part of virtually all widely used statistics packages, and their use will only increase as the information revolution brings us larger datasets

Table 10. The finished product quality data

x_1(°F)	x_2(psi)	y	x_1(°F)	x_2(psi)	y	x_1(°F)	x_2(psi)	y
80	50	50.8	90	50	63.4	100	50	46.6
80	50	50.7	90	50	61.6	100	50	49.1
80	50	49.4	90	50	63.4	100	50	46.4
80	55	93.7	90	55	93.8	100	55	69.8
80	55	90.9	90	55	92.1	100	55	72.5
80	55	90.9	90	55	97.4	100	55	73.2
80	60	74.5	90	60	70.9	100	60	38.7
80	60	73	90	60	68.8	100	60	42.5
80	60	71.2	90	60	71.3	100	60	41.4

with more and more variables. The demand for variable selection will be strong, and it will continue to be a basic strategy for data analysis.

ACKNOWLEDGMENT

This research was supported in part by Grant No. 06.1936, Grant No. 07.2036 and Grant No. 09.1014 from the Latvian Council of Science and the National Institute of Mathematics and Informatics of Latvia.

REFERENCES

Akaike, H. (1973). Information theory and an extension of the maximum likelihood principle. In B. N. Petrov, & F. Csaki (Eds.), *Proc. of the 2nd International Symposium on Information Theory* (pp. 267-281). Budapest: Akademia Kiado.

Benjamini, Y., & Hochberg, Y. (1995). Controlling the false discovery rate: A practical and powerful approach to multiple testing. *Journal of the Royal Statistical Society. Series B. Methodological*, *57*(3), 289–300.

Breiman, L. (1992). The little bootstrap and other methods for dimensionality selection in regression: X-fixed prediction error. *Journal of the American Statistical Association*, *87*(419), 738–754. doi:10.2307/2290212

Breiman, L. (1995). Better subset selection using the nonnegative garrote. *Technometrics*, *37*(3), 373–384. doi:10.2307/1269730

Chatterjee, S., & Hadi, A. S. (2006). *Regression Analysis by Example*, (4th ed.). Hoboken, NJ: John Wiley & Sons, Inc.

Clyde, M., & George, E. I. (1999). Empirical Bayes estimation in wavelet nonparametric regression. In P. Muller & B. Vidakovic (Eds.), *Bayesian Inference in Wavelet-Based Models* (pp. 309-322). New York: Springer-Verlag

Clyde, M., & George, E. I. (2000). Flexible empirical Bayes estimation for wavelets. *Journal of the Royal Statistical Society. Series B. Methodological*, *62*(4), 681–689. doi:10.1111/1467-9868.00257

Donoho, D. L., & Johnstone, I. M. (1994). Ideal spatial adaptation by wavelet shrinkage. *Biometrika*, *81*(4), 425–456. doi:10.1093/biomet/81.3.425

Draper, N. R., & Smith, H. H. (1981). *Applied regression analysis*, (2nd ed.). New York: Wiley.

Efron, B. (1983). Estimating the error rate of a predictive rule: Improvement over cross-validation. *Journal of the American Statistical Association*, *78*(382), 316–331. doi:10.2307/2288636

Efroymson, M. A. (1960). Multiple regression analysis. In A. Ralston, & H. S. Wilf (Eds.) *Mathematical Methods for Digital Computers* (pp. 191-203). New York: Wiley.

Foster, D. P., & George, E. I. (1994). The risk inflation criterion for multiple regression. *Annals of Statistics*, *22*(4), 1947–1975. doi:10.1214/aos/1176325766

Furnival, G. M., & Wilson, R. W. (1974). Regression by leaps and bounds. *Technometrics*, *16*(4), 499–511. doi:10.2307/1267601

Garthwaite, P. H., & Dickey, J. M. (1996). Quantifying and using expert opinion for variable-selection problems in regression (with discussion). *Chemometrics and Intelligent Laboratory Systems*, *35*(1), 1–34. doi:10.1016/S0169-7439(96)00035-4

George, E. I. (1999). Bayesian model selection. In S. Kotz, C. Read, & D. Banks (Eds.), *Encyclopedia of Statistical Sciences* (Vol. 3, pp. 39-46). New York: Wiley.

Gilmour, S. G. (1996). The interpretation of Mallows's C_p-statistic. *The Statistician, 45*(1), 49–56. doi:10.2307/2348411

Gong, G. (1986). Cross-validation, the jackknife, and the bootstrap: Excess error estimation in forward logistic regression. *Journal of the American Statistical Association, 81*(393), 108–113. doi:10.2307/2287975

Haughton, D. (1988). On the choice of a model to fit data from an exponential family. *Annals of Statistics, 16*(1), 342–355. doi:10.1214/aos/1176350709

Hocking, R. R. (1976). The analysis and selection of variables in linear regression. *Biometrics, 32*(1), 1–49. doi:10.2307/2529336

Hudson, D. J. (1964). *Statistics*. Geneva.

Hurvich, C. M., & Tsai, C. L. (1989). Regression and time series model selection in small samples. *Biometrika, 76*(2), 297–307. doi:10.1093/biomet/76.2.297

Hurvich, C. M., & Tsai, C. L. (1998). A cross-validatory AIC for hard wavelet thresholding in spatially adaptive function estimation. *Biometrika, 85*(3), 701–710. doi:10.1093/biomet/85.3.701

Johnstone, I. M., & Silverman, B. W. (1998). Empirical Bayes approaches to mixture problems and wavelet regression. Technical Report, University of Bristol, UK.

McClave, J. T., Benson, P. G., & Sincich, T. (1998). *Statistics for Business and Economics*, (7th ed.). Upper Saddle River, NJ: Prentice Hall.

Miller, A. J. (2002). *Subset selection in regression*, (2nd ed.). New York: Chapman & Hall/CRC.

Montgomery, D. C., & Peck, E. A. (1992). *Introduction to linear regression analysis*, (2nd ed.). New York: Wiley.

Moran, P. A. P. (1953). The statistical analysis of the Canadian lynx cycle, I: Structure and prediction. *Australian Journal of Zoology, 1*(2), 163–173. doi:10.1071/ZO9530163

Myers, R. L. (1992). *Classical and modern regression analysis*, (2nd ed.). New York: Wiley.

Narula, S. C., & Wellington, J. F. (1977). Prediction, linear regression and minimum sum of relative errors. *Technometrics, 19*(2), 185–190. doi:10.2307/1268628

Nechval, K. N., Berzins, G., Nechval, N. A., Purgailis, M., & Zolova, N. (2008a). Information criterion for variable selection in econometric models and its applications. In E. Kopytov, H. Pranevicius, E. Zavadskas, & I. Yatskiv (Eds.), *Proceedings of the International Conference on Modelling of Business, Industrial and Transport Systems* (pp. 24-32). Latvia, Riga: Transport and Telecommunication Institute.

Nechval, N. A., Berzinsh, G., Purgailis, M., & Nechval, K. N. (2008b). New variable selection criterion for econometric models. In R. Trappl (Ed.), *Cybernetics and Systems 2008* (Vol. I, pp. 64-69). Austria, Vienna: Austrian Society for Cybernetic Studies.

Nechval, N. A., Nechval, K. N., Purgailis, M., Rozevskis, U., Strelchonok, V., Moldovan, M., et al. (2009). Recognition of subsets of informative variables in regression. In V. Krasnoproshin, S. Ablameyko, & R. Sadykhov (Eds.), *Proceedings of the International Conference on Pattern Recognition and Information Processing* (pp. 371-376). Belarus, Minsk: University of Belarus.

Nechval, N. A., & Purgailis, M. (2008c). New variable selection criteria for econometric models and their applications. *Humanities and Social Sciences: Latvia, 57*(4), 6–26.

Newbold, P. (1995). *Statistics for Business & Economics*, (4th ed.). New Jersey: Prentice-Hall, Inc.

Rao, C. R., & Wu, Y. (1989). A strongly consistent procedure for model selection in a regression problem. *Biometrika*, *76*(2), 369–374. doi:10.1093/biomet/76.2.369

Rissanen, J. (1978). Modeling by shortest data description. *Automatica*, *14*(5), 465–471. doi:10.1016/0005-1098(78)90005-5

Schwarz, G. (1978). Estimating the dimension of a model. *Annals of Statistics*, *6*(2), 461–464. doi:10.1214/aos/1176344136

Shao, J. (1993). Linear model selection by cross-validation. *Journal of the American Statistical Association*, *88*(422), 486–494. doi:10.2307/2290328

Shao, J. (1997). An asymptotic theory for linear model selection. *Statistica Sinica*, *7*(3), 229–264.

Shibata, R. (1981). An optimal selection of regression variables. *Biometrika*, *68*(1), 45–54. doi:10.1093/biomet/68.1.45

Stone, M. (1977). An asymptotic equivalence of choice of model by cross-validation and Akaike's criterion. *Journal of the Royal Statistical Society. Series B. Methodological*, *39*(1), 44–47.

Stone, M. (1979). Comments on model selection criteria of Akaike and Schwarz. *Journal of the Royal Statistical Society. Series B. Methodological*, *41*(3), 276–278.

Thompson, M. L. (1978). Selection of variables in multiple regression: Part I. A review and evaluation. *International Statistical Review*, *46*(1), 1–19. doi:10.2307/1402505

Tibshirani, R. (1996). Regression shrinkage and selection via the lasso. *Journal of the Royal Statistical Society. Series B. Methodological*, *58*(2), 267–288.

Tibshirani, R., & Knight, K. (1999). The covariance inflation criterion for model selection. *Journal of the Royal Statistical Society. Series B. Methodological*, *61*(3), 529–546. doi:10.1111/1467-9868.00191

Tong, H. (1990). *Non-linear time series: A dynamical system approach*. Oxford: University Press.

Wei, C. Z. (1992). On predictive least squares principles. *Annals of Statistics*, *20*(1), 1–42. doi:10.1214/aos/1176348511

Ye, J. (1998). On measuring and correcting the effects of data mining and model selection. *Journal of the American Statistical Association*, *93*(441), 120–131. doi:10.2307/2669609

Zhang, P. (1992). Inference after variable selection in linear regression models. *Biometrika*, *79*(4), 741–746. doi:10.1093/biomet/79.4.741

Zheng, X., & Loh, W. Y. (1997). A consistent variable selection criterion for linear models with high-dimensional covariates. *Statistica Sinica*, *7*(3), 311–325.

KEY TERMS AND DEFINITIONS

AIC: The Akaike information criterion for selection of variables

BIC: The Bayesian information criterion for selection of variables

C_p: The Mallows criterion for selection of variables

$S_{\varphi(p)}$: The multiplicative criterion of parametrically penalized residual sum of squares

$S_{\varphi(p)}$);α: The multiplicative criterion of parametrically penalized residual sum of squares, which takes into account only stable subset models.

Variable Selection: Selecting input variables that are most predictive of a given outcome

Compilation of References

Adrot, O., Shahriari, K., & Flaus, J. M. (2004). Estimation of bounded model uncertainties. In *11th IFAC Symposium on Automation in Mining and Metal Processing*, Nancy, France.

Akaike, H. (1973). Information theory and an extension of the maximum likelihood principle. In B. N. Petrov, & F. Csaki (Eds.), *Proc. of the 2nd International Symposium on Information Theory* (pp. 267-281). Budapest: Akademia Kiado.

Albrow, M. (1997). *The global age.* Stanford, CA: Stanford University Press.

Amen, D. G. (2005). *Making a good brain great.* New York: Harmony Books.

American Heritage Dictionary 4th Ed. (2006). Boston: Houghton Mifflin Co.

Amsden, R. T., Ferratt, T. W., & Amsden, D. M. (1996). TQM: Core paradigm changes. *Business Horizons, 39*(6), 6–14. doi:10.1016/S0007-6813(96)90031-2

Anderson, J. R. (1993). *Rules of the mind.* Hillsdale, NJ: Erlbaum.

Anonymous. (n.d.). Appeared in numerous emails to authors and is available on dozens of Internet sites. Retrieved April 5, 2009, from http://www.gamedev.net/community/forums/topic.asp?topic_id=375056

Appelbaum, R. P. (1970). *Theories of Social Change.* Chicago: Markham.

Argyris, C. (1990). *Overcoming organizational defenses: Facilitating organizational learning.* Boston: Allyn and Bacon.

Argyris, C. (1993). *Knowledge for action: A guide to overcoming barriers to organizational change.* San Francisco: Jossey-Bass.

Argyris, C. (2005). Double-loop learning in organizations: A theory of action perspective. In K. G. Smith & M. A. Hitt (Eds.), *Great Minds in Management: The Process of Theory Development* (pp. 261-279). New York: Oxford University Press.

Arievitch, I. (2003). A potential for an integrated view of development and learning: Galperin's contribution to sociocultural psychology. *Mind, Culture, and Activity. International Journal (Toronto, Ont.), 10*(4), 178–288.

Armengol, J. (1999). *Application of Modal Interval Analysis to the simulation of the behaviour of dynamic systems with uncertain parameters*, PhD thesis, Universitat de Girona.

Arthur, W. (2002). The emerging conceptual framework of evolutionary developmental biology. *Nature, 415*, 757–764.

Ashby, R. (1960). *Design for a brain: The origin of adaptive behaviour.* New York: John Wiley.

Ashby, W. R. (1956). *An introduction into cybernetics.* New York: Wiley.

Ashby, W. R. (2004). Principles of the self-organizing system. *Emergence: Complexity and Organization, 6*(1-2), 103–126.

Atwater, L. E., & Wright, W. J. (1996). Power and transformational and transactional leadership in public and private organizations. [Article]. *Interna-*

tional Journal of Public Administration, 19(6), 963–989. doi:10.1080/01900699608525127

Augros, R., & Stanciu, G. (1987). *The new biology: Discovering the wisdom in nature.* Boston, MA: Shambhala.

Austin, J., Stevenson, H., & Wei-Skillern, J. (2006). Social and commercial entrepreneurship: Same, different, or both? *Entrepreneurship Theory and Practice, 30*(1), 1–22. doi:10.1111/j.1540-6520.2006.00107.x

Auyang, S. Y. (1998). *Foundations of complex-system theories in economics, evolutionary biology, and statistical physics.* New York, NY: Cambridge University Press.

Aveleira, A. (2004, Oct). Consciousness and reality: A stable-dynamic model based on Jungian psychology. *Metareligion.* Retrieved December, 2005 from http://www.meta-religion.com/Psychiatry/Analytical_psychology/consciousness_and_reality.htm

Avgouleas, E. (2009). (forthcoming). The Global Credit Crisis, Behavioural Finance, and Financial Regulation, In Search of a New Orthodoxy. *Journal of Corporate Law Studies, 9*(1).

Axelrod, R. (1997). *The Complexity of Cooperation. Agent-Based Models of Competition and Cooperation.* Princeton, NJ: Princeton University Press.

Babaali, M., & Egerstedt, M. (2005). Asymptotic observers for discrete-time switched linear systems. In *Proceedings of 16th IFAC World Congress,* Prague, Czech Republic.

Bacharach, S. B. (1989). Organizational theories: Some criteria for evaluation. *Academy of Management Review, 14*(4), 496–515. doi:10.2307/258555

Badouel, E., Caillaud, B., & Darondeau, P. (2002). Distributing Finite Automata Through Petri Net Synthesis. *Formal Aspects of Computing, 13,* 447–470. doi:10.1007/s001650200022

Bakken, T., & Hernes, T. (2006). Organizing is Both a Verb and a Noun: Weick Meets Whitehead. *Organization Studies, 27*(11), 1599–1616. doi:10.1177/0170840606068335

Bale, L. S. (1995). Gregory Bateson, Cybernetics, and the Social/Behavioral Sciences. *Cybernetics & Human Knowing, 3*(1), 27–455.

Balluchi, A., Benvenuti, L., Di Benedetto, M. D., & Sangiovanni Vincentelli, A. L. (2001). A hybrid observer for the driveline dynamics. In *Proceedings of the European Control Conference,* Porto, Portugal.

Barker, A., Nancarrow, C., & Spackman, N. (2001). Informed eclecticism: A research paradigm for the twenty-first century. *International Journal of Market Research, 43*(1), 3.

Bartlett, J. (1992). *Familiar Quotations: A Collection of Passages, Phrases, and Proverbs Traced to their Sources in Ancient and Modern Literature* (16 ed.). Toronto: Little, Brown.

Bartunek, J. M. (1988). The dynamics of personal and organizational reframing. In R. E. Quinn & K. S. Cameron (Eds.), *Paradox and transformation* (pp. 137-162). Cambridge, MA: Ballinger.

Bateson, G. (1967). Cybernetic explanation. *The American Behavioral Scientist, 10*(8), 29–32.

Bateson, G. (1979). *Mind in Nature: A Necessary Unity.* New York: Dutton.

Beaudouin-Lafon, M. (2000). Instrumental interaction: An interaction model for designing post-WIMP user interfaces. In *Proceedings of the 2000 ACM Conference on Human Factors in Computing Systems,* The Hague, Netherlands, (pp. 446-453).

Beer, S. (1959). *Cybernetics and management.* London: English University Press.

Beer, S. (1975). *Platform for change.* Chichester, UK: John Wiley & Sons Ltd.

Beer, S. (1979). *The heart of enterprise.* Chichester, UK: Wiley.

Beer, S. (1985). *Diagnosing the system.* Chichester, UK: Wiley.

Begley, S. (2007). *Train your mind change your brain: How a new science reveals our extraordinary potential to transform ourselves*. New York, NY: Ballantine Books.

Behe, M. (1996). *Darwin's black box*. New York: The Free Press.

Benjamini, Y., & Hochberg, Y. (1995). Controlling the false discovery rate: A practical and powerful approach to multiple testing. *Journal of the Royal Statistical Society. Series B. Methodological, 57*(3), 289–300.

Bennet D. & Bennet, A. (2008c). The depth of KNOWLEDGE: Surface, shallow and Deep. *VINE: The journal of information and knowledge management systems, 38*(4/December).

Bennet, A. & Bennet, D. (2006). Learning as associative patterning. *VINE: The journal of information and knowledge management systems, 36* (4).

Bennet, A., & Bennet, D. (2004). *Organizational survival in the new world: The intelligent complex adaptive system*. New York, NY: Elsevier.

Bennet, A., & Bennet, D. (2007). *Knowledge mobilization in the social sciences and humanities*. Marlinton, WV: MQI Press.

Bennet, A., & Bennet, D. (2008a). The decision-making process for complex situations in a complex environment. In F. Burstein & C.W. Holsapple, (Eds), *Handbook on decision support systems*. New York, NY: Springer-Verlag.

Bennet, D. & Bennet, A. (2008b). Engaging tacit knowledge in support of organizational learning. *VINE: The journal of information and knowledge systems, 38* (1).

Bennet, D. (2006). Expanding the knowledge paradigm. *VINE: The journal of information and knowledge management systems, 36* (2).

Bennet, D., & Bennet, A. (2009), Associative patterning: The unconscious life of an organization. In J.P. Girard, (Ed.), *Building organizational memories*. Hershey, PA: IGI Global.

Bennis, W. (2000). Leadership of change. In M. Beer & N. Nohria (Eds.), *Breaking the Code of Change* (pp. 113-121). Boston, Mass.: Harvard Business School Press.

Benson, J. K. (1977). Organizations: A dialectical view. *Administrative Science Quarterly, 22*(1), 1–21. doi:10.2307/2391741

Bereiter, C. (2003). Artifacts, canons, and the progress of pedagogy: A response to contributors. In B. Smith (Ed.), *Liberal education in a knowledge society,* (pp. 223-244). Chicago: Open Court.

Berkes, F. (2003). Alternatives to conventional management: Lessons from small-scale fisheries. *Environments, 3*(1).

Bernier, L., & Hafsi, T. (2007). The changing nature of public entrepreneurship. *Public Administration Review, 67*(3), 488–503. doi:10.1111/j.1540-6210.2007.00731.x

Bertalanffy, L. V. (1951). General systems theory: A new approach to the unity of Science. *Human Biology, 23*(Dec), 302–361.

Bilke, S., & Sjunnesson, F. (2002). Stability of the Kauffman model. *Physical Review E: Statistical, Nonlinear, and Soft Matter Physics, 65*, 016129. doi:10.1103/PhysRevE.65.016129

Bloomfield, B. P., & Coombs, R. (1992). Information technology, control, and power: The centralization debate revisited. *Journal of Management Studies, 29*, 459–484. doi:10.1111/j.1467-6486.1992.tb00674.x

Bødker, S. (1991). *Through the Interface: A Human Activity Approach to User Interface Design*. Hillsdale, NJ: Lawrence Erlbaum.

Bødker, S., & Andersen, P. B. (2005). Complex mediation. *Human-Computer Interaction, 20*, 353–452. doi:10.1207/s15327051hci2004_1

Boudon, R. (1986). *Theories of Social Change* (J. C. Whitehouse, Trans.). Cambridge, UK: Polity Press.

Boutellier, R., Baumbach, M. & Bodmer, C. (1999). Successful-practices in after-sales-management. *io Management, 68*(1/2), 23-27.

Bradbury, H., & Lichtenstein, B. M. B. (2000). Relationality in organizational research: Exploring The Space Between. *Organization Science, 11*(5), 551. doi:10.1287/orsc.11.5.551.15203

Bradley, D. M. (2007). Verhulst's logistic curve. In *Proceedings of the National Academy of Sciences (PNAS)*, (pp. 1-5). Retrieved October 22, 2008, from http://arxiv.org/PS_cache/arxiv/pdf/0706/0706.3163v1.pdf

Brandenburger, A. M., & Nalebuff, B. J. (1997). *Co-Opetition. 1. A revolutionary mindset that combines competition and cooperation. 2. The Game Theory strategy that's changing the game of business*. New York: Doubleday.

Braverman, H. (1974). *Labor and monopoly capital: The degradation of work in the twentieth century*. New York: Monthly Review Press.

Breiman, L. (1992). The little bootstrap and other methods for dimensionality selection in regression: X-fixed prediction error. *Journal of the American Statistical Association, 87*(419), 738–754. doi:10.2307/2290212

Breiman, L. (1995). Better subset selection using the nonnegative garrote. *Technometrics, 37*(3), 373–384. doi:10.2307/1269730

Brennan, R., & Ankers, P. (2004). In search of relevance: Is there an academic-practitioner divide in business-to-business marketing? *Marketing Intelligence & Planning, 22*(5), 511–519. doi:10.1108/02634500410551897

Briggs Myers, I. (2000). *Introduction to types: A guide to understanding your results on the Myers-Briggs Type Indicator*. Oxford, UK: CPP Ltd.

Bronfenbrenner, U. (1970). *Two Worlds of Childhood: U.S. and U.S.S.R.* Russell Sage Foundation.

Brown, T. L. (2003). *Making truth: Metaphor in science*. Chicago, IL: University of Illinois Press.

Brueck, T., Riddle, R., & Paralez, L. (2003). *Consortium benchmarking methodology guide*. Denver, CO: AWWA Research Foundation.

Bruner, J. (1987). Prologue in R. W. Rieber & A. S. Carton (Eds.), *The Collected Works of L.S. Vygotsky*, (Vol. 1, Problems of general psychology, pp. 1-16). New York: Plenum.

Buber, M. (1958). *I and Thou* (2d ed.). New York: Scribner.

Bubna-Litic, D. (2008). *Neophilia: A Consuming Passion Or Fabrication*. Paper presented at the ACSCOS 2008: The 3rd Australasian Caucus of the Standing Conference on Organizational Symbolism, Sydney.

Buchanan, M. (2004). Power laws and the new science of complexity management. *Strategy + Business, 34*(Spring), 70-79.

Burnes, B., Cooper, C., & West, P. (2003). Organisational learning: The new management paradigm? *Management Decision, 41*(5/6), 452. doi:10.1108/00251740310479304

Burrell, G. (1997). *Pandemonium: Towards a Retro-Organizational Theory*. Thousand Oaks, CA: Sage.

Burrell, G., & Morgan, G. (1979). *Sociological paradigms and organizational analysis*. Portsmouth, NH: Heinemann.

Butts, R., & Brown, J. (Eds.). (1989). *Constructivism and Science*. Dordrecht, Holland: Kluwer.

Byrnes, J. P. (2001). *Minds, brains, and learning: Understanding the psychological and education relevance of neuroscientific research*. New York, NY: The Guilford Press.

Calas, M., & Smircich, L. (2003). Introduction: Spirituality, management and organization. *Organization, 10*(2), 327. doi:10.1177/1350508403010002008

Calm, R., Sainz, M. A., Herrero, P., Vehi, J., & Armengol, J. (2006). Parameter identification with quantifiers. In *5th IFAC Symposium on Robust Control Design*, Toulouse, France.

Camp, R. C. (1989). *Benchmarking: The search for industry best practices that lead to superior performance*. Milwaukee, WI: Quality Press.

Campbell, D. T. (1960). Blind variation and selective retention in creative thought as in other knowledge processes. *Psychological Review, 67*(6), 380–400. doi:10.1037/h0040373

Campbell, D. T. (1983). Science's social system and the problems of the social sciences. In D. W. Fiske & R. A. Shweder (Eds.), *Metatheory in Social Science: Pluralism and Subjectivities* (pp. 108-135). Chicago: University of Chicago Press.

Čapkovič, F. (2003). The generalised method for solving problems of DEDS control synthesis. In P. W. H. Chung, C. Hinde & M. Ali (Eds.), *Developments in Applied Artificial Intelligence, Lecture Notes in Artificial Intelligence*, (Vol. 2718, pp. 702-711). Berlin: Springer.

Čapkovič, F. (2005). An Application of the DEDS Control Synthesis Method. *Journal of Universal Computer Science, 11*(2), 303–326.

Čapkovič, F. (2007). DES Modelling and Control vs. Problem Solving Methods. *International Journal of Intelligent Information and Database Systems, 1*(1), 53–78. doi:10.1504/IJIIDS.2007.013285

Čapkovič, F. (2007a). Modelling, analysing and control of interactions among agents in MAS. *Computing and Informatics, 26*(5), 507–541.

Čapkovič, F. (2008). A system approach to describing and analysing the behaviour of agents in MAS. In R. Trappl (Ed.), *Cybernetics and Systems 2008, Proceedings of the 19th European Meeting on Cybernetics and Systems Research, Vol. 1, Vienna, Austria, March 25-28, 2008* (pp. 70-75). Vienna, Austria: Austrian Society for Cybernetics Studies.

Capra, F. (1996). *The web of life: A new scientific understanding of living systems.* New York: Anchor Books Doubleday.

Castrodeza, C. (1978). Evolution, complexity, and fitness. *Journal of Theoretical Biology, 71*, 469–471. doi:10.1016/0022-5193(78)90174-1

Cavanagh, J., & Mander, J. (2002). Fixing the Rotten Corporate Barrel. *Nation*, pp. 22-24, from http://search.ebscohost.com/login.aspx?direct=true&db=aph&AN=8649666&site=ehost-live

Chapman, J. A. (2002). A framework for transformational change in organisations. *Leadership and Organization Development Journal, 23*(1/2), 16–25. doi:10.1108/01437730210414535

Charlton, B. G., & Andras, P. (2003). What is management and what do managers do? A systems theory account. *Philosophy of Management, 3*, 1–15.

Chatterjee, S., & Hadi, A. S. (2006). *Regression Analysis by Example*, (4th ed.). Hoboken, NJ: John Wiley & Sons, Inc.

Checkland, P. (1981). *Systems thinking, systems practice.* New York: Wiley.

Checkland, P., & Scholes, J. (1990). *Soft Systems Methodology in Action.* New York: Wiley.

Cheng, T., Sculli, D., & Chan, F. (2001). Relationship dominance - Rethinking management theories from the perspective of methodological relationalism. *Journal of Managerial Psychology, 16*(2), 97. doi:10.1108/02683940110380933

Chia, R. (1995). From modern to postmodern organizational analysis. *Organization Studies, 16*(4), 580. doi:10.1177/017084069501600406

Chia, R. (1999). A "Rhizomic" model of organizational change and transformation: Perspectives from a metaphysics of change. *British Journal of Management, 10*(3), 209. doi:10.1111/1467-8551.00128

Chittaro, L., & Serra, M. (2004). Behavioral programming of autonomous characters based on probabilistic automata and personality. *Journal of Computer Animation and Virtual Worlds, 15*(3/4), 319–326. doi:10.1002/cav.35

Choudhury, M. L., Zaman, S. I., & Nasar, Y. (2007). A knowledge-induced operator model,. *The Journal of Science, 12*(part 1, December).

Christiansen, E. (1996). Tamed by a rose: Computers as tools in human interaction. In B. Nardi (Ed.), *Context and Consciousness: Activity Theory and Human-Computer Interaction*, (pp. 175-198). Cambridge, MA: MIT Press.

Christos, G. (2003). *Memory and dreams: The creative human mind.* New Brunswick, NY: Rutgers University Press.

Church, D. (2006). *The genie in your genes: Epigenetic medicine and the new biology of intention.* Santa Rosa, CA: Elite Books.

Ciborra, C. C., Patriotta, G., & Erlicher, L. (1995). Disassembling frames on the assembly line. In W.J. Orlinkowski, G. Walsham, M. R. Jones, J. I. DeGross (Eds.) *Information Technology and Changes in Work* (pp. 397-418). New York: Chapman and Hall.

Cilliers, P. (1998). *Complexity and postmodernism: Understanding complex systems.* New York: Routledge.

Cilliers, P. (2005). Knowing complex systems. In K. A. Richardson (Ed.), *Managing organizational complexity: Philosophy, theory, and application* (pp. 7-19). Greenwich, CT: Information Age Publishing.

Clark, H. H. (1992). *Arenas of Language Use.* Chicago: University of Chicago Press.

Clarke, T. (2005). Accounting for Enron: shareholder value and stakeholder interests. *Corporate Governance: An International Review, 13*(5), 598–612. doi:10.1111/j.1467-8683.2005.00454.x

Clarke, T., & Clegg, S. (2000). Management Paradigms for the New Millennium. *International Journal of Management Reviews, 2*(1), 45–64. doi:10.1111/1468-2370.00030

Clarke-Hill, C., Li, H., & Davies, B. (2003). The paradox of co-operation and competition in strategic alliances: Towards a multi-paradigm approach. *Management Research News, 26*(1), 1. doi:10.1108/01409170310783376

Clegg, S. R., Cunha, J. V. d., & Cunha, M. P. e. (2002). Management paradoxes: A relational view. *Human Relations, 55*(5), 483.

Clemson, B. (1984). *Cybernetics: A new management tool.* Tunbridge Wells, UK: Abacus

Cleveland, H. (2002). *Nobody in charge: Essays on the future of leadership.* San Francisco, CA: Jossey-Bass.

Clyde, M., & George, E. I. (1999). Empirical Bayes estimation in wavelet nonparametric regression. In P. Muller & B. Vidakovic (Eds.), *Bayesian Inference in Wavelet-Based Models* (pp. 309-322). New York: Springer-Verlag

Clyde, M., & George, E. I. (2000). Flexible empirical Bayes estimation for wavelets. *Journal of the Royal Statistical Society. Series B. Methodological, 62*(4), 681–689. doi:10.1111/1467-9868.00257

Cocchiarella, N. (1991). Formal ontology, handbook of metaphysics and ontology. In B. Smith, H. Burkhardt, (Eds.), *Philosophia.* Munich, Germany: Verlag.

Cockburn, C. (1983). *Brothers.* London: Pluto Press. [Case: British Printers]

Cohen, J. (2002). *Posting to the Complex-M listserv*, 2nd September.

Cohen, J., & Stewart, I. (1994). *The collapse of chaos: Discovering simplicity in a complex world.* London: Viking.

Colclough, C., & Tolbert, C. M., III. (1992). *Work in the fast lane: Flexibility, divisions of labor, and inequality in high-tech industries.* Albany, NY: State University of New York Press.

Cole Wright, J. L. (2005). *The Role of reasoning and intuition in moral judgment: A Review.* Paper submitted as part of the doctoral studies comprehensive exam, Department of Psychology, University of Wyoming. Retrieved July 2008 from http://uwstudentfpweb.uwyo.edu/n/narvik/psychology/The%20Role%20of%20Reasoning%20and%20Intuition%20in%20Moral%20Judgments,%20Submitted%20Draft.doc

Collinson, D. L. (1992). *Managing the shopfloor: Subjectivity, masculinity and workplace culture.* New York: de Gruyter.

Colomy, P. (1991). Metatheorizing in a Postpositivist Frame. *Sociological Perspectives, 34*(3), 269–286.

Conger, J. A. (2000). Effective change begins at the top. In M. Beer & N. Nohria (Eds.), *Breaking the Code of Change* (pp. 99-112). Boston, Mass.: Harvard Business School Press.

Cooper, R. (2005). Peripheral Vision: Relationality. *Organization Studies, 26*(11), 1689–1710. doi:10.1177/0170840605056398

Cory, D. (1942). The transition from naïve to critical realism. *The Journal of Philosophy, 39*(10), 261–268. doi:10.2307/2017517

Cumming, J. F., Bettridge, N., & Toyne, P. (2005). Responding to global business critical issues: A source of innovation and transformation for FTSE 350 companies? *Corporate Governance, 5*(3), 42. doi:10.1108/14720700510604689

Cunningham, I. (1990). Openness and learning to learn. In O. Boyd-Barret, E. Scanlon, (Eds.) *Computers and learning*. London: Addison Wesley.

Curry, A., & Hodgson, A. (2008). Seeing in multiple horizons: Connecting futures to strategy. *Journal Future Studies, 13*(1), 1–20.

Czarniawska, B. (2001). Is it possible to be a constructionist consultant? *Management Learning, 32*(2), 353–266. doi:10.1177/1350507601322006

Daly, H. E. (1996). *Beyond Growth: The Economics of Sustainable Development*. Boston: Beacon Press.

Damasio, A. (2007). How the brain creates the mind. In Bloom, F.E. (Ed.), *Best of the brain from Scientific American: Mind, matter, and tomorrow's brain* (pp. 58-67). New York: Dana Press.

Daneke, G. A. (1999). *Systemic Choices: Nonlinear Dynamics and Practical Management*. Ann Arbor, MI: The University of Michigan Press.

David, E. (2009). *The rockets scientists of finance*. Retrieved April 29, 2009, from http://news.bbc.co.uk/2/hi/business/7826431.stm

Davis, A. S., Maranville, S. J., & Obloj, K. (1997). The paradoxical process of organizational transformation. *Research in Organizational Change and Development, 10*, 275–314.

Davis, G. B., & Olson, M. H. (1984). *Management information systems: Conceptual foundations, structure, and development*. New York: McGraw-Hill.

Davis, J. P., Eisenhardt, K. M., & Bingham, C. B. (2007). Developing theory through simulation methods. *Academy of Management Review, 32*(2), 480–499.

Davis, L. E., & Taylor, J. C. (1976). Technology, organization and job structure. In R. Dubin (Ed.), *Handbook of work, organization, and society* (pp. 379-419). Chicago: Rand McNally.

de Geus, A. (1988). Planning as learning. *Harvard Business Review*, March-April.

de Geus, A., & Scharmer, C. (1999). *Every institution is a living system*. Retrieved December 31, 2008, from http://www.management.com.ua/cm/cm015.html de Geus, A. (2007). Learning together for good decision making. *Reflections, 8*(1), 28 -35.

de Leeuw, E. (1999). Healthy cities: Urban social entrepreneurship for health. *Health Promotion International, 14*(3), 261–269. doi:10.1093/heapro/14.3.261

Dean, J. W. Jr, Yoon, S. J., & Susman, G. I. (1992). Advanced manufacturing technology and organization structure: Empowerment or subordination? *Organization Science, 3*(2), 203–229. doi:10.1287/orsc.3.2.203

DeBresson, C., & Amesse, F. (1991). Networks of innovators: A review and introduction to the issue. *Research Policy, 20*, 363–379. doi:10.1016/0048-7333(91)90063-V

December 31, 2008, from http://www.richardjung.cz/bert2.pdf.

December 31, 2008, from http://www.strategydynamics.com/products/oilprod.asp

Deetz, S. (1996). Describing differences in approaches to organization science: Rethinking Burrell and Morgan and their legacy. *Organization Science, 7*(2), 191–207. doi:10.1287/orsc.7.2.191

Dei Ottati, G. (1994). Co-operation and Competition in the Industrial Districts as an Organizational Model. *European Planning Studies, 4*(3), 463–483. doi:10.1080/09654319408720281

Dekkers. (2008). Adapting organizations: The instance of Business process re-engineering. *Systems Research and Behavioral Science, 25*(1).

Demazeau, Y. (2003) Y. MAS methodology. *Tutorial at the 2nd French-Mexican School of the Repartee Co-*

operative Systems - ESRC 2003, Sept. 29-Oct. 4, 2003. Rennes, France: IRISA.

Dembski, W. A., & Ruse, M. (Eds.). (2004). *Debating design. From Darwin to DNA*. Cambridge: Cambridge University Press.

Demetriou, A., Doise, W., & Van Lieshout, C. F. M. (1998). *Life-span developmental psychology*. New York: John Wiley & Son.

Dewey, J. (1952/1989). Modern Philosophy. In J. A. Boydston (Ed.). *John Dewey: The Later Works*, (Vol. 16, pp. 407-419). Carbondale: Southern Illinois University Press.

Diamond, J. (2005). *Collapse: How societies choose to fail or succeed.* New York: Viking.

Dice, L. R. (1962). *Natural communities.* Ann Arbor, MI: University of Michigan Press.

Dolan, C. (2007). *Feasability Study: The Evaluation and Benchmarking of Humanities Research in Europe*. Arts and Humanities research Council.

Domlan, E. A. (2006). *Diagnostic des Systmes Chamgement de Regime de Fonctionnement*, PhD thesis, Institut National Polythechnique de Lorraine.

Donaldson, L. (1995). American anti-management theories of organization: A critique of paradigm proliferation. *Cambridge Studies in Management, 25*. Cambridge, UK: Cambridge University Press.

Donaldson, L. (2001). *The contingency theory of organizations*. Thousand Oaks, CA: Sage.

Donoho, D. L., & Johnstone, I. M. (1994). Ideal spatial adaptation by wavelet shrinkage. *Biometrika*, *81*(4), 425–456. doi:10.1093/biomet/81.3.425

Draper, N. R., & Smith, H. H. (1981). *Applied regression analysis*, (2nd ed.). New York: Wiley.

Dubin, R. (1978). *Theory Building* (Rev. Ed.). New York: The Free Press.

Ducheneaut, N., & Bellotti, V. (2001). E-mail as habitat: An exploration of embedded personal information management. *Interaction*, *8*, 30–38. doi:10.1145/382899.383305

Dunphy, D., Griffiths, A., & Ben, S. (2003). *Organisational Change for Corporate Sustainability: A Guide for Leaders and Change Agents of the Future*. London: Routledge.

Durning, A. T. (1992). *How much is enough?* New York: Norton.

Duverger, M. (1972). *The Study of Politics.* London: Nelson.

Edelman, G., & Tononi, G. (2000). *A universe of consciousness: How matter become imagination.* New York: Basic Books.

Edwards, M. G. (2008). Where's the Method to Our Integral Madness? An Outline of an Integral Meta-Studies. *Journal of Integral Theory and Practice*, *3*(2), 165–194.

Edwards, M. G. (2010). *Organizational Transformation for Sustainability: An Integral Metatheory.* New York: Routledge.

Edwards, M., & Volkmann, R. (2008). *Integral Theory into Integral Action: Part 8.* Retrieved 11/03/08, 2008, from http://www.integralleadershipreview.com/archives/2008-01/2008-01-edwards-volckmann-part8.html

Efron, B. (1983). Estimating the error rate of a predictive rule: Improvement over cross-validation. *Journal of the American Statistical Association*, *78*(382), 316–331. doi:10.2307/2288636

Efroymson, M. A. (1960). Multiple regression analysis. In A. Ralston, & H. S. Wilf (Eds.) *Mathematical Methods for Digital Computers* (pp. 191-203). New York: Wiley.

Eisenhardt, K. M. (1989). Building theories from case study research. *Academy of Management Review*, *14*, 535–550.

Eisenhardt, K. M. (1991). Better stories and better constructs: The case for rigor and comparative logic. *Academy of Management Review*, *16*(3), 620–627. doi:10.2307/258921

Eisenhardt, K. M., & Graebner, M. E. (2007). Theory building from cases: Opportunities and challenges. *Academy of Management Journal, 50*(1), 25–32.

Elrod, P. D., & Tippett, D. D. (2002). The "death valley" of change. *Journal of Organizational Change Management, 15*(3), 273. doi:10.1108/09534810210429309

Emery, F. E. (Ed.). (1969). *Systems Thinking: Selected Readings.* New York: Penguin.

Engeström, Y. (1987). *Learning by Expanding: An Activity-Theoretical Approach to Developmental Research.* Helsinki, Finland: Orienta-Consultit.

Engeström, Y. (1999). Introduction. In Y. Engeström, R. Miettinen, & R-L. Punamäki (Eds.), *Perspectives on Activity Theory,* (pp. 1-16). Cambridge, UK: Cambridge University Press.

Engeström, Y. (2007). Enriching the theory of expansive learning: Lessons from journeys towards coconfiguration. *Mind, Culture, and Activity. International Journal (Toronto, Ont.), 14*(1), 23–39.

Epstein, M. J., & Hanson, K. O. (2006). *The Accountable Corporation*: Westport, Conn.: Praeger Publishers.

Espejo, R. (1996). *Organizational transformation and learning: A cybernetic approach to management.* Chichester, UK: Wiley.

Eysenck, H. J. (1957). *Fact and fiction in psychology.* Middlesex, UK: Pelican.

Fahrni, F., Völker, R., & Bodmer, C. (2002). *Erfolgreiches Benchmarking in Forschung und Entwicklung, Beschaffung und Logistik* [Successful benchmarking in research and development, purchasing and logistics]. München, Germany: Hanser.

Fairhurst, G. T., Green, S., & Courtright, J. (1995). Inertia forces and the implementation of a socio-technical systems approach: A communication study. *Organization Science, 6*(2), 168–180. doi:10.1287/orsc.6.2.168

Felde, J. (2004). *Supplier collaboration: An empirical analysis of Swiss OEM-supplier relationships.* Bamberg, Germany: Difo-Druck.

Ferguson-Smith, A. C., Greally, J. M., & Martienssen, R. A. (Eds.). (2009). *Epigenomics.* New York: Springer.

Fink, G. (2008, June). *Collective cultural shock, cultural stretch and hybridization.* Paper presented at IACCM conference, Management of Meaning in Organizations, Poznań, Poland.

Fiol, C. M. (2002). Capitalizing on paradox: The role of language in transforming organizational identities. *Organization Science, 13*(6), 653. doi:10.1287/orsc.13.6.653.502

Fisher, D., Rooke, D., & Torbert, B. (2003). *Personal and Organizational Transformations: Through Action Inquiry* (4th ed.). Boston: Edge\Work Press.

Fiske, D. W., & Shweder, R. A. (Eds.). (1986). *Metatheory in Social Science: Pluralisms and Subjectivities.* Chicago: University of Chicago Press.

Fitzgerald, R., & Findlay, J. (2004). A computer-based research tool for rapid knowledge-creation. In L. Cantoni & C. McLoughlin (Eds.), *Proceedings of World Conference on Educational Multimedia Hypermedia and Telecommunications,* (EDMEDIA) in Lugano, Switzerland. Chesapeake, VA: AACE.

Flood, R. L., & Carson, E. (1988). *Dealing with Complexity: An Introduction to the Theory and Application of Systems Science.* New York: Kluwer.

Flood, R. L., & Jackson, M. C. (Eds.). (1991). *Critical Systems Thinking: Directed readings.* Chichester, UK: Wiley.

Fonseca, S., Griss, M., & Letsinger, R. (2001). *Agent Behavior Architectures - A MAS Framework Comparison* (HP Labs Technical Report HPL-2001-332). Palo Alto, CA: HP.

Fontrodona, J., & Sison, A. J. G. (2006). The Nature of the Firm, Agency Theory and Shareholder Theory: A Critique from Philosophical Anthropology. *Journal of Business Ethics, 66*(1), 33. doi:10.1007/s10551-006-9052-2

Foot, K. (2002). Pursuing an evolving object: a case study in object formation and identification. *Mind, Culture, and Activity, 9*(2), 132–149. doi:10.1207/S15327884MCA0902_04

Forster, N. (2005). *Maximum Performance: A Practical Guide to Leading and Managing People at Work.* Cheltenham, UK: Edward Elgar.

Foster, D. P., & George, E. I. (1994). The risk inflation criterion for multiple regression. *Annals of Statistics, 22*(4), 1947–1975. doi:10.1214/aos/1176325766

Foucault, M. (1993). *Diskursens ordning.* (L'ordre de discourse). Stockholm/Steghag: Symposion.

Fowler, A. (2000). NGDOS as a moment in history: Beyond aid to social entrepreneurship or civic innovation? *Third World Quarterly, 21*(4), 637–654. doi:10.1080/713701063

Friedman, M. (1979, Sept. 13). The social responsibility of business is to increase its profits. *The New York Times Magazine.*

Friedman, M. (2007). The Social Responsibility of Business Is to Increase Its Profits. In W. C. Zimmerli, M. Holzinger & K. Richter (Eds.), *Corporate Ethics and Corporate Governance* (pp. 173-178). Berlin: Springer.

Furnival, G. M., & Wilson, R. W. (1974). Regression by leaps and bounds. *Technometrics, 16*(4), 499–511. doi:10.2307/1267601

Garfinkel, H. (1967). *Studies in Ethnomethodology.* New York: Prentice Hall.

Garrison, J. (2001). An introduction to Dewey's theory of functional "trans-action": An alternative paradigm for activity theory. *Mind, Culture, and Activity. International Journal (Toronto, Ont.), 8*(4), 275–296.

Garthwaite, P. H., & Dickey, J. M. (1996). Quantifying and using expert opinion for variable-selection problems in regression (with discussion). *Chemometrics and Intelligent Laboratory Systems, 35*(1), 1–34. doi:10.1016/S0169-7439(96)00035-4

Gasso, K. (2000). *Identification des systmes dynamiques non-linaires: Application Multi Modle.* PhD thesis, Centre de Recherche en Automatique de Nancy.

Geisler, E., & Ritter, B. (2003). Differences in additive complexity between biological evolution and the progress of human knowledge. *Emergence, 5*(2), 42–55. doi:10.1207/S15327000EM050206

Gentile, M. C., & Samuelson, J. F. (2005). The State of Affairs for Management Education and Social Responsibility. *Academy of Management Learning & Education, 4*(4), 496–505.

George, E. I. (1999). Bayesian model selection. In S. Kotz, C. Read, & D. Banks (Eds.), *Encyclopedia of Statistical Sciences* (Vol. 3, pp. 39-46). New York: Wiley.

George, J. M., & Jones, G. R. (2002). *Organizational behaviour.* Upper Saddle River, NJ: Prentice-Hall.

Georgescu-Roegen, N. (1971). *The Entropy Law and the Economic Process.* Cambridge, MA: Harvard University Press.

Georgescu-Roegen, N. (1976). *Energy and Economic Myths: Institutional and Analytical Economic Essays.* New York: Pergamon Press.

Georgescu-Roegen, N. (1977a). Bioeconomics: A new look at the nature of the economic activity. In L. Junker (Ed.), *The Political Economy of Food and Energy* (pp. 105-134). Ann Arbor, MI: University of Michigan.

Georgescu-Roegen, N. (1977b). Matter matters, too. In K. D. Wilson (Ed.), *Prospects for Growth: Changing Expectations for the Future* (pp. 293-313). New York: Praeger.

Georgescu-Roegen, N. (1979). The Role of Matter in the Substitution of Energies. In A. Ayoub (Ed.), *Energy: International Cooperation on Crisis* (pp. 95-105). Québec: Press de l'Université Laval.

Ghoshal, S. (2005). Bad management theories are destroying good management practices. *Academy of Management Learning & Education, 4*(1), 75–91.

Gibbons, M., Limoges, C., Nowotny, H., Schartzmann, S., Scott, P., & Trow, M. (1994). *The new production of knowledge: The dynamics of science and research in contemporary societies.* London: Sage.

Giddens, A. (1984). *The Constitution of Society.* Cambridge: Polity Press.

Gieryn, T. (2000). A place for space in sociology. *Annual Review of Sociology, 26*, 463–496. doi:10.1146/annurev.soc.26.1.463

Gifford, B., & Enyedi, N. (1999). Activity centered design: Towards a theoretical framework for CSCL. In *Proceedings of the 1999 Conference on Computer Support for Collaborative Learning,* (pp. 189-196). Stanford, California.

Gilbert, S. F. (1991). Induction and the origins of developmental genetics. In S. F. Gilbert (Ed.), *A conceptual history of modern embryology* (pp. 181–206). New York: Plenum Press.

Gilbert, S. F., Opitz, J. M., & Raff, R. A. (1996). Resynthesizing evolutionary and developmental biology. *Developmental Biology, 173*, 357–372. doi:10.1006/dbio.1996.0032

Gilmour, S. G. (1996). The interpretation of Mallows's C_p-statistic. *The Statistician, 45*(1), 49–56. doi:10.2307/2348411

Gioia, D. A., & Pitre, E. (1990). Multiparadigm perspectives on theory building. *Academy of Management Review, 15*(4), 584–602. doi:10.2307/258683

Giordano, L. (1992). *Beyond Taylorism: Computerization and the new industrial relations.* New York: St. Martin's Press. [Case: Pine Hill]

Glaser, B. G. (2002). Conceptualization: On theory and theorizing using grounded theory. *International Journal of Qualitative Methods, 1*(2).

Glaser, B. G., & Strauss, A. L. (1967). *The discovery of grounded theory: strategies for qualitative research.* New York: DeGruyter.

GMU. (2009). *John Nelson Warfield.* Retrieved from http://policy.gmu.edu/tabid/86/default.aspx?uid=87

Goffin, K., Lemke, F., & Szwejczewski, M. (2006). An exploratory study of 'close' supplier-manufacturer relationships. *Journal of Operations Management, 24*(2), 189–209. doi:10.1016/j.jom.2005.05.003

Gong, G. (1986). Cross-validation, the jackknife, and the bootstrap: Excess error estimation in forward logistic regression. *Journal of the American Statistical Association, 81*(393), 108–113. doi:10.2307/2287975

Goswami, A. (1993). *The self-aware universe – how consciousness creates the material world.* New York: Penguin Putnam.

Gould, S. J. (2002). *The structure of evolutionary theory.* Cambridge, MA: Harvard University Press.

Graham, M. B. W. (1986). A tale of two FMSs. In C. A. Voss (Ed.), *Managing advanced manufacturing technology* (pp. 353-366). London: Croon Helm. [Cases: FMSa and FMSb]

Graham, P. J. (2004). Theorizing justification. In M. M. O'Rourke, J. Campbell, H. Silverstein (Eds.) *Contemporary topics in philosophy 5: Knowledge and skeptics.* Cambridge, MA: MIT Press. Also see, http://www.csun.edu/~philos33/Theorizing_Just_Graham.pdf

Graham, P. J. (2005). Liberal fundamentalism and its rivals. In J. Lackey, E. Sosa (Eds) *The Epistemology of Testimony.* Oxford, UK: UP. Also see http://www.philosophy.ucr.edu/people/graham/Liberal_Fundamentalism.pdf.

Greenwich, CT: Information Age Publishing.

Grint, K. (1991). *The sociology of work: An introduction.* London: Polity Press.

Guba, E. G., & Lincoln, Y. S. (1989). *Fourth generation evaluation.* Newbury Park, CA: Sage.

Guberman, S., & Minati, G. (2007). *Dialogue about systems.* Milan, Italy: Polimetrica.

Gugaliya, J. K., Gudi, R. D., & Lakshminarayanan, S. (2005). Multi mode decomposition of nonlinear dynamics using fuzzy cart approach. *Journal of Process Control, 15*(4), 417–434. doi:10.1016/j.jprocont.2004.07.004

Guo, K. J. (2006). *Strategy for Organisational Change in State Owned Commercial Banks in China.* Unpublished doctoral thesis, under submission at John Moores University, Liverpool, UK.

Guo, K. L. (2007). The entrepreneurial health care manager: Managing innovation and change. *The Business Review, Cambridge*, *7*(2), 175–178.

Gupta, S., Lewis, M. W., & Boyer, K. (2007). Innovation-supportive culture: The case of advanced manufacturing technology. *Journal of Operations Management*, *25*(4), 871–884. doi:10.1016/j.jom.2006.08.003

Habermas, J. (1971). *Knowledge and human interests*. Boston: Beacon Press.

Habermas, J. (1987). *The theory of communicative action*, (Vol. 2). Cambridge, UK: Polity Press.

Halinen, A. & Tornroos, J. (2005). Using case methods in the study of contemporary business networks. *Journal of Business Research, 58*(9 - Special Issue), 1285-1297.

Hambrick, D. C. (2005). Just How Bad Are Our Theories? A Response to Ghoshal. *Academy of Management Learning & Education*, *4*(1), 104–107.

Hammond, D. (2003). *The Science of Synthesis: Exploring the Social Implications of General Systems Theory*. Boulder, CO: University Press.

Hampden-Turner, C. (1981). *Maps of the mind*. New York: MacMillan.

Hansson, T. (2002). Leadership by activity theory and professional development by social construction. *Systemic Practice and Action Research*, *15*(5), 411–436. doi:10.1023/A:1020129327695

Harder, J., Robertson, P. J., & Woodward, H. (2004). The spirit of the new workplace: Breathing life into organizations. *Organization Development Journal*, *22*(2), 79–103.

Hassard, J., & Kelemen, M. (2002). Production and Consumption in Organizational Knowledge: The Case of the 'Paradigms Debate'. *Organization*, *9*(2), 331–355. doi:10.1177/1350508402009002911

Hatchuel, A. (2001). The two pillars of new management research. *British Journal of Management*, *12*(Special Issue), S33–S39. doi:10.1111/1467-8551.12.s1.4

Haughton, D. (1988). On the choice of a model to fit data from an exponential family. *Annals of Statistics*, *16*(1), 342–355. doi:10.1214/aos/1176350709

Hawken, P., Lovins, A., & Lovins, L. H. (1999). *Natural capitalism: Creating the next industrial revolution*. New York: Little, Brown & Co.

Hawkins, J., & Blakeslee, S. (2004). *On intelligence: How a new understanding of the brain will lead to the creation of truly intelligent machines*. New York: Times Books.

Hayles, N. K. (1999). *How we became posthuman: Virtual bodies in cybernetics, literature, and Informatics*. Chicago: The University of Chicago Press.

Heath, T. L. (Ed.). (1853). *The Works of Archimedes*. Cambridge, MA: Cambridge University Press.

Hegel, G. W. F. (1904). *The Phenomenology of Mind*, (transl. J. B. Baillie). New York: Harper Row.

Heidegger, M. (1927). *Sein und Zeit*, also published as Heidegger, M., Stanbaugh, J., *Sight and Time*, 1996, New York: State University of New York Press.

Higgs, M. (2001). Is there a relationship between the Myers-Briggs type indicator and emotional intelligence? *Journal of Managerial Psychology*, *16*(7), 509–533. doi:10.1108/EUM0000000006165

Hirschhorn, L., & Mokray, J. (1992). Automation and competency requirements in manufacturing. In P. S. Adler (Ed.), *Technology and the future of work* (pp.15-45). New York: Oxford University Press. [Case: DEC]

Hirst, E., & Vadeboncoeur, J. (2006). Patrolling the borders of otherness: Dis/placed identity positions for teachers and students in schooled spaces. *Mind, Culture, and Activity. International Journal (Toronto, Ont.)*, *13*(3), 205–227.

Hocking, R. R. (1976). The analysis and selection of variables in linear regression. *Biometrics*, *32*(1), 1–49. doi:10.2307/2529336

Hodgson, A. (2007). Strategic thinking with scenarios. In S. Muralidaran (Ed.), *Business Environment Analysis* (p.

125). Hyderabad, India: Icfai University Press. Holland, J., Holyoak, K., Nisbett, R. & Thagard, P. (1986). *Induction: Processes of inference, learning and discovery.* Cambridge, MA: MIT Press.

Hodgson, A. (2007). Using Systems Thinking to Deepen Scenarios. *Systemist, 29*(2), 71–80.

Hodkinson, P., Biesta, G., & James, D. (2008). Understanding learning culturally: Overcoming the dualism between social and individual views of learning. *Vocations and Learning, 1*, 27–47. doi:10.1007/s12186-007-9001-y

Honey, P., & Mumford, A. (1986). *The manual of learning styles.* Berkshire, UK: Maidenhead. See also http://www.fae.plym.ac.uk/tele/course/cognition3.html

Horgan, J. (1995). From complexity to perplexity. *Science, 272*, 74–79.

Hout, T. M. (1999). Books in review: Are managers obsolete? *Harvard Business Review, 77*(2), 161–168.

Howard, R., & Schneider, L. (1988). Technological change as a social process: A case study of office automation in a manufacturing plant. *Central Issues in Anthropology, 7*(2), 79–84. doi:10.1525/cia.1988.7.2.79

Hubbard, B. M. (1998). *Conscious evolution: Awakening our social potential.* Novato, CA: New World Library.

Hudson, D. J. (1964). *Statistics.* Geneva.

Huff, A. S. (2000). Presidential Address: "Changes in Organizational Knowledge Production. *Academy of Management Review, 25*(2), 288–293. doi:10.2307/259014

Hughes, J. (1990). *The philosophy of science.* Golden, CO: Longhand Press.

Huitt, W. (1988). Personality differences between Navajo and non-Indian college students: Implications for instruction. [Retrieved]. *Equity & Excellence, 24*(1), 71–74. doi:10.1080/1066568880240110

Huitt, W. (1997). Individual differences. *Educational Psychology Interactive.* Retrieved May, 2005 from http://chiron.valdosta.edu/whuitt/col/intro/research.html

Humphreys, M., & Brown, A. D. (2002). Narratives of organizational identity and identification: A case study of hegemony and resistance. *Organization Studies, 23*(3), 421. doi:10.1177/0170840602233005

Hung, P. C. K., & Mao, J. Y. (2002). Modeling e-negotiation activities with Petri nets. In R. H. Spraguer, Jr. (Ed.), *Proceedings of 35th Hawaii International Conference on System Sciences HICSS 2002, Big Island, Hawaii,* (Vol. 1, pp. 26). Piscataway, NJ: IEEE Computer Society Press.

Hurvich, C. M., & Tsai, C. L. (1989). Regression and time series model selection in small samples. *Biometrika, 76*(2), 297–307. doi:10.1093/biomet/76.2.297

Hurvich, C. M., & Tsai, C. L. (1998). A cross-validatory AIC for hard wavelet thresholding in spatially adaptive function estimation. *Biometrika, 85*(3), 701–710. doi:10.1093/biomet/85.3.701

Huse, M. (2003). Renewing Management and Governance: New Paradigms of Governance? *Journal of Management & Governance, 7*(3), 211. doi:10.1023/A:1025004111314

Husserl, E. (1911). Philosophie als strenge Wissenschaft. *Logos* 1, 289-341. English translation by Quentin Lauer in Husserl, 1965, Philosophy as rigorous science. In *Phenomenology and the crisis of philosophy* (pp. 71-147). New York: Harper Collins.

Iles, P. A., & Yolles, M. (2001). Across the great divide: HRD, technology translation and knowledge migration in bridging the knowledge gap between SMEs and Universities. *Human Resource Development International, 4*(1), 1–35. doi:10.1080/13678860122995

Iles, P. A., Ramgutty-Wong, A., & Yolles, M. I. (2004). HRM and knowledge migration across cultures: Issues, limitations, and Mauritian specificities. *Employee Relations: International Journal of Human Resource Management, 26*(6), 643–662. doi:10.1108/01425450410562227

Iles, P., & Yolles, M. (2002). International joint ventures, HRM and viable knowledge migration. *International Journal of Human Resource Management, 13*(4), 624–641. doi:10.1080/09585190210125633

Iles, P., & Yolles, M. (2003a). International HRD alliances in viable knowledge migration and development: The Czech Academic Link Project. *Human Resource Development International*, *6*(3), 301–324. doi:10.1080/13678860210122652

Iles, P., & Yolles, M. I. (2003). Knowledge migration and the transfer of HRM knowledge in international joint ventures and HRD alliances in the Czech Republic and Bulgaria. *Estonian Business Review*, *17*, 82–97.

Ingvar, D. H. (1985). Memory of the future: An essay on the temporal organization of conscious awareness. *Human Neurobiology*, *4*, 127–136.

Interface Inc. (1997). *Interface sustainability report.* Corporate publication. See also the online version of this report at http://www.interfacesustainability.com.

International Futures Forum. (2009). *Ten things to do in a conceptual emergency.* Axminster, UK: Triarchy Press.

Ionescu, G. (1975). *Centripetal politics.* London: Hart-Davis, MacGibbon.

Iordache, M. V., & Antsaklis, P. J. (2006). *Supervisory Control of Concurrent Systems: A Petri Net Structural Approach.* Boston: Birkhauser.

Jackson, M. C. (1992). *Systems methodology for the management sciences.* New York: Plenum.

Jackson, M. C. (2000). *Systems approaches to management.* NewYork: Kluwer.

James, W. (1907). *Pragmatism.* New York: Meridian Books.

Janis, I. L., & Mann, L. (1977). *Decision making: A psychological analysis of conflict, choice, and commitment.* New York: Free Press.

Jantsch, E. (1980). *The self-organising universe: Scientific and human implications of the emerging paradigm of evolution.* New York: Pergamen Press.

Jaulin, L., Kieffer, M., Didrit, O., & Walter, E. (2001). *Applied Interval Analysis.* Berlin: Springer-Verlag.

Jick, T. D. (1979). Mixing qualitative and quantitative methods: Triangulation in action. *Administrative Science Quarterly*, *24*(4), 602–611. doi:10.2307/2392366

Jirapornkul, S. (2009). *Changing values of Thai managers and employees and its implications for Thai organizations.* Unpublished doctoral thesis, Institute of International Studies, Ranmkhamheng University, Bangkok.

Johansen, T. A., & Foss, B. A. (1995). Identification of non-linear system structure and parameters using regime decomposition. *Automatica*, *31*(2), 321–326. doi:10.1016/0005-1098(94)00096-2

Johnstone, I. M., & Silverman, B. W. (1998). Empirical Bayes approaches to mixture problems and wavelet regression. Technical Report, University of Bristol, UK.

Jones, B., & Scott, R. (1986). 'Working the system': A comparison of the management of work roles in American and British flexible manufacturing systems. In C.A. Voss (Ed.), *Managing advanced manufacturing technology* (pp. 353-366). London: Croon Helm. [Cases: Alpha and Turnco]

Jung, C. G. (1921). *Psychological types.* Princeton, NJ: Princeton University Press.

Jung, C. G. (1957-1979). *Collected Works*, Bollinger Series (vols. 1-20). New York: Pantheon.

Kandel, E. R. (2006). *The neuroscience of adult learning: New directions for adult and continuing education.* San Francisco: Jossey-Bass.

Kaplan, A. (1964). *The Conduct of Inquiry: Methodology for Behavioral Science.* San Francisco: Chandler Publishing Company.

Kaptelinin, V., & Miettinen, R. (2005). Perspectives on the object of activity. *Mind, Culture, and Activity*, *12*(1), 1–3. doi:10.1207/s15327884mca1201_1

Kaptelinin, V., & Nardi, B. (2006). *Acting with Technology: Activity Theory and Interaction Design.* Cambridge MA:The MIT Press.

Kauffman, S. (1995). *At Home in the Universe: The Search for Laws of Self-Organization and Complexity.* New York: Oxford University Press.

Kauffman, S. A. (1993). *The origins of order.* New York: Oxford University Press.

Kauffman, S. A. (1995). *At home in the universe.* London: Viking.

Kaufmann, L. (2008). *Laws of form – An exploration in mathematics and foundations* (Rough Draft). Chicago: University of Illinois. Retrieved December 31, 2008, from http://www.math.uic.edu/~kauffman/Laws.pdf

Kay, J. (2008, Winter). Drowning by numbers. *RSA Journal.* London: Royal Society of Arts.

Kercel, S. W. (2007). Entailment of ambiguity. *Chemistry & Biodiversity, 4*(10), 2369–2385. doi:10.1002/cbdv.200790193

Kestleloot, R. (1989). Introduction of computerised numerical control and the rationalisation of production. In A. Francis & P. Grootings (Eds.), *New technologies and work: Capitalist and socialist perspectives* (pp. 165-186). London: Routledge. [Case: VM]

Kets de Vries, M. F. R. (1991). *Organisations on the couch: Clinical perspectives on organisational behaviour and change.* San Francisco: Jossey-Bass.

Key, S. (1999). Toward a new theory of the firm: a critique of stakeholder "theory". *Management Decision, 37*(4), 317. doi:10.1108/00251749910269366

Knights, D. (1995). Refocusing the case study. *Technology Studies, 2*(2), 230–254.

Koestler, A. (1967). *The ghost in the machine.* London: Hutchinson.

Kolb, D. A. (1974). *Organisational psychology: An experiential approach.* Englewood Cliffs, NJ: Prentice-Hall.

Kolb, D. A. (1984). *Experiential learning: Experience as the source of learning and development.* Upper Saddle River, NJ: Prentice-Hall.

Kolev, L. V. (1993). *Interval Methods for Circuit Analysis.* Hackensack, NJ: World Scientific.

Korten, D. (2002, May). From mindless greed to civil society: Restoring an ethical culture and challenging a world consumed with the love of money. *Opportunity Knocks, 9.*

Korten, D. (2006). The great turning: From empire to Earth community. *YES! A Journal of Positive Futures, 38,* 12-18.

Koschman, T. (1996). Paradigm shifts in instructional technology. In T. Koschman (Ed.), *CSCL Theory and Practice of an Emerging Paradigm* (pp. 1-23). Mahwah, NJ: Lawrence Erlbaum.

Kubicek, H. (1975). *Empirische Organisationsforschung: Konzeption und Methodik* [Empiric organisational research: Conception and methodology]. Stuttgart, Germany: Poeschel.

Kuhn, T. (1970). *The Structure of Scientific Revolutions* (2nd ed.). Chicago: The University of Chicago Press.

Kuhn, T. S. (1970). *The structure of scientific revolutions.* Chicago: University of Chicago Press.

Kuntz, P. G. (1968). *The concept of order.* Seattle, WA: University of Washington Press.

Kurtzweil, R. (1990). *The age of intelligent machines.* Cambridge, MA: MIT Press.

Labarre, P. (2000, March). Do you have the will to lead? *Fast Company.*

Lachmann, R. (Ed.). (1991). *The Encyclopedic Dictionary of Sociology* (4 ed.). The Dushkin Publishing Group.

Lakoff, G. (2008). *The political mind: Why you can't understand 21st- century American politics with an 18th-century brain.* New York, NY: Viking.

Lakoff, G., & Johnson, B. B. (1999). *Philosophy in the flesh: The embodied mind and its challenge to western thought.* New York, NY: Basic Books.

Langley, P., Morecroft, J., & Morecroft, L. (2008). *Oil producers microworld.* Retrieved

Larsson, R. (1993). Case survey methodology: Quantitative analysis of patterns across case studies. *Academy of Management Journal, 36*(6), 1515–1546. doi:10.2307/256820

Laszlo, A. (2008). *Evolving with heart: Dancing the path of syntony*. Manuscript.

Laszlo, A. (2009). The nature of evolution. *World Futures*, *65*(3), 204–221. doi:10.1080/02604020802392112

Laszlo, A., & Laszlo, K. C. (2004). Strategic evolutionary advantage (S.E.A.). *World Futures*, *60*(1-2), 99–114. doi:10.1080/725289195

Laszlo, C., & Laugel, J. F. (2000). *Large-scale organizational change: An executive's guide*. Woburn, MA: Butterworth-Heinemann.

Laszlo, E. (1999). *Holos — The fabulous world of the new sciences: Explorations at the leading edge of contemporary knowledge*. Unpublished manuscript.

Laszlo, E. (2002). *Macroshift: Navigating the transformation to a sustainable world*. San Francisco: Berrett-Koehler.

Laszlo, K. C. (2003). The evolution of business: Learning, innovation, and sustainability for the 21st century. *World Futures*, *59*(8), 655–664.

Laszlo, K. C., & Laszlo, A. (2002, October). Evolving knowledge for development: The role of knowledge management in a changing world. *Journal of Knowledge Management*, *6*(4), 400–412. doi:10.1108/13673270210440893

Latour, B. (1994). On technical mediation: Philosophy, genealogy and sociology. *Common Knowledge*, *3*, 29–64.

Laurillard, D. (1987). Computers and the emancipation of students. In O. Boyd-Barret & E. Scanlon (Eds.), *Computers and learning*. Workingham, UK: Addison Wesley.

Lave, J. (1996). Teaching as learning, in practice. *Mind, Culture, and Society*, *3*(3), 149–164. doi:10.1207/s15327884mca0303_2

Lave, J., & Wenger, E. (1991). *Situated Learning: Legitimate Peripheral Participation*. Cambridge, UK: Cambridge University Press.

Lee, B. (1985). Intellectual origins of Vygotsky's semiotic analysis. In J.V. Wertsch (Ed.), *Culture, Communication, and Cognition: Vygotskian perspectives* (pp. 66-93). Cambridge, UK: Cambridge University Press.

Lenz, K., Oberweis, A., & Schneider, S. (2001). Trust based contracting in virtual organizations: A concept based on contract workflow management systems. In Schmid, B., Stanoevska-Slabeva, K., & Tschammer, V. (Eds.), *Towards the E-Society – E-Commerce, E-Business, and E-Government* (pp. 3-16). Boston: Kluwer Academic Publishers.

Leonard-Barton, D. (1990). A dual methodology for case studies: Synergistic use of a longitudinal single site with replicated multiple sites. *Organization Science*, *1*(3 - special issue), 248-266.

Leontev, A. (1978). *Activity, Consciousness and Personality*. Englewood Cliffs, NJ: Prentice Hall.

Letiche, H. (2006). Relationality and Phenomenological Organizational Studies. *Tamara: Journal of Critical Postmodern Organization Science*, *5*(3), 7–18.

Levin, T., & Wadsmanly, R. (2008). Teachers' views on factors affecting effective integration of information technology in the classroom: Developmental scenery. *Journal of Technology and Teacher Education*, *16*(2), 233–263.

Lewis, M. W. (1996). *Advanced manufacturing technology design: A multiparadigm study*. Unpublished dissertation, University of Kentucky, KY.

Lewis, M. W. (2000). Exploring paradox: Toward a more comprehensive guide. *Academy of Management Review*, *25*(4), 760–776. doi:10.2307/259204

Lewis, M. W., & Grimes, A. J. (1999). Metatriangulation: Building theory from multiple paradigms. *Academy of Management Review*, *24*(4), 672–690. doi:10.2307/259348

Lewis, M. W., & Kelemen, M. (2002). Multiparadigm inquiry: Exploring organizational pluralism and paradox. *Human Relations*, *55*(2), 251–275. doi:10.1177/0018726702055002185

Lichtenstein, B. B. (2000). Valid or vacuous? A definition and assessment of new paradigm research in management. *The American Behavioral Scientist*, *43*(8), 1334. doi:10.1177/00027640021955892

Lincoln, Y. S., & Guba, E. G. (2006). The only generalization is: There is no generalization. In R. Gomm, M. Hammersley & P. Foster (Eds.), *Case study method: Key issues, key texts* (pp. 27-44). London: Sage.

Ling, C., & Edgar, T. F. (1997). Real-time control of a water-gas shift reactor by a model-based fuzzy gain scheduling technique. *Journal of Process Control*, *7*(4), 239–253. doi:10.1016/S0959-1524(97)00001-2

Lissack, M. R. (1997). Mind your metaphors: Lessons from complexity science. *Long Range Planning*, (April): 294–298. doi:10.1016/S0024-6301(96)00120-3

Lissack, M. R. (1999). Complexity: The science, its vocabulary, and its relation to organizations. *Emergence*, *1*(1), 110–126. doi:10.1207/s15327000em0101_7

Ljung, L. (1999). *System Identification*. Upper Saddle River, NJ: Prentice Hall.

Locke, K. D. (2005). *Grounded theory in management research*. Thousand Oaks, CA: Sage.

Locker, A. (1997). *The present status of general system theory, 25 years after Ludwig von Bertalanffy's decease*. Kutna Hora, Czech Republic: Centre for Systems Research. Retrieved

Locker, M. (2006). *Reviving paradoxes: Transclassical systems theory as meta-theory for a science-faith dialogue*. Bryn Mawr, PA: Metanexus Institute. Retrieved March 30, 2009, from http://www.metanexus.net/conferences/pdf/conference2006/Locker.pdf

Louie, A. H. (2007). A Rosen etymology. *Chemistry & Biodiversity*, *4*(10), 2296–2314. doi:10.1002/cbdv.200790188

Lüscher, L. S., & Lewis, M. W. (2008). Organisational change and managerial sensemaking: Working through paradox. *Academy of Management Journal*, *51*(2), 221–240.

Luhmann, N. (1986). The autopoiesis of social systems. In G. Hofstede, & M. Sami Kassem, (Eds.) *Sociocybernetic paradoxes*. London: Sage.

Luscher, L., & Lewis, M. W. (2008). Organizational change and managerial sensemaking: Working through paradox. *Academy of Management Journal*, *51*(2), 221–240.

Luscher, L., Lewis, M. W., & Ingram, A. (2006). The social construction of organizational change paradoxes. *Journal of Organizational Change Management*, *19*(4), 491–502. doi:10.1108/09534810610676680

Ma, H. (2000, January). Of competitive advantage: Kinetic and positional. *Bryant College Journal*.

Maanen, J. V., Sørensen, J. B., & Mitchell, T. R. (2007). The interplay between theory and method. *Academy of Management Review*, *32*(4), 1145–1154.

MacIntosh, R., & MacLean, D. (1999). Conditioned emergence: A dissipative structures approach to transformation. *Strategic Management Journal*, *20*(4), 297. doi:10.1002/(SICI)1097-0266(199904)20:4<297::AID-SMJ25>3.0.CO;2-Q

Macrae, D. G. (1951). Cybernetics and Social Science. *The British Journal of Sociology*, *2*(2), 135–149. doi:10.2307/587385

Macy, J. (2006, September). The great turning as compass and lens. *YES! A Journal of Positive Futures, 38*.

Makower, J. (2002, December). Follow the leaders: How consumer product companies burnish their green credentials. *The Green Business Letter*.

Mander, J., Cavanagh, J., Anderson, S., & Barker, D. (2003). Alternatives to economic globalization. *Tikkun*, *18*(1), 39–41.

Marchese, T. J. (1998). The new conversations about learning: Insights from neuroscience and anthropology, cognitive science and workplace studies. *New Horizons for Learning*. Retrieved January 19, 2008, from www.newhorizons.org/lifelong/higher_ed/marchese.htm

Markides, C. (1999, Spring). A dynamic view of strategy. *Sloan Management Review*, 55–63.

Marshall, S. P. (1995). *Schemes in problem solving*. Cambridge, UK: Cambridge University Press.

Martin, J. (1992). *Cultures in Organization*. Oxford, UK: Oxford University Press.

Martin, J. (2000). Hidden gendered assumptions in mainstream organizational theory and research. *Journal of Management Inquiry*, *9*(2), 207–216. doi:10.1177/105649260092017

Marton, F., & Booth, S. (1997). *Learning and awareness*. Mahwah, NJ: Erlbaum.

Maruyama, M. (1965). Metaorganization of information: Information in a classificational universe, relational universe, and relevantial universe. *Cybernetica*, *8*(4), 224–236.

Maruyama, M. (1972). Non-classificational information and non-informational communication. *Dialectica*, *26*(1), 51. doi:10.1111/j.1746-8361.1972.tb01227.x

Maruyama, M. (1980). Mindscapes and science theories. *Current Anthropology*, *21*, 589–599. doi:10.1086/202539

Marx, K. (1990). *Capital: A Critique of Political Economy*, (Vol. 1). London: Penguin.

Masuch, M. (1985). Vicious circles in organizations. *Administrative Science Quarterly*, *30*(1), 14–33. doi:10.2307/2392809

Matthews, R. A. (1996). *Fordism, flexibility and regional productivity growth*. New York: Garland.

Maturana, H., & Varela, F. J. (1979). *Autopoiesis and cognition*. Boston: Boston Studies in the Philosophy of Science.

Maxwell, N. (2000). A new conception of science. *Physics World*, August, 17-18.

May 2005, from http://chiron.valdosta.edu/whuitt/papers/mbtinav.html

McClave, J. T., Benson, P. G., & Sincich, T. (1998). *Statistics for Business and Economics*, (7th ed.). Upper Saddle River, NJ: Prentice Hall.

McCormick, D. W., & White, J. (2000). Using One's Self as an Instrument for Organizational Diagnosis. *Organization Development Journal*, *18*(3), 49–63.

McElroy, M. W. (2000). *Managing for sustainable innovation*. Unpublished manuscript.

McIntosh, M., Leipziger, D., Jones, K., & Coleman, G. (1998). *Corporate citizenship: Successful strategies for responsible companies*. London: Financial Times Pitman Publishing.

McKelvey, B. (2002). Model-centered organization science epistemology. In J. A. C. Baum (Ed.), *Blackwell's Companion to Organizations* (pp. 752-780). Thousand Oaks, CA: Sage.

McKelvey, W. (2001). What is complexity science? It is really order-creation science. *Emergence*, *3*(1), 137–157. doi:10.1207/S15327000EM0301_09

McKenna, M. K., Shelton, C. D., & Darling, J. R. (2002). The impact of behavioral style assessment on organizational effectiveness: A call for action. *Leadership and Organization Development Journal*, *23*(6), 314–322. doi:10.1108/01437730210441274

Meadows, D. (1999). *Leverage points: Places to intervene in a system*. Hartland, VT: The Sustainability Institute.

Meadows, D. H., Meadows, D. L., Randers, J., & Behrens, W. W., III. (1972). *The limits to growth: a report for The Club of Rome's project on the predicament of mankind*. New York: Universe Books.

Meehl, P. E. (2002). Cliometric metatheory: II. Criteria scientists use in theory appraisal and why it is rational to do so. *Psychological Reports*, *91*, 339–404. doi:10.2466/PR0.91.6.339-404

Merton, R. K. (1968). *Social Theory and Social Structure*. New York: Free Press.

Miettinen, R. (1999). The riddle of things: Activity theory and actor-network theory as approaches to studying innovation. *Mind, Culture, and Activity. International Journal (Toronto, Ont.)*, *6*(3), 170–195.

Mikhailov, A. S., & Calenbuhr, V. (2002). *From Cells to Societies. Models of Complex Coherent Action*. Berlin: Springer.

Mikulecky, D. C. (1993) *Applications of network thermodynamics to problems in biomedical engineering.* New York: New York University Press.

Mikulecky, D. C. (2000). Robert Rosen: The well-posed question and its answer – Why are organisms different from machines? *Systems Research and Behavioral Science, 17*(5), 419–432. doi:10.1002/1099-1743(200009/10)17:5<419::AID-SRES367>3.0.CO;2-D

Mikulecky, D. C. (2001). Network thermodynamics and complexity: A transition to relational systems theory. *Computers & Chemistry, 25,* 369–391. doi:10.1016/S0097-8485(01)00072-9

Mikulecky, D. C. (2007a). Complexity science as an aspect of the complexity of science. In C. Gershonen, D. Aerts, & B. Edmonds (Eds.), *Worldviews science and us: Philosophy and complexity. (pp. 30-52).* Hackensack, NJ: World Scientific.

Mikulecky, D. C. (2007b). Causality and complexity: The myth of objectivity in science. *Chemistry & Biodiversity, 4*(10), 2480–2490. doi:10.1002/cbdv.200790202

Milanese, M., Norton, J., Piet-Lahanier, H., & Walter, E. (1996). *Bounding Approaches to System Identification.* New York: Plenum Press.

Miles, M. B., & Huberman, A. M. (1994). *Qualitative data analysis: An expanded sourcebook.* Thousand Oaks, CA: Sage.

Milkman, R., & Pullman, C. (1991). Technological change in an auto assembly plant. [Case: GM]. *Work and Occupations, 18*(2), 123–147. doi:10.1177/0730888491018002001

Miller, A. J. (2002). *Subset selection in regression,* (2nd ed.). New York: Chapman & Hall/CRC.

Minati, G. (20020. Ethics as emergent property of the behaviour of living systems. In Parra-Luna F. (Ed.), *Encyclopaedia of Life Support Systems (EOLSS),* (Vol. 1, Physical Sciences Engineering and Technology Resources, Systems Science and Cybernetics: The Long Road to World Sociosystemicity). Oxford, UK: EOLSS Publishers. Retrieved from http://www.eolss.net

Minati, G. (2004). Buying consensus in "free markets". *World Futures, 60*(1-2), 29–37. doi:10.1080/725289194

Minati, G. (2006a). Multiple Systems, Collective Beings, and the Dynamic Usage of Models. *Systemist, 28*(2), 200–211.

Minati, G. (2006b). Some Comments on Democracy and Manipulating Consent in Western Post-Democratic Societies. In G. Minati, E. Pessa & M. Abram (Eds.), *Systemics of Emergence: Research and Applications* (pp.569-584). New York: Springer.

Minati, G. (2007). Some new theoretical issues in Systems Thinking relevant for modelling corporate learning. [TLO]. *The Learning Organization, 14*(6), 480–488. doi:10.1108/09696470710825097

Minati, G. (2008). *New Approaches for Modelling Emergence of Collective Phenomena-The Meta-structures project.* Milan, Italy: Polimetrica.

Minati, G., & Brahms, S. (2002). The Dynamic Usage of Models (DYSAM). In G. Minati & E. Pessa (Eds.), *Emergence in Complex Cognitive, Social and Biological Systems* (pp. 41-52), New York: Kluwer.

Minati, G., & Pessa, E. (2006). *Collective Beings.* New York: Springer.

Minati, G., Penna, M. P., & Pessa, E. (1998). Thermodynamic and Logical Openness in General Systems. *Systems Research and Behavioral Science, 15*(3), 131–145. doi:10.1002/(SICI)1099-1743(199803/04)15:2<131::AID-SRES127>3.0.CO;2-O

Mintzberg, H. (2005). Developing theory about the development of theory. In K. G. Smith & M. A. Hitt (Eds.), *Great Minds in Management: The Process of Theory Development* (pp. 355-372). Oxford, UK: Oxford University Press.

Mirvis, P. H. (1988). On the crafting of a theory. In R. E. Quinn & K. S. Cameron (Eds.), *Paradox and transformation* (pp. 279-288). Cambridge, MA: Ballinger Publishing Co.

Mitroff, I. I. (1998). On the fundamental importance of ethical management: Why management is the most important of all human activities. *Journal of Management Inquiry, 7*(1), 68–79. doi:10.1177/105649269871011

Mitroff, I. I. (2003). Spiritual I.Q: The farthest reaches of human development. *World Futures, 59*(7), 485–494. doi:10.1080/713747072

Mitroff, I., & Linstone, H. (1993). *The unbounded mind: Breaking the chains of traditional business thinking.* New York: Oxford University Press.

Moll, L. (1990). Introduction. In L. Moll (Ed.), *Vygotsky and Education. Instructional Implications and Applications of Sociohistorical Psychology.* Cambridge, UK: Cambridge University Press.

Montgomery, D. C., & Peck, E. A. (1992). *Introduction to linear regression analysis,* (2nd ed.). New York: Wiley.

Montuori, A. (1989). *Evolutionary competence: Creating the future.* Amsterdam: J. C. Gieben.

Moon, J. A. (2004). *A handbook of reflective and experiential learning: Theory and practice.* New York: Routledge-Falmer.

Moore, J. F. (1997). *The death of competition: Leadership and strategy in the age of business ecosystems.* New York: Harper Business.

Moore, R. E. (1962). *Interval Arithmatic and Automatic Error Analysis in Digital Computing.* PhD thesis, Applied Mathematics and Statistics Laboratories, Report 25, Standford University.

Moore, R. E. (1966). *Interval Analysis.* Englewood Cliffs, NJ: Prentice Hall.

Moran, P. A. P. (1953). The statistical analysis of the Canadian lynx cycle, I: Structure and prediction. *Australian Journal of Zoology, 1*(2), 163–173. doi:10.1071/ZO9530163

Morgan, G. (1996). *Images of Organizations.* Thousand Oaks, CA: Sage.

Morgan, G. (Ed.). (1983). *Beyond method.* Newbury Park, CA: Sage.

Morris, G. W., & LoVerde, M. A. (1993). Consortium surveys. *The American Behavioral Scientist, 36*(4), 531–550. doi:10.1177/0002764293036004008

Mort, G. S., Weerawardena, J., & Carnegie, K. (2003). Social entrepreneurship: Towards conceptualisation. *International Journal of Nonprofit and Voluntary Sector Marketing, 8*(1), 76–88. doi:10.1002/nvsm.202

Murata, T. (1989). Petri Nets: Properties, Analysis and Applications. *Proceedings of the IEEE, 77*(4), 541–588. doi:10.1109/5.24143

Murray-Smith, R., & Johansen, T. A. (1977). *Multiple Model Approaches to Modelling and Control.* Danvers, MA: CRC.

Myers, R. L. (1992). *Classical and modern regression analysis,* (2nd ed.). New York: Wiley.

Nardi, B. (1996). Studying context: A comparison of activity theory, situated action models and distributed cognition. In B. Nardi (Ed.), *Context and Consciousness: Activity Theory and Human-Computer Interaction* (pp. 69-102). Cambridge, MA: MIT Press.

Nardi, B. (2007). Placeless organizations: Collaborating for transformation. *Mind, Culture, and Activity. International Journal (Toronto, Ont.), 14*(1/2), 5–22.

Narula, S. C., & Wellington, J. F. (1977). Prediction, linear regression and minimum sum of relative errors. *Technometrics, 19*(2), 185–190. doi:10.2307/1268628

Nattrass, B., & Altomare, M. (1999). *The natural step for business: Wealth, ecology, and the evolutionary corporation.* British Columbia: New Society Publishers.

Nechval, K. N., Berzins, G., Nechval, N. A., Purgailis, M., & Zolova, N. (2008a). Information criterion for variable selection in econometric models and its applications. In E. Kopytov, H. Pranevicius, E. Zavadskas, & I. Yatskiv (Eds.), *Proceedings of the International Conference on Modelling of Business, Industrial and Transport Systems* (pp. 24-32). Latvia, Riga: Transport and Telecommunication Institute.

Nechval, N. A., & Purgailis, M. (2008c). New variable selection criteria for econometric models and their applications. *Humanities and Social Sciences: Latvia*, *57*(4), 6–26.

Nechval, N. A., Berzinsh, G., Purgailis, M., & Nechval, K. N. (2008b). New variable selection criterion for econometric models. In R. Trappl (Ed.), *Cybernetics and Systems 2008* (Vol. I, pp. 64-69). Austria, Vienna: Austrian Society for Cybernetic Studies.

Nechval, N. A., Nechval, K. N., Purgailis, M., Rozevskis, U., Strelchonok, V., Moldovan, M., et al. (2009). Recognition of subsets of informative variables in regression. In V. Krasnoproshin, S. Ablameyko, & R. Sadykhov (Eds.), *Proceedings of the International Conference on Pattern Recognition and Information Processing* (pp. 371-376). Belarus, Minsk: University of Belarus.

Neumaier, A. (2001). *Introduction to Numerical Analysis*. New York: Cambridge University Press.

Newbold, P. (1995). *Statistics for Business & Economics*, (4th ed.). New Jersey: Prentice-Hall, Inc.

Nickles, T. (2009). *Scientific Revolutions*. Retrieved 04/23/2009, 2009, from http://plato.stanford.edu/entries/scientific-revolutions/

Nicolis, G., & Prigogine, I. (1989). *Exploring complexity: An introduction*. New York: W. H. Feeman and Co.

Nonaka, I. (2005). Managing organizational knowledge: Theoretical and methodological foundations. In K. G. Smith & M. A. Hitt (Eds.), *Great Minds in Management: The Process of Theory Development* (pp. 373-393). New York: Oxford University Press.

Nowostawski, M., Purvis, M., & Cranefield, S. (2001). A layered approach for modelling agent conversations. In T. Wagner & O. F. Rana (Eds.), *Proceedings of 2nd International Workshop on Infrastructure for Agents, MAS, and Scalable MAS, 5th International Conference on Autonomous Agents - AA 2001, Montreal, Canada, May 28-June 1, 2001* (pp. 163-170). Menlo Park, CA: AAAI Press.

Nutt, P. C., & Backoff, R. W. (1997). Facilitating transformational change. *The Journal of Applied Behavioral Science*, *33*(4), 490. doi:10.1177/0021886397334005

Olson, E. E., & Eoyang, G. H. (2001). *Facilitating Organizational Change: Lessons From Complexity Science*. San Francisco: Jossey-Bass/Pfeiffer.

Oreskes, N., Shrader-Frechette, K., & Belitz, K. (1994). Verification, validation, and confirmation of numerical models in the earth sciences. *Science*, *263*, 641–646. doi:10.1126/science.263.5147.641

Osborn, A. D. (1934). The philosophy of Edmund Husserl: In its development from his mathematical interests to his first conception of phenomenology. In *Logical Investigations*, New York: International Press.

Paris, C., Johnston, J. H., & Reeves, D. (1998). *A theoretical framework and measurement strategy for training team tactical decision making.* Paper presented at Proceedings of the Command and Control Research and Technology Symposium, Naval Postgraduate School, Monterey, CA.

Patton, M. Q. (2002). *Qualitative research evaluation methods.* Thousand Oaks, CA: Sage.

Pedler, M., Burgoyne, J., & Brook, C. (2005). What has action learning learned to become? *Action Learning Research and Practice*, *2*(1), 49–68.

Pert, C. B. (1997). *Molecules of emotion: A science behind mind-body medicine*. New York: Touchstone.

Petersen, K. J., Handfield, R. B., & Ragatz, G. L. (2005). Supplier integration into new product development: Coordinating product, process and supply chain design. *Journal of Operations Management*, *23*(3/4), 371–388. doi:10.1016/j.jom.2004.07.009

Peterson, J. L. (1981). *Petri Net Theory and Modeling the Systems*. New York: Prentice Hall Inc.

Pfeffer, J. (1993). Barriers to the advance of organizational science: Paradigm development as a dependent variable. *Academy of Management Review*, *18*, 599–620. doi:10.2307/258592

Pfeffer, J. (2005). Why Do Bad Management Theories Persist? A Comment on Ghoshal. *Academy of Management Learning & Education*, *4*(1), 96–100.

Pfeffer, J. (2007). A modest proposal: How we might change the process and product of managerial research. *Academy of Management Journal, 50*(6), 1334–1345.

Piaget, J. (1950). *The psychology of intelligence.* New York: Harcourt and Brace.

Pichault, F. (1995). The management of politics in technically related organizational change. *Organization Studies, 16*(3), 449–476. doi:10.1177/017084069501600304

Pinchbeck, D. (2006). *2012: The return of Quetzalcoatl.* New York: Tarcher/Penguin.

Ploix, S., Adrot, O., & Ragot, J. (1999). Parameter uncertainty computation in static linear models. *Decision and Control, 1999, Proceedings of the 38th IEEE Conference on, 2*, 1916–1921.

Plummer, R., & Fennell, D. (2007). Exploring co-management theory: Prospects for sociobiology and reciprocal altruism. *Journal of Environmental Management, 85*(4), 944–955. doi:10.1016/j.jenvman.2006.11.003

Poli, R. (2001). The basic problem of the theory of levels of reality. *Axiomathes, 12*(3-4), 261–283. doi:10.1023/A:1015845217681

Poli, R. (2005). Personal communication.

Poole, M. S., & Van de Ven, A. H. (1989). Using paradox to build management and organization theories. *Academy of Management Review, 14*(4), 562–578. doi:10.2307/258559

Popper, K. (2002). *The Logic of Scientific Discovery* (J. F. Karl Popper, L. Freed, Trans.). New York: Routledge Classics.

Popper, K., & Eccles, J. (1977). *The Self and its Brain.* Berlin: Springer-Verlag.

Porter, M. (1996, November/December). What is strategy? *Harvard Business Review.*

Punch, K. (2005). *Introduction to social research: Quantitative and qualitative approaches.* Thousand Oaks, CA: Sage.

Puschmann, T., & Alt, R. (2005). Successful use of e-procurement in supply chains. *Supply Chain Management: An International Journal, 10*(2), 122–133. doi:10.1108/13598540510589197

Quinn, R. E., & Cameron, K. S. (1988). *Paradox and Transformation: Toward a Theory of Change in Organization and Management.* Cambridge, Mass.: Ballinger.

Quinn, R. E., Kahn, J. A., & Mandl, M. J. (1994). Perspectives on organizational change: Exploring movement at the interface. In J. Greenberg (Ed.), *Organizational behavior: The state of science* (pp. 109-133). Hillsdale, NJ: Lawrence Erlbaum Associates.

Raeithel, A. (1996). *From coordinatedness to coordination via cooperation and co-construction.* Paper presented at the Workshop on Work and Learning in Transition, San Diego, CA.

Raff, R. A. (2000). Evo-devo: The evolution of a new discipline. *Nature Reviews. Genetics, 1*(1), 74–79. doi:10.1038/35049594

Ragot, J., Maquin, D., & Domlan, E. A. (2003). Switching time estimation of piecewise linear systems. application to diagnosis. In *Proceedings of the 5th IFAC Symposium on Fault Detection, Supervision and Safety of Technical Processes*, (pp. 669–704).

Rao, C. R., & Wu, Y. (1989). A strongly consistent procedure for model selection in a regression problem. *Biometrika, 76*(2), 369–374. doi:10.1093/biomet/76.2.369

Rashevsky, N. (1954). Topology and life: In search of general mathematical principles in biology and sociology. *The Bulletin of Mathematical Biophysics, 16*, 317–348. doi:10.1007/BF02484495

Ratey, J. J. (2001). *A user's guide to the brain: Perceptions, attention, and the four theaters of the brain.* New York: Pantheon Books.

Ray, P., & Anderson, S. R. (2000). *The cultural creatives: How 50 million people are changing the world.* New York: Harmony Books.

Reichel, A. (2008). Observing the next organisation. *UK Systems Society: Systemist, 30*(2).

Richardson, K. A. (2004). On the relativity of recognizing the products of emergence and the nature of physical hierarchy. In *Proceedings of the 2nd biennial international seminar on the philosophical, epistemological and methodological implications of complexity theory*, January 7th-10th, Havana International Conference Center, Cuba.

Richardson, K. A. (2005a). Simplifying Boolean networks. *Advances in Complex Systems*, *8*(4), 365–381. doi:10.1142/S0219525905000518

Richardson, K. A. (2005b). The hegemony of the physical sciences: An exploration in complexity thinking. *Futures*, *37*(7), 615–653. doi:10.1016/j.futures.2004.11.008

Richardson, K. A., Tait, A., Roos, J., & Lissack, M. R. (2005). The coherent management of complex projects and the potential role of group decision support systems. In K. A. Richardson (Ed.), *Managing organizational complexity: Philosophy, theory, and application* (pp. 433-458)

Richardson, M. K., & Keuck, G. (2002). Haeckel's ABC of evolution and development. *Biological Reviews of the Cambridge Philosophical Society (London)*, *77*, 495–528. doi:10.1017/S1464793102005948

Riedl, R. (1977). A systems analytical approach to macro-evolutionary phenomena. *The Quarterly Review of Biology*, *52*, 351–370. doi:10.1086/410123

Riedl, R. (1978). *Order in living systems*. New York: Wiley.

Riegler, A. (2001). The cognitive ratchet. The ratchet effect as a fundamental principle in evolution and cognition. *Cybernetics and Systems*, *32*(3/4), 411–427. doi:10.1080/01969720151033571

Riegler, A. (2008). Natural or internal selection? *Artificial Life*, *14*(3), 345–362. doi:10.1162/artl.2008.14.3.14308

Rigg, C. (2008). Action learning for organizational and systemic development: Towards a 'both-and' understanding of 'I' and 'we'. *Action Learning Research and Practice*, *5*(2), 105–116. doi:10.1080/14767330802185616

Rissanen, J. (1978). Modeling by shortest data description. *Automatica*, *14*(5), 465–471. doi:10.1016/0005-1098(78)90005-5

Ritzer, G. (1992). *Metatheorizing*. Newbury Park, California: Sage.

Ritzer, G. (2001). *Explorations in Social Theory: From Metatheorizing to Rationalisation*. London: Sage.

Ritzer, G. (2006). Metatheory. In G. Ritzer (Ed.), *Blackwell Encyclopedia of Sociology*. New York: Wiley.

Robbins, S. P. (2001). *Organizational behaviour*. Upper Saddle River, NJ: Prentice-Hall.

Robèrt, K. H. (1997). *The natural step: A framework for achieving sustainability in our organizations*. Cambridge, MA: Pegasus Innovations in Management Series.

Rogoff, B. (2003). *The Cultural Nature of Human Development*. New York: Oxford University Press.

Roller, D., & Roller, D. H. D. (1954). *The Development of the Concept of Electric Charge: Electricity from the Greeks to Coulomb* (Vol. 8). Cambridge, MA: Harvard University Press.

Rooke, D., & Torbert, W. R. (2005). 7 Transformations of Leadership. *Harvard Business Review*, *83*(4), 66.

Rosen, R. (1958). The Representation of biological systems from the standpoint of the theory of categories. *The Bulletin of Mathematical Biophysics*, *20*, 317–341. doi:10.1007/BF02477890

Rosen, R. (1972). Some relational cell models: The metabolism–repair system. In *Foundations of mathematical biology* (pp. 217-253). New York: Academic Press.

Rosen, R. (1973). On the relation between structural and functional descriptions of biological systems. In M. Conrad & M.E. Magar (Eds.) *The physical principles of neuronal and organismic behavior*. New York: Gordon and Breach.

Rosen, R. (1975). Biological systems as paradigms for adaptation. In R. H. Day & T. Groves, (Eds) *Adaptive economic models*. New York: Academic Press.

Rosen, R. (1985). *Anticipatory systems*. New York: Pergamon Press

Rosen, R. (1986a). Causal structures in brains and machines. *International Journal of General Systems, 12*, 107–126. doi:10.1080/03081078608934929

Rosen, R. (1986b). Some comments on systems and system theory. *International Journal of General Systems, 13*, 1–3. doi:10.1080/03081078608934949

Rosen, R. (1991). *Life itself.* New York: Columbia University Press.

Rosen, R. (1993). Drawing the boundary between subject and object: Comments on the mind-brain problem. *Theoretical Medicine, 14*, 89–100. doi:10.1007/BF00997269

Rosen, R. (2000). *Essays on life itself.* New York: Columbia University Press.

Rosenblueth, A., Wierner, N., & Bigelow, J. (1943). Behaviour, purpose and teology. *Philosophy of Science, 10*(S), 18-24.

Rosenbrock, H. H. (1990). *Machines with purpose*. New York: Oxford University Press. [Case: Esprit]

Ross, P. E. (2006). The expert mind. *Scientific American*, (August): 64–71. doi:10.1038/scientificamerican0806-64

Ross, S. N., & Glock-Grueneich, N. (2008). Growing the field: The institutional, theoretical, and conceptual maturation of "public participation," part 3: Theoretical maturation. *International Journal of Public Participation, 2*(1), 14–25.

Rößl, D. (1990). Die Entwicklung eines Bezugsrahmens und seine Stellung im Forschungsprozess [Development of a reference framework and its position in the research process]. *Journal für Betriebswirtschaft, 40*(2), 99–110.

Roth, W.-M. (2004). Activity theory and education: An introduction. *Mind, Culture, and Activity. International Journal (Toronto, Ont.), 11*(1), 1–8.

Roth, W.-M. (2007). Emotion at work: A contribution to third-generation cultural-historical activity theory. *Mind, Culture, and Activity. International Journal (Toronto, Ont.), 14*(1/2), 40–63.

Rothenberg, A. (1979). *The emerging goddess.* Chicago: University of Chicago Press.

Rowland, G. (1992, November/December). Do you play Jazz? *Performance & Instruction.*

Rueda, R., Gallego, M., & Moll, L. (2000). The last restrictive environment: A place or a context? *Remedial and Special Education, 21*(2), 70–87. doi:10.1177/074193250002100202

Rydberg, T., & Christiansen, E. (2008). Community and network sites as technology enhanced learning environments. *Technology, Pedagogy and Education, 17*(3), 207–219. doi:10.1080/14759390802383801

Saint-Voirin, D., Lang, C., & Zerhouni, N. (2003). Distributed cooperation modelling for maintenance using Petri nets and multi-agents systems. In *Proceedings of 5th IEEE Int. Symp. on Computational Intelligence in Robotics and Automation, CIRA'03, Kobe, Japan, July 16-20,* (Vol. 1, pp. 366-371). Piscataway, NJ: IEEE Press.

Sarker, S., & Lee, A. S. (1999). IT-enabled organizational transformation: a case study of BPR failure at TELECO. *The Journal of Strategic Information Systems, 8*(1), 83–103. doi:10.1016/S0963-8687(99)00015-3

Saunders, P. T., & Ho, M.-W. (1976). On the increase in complexity in evolution. *Journal of Theoretical Biology, 63*, 375–384. doi:10.1016/0022-5193(76)90040-0

Scarbrough, H., & Corbett, J. M. (1992). *Technology and organization: Power, meaning and design.* New York: Routledge.

Schmalenbach, E. (1911). Die Privatwirtschaftslehre als Kunstlehre [The subject of private economy as craft = Business administration as applied science]. *Zeitschrift für handelswissenschaftliche. Forschung, 6*, 304–316.

Schofield, J. W. (2006). Increasing the generalizability of qualitative research. In R. Gomm, M. Hammersley & P. Foster (Eds.), *Case study method: Key issues, key texts* (pp. 69-97). London: Sage.

Schön, D. A. (1991). *The Reflective Turn: Case Studies In and On Educational Practice*. New York: Teachers Press.

Schrödinger, E. (1944). *What is life?* Cambridge, UK: Cambridge University Press.

Schutz, A., & Luckmann, T. (1974). *The structures of the lifeworld*. London: Heinamann.

Schwaninger, M. (2001). Intelligent organisations: An integrative framework. *Systems Research and Behavioral Science*, *18*, 137–158. doi:10.1002/sres.408

Schwaninger, M. (2001). System theory and cybernetics: A solid basis for transdisciplinarity in management education and research. *Kybernetes*, *30*(9/10), 1209. doi:10.1108/EUM0000000006551

Schwartz, P. (2003). *Inevitable surprises: Thinking ahead in a time of turbulence*. New York: Penguin Group, Inc.

Schwarz, E. (1994, April). A metamodel to interpret the emergence, evolution and functioning of viable natural systems. In R. Trappl (Ed.), *Cybernetics and systems '94*, (pp.1579-1586). Singapore: World Scientific.

Schwarz, E. (1994, September). *A trandisciplinary model for the emergence, self-organisation and evolution of viable systems*. Paper presented at the International Information, Systems Architecture and Technology, Technical University of Wroclaw, Szklaska Poreba, Poland.

Schwarz, E. (1997). Towards a holistic cybernetics: From science through epistemology to being. *Cybernetics & Human Knowing*, *4*(1), 17–50.

Schwarz, E. (2001, August). *Anticipating systems: An application to the possible futures of contemporary society*. Invited paper presented at CAYS'2001, Fifth International Conference on Computing Anticipatory Systems, Liege, Belgium.

Schwarz, E. (2005). Personal communication.

Schwarz, G. (1978). Estimating the dimension of a model. *Annals of Statistics*, *6*(2), 461–464. doi:10.1214/aos/1176344136

Schweikert, S. (2000). *Konsortialbenchmarking-projekte: Untersuchung und Erweiterung der Benchmarking-methodik im Hinblick auf ihre Eignung, Wandel und Lernen in Organisationen zu unterstützen* [Consortial benchmarking projects: Analysis and amplification of this benchmarking method what concerns the suitability to support change and learning in organisations]. Flein, Germany: Verlag Werner Schweikert.

Scott, B. (2001). Cybernetics and the social sciences. *Systems Research and Behavioral Science*, *18*(5), 411. doi:10.1002/sres.445

Scribner, S. (1985). Vygotsky's uses of history. In J.V. Wertsch (Ed.). *Culture, Communication, and Cognition: Vygotskian Perspectives* (pp. 119-145). Cambridge, UK: Cambridge University Press.

Senge, P. (1993). *The fifth discipline: The art and practice of the learning organization*. New York: Doubleday Currency.

Senge, P. M., Lichtenstein, B. B., Kaeufer, K., Bradbury, H., & Carroll, J. S. (2007). Collaborating for Systemic Change. *MIT Sloan Management Review*, *48*(2), 44–53.

Senge, P., Kleiner, K., Roberts, S., Ross, R. B., & Smith, B. J. (1994). *The Fifth Discipline Fieldbook: Strategies and Tools for Building a Learning Organization*. New York: Currency Doubleday.

Shahriari, K. (2007). *Analyse de Surete de Procedes Multi Mode par des Modeles a Base d'Intervalles*. PhD thesis, Joseph Fourier University.

Shahriari, K., & Tarasiewicz, S. (2008). Linear time-varying systems: Model parameters characterization using intervals analysis. *International Journal of Mathematics and Computer in Simulation*, *1*(2), 54–62.

Shahriari, K., Adrot, O., & Flaus, J. M. (2006a). Multi mode modeling with linear dynamic models using set-membership tools. *The 11th Information Processing and Management of Uncertainty in Knowledge-Based Systems International Conference*.

Shahriari, K., Flaus, J. M., & Adrot, O. (2006). Linear multi-mode modelling using set-membership approach. In *5th IFAC Symposium on Robust Control Design.*

Shaiken, H. (1986). *Work transformed: Automation and labor in the computer age*. New York: Holt, Rinehart, and Winston. [Case: Ford]

Shank, G. D. (2002). *Qualitative research: A personal skills approach*. Upper Saddle River, NJ: Merrill/Prentice Hall.

Shao, J. (1993). Linear model selection by cross-validation. *Journal of the American Statistical Association*, *88*(422), 486–494. doi:10.2307/2290328

Shao, J. (1997). An asymptotic theory for linear model selection. *Statistica Sinica*, *7*(3), 229–264.

Shareef, R. (2007). Want better business theories? Maybe Karl Popper has the answer. *Academy of Management Learning & Education*, *6*(2), 272–280.

Sharpe, B., & van de Heijden, K. (2007). *Scenarios for success – Turning insights into action.* Chichester, UK: John Wiley & Sons Ltd.

Sheard, S. (2007). Devourer of our convictions: Populist and academic organizational theory and the scope and significant of the metaphor of 'revolution'. *Management and Organizational history, 2*(2), 135-152.

Shibata, R. (1981). An optimal selection of regression variables. *Biometrika*, *68*(1), 45–54. doi:10.1093/biomet/68.1.45

Shotter, J. (2004). *Dialogical Dynamics: Inside the Moment of Speaking.* Retrieved June 18, 2004, from http://pubpages.unh.edu/~jds/thibault1.htm

Shotwell, J. M., Wolf, D., & Gardner, H. (1980). Styles of achievement in early symbol use. In F. Brandes (Ed.), *Language, thought, and culture* (pp.175, 199). New York: Academic Press.

Siggelkow, N. (2007). Persuasion with case studies. *Academy of Management Journal*, *50*(1), 20–24.

Simon, H. A. (1969). *The sciences of the artificial.* Cambridge, MA: MIT Press.

Skinner, Q. (1985). Introduction. In Q. Skinner (Ed.), *The Return of Grand Theory in the Human Sciences* (pp. 1-20). New York: Cambridge University Press.

Smith, K. G., & Hitt, M. A. (Eds.). (2005). *Great Minds in Management: The Process of Theory Development.* Oxford, UK: Oxford University Press.

Smith, M. E. (2003). Changing an organisation's culture: correlates of success and failure. *Leadership and Organization Development Journal*, *24*(5), 249–261. doi:10.1108/01437730310485752

Solomon, R. C. (1999). *A better way to think about business: How personal integrity leads to corporate success.* New York: Oxford University Press.

Solomon, R. C., & Hanson, K. R. (1983). *Above the bottom line: An introduction to business ethics.* New York: Harcourt Brace Jovanovich.

Sorokin, P. A. (1937-1942). *Social and cultural dynamics*, (Vols. 1-4). New York: American. Book Co.

Soros, G. (2006). *The Age of fallibility: Consequences of the war on terror.* New York: Public Affairs.

Soros, G. (2008). The crisis & what to do about it. *The New York Review of Books*, *60*(19), 63–65.

Southerland, J. W. (1975). *Systems: Analysis, administration, and archetectura.* New York: Van Nostrand.

Spencer Brown, G. (1969). *The laws of form.* London: Allen and Unwin.

Stacey, R. (2005). Organisational identity: The paradox of continuity and potential transformation at the same time. *Group Analysis*, *38*(4), 477–494. doi:10.1177/0533316405058540

Stacey, R. D., Griffin, D., & Shaw, P. (2000). *Complexity and Management: Fad or Radical Challenge to Systems Thinking.* New York: Routledge.

Staehle, W. H. (1984). Job design and automation in the Federal Republic of Germany. In F. Butera & J. E. Thurman (Eds.), *Automation and work design* (pp. 208-232). New York: Elsevier. [Case: PCB Co.]

Stake, R. E. (1995). *The art of case study research.* Thousand Oaks, CA: Sage.

Stake, R. E. (2005). Qualitative case studies. In N. K. Denzin & Y. S. Lincoln (Eds.), *The Sage handbook of qualitative research.* (pp. 443-466). Thousand Oaks, CA: Sage.

Stake, R. E. (2006). The case study method in social inquiry. In R. Gomm, M. Hammersley & P. Foster (Eds.), *Case study method: Key issues, key texts* (pp. 19-26). London: Sage.

Stapleton, I., & Murphy, C. (2003). Revisiting the Nature of Information Systems: The Urgent Need for a Crisis in IS Theoretical Discourse. *Transactions of International Information Systems, 1*(4).

Starbuck, W. H. (2003). Shouldn't organization theory emerge from adolescence? *Organization, 10*(3), 439–452. doi:10.1177/13505084030103005

Starkey, K., & Madan, P. (2001). Bridging the relevance gap: Aligning stakeholders in the future of management research. *British Journal of Management, 12*(Special Issue), S3–S26. doi:10.1111/1467-8551.12.s1.2

Steffy, B. D., & Grimes, A. J. (1986). A critical theory of organization science. *Academy of Management Review, 11*, 322–336. doi:10.2307/258463

Steier, F. (1991). *Research and Reflexivity.* London: Sage Publications.

Steingard, D. S. (2005). Spiritually-Informed Management Theory: Toward Profound Possibilities for Inquiry and Transformation. *Journal of Management Inquiry, 14*(3), 227–241. doi:10.1177/1056492605276841

Steingard, D., & Fitzgibbons, D. E. (2004). Towards a spiritually integral theory of management. *Journal of Management. Spirtuality and Religion, 1*(2), 145–175.

Steinle, C. (2005). *Ganzheitliches Management: Eine mehrdimensionale Sichtweise integrierter Unternehmungsführung* [Integral Management. A multi-dimensional view of holistic business administration]. Wiesbaden, Germany: Gabler.

Stephens, J. R., & Haslett, T. (2005). From Cybernetics and VSD to Management and Action. *Systemic Practice and Action Research, 18*(4), 395. doi:10.1007/s11213-005-7170-x

Sternberg, R. J. (1996). *Cognitive psychology.* New York: Harcourt Brace College Publishers.

Stinchcombe, A. L. (1987). *Constructing Social Theories.* Chicago: University of Chicago Press.

Stokes, P. (2006). Personal communication.

Stone, M. (1977). An asymptotic equivalence of choice of model by cross-validation and Akaike's criterion. *Journal of the Royal Statistical Society. Series B. Methodological, 39*(1), 44–47.

Stone, M. (1979). Comments on model selection criteria of Akaike and Schwarz. *Journal of the Royal Statistical Society. Series B. Methodological, 41*(3), 276–278.

Stonier, T. (1992). *Beyond information: The natural history of intelligence.* London: Springer-Verlag.

Stonier, T. (1997). *Information and meaning: An evolutionary perspective.* London: Springer-Verlag.

Strauss, A. L., & Corbin, J. (1998). *Basics of qualitative research: Techniques and procedures for developing grounded theory.* Thousand Oaks, CA: Sage.

Strauss, L. (1964). *The city and man.* Chicago: The University of Chicago Press.

Sugeno, M., & Kang, G. T. (1988). Structure identification of fuzzy model. *Fuzzy Sets and Systems, 28*(1), 15–33. doi:10.1016/0165-0114(88)90113-3

Sunaga, T. (1958). Theory of interval algebra and its application to numerical analysis. *RAAG Memoirs, Ggujutsu Bunken Fukuy-kai,* Tokyo, 2(29–46), 547–564.

Sundaramurthy, C., & Lewis, M. W. (2003). Paradoxes of governance: Managing control and collaboration. *Academy of Management Review, 28*(3), 397–415.

Sutton, R. I., & Staw, B. M. (1995). What theory is not. *Administrative Science Quarterly, 40*(3), 371–384. doi:10.2307/2393788

Tainter, J. A. (1990). *The collapse of complex societies.* Cambridge, MA: Cambridge University Press.

Takagi, T., & Sugeno, M. (1985). Fuzzy identification of systems and its applications to modeling and control. *IEEE Transactions on Systems, Man, and Cybernetics, 15*, 116–132.

Takahara, Y., & Mesarovic, M. D. (2004). *Organization Structure: Cybernetic Systems Foundation*, (IFSR International Series on Systems Science and Engineering, Vol.22). New York: Springer.

Taleb, N. (2007). *The black swan: The impact of the highly improbable.* New York: Random House.

Taylor, J., & Every, E. (2000). *The Emergent Organisation: Communication as its Site and Surface*. Mahwah, New Jersey: Lawrence Erlbaum Associates.

Teunissen, J. (1996). Paradoxes in social science and research. In W. Koot, I. Sabelis, & S. Ybema (Eds.), *Contradictions in context* (pp. 17-38). Amsterdam: VU University Press.

TFPL. (1999). *Skills for knowledge management: A briefing paper.* London: TFPL, Ltd.

Theobald, R. (1997). *Reworking success: New communities at the millennium.* Stony Creek, CT: New Society Publishers.

Thomas, R. J. (1994). *What machines can't do.* Berkeley, CA: University of California Press. [Case: AutoParts]

Thompson, M. L. (1978). Selection of variables in multiple regression: Part I. A review and evaluation. *International Statistical Review, 46*(1), 1–19. doi:10.2307/1402505

Tibshirani, R. (1996). Regression shrinkage and selection via the lasso. *Journal of the Royal Statistical Society. Series B. Methodological, 58*(2), 267–288.

Tibshirani, R., & Knight, K. (1999). The covariance inflation criterion for model selection. *Journal of the Royal Statistical Society. Series B. Methodological, 61*(3), 529–546. doi:10.1111/1467-9868.00191

Tong, H. (1990). *Non-linear time series: A dynamical system approach.* Oxford: University Press.

Torbert, W. R. (1994). Cultivating postformal adult development: Higher stages and contrasting interventions. In M. E. Miller & S. R. Cook-Greuter (Eds.), *Transcendence and mature thought in adulthood: The further reaches of adult development* (pp. 181-203). London: Rowman & Littlefield.

Tranfield, D., Denyer, D., Marcos, J., & Burr, M. (2004). Co-producing management knowledge. *Management Decision, 42*(3/4), 375–386. doi:10.1108/00251740410518895

Trim, P. R. J., & Lee, Y. (2004). A reflection on theory building and the development of management knowledge. *Management Decision, 42*(3/4), 473–480. doi:10.1108/00251740410518930

Tsoukas, H., & Chia, R. (2002). On organizational becoming: Rethinking organizational change. *Organization Science, 13*(5), 567. doi:10.1287/orsc.13.5.567.7810

Tuomi-Gröhn, T., Engeström, Y., & Young, M. (2003). From transfer to boundary-crossing between school and work as a tool for developing vocational education: An introduction. In T. Tuomi-Gröhn & Y. Engeström, (Eds.), *Between School and Work: New Perspectives on Transfer and Boundary-crossing,* (pp. 1-15). Kidlington, UK: Elsevier Science.

Tyre, M. (1991). Managing innovation on the factory floor. [Case: Italian Finishing]. *Technology Review,* (October): 59–65.

Uhl-Bien, M., & Marion, R. (2008). *Complexity leadership.* Charlotte, NC: Information Age Publishing.

Umpleby, S. (2007). Reflexivity in social systems: The theories of George Soros. *Systems Research and Behavioral Science, 24*, 515–522. doi:10.1002/sres.852

Updated Edition: Why the Future of Business is Selling Less of More. New York: Hyperion.

Upton, D. (1990). *John Crane UK Limited: The CAD-CAM link.* Boston, MA: HBS Case Services. [Cases: JC Reading and JC Slough]

Upton, D., & McAffee, J. (1998). Computer integration and catastrophic process failure in flexible production: An empirical investigation. *Production and Operations Management, 7*(3), 265–281.

Vallas, S. P., & Beck, J. P. (1996). The transformation of work revisited: The limits of flexibility in American manufacturing. *Social Problems*, *42*(3), 339–362. doi:10.1525/sp.1996.43.3.03x0142l

van de Heijden, K. (2005). *Scenario planning – The art of strategic conversation*. Chichester, UK: John Wiley & Sons Ltd.

Van de Ven, A. H. (2007). *Engaged Scholarship: A Guide for Organizational and Social Research*. Oxford, UK: Oxford University Press.

Van de Ven, A. H., & Poole, M. S. (1995). Explaining development and change in organizations. *Academy of Management Review*, *20*(3), 510–540. doi:10.2307/258786

van Eijnatten, F. M., van Galen, M. C., & Fitzgerald, L. A. (2003). Learning dialogically: The art of chaos-informed transformation. *The Learning Organization*, *10*(6), 361–367. doi:10.1108/09696470310497203

van Gelder, S. (1998, Fall). The natural step: The science of sustainability. *YES! A Journal of Positive Futures*, *7*, 50-54.

Van Maanen, J., & Barley, S. R. (1984). Occupational communities. *Research in Organizational Behavior*, *6*, 287–365.

Van Oers, B. (1998). The fallacy of decontextualization. *Mind, Culture, and Activity. International Journal (Toronto, Ont.)*, *5*(2), 135–142.

Varela, F., Thompson, E., & Rosch, E. (1991). *The embodied mind*. Cambridge, MA: MIT Press.

Venkat, A. N., Vijaysai, P., & Gudi, R. D. (2003). Identification of complex nonlinear processes based on fuzzy decomposition of the steady state space. *Journal of Process Control*, *13*(6), 473–488. doi:10.1016/S0959-1524(02)00120-8

Vince, R. (2004). Action learning and organizational learning: Power, politics and emotions in organizations. *Action Learning*, *1*(1), 63–78. doi:10.1080/1476733042000187628

Vince, R., & Broussine, M. (1996). Paradox, defense and attachment: Accessing and working with emotions and relations underlying organizational change. *Organization Studies*, *17*(1), 1–21. doi:10.1177/017084069601700101

von Bertalanffy, L. (1950). An outline of general system theory. *The British Journal for the Philosophy of Science*, *1*(2), 134–165. doi:10.1093/bjps/I.2.134

von Foerster, H. (1984). Principles of self-organization in a socio-managerial context. In H. Ulrich & G. J. B. Probst (Eds.), *Self-organization and management of social systems* (pp. 2-22). Berlin: Springer.

von Foerster, H. (1995). Ethics and second order cybernetics. *Stanford Humanities Review 4*(2), 308-319. Retrieved March 30, 2009, from http://www.stanford.edu/group/SHR/4-2/text/foerster.html

von Ghyczy, T. (2003, September). The fruitful flaws of strategy metaphors. *Harvard Business Review*, 86–94.

von Glasersfeld, E. (1995). *Radical constructivism: a way of knowing and learning*. London: Falmer Press.

Vygotsky, L. (1986). *Thought and Language*. Cambridge, MA: MIT Press.

Vygotsky, L. (1987). Thinking and speech. In R. W. Rieber & A. S. Carton (Eds.), *The Collected Works of L. S. Vygotsky*, (Vol. 2, The fundamentals of defectology, pp. 122-138). New York: Plenum.

Vygotsky, L. (1994). The socialist alteration of man. In R. van der Veer & J. Valsiner (Eds.), *The Vygotsky Reader*. Oxford, UK: Blackwell.

Vygotsky, L. (1997). *Educational Psychology*, (transl. R. Silverman). Boca Raton, FL: St Lucie Press.

Vygotsky, L. (1998). Pedagogy of the adolescent. In R. Rieber (Ed.), *The Collected Works of L. S. Vygotsky*, (Vol. 5, Child psychology, pp. 31-184) (transl. M. J. Hall). New York: Plenum

Vygotsky, L. (1999). Consciousness as a problem in the psychology of behavior. *Undiscovered Vygotsky: Etudes on the pre-history of cultural-historical psychology*, (Vol 8, pp. 251-281). New York: Peter Lang.

Vygotsky, L. (2004). The historical meaning of the crisis in psychology: A methodological investigation. In R.W. Rieber & D.K Robinson (Eds.), *The Essential Vygotsky* (pp. 227-357). New York: Kluwer Academic.

Wack, P. (1985a). Scenarios: uncharted waters ahead. *Harvard Business Review, 63*(5), 73–89.

Wack, P. (1985b). Scenarios: Shooting the rapids. *Harvard Business Review, 63*(6), 139–150.

Waddington, C. H. (1957). *The strategy of the genes*. London: Allen and Unwin.

Waddock, S. (2005). Hollow Men and Women at the Helm... Hollow Accounting Ethics? *Issues in Accounting Education, 20*(2), 145–150. doi:10.2308/iace.2005.20.2.145

Walker, D., & Nocon, H. (2007). Boundary-crossing competence: Theoretical considerations and educational design. *Mind, Culture, and Activity. International Journal (Toronto, Ont.), 14*(3), 178–195.

Wallis, S. E. (2006a, July 13, 2006). *A sideways look at systems: Identifying sub-systemic dimensions as a technique for avoiding an hierarchical perspective.* Paper presented at the International Society for the Systems Sciences, Rohnert Park, CA.

Wallis, S. E. (2006b). *A Study of Complex Adaptive Systems as Defined by Organizational Scholar-Practitioners.* Unpublished Theoretical Dissertation, Fielding Graduate University, Santa Barbara.

Wallis, S. E. (2008). Emerging order in CAS theory: Mapping some perspectives. *Kybernetes, 37*(7), 1016–1029. doi:10.1108/03684920810884388

Wallis, S. E. (2008b). From Reductive to Robust: Seeking the Core of Complex Adaptive Systems Theory. In A. Yang & Y. Shan (Eds.), *Intelligent Complex Adaptive Systems*. Hershey, PA: IGI Publishing.

Wallis, S. E. (2008c). *The integral puzzle: Determining the integrality of integral theory.* Retrieved 07/14, 2008, from http://www.integralworld.net/wallis.html

Wallis, S. E. (2008d). Validation of theory: Exploring and reframing Popper's worlds. *Integral Review, 4*(2), 71–91.

Wallis, S. E. (2009a). The Complexity of Complexity Theory: An Innovative Analysis. *Emergence: Complexity and Organization, 11*(4).

Wallis, S. E. (2009b). *From reductive to robust: Seeking the core of institutional theory.* Under submission - available upon request.

Wallis, S. E. (2009c). Seeking the robust core of organizational learning theory. *International Journal of Collaborative Enterprise, 1*(2). doi:10.1504/IJCENT.2009.029288

Wallis, S. E. (2009e). *Theory of peak performance theory.* Under submission - available upon request.

Wallis, S. E. (2009f). *Towards a robust systemization of Gandhian ethics*. Under submission - available upon request.

Walter, E., & Pronzato, L. (1997). *Identification of Parametric Models: From Experimental Data*. Berlin: Springer-Verlag.

Warmus, M. (1956). Calculus of approximations. *Bulletin de l'Academie Polonaise de Sciences, 4*(5), 253–257.

Wartofsky, M. (1979). *Models*. Dordrecht: Riedel.

Weber, M. (2003). Personal Communication.

Weed, L. (2002). Kant's noumenon and sunyata. *Asian Philosophy, 12*(2), 77–95. doi:10.1080/0955236022000043838

Wei, C. Z. (1992). On predictive least squares principles. *Annals of Statistics, 20*(1), 1–42. doi:10.1214/aos/1176348511

Weick, K. E. (1990). Technology as equivoque: Sensemaking in new technologies. In P. S. Goodman & L. S. Sproull (Eds.), *Technology and organizations* (pp. 1-44). San Francisco: Jossey-Bass.

Weick, K. E. (1993). The collapse of sensemaking in organizations: The Mann Gulch disaster. *Administrative Sci-*

ence Quarterly, *38*(4), 628–652. doi:10.2307/2393339

Weick, K. E. (1995). *Sensemaking in organizations*. Thousand Oaks, CA: Sage.

Weick, K. E. (2005). The experience of theorizing: Sensemaking as topic and resource. In K. G. Smith & M. A. Hitt (Eds.), *Great Minds in Management: The Process of Theory Development* (pp. 394-413). New York: Oxford University Press.

Weick, K. E. (2007). The generative properties of richness. *Academy of Management Journal*, *50*(2), 14–19.

Weinberg, G. (1975). *An introduction to general systems thinking*. New York: John Wiley.

Weisbord, M. R. (1987). *Productive Workplaces: Organizing and Managing for Dignity, Meaning, and Community*: Jossey-Bass.

Wells, G. (2007). The mediating role of discoursing in activity. *Mind, Culture, and Activity. International Journal (Toronto, Ont.)*, *14*(3), 160–177.

Wertsch, J. (1998). *Mind as Action*. New York: Oxford University Press.

Westenholz, A. (1993). Paradoxical thinking and change in frames of reference. *Organization Studies*, *14*(1), 37–58. doi:10.1177/017084069301400104

Wheatley, M. J. (1992). *Leadership and the New Science*. San Francisco: Barrett-Koehler.

Whitehead, A. N., & Russell, B. (1910). *Principia mathematica*. Cambridge, MA: Cambridge University Press.

Wilkinson, B. (1983). *The shopfloor politics of new technology*. London: Heinemann. [Case: Plating Company]

Wilson, E. J., & Vlosky, R. P. (1997). Partnering relationship activities: Building theory from case study research. *Journal of Business Research*, *39*(1), 59–70. doi:10.1016/S0148-2963(96)00149-X

Winograd, T. (Ed.). (1996). *Bringing Design to Software*. New York: Addison Wesley.

Winter, W., & Thurm, M. (2005). Second-order cybernetics! In systemic management thinking? *Kybernetes*, *34*(3/4), 419. doi:10.1108/03684920510581602

Wollheim, R. (1999). *On the emotions*. New Haven, CT: Yale University Press.

Wood, D., Bruner, J.S., & Ross, G. (1976). The role of tutoring in problem solving. *Journal of Psychology and Psychiatry, 17*.

Woodside, A. G., & Wilson, E. J. (2003). Case study research for theory-building. *Journal of Business and Industrial Marketing*, *18*(6/7), 493–508. doi:10.1108/08858620310492374

Wright, P., Mukherji, A., & Kroll, M. J. (2001). A reexamination of agency theory assumptions: Extensions and extrapolations. *Journal of Socio-Economics*, *30*(5), 413. doi:10.1016/S1053-5357(01)00102-0

Wytenburg, A. J. (2001). Bracing for the future: Complexity and computational ability in the knowledge era. *Emergence*, *3*(2), 113–126. doi:10.1207/S15327000EM0302_08

Yager, R. R., & Filev, D. P. (1993). Unified structure and parameter identification of fuzzy models. *IEEE Transactions on Systems, Man, and Cybernetics*, *23*(4), 1198–1205. doi:10.1109/21.247902

Yaroshevsky, M. (1989). *Lev Vygotsky*, (transl. S. Syrovatkin). Moscow: Progress.

Ye, J. (1998). On measuring and correcting the effects of data mining and model selection. *Journal of the American Statistical Association*, *93*(441), 120–131. doi:10.2307/2669609

Yen, J., Yin, J., Ioerger, T. R., Miller, M. S., Xu, E., & Volz, R. A. (2001). CAST: Collaborative agents for simulating teamwork. In B. Nebel (Ed.), *Proceedings of 17th International Joint Conference on Artificial Intelligence - IJCAI' 2001, Seattle, WA* (Vol. 2, pp. 1135-1142). San Francisco, CA: Morgan Kaufmann Publishers.

Yin, R. K. (1981). The case study crisis: Some answers. *Administrative Science Quarterly*, *26*, 58–65. doi:10.2307/2392599

Yin, R. K. (2003). *Case study research: Design and methods*. Thousand Oaks, CA: Sage.

Yolles, M. (2006). Knowledge cybernetics: A new metaphor for social collectives. *Organizational Transformation and Social Change*, *3*(1), 19–49. doi:10.1386/jots.3.1.19/1

Yolles, M. (2007). Exploring cultures through knowledge cybernetics. [JCCM]. *Journal of Cross-Cultural Competence and Management*, *5*, 19–74.

Yolles, M. I. (1999). Management systems: A viable approach. *Financial Times*. London: Pitman.

Yolles, M. I. (2000). From viable systems to surfing the organisation. *Journal of Applied Systems*, *1*(1), 127–142.

Yolles, M. I. (2000b). The theory of viable joint ventures. *Cybernetics and Systems*, *31*(4), 371–396. doi:10.1080/019697200124757

Yolles, M. I. (2001). Viable boundary critique. *The Journal of the Operational Research Society*, *51*(January), 1–12.

Yolles, M. I. (2002). Introduction to knowledge profiling, In G. Ragsdell, D. West, & J. Wilby (Eds.), *Systems theory and practice in the knowledge age*. New York: Kluwer Academic/Plenum Publishers.

Yolles, M. I. (2003). The political cybernetics of organisations. *Kybernetes*, *23*(9/10), 1253–1282. doi:10.1108/03684920310493242

Yolles, M. I. (2004). Implications for Beer's ontological system/metasystem dichotomy. *Kybernetes*, *33*(3), 726–764. doi:10.1108/03684920410523670

Yolles, M. I. (2005). Revisiting the political cybernetics of organisations. *Kybernetes*, *34*(5/6), 617–636. doi:10.1108/03684920510595328

Yolles, M. I. (2006). *Organisations as complex systems: An introduction to knowledge Cybernetics*. Greenwich, CT: Information Age Publishing.

Yolles, M. I. (2007a). The dynamics of narrative and antenarrative and their relation to story. *Journal of Organizational Change Management*, *20*(1), 74–94. doi:10.1108/09534810710715298

Yolles, M. I. (2009). (in press). Migrating personality theories Part 1: Creating agentic trait psychology? *Kybernetes*, *36*(6).

Yolles, M. I., & Frieden, R. (2005). A metahistorical information theory of social change: The theory. *Organisational Transformation and Social Change*, *2*(2), 103–136. doi:10.1386/jots.2.2.103/1

Yolles, M. I., & Guo, K. (2003). Paradigmatic metamorphosis and organisational development. *Systems Research and Behavioral Science*, *20*, 177–199. doi:10.1002/sres.533

Yolles, M. I., & Ye, Z. (2005, July). *Taoist viable systems*. Presented at the International Society for Systems Science Conference, Cancun, Mexico.

Yolles, M., & Guo, K. (2004, July). *Cybernetic organisational development*. Presented at the International Society of Systems Science Conference, Pacific Grove, Monterey, CA.

Yolles, M., & Guo, K. (2005, July). *Understanding coherence and pathology in Chinese state owned commercial banks*. Presented at the International Society of Systems Science Conference, Cancun, Mexico.

Young, R. C. (1931). The algebra of multi-valued quantities. *Mathematische Annalen*, *104*, 260–290. doi:10.1007/BF01457934

Young, W. H. (1908). Sull due funzioni a piu valori constituite dai limiti d'una funzione di variable reale a destra ed a sinistra di ciascun punto. *Rendiconti Academia di Lincei. Classes di Scienza Fiziche*, *17*(5), 582–587.

Zell, D. (2003). Organizational Change as a Process of Death, Dying, and Rebirth. *The Journal of Applied Behavioral Science*, *39*(1), 73–96. doi:10.1177/0021886303039001004

Zhang, P. (1992). Inference after variable selection in linear regression models. *Biometrika*, *79*(4), 741–746. doi:10.1093/biomet/79.4.741

Zheng, X., & Loh, W. Y. (1997). A consistent variable selection criterion for linear models with high-dimensional covariates. *Statistica Sinica*, *7*(3), 311–325.

Zsolnai, L. (2006). Extended stakeholder theory. *Society and Business Review*, *1*(1), 37–44. doi:10.1108/17465680610643337

Zuboff, S. (1988). *In the age of the smart machine*. New York: Basic books. [Case: Piney Wood]

About the Contributors

Steve Wallis is a Fellow of the Institute for Social Innovation which helps individuals and organizations address societal problems via research, leadership, and organizational development. As an organization development consultant he has a decade of experience in Northern California across a wide range of industries. He earned his Ph.D. in 2006 from Fielding Graduate University. As the founder and director of the Foundation for the Advancement of Social Theory (FAST), a non-profit venture under the auspices of ISI and Fielding, Steve is dedicated to supporting scholars and practitioners as they identify and pursue objective methods for advancing theory across the spectrum of the social sciences. His papers and chapters serve to advance the metatheoretical conversation and identify innovative paths for advancing social theory. He is the editor of "*Cybernetics and Systems Theory in Management: Tools, Views and Advancements*" (in press). Applying those metatheoretical methods, publications include analyses in topic areas of complexity theory, CAS theory, organizational learning theory, social entrepreneurship theory, and others.

* * *

Alex and David Bennet are co-founders of the Mountain Quest Institute, a research and retreat center nestled in the Allegheny Mountains of West Virginia focused on achieving growth and understanding through questions for knowledge, consciousness and meaning. See www.mountainquestinstitute.com The Bennets are co-authors of the seminal work, *Organizational Survival in the New World: The Intelligent Complex Adaptive System* (Elsevier, 2004), a new theory of the firm based on research in complexity and neuroscience and incorporating networking theory and knowledge management. More recently they worked with the government of Canada to co-author and publish Knowledge Mobilization in the Social Sciences and Humanities: Moving from Research to Action (MQIPress, 2007). **Alex** served as the Chief Knowledge Officer for the U.S. Department of the Navy (DON), and was co-chair of the Federal KM Working Group. She is the recipient of the DON Distinguished and Superior Public Service Awards. Dr. Bennet has degrees in Human and Organizational Systems, Human Development, Management for Organizational Effectiveness, English and Marketing. **David**'s experience spans many years of service in the Military, Civil Service and Private Industry, including fundamental research in underwater acoustics and nuclear physics and frequent design and facilitation of organizational interventions. Most recently, he was CEO, then Chairman of the Board and Chief Knowledge Officer of a professional services firm. Dr. Bennet has degrees in Physics, Mathematics, Nuclear Physics, Human and Organizational Systems, Human Development, and Liberal Arts. The Bennets may be contacted at alex@mountainquestinstitute.com

František Čapkovič, In 1972 he received his master degree from the Faculty of Electrical Engineering, Slovak Technical University, Bratislava, Slovakia. Since 1972 he has been working with the Slovak Academy of Sciences (SAS), Bratislava - in 1972–1991 at the Institute of Technical Cybernetics, in 1991–2001 at the Institute of Control Theory and Robotics and in 2001 to the present at the Institute of Informatics. He received the PhD from SAS in 1980. Since 1998 he has been the Associate Professor. Now he works in the area of modelling, analysing and control of Discrete-Event Systems (DES) and Multi Agent Systems (MAS). He is the leader of research projects. Since 1991 he has been a head of 7 national projects as well as a head of the Slovak participation in 12 international projects. He is the author of more than 160 publications of different kinds – journal papers, book chapters and conference proceedings.

Mark Edwards is a lecturer at the Business School, University of Western Australia. He teaches in the areas of business ethics, organizational change and transformation and integrative metatheory. He has published in scholarly journals on a variety of topics including organizational development, organizational learning, sustainability, futures studies, cultural evolution, disability studies, metatheory development and integrative metastudies. Mark's PhD thesis was awarded with distinction and will be published by Routledge in 2009 in a series on business ethics. The book will be titled, "Organizational Transformation for Sustainability: An Integral Metatheory". Mark's articles have appeared in several academic journals including "*Leadership and Organizational Development Journal*", "*Journal of Organizational Change and Management*", "*Integral Leadership Review*", "*The Learning Organization*", "*Futures*", "*ReVision*" and "*Journal of Integral Theory and Practice*". He has also contributed chapters to books dealing with such topics as 21st century management, integral metatheory, management education, cybernetics and corruption and globalisation. He is also a member of the European research network SUSTAIN which looks at innovative approaches to sustaining work. He is a registered psychologist. Before working as an academic, Mark worked for many years with higher education students with disabilities in the role of disability services coordinator. These experiences continue to inform his approach to both personal and organisational change and transformation.

Thomas Hansson used to be an upper secondary school teacher for twenty years. He received a PhD at *Luleå University of Technology*, Centre for research in teaching and learning in 2001. Then TH worked as developmental leader in teacher education at *Mälardalen University* for a year, educational consultant/lecturer at *University of Southern Denmark* for five years and currently as Docent in Pedagogy at *Blekinge Institute of Technology*. TH initiated, participated in and assessed several EU-projects in the role of leader, consultant and expert. Research interests are on collective, digital and workplace learning, human activity systems/systems thinking, organizational learning/learning organizations, action research and cultural historical activity theory.

Anthony Hodgson, B.Sc., A.R.C.S., F.R.S.A.: Anthony is the founder of Decision Integrity Limited, a research company pioneering ways to facilitate better decisions through application of holistic thinking, systems mapping, cybernetics, integrative group processes and sustainable values. His career long consulting experience has included international corporations including 3M, Agilent Technologies, BP, BT, Boots, Fujitsu, General Motors, Hewlett Packard, the Shell Group, StatoilHydro, and Unilever. A graduate of the Royal College of Science, Imperial College, London, he has taught on the Executive MBA at The London Business School. He helped the international development of the Society for Organisational Learning. He is a founder member of the International Futures Forum and a contributing member of the Oxford Futures Forum. He is a Fellow of the Royal Society of Arts, he has published papers on aspects of educational technology, systems thinking in management and health care, cognitive facilitation and co-authored books on strategy and scenario method.

Stefan Krummaker is a senior lecturer and senior research associate in leadership and organizational behavior at the Leibniz University of Hannover. He earned his PhD in management from the Leibniz University of Hanover in 2007. Besides management research, his current research interests include followership/follower-centered perspectives on leadership and collaborative research. Stefan has authored and co-authored several books, journal articles and conference papers. He also works as a management trainer and as an executive coach. Before entering academia, Stefan has worked more than 11 years for an international tourism company.

Alexander Laszlo, Ph.D., is co-founder and President of Syntony Quest and former Director of the Doctoral Program in Management at the Graduate School of Business Administration & Leadership (ITESM), Mexico. Currently, he teaches on evolutionary leadership, collaboration, and systems thinking at a variety of MBA and Doctoral programs internationally. He has worked for UNESCO, the Italian Electric Power Agency, and the U.S. Department of Education, has held visiting appointments with the London School of Economics and the European University Institute, and has been named a Level I Member of the National Research Academy of Mexico (SNI). He is on the Editorial Boards of *World Futures, Systems Research & Behavioral Science, Organisational Transformation & Social Change* and *Latin American Business Review,* recipient of the Sir Geoffrey Vickers Memorial Award, active member of several systems science societies, and author of over fifty journal, book, and encyclopedia publications.

Kathia Castro Laszlo, Ph.D., is co-founder and Executive Director of Syntony Quest, an educational, research and consulting organization that empowers businesses and communities to work and learn in ways that embody social and environmental integrity, with offices in San Francisco and Monterrey, Mexico. She is also professor at MA and Ph.D. levels at various universities internationally in the fields of systems thinking, leadership, strategy and organizational development. Her work bridges scholarly understanding with practical application in areas of organizational change, leadership and development of human and social capital for sustainability. A Fulbright Scholar from Mexico, she is author of numerous peer reviewed publications on topics ranging from educational change to sustainable development, innovation and knowledge management, as well as the forthcoming book *Education and Beyond: An introduction to the design of Evolutionary Learning Community.*

Marianne W. Lewis is an associate professor of management at the University of Cincinnati. Her research explores systemic tensions, conflicts, and paradoxes that both impede and enable innovation. In particular, her work addresses the challenges of developing new products, implementing technological and organizational change, and building organization theory. Representative articles appear in the *Academy of Management Review, Academy of Management Journal, Journal of Operations Management, Human Relations* and *Journal of Management Education.* Her paper, "Exploring paradox: Toward a more comprehensive guide" received the *AMR* Best Paper Award in 2007. She earned her Ph.D. in Management from the University of Kentucky, and MBA from Indiana University.

A native of Illinois,**Don Mikulecky** received his PhD in physiology from the University of Chicago in 1963 while serving as a Lieutenant in the US Marine Corps Reserve. The subsequent 10 years saw him spend time as a postdoctoral student in Rehovot, Israel, as faculty at SUNY, as visiting scholar at Philander Smith College in Little Rock, AR, as visiting lecturer at Harvard Medical School, and as director of the Division of Neurosciences and Molecular Biology at Meharry Medical School in Nashville. He arrived at Virginia Commonwealth University in 1973 to begin a career of nearly 30 years as a professor of physiology and biomedical engineering. He has enjoyed sabbaticals at the College de France at the University of Paris, the Max Planck Institute for Biophysics in Frankfurt, Germany, and at the University of Rouen in France. He has authored over 100 publications, including a book on Network Thermodynamics. A pioneer in the use of computer modeling systems in the life sciences, Dr. Mikulecky is presently a Senior Fellow in the VCU Center for Biological Complexity. His website and blog reveal his passion for changing the way in which we view and study living systems. In October 2007 he was editor of and contributing author to a special edition of the journal "Chemistry and Biodiversity" entitled "System Theory and Biocomplexity: In Memoriam Robert Rosen".

Gianfranco Minati graduated in Mathematics from the University of Milan, Italy. He has switched from a position as executive in a large industrial-financial Italian group (1979-1984) to Research. He is founder and president of the *Italian Systems Society,* vice-president of the *Systems Science European Union* and doctoral lecturer at the Polytechnic University of Milan. He is author, co-author and editor of several academic publications (18 books like *New Approaches for Modelling Emergence of Collective Phenomena - The Meta-structures project*, Polimetrica, Milan, 2009;*Processes of emergence of systems and systemic properties*, World Scientific, Singapore, 2008; *Dialogue about systems*, Polimetrica, Milan, 2007; *Collective Beings*, Springer, New York, 2006; *Systemics of Emergence*, Springer, New York, 2006; *Emergence in Complex Systems,* Kluwer, New York, 2002 and 58 peer-reviewed articles). His current research interest focuses on modelling processes of emergence by using *meta-structures.*

Konstantin N. Nechval has the PhD degree in automatic control and systems engineering. He is an Associate Professor in the Department of Applied Mathematics at the Transport and Telecommunication Institute (Riga, Latvia). His research interests include mathematics, stochastic processes, pattern recognition, operations research, statistical decision theory, and adaptive control.

Nicholas A. Nechval has the PhD degree in automatic control and systems engineering, and the DSc degree in radio engineering. In 1992, Dr. Nechval was awarded a Silver Medal of the Exhibition Committee (Moscow, Russia) in connection with research on the problem of Prevention of Collisions between Aircraft and Birds. He is the holder of several patents in this field. His book, 'Improved Decisions in Statistics' (co-authored with E.K. Vasermanis), was awarded the '2004 Best Publication Award' by the Baltic Operations Research Society. His research interests include mathematics, stochastic processes, pattern recognition, multidimensional statistic detection and estimation, multiresolution stochastic signal analysis, digital radar signal processing, operations research, statistical decision theory, and adaptive control. At present, Dr. Nechval is a Professor of Mathematics and Computer Science at the University of Latvia (Riga, Latvia).

Maris Purgailis (PhD) is a Dean of the Faculty of Economics and Management at the University of Latvia (Riga, Latvia). His research interests include economics and management, operations research, statistical decision theory, and adaptive control. Professor Purgailis is a professional member of the Latvian Statistical Association.

Kurt A. Richardson is the Associate Director for the ISCE Group and is Director of ISCE Publishing, a publishing house he founded in 2004 that specializes in complexity-related publications. He has a BSc(hons) in Physics (1992), MSc in Astronautics and Space Engineering (1993) and a PhD in Applied Physics (1996). Kurt's current research interests include the philosophical implications of assuming that everything we observe is the result of complex underlying processes, the relationship between structure and function, analytical frameworks for intervention design, and robust methods of reducing complexity, which have resulted in the publication of over forty journal papers and book chapters, and ten books. He is the Managing/Production Editor for the international journal *Emergence: Complexity & Organization* and is on the review board for the journals *Systemic Practice and Action Research, Systems Research and Behavioral Science*, and *Tamara: Journal of Critical Postmodern Organization Science*. Kurt is the editor of the recently published *Managing Organizational Complexity: Philosophy, Theory, Practice* (Information Age Publishing, 2005) and is coeditor of the forthcoming book *Complexity and Knowledge Management: Understanding the Role of Knowledge in the Management of Social Networks* (due August 2008). Kurt is also a fully qualified spacecraft systems engineer, and is currently developing a software environment to support the integration and testing of complex engineered systems.

Alexander Riegler obtained a PhD in Artificial Intelligence and Cognitive Science from Vienna University of Technology in 1995 with a dissertation on Artificial Life. He worked in the Institute of Software Technology at the Vienna University of Technology, the Department of Theoretical Biology at the University of Vienna, the Department of Computer Science at the University of Zurich, the Leo Apostel Center for Interdisciplinary Studies at the Free University of Brussels, and the Institute of Philosophy at the University of Leuven. Riegler's interdisciplinary work includes diverse areas such as knowledge representation and anticipation in cognitive science, post-Darwinian approaches in evolutionary theory, and constructivist and computational approaches to epistemology. He is the editor-in-chief of the journal *Constructivist Foundations*, http://www.constructivistfoundations.info

Uldis Rozevskis (PhD) is an Associate Professor at the University of Latvia (Riga, Latvia). His main research interests include the network design and optimization, stochastic models, teletrafic theory and performance analysis, high-speed network dynamics. Dr. Rozevskis is a professional member of the Latvian Statistical Association.

Holger Schiele (born 1969) has earned both, his PhD and his habilitation (venia legendi) from the University of Hanover, Germany. He now holds the chair of Technology Management at the University of Twente, The Netherlands. Besides academic work, Holger Schiele has a substantial practical experience of more than ten years, working with Dresdner Bank AG, in the strategy department of Preussag AG and as consultant and project manager for PricewaterhouseCoopers and h&z business consulting. He is author of three books and several journal papers, published in English-language journals such as Research Policy, European Planning Studies, Industrial Marketing Management, Journal of Purchasing and Supply and Journal of Business Strategy.

Kyarash Shahriari finished his B.Sc. degree at the engineering school of Shahid Bahonar University in electronics engineering in 1999. For two years, he collaborated with Kerman Tablo Co. and Ansaldo Energia as electronics and instrumentation and control engineer. He then joined Laboratoire d'Automatique de Grenoble (LAG) in 2001 from where he received his M.Sc. and Ph.D. degrees in control engineering in 2003 and 2007 respectively. After finishing his PhD, he jointed Atkins Rail in 2007 as systems theory researcher. From Feb. 2008 to August 2009, he has been postdoctoral fellow at Laboratory of Complex Automation and Mechatronics (LACM), Laval University. He is now with Centre de Recherche Industrielle du Québec (CRIQ). His research interests are control theory, systems identification, optimal control, interval analysis, and surety (safety/security) analysis of complex dynamic systems/processes.

Maurice Yolles is professor of management systems, a title which he gained during his tenure at Liverpool Business School, Liverpool John Moores University. He recently took early retirement from this university. A fellow of the Cybernetics Society, he gained a doctorate in political science in 1980 and a *Doctor Honoris Causa* in 2008 for his work in Social Cybernetics. He has also given numerous keynote presentations around the world, and received awards for individual research papers. Yolles can point to about 200 publications, including academic papers in learned journals and numerous conferences, 2 research monographs and other texts. These have cut across a number of disciplinary areas. He also edits the international *Journal of Organisational Transformation and Social Change.* For a number of years he was vice president for Research and Publications of the International Society for Systems Science. He currently teaches as a visiting professor at Ramkhamhaeng University in Bangkok. Most of his history of teaching and administrative experience has been in relation to postgraduate studies.

Index

M

N

O

P

Q

R

S

T

V

W